P9-DHM-647

ILLINOIS PRAIRIE DPL

OTHER BOOKS BY WILLIAM LEE MILLER

The Protestant and Politics

Piety Along the Potomac

The Fifteenth Ward and the Great Society

Of Thee, Nevertheless, I Sing: An Essay on American Political Values

Yankee from Georgia: The Emergence of Jimmy Carter

The First Liberty: Religion and the American Republic

The Business of May Next: James Madison and the Founding

ARGUING ABOUT SLAVERY

ARGUING ABOUT SLAVERY

The Great Battle in the United States Congress

WILLIAM LEE MILLER

New York Alfred A. Knopf

1996

THIS IS A BORZOI BOOK
PUBLISHED BY ALFRED A. KNOPF, INC.

Published in the United States by Alfred A. Knopf, Inc., New York, and simultaneously in Canada by Random House of Canada Limited, Toronto. Distributed by Random House, Inc., New York.

Library of Congress Cataloging-in-Publication Data
Miller, William Lee.
Arguing about slavery: the great battle in the United States Congress / William Lee Miller. — 1st ed.
p. cm.
Includes bibliographical references and index.
ISBN 0-394-56922-9
1. United States—Politics and government—1815–1861.
2. Slavery—United States—History—19th century.
3. United States. Congress—Freedom of debate.
4. Adams, John Quincy, 1767–1845.
I. Title.
E338.M65 1996
973.5—dc20 95-35075
CIP

Manufactured in the United States of America
Published January 19, 1996
Second Printing, March 1996

to L.C.M.M.

Contents

PART IV: SHUT THE DOOR IN THEIR FACE

PART V: THE FIRST SON OF THE REPUBLIC

PART VI: THE TEDIUM AND SUBLIMITY OF REPUBLICAN GOVERNMENT

PART VII: THE MOST IMPORTANT QUESTION EVER TO COME BEFORE THE HOUSE

PART VIII: WELCOME TO THE TWENTY-FIFTH CONGRESS OF THE UNITED STATES

PART IX: THE GREAT MORAL MONUMENT

PART X: THE TRIBULATION OF THE WHIGS

PART XI: THE TRIALS

PART I

INTRODUCTIONS

1 / A PERSONAL INTRODUCTION

I DISCOVERED THE TRUE STORY told in these pages while I was working on something else—on "America's moral and intellectual underpinnings," as I rather grandly put it. I had decided to deal with that subject, not a small one, by telling stories. When I came across this one it grabbed me by the collar, threw me upon the floor, sat upon my chest, and insisted on being told.

The other narratives in my project, the ones I had planned to do beforehand, were all quite well known, and perhaps rather obvious: Abigail and John Adams corresponding while John was in Philadelphia getting a new nation started; young James Madison writing memos to himself about the foundations of republicanism;* Abraham Lincoln engaging in relentless moral reasoning. But now I had, sitting, as I say, upon my chest, and pointing an insistent finger at me like Uncle Sam in the World War I recruiting poster, a story that certainly is not well known, yet nevertheless seemed to me to be as heavily weighted with significance as these others.

It deals, as the reader will learn, with the great central test of the American nation, the struggle to end American slavery without destroying the American Union. But it does not deal with the "terrible scourge of war" to which that struggle finally led. This is not a book about the Civil War. The extended occurrence it re-creates took place some years before that war, even before it was clear there would be a war. The preeminent historian of the South's role leading up to the war, William Freehling, has called the events recounted here "the Pearl Harbor of the slavery controversy," but it was part of its compelling attraction that at this Pearl Harbor there were no bombs. Instead, there were arguments.

The exchange of moral, intellectual, and rhetorical firepower would reveal what the war with real bullets one day would mean, as the march of armies and the spilling of blood and the strategy of arms do not.

*This one has been published: *The Business of May Next: James Madison and the Founding* (Charlottesville: University Press of Virginia, 1992).

Soldiers and their generals fight for many causes, worthy and unworthy, and when it comes to the battlefield the considerations may be pretty much the same, whatever the cause. The generals study each other's tactics across the battle lines, often with admiration. They are the technicians of warfare. The soldiers of the contending armies display courage (and sometimes cowardice), and the people they fight for make heroic sacrifices (or exploit the war for gain) on both or all sides, although perhaps to different degrees and in different ways. To learn what the fighting and the courage and sacrifices meant one must look elsewhere, behind the physical contest to loyalties and emotions, thoughts and ideas, moral convictions and arguments. One must ask what moral and mental content shaped the decisions that brought these people to the battlefield. Of no war is that more true than the American Civil War.

That war was not a contest initiated by monarchs, nobles, generals, or magistrates simply for some reason of state. When one has said all there is to say about old-fashioned power politics in the American Civil War, there is still an enormous remainder. That war was, in a defining way, a clash of moral ideas and loyalties, both sides claiming descent from the American Revolution.

It was certainly a part of the attraction of this "Pearl Harbor" to me that it took place mostly on the floor of the House of Representatives. This was not simply a discussion among the locals around the stove in the general store, important though such discussions, in a republic, may sometimes be; this was formal debate on the House floor on the part of the representatives the people had chosen and the Constitution had empowered to make law.

I found the records for this nine-year contest in the House to be full and rich and very lively. (Notice that I do not say "accurate.") Perhaps you would be tempted to say, as popular prejudice surely would say, that nothing could be duller than the written record of congressional debates (unless possibly the debates themselves); you could, of course, compose your own jokes on that well-worked topic. But that was not the general attitude in the early years of the republic, and it was not mine when I read the pages of the *Congressional Globe*, even with the ink smudges and small type.

For a citizen of the second quarter of the nineteenth century the closely printed columns of the *Globe*, or, more likely, of his own local penny paper reprinting long congressional speeches, were a more potent equivalent of today's C-Span. There were not many competitors. Politics was your baseball and maybe your situation comedy as well. The rhythms of life allowed you, still, to read the full text of a many-columned speech. And you had not yet come to take for granted this fragile new continent-sized republic; you had not yet developed the modern forms of cynicism about the legislative bodies at its center. What happened in Congress mattered.

For my part, reading the record of these ancient debates was the opposite of dull; I kept wanting to quote more than was practicable. The record, as I say, was not perfect on the point of accuracy, but the flaws in that regard helped to remind the reader that not only had real people spoken these words (or something close to these words); real people, present at that moment, had tried to record them.

The *Congressional Record* of today did not yet exist in the 1830s and 1840s. The *Congressional Globe* and its sometime competitor the *Register of Debates* were records of the debates in the House and the Senate kept by private printing firms—Blair and Rives, Gales and Seaton—that competed for selection as official printer. They had partisan and factional alliances, and sometimes these would show through in the record. They would send a reporter to the chamber to copy down what he could; if his attention wandered, some solon's great flight of oratory might be lost to history. Congressmen would often hand a full copy of their remarks to the reporter, or carry it around to the printer's office the next morning, and in that case the full speech text would spread itself on the page. The reporter making his own effort to get down what was said might scramble to reproduce it all as best he could, in the congressman's voice, or he might shift without warning into third person: "He said . . ." Or he might just give a swift reporter's summary: "The congressman spoke at great length on the petition question, mentioning the Magna Carta." Long speeches would receive short summary; short exchanges would be captured in full. A sleepy reporter would confuse one congressman from Massachusetts with another, and the printer's office, in haste, would get the date wrong. Sometimes the reporter would simply characterize what was happening on the floor, without trying to record its substance: "After a very long and noisy discussion"; "interrupted by deafening cries to order"; "great agitation in the House"; "Great confusion here prevailed, so that it was impossible to hear with distinction." The confession that the reporter could not hear was spread upon the record, apparently without embarrassment, fairly often: "Some remarks were here made by the Speaker not heard by the Reporter"; "Mr. Everett offered some remarks which were not sufficiently understood by the Reporter to enable him to give them"; "Mr. Weller and Mr. Holmes conversed across each other, but of what passed the Reporter has no idea." Paradoxically, the limitations and errors and personal touches reassure the reader of the essential value of the record, by reminding him that the reporter, an actual human being, was really there, trying to record what he heard and saw.

And in the printed result of his scribblings I could discern a tremendous argument and parliamentary battle. As I read, a century and a half later, what these congressmen said, I could feel the steam rising from the pages, and with those delusions of grandeur with which an excited writer sometimes begins a new project, I decided that I would *re-create* that nine-year battle—not simply to summarize and report it, but to show it happening.

There was more than Congress in this story; the "people" were there, too, in the form of signatures scribbled on thousands of petitions, with which they inundated Congress. As a republican would understand this new government, Congress is not an entity enclosed within itself, but is representative and (to whatever degree) responsive, moved and shaped in the end by currents in the people's understanding.

And this episode had, as stories ought to have, something of a hero. He might even be presented as a profile in courage of a man for all seasons. Or almost all seasons. This rather unlikely hero was John Quincy Adams, an ex-president of the United States, an old man in his late sixties and his seventies. In addition to his other virtues, he was a world-class journal keeper, and the multiple volumes of his daily record made another rich source for the re-creating of this story. He does not appear immediately in what follows but will appear in due time, and his heroism, such as it may be, will I hope be apparent to the reader. But this is not primarily the story of a hero, or of multiples of heroes and heroines, nor to be sure of villains either, but of institutions and ideas, and of the underpinnings of American democracy.

The fact that I had not known about this historical episode was, I confess, one reason it placed a claim on me. Although it was (as it seemed to me) of considerable historical significance, in what it led to and certainly in what it displayed, it was scarcely known, even to the well-read. Once you know what the story is, you can make your own test in the circles of your acquaintance, to see whether even the most elementary facts about it are known.

As I rounded into the home stretch in the writing of this book, William Freehling published his book *Road to Disunion*, which has a section on this episode, as it fit within his topic. In introducing that section, Freehling, by his exclamations about the ignorance of it on the part even of Civil War buffs and professional historians, gave authoritative support to my sense that this is a little-known event. "Antebellum specialists who can explain picky details of the Kansas-Nebraska and Fugitive Slave controversies," he wrote, "might flunk an exam" on this controversy. Contemporaries, however, had no such vacuum of knowledge: they knew about it in detail, and recognized its importance.

Why has this story come to be so little known? Let us cite several reasons, as speculation. Because the great preoccupation with the Civil War soaks up, or overwhelms, everything that falls just outside its boundaries. Because, republican principle notwithstanding, we are a great deal better at writing about, and a great deal more interested in reading about, battles with blood and bullets on the battlefield than contests with arguments and speeches in legislative halls. (One of the testing features of the present book—a challenge indeed—is to try to make an extended legislative battle interesting to a general reader.) Because after 1876 the impulse toward healing and reconciliation between the North and the white South thrust into the shadow of forgetfulness the contentious events *before* the war, in which the arguments against the evils of slavery were continuously put forward, and the evil effects of slavery on the body politic were blatantly displayed; one wanted to forget all that. Because in the twentieth century popular culture, from *The Birth of a Nation* to *Gone with the Wind*, accepted myths that shifted values, and put the long, difficult, honorable struggle against slavery out of the picture—or, worse, into distortion and caricature.

Even now, with the changes that have occurred in the studying and writing of history since the 1960s, I wonder whether this episode can be given its value and its weight. The recovery of the history of American slaves, and of, as we now say, African-Americans, is an immensely important and worthy development, but it will not necessarily lead to the uncovering of a story like this one, in which virtually all the participants are free and white. The enormous shifting of vision so that social and domestic life, and in particular the role of women, comes into view is of great importance and value, too, but will not necessarily lead to the center of this story. Women play a large role in it, but not at its center, which is all male. The recovery of the peoples at the margins, outside the usual high history of top political figures and events—of the peoples on the fringe instead of the "establishment"—is also an important and worthy recent development, but although there are important characters originally on the edge of society, this story does not deal, primarily, with the margins or the fringe. Paradoxically, this hidden story takes place, principally, smack in the middle of the establishment. So to include it in your picture of America's past you have to widen your lens in a different way from these salutary recent enlargements. You have to focus on republican institutions, and what they mean.

2 / A FORMAL INTRODUCTION: COMPLETING THE WORK OF THE FOUNDERS

Before the Time Before the War

IT IS UNDERSTANDABLE THAT Americans in the years since it ended, very much including the bloody twentieth century, have been preoccupied with the Civil War. It stands as an obvious giant fact in our common experience and national collective memory. The wounds went deep, the legends are abundant, the romance is thick, the stakes were very high, and the scars are still with us more than a century and a quarter, and several other wars, later. It was, as is often said, the first "modern" war, with conscription on both sides, and with grisly pitched battles that would grind away the lives of thousands in an afternoon. In the end, 620,000 American combatants, on both sides, died—as the historian James McPherson observes, more than have been killed in all other American wars, including the two world wars of the twentieth century and Korea and Vietnam, *combined.* And this was at a time when the total population of the United States was fewer than 32 million people.

The Civil War cut through American life like a ragged blade and had lasting effects not only in the obvious ways, on America's history and politics and world role, but in myriad less obvious ways. The looming mountain of the Civil War, in our memory more than a century later, casts an obscuring shadow on the contest over the institution of slavery in the years before the war came.

But for the purposes of this story, take a giant step in imagination back over the war—or two giant steps—into the time before it came, and before anyone was aware that it would come. The historian David Potter, in his book *The Impending Crisis,* notes the difficulty under which historians labor (he might have said citizens, too) in understanding the stretch of time with which he deals—from the end of the Mexican War in 1848 to the outbreak of the Civil War in 1861—because they know that the Civil War, with all its consequences, will come. They (we) interpret "antebellum" America as exactly that: before-the-war America. And because we know what it is "before," we bend our interpretations to fit that outcome and have great difficulty fathoming the situation, and the choices, of those who were living at that time.

We know, as they did not, not only that there would come the terrible scourge of war but also that there would be an Emancipation Proclamation in 1863, and a Thirteenth Amendment in 1865, and two more post–Civil War amendments, and that the day of jubilee would come and that slaves would be emancipated and that the land of the free, however imperfect in other regards, would thereafter and presumably forever be a land in which there could constitutionally be no bondage, no involuntary servitude, none of that blight that the Constitution-writers of 1787 deliberately kept themselves from naming. We know that the time would come when all who dwelt in this land thenceforth would be forever free. But the Americans in the years before the war did not know that.

Imagine the situation not in the 1850s or late 1840s, after the Mexican War, when the leaves already were whirling and the trees already bending with the strong winds which would culminate in the hurricane of Civil War (that period really was "antebellum"), but in the 1830s and early 1840s, when a new breeze was arising among many currents in the political weather. Shift the focus of attention from that war-to-come, and ask instead about the institution of slavery itself. In the 1830s one did not know that a cataclysmic Civil War would come, but one did know that the apparently invincible institution of American slavery was an inescapable present reality.

"Slavery Can Never Be Abolished"

Imagine how formidable the institution of slavery then appeared—how impossible to eliminate. Think how securely it would have seemed to be woven into the fabric of the nation's life. Slavery had become, by the second quarter of the nineteenth century, an immense, rooted institution. American slavery, many believed, and a congressman from South Carolina argued at length on the floor of the U.S. Congress, could *never* be abolished.

This congressman, James Henry Hammond, who will make a brief but pivotal appearance in the story to come—perhaps one can say that he was in the lead airplane at this rhetorical Pearl Harbor, and dropped the first parliamentary bomb—argued his point at great length on the House floor on February 1, 1836. One reason Hammond said slavery could not be abolished dealt in the terms that a later century would particularly understand, economics. When making the point that emancipation by government action was economically unfeasible, he cited these figures:

> **[Hammond]:** There are about 2,300,000 slaves at this moment in the United States, and their annual increase is about 60,000. Sir, even the British Government did not dare to emancipate its enslaved West India subjects without some compensation. They gave them [the owners] about sixty percent of their value. It could scarcely be expected that this Government would undertake to free our slaves without paying for them. Their value, at $400, average, (and they are now worth more than that) would amount to upwards of nine hundred millions. The value of their annual increase, alone, is twenty-four millions of dollars; so that to free them in one hundred years, without the expense of taking them from the country, would require an annual appropriation of between thirty-three and thirty-four millions of dollars. The thing is physically impossible.*

Gigantic, unthinkable figures at a time when the total annual receipts of the federal government, from all sources and for all purposes, were not more than the figure Hammond cited; in 1830 they had been only $24,844,000.

Abraham Lincoln, making speeches in New England twenty-four years after Hammond's speech, used a story to illustrate how such big money interferes with understanding. There was, said Lincoln, an argument between two pastors. One pointed to a word in the Bible. "Do you see that word?" "Yes, of course." Then the first pastor put a gold coin over the word. "Do you see it now?" Lincoln's New England audiences, like one at New Haven, would begin to laugh in anticipation of his application of this joke even before he stated it.

"Whether the owners of this species of property [slaves] do really see it as it is," Lincoln went on, "it is not for me to say, but if they do, they see it as it is through 2,000,000,000 of dollars, and that is a pretty thick coating." The audience laughed. "Certain it is," Lincoln continued, "that they do not see it as we see it. Certain it is, that this two thousand million of dollars, invested in this species of property, all so concentrated that the mind can grasp it at once—this immense pecuniary interest, has its influence upon their minds."

*The quotations from congressmen in this book have been taken from the *Congressional Globe*, with the date specified in the text, except where noted otherwise. Some quotations come from the rival congressional publication during part of this period, the *Register of Debates*; where that is used the text will say so.

The pecuniary interest was by no means confined to the South. The slave trade, although formally declared illegal in 1808, had been carried on—as Southern apologists regularly pointed out—by Northerners. The Northern textile industry, among many others, had strong ties to a Southern slave-based economy.

Suppose today some dominant industry, built into the lives and fortunes of a great many people—to a degree of the whole nation—were found to be morally repugnant; what difficulties there would then be in extracting it from the nation's life! Think how difficult it has been today to win victories over the tobacco industry, when the deleterious effects of tobacco are known and officially promulgated, and when the larger self-interest, the self-interest of millions—of all citizens in the end—is engaged on the opposite side to the evil. In the case of slavery the respective roles of self-interest and of disinterested conscience were differently distributed, with comparatively little immediate mass self-interest (among the relevant, voting white public) available to the evil's opponents. The tobacco industry is much smaller proportionately, and more narrowly located geographically, and much less powerful (powerful though it is), than was the institution of slavery.

Slavery was not only an immense industry in itself, but had fundamental ties to other industries—cotton, rice, indigo, and tobacco and others directly, many others less directly. Slavery was integral to the life and culture, as John C. Calhoun kept saying, of an entire region, of eleven states (in 1835) of the Union—of almost half of the nation. When a "pecuniary interest" has that magnitude, it is a formidable opponent indeed. Rationalizations are supplied, positions are softened, conflict is avoided, compromises are sought, careers are protected, life goes on. Don't try to change what can't be changed. Adapt to it.

There were, in addition, in the case of the slave industry, unique elements of fear. What would happen if the slaves were freed? Millions of systematically mistreated people would suddenly be out from under the social control that slavery provided. North and South, this point exercised no small influence on popular attitudes.

The apprehensions about what it might mean were heightened by the all too familiar complex of guilt, prejudice, and disdain that accompanies the cruel distinctions of race. Unfortunately, Americans at all times in our history have known the powerful undertow of that irrational current. At the end of the twentieth century, although there have been enormous changes, there still are discernible patterns of what has come to be called "racism." The changes have been sizable enough, however, for an effort of imagination to be required in order to grasp just how much worse the "racism" was in the days of slavery. Extrapolate backward from today's worst white attitudes, and multiply by a large number. If one reads the Lincoln-Douglas debates from 1858, for one accessible example, one finds in the speeches of Stephen Douglas, a respected mainstream politician soon to be a major party's candidate for president, remarks about blacks that would not be uttered in the late twentieth century even by marginal demagogues like David Duke. No code words were necessary then; blatant racial stereotypes were common currency. Douglas repeatedly made a pseudo-clever remark comparing Negroes to crocodiles, for which Lincoln rebuked him, that was greeted by laughter and cheers from his audience. In 1864, in the midst of the Civil War, the Democratic Party's campaign for the presidency used racial stereotypes and fears as its central strategy, with a "vulgarity"—James McPherson observes—that can scarcely be believed. It was in that campaign that the word "miscegenation" was invented, with a great deal of oratory about the alleged threat to white women—one's daughters, typically—posed by Negro (or "nigger") males. That was not on the fringes; that was a major party's campaign.

In the middle of the twentieth century, when some states still had racial segregation by law, the way racial discrimination and racial prejudice mutually reinforced each other was seen by analysts to be a vicious circle. Most people take their cues from what they see, and what is said, around them. They take uncriticized, as a given, the world as it is. In the 1930s and 1940s and early 1950s, one would see African Americans on the less desirable side of the tracks, in what would come to be called "ghettos," in shacks and in slums, in menial positions and stereotyped roles; that in turn encouraged and supported the disdain and exclusion, the jokes, the thoughtless dismissal, the prejudiced attitudes that, again in turn, gave powerful support to the maintenance of the exclusionary social patterns. The line in the mind and the line in society reinforced each other. Imagine then how much worse it would have been when the line in society was not just racial segregation but *slavery*. Try to imagine how all the images of that terrible institution would have reinforced racial stereotypes and disdain—and what a vested interest there would have been in maintaining and reinforcing that "racist" combination.

There was a melancholy democratic paradox in American political culture, becoming more and more evident exactly in the days of our story, with the spread of "Jacksonian democracy." Government of, by, and for the people, celebrating the virtues of the common man, was the great moral core and practical triumph of the new nation. But that democratic government, and aspects of its ethos, worked perversely with respect to American slavery and race—with respect, that is, to those who had been radically excluded at the outset, marked, and subordinated. Spreading democracy broadened the majority rule of a citizenry that was almost altogether white, and very heavily prejudiced on race. American democracy came very close to making itself a racially exclusive "democracy" for "democratic" reasons.

IN ADDITION TO THESE facts of enormous power—economic interest and racial fear, exclusion, and disdain—there were in the United States in the early days potent *political* facts, in two forms. One form was the political power of the slaveholders. Slavery was an enormous *present* interest in the United States, not only in that millions of black slaves were a large part of the population, arousing racial fears, but also in that their *owners* were a major and very powerful part of the population, too, strategically located, already from the outset in the highest places. The Constitution had made its original compromises. In place of a king the nation had had as its first chief executive and symbol a hero-president who was a slaveholder; in the story to be told here, a Virginia congressman, in the midst of debate, will point triumphantly to George Washington's picture hanging in front of the House of Representatives itself. There he is! A slaveholder! Five of the first seven presidents were slaveholders; for thirty-two of the nation's first thirty-six years, forty of its first forty-eight, fifty of its first sixty-four, the nation's president was a slaveholder. The powerful office of Speaker of the House was held by a slaveholder for twenty-eight of the nation's first thirty-five years. The president pro tem of the Senate was virtually always a slaveholder. The majority of cabinet members and—very important—of justices on the Supreme Court were slaveholders. The slaveholding Chief Justice Roger Taney, appointed by the slaveholding President Andrew Jackson to succeed the slaveholding John Marshall, would serve all the way through the decades before the war into the years of the Civil War itself; it would be a radical change of the kind the slaveholders feared when, in 1863, President Lincoln would appoint the antislavery politician Salmon P. Chase of Ohio to succeed Taney. But by then, even *having* a President Lincoln had been the occasion for the slaveholders to rebel, to secede, and to resort to arms.

One cites these facts about the formidable presence of the slave interest—to which, of course, dozens more could be added—not as later unhistorical moralizers sometimes do, as an indictment of the nation, but for almost the opposite purpose: to dramatize the immense power of the interest that the nation would nevertheless overcome.

In addition to the domination by slaveholders at the center of government, there was in the case of American slavery a further major difficulty that flowed from the original American political arrangements. It is important to remind ourselves how much more difficult it was to end slavery in the United States than in England or France. The emancipationists in England, who managed finally in 1833 to obtain a vote in Parliament ending slavery in the West Indies, just before the events to be recounted in this book (and as one cause of those events, England showing the way to its former colonies across the water), had two enormous advantages over their American counterparts: the slaves they emancipated were all safely outside the sceptered isle of England, and the decision to emancipate could unquestionably be made by the one central organ of government. So it had been also for the French revolutionaries in the eighteenth century, who on coming into power proclaimed the end of serfdom throughout France. That point is sometimes presented as evidence of the superiority of the French Revolution to the American, but before we agree we should look at the radically differing circumstances.

In the United States the contrasting disadvantages were closely interwoven. The slaves to be freed were not to be found in some distant islands or colonies but were a very large reality very much present within the body politic—one-sixth of the population at the time of the Revolution, one-eighth at the time of the Civil War. Moreover, they were, as Lincoln said in his Second Inaugural, "not distributed generally over the Union, but localized in the Southern part of it." And this American nation was no ancient unitary kingdom but a recently formed and still fragile "union" of former colonies, now states, in which the individual states could plausibly claim to be "sovereign." They could claim to have preexisted that union and to have formed it, and could claim to retain all powers not expressly given over to it. At the extreme they could claim even the right to "nullify" federal laws, or to "interpose" state sovereignty between the federal authority and the people, as South Carolina had done, in the Nullification Crisis, just a few years before the events to be told here.

The new nation had a written constitution composed by delegates from, and ratified by conventions in, those states; that constitution had in it fundamental compromises on slavery, fundamental protections of "property," and fundamental protections of state authority and limitations on federal authority. States' rights and strict construction of the Constitution were plausible arguments against any interference with slavery in the Southern states, and Northern politicians or citizens who wanted to steer clear of that explosive subject could justify doing so with constitutional scruples. Even citizens much distressed by slavery could believe they had to say: it's in the bond. We agreed to a union with states in which slavery was an important existing institution. Interfering with slavery in the slaveholding states is constitutionally impermissible.

This *federal* aspect of the new nation could furnish Northerners both an excuse (what happens in South Carolina is not our responsibility in Massachusetts; we made an agreement) and also a threat (attacks on slavery will destroy the union). So for that reason, too, ending slavery in the United States was an enormously more difficult task than in England or France. It was a huge cancer that had been present already in the American body politic at its birth, intertwined throughout all its original organs.

THINKERS AND STATESMEN AND leaders and realistic politicians of all stripes and attachments believed that American slavery could not be ended—not by deliberate human action. Those who supported slavery belligerently asserted that it could not be done; those who deplored slavery sorrowfully granted that it could not be done; those who had unsorted mixtures of opinions—the great majority, let us guess—felt that it could not be done, and did not want to hear about it. You know how it is with an unpleasant subject in public affairs, remote from you, that you don't know what to think about; you would just as soon not hear about it, and you become annoyed with those who insist on bringing it up.

Many consoled themselves with the belief that the end of slavery would come about somehow and eventually, by the gradual unfolding of historical forces—by the expansion of the nation westward, into land whose climate and resources made slavery economically unprofitable. Daniel Webster was one who propounded this convenient view: slavery's demise was inevitable, so we would not have to do—*should* not do—anything to make it happen. Some scholars down to at least the middle of the twentieth century echoed this notion: slavery could have been ended just by the passage of time. In the twentieth century, white citizens often expressed a comparable attitude about the Jim Crow system that had hardened into place in the late nineteenth: time will change it—and *only* time will change it. Those who expressed this view were often suspiciously quick to insist that no positive human action—particularly no law—could hasten the slow workings of time against racial segregation. "You can't change hearts by law," it was said, and racial discrimination could be ended only by a "slow process of education," and not by any action whatever. Many who said that not only did no such educating, but used the insistent passivity of these ideas to oppose ("too fast") any effort to educate. It is a revealing curiosity of American popular attitudes that a people so practical, so optimistic, so energetic, so direct, so quick to say that anything can be done by an effort of will—the impossible takes a little longer—on other topics, have regularly and abruptly turned to the opposite extreme on issues of slavery and race: nothing can be done. Leave it alone. Don't meddle. It cannot be fixed. American slavery and racial injustice cannot be ended by direct human decision and action.

The Double Legacy of the Founders

This deeply perplexing national plight and scandal had one of its roots in the work of those great men, the American founders. They had not really distinguished themselves on the appalling subject of slavery, although they did better than subsequent generations, living in a wholly different setting, would sometimes grant.

They left to the nation they founded a double legacy. In their declaration to a candid world they had explicitly grounded their claim to liberty in the universal moral order, explicitly tied it to *equality*, and explicitly extended it universally. All men are created equal, they said. From that equal creation all human beings derived an inalienable right to liberty. And this affirmation of liberty, and also of equality, was by no means a peculiarity of Thomas Jefferson's, or of the Declaration; it was a defining component of the Revolution and of the founding throughout. But at the time they proclaimed these things, the founders were themselves denying equal liberty to 697,000 human beings, or one-sixth of the population.

The principal founders were aware of the contradiction between slavery and the nation's moral substance, and they did make some important statements, and take some important actions, against it. One may emphasize what they accomplished with respect to slavery or what they failed to accomplish, but in any case they left to the new nation an unstable mixture of the accomplishments and the failures—to be resolved after they were gone. They bequeathed a double doubleness: two sections, North and South, differing significantly, and two claims about slavery, denouncing it and at least implicitly accepting it.

At the beginning the two sets of two had not entirely coincided. Both slavery as an institution and antislavery as a sentiment had existed in all the colonies. There was antislavery sentiment in the South, particularly in Virginia and the upper South, and there were slaves in the North along with some defense of the institution. But in the half-century that followed the founding, each element of each pair came to be associated primarily with one element of the other—the sorting of which was sharply accentuated at the time we will deal with here.

When the quarrel with England started in the middle of the eighteenth century, *all* the colonies of British America had slaves. Slaves constituted 14 percent of the population in New York, 7.5 percent in New Jersey, 10 percent even in the New England colony of Rhode Island—not trivial percentages. The ending of slavery in the *North* was a significant accomplishment of the idealism of the American Revolution—one that has been forgotten because Americans have no memory that it even needed to be done.* Abolishing Northern slavery was a result of "the Contagion of Liberty," as Bernard Bailyn called it: the spread of the ideas of the Revolution. Ending slavery in the North was not easy, and should not be taken for granted. But the result of that major accomplishment was to isolate slavery in the South, as the peculiar institution of that region.

The same thing happened with respect to the territories. Defenders of Thomas Jefferson against critics of his conduct on race and slavery cite as the most clear-cut of his actions against slavery his authorship, while he was a member of Congress under the Articles in 1784, of a provision that would have excluded slavery from all of the territory to the West—the land that would become Alabama and Kentucky, as well as Ohio and Indiana. But that provision failed in Congress by one state's vote, which in turn was changed, as he lamented, by the illness of one delegate. In the Northwest Ordinance of 1787, then, slavery was excluded only from the territory north of the Ohio River—another significant accomplishment, not to be taken for granted, but one which again had the effect of isolating slavery in the southern portion of the country.

The founding doubleness that had already been present in the colonies was manifest as well in the federal Constitution of 1787, the fundamental law of the new nation. The Constitution did recognize slavery, and yet at the same time it did not.

Although one may skip quickly over them, there are in the Constitution three clauses dealing specifically, although not by name, with slavery. The reader will find one of them very early, probably on the first page of the consulted copy, in Article I, section 2, paragraph 3. If it were not such a serious subject, the circumlocutory verbosity would be comic: "Representatives and direct taxes shall be apportioned among the several States which may be included within this Union, according to their respective numbers, which shall be determined by adding to the whole number of free persons, including those bound to service for a term of years, and excluding Indians not taxed, three-fifths of all other persons." Discard the window dressing about direct taxes, which gave the provision the appearance of a sectional compromise, but which in practice proved to be mean-

*Vermont in 1777, on becoming a state, was by its own constitutional prohibition the first state without slavery; Massachusetts, by constitutional interpretation, was next, in 1781. In most other states, emancipation was gradual. New Jersey, in 1804, enacted the last emancipation act of a Northern state.

ingless: there were no "direct taxes" thus to be apportioned among the states. This is a provision for determining the number of representatives in the House that there shall be from each state. Those representatives are to be apportioned to population. To determine the population of a state for this purpose, count the free persons (implication: there are some others who are *not* free). Include the persons—indentured servants—"bound to service for a term of years" (implication: there are others bound to service whose "service" has no term). Exclude Indians not taxed. And—count three-fifths of the "other persons" who are left by this curious roundabout residual method. These unnamed other persons are slaves. This is the infamous three-fifths clause, the "federal ratio," the point of which is sometimes today slightly misunderstood. It has to do not with the rights or moral worth of black persons but with the respective power of slave and free states in the House of Representatives. The slave states would have been happy to have replaced the fraction with the whole number, "equality," if you will; the free states would have preferred that it be not three-fifths but zero.

Since the number of votes a state has in the electoral college, the constitutional invention that chooses presidents, is determined by the number of senators plus the number of House members allocated to that state, the three-fifths addition to the slave states' House delegations augmented also their votes for president—which may have had more than a little to do with the fact, noted above, that for forty of the first forty-eight years of the nation's life there were slaveholders from slave states in the office of president. One of those who particularly resented the role of the three-fifths clause in warping electoral college votes was John Adams, who would probably have been reelected president over Thomas Jefferson in 1800 if the three-fifths ratio had not augmented the vote of the Southern states.

The other two specific constitutional provisions have something of the same quality of morally embarrassed circumlocutory prose to avoid using the word "slave." One of them, the fugitive slave clause, added without much debate late in the convention as the result of some offstage deal, is morally embarrassing in every way; it committed the whole country to the return of slaves to their owners. The other, the clause permitting the ending of the slave trade after twenty years (but not allowing it to be ended until that time), is morally ambiguous: you may emphasize what it permitted, or what it denied.

In addition to these three provisions dealing specifically with slavery, there were other parts of the Constitution that, from the facts of the time, implicitly absorbed and protected it—a right to *property,* for the most important example, in which property in slaves was presumed to be included, on the same footing as all the other rights and liberties protected by the Constitution. And there were the various provisions for the common defense and security: presumably Vermont's Green Mountain fighters for freedom could be called out to defend against an insurrection, in behalf of freedom, by the slaves of South Carolina. This last point would loom ominously over the horizon fairly often in the speeches and arguments and worries of the story told in these pages.

Why did the framers, designing their charter of liberty, agree to these pernicious provisions? Most of the founders—all of the great ones—disapproved of slavery. But that disapproval was neither their primary commitment nor the object of the great meeting in Philadelphia in May of 1787.

That meeting took place in the real world. Its purpose was to form a more satisfactory government for the Union of the American States—an extremely delicate and difficult undertaking, as events would prove, enough so that quite sober men were moved to attach to its successful completion the word "miracle." And the states with which they were trying to carry off this enormously delicate and sensitive task had all once been, and were almost all still, slaveholding communities (as we have said, even in the North, although that was rapidly changing). They were also "sovereign." Or claimed to be.

It was necessary to negotiate with these "sovereign" slaveholding states as they presented themselves in the form of delegates there in a room in the Pennsylvania State House, in order to get the votes (the votes of *states*) to produce a constitution, and it would be necessary to deal with them again in the form of delegates to the ratifying conventions in the states in order to get this new ship of state under sail. So the delegates in Philadelphia who said they saw slavery to be a moral evil—as almost all of them who spoke about it said they did—faced a difficult situation. They were trying to form a government among a group of states that included at least two that insisted absolutely that no constitution could be ratified that contained a restriction on slavery. When James Madison wrote to Jefferson in Paris about the Constitutional Convention, he included in all the many pages of his report only one brief paragraph touching on slavery, and that as an aspect of "the adjustment of the different interests of different parts of the Continent." This brief passage—Madison writing to Jefferson about the Constitutional Convention!—describes the conflict and the compromise over regional differences, and concludes with its only words about slavery: "S. Carolina and Georgia were inflexible on the point of slaves."

South Carolina and Georgia were inflexible, we might say—and the rest of the country was flexible. We can cite the very real limits on what the framers could possibly have done on this subject, but it has to be said also that their commitment was not overwhelming. Suppose Madison and those who worked with him had put the restriction of slavery as high on their list of things they would fight for as he and Jefferson had put religious liberty in the long struggle that led to the adoption of Jefferson's great Virginia Statute for Religious Freedom, with its ringing declaration that "Almighty God hath created the mind free," and its separating of church from state. On that issue they took the lead, and were well ahead of opinion, and made alliances and fought hard—Jefferson was to say toward the end of his life that it was the severest fight he ever engaged in. Or suppose that Madison and others in Philadelphia had cared as much about, and fought as hard on, issues respecting slavery as they did on the issue of state equality in the Senate—on which issue they almost broke up the Convention. But they did not fight against South Carolina and Georgia and the other slave states with anything like the principled persistence with which they resisted Delaware and New Jersey and the other small states. On slavery they did not have the resolute strength that their opposition did. The historian Don Fehrenbacher writes that at the Constitutional Convention and for the first half century of the nation's life, slavery was an *interest* ("concentrated, persistent, practical, and testily defensive") whereas antislavery was only a *sentiment* ("diffuse, sporadic, moralistic, and tentative"). The failure of the founders, and particularly the framers, to do more to restrict slavery stems not only from the realities of their situation—limiting enough—but also from the contrast those two terms imply—the weakness of the "sentiment" on the one side and the brute strength of the "interest" on the other.

But that is not the end of what is to be said about the founders on slavery. We said they left a double legacy. In addition to the compromises there were those other actions by the framers that would enable, for example, Abraham Lincoln, in his speeches in the 1850s, to argue plausibly that they not only disapproved of slavery as a moral evil but intended to set it on the road to extinction. Even the specific constitutional provisions admit of some mitigating interpretation. It is possible to interpret the clause on the slave trade as antislavery, because it did allow Congress by 1808 to end it—and Congress, at the initiative of President Jefferson, did end it on the first day of 1808. That, again, is an accomplishment that is not to be taken for granted. In fact, William Freehling has written that this ending of the slave trade was "probably the most important slavery legislation Congress ever passed and among the most important American laws on any subject."

And there is something else to be said about the specific wording of the Constitution—about what is not there. The use of elaborate euphemisms and circumlocutory verbal devices to avoid the words "slave" and "slavery," at considerable cost at least to brevity and possibly to clarity, had an important purpose. It was explicitly designed to keep the Constitution from recognizing, as James Madison put it, that there could be "property in men." In its silent way it was rather a touching appeal to future generations to do what the framers themselves were not able to do. They would not speak the word, not in this document.

It is certainly true that the framers might have written different words, not only with respect to slavery but also with respect to race. The framers had extracted the three-fifths "federal ratio" from an act of Congress under the Articles of Confederation, which said that the formula for counting people in the states would be "the whole number of *white* and other free citizens and inhabitants of every age, sex & condition" (my emphasis). The framers, with that precedent from the old Congress as their source—for the rest of it they followed that act almost verbatim—nevertheless took out the word "white." By that significant editing the repugnant notion that this would be a "white man's country" lost any constitutional foothold.

To see what might have been written on slavery, instead of the framers' awkward but worthy circumlocutory silence, we may look forward seventy-four years to the blunt explicitness of the Constitution of the Confederate States of America. With none of the framers' moral qualms, the Confederates would use the words "slave" and "slavery" throughout, and would show no reluctance to employ racial categories in their national instrument; they would refer, for example, to "the importation of negroes of the African race." They would add to the text of the U.S. Constitution, which in general they followed closely, this striking new civil right (my emphasis): "No bill of attainder, *ex post facto* law, *or law denying or impairing the right of property in negro slaves*, shall be passed."

The framers of 1787 avoided anything like that, and their deliberate avoidance of the words "slave" and "slavery" (and "negro" and "African" and "white") is significant. Don Fehrenbacher minted a good figure of speech to describe the framers' doubleness, their specific reluctant provisions about slavery but their refusal to name it: "It is as though the Framers were half-consciously trying to frame two constitutions, one for their own time and the other for the ages, with slavery viewed bifocally—that is, plainly visible at their feet, but disappearing when they lifted their eyes."

A Nation-Defining Argument

But that is not all. The founders bequeathed more than compromises with slavery, more than their "sentiment" against slavery, with its comparative weakness and lack of persistence, more than their meticulous avoidance—lifting their eyes to the future—of any explicit verbal recognition that there could be "property in men." They also left to the new nation the institutions of representative government. Although the institutions of civil liberty and representative government had no explicit link to the issue of slavery, they provided the openings through which such a manifest injustice could be combated. (To be sure, they also provided the openings through which it could be *defended*, and the defenders almost won.)

Today many Americans dealing with this point would jump instantly to the Bill of Rights, slighting the importance of representative republican government as a whole. But the core accomplishment of the revolutions in England that fed their institutions and their ideals into the makeup of America (the Puritan movement and the Glorious Revolution of 1688) was parliamentary government. Representative government. The forefathers of our forefathers gave a discriminating answer to the question about how a people shall be governed. Not by raw authority or command. Not by deference to inherited privilege. Not by the arm-wrestling and bargaining of great chieftains. Not by blind custom and inertia and impulse. They shall be governed instead by a debating society of their own choosing. They shall be governed by themselves—"self-government"—by the instrument of their chosen representatives. That is to say also that they shall be governed by deliberation—by mutual argument and persuasion.

And then the founders did leave to their heirs also the written protections of their civil liberties—in the bills of rights in the states, and then in the federal Bill of Rights and particularly in the First Amendment. The people shall choose those who shall speak for them, and in an institution—a legislature—in which the members' freedom to speak shall be protected in order that they can dispute and reason and argue and determine the law of the land. Many of our fundamental public freedoms began as freedoms for parliament, for the people's legislature.

The people were guaranteed freedom of "conscience," first of all, and freedoms by which that conscience might be expressed: freedom of speech and freedom of the press. They were guaranteed also another freedom, particularly important in the story to follow, that not many today would think of so quickly: the right of petition, the right to ask one's representatives for redress of grievances. By pulling on the string of this one among the bundle of liberties—the right of petition—the new nation, in the story to be told here, would manage to show itself that in the end those liberties are tied together; they are part of a single construct of liberty of thought and argument. The new nation also would demonstrate to itself that civil liberty was incompatible with the tragic deposit of its colonial past: human slavery.

The founders had left to the nation that possibility. They left not only the unsavory institution of slavery, with their own disapproval hovering over it, but also these other institutions—representative government, government by mutual deliberation, freedom of public argument and of appeal to one's representatives—by which it might be combated and one day overcome.

THE FOUNDERS LEFT YET more than that. If their opposition to slavery was not as robust and consistent and central as one would wish it to have been, they at any rate bequeathed the larger principles out of which their heirs, in a different setting, might develop a more persistent opposition. In other words, they left as a legacy not only the institutions but also the ideals out of which the ending of slavery could be brought about.

The United States had been, to an unusual degree, deliberately founded on universal social ideals. The glue that held it together was not blood or soil or a common religion or a long mythic history but a shared set of principles for the arrangement of society.

Those principles—the nation's moral essence—had been captured most memorably in the most familiar paragraph of the Declaration of Independence, a document that grew in prestige and centrality through the nation's early years. This new people stepped upon the great stage of history, and declared to "a candid world" its reasons: liberty, equality, self-government. The most consequential paragraph of this most potent document set forth self-evident truths that "we hold." The very first of these truths is that all members of the human family are created equal. And "from that equal creation" certain human rights are derived. Those rights are inherent—they cannot be "alienated"—and they are universal. Through the Continental Congress, using Jefferson's pen, the new Americans took the case straight to the *creation*, and to *nature*, and explicitly tied it to *equality* and extended it to all humankind.

These sweeping assertions placed on the defensive any lingering half-suggested subliminal notion that the relevant liberties were really just those of the colonists in British America, or of Englishmen, or of whites, or of property holders, or of males—that the equality we asserted did not extend to servants or the poor or women or the black residents of this or of other continents, that self-government and human rights applied only in a limited sphere. Whatever the limitations in the application that Jefferson and other founders themselves might have made in their own time and place, they wrote better than they knew. Their universal ideals held the promise of an enlarging application in the nation's continuing life. And they themselves knew that the institution of human slavery in their midst was a radical contradiction to those ideals.

Those ideals confronted that institution in the little-known episode to be re-created in the pages that follow. This episode was the first explicit and extended struggle between American slavery and what would be called, in a later century, the American Creed. It was the articulate beginning of a national fork-in-the-road choice between inherited despotism and developing democracy. Or between tragic evil and human ideals.

On the one hand, there was in the new United States, as we have said, human slavery as a rooted institution, growing, powerful. On the other hand, there were the Bill of Rights and the ideas of freedom of conscience and of debate from which it grew, and more broadly there was republicanism—democracy as we should now say—both as constitutional institutions and as ideal. This is a story about a great nation-defining argument between these two parts of the founders' legacy.

PART II

IMMEDIATE REPRESENTATIVES

3 / AN INDIGNANT REBUKE TO THE FANATICS OF THE NORTH

On December 16, 1835, an otherwise undistinguished thirty-eight-year-old congressman named John Fairfield, from York County, Maine, rose upon his legs in the United States House of Representatives to present the first of that session's petitions for the abolition of slavery in the District of Columbia. He was one of the 242 congressmen from the twenty-four states then in the Union. They were gathered—such of them as were present—not in today's House chamber, which did not yet exist, but in the old one, the large semicircular room with the high ceiling and the twenty-four Corinthian columns that one can still find on the second floor of the Capitol, now filled with appalling statues and known as "Statuary Hall."

This first session of the Twenty-fourth Congress—beginning, as sessions then did, in early December—had just started on December 7. While tardy members were gradually making their way to the capital city, the House had chosen its speaker, adopted its rules, appointed its official printer, filled its committees, and bickered over whether congressmen should be allowed to wear hats in the chamber. December 16 was the first day anything noteworthy happened.

According to House rules, the first thirty days of a congressional session were all petition days. Each day's proceedings started off, after an interlude, with the people's representatives hearing what the people wanted to intercede and remonstrate about. Thereafter, as the House got down to business, only every other Monday was a petition day.

Several of the other congressmen, especially from Massachusetts and Vermont and Pennsylvania, were waiting with petitions upon their desks similar to the one Fairfield had in his hand. Fairfield was the first to present such a petition not from any uniqueness in the particular petition he brought forward, nor from any particular eagerness on his part, but rather by the accident of geography and of House procedure. On petition days the clerk would call the roll of the states not in alphabetical order but, by the quaint early House practice, in a geographical order, starting in the North with the state of Maine. And when his state was called, a congressman would rise to present such petitions and resolutions as he wanted to, or felt he had to. So in December of 1835 Maine was called, and it fell to Mr. Fairfield unintentionally to initiate one of the extraordinary passages in the annals of American government.

Introducing a petition did not mean that one necessarily agreed with the petition's point, any more than one necessarily agreed with a speaker or a newspaper whose guaranteed freedom one affirmed. Congressman Fairfield was careful to explain that he did not himself concur in the "prayer" of this petition he presented; he was simply doing his duty for the 172 ladies in his district who had signed it and sent it to him.

A petition asking for the end of slavery in the District of Columbia was nothing new, and not particularly rare. The House had been sporadically receiving petitions for an end to slavery and/or the slave trade since the First Congress, which received such a petition from a group of Philadelphia Quakers. After the establishment of the new federal city in 1800, antislavery petitions had begun to concentrate on the presence of slavery and slave trading in the nation's newly built capital city. Slavery in the District not only was particularly offensive to opponents of slavery, but could not be so plausibly defended by its supporters, who in this case could not invoke states' rights or the original constitutional agreements; the District was not a state, and had not existed when the Constitution was written. Slavery in the District was said, by the classically educated petitioners, to be the Achilles' heel of slavery in the nation. Defending slavery in the District was correspondingly said, by the great opponent of these petitions, John C. Calhoun, who was also classically educated, to be the Thermopylae of Southern civilization.

On this December afternoon, however, the nation's representatives, generally speaking, displayed no eagerness either to attack slavery at its Achilles' heel or to defend Southern civilization at its Thermopylae. The much more prevalent inclination was to wish that the whole subject would go away. The Democratic Party, which held both the office of president and control of Congress, and which was about to enter a presidential election year—1836—without its great hero Andrew Jackson at the head of the ticket, was particularly lacking in eagerness to consider the subject. Its success under Jackson, and its prospects of continuing that success under his vice-president and proposed successor, Martin Van Buren, were founded on an alliance between Southern planters and Northern common folk that excessive concentration on the subject of slavery would threaten.

The new Whig Party, too, had Northern and Southern branches, and in fact its components may have been more deeply divided on the topic of slavery than the Democrats. The history of the next two decades would certainly prove that concentrating on the subject would not be healthy for the Whig Party.

As with the parties, so with the public they represented: the subject of slavery was a great toothache in the national polity that most Americans did not want to hear about or think about. And so it might have been expected that this petition of Fairfield's, and all the others waiting on various Northerners' desks, would be respectfully encouraged to vanish.

The usual practice with petitions on this touchy subject (and often with petitions on other matters as well) had been respectfully to receive them, respectfully to print them, respectfully to assign them to an appropriate committee, and respectfully to allow them to slide thereafter unnoticed into oblivion. Sometimes Congress had been so respectful as to give the abolitionist petitions an answer (invariably the answer, of course, was no). But in the winter of 1835–36 all of this respectfulness was about to wear out.

This was to be the moment, the disinclination of most congressmen and much of the public notwithstanding, when at last the nation's complicated legacy on the subject of African slavery was to force itself into the nation's major forum. The House by its nature could not insulate itself from the currents of public feeling, and the currents on the subject of slavery were now about to become, in some circles, intense.

The more potent intensity in the House was not, as one might expect looking back from the twentieth century, that of the new abolitionists; though they were passionate, they were not powerful, and they were almost nonexistent in the House. The potent new intensity was that of militant slaveholders; their militancy was grounded in what a journalist of the time, Duff Green, called a "morbid sensitivity" that had been provoked by a series of recent events.

The deep mixture of fear and guilt that focused on the possibility of slave revolts had been furnished not long before this session of Congress with an actual instance. The reports of the slave upheavals in Santo Domingo in the Caribbean in the 1790s had been frightening enough, and Denmark Vesey's aborted slave conspiracy in the summer of 1822 had been frightening particularly to the South Carolina low country, but in 1831 in Southampton County, Virginia, the insurrection led by Nat Turner, in which about sixty white people, including women and children, were killed, had escalated those fears across the South.

Many today surveying the whole record remark on the *paucity* of American slave rebellions and slave revolts, given two, three, four million people held in bondage; but a white resident of a slave state in 1835 did not have the luxury of broad historical surveys. There had been, in the recent past, at least one undeniable rebellion, and at least one undeniable conspiracy to rebel, and these were multiplied manyfold in apprehensive Southern imaginations.

It was a staple in Southern polemic that the disgusting abolitionist pamphlets from the North, which had just this year flooded the South, would instigate further slave rebellions. In the debate that was to come in the first session of the Twenty-fourth Congress, one of Mr. Fairfield's colleagues, James Garland, who came from Ivy Depot in Albemarle County, Virginia—Thomas Jefferson's home county—would make this characteristic appeal (on December 23) to his fellow statesmen from the North to understand the plight of Southern males:

> **[Garland]:** We appeal to our brethren of the North in behalf of our wives and of our children . . . for their protection and security against the instigators of midnight murder and assassination.

It may be no serious matter to such Northern folk . . .

> **[Garland]:** . . . to contemplate our plains drenched with blood, in a servile war; they are absent and secure; but to us, who are husbands and fathers, who must be in the midst of it, it is with no slight concern, no ordinary emotion, that we can contemplate, or could see the blood reeking from the bosoms of our wives and children, pouring from wounds inflicted through the instigation of these disturbers of our peace, and enemies of our lives and liberties.

Mr. Garland, no longer appealing for sympathy, followed that characteristically bloody passage with a comment that indicates something of the temper that underlay, in some quarters, the events in this Congress:

> **[Garland]:** . . . we should revenge to the utmost their blood, upon the heads of those who shed it.

Garland's speech represented one new variety of militancy; the cascade of new petitions there on the desks of—among others—Congressmen Fairfield of Maine and Jackson and Briggs of Massachusetts and Slade and Janes of Vermont represented another. John C. Calhoun, the great opponent of the abolitionists, said in the Senate that "[these petitions] do not come as heretofore, singly and far apart, from the quiet routine of the Society of Friends or the obscure vanity of some philanthropic club, but they are sent to us in vast numbers from soured and agitated communities."

So underneath the surface calm of the beginning of the Twenty-fourth Congress, debating whether Congressmen could wear hats or not, a seething argument about slavery was waiting to break through.

Although it had simmered throughout the short history of the new republic, it had come to a boil only once before, in the period 1819–21, when Congress had debated "the Missouri Question"—whether to admit Missouri as a slave state. The wide-ranging debate in that instance, the famous firebell-in-the-night of the history texts, had frightened many with its revelation of the deep fault in the moral and political geology of the new union. Among its most frightening aspects, to South Carolinians and other white residents of the slaveholding states, had been the awareness that the free black Denmark Vesey had been moved to plan his slave revolt in Charleston by reading the arguments in Congress on the Missouri Question. That was what came of unrestrained discussion of human rights in any setting in which slaves and blacks could overhear.

The Missouri matter had been settled with the famous compromise, and the subject of slavery had been put back to sleep in the nation's councils. But now it was to be awakened once more, and this time it would not be put to sleep again.

CONGRESSMAN FAIRFIELD, unwittingly holding in his hand the harbinger of great events, moved that the petition from the 172 women in Maine be referred to the Committee on the District of Columbia. That was the routine. That had been the usual action, back in those days of respectfulness; it would have started the petition, as many before it, on its quiet trip to oblivion. But some in the House now wanted a swifter, surer, and less respectful trip. Congressman Cramer, a Democrat from Martin Van Buren's home state, New York, moved that the petition be laid on the table—that familiar parliamentary device, not debatable, that abruptly stops debate and if successful puts the motion onto that much overloaded and very metaphorical table, from which it probably—certainly in this case—will never return. Tabling the petition would prevent its being referred to a committee, which had always been a little dangerous; in transit through the House's procedures a petition might leak some discussion of its subject out upon the floor. Now that possibility was to be sealed off. And the House did decide, by a voice vote, to table Mr. Fairfield's petition. So much for the 172 ladies from Maine.

Congressman Fairfield, still doing his duty for his constituents, then presented another petition of the same kind, this time from the same number—172—of gentlemen praying for the same thing: abolition of slavery in the District. No doubt sensing, from the previous action, the mood of the House, this time Fairfield himself moved that the petition be laid on the table. John Y. Mason of Virginia, presumably desiring to make clear the mood of the House, and perhaps also to identify the villains who could pay the slightest attention to such a petition, called for a count of the yeas and nays, which was ordered, and the House then voted by the lopsided vote of 180–31 to "lay the memorial on the table." No discussion. No reference to committee. No response to the petition. The desire to treat these petitions with a more vigorous repudiation than hitherto was clearly gathering strength, and winning victories.

But another viewpoint was also, if not gathering strength, at least showing a new persistence. Congressman William Slade of Vermont, who was one of the very few among the 242 Congressmen then in the House who might be suspected of having some actual sympathy with these petitions, moved that this one, despite its tabling, be printed. He argued that if the petitioners were like others whom he knew personally, then they were very respectable people, and not members of "the Abolition society," and that "they were entitled, as a matter of common courtesy to a respectable hearing," and moreover, as "a matter of common right, as well as of common courtesy," that their petition should be printed for the information of members of the House.

But the House was not interested in that information, and not disposed to that courtesy. Another Democrat from New York, a leader of the House named Aaron Vanderpoel, a friend and colleague of the party's new leader, Vice-President Van Buren, remarked that this discussion was quite unprofitable—a sentiment that would be echoed many times in the sessions to come—and insisted that House members already knew all they needed to know about what was in these petitions. He therefore moved that the motion to print also be laid on the table, and his motion passed by another overwhelming vote, 168–50. So it was further decided: no printing. The petition, promptly laid on the table without discussion, reference to committee, or response, was not even to be made available to those who wanted to read it. That would seem to have been enough to satisfy even the most ardent opponent of these petitions, and to seal off the subject, and to provide the method for vaporizing any subsequent petitions of the same kind. But given the feelings in some Southern breasts, even this was not enough.

And given the feeling in a few Northern breasts, those overwhelming negative votes were not enough to stop the presentation of further petitions. Two days later, after the roll call of the states had reached Massachusetts, Congressman William Jackson of that state offered yet another. Such persistence in what the excitable young South Carolinian James Henry Hammond regarded as fanaticism provoked from him a motion that lifted the parliamentary conflict another step above a mere skirmish to the higher plane of major parliamentary warfare. He moved that Jackson's petition *not be received*. Later he altered the wording of his motion to say that the petition be *rejected*. That was a new idea, and set off a month of fireworks. Or nine years of fireworks.

Hammond's stunning remarks on this portentous occasion (Friday, December 18) were reported as follows in the *Congressional Globe*:

> **Mr. Hammond** moved that the petition be not received. The large majority by which the House had rejected a similar petition [Mr. Fairfield's] a few days ago had been very gratifying to the whole South. He had hoped it would satisfy the gentlemen charged with such petitions, of the impropriety of introducing them here. Since, however, it had not had that effect, and they persisted still in urging them upon the House and upon the country, he thought it was not requiring too much of the House, to ask it to put a more decided seal of reprobation on them, by peremptorily rejecting this [one].

The Speaker of the House, the future president of the United States, James K. Polk of Tennessee, perhaps a little disconcerted, explained that there was no precedent for such an action as *that*—that a petition, duly presented by a member, not even be *received*. There were various ways a petition could be answered in the negative, or allowed to slip by in silence, but to vote explicitly not to *receive* it—in effect to throw it back indignantly in the face of the petitioners—that was new.

Mr. Hammond, however, had a reason for his motion:

> **Mr. Hammond** . . . did think it due to the House and the country, to give at once the most decisive evidence of the sentiments entertained here upon this subject. He wished to put an end to these petitions. He could not sit there and submit to their being brought forward until the House had become callous to their consequences. He could not sit there and see the rights of the Southern People assaulted day after day, by the ignorant fanatics from whom these memorials proceed[ed].

Did Hammond make this novel motion on his own spontaneous initiative? Later on in life he wrote that he did, and the leading relevant history now says that he did. But some inferred otherwise, and the inference rested on two considerations: congressional living arrangements, and the intellectual force of the great figure from Hammond's own state, John C. Calhoun.

As to the living arrangements, in those days most congressmen, and senators, too, who came to the nation's capital for their winter in the mud lived together in congenial clumps in the boardinghouses that ringed the Capitol. They not only slept in these places; they ate their meals there as well, usually at one long table in a common "mess." These lodging houses, we may assume, were hotbeds of political conversation and conniving, and they tended to be sorted by section, by ideology, and even by state; they may well have reinforced provincial attitudes more than living in Washington modified them.

One such house, on Capitol Hill, was run by a Mrs. Lindenberger, and had as its lodgers for the winter of this first session of the Twenty-fourth Congress—this is the entire list—Congressman James Henry Hammond of South Carolina, with whom we are now acquainted; another new member in this session of Congress named Waddy Thompson, Jr., who came from the South Carolina upcountry—from John Calhoun's district, in fact, around Pendleton; Senator William C. Preston of South Carolina; Congressman Francis W. Pickens, a cousin and close associate of John Calhoun's, another young South Carolina politician who would have a long career; and John C. Calhoun himself, now the other senator from South Carolina. In other words, the entire group was from South Carolina, and of a Calhounite persuasion—or perhaps even further "right." One would guess that anyone suspected of sympathy for abolition would have had a hard time getting the bread passed to him at Mrs. Lindenberger's mess.

It has been suggested by scholars in the past that Hammond's motion in the House was cooked up there, with John Calhoun playing the leading role. Whether that is the way it happened is one of those fine points that scholars discuss; some infer that Calhoun, the much older and much more accomplished man—a former vice-president and cabinet member and serious possibility for president, a leading political figure, and a man of great personal and intellectual power—must have put the ambitious young Hammond up to his motion, that Hammond was Calhoun's agent in the House. Others insist that James Henry Hammond, who was no shrinking magnolia, needed no help in conceiving measures to protect the slaveholding South. Perhaps we may infer, from knowledge of like situations, that those articulate South Carolina leaders, sharing those suppers, reinforced each other's opinions and shared ideas.

Certainly Hammond's motion in the House did reflect Calhoun's position, and Calhoun's attitude, even before Calhoun gave voice to it over in the other wing of the Capitol in January: *reject* those petitions. The strategy of that position was dramatized with two metaphors, one of frontiers and outposts and the other of thresholds. In this climactic battle for the life of Southern civilization—this Thermopylae—Calhoun and Hammond and others would say, we must meet the abolitionist fanatics at the *threshold;* we must hold against them the farthest outpost. If that outpost is yielded, if that threshold once is crossed, then all will be lost.

CALHOUN AND HAMMOND DID have rational arguments for their position—arguments that could be stated in the quiet tones of civic discourse. They held that for Congress to reject the petition was not to infringe the petitioners' right, protected in the First Amendment, because the petitioners had assembled, and written their petition, and had sent it to the congressional bodies, and that therefore their right to petition had in no way been restricted. But, said Calhoun and Hammond, Congress had every right to decide what to do with the petition. It had no obligation to receive it; peremptorily rejecting a petition outright was one of the alternative ways that parliamentary bodies might choose to respond.

And, they said, these particular petitions should be rejected for the soundest of reasons. Congress had no constitutional right to abolish slavery in the District, or for that matter even to discuss slavery anywhere, and therefore Congress should summarily reject petitions on that subject. Their prayer lay outside the powers of Congress. The petitioners were, one might say, like parched farmers petitioning for rain; they were asking for something Congress had no power to grant.

But this assertion about Congress's alleged lack of power was troublesome to many, however stirring it may have sounded at Mrs. Lindenberger's mess. That there was no constitutional right to touch slavery in the original *states* was generally agreed, even by antislavery forces, and there were the specific provisions and compromises in the Constitution that gave that agreement a plausible foundation. But the District? The District of Columbia had not even existed when the Constitution was written. It was the federal city, the city of all the states and all the citizens, of Massachusetts and Maine as much as of South Carolina and Georgia. Moreover, the Constitution did specifically provide, in Article I, Section 8, Paragraph 17, that "[Congress shall have the power to] exercise exclusive legislation in all cases whatsoever over such district (not exceeding ten miles square) as may, by cession of particular states and the acceptance of Congress, become the seat of the Government of the United States."

Why would the framers have used that sweeping phrase "in all cases whatsoever" unless they meant it? Hammond and Calhoun and the most overheated Southerners had an uphill case with that one, and their support dropped off. Almost nobody in Congress proposed actually to *do* anything about slavery in the District, despite all the petitions; but to deny that Congress had the constitutional power to touch slavery in the District if it should choose to—that went too far. It raised the question of whether we were a union after all.

IN THE VOICES OF the Southern members, and some others as well, one could hear something more than an effort to win a rational argument or to establish a formal position. There is passion rising from the closely printed pages of the old *Congressional Globe* like the steam from a geyser about to erupt.

The proposal that Hammond put forward, for all the careful reasoning that Calhoun might later adjoin to it, was intended to give vent to passionate indignation. Its purpose was, as Hammond himself said, to "put a more decided seal of reprobation" on the petitions brought forward by these "ignorant fanatics."

One of Hammond's South Carolina messmates at Mrs. Lindenberger's, Waddy Thompson, Jr., on December 21, 1835, put this point in terms of what was needed to satisfy the *feelings* of the South:

> [**Thompson**]: In my opinion nothing will satisfy the excited, the almost frenzied South, but an indignant rejection of these petitions; such a rejection as will at the same time that it respects the right of petitioning, express the predetermination, the foregone conclusion of the House on the subject—a rejection, sir, that will satisfy the South, and serve as an indignant rebuke to the fanatics of the North.

The use of the word "fanatics" to describe the petitioners became so constant as to verge on the automatic—and therefore to lose its edge. So it was necessary to sharpen it again. Hammond was not alone in joining ignorance to fanaticism: these petitioners were *ignorant* fanatics. In their ignorance they were (among the tamer charges) "misguided," "rash and misguided men," "misguided, deluded and infatuated men." To Francis Thomas of Maryland, they were *headstrong* fanatics. To Hammond and Benjamin Howard of Maryland, their fanaticism had a geography: they were "fanatics of the North." To John Jones and John Patton of Virginia, they were "agitators and fanatics of the North."

On a couple of the most interesting occasions of that turbulent winter session, a speaker would explicitly discard the now well-worn word and by discarding it, and substituting a stronger word or phrase, try to recapture the original intensity. Thus Waddy Thompson, after putting to himself, rhetorically, the notion that certain Northern opinions ought to be conciliated, responded to his own question in this way:

> **[Thompson]:** Who is it in the North that we are to conciliate? The fanatics? Fanatics, did I say, sir? Never before was so vile a band dignified with that name. They are murderers, foul murderers, accessories before the fact, and they know it, of murder, robbery, rape, infanticide.

To call this vile band of foul murderers, these *knowing* accessories *before* the fact—itself an imaginative conception—of murder, robbery, rape, and infanticide by so pale a term as "fanatics"—to group them with other, as it were, garden-variety, or everyday, fanatics—would be in fact to *dignify* them because it would so far miss the mark of the evil they represented.

James Garland explicitly discarded not only the term "fanatics" but also the figure that another member had contributed, that of "blood-hounds," thus building a little pile of rejected alternatives on top of which to situate his own replacement:

> **[Garland]:** [L]ast summer's campaign of a few fanatics, my colleague called them blood-hounds, but the term is too mild. I call them *fiends of hell*. . . .

Of course these fiends of hell provoked flowing Southern metaphors of anguish. Thus Francis Thomas of Maryland lamented that

> **[Thomas]:** [t]hese fanatical crusaders against evils abroad, who have, no doubt, vices enough at their own doors to exhaust, in their correction, that overflowing Christian charity of which they boast so much, and manifest so little, nothing daunted, continue to pour their poisons into that national chalice, from which the whole people of the United States have so long quaffed the sweet waters of Concord and Union.

There were already at this early date threats that the slave states would leave the Union. And there were proud threats from individuals that they personally would leave the hall, leave Congress, leave Washington—if these insults to the South continued. The fierce and fiery young Henry A. Wise, from Accomac County on the Eastern Shore of Virginia, who during his ten years as a congressman—just now barely begun—would speak as often as any member of that body, said of the prayer of these petitions against slavery in the District:

[Wise]: If it was the opinion that Congress had the right to interfere in this question, let the South know it at once, and it would know what to do. Their predecessors had told them what to do. They had no longer any business there. Their business was at home, to report to their people. He would go home, never to return there again, if that House were to say, directly or indirectly, that Congress had the power [to deal with slavery in the District].

As the discussion ranged across the whole field of slavery and race, there were blunt appeals to those feelings that a much later generation would call "racism," simply taking for granted (not without reason) that one's hearers, North and South, would share the prejudice. Thus Hammond would say:

[Hammond]: Although I am perfectly satisfied that no human process can elevate the black man to an equality with the white—admitting that it could be done—are we prepared for the consequence which then must follow? Are the people of the North prepared to . . . place their political power on an equality with their own? Are we prepared to see them mingling in our legislatures? Is any portion of this country prepared to see them enter these halls and take their seats by our sides, in perfect equality with the white representatives of an Anglo-Saxon race—to see them fill that chair—to see them placed at the heads of your Departments; or to see, perhaps, some Othello, or Toussaint, or Boyer, gifted with genius and inspired by ambition, grasp the presidential wreath, and wield the destinies of this great republic? From such a picture I turn with irrepressible disgust.

Mobs North and South could give vent to their appraisal of these fanatics, these bloodhounds, with *action:* by tarring and feathering, by blacking the offending fanatics' faces and putting them on the next train, by breaking up abolitionist meetings and running the speakers out of town, by looting Lewis Tappan's home in New York and burning his furniture in the square. Congressmen in the House, usually (not quite always) denied the satisfaction of expressing themselves with fists, fire, knives, clubs, stones, and guns, ordinarily had to make do with words. But they could at least echo on the House floor the kinds of statements that were then being promulgated by local vigilante groups all over the South, about what they would do if they caught one of these fiends in their locality. James Henry Hammond, at the end of the long speech he would make on February 1, 1836, rose to this peroration:

> **[Hammond]:** And I warn the abolitionists, ignorant, infatuated, barbarians as they are, that if chance shall throw any of them into our hands he may expect a felon's death. No human law, no human influence, can arrest his fate. The superhuman instinct of self-preservation, the indignant feelings of an outraged people, to whose hearth-stones he is seeking to carry death and desolation, pronounce his doom; and if we failed to accord it to him we would be unworthy of the forms we wear, unworthy of the beings whom it is our duty to protect, and we would merit and expect the indignation of offended Heaven.

This was the climax to his carefully worked-out speech. Note its startling assertion: that it would be an offense against heaven not to kill any available abolitionist. In a private letter the previous summer, Hammond had put the point more succinctly. Abolitionism, he wrote, could be "silenced in but one way—Terror—Death."

Since for the most part the weapons necessary to carry out that program—Terror, Death—were not available to congressmen in a deliberative body doing the public's business in a civilized republic, under the auspices of law grounded in a constitution that protected civil liberty, was there not some way in that setting that the intensity of one's feeling, the severity of one's disapproval, the gravity of the danger as one saw it, could be more satisfactorily expressed than by speeches, arguments, epithets alone? Hammond and Thompson and Henry Wise and those who shared their point of view came as close as they could to that objective with the parliamentary device that Hammond put forward, insisting that the House should indignantly rebuke the petitioners by *rejecting* those petitions. Their proposal and defense of that action triggered an exploration of the meaning of civil liberty in the new republic. Of the meaning, indeed, of the new country itself.

EVEN SOME WHO WERE very strongly against abolition—as almost all congressmen were—nevertheless had reservations about this proposed new way of treating the petitions, as an insult to be thrown back in the face of petitioners. There might be a constitutional issue in such a course of action. There certainly could be what later generations would call a public relations problem. Mingled in the speeches of congressmen that winter with the many and varied denunciations of the abolitionist fanatics (almost nobody spoke in their defense), there was an uneasy discussion about the "sacred" right of petition. Caleb Cushing, a distinguished new congressman from Massachusetts, would explain in a learned historical review that the right went back to the Magna Carta; was, after all, guaranteed by the First Amendment to the United States Constitution, and by many state bills of rights as well; was part of the bundle of civil liberties that *defined* the new republic. One could argue that any of the other ways of dealing with petitions—except perhaps laying them on the table without discussion—was sufficient to respect that sacred right, even if nothing whatever was done in response to the petition respectfully referred to committee. But throwing the petition back in the petitioners' faces stamped *rejected*—surely that was not a proper response to the exercise of a sacred right. (Of course, Hammond and Calhoun made clear that they *wanted* the treatment to be disrespectful; that was exactly the point, to show these ignorant fanatics that their petitions were an *insult* to the *honor* of the South, and to make them stop.)

At least many congressmen were uneasy about Hammond's motion—enough to prevent its passage. The earlier, already extreme device of whisking Congressman Jackson's petition into the oblivion of the table—which had seemed extreme enough just two days before, but which was now reduced to comparative moderation by Hammond's (or Calhoun's) superextreme alternative—could not be passed, either. The House got itself into one of those tangles to which parliamentary bodies are subject, in which competing efforts to save time actually waste it, and competing efforts to straighten things out actually produce more snarls. By now one, now another, now a third congressman insisting that no one wanted to talk about the subject of slavery—they talked about it. And by now a Southerner, now a Northerner, now a Westerner; now a Democrat, now a Whig, all saying that no one wanted to disturb the harmony and concord of the body—they disturbed it. They disagreed not, apparently, on the great subject of slavery itself—at least not until December 23, 1835—and not in theory on the right of petition, which they all repeatedly called "sacred" (even those who most wanted to squelch it in this case called it sacred while doing so), but rather on the best method to combine their deep respect for the right of petition in general with their detestation of this set of petitions, and this group of petitioners, in particular. Should they flatly reject petitions on this subject, at the door of the House, as it were, as Hammond (and Calhoun) proposed? Should they, rather, cautiously allow them just barely through the door (honoring the sacred right of petition) but then immediately lay them on the table—nail them to the table, as one congressman said—without printing, referral, or discussion? Or should they be very brave, as was proposed by a few congressmen, including at this stage a border-state Southerner or two, and assign all the petitions on this subject to a select committee—a special committee—with instructions to answer them all at once, carefully and forever, explaining why their prayer that slavery and the slave trade in the District be ended could *not* be granted? A couple of the congressmen referred to the experience with the Sunday mail controversy a few years before. (This controversy, arising out of the same evangelical Protestant reform impulse that had given abolition a shot in the arm, had to do with the desecration of the Sabbath by the delivery of mail.) There had been *floods* of petitions on that subject, too. And what had the House done? It had sent them all to a select committee, which had composed so cogent an all-purpose response as to quiet the controversy forever. But perhaps the House suspected that this slavery matter was going to cut deeper than the issue of Sunday mail.

There were old motions, new motions, motions to put on the table, rulings by the chair, appeals from rulings by the chair, points of order, calls for the previous question, and inquiries as to just what question was before the House. Such was the parliamentary confusion that the strict South Carolina spokesmen were embarrassed to discover that a petition essentially like those against which they had been so valiantly fighting had already been successfully introduced by Congressman George Briggs of Massachusetts—Jackson had not been the first congressman to rise when Massachusetts had been called—and had absentmindedly been referred, in the heretofore routine procedure of the House, to the Committee on the District of Columbia.

One can imagine how that might have been. The clerk on each of these petition days would drone out the names of the states, beginning, as we said, in the North with the state of Maine and working southward. A congressman from the given state could then rise, and race through a brief description of a petition and move its referral to a committee, and a vote would be taken, and that would be that. Most petitions were utterly routine; many dealt with purely individual grievances. One may certainly infer that there was much mumbling and hasty routine in the receiving of them: is-there-a-second-as-many-as-are-in-favor-opposed-so-ordered. Not every congressman was present at the start of every session, or later either. The nineteenth-century United States House of Representatives was by no means the most orderly parliamentary body there has ever been. So it was not perhaps surprising that Congressman Briggs's petition had slipped out into the bloodstream of the House before the South Carolinians had their antidote ready to stop it. Young Congressman Hammond, on making this disconcerting discovery, sprang to his feet to say that had he known he would have moved to reject Briggs's petition, too.

But parliamentarily speaking, it was now too late for that. What to do? It was decided to make an effort—in a revealing perfectionism that reflected their intensity—to recover Briggs's petition so that it could be more satisfyingly strangled by one of the new methods. But in order to silence it properly it was necessary to get the thing back before the House—to reconsider it. By trying thus to go back and perfect their silencing of every single one of the abolitionist petitions, the more extreme Southern spokesmen shot themselves in the foot, as indeed they would do repeatedly throughout the controversy's nine-year life. The discussion of slavery that flowed on through December 1835 had as its parliamentary foundation the motion to reconsider the referral of Congressman Briggs's petition to committee. Moving to *reconsider* the referral of the Briggs petition to committee opened the floor to exactly that discussion of slavery they had been endeavoring to prevent.

Or they alleged they wanted to prevent. Some Democrats and some Northerners and some Southerners from other states, too, suspected that the Highest of the High Carolinian purists had reasons not to object altogether to a parliamentary situation that clogged the wheels of a government they opposed, and put pressure on other Southerners to join them in a united front, under Calhoun's leadership, out there at the furthest outpost of the defense of Southern civilization.

But it is one of the annoying features of representative government in a free republic that a parliamentary situation that allows some representatives to hold forth against accessories before the fact of murder, robbery, rape, and infanticide, against those for whom the word "fanatic" is too mild, also gives other representatives, who might take a different view of these matters, their chance to speak, and to present a different view. Were there any such congressmen? There certainly were not many.

4 / HERE THE PEOPLE RULE

THE INSTITUTION IN WHICH these events took place, the United States House of Representatives, had assembled for the very first time not so long before these events—on April 1, 1789, in New York City. Frederick Muhlenberg of Pennsylvania had been the Speaker, James Madison of Virginia "first man" and leader, and the tart-tongued Federalist Fisher Ames of Massachusetts the member whose diary would be most often quoted by historians (he wrote that the reciprocal opening addresses between President Washington and respondents for the houses of Congress had in them a good deal of "divine molasses"—a continuing American tradition). That first House theoretically had sixty-five members, but at the time of its first meetings, Rhode Island and North Carolina had not yet ratified the Constitution, and three of New York's six members, even though Congress met in New York City, had not yet arrived.

The United States government got under way, with the House playing a major role in those first days, and with vicissitudes rolled on through forty-six years, and twenty-three Congresses, to the moment Congressman Fairfield introduced his petition and this story began. During those forty-six years, representatives chosen by popular vote would gather in the capital city—New York City first, and then Philadelphia, and, after 1800, in the new place in the mud along the Potomac River—to enact, in collaboration with the Senate, the nation's laws. Five reapportionments had expanded the total number of congressmen to 242 members. There were now twenty-four states. Two new ones, Arkansas and Michigan, would be added during this Twenty-fourth Congress. The total population in 1789 had been about four million; the 1830 census had found almost thirteen million, and the 1840 census would find seventeen million, a considerable jump.

In those early days, the House of Representatives assembled for the commencement of a session of Congress each year, as this first session of the Twenty-fourth Congress had done, early in the month of December, after the fall harvest was complete. In the short sessions which ended in the odd-numbered years, they adjourned on March 3, before spring planting began, and in inaugural years before the new presidential term began, as it then did, on March 4. The long session, the first regular session of each Congress, like the one that started off with Fairfield's petition, would begin in December of an odd-numbered year and last into the early summer of the following even-numbered year. The congressmen would "winter" together, as one might somewhat anachronistically and euphemistically put it, in muddy, tobacco-tinctured Washington.

The relationship of elections to these early sessions of Congress is confusing to a modern reader, and perhaps was so as well to a voter of the time, because of the lame duck feature: congressmen you had just voted out of office would promptly head off to Washington to make laws again, in a lame duck session; congressmen you had just elected in November (although not necessarily in November—states still set the election dates, and these varied) would not take office for *thirteen months,* not until December of the following year. This curious feature of the American Constitution would not be corrected until the ratification of the Twentieth Amendment in 1933—long after the events of concern to us here.

Sometimes presidents would exercise their constitutional power to call an extra session, in which case the congressmen would be privileged to enjoy, in the summertime or the early fall, the heat as well as the mud of the newly built capital city. President Martin Van Buren would call a special session in September of 1837 to deal with the financial panic of that year, and newly inaugurated Whig president William Henry Harrison would call a special session for May of 1841. (By the time it met, President Harrison had died.)

Even so, being a congressman was not the full-time Washington-based job that it would become in the twentieth century. Most congressmen came to the capital alone, leaving their wives and families back home; they were not paid enough to do otherwise. Most of them lived in raw masculine isolation in lodging houses like Mrs. Lindenberger's. It tells you something about the development of the city that streets were still insufficiently laid out for there to be firm numbered addresses, so the location of the lodgings would often be indicated by landmarks, even in the official directory of the nation's legislators. Gadsby's Hotel and Brown's Hotel were well enough known not to need addresses; other places could use them as landmarks.

The congressmen lived in their little village on the hill, separated by a long stretch of mud from another little village clustered around the President's House at the other end of Pennsylvania Avenue. They were, indeed, separate branches, inconveniently distant from each other. It is one of the themes of *The Washington Community: 1800–1828*, by James Sterling Young, that the layout of the capital city, and the living arrangements that grew around that original plan, reflected the constitutional separation of powers.

The abolitionist Theodore Weld, writing to his abolitionist wife, had a different explanation for the city's distances: "Who but a slaveholder," he wrote, "in laying out the plan of the national buildings would have dreamed of locating all the departments and offices of the government in which are employed at least one thousand clerks, assistants, etc., at such a great distance from the capitol! Thousands of dollars are spent every year and *years* of time lost in going and sending from the Offices to the Capitol and vice versa. All of which might have been saved if they had been located in each other's vicinity."

The number of lawyers in the House, then as now, was large, and the number of congressmen who would make a lifelong career in public office, then as now, was also large, but the difference was this: they usually did not make that career in Congress or in Washington.

In the late twentieth century there is much hand-wringing about the power of incumbency in the House: a congressman gets elected, and reelected, and reelected, and gains seniority on the mohair-allotment subcommittee, and receives campaign funds from the Mohair Political Action Committee, and buys a house in Chevy Chase or Fairfax County and stays on forever. In the first half of the nineteenth century it was not like that at all. The turnover was then very high. A counting by James Sterling Young of the earliest Congresses—the First through the Twenty-second—shows that almost a third (32.4 percent) of the House members did not return in the session with the *lowest* turnover; turnover once reached 63.1 percent (after Congress voted a pay raise for itself—this issue seems never to go away, and to anger citizens of all centuries); and in another case was 52 percent.

If you joined the House in the Twenty-second Congress in 1831, you were one of eighty-nine freshman congressmen, in a House of 213 members; only forty-six of these would return for a second term—we learn from historian Leonard L. Richards—and only twenty-six for a third. In the Twenty-third Congress, beginning in December of 1833, as a result in part of the enlargement of the total number from 213 to 242 in the reapportionment based on the census of 1830, a congressman would have had 152 new colleagues. In the agitated Twenty-fourth Congress, with which the story told here has begun, there were 115 new congressmen, including the excitable Waddy Thompson, Jr., the learned Caleb Cushing (the Massachusetts expert on the Magna Carta) and James H. Hammond. Francis Pickens had come from South Carolina in the middle of the Twenty-third Congress in 1834; Henry A. Wise from Virginia at the start of that Congress in 1833.

Seniority did not count for as much as it would later in the history of the House. New members would speak and participate soon after arrival, if they had the voice and the temperament to do it in front of two hundred contentious critics. The talented politician Henry Clay had been elected Speaker of the House in his *first* term, something that would be unthinkable in later Houses. Men would serve a term or two and then return to their home states to continue a political career in a state or local office, or they would be elected to the Senate, or they would be appointed to offices in the federal or state government. Being a congressman was more often an interlude or variation in a public career than it is now; recall Abraham Lincoln's proposed rotation, in the next decade, with two other Illinois Whigs, and his service for only one term. The number of resignations was high, much higher than today, and so was the number of members who did not choose to run again.

There was no problem of a mentality developed "inside the Beltway," separate from the country. The members of the Twenty-fourth Congress would have had a hard time imagining a Washington that would require a beltway, and their own lines of influence ran straight to their home states and districts—too much so, some might say. Living and eating in those often ideologically and geographically segregated lodging houses meant that voices from home were there every night at supper, as we have inferred to be the case at Mrs. Lindenberger's.

The Speaker of the House appointed the committees and the chairmen of committees, and was a powerful figure. House committees were not then as important as they would one day become and are now—not yet little legislatures—and the activity on the floor was correspondingly more important. The committees usually would meet in the forenoon, and the House would assemble at noon and meet into the middle of the afternoon, or the late afternoon, six days a week. Occasionally the House would go on into the evening, or even—as this Congress would do when considering the admission of Arkansas—all night.

Each member then had a desk on the floor, which served as his office; his staff consisted of himself. A little later in the nineteenth century that desk on the floor would become an issue. It would be claimed that it encouraged members to sit there attending to personal business instead of listening; the House, it was said, ought just to have benches, like the House of Commons.

An early-nineteenth-century congressman would occasionally refer to himself as the "immediate representative" of the people in his district, implicitly contrasting himself especially to senators, who represented states and were chosen at the time by state legislatures. Perhaps he would also be implying a contrast to presidents, who were chosen by the complicated method of "electors" from the states, and to federal judges, who were appointed. Members of the House alone were chosen directly by the people.

THIS "CONGRESS," TO GO back to basics, was, with all its warts, the institution with which the American government began. And the shaping of new governments was the act with which the American *nation* began.

Representatives of the British colonies in America gathered in Philadelphia in September of 1774 and called themselves a "Congress" (like the Congress of Vienna) and met again the next spring and, in the year after that, 1776, moved from grievance to independence and war, and the "Congress" conducted the war and negotiated the peace, and devised a first try at continental government.

That Congress under the Articles of Confederation accomplished more than later American history sometimes grants, but still it came to show severe faults. The newly independent Americans thereupon had another deliberative gathering in Philadelphia in the summer of 1787, and out of that came a three-pronged and multilayered second try under a written constitution, in which the first and longest article enumerates the powers of Congress. The caterpillar that had begun in 1774 grew and changed and gathered strength and sprouted wings (perhaps you had not thought of Congress as a butterfly) and burst upon the world as the center of the new government.

It is true that the new federal government had three separate branches, and two houses in the legislative branch, but none of the other parts of it reached, as purely as did the House, the essence of the sort of "republican" union the founding generation had intended. Unlike an "executive," the representatives had to give reasons, and make arguments, for their positions, in the presence of those of equal status who might disagree and give contrary arguments. And they were supposed to carry on that argument as the "immediate representatives" of the people who elected them, who might instruct them, and who might replace them.

The legislature was the defining branch of the new government, and the House of Representatives was its most fundamental unit: representative of the people, continuous with the popular houses of the state and colonial legislatures and with the House of Commons in England, conducting the people's business, chosen in freedom by the people, locked in argument.

As a longtime member of the House of Representatives named Gerald Ford would say, many, many years later, when as a new president in a tight moment he addressed, along with the whole nation, his old colleagues in that House: "Here the people rule."

A READER IN THE days of the 104th or 105th or 106th Congress would be inclined to be ironical about the people ruling, when he (or particularly she) thought about who was, and who was not, allowed to serve as, and to vote for, one of those "immediate representatives" back there in the Twenty-fourth. Every one of the 242 representatives, bustling about the desks in that hall, calling out "Mr. Speaker! Mr. Speaker!" or making a windy speech or answering letters or dozing at his desk or chatting with a colleague or erupting into vituperative argument, doing, so he said, the people's business, was a male, and was (or passed for) white. The institution did not, to borrow a phrase from a vastly different time more than a century and a half later, "look like America."

Of course it did not look like the unimaginably different America of the late 1990s. The concept "Asian-American," for just one example of many that could be chosen, would probably have been almost as difficult for them to conceive of as the concept "beltway." America did not yet encompass most of the territory from which Hispanic Americans would one day come. It would be safe to guess that the Twenty-fourth Congress, although loaded with all the varieties of the Protestantism of the British Isles, and most of those of the European continent, included very few Catholics, virtually no Jews, and absolutely no Buddhists, or Muslims, or Hindus. The concept of a "white ethnic" would have been strange, though the forebears of some who would later be assigned to that category were beginning to arrive in the country.

But this House did not reflect the America of its own time, either, and the two most noticeable exclusions both figure in the story to be told here. There were then no women in the House, and there were no women in the voting constituency of the men who held every seat in the House. That the signers of Fairfield's petition, and many of the other abolitionist petitions, were women had this added significance: the signers were thus by this modest action entering into a civic life that was otherwise closed to them.

The other mammoth exclusion is at the center of the historical episode to be re-created in these pages, although the actual human beings who are unrepresented, whom we now call African-Americans, are, for that reason, not on the stage. This is a story of a fight among whites about extending democracy to blacks—about the first tiny steps toward possibly considering extending democracy to black persons.

This excluded group was not small. The reader may remember the figure Congressman Hammond cited, in 1836, for the number of American slaves: 2,300,000. The census in 1830 had counted, as we have said, somewhat under thirteen million Americans, of whom about two million were slaves. By 1840, in the total population of seventeen million there were almost 2,500,000 slaves.

The slaves were not only *not* represented; they were, one might say, *perversely* represented in this House. They were counted (fractionally) to augment the representation for the interests *adverse* to their own, the white slave state population dominated by slaveholders. This perverse anti-representation, as it might be called, was the result of the unsavory constitutional compromise mentioned in an earlier chapter, the three-fifths ratio.

As we have already said, this concession to the slaveholding South in the compromises at the Constitutional Convention in 1787 meant that slaves—despite their owners' insistence in other venues that they were simply property—were to count, fractionally, as part of a state's population when the number of House members was allocated to that state. The fact that the slaveholding states derived extra representation in the House according to how many slaves they held led to many victories in votes, and therefore in laws, and in all the shadows that such power casts in all directions. In 1820, for just one example, the House of Representatives killed the Tallmadge amendments, which would have kept slavery out of Missouri, by the votes of the South's extra representation, which effectively turned a minority into a majority.

Those in the free states who objected most strongly to this warp in the House's composition cited the numbers—from twenty to forty, and growing—of "extra" votes the slaveholding states gained by this provision. The magnitude of this most egregious of the framers' compromises is evident in the following statistics: by 1860, the seven largest slave states, with a free population of 3,298,000, had forty-five representatives in the House; while the state of New York, with a free population of 3,831,590, had only thirty-one.

There were about 320,000 free blacks in the 1830 census; 385,000 in 1840. A sprinkling could vote, in five upper North states, but these black voters were so few and so marginal as to have no political effect.

The composition of the electorate determines outcomes. James Madison made some jottings (never published) in the winter of 1791–92 about the limitations of republicanism in Virginia by an implicit republican standard of majority rule: "At present the slaves and non-freeholders amount to nearly ¾ of the State. The power is therefore in about ¼." (Property restrictions, limiting the franchise to freeholders or men with a certain amount of property, were another limitation of the early Houses, but on the way to being ended in the time of our story.) If Madison had considered the exclusion of women he would have made the fraction that held power even smaller. An experienced politician, he knew, moreover, that a shift in the base of power shifts policy: "Were slaves freed and the right of suffrage extended to all," he wrote, "the operation of government might be very different."

MUCH OF THE POLITICS of the United States—"these states," as Walt Whitman would affectionately call them—was, particularly in these early years, and not surprisingly, a politics of *states*. And the question above all others for our *national* life as the U.S.A. grew was, how many slave states and how many free states would there be to determine the nation's course?

Of the fifty-five members of the House who were actually present when the First Congress began meeting in 1789, twenty-five came from the states that would be slave states in 1835. That number would be augmented in the following session when North Carolina's four members arrived.

Thirty of the first fifty-five congressmen came from states that would be free states in 1835. To this number of free-state congressmen there would be added during the first session New York's missing three, and in 1791 Rhode Island's one. In other words, the division between representatives from slave and free states at the start was almost even, but with a slight advantage on the side of the states that were already, or were soon to be, free.

If you were an antislavery citizen of Massachusetts or Pennsylvania you probably would have expected this free-state advantage to grow, while the slave-state component of the House would remain static, confined to those original states. You probably would have expected the slave state proportion to decline markedly in proportion as population grew and new territories and states were added to the West. Perhaps you would have expected that before too long the anachronistic distinction between "free" and "slave" states would no longer apply in the people's House, or anywhere else in a free republic.

But you would have been disappointed. If you had been brought around to supporting the ratification of the Constitution in 1787 or 1788 by reassurances that the concessions to slavery in that document were simply a temporary expedient, and that slavery—so plainly contradictory to the meaning of the American Revolution—would soon end, as it was indeed being ended in the Northern states, you would by 1835 be disillusioned indeed. The early Congresses made decisions that continued and expanded the concessions to slavery in the Constitution—a fugitive slave law in 1793, for example.

The most damaging concession was the admission of new slave states, starting with Kentucky in 1791. The abolitionists would regard that as a fateful precedent and a missed opportunity: Congress theoretically could have decided—whether or not this was possible in real-world politics—that no new slave state would be admitted to the Union. But the precedent set with Kentucky continued with Tennessee in 1796, and then, after the Louisiana Purchase, with Louisiana, Mississippi, Alabama, and, after the fierce battle in Congress over the "Missouri Question," with Missouri. Half of the twenty-four states in 1835 were slave states. Six of the twelve slave states were original states, and six had been added in the years since the founding.

In the years thereafter the proportion of slave-state to free-state representation in Congress would be much affected by the original constitutional provisions. One might say that the Constitution conceded enough power to the slave states for them to continue to protect their peculiar interest, in Congress as elsewhere. Each state, of course, had two senators, so that as the Northern centers of population grew—in New York, Pennsylvania, Massachusetts, and other states—the disproportion in the senatorial representation of free- and slave-state populations increased: a slave-state senator would represent proportionately fewer and fewer citizens, compared to a free-state senator, because the population in the

Northern states, on the average, was growing faster than that in the South. And in the House, supposedly based on population to balance the Senate, the three-fifths rule warped the representation in the way we have described.

This House was, then, a severely distorted sample of republican government. But it was such a sample all the same. A restricted but real mutual deliberation took place among representatives of a restricted but expanding electorate, in an atmosphere of restricted but real civil liberty. This is a story of the use of the freedom and the ideals that this House in its crippled way did embody to challenge the evils in the society that the House itself reflected.

5 / THE RAMPARTS OF THE GREEN MOUNTAINS

On December 23, 1835, a week further along into the excitements of the Twenty-fourth Congress generated by Congressman Hammond's motion, the representative from Vermont, William Slade, who earlier had moved, against the grain of House opinion, that John Fairfield's petition be printed, now rose to give—with no desire to offend anyone, but out of the duty he felt to his constituents and to the republic—his views on the topics under discussion. His views were such as to infuriate Northerners and drive Southerners out of the hall.

At first he talked about the right of petition, which he thought deserved something more than the mere lip service it had so far received:

> **[Slade]:** The great purpose . . . of most of those who have hitherto spoken upon this subject seems to be to get rid of the petitions. The gentleman from New York (Mr. Beardsley) wished to have them all laid on the table, as fast as presented, and "nailed" there; and yet he is exceedingly regardful of the "sacred right of petitioning," which must on no account whatever, be impaired!

This Congressman Beardsley—Samuel Beardsley—from New York was a Democrat and friend of President Jackson's who had come to this session of Congress fresh from the triumph of saving the city of Utica from the "disgrace" (his word) of allowing the antislavery societies to hold their state convention in that city. He had been the leader of the group of concerned citizens—unkind commentators used the word "mob"—that prevented the disgrace. "Sacred" rights to assemble and petition were all very well in their place, but allowing abolitionists to meet in Utica was going too far.

> **[Slade]:** The gentlemen from South Carolina (Messrs. Hammond, Pickens, and Thompson) are most consistent. They profess to regard the petitions as disrespectful, and the petitioners as officious meddlers with that which does not concern them. They, therefore, would have the petitions rejected. There is, in this, the merit, at least, of consistency, and the gentlemen have my thanks for evincing a disposition to meet the question fairly.

But Mr. Slade's way of meeting the question fairly came to the opposite conclusion. His purpose was not, like almost everybody else's, simply to get rid of these petitions, nor yet was it simply to have them treated courteously, although he certainly wanted that; he went much further. He wanted the House to act upon them! Not only that—he wanted the House to act upon them *favorably*!

> I sir, said **Mr. S.**, am in favor of the prayer of the petitioners. I believe that Congress has a right to legislate on this subject, and that the time has come when it ought to legislate.

This was so far from anything being proposed by any other congressman, and so offensive to some of them, that it must have been here that the Southern members began to depart. At a later stage of these deliberations one of the gentlemen from the South would say that the moment a proposal to end slavery in the District was actually debated on the floor of Congress—at that moment, the Union would be dissolved. Slade was undeterred.

> **[Slade]:** What do the petitioners ask at our hands? Why, sir, simply that measures may be taken to put an end to slavery here, and especially that here, where the flag of freedom floats over the Capitol of this great Republic, and where the authority of that Republic is supreme, the trade in human flesh may be abolished. These are the questions which gentlemen are called on to meet, but which they do not meet, either by calling the petitioners "ignorant fanatics" or denouncing them [as] "murderers and incendiaries."

Who was this fellow Slade? Nobody else was making speeches like that. Was he himself one of those "ignorant fanatics," as James Hammond put it? Or worse than fanatics, as Waddy Thompson put it? In other words, an *abolitionist*? Not quite.

> **[Slade]:** I have said, sir, that I am in favor of the prayer of the petitioners. Let me not be misunderstood. The abolition of slavery which I would advocate, is a gradual abolition. I believe the immediate and unqualified abolition of slavery, to be inconsistent with a just regard, both to the best interests of the community, and the highest welfare of the slave. The philanthropy which aims at such an abolition, whatever I may think of its purity, I cannot commend for its intelligence or discretion.

Those were the terms of dispute in the world of antislavery journals and agitation—very remote from the mainstream and from these congressmen. Were you an "immediatist"? Did you believe in "immediate abolition, gradually accomplished"? Or did you endorse "gradual abolition, immediately decided upon"? Did you hold that slavery, being sinful, should be ended forthwith, and that slaveholders, as sinners, should not be compensated? Many new abolitionists held that view, but Slade did not. Not quite. But he was so close to it as to be the same thing to the astonished Southerners listening to him:

> **[Slade]:** . . . though I would have abolition advance by a gradual progress, towards its final consummation, I would have the work begin immediately. Sir, I cannot stand here as a freeman, without declaring, in the face of this House, and of the world, that the right to hold men as goods and chattels, subject to sale and transfer, at the will of a master, should cease, and be discontinued instantly and forever.

So Slade admitted that the "immediate and unqualified" abolition of slavery was not practical; the same was not true, however, of the slave *trade* in the District.

> **[Slade]:** . . . Mr. Speaker, while I thus repudiate the doctrine of the immediate and unqualified abolition of *slavery*, I maintain the duty of *immediately*, and *absolutely* abolishing the *slave trade* within the limits of this District. And here I come to a part of the subject which gentlemen do not choose to approach, but manifestly desire to avoid. In this I commend their prudence. The slave trade is an evil for which they well know there is no defence and no palliation.

Slade had been born and reared in Vermont, and had gone to Middlebury College, been admitted to the bar, practiced law in Middlebury, established a political newspaper, and served in various bureaucratic capacities, all inside his native state. But that had not quite been the whole of his experience. In 1824, at age thirty-eight, he became one of the seven clerks in the Department of State, in Washington. The nation's capital was a very long way, then, from northwestern Vermont—much farther than it is today, not only in transportation time but in ethos and atmosphere. Washington was very much a Southern city, and that meant a city in which slavery, and the trade in slaves, was a visible institution. One may surely read between the lines of his remarkable speech in December of 1835 that William Slade, during his earlier service in Washington, had been shocked to his New England core.

> **[Slade]:** I am well assured that the trade is actively carried on in the cities of Washington and Alexandria, especially in the latter, where is a large receptacle for the securing of slaves purchased in this District and the surrounding country; from which they are, from time to time, shipped to supply the markets in the Southern and Southwestern ports of the United States. I need not say that, what is usually connected with the slave trade elsewhere, is connected with it here—the forced and final separation of parents and children, of brothers and sisters, of husbands and wives—the utter annihilation of all the endearing relations of human life, and the substitution of the single relation which *property* bears to its *absolute proprietor*.

Slade even accompanied his speech with advertisements from the local newspapers. What must have been his tone of voice as he read out the following to his colleagues in the House:

> **[Slade]:** CASH FOR 200 NEGROES Including both sexes, from twelve to twenty-five years of age. Persons having servants to dispose of will find it to their interest to give me a call as I will give higher prices, in cash, than any other purchaser who is now in this market. . . .

He went on:

> **[Slade]:** Sir, shall this trade in human flesh be permitted to continue in the very heart of this republic? . . . Sir, this subject demands a searching investigation. Will gentlemen deny such investigation? Shall the petitions which ask for it be "nailed to the table," or "buried in the tomb of all the Capulets"?

The condemnation of slavery in religious categories was a considerable annoyance to believers, and unbelievers, in the slaveholding South, and called forth books and pamphlets and sermons and speeches and biblical interpretations and theological doctrines intended to refute the misguided, fanatical claims issuing from the North. In his speech on December 22, Congressman John W. Jones of Virginia had expressed horror that anything so appalling as this abolitionism should be thought to have emanated from religion:

> **[Jones]:** And, as if to add insult to injury, there were those . . . who had the charity to believe that they were influenced in their conduct by humane and religious motives. If, indeed, this most uncalled for, officious, and dangerous intermeddling with the rights of others, be dictated by religion, he would say it was not the religion which was inculcated by the Saviour of the world, or taught his disciples.

But, once again, in the inescapable logic of a republic—a "free society"—it had to be granted that if Jones expressed that view, then others could express, in response, a different view. The debate about what Christianity implied with respect to African slavery in America was to be one of the most important debates in the history of the country.

> **[Slade]:** I was not prepared for an intimation that religion justified the holding of human beings as *property*. Why, sir, what is the great leading moral precept put forth by that Saviour, whose name is thus invoked to sanction the practice of slavery?
>
> "All things whatsoever ye would that men should do unto you, do ye even so to them . . ."
>
> Now, sir, let gentlemen show me that Africans are not "men," and I will give up the argument. But, until that is done; until the declaration is blotted from the Book of Revelation, that "God hath made of one blood all nations of men, to dwell on all the face of the earth;" and until this great truth ceases to find a response in every human bosom, shall slavery stand rebuked by this all comprehensive and sublime precept of the Saviour of men. The Saviour . . . came to redeem men from sin—*to write the law of LOVE upon their hearts*—to establish principles and proclaim precepts, before whose searching and all-pervading influence the time-honored systems of injustice and oppression shall melt away.

Slade quoted Southerners and slaveholders themselves, and others closer to and more familiar with the peculiar institution than anyone from Middlebury, Vermont, could be. He caused to be read a petition that had been submitted to the House back in 1828 by eleven hundred residents of the District of Columbia, which petition vividly described the evils of the trade being conducted "at the capital of the freest Government on earth." He read excerpts from the debate on slavery and gradual emancipation and colonization that had taken place in the General Assembly of Virginia as recently as 1832, inspired by Nat Turner and fears of insurrection and racism and economic woes but condemnatory of slavery "in the abstract" as well. One year earlier, the Maryland legislature had, after much discussion of the slavery question, adopted a more effectual program to bring about emancipation and establish a white free-labor utopia: compulsory, state-financed colonization of black freedmen. Whatever the motives of these "reformers," their antislavery terminology had been fairly strong: slavery was a "mildew" and an "incubus," a sort of albatross around Virginia's neck, a lump in Maryland's throat. Slaveholding legislators in both states had borrowed the language of the abolitionists to denounce slavery while subscribing to racist ideals; now Slade could borrow their language in turn, returning the favor, to make his point, that these legislators in slaveholding states had, after all, condemned slavery, and very recently, too.

Slade also quoted from editorials in Southern papers written in those days when it was still possible to debate abolition in the South. He quoted the *Richmond Whig* as having declared at the time of those Virginia debates that "the great mass of Virginia herself triumphs that the slavery question has been agitated, and reckons it glorious that the spirit of her sons did not shrink from grappling with the monster." Slade then asked, rhetorically, in his own right, a question that would echo through nine years of sessions in this free republican deliberative body:

> **[Slade]:** Mr. Speaker, if it was "glorious" and safe for Virginia to "grapple with the monster" in 1832, is it inglorious and unsafe for the Congress of the United States to grapple with the same monster now?

Slade then turned to the answering of a fellow congressman whose presence, like his own, would run through the story here begun almost, but not quite, to the end, and whose speeches would outnumber almost, but not quite, all the others. This congressman was Henry A. Wise from Accomac on Virginia's Eastern Shore, a young man in his early thirties, talented, passionate, unpredictable, very articulate and very volatile, a Virginian who had already joined the South Carolinians in slavery's defense and who had given the first full-length and thorough constitutional and legal attack upon the vile petitions. Slade now answered Wise's constitutional and other arguments with a matching thoroughness.

To Wise's claim that slavery in the District was the proper concern only of citizens of the District, Slade answered that

> **[Slade]:** . . . the people who signed those petitions regard themselves as citizens, not only of the particular States in which they reside, but of the *republic*. Every interest within the scope of legislation of Congress is their interest. Every thing which concerns this Territory concerns them—its police; the value and security of the public property within its limits; and the safety of the representative bodies annually assembled here.
>
> This is the growing capital of a great republic. . . . [I]s it of no importance to our country whether its capital shall be surrounded by a mass of hardy independent *freedmen*, ready to peril their lives defending it, as well as themselves, from the invasion of a foreign power, or whether it shall be guarded by 60,000 *slaves*, who, instead of rallying in its defence, may hail the invader as an angel of deliverance from their bondage?
>
> And is not the subject invested with additional interest, when it is considered that the *Congress of the United States* will be surrounded by such an amount of such a population? Have the petitioners, then, as a part of the American people, no interest in this question?
>
> And then, too, there is the *character of the country* as it may be affected by the institutions within the territory, where the legislative power of that country is supreme. Is slavery tolerated in this district? The petitioners feel themselves, in some sense, responsible for it. Is *merchandise* made of men, within sight of the Capitol in which their Representatives are assembled, and on whose summit wave the stripes and the stars of freedom? As Americans, they keenly feel the reproach, and instinctively reach forth their hands to wipe out the stain from the escutcheon of their country.

To Wise's claim that Congress had no constitutional power to legislate about slavery, Slade answered, yes, it did have that power: if it could pass laws to abolish the traffic in slaves with Africa, even to the point of the penalty of *death*, how could it be that Congress was "powerless to reach the same evil in the very heart of the republic"?

To Wise's claim that Congress had no constitutional power over slavery in the *District*, he answered, yes, it did have that power, in the explicit grant to Congress in Article I, section 8 of *exclusive* (no other body has any) authority over the District "in all cases whatsoever."

To Wise's claim upon the "privileges and immunities" clause, as lawyers call it, and upon provisions requiring equal treatment of states, and upon various limitations on legislative power (banning *ex post facto* laws, and affirming the First Amendment freedoms), Slade responded that although of course these constitutional limitations on what Congress could do applied to congressional legislation in the District, those limitations, applying to all subjects, did not negate its power to legislate about slavery.

To Wise's claim upon the constitutional stipulation about fugitive slaves, Slade again responded that although this, too, must apply in the District as everywhere, it did not prevent Congress from abolishing slavery in the District, as the Northern free states in which it also applied had done.

To Wise's claim that the cession of the land that became the District by the slave states of Virginia and Maryland made it therefore necessarily a slave district, Slade answered, no, it did not. The language of the cession specifically refers to Congress's power in Article I, section 8, and if those two states themselves had the power to abolish slavery (not exercised—but as all other states had it, and others have exercised it), then how could that power be denied to the District erected on soil they had ceded?

Wise, a lawyer, had made a thorough and detailed lawyer's argument, in the way lawyers do, squeezing the juice from every possible provision of the Constitution, and from other documents and legal considerations, to make every possible argument against Congress's power over slavery in the District. Slade, also a lawyer, answered every one of his points in the same fashion.

But behind this maneuver of refined lawyerly argument there was a simpler political combat going on, and a plain moral argument also. Whose country is this, anyway? Whose is it going to be? What is it going to stand for?

This argument about slavery in the District anticipated the argument over slavery in the territories which would preoccupy the nation for more than a quarter of a century. There are slave states and free states joined together (how firmly?) in a union. There is a domain between them to which they both have claims: new territory, and the district of their common capital. Who will prevail? Or rather, which principles will prevail?

THERE MUST HAVE BEEN quite a scene when Slade brought this address to a close, two days before Christmas 1835, in a chamber dominated by Southerners of a different stripe from the Virginia debaters he had quoted. He finished thus:

> **[Slade]:** Sir, we must not bury these petitions. And let me say to [you] gentlemen, that such a policy will certainly defeat itself. You cannot smother investigation of this subject. Sir, the spirit of free inquiry is the

> master spirit of the age: it bows to the authority of truth and reason and revelation; but it bows to nothing else. It must have free course, and it will have it; giving life and soul and energy to the march of liberal principles, and destined to shake every institution on earth, which does not recognize the "inalienable rights" of man, and bow to the supremacy of just and equal laws. And, sir, it shall move onward and onward and onward, until every kindred and tongue and people under Heaven shall acknowledge and glory in the great truth that "ALL MEN ARE CREATED EQUAL."

If you read through the other speeches in that session of Congress you will realize just how unusual this one was. Most of the speechmaking was done by Congressmen from the eleven slave states. Most Northerners who did speak were quick to retreat, like Fairfield, or to reassure and assist their Southern colleagues, as Aaron Vanderpoel of New York and the future president Franklin Pierce of New Hampshire and others had done.

In a historical summary of these matters written much nearer the time (in 1897), a book called *The Middle Period* (what period is the "middle" changes), the author, a professor of political science and constitutional law at Columbia named John W. Burgess, gave the following description of Slade's speech and the response to it: "Mr. Slade . . . delivered an anti-slavery speech . . . such as had never before been heard upon the floors of Congress. He not only vindicated the power of Congress over the question of slavery in the District, but he discussed the whole question of slavery upon its merits. His words were simply a declaration of relentless war upon slavery in the halls of Congress. They created indescribable consternation in all parts of the House, and roused the resentment and anger of the slaveholders to a veritable fury."

FURY OR NOT, SOMEONE had to respond to Slade. After considerable confusion on the floor, this task fell to another Virginian, whom we have already quoted, James Garland.

Speaking in the aftermath of Slade's performance on December 23, Garland waxed sarcastic about the alleged benevolence of what the congressmen had just heard:

> **[Garland]:** The honorable gentleman professes great kindness for us, his benevolence for us is very expanded! He means no offence! He does not mean to call us land-pirates and man-stealers! Oh, no! But then, says the gentleman, that system among you is a system of land-piracy! a merchandise in human flesh! The gentleman does not mean to hurt us, oh, no, but

> he means to assail our rights, and destroy our property, out of mere benevolence, mere kindness to us. While he smiles in our faces, he drives the dagger to our hearts!

As is usual with benign modern reformers, Slade had sought to locate the evil he denounced not in the human beings he was opposing but in the *system* they defended. Garland was having none of that.

> **[Garland]:** You, he says, are not pirates and man-stealers, but your system of slavery is, in every mien and in every form, a system of piracy and man-stealing, accompanying the charge with every opprobrious epithet, which the honorable member could string together. This, sir, is kindness with a vengeance, for which we have no thanks to return to the honorable member from Vermont. . . .

Garland returned to the peril of the slave South, contrasted with the calm security of Vermont:

> **[Garland]:** Sir, these abolitionists, (I class them all together,) have excited a feeling of alarm in the South which cannot easily be quieted. The safety of our wives and our children is endangered by their mischievous and incendiary attempts to produce a servile insurrection among our slaves. But oh, says the gentleman from Vermont, you are in no danger; all will be effected peaceably and quietly! Sir, will the gentleman permit us to judge for ourselves. We are in the very midst of the slave population, while he is securely sheltered behind the ramparts of the Green Mountains of the North.

Congressman Garland mentioned the tour of the United States undertaken by the English abolitionist George Thompson, implying that Thompson had had something to do with the outrageous opinions of his colleague Slade and his Vermont constituency. Slade interrupted to note, in a laconic New England way, that Thompson had never been to Vermont. It was as though to say we did not need any Englishman to show us how to be antislavery in Middlebury.

Responding to an ironical Northern reference to "the sublime merits of slavery," Mr. Garland had the opportunity to use a visual aid—the portrait of George Washington hanging in the hall:

> **[Garland]:** Let me ask the gentleman, when he speaks of the "*sublime merits* of slavery" in the ironical sense . . . to cast his eyes upon that picture, (pointing to the portrait of General Washington) of the Father of

> his country, and stand rebuked by the recollection of his virtues and his deeds. When the people of the North were weak and assailed by a cruel and unrelenting enemy, and struggling for their rights . . . he and his companions in arms left their wives, their children, their domestic firesides, their farms, their all, risked all they possessed, hazarded all they held dear, and periled their lives and fortunes, to espouse the cause of the northern people, and in defence of northern liberty. Sir, that man was a slaveholder, and his southern companions were slaveholders.

Mr. Garland explained why "a more decided method" was now required to dispose of these petitions:

> **[Garland]:** . . . the House, by a decided vote, refused even to honor these memorials [Fairfield's] with the customary respect of ordering them to be printed. And what has been the result? Why, sir, the very next moment comes another memorial, and then another; till at length they come so thick that the attention of the House could not keep pace with them; and the very memorial now before us [Briggs's petition—all of this debate is on the question of reconsidering the referral of that petition to committee] was presented and got a reference to one of the standing committees without attracting the attention of the House, which I am quite sure, the House never designed. Nor was this all. Why, sir, the gentleman from Vermont (Mr. Slade) tells us he is charged with numerous petitions of the same character. Sir, when are we to have an end of them? This House has decided they will not print them; it has decided they will not consider them further than to lay them on the table, and yet they came and are to come, in shoals upon us. Sir, it is time now that this house should take a more decisive stand; should adopt a more definitive course, should decisively rebuke these intermeddlers with the property of others.

He linked the "more decided method" with recent events, and characterized the abolitionists in no uncertain terms.

> **[Garland]:** Sir, there is another reason why the action of Congress should be more decisive now than at any former period; and why the people of the South should call for a more direct expression of the sentiments of this House than heretofore. On former occasions there was no extraordinary feeling of alarm, no excitement, no apprehension of danger spread through that section of the country. The spirit of insurrection and insubordination was not then abroad.

But the spirit of insurrection and insubordination was now abroad, and the slaveholders, said Garland, intended to face it with resolution.

> **[Garland]:** Mr. Speaker, we may suffer much in the conflict with which we are threatened; but be assured, that unless God, in his providence, has determined our fate otherwise, we shall drive back the storm—we will maintain our rights—keep our slaves in subjection, and drive back, with a signal overthrow, these intruders upon our rights.

After Garland had quite finished, a New York member moved the previous question, which the House promptly voted. One might expect that few, by that time, knew that the previous question was the reconsideration of the referral of Mr. Briggs's petition to committee, but be that as it may, the members now voted in favor of it.

So the referral of Briggs's petition was the question once more before the House—to be reconsidered. And the House (promptly once again; like all such bodies after hours, or weeks, of tedious going, when enough members wanted to or were tired enough, it could suddenly move very swiftly) voted to lay Briggs's petition on the table. So that petition had been retrieved, after using up all the shopping days before Christmas to do it, and had been denied the dignity of referral to committee, or discussion, or response. But it had *not* been subject to that last indignity—being *rejected*, stamped with Mr. Hammond's "seal of a more decided reprobation."

The House, in its day of swift action at the end of 1835, did not go quite that far. It simply laid Mr. Briggs's petition on the table, along with all the others. Before this episode was over it would be joined by many more.

PART III

THE FIENDS AND THEIR WORK

6 / FIENDS OF HELL, EAST

WHO SIGNED THE PETITIONS that so exasperated James Henry Hammond? Who were the ignorant, infatuated barbarians whose right to petition Slade presumed to defend? Who were these foul murderers, bloodhounds, incendiaries, agitators, instigators of midnight murder? These disturbers of our peace and enemies of our lives and liberties? These cold-hearted, base, malignant libelers and calumniators? These knowing accessories to murder, robbery, rape, and infanticide? In short, who were these fiends of hell? Churchwomen, mostly. Churchwomen and preachers, and Quakers, and a few teachers and lawyers and journalists—a powerless and marginal handful of practitioners of a new sort of reform.

The leaders of the movement that produced these petitions were men like—to start with one Eastern example—John Greenleaf Whittier. Whittier, whose middle name evokes his distinguished Puritan ancestry, was a tall, shy, talented Massachusetts Quaker, a writer of poems which his sister first sent off for publication without his knowledge, who was later to become one of the most acclaimed of American poets. It is still possible to encounter in older anthologies Whittier's "Snow-bound"—once one of America's most widely known and admired poems. Occasionally someone even now will quote, as did the chief justice of the United States Supreme Court in the flag-burning case of 1989, these lines from Whittier's "Barbara Frietchie":

> "Shoot, if you must, this old gray head,
> But spare your country's flag," she said.

And this couplet from his "Maud Muller" is still floating around in the community's storehouse of quotable observations:

> For of all sad words of tongue or pen,
> The saddest are these: "It might have been!"

Whittier's eminence, faded now, was such that Quaker settlers would one day give his name to a new town in California, in which many years later the man who would become the thirty-seventh president of the United States would spend his early days, listening to train whistles.

The Quaker books in the farmhouse in which Whittier grew up helped to form his original antislavery convictions, but in the early 1830s those latent convictions were given so much sharper a form and so much greater an intensity and so much higher a priority as to make of them a new ideology altogether. That happened to many young people in the late 1820s and early 1830s, and to a few not so young. It was one of those moments when a new moral perception swept through the community and a new movement was born. This one was to be the greatest such movement in American history.

A significant number of Americans underwent a kind of moral conversion. The new moral perception was not only that slavery was wrong—many had been saying that for years—but that its wrongness had the highest priority, and that the ways its wrongness had been opposed heretofore had been profoundly inadequate.

That may not sound like much of a difference to us, but in context the difference was enormous. It matters a great deal not only what position a participant in the public debate may take on an issue, but also how salient he (or now, she) makes it—whether down on the list as point 27 to be mentioned only if asked, or whether up at the top, featured at the center of the speaker's argument. Most of the American founders—as we have said, all of the great ones—had been formally opposed to slavery, but opposing slavery had been subordinated to the contingencies of forging a government and a union. Now opposition to slavery was to be the center not just of these crusaders' argument, but of their daily work. As they would say, of their lives.

In the case of the talented and ambitious young Whittier, that meant giving up (as he then thought) his already well-begun careers as an editor of newspapers, as an aspiring politician, and (most important) as a poet. Although he was only twenty-five when "converted" to abolitionism, he had already published two books of poems, more than his hero Robert Burns had published at that age. One of Whittier's biographers quotes, as applying to Whittier himself, lines the poet would dedicate to an abolitionist leader of a later generation, Charles Sumner:

> "Forego thy dreams of lettered ease,
> Put thou the scholar's promise by.
> The rights of man are more than these."
> He heard, and answered: "Here am I!"

Putting aside his own lettered ease and promise as a poet, Whittier answered, "Here am I," and in 1833 (when he was twenty-six) published a pamphlet called *Justice and Expediency,* which was full of ringing sentences pushing for "the only practicable, the only just scheme of emancipation: immediate abolition of slavery."

"IN THE GRAY TWILIGHT of a chill day of late November" in 1833, Whittier remembered forty years later, a good friend of his from Boston "made his appearance at the old farm house in East Haverhill" (the domicile that was to be the scene of "Snow-bound") to inform young Whittier of his appointment as a delegate to the convention that was to be held in Philadelphia that December to form the American Anti-Slavery Society.

This friend was William Lloyd Garrison, a slightly older product of Newburyport who had himself been converted from gradualism to "immediatism," and who had in turn, by his writing and his conversation and his encouragement, helped to convert Whittier.

Garrison was a journalist, an editor, a "publicist" who was already on his way to becoming the best-known of the abolitionists (of the white abolitionists, it should be said in the late twentieth century, as Frederick Douglass has become the best-known of black abolitionists). Garrison had been the very young editor who, before the conversion of either one of them, had first accepted a poem of Whittier's for publication in his short-lived paper the *Newburyport Free Press*. A man named Benjamin Lundy, a gentle and devoted Quaker opponent of slavery from the previous generation, in Boston on a speaking tour, persuaded Garrison, already a reformer, to concentrate his efforts on opposition to slavery. (Lundy converted Garrison, Garrison converted Whittier; that is the way it often went.) In 1828, Garrison, having moved to Bennington, Vermont, to edit another of the short-lived little papers of the time, would be an active participant in a campaign to collect petitions against slavery and send them to Congress that year. Then for a time he went to work on Lundy's antislavery paper, published in Baltimore, which had the quaint title *Genius of Universal Emancipation*. In Baltimore, Garrison met, through Lundy, free black people who were fiercely opposed to "colonization" as the remedy for slavery.

Lundy's gradualism eventually proved too restrained for the passions of Garrison, and he left Baltimore to establish in Boston a paper of his own, devoted to "immediatism": the *Liberator*. The first day of its publication, January 1, 1831, is often taken as the point of departure for the new abolitionism.

Nat Turner's slave rebellion in Southampton County, Virginia, occurred in August of that same year; David Walker's "Appeal . . . to the Colored Citizens . . . of the United States," a fierce condemnation of slavery from the perspective of a free black person, and including a call to rebellion, had been published in Boston late in 1829. These events were often linked, not only later by historians, but at the time by what Waddy Thompson called "the excited, the almost frenzied South." Garrison and his new publication came to be notorious—condemned and denounced particularly in the South—in part by confusion and association with these events by which its beginning was bracketed. He and the *Liberator* suddenly became well known as leading indicators of the new atmosphere with respect to slavery.

Governors of Southern states asked the governor of Massachusetts please to make Garrison shut up. But in a society formally pledged to civil liberty it would have been hard for the governor of Massachusetts to comply with that request, which he did not try to do. That would be one of many examples of the difficulties under which slavery's attempt to erect intellectual barricades would labor in a society formally committed to freedom. Still, the circulation of Garrison's newspaper remained very small.

So Garrison had already achieved a certain notoriety when he came to the Whittier farm in Haverhill in November of 1833 to ask Whittier to attend the convention in Philadelphia the following month. The poet, writing many years later, remembered that he had been apprehensive about this trip to Philadelphia. He was timid, and did not much enjoy traveling; the political atmosphere was disturbing. The "few abolitionists were everywhere spoken against, their persons threatened, and in some instances a price set on their heads by Southern legislators." And, for this Upper New Englander, going to Pennsylvania was going *south*. "Pennsylvania was on the borders of slavery," Whittier wrote, "and it needed small effort of imagination to picture to one's self the breaking up of the Convention and maltreatment of its members."

Nevertheless Whittier did, in the end, make the trip down South to Philadelphia. On the morning the convention began, ". . . we repaired to the Adelphi Building, on Fifth Street, below Walnut, which had been secured for our use. Sixty-two delegates were found to be in attendance. Beriah Green, of the Oneida (New York) Institute, was chosen president. . . . Lewis Tappan and myself took our places at his side as secretaries. . . . Looking over the assembly, I noticed that it was mainly composed of comparatively few young men, some in middle age, and a few beyond that period. They were nearly all plainly dressed, with a view to comfort rather than elegance. Many of the faces turned towards me wore a look of expectancy and suppressed enthusiasm; all had the earnestness which might be expected of men engaged in an enterprise beset with difficulty and perhaps with peril."

Through the mist of memory, Whittier remembered, and named, and described, some of the sixty-two who were delegates. One was an older Quaker who "for thirty years had been the protector of the free colored people of Philadelphia, and whose name was whispered reverently in the slave cabins of Maryland as the friend of the black man, one of a class peculiar to old Quakerism, who in doing what they felt to be duty, and walking as the Light within guided them, knew no fear and shrank from no sacrifice. Braver men the world has not known."

Another delegate who attracted Whittier's notice was ". . . the young professor of a Western college, who had lost his place by his bold advocacy of freedom, [and] with a look of sharp concentration in keeping with an intellect keen as a Damascus blade, closely watched the proceedings through his spectacles."

That was Elizur Wright, Jr., who in the late summer had left his teaching post at Western Reserve College to become (with a subsidy from Arthur Tappan) the corresponding secretary—the full-time employee, and in effect office manager—of the emerging organization; the invitations to all the meetings, including this first one, would have his name on them. For the next six years he would closely watch the proceedings through his spectacles, and administer them with his Damascus-blade intellect.

Twenty-one of the sixty-two delegates, we are told, were Quakers; at least one, Samuel May, was a Unitarian minister; most of the rest were Congregationalists or Presbyterians, products of a new religious atmosphere. There apparently were three black men at the convention who signed its declaration. And although formal participation in public life was then reserved for males, there were four women invited to the Adelphi as "listeners and spectators." The time would soon come when they would do much more than listen.

In a still later reminiscence, on the fiftieth anniversary of the Philadelphia convention, Whittier as an old man described the group that had gathered there in his youth: "Looking back over the long years of half a century, I can scarcely realize the conditions under which the convention of 1833 assembled. Slavery was predominant. . . . Our convention, with few exceptions, was composed of men without influence or position, poor and little known, strong only in their convictions and faith in the justice of their cause. To onlookers our endeavor to undo the evil work of two centuries and convert a nation to the 'great renunciation' involved in emancipation must have seemed absurd in the last degree. Our voices in such an atmosphere found no echo. We could look for no response but laughs of derision or missiles of a mob."

Nevertheless, committees were appointed, as they always are, and officers chosen, as they always will be. The three-person committee charged with drafting a declaration, of which Whittier himself was a member, sublet the task to Garrison. In a reminiscence of Garrison many years later, Whittier wrote: "I love to think of him . . . as I found him in the gray December morning in the small attic of a colored man, in Philadelphia, finishing his night-long task of drafting his immortal *Declaration of Sentiments* of the American Anti-Slavery Society."

THE DECLARATION THAT RESULTED from Garrison's night-long labors was a rip-roaring and uncompromising document, loaded with hyperbole and rhetorical flourish, sprinkled with insistent capitals, and spiced with italics. It condemned root and branch not only American slavery but also all slaveholders, and all strategies other than immediatism.

It began, not surprisingly, with references to another declaration written fifty-seven years before in the same city and not far from the same spot (Jefferson had done his drafting in his rooms at 7th and Market; Adelphi Hall was nearer to 5th and Market): "More than fifty-seven years have elapsed since a band of patriots convened in this place to devise measures for the deliverance of this country from a foreign yoke. The cornerstone upon which they founded the TEMPLE OF FREEDOM was broadly this—'that all men are created equal; that they are endowed by their Creator with certain inalienable rights; that among these are life, LIBERTY, and the pursuit of happiness.' " (Capitals in the original.)

The task undertaken by the group in the Adelphi was then compared to that of the founding fathers, and contrasted to it—favorably:

"We have met together for the achievement of an enterprise, without which that of our fathers is incomplete, and which, for its magnitude, solemnity, and probable results upon the destiny of the world, as far transcends theirs as moral truth does physical force."

The 1833 declaration proceeded through three paragraphs contrasting (with Garrison's italics) *their* principles, measures, grievances—that is, those of the American patriots of 1776—to *ours*—that is, those of the sixty-two reformers gathered in the Adelphi Building in Philadelphia in 1833. The superiority of the latter that Garrison had in mind came, in part, from the new group's pacifist or nonviolent principles:

"*Their* principles led them to wage war against their oppressors, and to spill human blood like water, in order to be free. *Ours* forbid the doing of evil that good may come, and lead us to reject, and to entreat the oppressed to reject, the use of all carnal weapons. . . .

"*Their* measures were physical resistance—the marshaling in arms—the hostile array—the mortal encounter. *Ours* shall be such only as the opposition of moral purity to moral corruption. . . ."

In addition, Garrison contrasted the respective sufferings:

"*Their* grievances, great as they were, were trifling in comparison with the wrongs and sufferings of those for whom we plead. Our fathers were never slaves—never bought and sold like cattle. . . ."

One might have asked, at least as a matter of rhetorical strategy, whether it was wise to start a new movement of reform in the America of the 1830s (or any other decade, for that matter) by claiming that the American founders' grievances were (comparatively) "trifling." And one might further have questioned such an approach when the sufferings in comparison to which the founders' are judged to be trifling are those not of the declaration-signers themselves—who also have not been bought and sold like cattle—but of third parties—"those for whom we plead"—the moral prestige of whose suffering the signers of the document implicitly borrow for themselves. But one suspects that hints about possible self-righteousness in the tone of the document would not have been well received in the Adelphi.

The declaration did indeed put forward a stinging and thorough and unrestrained condemnation of American slavery: ". . . the guilt of [this nation's] oppression is unequalled by any other on the face of the earth." It called for immediate emancipation: "[This nation] is bound to repent instantly, to undo the heavy burden, to break every yoke, and to let the oppressed go free. . . . the slaves ought instantly to be set free, and brought under the protection of the law. . . . [A]ll those laws which are now in force, admitting the right of slavery, are . . . before God null and void. . . ."

There was no reluctance about calling slaveholders names: "every American citizen, who retains a human being in involuntary bondage, as his property, is [according to scripture] a MAN-STEALER."

The document used a verb about the action of these man-stealers that one is not likely to see often: to "imbrute" ("no man has a right . . . to imbrute his brother").

In the midst of all of the unrestrained sentences one found just one significant concession, qualified by portentous italics: "We concede that Congress, *under the present national compact*, has no right to interfere with any of the slave states, in relation to this momentous subject."

On the other key points at issue the declaration gave clear, and extended and unequivocal, answers. No gradualism. No colonization ("delusive, cruel, and dangerous"). No compensation.

On this last matter Garrison produced an oratorical series of points beginning with the word "because," and rising in one case to indignant capitals. Man-stealing slaveholders are not to be compensated:

"BECAUSE SLAVERY IS A CRIME, AND THEREFORE IT IS NOT AN ARTICLE TO BE SOLD;

"Because immediate and general emancipation would only destroy nominal, and not real property. . . ."

And finally there was this sharp twist:

"Because if compensation is to be given at all, it should be given to the outraged and guiltless slaves, and not to those who have plundered and abused them."

The delegates adopted the declaration pretty much as Garrison had written it, and affixed their signatures to it. The paper that they signed ended—the very last phrase—with a characteristic assertion of a willingness if necessary "to perish untimely as martyrs in this great, benevolent, and holy cause."

THE ESSENCE OF THE agenda with which these potential martyrs in a holy cause went out to face a hostile country was not only the immediate end of the sin of slavery but also rejection of the American Colonization Society.

Readers today, because the subject has lost all its fire, may not understand the importance of this last point, but in its time that was where the real debate lay. When Whittier was "converted," in his early twenties, on the subject of slavery, he, like almost all of the other abolitionists, was converted from "colonization" to "immediatism." His first fiery pamphlet, *Justice and Expediency,* was not only a thorough statement of the intrinsic evil of slavery but also a specific attack on the colonization movement as a deceptive and mistaken attempt to deal with it.

The American Colonization Society had since 1817 been promoting a polite form of antislavery. Its program was gradual emancipation—solely at the discretion of the slaveholders—and the emigration of the freed slaves to another place, a colony (hence the name) in the West Indies, in South America, or, as it developed, in Africa, and specifically to the newly established nation of "Liberia" with its capital of "Monrovia" (named for President Monroe). That program was loaded with convenient ambiguities, and was therefore ideal for politicians and public leaders caught in a hard spot either with their constituencies or with their consciences.

Colonization attracted the support of many of the nation's worthiest citizens. The talented straddler Henry Clay was one of the founders of the society. His young admirer out in Illinois, Abraham Lincoln, supported the idea almost all his life, right up into the President's House. Thomas

Jefferson in his old age supported it; James Madison in his old age was head of it; many of the nation's "most eminent divines," as they used to be called, and statesmen and public benefactors, supported it, too. It was the acceptable way of opposing slavery—not acceptable in South Carolina or in other centers of the fire-eating defense of slavery, but acceptable, and often comforting, elsewhere.

The colonization idea could be presented, because of its useful ambiguity, in radically different ways. It could represent a genuine effort, however misguided, to bring an end to slavery. Many abolitionists—that is, immediatists—started as colonization people. Whittier, as we have seen, did; even Garrison, if one goes far enough back, did. James Birney, later to be the abolitionists' candidate for president, had been a paid agent of the colonization society, and that was radical enough to cause him to be shunned in his hometown of Huntsville, Alabama. Colonization was sufficiently antislavery to draw the ire of the most excitable defenders of slavery. Proposals in the 1820s that Congress appropriate funds to support colonization were one item in the list of frightening developments that caused the atmosphere in South Carolina to be, as Waddy Thompson said, frenzied.

But colonization could at the same time be presented as a way to rid the nation of free Negroes (an anomaly, embarrassment, and danger, from the point of view of a race-based slavery) and also as a way to deflect antislavery agitation.

The colonization movement included under its great tent of ambiguity a wide range of opinion on slavery and race. It also corresponded to that mixture that a great many Americans, then and now, have within themselves with respect to the emotion-fraught issues of race and slavery: to want to end injustice—but not too soon. To want to see evils overcome—but not with any disruption. To want a better world for everybody—but *gradually*. Not too fast. What would happen if slavery were ended tomorrow? Can you imagine it? The well-disposed portion of the broad American ("white") public had in it a very great tendency to evade this difficult complex of issues. To keep it ambiguous. The American Colonization Society suited this inclination.

And the new proponents of "immediatism" opposed that inclination to ambiguity and postponement. American abolitionists were influenced in this regard by the example of their English counterparts—Wilberforce and the others—who had finally succeeded, in 1833, as we have said, in achieving by a vote in Parliament the abolition of slavery in the British possessions in the West Indies. That vote had several results in the United States: it furnished both an example and a moment of beginning (the American organizers waited until word of the vote arrived from England to go to Philadelphia to form the American Anti-Slavery Society) and it freed English campaigners now to come and be mobbed in the United States.

And it was one source of the lesson opposing any kind of procrastination. As Martin Luther King and his cohorts fighting against racial segregation in the twentieth century had had repeatedly to explain "Why We Can't Wait" (the title of one of his books), so in the previous century the English abolitionists, in their long struggle, had finally come to see that they had to say "immediately"—because anything gradual stretched out into never. If you were serious about ending slavery, history had shown, you had to cut through that endless self-deceiving delay.

But the new abolitionism had other very important differences with the colonization movement—beyond the issue of gradualism—that should be underlined for twentieth-century understanding. Many immediatists affirmed racial equality and what the later century would call an "integrated" society; the colonizers by definition rejected the second, and implicitly, and often explicitly, rejected the first. The premise of the proposed removal of freed black persons from this country could include not only implicit but also explicit versions of what the late twentieth century calls "racism."

So the issue was not just one of timing: "immediate" versus gradual. The issue was also one of the vision of America and the concept of justice, and therefore no small thing. Many immediatists were "integrationists;" the colonizers were not. The immediatists affirmed a biracial society; the colonizers did not. It was not just a little factional quarrel between two reform groups with different emphases or strategies; it was a switching point in the understanding of what this country was to be, and of the pattern of justice upon which it was to rest.

An argument of the immediatists, at a different level, against colonization was simply that it would never work. It was insulting, misguided, and doomed to failure. Black leaders would explain, from time to time, including ultimately at a meeting in the White House with President Lincoln himself, that the United States was their country, that they had no connection with any other and did not want to go to any other.

And it was not going to work. Whittier made this dramatic computation in *Justice and Expediency,* the pamphlet that declared his immediatism:

> Let facts speak. The Colonization Society was organized in 1817. It has two hundred and eighteen auxiliary societies. The legislatures of fourteen states have recommended it. Contributions have poured into its treasury from every quarter of the United States. Addresses in its favor have been

heard from all our pulpits. It has been in operation sixteen years. During this period nearly one million human beings have died in slavery, and the number of slaves have increased more than half a million, or in round numbers, 550,000;

The Colonization Society has been busily engaged all this while in conveying the slaves to Africa; in other words, abolishing slavery. In this very charitable occupation it has carried away of manumitted slaves: 613.

Balance against the society: 549,387!

The compensation of slaveholders would also never work: the country would go broke buying slaves. This was a point on which the new abolitionists and James Henry Hammond, from their opposite premises, agreed. But the abolitionists were against compensation for other reasons as well. We have seen the blast against compensation of slaveholders in Garrison's *Declaration of Sentiments*. Slaveholders should not be compensated "because emancipation would destroy only nominal, not real property; and because compensation, if given at all, should be given to the slaves."

If you think about that last proposition for a moment, you will see how far from the centers of power these people had to be. One of Congressman Hammond's reasons why slavery could never be ended was that the compensation of the owners would simply be too costly to be borne. These immediatists responded that there need be no compensation whatever because that property, millions of dollars' worth though it was on this world's books, was not real, because it was not just; its owners deserved no compensation whatever. And not only that: if you were going to talk about compensation, how about compensating the *slaves*?

The sixty-two delegates spent three days in Philadelphia and at the end had a solemn signing of the declaration. Given the fiercely hostile atmosphere and the impossibility of their task, Whittier was not wrong to touch with drama the signing of this document, as he remembered it many years later. The delegates were called by name to the front of the room. "One after another passed up to the platform, signed, and retired in silence. All felt the deep responsibility of the occasion: the shadow and forecast of a life-long struggle rested upon every countenance."

THE AMERICAN ANTI-SLAVERY SOCIETY now set about persuading the nation, and particularly slaveholders, to renounce their sin. Their program, announced in the declaration from the Philadelphia meeting, was to establish local societies everywhere, to send traveling evangelist-persuaders ("agents") everywhere, and to spread pamphlets and books everywhere. But the South clamped shut against all of these efforts. "Everywhere" turned out to be the North. Or rather, some parts of the North.

The antislavery societies that had once existed in the South disappeared, and a quite different kind of society, opposite in purpose, developed instead, and spread throughout the region: the Committee of Public Safety or Committee of Vigilance. These local watchdog groups of eminent citizens took charge of tarring and feathering Northern traveling book salesmen who were suspected of being abolitionists; made sure no one read the *Liberator* or the *Slave's Friend*; and put prices on the heads of noted signers of that shocking declaration up in Philadelphia—$100,000 for Arthur Tappan. Unofficial but socially accepted censorship-and-intimidation councils, the committees would last straight through to the Civil War, growing more and more powerful as the years went by. They were precursors to the Ku Klux Klan.

Although in the very early 1830s some abolitionist-evangelists had risked their necks on tours of the South, it was apparent by the middle of the decade that there were groups of men in virtually every Southern county seething with eagerness to kill any abolitionist who ventured into the neighborhood. We have seen that James Henry Hammond could solemnly and explicitly declare in the oratorical climax to a carefully written major speech on the floor of the United States House of Representatives that it would be a violation of duty to God, and—perhaps worse—of HONOR, for any Southern gentleman to fail to kill any abolitionist who made himself available for that purpose in the South. So the prospects were not bright, after 1833, for traveling abolitionist speakers in the South. They were in fact being mobbed in the *North*.

The vast bulk of the American people, in the North as well as the South, found the abolitionists at least as repugnant as did their representatives in the Capitol in Washington. They were, in the 1830s, not just a minority, but a very small minority that was despised, scorned, and actively opposed. The constraints that kept this opposition (just barely) within bounds on the floor of the House of Representatives—that confined it for the most part to epithets, shouts, grinding of teeth, angry speeches, threats to go home, and furious parliamentary maneuvers, rather than physical violence—did not always operate among the public at large.

Throughout the North in 1834 and 1835, abolitionist speakers were greeted with rocks, eggs, threats, cancellation of arrangements, the breakup of meetings, editorial calls for repression by leading newspapers, condemnation by leading citizens. When it was announced that an Englishman, the "notorious miscreant" (as hostile congressmen called him)

George Thompson (the one who had not been to Middlebury), would speak to the Boston Female Anti-Slavery Society in the fall of 1835, eminent Boston leaders called a mass meeting in Faneuil Hall to discuss measures to keep this terrible event from happening. (Faneuil Hall had been a principal meeting place of the patriots during the American Revolution, a symbol to this day of the fight for liberty, but perhaps not a good one during the meeting in August of 1835.) The New Jerusalem Church, where Thompson was to have spoken, demanded a prohibitive $20,000 bond as protection against mobs; a second place refused to take the meeting at all. When Thompson actually showed up, on October 21, 1835 (that is, about six weeks before the beginning of the congressional session at which Fairfield would introduce his petition and Hammond his motion), he was met by a mob, which included many of Boston's most eminent citizens. They were "gentlemen of property and standing," a phrase which has woven itself into memory; this was the first of what the abolitionists themselves called "respectable mobs"—"respectable" perhaps with sarcasm. The aggressive gathering of Boston eminence searched for Thompson, but he got away, and they seized William Lloyd Garrison instead, bound him, and paraded him through the streets.

When the Anti-Slavery Society of New York State proposed on that same day, October 21, 1835, to hold its state convention in Utica, the leader of the anti-abolitionist meeting that called for measures to stop it was the local congressman, the Democrat of note and friend of President Jackson to whom Congressman Slade had referred, his colleague Samuel Beardsley. Beardsley said at this meeting, according to an abolitionist witness, that "the disgrace of having an Abolition Convention held in the city is a deeper one than that of twenty mobs, and that it would be better to have Utica razed to its foundations, or to have it destroyed like Sodom and Gomorrah, than to have the convention meet here." Clearly he felt strongly. The Utica mob, spurred by its congressman to prevent this disgrace, kept the convention out of the meeting room the council had granted them; broke up their meeting at the Second Presbyterian Church to which they fled; then, to let off steam, sacked the offices of an antislavery newspaper. The fleeing convention delegates, meanwhile, adjourned on invitation to the private home of a wealthy citizen named Gerrit Smith, who lived in nearby Petersboro.

Smith had been a colonizer; witnessing the Utica mob and its congressional leader in action changed his mind, and he was thenceforth a stalwart immediatist. These violent attacks upon the freedom of speech and of assembly of abolitionists often had that result on sympathetic but not yet committed witnesses: Wendell Phillips, the Boston Brahmin who was to be one of abolition's great orators, was "converted" to undiluted abolition by watching that mob of respectables parade through the streets with Garrison bound up in rope.

Another mob, summoned by a notice that read, "All citizens who may feel disposed to manifest the true feelings of the state on this subject are requested to attend," had driven the New York City Anti-Slavery Society from its planned meeting place in October of 1833 and manifested the allegedly true feelings of the state on July 10, 1834, by attacking Lewis Tappan's house in New York City, where the abolitionist leaders often met, breaking up a meeting, taking Tappan's furniture out in the yard and burning it, and gutting several churches and businesses and many homes owned by blacks.

Utica's repression is notable because it was led by a congressman, Boston's because it was Boston, and New York City's because it was New York City and one of the longest and worst. But dozens of cities across the North had episodes of the same kind in the years following the organization of the American Anti-Slavery Society. There were physical efforts to suppress speakers in all of the New England states in those years, and in Pennsylvania, New York, and Ohio as well. New York City and the state of Ohio were particular Northern centers of anti-abolitionist violence, because each contained a particularly volatile mixture of groups and opinions. In many of these places in the North there was significant violence well into the 1840s.

New Jersey and Connecticut, among states in the North, record far fewer mob actions than other Northern states in the 1830s not because they were more hospitable to abolitionists but for the opposite reason: they were more hostile and shut the door more effectually.

When the new association began to send "agents" across the North, some of them wore "storm suits" of old clothes when they spoke, because they could not afford, on an abolition agent's very small salary, to keep replacing clothes. Occasionally there were stonings or clubbings or lashings. The advice given to antislavery agents in their training period about how to conduct themselves in the presence of a mob calls to mind the backbone-strengthening, cutting-the-threat-down-to-size talks that civil rights leaders like Andrew Young would give in the twentieth century to young demonstrators facing down the Birmingham police.

When there would come an abolitionist martyr, it would be, in the fall of 1837, the preacher-editor Elijah Lovejoy, killed by a mob out in Alton, Illinois, while defending his press. Mobs had already destroyed three of his presses; trying to defend the fourth, he brandished a pistol, and was killed. Some abolitionists, although of course honoring him in some ways, nevertheless condemned his threatened use of that "carnal weapon."

And if this was the story in the North, antislavery evangelizing of the South was out of the question. Perhaps it had once been imagined that they could send abolitionist-evangelists south to preach abolition for the conversion of slaveholders. But the result was otherwise: instead of Northerners going south, Southern opponents of slavery, fleeing or driven out, came north. They became important operatives in Northern antislavery activity. These included James A. Thome of Augusta, Kentucky, and William T. Allan of Huntsville, Alabama, sons of slaveholders, whom we will meet again in the next chapter. They also included James Birney, also from Huntsville, whom we have already mentioned as a particularly big catch for the immediatists because he had been a prominent agent for the colonizers; when in the fullness of time there would come an abolition party—the Liberty Party—he would be its candidate for president. But perhaps the most potent of all the Southerners who moved north were the sisters Angelina and Sarah Grimké, who came from a distinguished family in Charleston, South Carolina, the heart of the strongest resistance to abolition. They left Charleston for Philadelphia, the Episcopal Church for the Society of Friends, and a slave-owning family for active work for the abolition of slavery, and were to be a mystery and a torment to their family back in Charleston all their lives.

7 / FIENDS OF HELL, WEST

THE PORT CITIES ON the coast (like Boston and the Newburyport of Whittier, Garrison, and Congressman Caleb Cushing) were centers not only of reform but also of banking, commerce, and conservatism—in Newburyport's case, especially of shipping. Not many decades earlier, some of these cities had been, as they were to be continually reminded, centers of the slave trade. The Whigs in Boston would one day come to be divided into "Conscience Whigs" and "Cotton Whigs," the latter—textile manufacturers and others—catering to commercial interests with opinion-softening ties to the South. Senator Charles Sumner would one day coin a slogan, presumably not much appreciated by many textile manufacturers in eastern Massachusetts, linking in infamy the "lords of the loom" with the "lords of the lash."

But there weren't many of either of these in Ashtabula County, Ohio. Nor were there many in the smaller towns and rural parts of Massachusetts, where the Puritan dispensation lived on in its American home base, relatively undiluted by the cosmopolitanism and commercial ties that qualified it in the cities. Vermont, a capsule of rural and small-town New England, the first new state to join the original thirteen, was proud also to be the first never to have had slavery within its boundaries.

The new abolitionism had its most energetic support in the areas where the revivalism of the time was strongest, which were also the areas to which Protestant New Englanders had migrated: in the famous "burned-over district," a band of counties in upstate New York (burned over by multiple revivals and religious movements); in western Pennsylvania; in the Western Reserve of northern Ohio; and in certain pockets of New England and Quakerdom farther west. Most of the New Englanders who moved toward the West were the citizens of small towns, not lords of anything.

The Western Reserve is a strip of the old Northwest Territory, now of the state of Ohio, running for 120 miles along Lake Erie, that the state of Connecticut "reserved" to itself in 1786, after already having ceded to the Union its claim to Western territory in 1781. This cession was part of the interstate politics of the time; specifically, it was part of the effort to persuade Maryland, which had no Western land, to ratify the Articles of Confederation. Connecticut agreed to the terms of the Articles, but then five years later decided to retain part of the Western land that had been granted in its original royal charter—to compensate for its small size, on the one hand, and to compensate its citizens who had incurred severe losses during the Revolutionary War, on the other. Connecticut immigrants streamed into this "reserved" section of what would become northern Ohio, which thus remained a little nugget of transplanted New England. When Connecticut did finally cede the reserve to the Union in 1800, it made the provision that the land titles already granted by the state be protected.

To its encomiasts the Western Reserve was a kind of filtered, and improved, New England, with a change in manner toward openness and forthrightness, and a disentangling from the moral encumbrances of the commercial ties of the wealthy centers—a satisfactory hybrid of New England and the Midwest. It was in any case prime territory for the development of antislavery convictions. The prohibition of slavery by the Northwest Ordinance of 1787 made escape from, or avoidance of, that institution a motive in migration to all of the old Northwest, and first of all to the state of Ohio, and in particular to the Western Reserve.

The Western Reserve, along with the burned-over district in New York and the other areas mentioned above, was a center as well of the "Second Awakening" (the nineteenth century's wave of religious revivals), and partly for that reason, also of opposition to slavery.

At the center of the new abolitionism were young Presbyterian and

Congregational ministers of a trailblazing sort: Theodore Weld, Joshua Leavitt, James Thome, William Allan, Elijah Lovejoy, Amos Phelps, John Rankin, Jonathan Blanchard, Hiram Foote, Samuel Crothers, Huntington Lyman, Charles W. Dennison, John Watson Alvord, Simeon Jocelyn, Beriah Green, James Dickey, the Chillicothe Presbytery. Histories of abolition tend to become honor rolls.

But perhaps "ministers" is not the right word for them. Many were indeed converted in some high-octane religious setting; did go to seminaries; were ordained. They all did make their antislavery case in distinctly Christian terms—very much so. They did indeed have the style and approach of the preacher or evangelist. Nevertheless they characteristically did not serve churches. They traveled; they spoke; they wrote; they distributed tracts; they edited journals; they agitated; they were mobbed. They did those things full-time. That was their job. That was almost their denomination, their community of faith. When asked our identity in the settled modern world we usually answer with our occupation; in olden times one answered with some connection of place or of family. This new breed of the 1830s might have answered, after the manner of another—minority—modern tradition, with their "cause." Who are you? An "abolitionist." A "reformer."

The minister-reformers among them were joined by, or overlapped with, some who might fit partly into more conventional categories as journalists (Garrison; Stanton; Leavitt; Lovejoy), although on religious, reform, abolitionist journals—journals of the "movement" (a term used in the nineteenth century, as in the twentieth). They were joined also by an occasional former professor or educational administrator (Wright; Green), or lawyer (Birney; Sterling; Stewart; Wendell Phillips). They were supported by a few unusual merchants and men of wealth (the Tappan brothers; Gerrit Smith; the "Association of Gentlemen" in New York), who were angels as well for other aspects of the "Benevolent Empire" of Protestant do-goodish and evangelical undertakings. Those who were technically laymen rather than ministers, like Elizur Wright, Jr., and Henry B. Stanton, characteristically came from the same evangelical Protestant world, and spoke the same language, as those who were ordained.

There is no great symbolic figure for this American abolitionism in the nineteenth century to match Martin Luther King, Jr., for the twentieth-century civil rights movement—a figure, that is, whose worth must later be acknowledged, for public purposes at least, and however grudgingly, even by those who were once on the opposite side. To some extent it may be said that the apotheosis of Abraham Lincoln fills the slot in America's Mount Rushmore of memory for which an abolitionist might be a candidate. But Lincoln has many facets and many meanings in America's collective mind, transcending and qualifying as well as including antislavery, and he is not a symbol for anyone else who worked in that vein. In the case of Martin Luther King, Jr., our collective memory, though honoring King as an individual, is also subconsciously—perhaps consciously—honoring a great cadre of civil rights leaders, and an entire movement. There is no such extension of the warmth and approbation for Abraham Lincoln, "the Great Emancipator," out onto the lesser emancipators, like the traveling evangelical abolitionists of the 1830s and afterward. They remain "controversial" not only among members of the public but among scholars as well; to this day, one's appraisal of them tends to reflect one's own political philosophy.

One may ask, with the perspective of the late twentieth century, why Frederick Douglass, or some other black abolitionist, might not be the abolitionists' equivalent of King. The answer is that the very structures and attitudes against which they fought left black persons too far from any levers of power and too far from the central stream of the society to become key leaders, and hence symbols, to the whole nation, the way King could be in the next century. Douglass was still a slave while the events we have so far described took place. He did not escape from slavery until 1838; he did not give a public speech until 1841; thereafter he was a lecturer and a writer, with a complicated relationship to the white abolitionists. His great personal story has its own historical significance, but he is not likely to become a comprehensive symbol for the entire nation of the whole movement to abolish slavery.

There is another candidate who is not going to be accorded that place, either, but who deserves to be closer to it than he has been. The greatest of the new group of preacher-abolitionists, and the one who makes the most solid link to the West, was Theodore Weld, who has pretty much slipped out of America's consciousness, insofar as he was ever in it in the first place. His own extreme reticence and modesty are partly responsible for his obscurity. He did not sign his name to his productions; he did not like to go to conventions; he did not claim credit for his accomplishments; he did not write any book explaining what he had done; he did not edit a journal; for the most part (not entirely) he stayed clear of the disputes among the abolitionists. Weld would never have produced any swaggering personal assertion like Garrison's famous salute in the *Liberator*: "*I* am in earnest. *I* will not equivocate; *I* will not excuse; *I* will not retreat a single inch; and *I* will be heard!" (my emphasis). That assertion was to be quoted in modern times, rather incongruously, by John F. Kennedy, who did on occasion equivocate and excuse and retreat more than a single inch, sometimes to his credit. Weld would not have expressed himself in that self-dramatizing way. Nevertheless he was heard.

. . .

When Weld was a college boy at Hamilton College in New York he encountered the high-powered lawyer-turned-evangelist Charles Grandison Finney, the most important single figure in the outburst of revivals called the Second Awakening. At first Weld had said, dismissively, in response to Finney's impassioned appeals, "My father is a *real* minister" (meaning that Finney, the fiery ex-lawyer and traveling evangelist, was not). But the story of young Weld's encounter with Finney of course ends, as these stories always do end, with Weld being converted after all, falling on his knees together with Finney, the two of them "crying and praying" together.

Converted to what? Converted to a more intense expression of Christianity, to be sure, but to what worldly effect? There are more intense expressions of Christianity recurring throughout the history of Christendom, with widely differing political effects, direct and indirect; often the indirect are the more important. The effects of the First Awakening of the 1730s and 1740s on the politics of the subsequent decades—the revolt of the colonies of British America, and their setting up of a new nation—were certainly large; scholars debate how large, and what they were. But they were indirect. Jonathan Edwards and George Whitfield and the Tennant brothers—leaders of that awakening—did not make much of a direct application of their preachings to the actual social world around them, and moreover they were still enough within a Reformation mold to insist that it was God's grace and not human effort that did all the converting and the history-changing.

But the Second Awakening in the first half of the nineteenth century was no more like the First than the Second World War was like the First. The intervening century had brought a new nation, a widespread and growing democratic impulse, a further spread of the ideology of the Enlightenment, a Romantic movement, and an erosion or development, depending on how you look at it, of ancient Reformation theological points. Charles Finney was more than willing to give God some help in bringing sinners to repentance; he is famous for his "New Measures" to that end, and for the "anxious seat" that exposed the prospective convert to intense public pressure. And he was willing also to make more explicit references to the present real world than the evangelists who went before him. "Disinterested benevolence"—Jonathan Edwards's conception of the core of Christian life—was now to be given a more practical, immediate, and specific application than hitherto. In this "Awakening," there were to be significant *direct* effects on society—a long list of social reforms (prison reform; the public school system; reform of mental hospitals; "temperance") and a string of more specifically religious movements, like those for Sunday schools, missions around the world, and the distribution of Bibles and tracts. Theodore Weld's conversion by Charles Finney, in this setting, thus included a large dose of world-changing activism.

First the freshly reconverted Weld toured with Finney's "holy band" of traveling preachers. Already in that activity he made a startling innovation: he encouraged women to speak in meetings! Except among Quakers, that was not done; it violated custom and specific injunctions from Saint Paul.

Then Weld, an effective speaker and much in demand, specialized in two others in the potpourri of causes in that world of active benevolence: temperance, and "manual labor education." This last was a movement promoting colleges and seminaries at which students, along with their "literary" studies, earned their keep and learned to work with their hands. When a little later Weld went on to be trained for the ministry (perhaps), he went to the Oneida Institute in New York, which was one of the centers of that evangelically flavored manual labor education (up at four for prayers; breakfast at six; take the swill to the pigs; then to class; more chores; more classes; mostly bread and milk, codfish and potatoes for the occasional big dinner, a strip of meat once in a while for those few who were not vegetarians; more chores; more classes; more prayers; seven hours in bed at night). At Oneida, Weld came to be mentor for the two sons of Lewis Tappan, and through them became a friend of Tappan himself, and thus was linked to the enterprises Tappan and his brother supported with their silk-importing and dry-goods-store money. Lewis Tappan and Finney himself and Lyman Beecher, recognizing the young man's talents, urged various pastorates on him, but he refused them all. Instead in the early 1830s he toured the South as a promoter of manual school education and a temperance lecturer. Along the way, he talked to people about slavery.

Meanwhile, in that evangelical Protestant reform world he had become the friend of an Englishman named Charles Stuart, a veteran of the English battle over slavery, who sent him pamphlets and arguments on the subject. On his tour as a temperance lecturer, he came to Western Reserve College, in a town near Cleveland. Smack in the territory it was named for, Western Reserve was supposed to be a sort of a Yale of the West for this new Connecticut in Ohio. It had been founded by the transplants just in 1826, so that they would not have to send their sons back East, and so that the Presbyterian and Congregational churches of the settling frontier would have preachers. The president of the college when Weld visited was a man named Charles Storrs; the professor of mathematics was Elizur Wright, Jr., whom we have already met. The professor of sacred literature was the Reverend Beriah Green, who a year later would become president of that interracial manual labor institute/seminary at Oneida, New York, where the students took the swill to the pigs, and become, not long after that, the president, sitting up in front there in Whittier's description, of that 1833 founding meeting of the Anti-Slavery Association in Philadelphia.

Back at the time of Weld's visit to the college in 1832, these three, to the distress of the colonizer trustees and the rest of the faculty, were already an immediatist cadre, and talked to Weld. Biographers and historians infer that Weld now underwent yet another conversion—it was the time and place of many conversions—to the immediate abolition of slavery as the primary claim upon his life. It was like the conversion that Whittier underwent at about the same time, and that Garrison had undergone a little earlier, and that a number of other young Americans were undergoing. Weld had been ripe. He had been nominally a colonizer, but no longer. Henceforth his active expression of disinterested benevolence was to be sharply focused on the grave evil of slavery. By 1832, at age twenty-nine, he was almost a full-time abolitionist (two years later the "almost" could be stricken), and he swore to give his life to that cause, which he very nearly did.

NEW YORK CITY CAME to be the headquarters of the American Anti-Slavery Society founded at the meeting Whittier attended in Philadelphia, and, odd as it may seem to later geographical sensibilities, tended to be associated with the efforts in the "West" in contrast to the Eastern efforts centered in Boston.

The great benevolent organizations had their headquarters in New York and held their annual joint gatherings there each May. And New York was already the center of money and fund-raising. We have mentioned the Tappan brothers—Arthur, for whose head $100,000 was to be offered in the South, and Lewis, whose furniture had been smashed in the North. (Arthur Tappan, not generally given to humor, nevertheless remarked, when he heard the sum offered for his head, that if they would deposit it to his name in the bank he might consider turning himself in.) They were, as we have said, silk importers and dry goods merchants; their store sold for fixed prices—no haggling—and hard cash, and made money by low markups and high volume. They became leading benefactors in the Empire of Benevolence that dealt with all the social reforms, and with the more distinctly religious ones as well. (The phalanx of Protestant voluntary societies that took on these causes was to be much admired at just this time by the young Frenchman who visited this country and wrote a great book about it, Alexis de Tocqueville.) In addition to their efforts to reform the world in other regards, the Tappans led and financed multiple antislavery activities. Whenever you read about an abolitionist project, you find that one of the Tappans was furnishing the money.

The Tappans asked their able new friend Weld to help them with one of their great projects: to pick the site for an institution that would train men to evangelize the rugged West. Rochester was first considered, but then Cincinnati was chosen, and Lane Seminary was born. The great Lyman Beecher, the leading clergyman of the age, was persuaded (with the help of money from Arthur Tappan) to leave his powerful post in the East to move to Cincinnati and assume the presidency of this place, full of hope and promise.

The cream of the crop of Finney's converts were invited to come as students; they were not raw college graduates but in many cases older men. Weld, who was now thirty-one, brought with him from the Oneida Institute some of the ablest of Finney's followers and some of his own, too. An attack on the student debates that will be described below, written by a man named Hall and published in a Cincinnati magazine in the following spring, arguing that the young students should stick to their books and that the budding preachers should stay out of politics, called them, condescendingly, "boys at school"; "precocious undergraduates"; "embryo clergymen." Weld, responding to this attack, gave a few statistics: "Thirty of the theological class are over twenty-six years old, fourteen are over twenty-eight, and nine are between thirty and thirty-five. Two of the class were members of colleges seventeen years ago. . . . One of the class was a practicing physician for ten years. . . . six of the class are married men; three of them have been so for nearly ten years. . . . So much for the babyhood of the theological students." These mature students were to make a mark in abolition history.

The main stated aspiration for this new place, which opened in the autumn of 1833 in Walnut Hills, was for it to become a center of the new Finney-style evangelism, aimed at converting the "West." But the students were to give that expectation a twist. Weld saw Lane as a possible center of abolition.

And so there would come about in the very early days of Lane Seminary, in February of 1834, the most extraordinary episode of student "activism" in this nation's history. Weld was the planner and central figure in that event, a "teach-in" of the highest magnitude. These student activists broke no windows and threw no bombs, blocked no one's way and spit in no one's face, and shouted down no speakers; the method of their action was talking, arguing, sorting out their own ideas, converting others—converting *themselves*—by argument. Irenically, throughout: "Every student in the seminary," Weld wrote, in response to Hall's attack, "will testify that courtesy and kindness pervaded the whole debate."

Full academic freedom had been a founding point of the seminary. This very mature student body, exercising that freedom, organized extracurricular discussions about temperance and other issues of the day, and then, with Weld in the lead, on slavery.

Or rather, on the better way to end slavery. Among the Lane students, antislavery opinions of some kind were widespread, perhaps universal (colonizers, of course, regarded themselves as antislavery), but most students' positions had not yet reached the point of "immediatism." Apparently there was on the faculty only one full sympathizer with Weld and immediatism, a man named Morgan, and one partial sympathizer, Calvin Stowe, and only one sympathetic trustee; others ranged across the spectrum to strong opposition, with one faculty member, named Briggs, and many trustees fiercely opposed to the new abolitionists.

Cincinnati was a growing, changing, mixed, Western but Southern city—almost a Southern city on free soil, just across the river from slavery. Between 1820 and 1829 the entire population doubled, and the free black population multiplied tenfold. The Underground Railroad was going strong. But the larger flavor of the city was that of a community of Southern sympathizers. As the upper South was different from the deep South, so the upper North was different from the lower North, and Cincinnati was very low North indeed. The city was explosive; there had been a race riot in 1828.

At Lane, up on Walnut Hills, Weld had begun already, when the school commenced in the fall, planning an open, school-wide discussion of abolition. At first it was to have been held at almost exactly the time that the sixty-two delegates were meeting in Philadelphia to form the American Anti-Slavery Society, but after Weld talked with some of the faculty and students of colonizer persuasion, the Lane discussion was postponed until February of 1834. Weld, meanwhile, invited by a circular from Arthur Tappan, Joshua Leavitt, and Elizur Wright, Jr., to attend the Adelphi meeting in Philadelphia, wrote (from "Lane Seminary, Walnut Hills, Ohio") that he had to decline but that "My whole heart is with you." Asked to express his views, he did so: "I am deliberately, earnestly, solemnly, with my whole heart and soul and mind and strength, for the immediate, universal, and total abolition of slavery."

Weld and his fellow planners out in Cincinnati proposed that the faculty participate in their grand debate on slavery, and at first Beecher was disposed to do it, and to present his (rather characteristic) view that immediatism and colonizing need not be opponents but could go along side by side. But others in the faculty and the trustees were made uneasy by the whole event, in explosive Cincinnati, and proposed postponement yet again. This time, however, Weld and the students said they would go ahead, and the faculty, though apprehensive, agreed not to interfere.

The "debates" (as we may call them, although they were not debates exactly) went on for eighteen evenings, two and a half hours an evening. They were divided nine evenings each for the two topics, which in context came to almost the same thing: "Ought the people of the slaveholding states to abolish slavery immediately?" and "Are the doctrines, tendencies, and measures of the American Colonization Society, and the influence of its principal supporters, such as render it worthy of the patronage of the Christian public?"

There is no direct record of the speeches during the Lane debates, but there are indirect reports and much evidence of the effects. James Thome, a key figure, gave a report at the next annual meeting—the first anniversary meeting—of the Anti-Slavery Society which was printed in its journal. Weld himself gave an indirect picture in a vigorous answer he wrote, later in the spring, to Hall's patronizing and dismissive attack.

When the portentous event actually came, Weld spoke first, and although one cannot recapture speech-making from before the days of recording, by all reports Weld was an extraordinarily powerful advocate; in his writings one does get a sense of great rhetorical force. He was followed by a man who was to play an almost equally large role in the petition campaign and the abolition movement, Henry B. Stanton. (Stanton, a descendant of the William Brewster who arrived on the *Mayflower,* had been converted by Finney and then by Weld, had studied at Oneida and come on from there to Lane, and was to go on to be the second-greatest—after Weld—of the traveling agents of abolition, and then to a career in the later politics of antislavery; in the long history of the nation he has come to be perhaps best known, however, for being the spouse of Elizabeth Cady Stanton.)

Then came the Southern speakers. In preparation for the debates, Weld had softened up some of the participants, in particular the key Southerner William T. Allen. Allen was the son of a slaveholder and heir to slaves from Huntsville, Alabama, with whose family Weld had stayed, and discussed slavery, on his trip through the South, and Allen spoke first, followed by other Southerners. These speakers apparently had the most powerful effect of all. One of them was a black man named James Bradley, an ex-slave, who was said to have brought the audience to tears. (Oneida had had a few black students, and now Lane did: perhaps these were the first American interracial student bodies.) Another son of slaveholders who had crossed both the Ohio River and the ideological Rubicon was

James A. Thome of Augusta, Kentucky; he, like many others, was converted by these debates to immediatism.

"Converted" is the operative word. This was a teach-in on slavery, but it was a revival meeting, too, though a revival with a much more specific and consequential worldly outcome than revivals generally had. Thome, like most of the others, like most of the faculty and the trustees and the eminent divines, had been a colonizer; the eighteen evenings brought him to believe that colonization simply served to soften his sense of the evil of slavery and increase his prejudice against black persons. He cast this change of conviction in the stark and personal terms of revivalistic evangelism; he came to see the "sin" of slavery, and himself as "sinner" specifically in this regard. The sin of slavery, he said, placed the phrase "Thou art the man" upon "the forehead of every oppressor."

In the eighteen evenings in Walnut Hills there was evidently a good deal of this personal intensity. It was an atmosphere familiar in Christian history, especially in its evangelical Protestant manifestation: emotional, confession-personal, testimony-filled, self-examining (and perhaps other-examining: to critics perhaps including some emotional bullying), but now applied, with a sharply drawn moral point, to a quite specific social institution. Categories were collapsed: slavery became "sin," and all the immediacy urged against colonization was impelled by that loaded religious word, and the other loaded words and patterns of a high-powered religious conversion.

Weld came on again at the end, to nail down with argument the case against the colonizers. One man, John T. Pierce, who had come from Oneida to Lane and who was a strong colonizer, had refused to attend the debates, but relented in time to go to the last two evenings, heard what was called Weld's great speech closing the debate, was, of course, converted, and went on to glory as an immediatist agent later on—abolitionist histories are full of stories of this kind. By the end almost the entire group had been persuaded to abandon the ambiguous and slippery gradualism of the colonizing movement, and instead to oppose slavery root and branch, with African Americans still here in an integrated, biracial society.

BUT THAT GROUP CONVERSION would not have had such lasting significance had it not been for the sequel. The trustees opposed what the students did about it, and the students, en masse, withdrew from the school. And went on from there.

This did not happen right away. The students, glowing from those eighteen nights, formed an antislavery association with explicit immediatist principles: not only "immediate emancipation of the whole colored race, within the United States"—"immediate" and "within the United States" were the cutting points that the colonizers would not have accepted—but also (the colonizers would not have said this, either) the emancipation "of the free colored man from the oppression of public sentiment."

It is to be noted that the Lane rebels opposed not only slavery but, as the late twentieth century would call it, "racism." It is also to be noted that Weld in particular, in those days when Jacksonian democracy celebrated the voice of the people, made no bones about appealing against public sentiment, against public opinion. On this subject public sentiment needed to be challenged and changed. The black person, the statement avowed, in contrast to what "public sentiment" held, was created by God as "a moral agent, the keeper of his own happiness, the executive of his own powers, the accountable arbiter of his own choice."

The Lane students after their debate proposed, further, "the elevation of [slave and free black] to an intellectual, moral, and political equality with the whites," and in the service of this purpose began an activity that may have been even more offensive to angry Cincinnati opponents than their statement of principles. Several Lane students, including Weld, undertook to conduct schools, libraries, Bible classes, "lyceums," and other uplifting activities—a kind of 1830s poverty program, except with more religion in it—in Cincinnati's "Little Africa." In doing that they stayed in the homes of, and in other ways associated "socially" with, the free black population. Weld was later to write: "While I was at Lane Seminary my intercourse was with the Colored people at Cincinnati, I think I may say exclusively. If I ate in the City it was at *their* tables. If I slept in the City it was at *their* homes. If I attended parties, it was *theirs*—weddings—*theirs*—Funerals—*theirs*—Religious meetings—*theirs*—Sabbath schools—*theirs*—Bible classes—*theirs*. During the eighteen months that I spent at Lane Seminary I did not attend Dr. Beecher's church once."

Two students dropped out of school to conduct the educational program among Cincinnati blacks; others continued to participate despite the opposition of the administration and the trustees. Both these activities, and the students' announcement of principles, and particularly the social fraternization, drew heavy fire in Cincinnati. The faculty asked Weld to use his influence to persuade the students, for strategic reasons—money-raising, and injury to the public reputation of the seminary—to stop for a time this associating with free blacks as equals. Weld flatly refused, on practical and on principled grounds: staying in the homes of black people was indispensable to gaining trust, and furthermore "any reference to color, in social intercourse, is an odious and sinful prejudice." That was in 1834.

President Beecher admired Weld, but he was caught, as such administrators in other places have been caught. And as such administrators always must, he made a fund-raising trip. Often in this controversy, in the cautions of the faculty and the later demands of the trustees, the Weldites were told: Stop! You will dry up our sources of money for the school! But the Weldites did not stop. Weld himself contemptuously responded to the argument that their activities would "decrease the patronage" of the institution: "What! are our theological seminaries to be awed into silence upon the great questions of human duty? Are they to be bribed over to the interests of an unholy public sentiment, by promises of patronage or by threats of its withdrawal? Shall they be tutored in passivity, and thrown to float like dead matter in the wake of the popular will, the satellite and slave of its shifting vagaries? Are theological students to be put under a board of conservators, with special instructions to stifle all discussion, except upon the *popular side*?"

While in the summer poor President Beecher was in the East raising funds and attending the great annual confab of benevolent societies, and while the two sympathetic faculty also were gone on vacation, the executive committee of the board of trustees of Lane Seminary staged a little coup. They ordered the students to disband their antislavery society. They decreed that there should be no more discussions (not even "communications with the students at their meals or when assembled on other ordinary occasions") without faculty approval. Students who disobeyed would be expelled, on trustees' order, with no hearing. Professor John Morgan, who shared the students' views, was not to be rehired.

Weld, still in Cincinnati working in the free-black poverty program, wrote to the constantly compromising Beecher, appealing to him to return to deal with these outrages, and Beecher started back west—but then swerved north for more engagements. Poor Beecher was angry at what the executive committee of the trustees had done—their restrictions enacted in his absence went too far—but he was angrier still at the ungovernable Weldites. Like many administrators in his position, he had enemies on both sides.

A view of these events less equivocal than Beecher's, and a sample of what he had to deal with on one wing, was offered by a Cincinnati religious leader who wrote a definition, for a theological dictionary no less, of a word we have already used, coined in the heat of that Cincinnati summer: "Weldite." "This is the name of a most deluded sect, the leader of which was a fanatic by the name of Theodore D. Weld. . . . In the year

1834, by the aid of a few men of some note in the religious world, he excited a great tumult on the subject of abolishing slavery at once, amalgamating blacks and whites, overturning the order and peace of the country, for the sake of giving liberty and equality to a set of men who were incapable of self-government."

It is to be noted that the charge included equality and amalgamating the races. It is to be noted further that once again the opponents of the abolitionists became also the opponents of civil liberty: you students should disband, stop meeting, leave politics alone, stop discussion. Or we will expel you.

Weld wrote a ringing "Statement of Reasons" why they "seceded" from the school, signed by fifty-one of the students and released to the public in January of 1835, full of lamentation about the bright hopes now gone dim. The very first reason was that "free discussion, with correspondent effort, is a DUTY, of course a RIGHT." "Better, infinitely better, that the mob demolish every building or the incendiary wrap them in flames; and the young men be sent home to ask their fathers 'what is truth?'—to question nature's million voices—her forests and her hoary mountains 'what is truth?' than that our theological seminaries should become Bastilles, our theological students thinkers by *permission*, and the right of free discussion tamed down into a soulless thing of gracious, condescending sufferance." Rather than be "thinkers by permission" in a seminary that was a Bastille, the students withdrew.

THERE IS ANOTHER CHAPTER. In the Western Reserve there was a new and struggling institution of higher learning, a product of the same Tappan support and Finney impulses that had led to the founding of Lane, with the added feature that Finney himself had signed on as its professor of theology. This was Oberlin. Among its other distinctions it admitted women—the first American college to do so. Although some of the Lane rebels stayed in Cincinnati to run the schools among free blacks, and Weld himself hit the abolition trail as a speaker, many of the Lane rebels removed to Oberlin, and became thus the Lane/Oberlin rebels (some of them Oneida/Lane/Oberlin rebels), famous in the histories of abolition and American reform. When a year and a half later the Anti-Slavery Society asked Weld to put together a band of seventy "agents"—they tried to make it that number, for biblical reasons—that band of seventy, which was to become another abolitionist legend, included many who had Oberlin in their background, some who went clear back to Oneida; at its core were the Lane rebels.

From that extraordinary argument over eighteen nights in the chapel of a new little institution in Ohio, and the subsequent student rebellion, there would come a cadre of antislavery leaders who would persist (not all student rebels persist) to evangelize the nation for abolition. So the legend goes. The careful critic may want to qualify: "the nation" means the North; "the North" means mainly, although not exclusively, the upper North; the upper North means mainly, although not exclusively, the smaller towns and rural areas of the upper North—they were not as successful in the cities, and Weld for one stuck mostly to smaller places. And in those towns they reached, of course, only a particular part of the population, and a minority. They would "abolitionize" a slice of the people in certain sections particularly of rural and small-town upper Ohio, Pennsylvania, New York, and New England. But still that accomplishment, restricted though a more sober view would see it to be, would be the indispensable ingredient in the eventual "abolitionizing" of the nation.

And one fruit of their abolitionizing would be petitions, piling onto the desks of congressmen.

8 / YES, SIR, WORKED BY STEAM

THE FIENDS OF HELL sent their agents across the North, making speeches and facing mobs. But the slaveholders who needed to be converted were in the South. Was there no way to reach them? Sending abolition agents there was going to produce not freed slaves but dead agents, and any societies formed there were now going to be on the opposite side from the abolitionists. But there was another device for attempting to penetrate the heart of the slaveholder: the printed word.

The 1830s was the decade of the emergence of a new and much more efficient means of printing, a new technology of influence, the steam-driven press, and off those presses before long every day up in New York there would roll hundreds and thousands of abolitionist horrors. Here is a summary given by Congressman John W. Jones of Virginia, in his speech in the House on December 22, 1835:

> [Jones]: Was it not known to every gentleman upon this floor, that numerous abolition societies had been formed in the Eastern and Northern States, frowned upon, indignantly frowned upon, he believed, by the intelligent, the well-informed, and respectable portions of these communities. But could they shut their eyes to the fact, that these societies existed,

> that they had gone on to collect large sums of money, and had put into operation printing presses, which were worked by steam? Yes, sir, worked by steam, with the open and avowed object of effecting the immediate abolition of slavery in the Southern States. That by means of these two great revolutionizers of the world, he meant steam power, and the press, they had caused to be printed, and by means of the public mails, circulated throughout the slaveholding States, large numbers of newspapers, pamphlets, tracts, and pictures, calculated, in an eminent degree, to rouse and inflame the passions of the slaves against their masters, to urge them on to deeds of death, and to involve them all in the horrors of a servile war.

The new breed of abolitionists did not intend to urge anyone on to deeds of death, or to involve anyone in the horrors of a servile war, but they did indeed send publications printed on steam-driven presses in great foolish bundles to clergymen and postmasters in the South, with the expectation that these worthies would carry out a further distribution to editors, to governors, and to public officials. The pamphlets were to be distributed free of charge "by strewing the wayside, the parlor, the bar room, the stage coach, the rail car, and the boat dock."

This program, it may be safely said, was not a great success in the South. In July of 1835—the summer before the start of the session of Congress in which Fairfield introduced his petition and Hammond his motion—a group of highly motivated citizens of Charleston broke into the post office, tore open the mail sacks, extracted the offending matter, and burned the pamphlets in the public square. For good measure, with their fires raging, they burned Arthur Tappan in effigy.

Groups of citizens in other towns emulated this example of civic discourse. Postmasters, with the encouragement of the postal authorities in Washington, took it upon themselves to suppress the pamphlets; the postmaster in New York, with that same encouragement, extinguished the conflagration of pamphlets at its source.

So that summer blaze of pamphlets had been quickly stamped out; there was, however, smoke and heat and an afterglow hanging over the next session of Congress.

The pamphlets did furnish to congressmen, straining to communicate and to persuade, what later generations would call "visual aids": they could hold up an actual physical sample of this disgusting incendiary material so their colleagues could actually see it and deplore it in the concrete. Thus Congressman Garland, quoted in an earlier chapter—this pamphlet campaign was what he meant by "the events of last summer"—displayed before the very eyes of his fellow public servants an example of

> **[Garland]:** . . . such beautiful hieroglyphical calumnies as the one I now hold in my hand, pictures and cuts representing southern men and southern women in the most odious and disgusting form which it is possible for human ingenuity and devilish purpose to invent.

The reporter from the *Congressional Globe* made this parenthetical effort to describe what Congressman Garland was exhibiting on the House floor:

> [The paper **Mr. G.** held in his hand was a large sheet, printed on one side, and illustrated with cuts representing the pretended cruelties inflicted on the negroes of the South.]

The congressman was provoked by this sheet to a particularly rich and hearty flow of epithets:

> **[Garland]:** The authors of such papers are cold-hearted, base, and malignant libelers and calumniators, and deserve the bitterest execrations of every good and patriotic heart—they should be scouted from society.

Later in the session, on February 1, 1836, James Henry Hammond, in the long and carefully prepared speech I have already quoted more than once, covered in detail the recent history of the antislavery movement, and made more extensive use of the actual presence, in their midst, of the offensive incendiary materials. "I hold in my hand . . ." he would say, anticipating by 115 years the memorable use of that phrase by another legislator, Senator Joseph McCarthy. What Hammond held in his hand were various publications of the American Anti-Slavery Society—reports, but also pieces of propaganda.

> **[Hammond]:** Here, sir, is a number of the paper entitled "Human Rights"—a neat, well-printed sheet.

The neatness of the printing seems to have augmented the offensiveness of the "sheet," because it indicated that these incendiary fanatics had resources. Of other publications Hammond would observe "a large and handsome paper," and "of very respectable size."

An issue of this paper, *Human Rights* (Elizur Wright, who did most of the work, in a private pun, called it "Human Wrights"), had been among the items burned by the mob, or group of concerned citizens, in Charleston; Hammond noted that a copy was "committed to the flames" by William Wertenbaker, the librarian of the University of Virginia (the institution of higher learning founded by Thomas Jefferson, surrounded on all sides by quotations from Jefferson asserting the freedom of the human mind).

Hammond's inventory on the House floor of these shocking exhibits continued:

> **[Hammond]:** Here are several numbers of the "Anti-Slavery Record"; on the outside of each is a picture representing a master flogging naked slaves, and each of which contains within pictures equally revolting. Here is a handful of the little primer called the "Slave's Friend." On the covers and within each of these are also pictures calculated to excite the feelings and to nurture the incendiary spark in the tender bosom of the child. . . .

The Slave's Friend, as Hammond said, intended for children, was another of the items the watchful Charleston citizens, clearly not wanting to nurture that incendiary spark in tender bosoms, had consigned to the flames.

> **[Hammond]:** Here is a pamphlet entitled "Anti-Slavery Hymns," of which there are nineteen. They purport to be for the use of the "monthly concerts for the enslaved" in the city of New York, and the publication of a more copious collection in Boston is announced. Here is a small book entitled "Juvenile Poems." It contains, besides a great number of doggerel articles of the most inflammatory character, some nine or ten disgusting prints; all of which are designed "for the use of free American children of every complexion." Here is a pamphlet written by a "Man of Color," and here are a quantity of sermons, essays, reports, letters, &c., all intended for the same incendiary purposes.

This was by no means the end of Hammond's inventory of offensive materials. He must have had a large stack of them there upon his desk. It was common then for speeches to consume hours and sometimes days. Hammond, on February 1, took up much of the afternoon.

The fiends of hell were using illustrations in a new way that clearly frightened these congressmen; indeed, the pictures seem to have been the most offensive, and perhaps by inference the most effective, parts of the abolitionists' publication campaign. For one thing, the public eye was not yet accustomed to daily onslaughts of the "visual media." For another, pictures—even these crude engravings—might be especially effective with the illiterate, which almost all slaves were, and therefore especially dangerous. Congressmen Jones, Garland, and Hammond, and the *Globe* reporter, all referred to the prints in the quotations we have cited: "[P]ictures, calculated, in an eminent degree, to rouse and inflame the passions of the slaves against their masters"; "[S]uch beautiful hieroglyphical calumnies as the one I now hold in my hand, pictures and cuts representing southern men and southern women in the most odious and disgusting form which it is possible for human ingenuity and devilish purpose to invent"; "[C]uts representing the pretended cruelties inflicted on the negroes of the South"; "[D]isgusting prints." The use of illustrations, a harbinger of a world to come, was evidently a form of argument with which the old full-throated oratory found it hard to deal.

It was also clearly part of the danger that these bloodhounds, these firebrands, these fiends of hell, represented to Southern spokesmen, that they had money as well as growing numbers. More than one of the Southern representatives in that "exciting" winter (they themselves used the word "exciting" in that antique way) told the story of the growth of the new abolitionist societies, from the founding of the *Liberator* in Boston in 1831 by William Lloyd Garrison, through the arrival in America of the British antislavery activist George Thompson ("the notorious Thompson"; "the miscreant Thompson") after Parliament had ended slavery in the West Indies in 1833, through the formal founding of the American Anti-Slavery Society in Philadelphia in that same year, down to the pamphlet campaign of the previous summer. Gloomy speeches dwelt particularly upon the growing numbers of these societies—250, next year 350—and of members, thousands of them, and upon the money and resources available to them. Southern leaders read, and took seriously, the reports of the American Anti-Slavery Society in a way that few Northern congressman were likely to do. They knew, as surely not many people in the country did, the address in New York City from which the society mailed its materials—130 Nassau Street, and then 143 Nassau Street—and used "Nassau Street" as a fearsome metonymy. They acquired copies of Garrison's paper the *Liberator* (from Garrison in Boston) and of the society's paper the *Emancipator* (from Nassau Street), and studied them with much "excitement." In the early days, it is said, the subscribers to the *Liberator*—a very small number of people—consisted almost exclusively of free black people in the North and opponents reading it to goad their anger in the South.

PRESIDENT ANDREW JACKSON, A Tennessee slaveholder, in the annual message with which he greeted this Twenty-fourth Congress in December of 1835, called for severe penalties against the "unconstitutional and wicked" activities of the abolitionists, meaning their incendiary pamphlets and their inflammatory speakers. He specifically called for a federal law prohibiting the circulation of their publications:

> **[President Jackson]:** I would . . . respectfully suggest the propriety of passing such a law as will prohibit, under severe penalties, the circulation in the southern States, through the mail, of incendiary publications, intended to instigate the slaves to insurrection.

In the wake of this presidential request there arose a constitutional disagreement between two stubborn figures who had already clashed on Nullification, President Andrew Jackson and Senator John C. Calhoun. The point at issue in their curious constitutional confrontation, with their Scotch-Irish chins jutting at each other, was this: should there be a *national* censorship law, as Jackson proposed, or a series of *state* censorship laws, as Calhoun insisted?

In the Senate on December 21, Calhoun indicated that he certainly agreed with the president that the fanatics' activities—including sending those publications to the South—were "unconstitutional and wicked." The question was what to do about it. He moved that a select committee be appointed to deal with that passage in the president's message.

Proposing a *select* committee was significant, and it was significant, further, that the Senate accepted his proposal. Calhoun candidly explained that the standing committees to which such a proposal might ordinarily be expected to be assigned, including the Committee on the Post Office and Post Roads, had too few members from that "section that was most deeply interested in the matter"—that is, the slaveholding South. The committee, Calhoun claimed, should have a majority from that section, and this theory of committee membership was accepted. The resulting five-member committee had four from slave states and one from Massachusetts, with Calhoun as chairman—not only as chairman but as altogether dominant voice.

And so during that winter, while the House was coping with the first of the season's petitions, the Senate was discussing alternative methods—Jackson's and Calhoun's—of coping with the "unconstitutional and wicked" circulation of abolitionist publications, with their odious prints.

Each side in the conflict over that matter opposed the other's proposal for that reason of general principle and precedent, and possible application someday to oneself, that sometimes does provide at least a backhanded and minimal support for civil liberties. (Next time, if this principle be allowed, they may suppress *my* freedom.) The Calhoun Nullifiers, extreme states'-rights people, asked themselves: Do we really want the *federal government* censoring the mail? The Jackson Democrats, having felt the sting of South Carolinian resistance in the Nullification Crisis (when South Carolina claimed it could "nullify" a federal law), asked themselves: do we really want the *states* to decide which portions of the U.S. mail can be delivered and which cannot?

On February 4, 1836, Calhoun's committee reported, in place of the federal law suggested by President Jackson, Calhoun's own proposed bill. It was radically, one might almost say comically, a states'-rights bill. It subordinated the United States postal authorities absolutely to the will of the states in which they resided; what that state said should be delivered through the mail should be; what that state said should not be delivered should not be, under pain of fines and dismissal.

Calhoun's defense of his bill in the committee report and on the floor of the Senate carried the ironies of this moment in the history of American civil liberty one step further. In rebuking the proposal made by President Jackson, Calhoun invoked sound and fundamental principles—freedom of the press and freedom of the mails. But after having cogently argued against the federal suppression of fundamental freedoms, he concluded that only South Carolina ought to be allowed to suppress them. He made the case for liberty with point and force as it applied to the federal government—only to turn around and insist that the slaveholding states should and must interfere with it.

While he was defending liberty, Calhoun made the pertinent point that the free flow of ideas may be inhibited as effectively by blocking circulation as by prohibiting publication.

> **[Senator Calhoun]:** The object of publishing is circulation, and to prohibit circulation is, in effect, to prohibit publication. They both have a common object, the communication of sentiments and opinions to the public, and the prohibition of one may as effectually suppress such communication, as the prohibition of the other, and, of course, would as effectually interfere with the freedom of the press, and be equally unconstitutional. . . .

That would seem to be the solid argument of a sound civil-libertarian, would it not? Calhoun went on to ground his argument in the centrality of freedom of the press and of argument in the nation's past:

> **[Senator Calhoun]:** . . . it must be apparent, that to prohibit publication on one side, and circulation through the mail, on the other, of any paper

> on account of its religious, moral, or political character, rests on the same principle, and that each is equally an abridgement of the freedom of the press, and a violation of the Constitution.

He then made reference to the "sedition" part of the nation's first great contest over civil liberty, the episode of the Alien and Sedition Acts that had been enacted by the Federalist administration in 1798, and had been opposed, in the famous Virginia and Kentucky Resolutions, by the leaders of the opposing party, and of the South, Jefferson and Madison.

> **[Senator Calhoun]:** It would indeed have been but a poor triumph for the cause of liberty, in the great contest of [17]99 had the Sedition Law been put down on principles, that would have left Congress free to suppress the circulation through the mail of the very publications, which that odious act was intended to prohibit.

And yet after having called the sedition law an "odious act," as it applied to the federal government, Calhoun's report then said in effect that its odious objective should now be carried out by South Carolina.

In a later Senate speech (on June 8) defending his bill, Calhoun said that a federal law of the sort that President Jackson proposed was clearly unconstitutional:

> **[Senator Calhoun]:** It would be directly abridging the liberty of the press for Congress to pass such laws as the President recommended.

But then he also said, with inadvertently comic explicitness:

> **[Senator Calhoun]:** We [members of Congress] do not pass a law to abridge the freedom of the press, or to prohibit the publication and circulation of any paper whatever—this has been done by the States already.

Although the limits on the federal government in his view were severe indeed, there apparently were for Calhoun no civil-libertarian limits—perhaps no limits of any kind—on the *states,* "who possessed full power to pass any laws they thought proper."

Calhoun also argued—rightly, as one would surely believe—that President Jackson's proposed federal law was unconstitutional and wrong because it would grant to governmental authorities the right to determine which publications are "incendiary" and which are not, in order to exclude the former. But it developed, again, that Calhoun saw the fault in this grant of authority to be not that such a thing should not be done by *any* government—but rather that the federal government in particular had no constitutional power to do it. And that the federal government wouldn't do it *right*. Invading the people's liberties was apparently for him one of the powers reserved to the states.

The federal authorities, under such a bill as Jackson's, Calhoun noted significantly, would have the power not only to determine which publications were excludably incendiary, but which were not, and could enforce the delivery of the latter. Responding to criticism from Senator King of Georgia, Calhoun made the point plain: the federal government would have the right not only to brand some publications "incendiary" and exclude them, but also "to enforce the circulation of such as it may determine not to be incendiary even against the law of Georgia that might prohibit their circulation."

What is "incendiary"? Who is to decide? One can guess what Calhoun feared. There would be a federal Board of Incendiariness, with some people on it from places like Vermont and Massachusetts and Ohio, and they would pick up a copy of *The Slave's Friend*, and leaf through it, and decide that, whatever its merits otherwise, it was not any immediate danger to the republic: they might look through these nineteen antislavery hymns and hold that although they were not very good hymns, they did not constitute a call to insurrection against which the nation had to arm itself. Even Garrison's *Liberator*, shrill and intemperate though much of the material in its closely printed columns certainly was, might pass a federal board. If one had started suppressing publications that were shrill and intemperate, in this first decade of the penny press, one would have pretty well wiped the board clean.

Even if one should grant that a direct call to arms addressed to black Americans could legitimately be suppressed, the publications with which Nassau Street and its steam press were favoring a mostly resistant world would not be excludable. The abolitionists, by and large middle-class white evangelical Protestants, were appealing (mostly) to the conscience of their white fellow believers, not to the revolutionary ardor of oppressed black people. They grounded their appeals in Christian ethics and in American ideals, not in violent revolutionary ideology. And they were not calling anybody to arms; the main leaders and publications of 1830s abolitionism were pacifists, and, furthermore, in some cases—Garrison and others—were even opposed to government itself because of the coercion inherent in it.

So was the definition of "incendiary" broader than a call for slaves to murder their masters? It certainly was as far as Calhoun was concerned, and in Hammond's speech in the House, and in those of many others. Was a tract explaining that slavery was contrary to Christian teaching "incendiary"? A Northern congressman would later exclaim that even the speeches he and his colleagues might give in the House could be regarded as "incendiary." Would it then be impossible to circulate in the South the proceedings of Congress itself?

So what to do? Suppress such discussion in Congress? Prevent the circulation of congressmen's speeches? Insist that only the proslavery, and not the antislavery, side of the argument be presented? Should tracts purporting to prove—in contradiction to many books on the other side—that the Bible opposed slavery be suppressed as "incendiary"? Again—should only one side be heard, and not the other?

And what then about the most fundamental American documents themselves—the Virginia Declaration of Rights and the many bills and declarations that followed it, in the South as well as the North, and the great English documents and writings from which they drew—the many assertions of Liberty and Equality in the American heritage? The many assertions that human beings are by nature free and by nature equal—were those, too, to be suppressed? Above all, what about the Declaration of Independence, the document by which the nation was given its soul? Was Thomas Jefferson's Declaration of Independence not to be circulated in Virginia, for fear it would give the slaves, or tender-minded white youths, the wrong ideas?

What Calhoun proposed was that the federal authorities defer to state authorities and state laws for the definition of incendiariness—for the decision about what could or could not be delivered through the mail—but then cooperate with the states in enforcing their decisions. U.S. postmasters in the slave states would be instructed, under penalty of fines and dismissal, to remove from the mail anything "touching the subject of slavery" that state laws forbade. It was states' rights carried to new heights.

A winked-at suppression that did not need laws had already begun in the year before this contest in the Senate. When the flood of publications began rolling south from Nassau Street, President Jackson's close political associate Amos Kendall was postmaster general, and, in the summer of 1835, had not discouraged Southern postmasters from refusing to deliver materials to which the condemnatory adjectives could be applied. He seemed on one occasion even to apply a curious version of the doctrine of the Higher Law, to which, when later in a famous speech by William Seward the Higher Law would be on the other foot, the proslavery forces would have the most indignant objection. "We owe an obligation to the laws," Kendall wrote to the Charleston postmaster, "but a higher one to the communities in which we live." In another letter he said that although the abolitionist materials were technically within the letter of the postal regulations, they violated their spirit, which justified "any measure necessary to effect their exclusion." Kendall let postmasters know that they did not need to be scrupulous about the laws protecting the mails and that they could feel free to exclude antislavery material, and so they did. The postmaster in New York City was able to render the further service of excluding this material at its point of origin.

Some commentators and editorialists were made uneasy, as well they might have been, by this invitation from a federal official to local officers, or local community action groups, to go ahead and violate the laws he was supposed to administer. President Jackson's proposal in his December message may be seen as an effort to put the sanction of federal law behind those winks and hints from his postmaster general, and the suppressions by Southern vigilantes. Senator Calhoun's absolute states'-rights proposal in February may be seen as a competing effort in the same cause.

NEITHER PRESIDENT JACKSON'S PROPOSAL nor Senator Calhoun's was passed, because of the interesting cross-checking fears and convictions already described. Formal censorship by law foundered on this rather extraordinary example of conflicts in federalism.

And Northern opinion shifted somewhat. The onslaught of pamphlets in 1835, like the rest of the abolitionist program, had not been met with favor by the general Northern public. And therefore Amos Kendall's acquiescence in, or encouragement of, the suppression of the publications by Southern postmasters and even by vigilante groups at first met with some visible and audible approval in the North. But as the breadth and vagueness of the definition of "incendiary" in Southern laws and Calhoun's bill became apparent, and as the span of the materials that might be inspected, and the officials who might do the inspection, under Calhoun's bill sank in (do you want a deputy postmaster in a Southern town opening your private letters to see whether they contain any incendiary matter?), second thoughts about precedent and civil liberty set in. This was one piece of the larger story: as it was made apparent that the defense of slavery included an abrogation of civil liberty, including civil liberties of citizens of the free states, the opinion opposed to the "slave power" began to grow.

As the British government in 1765 had not been wise to enact a measure, the Stamp Act, that singled out for particular disadvantage two groups—journalists and lawyers—who were particularly well situated to fight back, so the Southern slave interest was not wise in these years to propose or enact measures or take steps that carried, or threatened to carry, their interference with the mails deep into the general flow of communication. For an angry mob to burn copies of *The Slave's Friend* in Charleston's square was one thing; for U.S. postmasters to refuse to deliver the *Boston Courier* and the *Philadelphia Saturday Evening Post* and the *Greenfield Gazette* was quite another. The suppressed publications included not only journals devoted to abolition, like the *Emancipator* and the *Liberator*, but also religious journals, general magazines, and big-city Northern newspapers which sometimes discussed slavery a little too candidly. Writers of newspaper editorials, at least, could certainly see what was wrong with that, and could help the public to see, and did. Not a small part of the negative reaction in the North appeared in the press, and related freedom of the mails to freedom of the press.

So the pamphlet controversy in that winter of 1835–36 first showed to the broad public of the new nation that the defenders of slavery were proposing an intellectual blockade. And it began to suggest, therefore, that that institution, even if confined to the South, was incompatible with republican government. Not only was the enslaved black person denied every freedom, but now the white person was to be denied the freedom to talk about it.

In the spring of 1836, the House of Representatives, partly in response to the apprehensions about the suppression of the press that this controversy had generated, passed a bill prohibiting any postmaster from detaining publications or preventing their delivery. And the Senate, after having defeated Calhoun's bill 25–19, acquiesced in this House bill, with minor changes. So the tender bosoms of the South were, so far as the federal law was concerned, left exposed to the vile influence of *The Slave's Friend* and other such publications.

That does not mean, however, that in the real world these pamphlets and hymns and children's books were allowed to do their nefarious work unhindered. The Southern states found old laws, or passed new ones, in which the words "incendiary" and "insurrection" figured large, which provided an apparent legal sanction for suppressing antislavery materials, and acted upon the Calhounite notion that once the U.S. mail arrived in the local post office, state law took over, and became absolute, and could therefore pick and choose what to deliver, never mind what federal law said. The result was a *de facto* nullification with respect to the U.S. mail service that continued right up to the Civil War. Informal and extralegal suppression proved to be every bit as effective as formal and legal exclusion could have been.

Not long before that winter, there had been abolition societies and open discussions of slavery in the slave states as well as the free states. A debate on emancipation—more or less on emancipation—had taken place in the Virginia House of Delegates, as Congressman Slade had noted, as late as 1832. The greatest figures in the development of an American understanding of civil liberty in the founding period a half century earlier

had been two young Virginia slaveholders who deplored sl
Jefferson and James Madison. But there were now to be c
more Jeffersons or Madisons, and no more such debates or
not in the South, and if the slave states could manage it, not in the
either.

Meanwhile the suppression of the incendiary publications flowing South from those steam-driven presses had shunted the energies of the abolitionist bloodhounds in another direction. They began to concentrate more and more on petitioning Congress.

9 / SUFFER US WE PRAY YOU, FATHERS AND RULERS OF OUR COUNTRY

IT IS NOT LIKELY that many of us today, asked to itemize the rights protected in the Bill of Rights, would get around to the right of petition very soon, if we would remember it at all. When students in a late-twentieth-century American classroom are asked to list the five rights protected by the First Amendment, the right of petition invariably finishes fourth or fifth—the related right of assembly being the other stumper. And when in the spring of 1989 the students in Beijing's Tiananmen Square demonstrated mostly for something very like the right to petition—to have their grievances respectfully heard by their rulers—the American reporters often translated their position into rights nearer to their own hearts and understanding, freedom of the press and freedom of speech. As the years have rolled on in American constitutional jurisprudence the right of petition has more or less been swallowed by the cognate right of assembly, and the cases and the arguments have mostly concentrated on those assemblies—where and when and how they can be held—and with the form in which the "petition"—metaphorically extended, as everything in the vicinity of those rights comes to be—can be presented. Here one would enter the realm of confrontations and bullhorns; of pickets, handbills, and billboards; of sidewalks, private lawns, prison courts, and public parks.

Today the right of petition looks rather pale beside those robust rights that have distinct constituencies, sharp disagreements, and sensational cases—freedom of the press, certainly, and religious liberty, and freedom of speech, or the cluster of rights in the middle articles of the Bill of Rights that protect the accused. But in the early days of the republic, before telephones, telegrams, talk shows, political action committees, lobbyists, public opinion polls, weekend trips back to the home district, and campaigns to write your congressman, and before popular campaigning had swollen to its later bloated condition, and before political parties achieved their later prominence, and before giant news organizations had arisen to identify their interests with those of the public, and perhaps before the nation had marinated itself in modern cynicism about republican government, the modest exercise of signing a petition was a chief way the public made known its sober will to its representatives.

There had been a long history of petitioning in the history of republics, particularly in England and in its American colonies, leading up to the protection of that right in the First Amendment of the American Bill of Rights. As Congressman Cushing said, it ran all the way back to the Magna Carta, and included a series of famous Remonstrances and Memorials and Petitions in the history of Liberty, much celebrated by the early American leaders.

The right of petition represented the openness of the governors to the mind and will of the governed that was the new country's essence. One instance of the arrogance of kings and nobles and royal administrations—as that of George III—was their dismissive refusal to listen to the formal pleas of their subjects. John C. Calhoun made a rhetorical mistake when he tried to argue that the right to petition was no longer of great importance, once *representative* government was instituted. Many of the petitioners in the episode out of which his comment came—women—could not vote for their representatives, and the men who could vote nevertheless believed that they retained their further right to inform, to plead with, and on occasion to *instruct*, their representatives by means of petitions.

When James Madison proposed, in the First Congress in the summer of 1789, what would eventually become the federal Bill of Rights, he described this particular freedom this way: "The people shall not be restrained from peaceably assembling and consulting for their common good; nor from applying to the legislature by petitions, or remonstrances for redress of their grievances."

The First Amendment, which was shaped by the legislative process out of that Madisonian beginning, ensures, in addition to those freedoms you would be more likely to name, that Congress shall make no law abridging the right of the people peaceably to assemble (the Constitution writers scrupulously avoided the split infinitive) and to petition the government for a redress of grievances. Linking an assembled citizenry's appraisal of the public good to mutual deliberation by its elected representatives, the right of petition might almost be taken to be the summary and foundation of the whole structure of civil liberty, or even of republican government, for which the founding generation had fought.

Petitioning had played a particularly large role in the campaign against slavery in England; the Americans learned a great deal from their English counterparts in this as in other regards. With its extraparliamentary, voluntary aspect, and its element of testimony, it was particularly compatible with the ethos of evangelical Protestantism, in England and in the United States. And it fit particularly well with the atmosphere of voluntary effort for social change by sheer moral suasion that spilled out of the Second Awakening.

In 1828–29 there had been a nationwide movement to petition Congress to end slavery in the District of Columbia. One part of that movement was the petition from eleven hundred residents of the District itself—the "monster" petition, as it was called—from which William Slade had read to the House in December of 1835. Petitions came in numbers from Pennsylvania, New York, and Ohio. There were even a few petitions from the border states. Vermont had the largest number from a New England state, in part because of the efforts of William Lloyd Garrison, who was then editing the *Journal of the Times*, at Bennington. Garrison sent out form petitions to postmasters, who could send mail free, asking them to secure names and return them; forty-one postmasters did.

The petitions of 1828 had been sufficiently successful to prod Congress into the sort of response that many would recommend again in 1835 and after: a select committee had been appointed, to which all the petitions were referred, which committee did bring in a report. The report, which explained why emancipation in the District was inexpedient, was eventually adopted, but not before it opened the floor to an acrimonious debate. And that open, angry debate would be one of the reasons why Southern leaders, and leaders of the administration, would not want to adopt that same procedure with the petitions that began to cascade into Congress six and seven and eight years later.

As we have observed, the atmosphere, and the numbers, were quite different by 1835. In the towns of Massachusetts and Maine and upstate New York and western Pennsylvania and the Western Reserve of Ohio—in that band of counties across the nation's upper middle to which New Englanders, moving west, had gone, and in which the evangelical revivals had been most successful, and to which now Theodore Weld and the others would come on their speaking tours—there was a wider constituency for a more insistent sort of opposition to slavery. And therefore for a much larger number of more insistent petitions.

Presbyterian-Congregationalist Lane Rebel traveling agents and New England reformers coming into town and waxing eloquent about the sin of slavery would offend many, and would be heckled and have eggs thrown at them. But they would persuade some, too. Antislavery societies would be formed, and female "auxiliary" societies, like the one the miscreant George Thompson was prevented from addressing in Boston. These antislavery societies with their auxiliaries would build up little libraries of *The Slave's Friend* and the *Emancipator* and the *Anti-Slavery Record,* disgusting prints and all, and they would sponsor and listen to antislavery speakers. And they would circulate antislavery petitions. The petitions were left in the shops of sympathetic shopkeepers, circulated at county fairs, made available at church and camp meetings. Most of all they were carried from door to door by volunteers. These volunteers were, in large numbers, women, as they had been in England. They would stir the conscience of the nation with *petitions*. They would inundate the "fathers and rulers" with petitions bearing hundreds of names, eventually thousands of names.

In December of 1834 the year-old American Anti-Slavery Society had begun, along with its other activities (the "incendiary" publications, and the speakers traveling about to face down mobs), a petition drive. It was not yet as organized as it would later become, but its proponents did now have that center of action in New York—Nassau Street—that so frightened some Southern congressmen. Nassau Street sent out petition forms to the local societies requesting that these forms, or some locally produced equivalent, be circulated; from there on—at that stage—the effort was left to the grass roots. The petitions would be sent either to the congressman from their own district (like Fairfield and Briggs) or sometimes to a sympathetic congressman from another district, like William Slade.

Some of the locally produced petitions at this stage were worded in a harsh and offensive manner. There were forged names, and long lists of names in the same hand, on some petitions. Petitions which spoke of the "villainous enslavers of souls" and the "foul stain of legalized plunder" furnished to congressmen who did not want to present them an excuse not to do so. These were all faults that Nassau Street would later try to correct.

Like so many things in modern life, the petitions that were sent out from New York came in a short form and a long form. The short form—a one-sentence shot—would be deployed later, when the petition battle had settled into trench warfare. The long form most widely circulated, famous in its time as the "Fathers and Rulers" petition, was composed in 1834, probably in November, but used repeatedly in the years that followed. Its author was Theodore Weld, to whose adventures we may for a moment return.

. . .

WHEN WELD LEFT LANE Seminary in the fall of 1834, he took to the road, accepting an appointment as the agent of the Anti-Slavery Society for the state of Ohio that he had been offered back in January of that year, a month after the society had been formed in Philadelphia, and before the Lane debates took place. On his belated acceptance of the assignment he became unequivocally, and exclusively, an abolition orator. In the late fall and winter and spring of 1834–35 he lectured eleven times in Ripley, Ohio, just across the river from Kentucky; in West Union; in Hillsborough and Greenfield; in Concord (five times, by his own report) and Oldtown (seven times) in Ross County; around Circleville (fourteen times) and Bloomingburg (nine times); and then, after setting up a first meeting of the Ohio Anti-Slavery Society in Putnam, and going over into Pennsylvania to Pittsburgh to expand the abolitionist beachhead at the Presbyterian General Assembly, he lectured in the Western Reserve—Cleveland, Ravenna, Elyria, Oberlin. Often he left an antislavery society behind him. He moved on to western Pennsylvania, and then, at Nassau Street's request, he opened up new territory in upstate New York.

He traveled mostly alone, dressed simply, stayed most often at the home of a local sympathizer. Some crowds would exhibit only "a good deal of squirming"; others would pelt him with various objects. He went to Circleville expressly because he heard it was "violent in the extreme against abolition." The Presbyterian pastor there was an opponent, warning his congregation against Weld and closing his church to him. Finally, when Weld was able to speak in the vestry of the Episcopal church, at the second lecture he was hit in the head with a rock tossed through the window, and was stunned for a moment. Weld described what happened after that in a report to Elizur Wright:

> Paused a few minutes till the dizziness had ceased, and then went on and completed my lecture. Meanwhile, some of the gentlemen had hung their cloaks up at the window, so that my head could not be so easily used as a target. The injury was not serious, though for a few days I had frequent turns of dizziness. The next day the mob were so loud in threats that the trustees of the church did not feel at liberty to grant the use of the vestry, but some of them very cheerfully united with other friends, and procured a large room in the centre of the village, recently fitted up for a store and counting room. This would hold comfortably one hundred persons.
>
> The next night I lectured there. Room full. Stones and clubs flew

> merrily against the shutters. At the close as I came out, curses were showered in profusion. A large crowd had gathered round the door. Lamp black, nails, divers pockets full of stones and eggs had been provided for the occasion, and many had disguised their persons, smeared their faces, etc., to avoid recognition. But the Lord restrained them—and not a hair of my head was injured. Next evening same state of things, with increase of violent demonstrations. The next, such was the uproar that a number of gentlemen insisted upon forming an escort and seeing me safe to my lodgings. . . .
>
> This state of things lasted till I had lectured six or seven times, then hushed down and for the latter part of the course had a smooth sea. I lectured fourteen times. God owned his truth—confounded those who rose up against him—filled gainsayers with confusions, and now Circleville may be set down as a strong abolition center. A society was formed immediately, embodying the most respectable citizens of the place.

At some point early in these adventures in Ohio, Weld composed, for the use of female petitioners in the auxiliaries that he left behind, the Fathers and Rulers petition. Originally it was shaped for use in that state, but later was used elsewhere. We should print just this one among the petitions, in order that the reader may judge its incendiary character.

> Petitions of Ladies resident in ______ County, State of Ohio.
>
> *Fathers & Rulers of our Country*,
> Suffer us, we pray you, with the sympathies which we are constrained to feel as wives, as mothers, and as daughters, to plead with you in behalf of a long oppressed and deeply injured class of native Americans, residing in that portion of our country which is under your exclusive control.

That is, the District of Columbia. This was a petition solely for the end of slavery in the District.

> We should poorly estimate the virtues which ought ever to distinguish your honorable body could we anticipate any other than a favorable hearing when our appeal is to men, to philanthropists, to patriots, to the legislators and guardians of a Christian people. We should be less than women, if the nameless and unnumbered wrongs of which the slaves of our sex are made the defenceless victims, did not fill us with horror and constrain us, in earnestness and agony of spirit to pray for their deliverance. By day and by night, their woes and wrongs rise up before us, throwing shades of mournful contrast over the joys of domestic life, and

> filling our hearts with sadness at the recollection of those whose hearths are desolate.

The petition joined Jefferson and the Bible, in the hallowed American way.

> Surely then, as the representatives of a people professedly christian, you will bear with us when we express our solemn apprehensions in the language of the patriot Jefferson "we tremble for our country when we remember that God is just, and that his justice cannot sleep forever," and when in obedience to a divine command "we remember them who are in bonds as bound with them." Impelled by these sentiments, we solemnly purpose, the grace of God assisting, to importune high Heaven with prayer, and our national Legislature with appeals, until this christian people abjure forever a traffic in the souls of men. . . .

The ladies of ______ County, Ohio, did not ask the end of slavery everywhere but only where Congress could do it:

> . . . we do conjure you to abolish slavery in the District of Columbia where you exercise exclusive jurisdiction. In the name of humanity, justice, equal rights and impartial law, our country's weal, her honor and her cherished hopes we earnestly implore for this our humble petition, your favorable regard. If both in christian and in heathen lands, Kings have revoked their edicts, at the intercession of woman, and tyrants have relented when she appeared a suppliant for mercy, surely we may hope that the Legislators of a free, enlightened and christian people will lend their ear to our appeals. . . .

The editors of the collected letters of Weld and the Grimké sisters remark that "This was by far the most popular form for 'female petitioner' until 1840. Tens of thousands are in the files of the House of Representatives (boxes 85–126) in the Library of Congress."

A committee of the House that was not sympathetic to the petitioners (the Pinckney Committee, of which more below) would report that in this session—the 1835–36 session of Congress—there were presented 176 petitions praying for the end of slavery in the District with the number of signatures "a little rising 34,000 nearly 15,000 of whom were females"—short of the 40,000 Nassau Street hoped for, but not bad either.

And perhaps there had been more. The board of managers of the Massachusetts Anti-Slavery Society, looking back on this explosive year and citing these figures, insisted that, large as they were, they were an undercount. "It is not to be supposed that a Committee so hostile to the prayer of the petitioners, so desirous to make them a contemptible body, would condescend to count minutely and accurately the number of petitions and signatures, either for the sake of doing them justice, or revealing their real strength." Early in the session, "Washington letter writers" (that is, what we today would call "correspondents"—newspaper reporters) estimated that not less than three hundred such petitions had already been sent to Congress. They came in, according to this report of the Massachusetts abolitionists, in such numbers as to provoke a temporary alteration in the order of calling the states, so that for a brief interlude the roll for that session would not begin with Maine, followed soon by Massachusetts. This report, looking back at the turbulent session we have been describing, estimated that by the end of the session the number of petitions would have been not less than five hundred, and the number of signatures 75,000 to 100,000. But—said this committee, about that session's petition-work—even if the numbers were only as the House committee reported them, "seldom has so large a number ever asked the action of Congress on any subject whatever."

PART IV

SHUT THE DOOR IN THEIR FACE

10/I WOULD HAVE MY HEAD DISSEVERED FROM MY BODY

THE UNITED STATES SENATE, which met over in the east wing of the unfinished Capitol building, was a much smaller body than the House of Representatives. There were in 1836, before the admission of Michigan and Arkansas, only forty-eight senators, compared to the unruly 242 congressmen. The two senators from each state were chosen for a longer term (six years as opposed to two years) and—the one point that is different today—they were chosen not by the populace but by the state legislatures. There was some sense that senators represented the state as a unit rather than the people as a cluster of discrete beings. The Senate, with its smaller numbers, longer terms, unlimited debate, and greater distance from popular fashions, was intended—in a famous and serviceable metaphor—to be the saucer in which to cool the hot tea of the popular body's passions. But on the subject of slavery no tea was cooled in the Senate.

Among the members of this eminent body—joining Daniel Webster and Henry Clay in what schoolchildren used to be taught was a banner group—was a man who had a short time before presided over it as vice president of the United States and was now the messmate of the South Carolinians at Mrs. Lindenberger's, John C. Calhoun. We have already seen him on the floor of that august body, fighting against the pernicious flood of incendiary pamphlets.

Calhoun was a major figure not only in South Carolina but in national politics as well. The modern historian David Potter has called him "the most majestic champion of error since Milton's Satan." The English reformer Harriet Martineau, who became acquainted with him on her visit to the United States in 1835, wrote—a famous quotation—that Calhoun was "a cast-iron man, who looks as if he had never been born and never could be extinguished." James Henry Hammond, who hoped to be the Calhoun of his generation, said in Charleston on the occasion of Calhoun's death in 1850 that "Mr. Calhoun had no youth, to our knowledge. He sprang into the arena like Minerva from the head of Jove, fully grown and clothed in armor: a man every inch himself, and able to contend with any other man."

Hammond's eulogy, claiming almost every virtue for his subject, did twice concede that Calhoun had no wit or humor. The historian Merrill Peterson, writing in the late twentieth century, said of Calhoun: "Intensely serious and severe, he could never write a love poem, though he often tried, it was later said, because every line began with 'whereas.' "

Calhoun had an intellectual force, a capacity to think down to first principles with clarity, that has been rare in this country, and particularly rare among active politicians. His moral and intellectual characteristics resembled not only those of the various Greeks to whom Hammond compared him but also those of his chief adversaries, the New England Puritans. Calhoun had not attended the new Carolina College in Columbia, a hotbed of raw Carolinian ideology, to which many of his younger associates—James Henry Hammond, for one—would go; he had instead, by his own youthful choice, gone north to Yale, and after that had studied law, a lonely Jeffersonian in the midst of Yankee Federalism, at a famous law school in Litchfield, Connecticut. It is sometimes said of him that he acquired his separatist strict-construction principles not in the South but in the New England that would hold the Hartford Convention to resist the War of 1812. Merrill Peterson observed of him, as many have done, that "[m]orally and temperamentally, he was more Puritan than the Puritans."

SENATOR CALHOUN REGARDED THE influx of abolitionist petitions into Congress in 1835–36 as an even greater threat than those incendiary pamphlets he was leading the fight against at that same time. And as with the pamphlets, so now with the indigestible petitions, Calhoun worked out a distinctive line of practical action—the line that his young messmate James Henry Hammond had already dramatically demonstrated in the House before the occasion arose for Calhoun to articulate it in the Senate.

The Senate, presumably because it was not the popular body and its members were not the people's "immediate representatives," received fewer of the petitions than did the House. And from the smallness of its membership if from no other cause there was not in the Senate the equivalent of the handful of Northern members who were willing to introduce them.

There was, however, at least one—Thomas Morris of Ohio—who was willing. When he did so, on January 7, 1836, Calhoun finally had an opportunity to apply the theory which he and young Hammond, together or separately, had developed. He responded to the presentation of two petitions by Morris with a full statement of his position; the gist of it, the reader will not be surprised to learn, was: Stop them at the *threshold*. Do not even *receive* them.

Why not just lay them on the table? Was that not dismissal enough? The answer was forthright:

> **[Calhoun]:** [T]he Senator from North Carolina [Bedford Brown] objects to a refusal to receive these slanderous and abusive petitions, for fear it should cause excitement and agitation. To avoid this, he recommends that they should be received and laid on the table, there to slumber quietly. He . . . well knew that there were two modes to prevent agitation, which, according to the difference of temperament and character, were resorted to: the one to receive and quietly pocket the insult, and the other by repelling it promptly and decisively. Now, he would ask the Senator whether, if one should petition him, and pronounce him in his petition to be a robber, kidnapper, pirate, with all the other abusive terms used in these petitions, to which of the two modes would he resort? Would he quietly take the petition and put it in his pocket, (lay it on the table,) or would he knock the scoundrel down? I am sure I need not wait an answer.

How much more for his *state* than for his personal honor was he duty-bound to knock the scoundrel down. The prayer of these petitions, no matter how deferentially and respectfully expressed, was an *insult* to the South. Just by proposing such a thing you insulted the *honor* of the South—of eleven sovereign states, as Calhoun would say. And the appropriate response to that was the legislative equivalent of knocking the scoundrel down.

The Senate did not follow Calhoun's lead all the way to this furthest outpost of indignation. When in March of 1836 the issue at last came to vote—"shall this petition be received?"—only nine other senators voted no with Calhoun: his South Carolina colleague (and messmate at Mrs. Lindenberger's) William C. Preston and eight others, all four of the Southern Whigs and four of the Southern Democrats. But four other Southern senators, all Democrats, voted against him: Senator John King of Georgia (who would mortify him with his tactics, as reported below); another Senator King, William R. King, from Alabama; Bedford Brown of North Carolina, to whom he had explained the necessity for knocking the scoundrel down; and Felix Grundy of Tennessee, an administration (Jackson–Van Buren) leader. With not a single vote from Northern senators, Calhoun's proposal was defeated 36–10.

There had been an alternative position before the Senate, marginally more hospitable to the petitions only by contrast to Calhoun's implacable one, which had been presented by the senator from Pennsylvania and future president James Buchanan. Buchanan was very far from being an antislavery man, as history would certainly prove, but he came from a state in which sentiments were mixed and from a party—the Jackson–Van Buren Democrats—which needed to hold together various constituencies, both North and South, in order to stay in power and to govern, and from a country in which the "right to petition" could be a potent symbol. The problem for the Democrats was not how to express the highest of high dudgeon against the abolitionists, but rather how to hold together disparate sections and reconcile multiple opinions. Buchanan the good Democrat proposed that the petitions be received (protecting the right of petition as Calhoun would not have done) but then that their prayer (for the abolition of slavery in the District) be immediately rejected, without any consideration (thus demonstrating how completely out of bounds it was).

Buchanan's proposal came to a vote a few days after the vote on Calhoun's, and the notable point about it is Calhoun's response. The motion, to reject the prayer of the abolitionist petition which had already been "received," carried overwhelmingly, 34–6. The six minority votes, representing one wing of opinion, came from Northern Whigs, including Daniel Webster, who did not believe the prayer should be so summarily rejected. One of these minority six, Senator Prentiss of Vermont, complained that to do that was almost as disrespectful to the petitions as the Calhoun treatment, rejecting the petition itself.

But Calhoun himself clung to an opinion that was a very long distance in the opposite direction—such a great distance that it was out of the range of the current question facing the Senate. He did not condescend to vote with the majority to reject the prayer of this petition for abolition; he condemned such a vote. But of course he did not vote on the other side either; that surely would put him, as he said, in a false position. He insisted that the balm that Buchanan's procedure was supposed to give to the wound of the slaveholding South—by immediately rejecting the petition's prayer, without assigning it to a committee or discussing it—actually worsened that wound. Why? It wouldn't stop the petitioners, but it might throw the South off guard. And the decisive principle had already been yielded: the great damage had been done even in admitting such a petition into the Senate's business. To vote to do that—to receive the petition—had been "a vote to give a fatal stab to the rights of the slaveholding south." After it had been thus acknowledged by the Senate, acting upon the petition, even negatively, made the situation worse. To take up such a petition and vote on it, even summarily to reject it, was a "decision pregnant with consequences of a most disastrous character." And so what Calhoun announced that he would do and then did do was—not to participate at all. When the roll was called, on March 11, 1836, His Satanic Majesty John C. Calhoun, rather than vote either way on a proposal he thought ought not even to be entertained by the Senate, rose and stalked out of the chamber alone.

AS TIME WENT ON, the Senate followed neither Calhoun's nor Buchanan's method of disposing of the petitions but yet another, an ingenious semicompromise that was happened upon inadvertently, and used in both branches of the legislature—in the Senate exclusive of any other, but only intermittently in the House. It was the kind of arrangement politicians appreciate. This method was for the question of a petition's reception to be raised, and then—before anyone had to commit himself one way or the other on the matter—for there to be a motion to lay on the table not the petition itself (which would be for some too respectful) but *the question of whether to receive the petition*. Then senators could vote, for widely differing reasons, to lay on the table the motion not to receive the petition.

That double-decker parliamentary arrangement was complex enough, and confusing enough, that a statesman in difficulty with a diversified constituency could place the emphasis now here, now there, according to need. The ideologically freighted issue of reception would never be broached—you would not have to vote on it, one way or the other. The petition itself would be left dangling in some limbo of parliamentary indefiniteness, from which it would never return.

Any politician can see the advantages of this majestically indirect method of treating the petitions. The Senate used it, as noted, thenceforth. The spirit of Calhoun's even more extreme attitude lived on, however, in the House.

IF YOU HAD BEEN a modern political consultant or public relations expert conferring with the most extreme members of the Twenty-fourth Congress from the slaveholding South—rather an incongruous conception—you almost certainly would have counseled against the line taken by Calhoun and Hammond. You would have counseled against that line even if—perhaps especially if—you took as a given the expressed desire of your clients to preserve unchanged the peculiar institution of their region, human slavery. Even if you were an amoral hired gun whose only purpose was to achieve what your clients said they wanted, you would have told them, Don't pursue the Calhoun/Hammond line. Keep cool. Keep your ties to sympathetic Northerners. Keep some ties to the Jackson administration and the Democratic Party. Play down the issue of the right of petition. Find the best way to whisk the petitions out of sight without any outcry. Don't stand on abstract shadow-boxing and symbol-juggling about whether the petitions have been "received" or not. Be "pragmatic" (not a word yet in use, but an outlook that already existed when men and women lived in caves). Be *prudent* (to use an older and better word). Don't hand your opponents the issue of civil liberties on a platter. Don't let them cast themselves as the defenders of the ancient hallowed Anglo-Saxon tradition of free debate and of the "sacred" republican right of petition, while you are cast as the opponent.

Nobody, you would have said—or almost nobody—really wants to give the petitions the time of day—petitions signed and waxed together in interminable strips and mailed to Washington by neurotic New England church ladies. There are well-worn and familiar devices for dispatching such petitions. One could refer them to the Committee on the District of Columbia with instructions to report negatively; one could refer them to the District Committee to allow it conveniently to lose them in the shuffle; one could set up a select committee to make one grand negative report on the whole subject, to silence these fanatics once and for all; one could even instantly reject the prayer of the petitions without assigning them to any committee, standing or select. That last procedure, worked out by Buchanan in the Senate, served the purpose—or purposes—quite well. Or one could join in that even more ingenious method, devised in the Senate, to vote to lay on the table a motion not to receive the petition—so that no one would have to vote even on receiving it, and the petition would disappear in a cloud of parliamentary ambiguity. All but the last two of these could certainly be presented as a respectful treatment of the petitions, and perhaps the last two could as well, if you were eager to believe it was, as many senators and congressmen were.

But immediate *rejection* of the petition itself clearly could not be construed as respectful. The problem with rejection was that it was *intended* to be *disrespectful*. Its purpose was, as Hammond said, to stamp the petitions with a seal of disapproval. To respond to an *insult*. To knock the scoundrel down. To shut the door in the petitioner's face. But—you would say—although that course might suit South Carolina it was not very shrewd with respect to the politics of the whole country. It lent the petitioners a sympathy they would not otherwise receive. The support for abolition was minuscule; the abolitionist orators were being stoned and mobbed even in the North; the poll results (if polls had existed in those days) would have shown very meager support for trying to abolish slavery even in the District of Columbia, and overwhelming detestation personally for those obnoxious abolitionists, who tried to force people to think about subjects they did not want to think about. They didn't have any support. Civil liberty, on the other hand, free debate and free press and the sacred right of petition, taken in the abstract at least, had wide and strong support. These were the "bulwarks" of republican government, the "palladiums" of liberty our founding fathers had fought for, celebrated in song and story and ballad and bills of rights and the First Amendment and increasingly now in Fourth of July orations. To take action that seemed to contravene these fundamental American liberties was not very prudent.

Senators, including Southerners, did say to John C. Calhoun what you would have said as his political consultant: his position was a boon to the antislavery forces, unnecessarily surrendering the issue of civil liberty to them. Thus Senator John King, the Democrat from Georgia we mentioned above as one who would disagree with Calhoun's tactics, said in February of 1836 that Southern senators who supported the Calhoun/Hammond position could not have served the purposes of "Nassau Street" any more effectively if they were paid to do so.

Why then did Calhoun and Hammond and Wise and the others persist in it? Some Democrats, supporters of Jackson and his chosen successor Van Buren, suggested that they had partisan and personal motives: to damage Jackson, and to promote Calhoun as the candidate of a sectional Southern party. And to be sure, in active politics it is usually hard to separate motives of personal and party advantage from motives of conviction; cynicism to the contrary notwithstanding, and pure idealism to the contrary notwithstanding, these disparate motives, in varying proportions, usually blend.

It is true that the entire Calhoun group was opposed to Jackson—either members of the new party formed exactly to oppose Jackson, the Whigs, or South Carolina Nullifiers, furious with Jackson over the Nullification Crisis and just now in alliance with the Whigs, or Southern states'-rights Democrats or former Democrats in that same condition and same alliance. If you were a supporter of Jackson and Van Buren and the administration, even though a Southerner, the chemistry of your opinions would have led you in a different direction. You would have had some identification with the national problem of governing—and the party problem of getting reelected. So you would have shared something like the outlook of the political consultant, and you would have preferred one of those other more prudent ways of handling the petitions, keeping them out of the limelight, preventing a hullabaloo, not sharpening the edges of conflict. But the Calhounites and the gamut of Whigs did not have those motives.

They were not governing the country. They did not want to protect Jackson or elect Van Buren. Which comes first? On which side? We hold opinions because of our party and our personal ambitions, and we join a party and have one set of ambitions rather than another because of our convictions. On both sides. In varying degrees.

Calhoun and his followers indignantly repudiated the charges that they had "political" motives, in the narrow sense, for their course of action. Calhoun himself, on the Senate floor, insisted that personal hostility to Jackson had nothing whatever to do with his attack on the president's proposed remedy for the wicked and unconstitutional pamphlets. And his followers shouted down the hint that Calhoun was furthering his own interests with an extreme position on the petition matter.

Congressman Francis Pickens—Calhoun's cousin, messmate, and closest friend in the House—had risen on December 28, 1835, before Calhoun had even made his speeches in the Senate, but with hints and rumors already circulating on account of Hammond's motion, heatedly to reject on the House floor the suggestion that some Southerners actually wanted a fight on this question in order to advance the fortunes of "a particular individual."

> **Mr. Pickens** said . . . he would confine himself to what had been thrown out by the gentleman from New York [this was Samuel Beardsley, the hero of the battle for Utica's purity]. That gentleman had asked, why was it that discussion [of the petition] was desired upon that floor? And [he] intimated that certain fanatics, as well in the South as in the North, desired to agitate this question.

The notion that there might be some fanatics in the *South* as well as the North was vehemently denied by Congressman Pickens. Did the gentleman from New York not know that "fanatics," by definition, came from the North?

> **[Pickens]:** He had heard some insinuations . . . that certain gentlemen of the South . . . desired the discussion of this question [i.e., antislavery petitions] to advance the interests of a particular individual, and he would again repeat that it was a foul and infamous calumny. . . .
>
> Mr. Pickens desired to take [the] opportunity to throw back the insinuation with scorn and contempt. Sir, said Mr. Pickens, we do desire to agitate this question. We desire it because we believe we have been foully slandered before the world; I stand here prepared, at any time the question shall come up, to vindicate the institutions of the people I have the

> honor in part to represent, from the foul aspersion and calumny thrown upon them. These are the motives which prompt us to desire discussion.

Pickens's multiple use of the word "foul" in the House resembled the use of the word by Calhoun in the Senate, speechifying after the New Year—foul slanders, foul petitions, foul aspersions, foul calumny. One would guess that the word "foul" echoed around the table at Mrs. Lindenberger's mess.

The subtler foul charge was that Calhoun took an uncompromisingly extreme position in order thereby to unite the South—with himself as the likely leader of any Southern movement or party. He and his defenders would agree that he did indeed believe the South should stand united—he affirmed that, and insisted upon it—but would vigorously reject the foul implication that he believed it for reasons of personal ambition.

Thus on February 12, 1836, Calhoun told the Senate that he heard "with deep mortification and regret" the speech by John King of Georgia, criticizing his position on those petitions, because King's speech would have "a tendency to divide and distract the Southern delegation on this, to us, all momentous question."

> **[Calhoun in the Senate]:** We are here but a handful in the midst of an overwhelming majority. It is the duty of every member from the South, on this great and vital question . . . to avoid everything calculated to divide and distract our ranks.

Shortly before Calhoun made that speech in the Senate, as we shall see, a South Carolina congressman, Henry Pinckney—not a lodger at Mrs. Lindenberger's—had in fact "broken ranks" and taken a position that from Calhoun's point of view would divide and distract the Southern members exceedingly. Calhoun's remarks in the Senate may be interpreted as directed toward that recalcitrant member of the other house, as well as his fellow senators.

But though he certainly did urge that the South stand united with respect to the petitions, the incendiary publications, and the underlying constitutional point—that the national legislature could not touch the subject of slavery—he did not do so (his followers insisted) from any personal motive. Indeed, Calhoun's admirers across many decades have attributed to him an unusually flinty integrity, on the basis of which he acted to the detriment of his personal political career, which might otherwise have culminated in accession to the President's House itself.

Such a man, one might say, would disdain even the idea of a political consultant or public relations expert. So if we accept that most insistent Carolinian view, that it was not for reasons of personal ambition, blatant or subtle, that Calhoun and his allies took their stand, what then were their reasons?

ONE REASON DEALT WITH practical effects. Calhoun believed, or said he believed, that his position would silence the petitioners: "show these fanatics, by a decided refusal, by shutting the door in their face, that they have nothing to hope by agitation, and they will soon cease to agitate." That was not an accurate prediction. For nine years there would be repeated shuttings of the door in the fanatics' faces, shutting it and shutting it and shutting it, and in the end there would be far more "fanatics" than at the beginning and the door would be open.

Calhoun's home territory, however, was not a pragmatic ground dealing with effects, but the loftier ground of principle. Any treatment of the petitions other than outright rejection might be taken implicitly to concede, however minimally and with however little likelihood of practical result, the legitimacy of congressional consideration of slavery. Calhoun denied that legitimacy; that was the outpost not to yield, the threshold not to allow the fiends to cross. Even answering no was giving an answer. Was acknowledging the question. And if the answer today is no—tomorrow or some future day it might be yes. So do not even admit that the question can properly be asked.

An exchange with future president John Tyler, who in this winter of 1835–36 was a senator from Virginia, is instructive. Historian Merrill Peterson has linked these two—Calhoun with Tyler—in that each could "profess high principles to the point of absurdity." Tyler's highness of professed principle led him to object to Calhoun's position on the petition matter in the Senate, according to Calhoun's reply on January 7, because "to refuse to receive the petition is not strong enough; it is not, to use his expression, up to the occasion." That, one might say, was an objection after Calhoun's own heart—none of this weak-kneed expediency or prudence but the protestation that *his* (Calhoun's) position was too weak!

Calhoun was much pleased by what Senator Tyler had said. He rejoiced to hear that the honorable gentleman from Virginia was in favor of stronger measures than had hitherto been taken; doubly rejoiced to hear that the District Committee unanimously disavowed any constitutional power on the part of Congress over slavery in the District; triply rejoiced—he really was delighted with Tyler—to hear that there would be near-unanimity on that question in the Senate itself.

But Calhoun, of course, in his turn, for all his exponential rejoicing, thought Tyler's high principles not high enough. Tyler favored referring the petitions to the Committee on the District of Columbia because he knew that the committee would *unanimously* deny any constitutional power to legislate on slavery in the District. But in Calhoun's view, even that emphatic unanimity would not be "up to the occasion." The Tyler-Calhoun dispute was a clash of antlers between two contrasting specimens of absurdly high principle.

Calhoun proposed a combination: let the Senate, by a unanimous rejection of these vile insults to the slaveholding states, show a just indignation at the slander they contained; and let that indignant rejection be followed by the passage of a *resolution*, with all of the further unanimity that Senator Tyler promised, denying the power of Congress even to consider emancipation in the District. By such a course much, very much, would be done to put down agitation, to restore confidence to the South, and to preserve harmony in the Union. But meanwhile let no petition sully the Senate floor. Thus the two mighty elks could brandish their antlers in the same direction.

The course of action proposed by Senator Tyler, adamantly anti-abolition though he was, would nevertheless give the whole game away, according to Calhoun. Why? Even though there would be a *unanimous* vote in the Committee on the District, and a near-unanimous vote in the whole Senate, flatly informing these petitioners that it was unconstitutional for Congress to touch slavery in the District, it would nevertheless, in those unanimous votes, be favoring the petitioners with an answer. Saying anything implies that they deserve an answer. I answer you; therefore you exist. From the point of view of the Constitution, as Calhoun constructed it, these petitioners should be regarded not just as wrong and wrongheaded but as nonexistent. They should not be answered. Their existence should not be in any way acknowledged, because constitutionally speaking they should not exist.

And drawing that line was of absolute importance; there were no gradations or fallback positions. To allow the petitioners to infiltrate the procedures of Congress, even if then to repudiate them roundly, was to concede everything the abolitionists wanted. Calhoun held not only that what the petitions proposed was unconstitutional, but also that *discussing* the subject they dealt with was unconstitutional, and even that admitting the petitions into a parliamentary position from which they *might* be discussed (even though nobody would do it) was unconstitutional.

He had a tightly screwed constitutional theory, stricter than strict, that found no power for the subject of slavery ever to cross Congress's mind. It was the intellectual blockade at its height, applied to the procedures of Congress. He had also a strategic point, to accompany this tightly screwed constitutional theory: attacking slavery in the District would be abolitionism's opening wedge, in theory and in practice. Any theory that allowed Congress to discuss the possibility of ending slavery in the District could then be extended to discuss ending it in the states—even in South Carolina itself! It would be the abolitionists' entry point. So—stop them at the frontier.

Stop the *discussion* at the frontier. A modern reader needs to be reminded how far any of this was from any actual policy. Nobody in a position of power was proposing actually to end slavery, or even the slave trade, even in the District. But there were a few who felt that, given the commitment of the new republic to free debate, those powerless few who wanted to sound off about such a subject ought to be allowed to do so.

Calhoun disagreed. His argument against free speech at this point is interesting. Even the least reproachable, best-established institutions can be rendered suspect, he said, by constant criticism and attack. Therefore protect them from such an attack.

This proposition would have troubled you as his (unemployed) political consultant; how was he going to square that idea with the nation's commitment to free speech, free press, free debate? Jefferson, Calhoun's great original mentor, had said that truth is great and will prevail, and that it needs against error no weapons except its own—free argument and debate. But now here was the sometime Jeffersonian John C. Calhoun saying that if you talked negatively too much you could endanger worthy institutions—you should be silenced, and your very existence denied. Somehow it did not sound very Jeffersonian. It did not sound very "republican."

Calhoun would also present, in a long speech on March 9, 1836, what we may call the nutritional theory of the rights of legislative bodies. They must choose their own diet, avoiding the fat and cholesterol and sodium of greasy and unhealthy petitions:

> **[Calhoun]:** [This claim that legislatures may reject petitions] may be compared to the function of the animal economy, with which all living creatures are endowed, of selecting, through the instinct of taste, what to receive or reject, on which the preservation of this existence depends. Deprive them of this function, and the poisonous as well as the wholesome would be indifferently received into their system. So with deliberative bodies; deprive them of the essential and primary right to determine at their pleasure what to receive or reject, and they would become the passive receptacles, indifferently, of all that is frivolous, absurd, unconstitutional, immoral and impious, as well as what may properly demand their deliberation and action. Establish this monstrous, this impious principle

> (as it would prove to be in practice,) and what must be the consequence? To what would we commit ourselves?

Somehow that doctrine, of the fastidious choosiness by legislatures as to the topics citizens might raise in petitions, also did not sound very Jeffersonian. Had Jefferson not written, echoing Locke and Milton, that we should let Truth and Error grapple, in an arena of freedom?

These general arguments on the abstract issue of petitioning got their emotional force from arguments of another kind, which dealt with the effects of this particular body of petitions on the South and Southerners, in particular the senators themselves. Two days later in that turbulent spring, on March 11, the most distinguished Southern senator struck rather a plaintive note:

> **[Calhoun]:** Under the decision of the Senate, we of the South are doomed to sit here and receive in silence, however outrageous or abusive in their language towards us and those whom we represent, the petitions of the incendiaries who are making war on our institutions. Nay, more, we are bound, without the power of resistance, to see the Senate, at the request of these incendiaries, whenever they think proper to petition, extend its jurisdiction to the subject of slavery over the States as well as this District. Thus deprived of all power of effectual resistance, can any thing be considered more hopeless and degrading than our situation; to sit here, year after year, session after session, hearing ourselves and our constituents vilified by thousands of incendiary publications in the form of petitions, of which the Senate, by its decision, is bound to take jurisdiction, and against which we must rise like culprits to defend ourselves, or permit them to go uncontradicted and unresisted? We must ultimately be not only degraded on our own estimation and that of the world, but be exhausted and worn out on such a contest.

Beyond the general theories about petitioning there was this strong emotional undercurrent, pulling strategy in the direction of absolutism and uncompromising extremes. "We must rise like culprits to defend ourselves"; "We must ultimately be . . . degraded on our own estimation and that of the world."

This irrational and personal element found expression in the theme of *honor*, and the related themes of insult and slander and libel, that appear constantly in Calhoun's speeches, and in Hammond's and Waddy Thompson's and Henry Wise's and others'. Nothing was more central to their indignant response than this: the petitions (and the incendiary pamphlets) were an insult to Southern honor. In his first speech in the Senate about petitions (on January 7, 1836), Calhoun added the concept of slander: these petitions contained a "gross, false, and malicious slander on eleven states represented on this floor." As the Senate would not receive a petition reflecting on an individual congressman, so it should not receive petitions that "willfully, maliciously, almost wickedly" slander so many sovereign states. Later he added libel: "so base a libel on the state he represents, as well as the entire South"; "these vile and libelous attacks on nearly half of the states of this Union."

In his exchange with Senator King of Georgia, on February 12, 1836, Calhoun conveyed the amplitude of his feeling that, "right of petition" notwithstanding, no Southerner should countenance these slanderous and unconstitutional petitions even being received:

> **[Calhoun]:** Let us change the question, to test the principle on which the Senator acts. He [King] admits the constitutional power of Congress over the subject, whether in this district or in the States, to be the same. I ask him, then . . . is he prepared, as a Senator from Georgia, to vote to receive a petition for the abolition of slavery in that State—a petition, too, for his principles go to that extent, couched in the most abusive and slanderous language against the State and its institutions?
>
> (**Mr. King** replied, yes.)
>
> All, then, (said **Mr. Calhoun**) that I can say is, that the Senator and myself are so organized as to have feelings directly dissimilar. Rather than receive such a petition against South Carolina, against those whom I represent, I would have my head dissevered from my body.

George Mason was reported to have said, in the closing days of the great Convention of 1787 that wrote our Constitution, that he would *cut off his hand* sooner than he would sign his name to the defective document the convention had produced, with its omission of a bill of rights and its other faults as Mason saw them. Drawings of a bleeding severed hand, and doggerel verses about it and editorial references to it, figured large in the propaganda of the first popular debate about ratifying the proposed Constitution that fall in the state of Pennsylvania. The subsequent debates on ratification produced a good deal of imagery about what one would cut off one's hand rather than do. Then in the Virginia ratifying convention of the following summer, Edmund Randolph, who, like Mason, had declined to sign the Constitution in September of 1787, but who now, partly through the careful arguments of James Madison and partly through the influence of the other states' ratifications, had come around to the other side, raised the ante on the mere cutters-off of hands. He said, in June of 1788, that he would "assent to the lopping of his *limb* [indicating his arm] before I will assent to the dissolution of the union." Now, forty-eight years later, in the United States Senate, John C. Calhoun raised the proposed self-dismemberment to a still higher pitch, the highest, so far as the present author knows, in America's rich rhetorical history: "Rather than receive such a petition against South Carolina, against those whom I represent, I would have my head dissevered from my body."

11 / THE GREATEST OF ALL THE GREAT BLESSINGS

WHAT WAS THE VILE slander and malicious libel against the South that made Calhoun stalk out of the chamber and Hammond call for "Terror-Death"? The epithet "land pirates" seems to have been particularly offensive, and also "man-stealers" and "dealers in human flesh." But most of the petitions (as distinguished from abolitionist tracts and speeches) now included no such terms. Might one surmise that, in the angry outlook of Calhoun, Hammond, Waddy Thompson, Francis Pickens, and Henry Wise, there was no such thing as a *respectful*, nonabusive petition for the abolition of slavery? No matter how mild or neutral or gentle the language might be, no matter how carefully it might restrict itself to policy—would it still be a slander, a libel, an insult to the honor of the South?

When the House on December 21 was discussing the reconsideration of that slippery petition presented by Congressman Briggs of Massachusetts, Congressman Bouldin of Virginia suggested that there were in that petition "many disrespectful slurs thrown over the people of the South." Briggs had broken in to say that, no, the gentleman from Virginia labored under a mistake, and asked that the petition, which was very short, be read.

When that was done, Congressman Bouldin admitted that he "was pleased to find it not as bad by any means as others. Yet," he said, "it contained nearly the same in substance."

> **[Bouldin]:** All these petitions took a swaggering stand over the South, and proposed a kind of guardianship over their morals, and were dreadfully afraid that holding negroes had made us vastly corrupt, and would make us more so.

Then Bouldin engaged in comparative moral reflection, with biblical allusions. Let him who is without fault cast the first stone. "We thank God that we are not as other men, whoremongers and adulterers." This pharisaical self-righteousness condemned in the Bible, said Bouldin, was the language of these petitions—all of them. They might have a thin gauze over them, he admitted, such as this: they might say they did not presume to dictate to the South. They might say they did not mean to disparage their sister states, or dictate to them. But these petitions, said the Virginia congressman, nevertheless let it be known that the acts the Southerners committed were such as to call down the vengeance of heaven upon them.

Was there any way that a condemnation of slavery could have been written, in 1836, that did not seem to Southern congressmen to make such invidious moral comparisons? That did not seem to call down the vengeance of heaven upon the sister states to the South—to "take a swaggering stand" over the South?

The antislavery movement would eventually acquire a political leader who would throughout his career go out of his way repeatedly to insist, to his Northern audiences, that their Southern brethren were "just as we would be" in the same circumstances—who projected a note of humility, an absence of self-righteousness, individual or collective, of a sort that is very rare in any politician on any side of any question in any era. But did that absence of all sanctimony, that disavowal of all moral "swaggering," on the part of Abraham Lincoln alter the appraisal of him in the South? Not in the least. His election alone was enough to trigger rebellion.

Any moral condemnation of slavery from the 1830s onward would have been taken to have that element of self-righteousness, whether or not it did have it. And it would be taken to have that tone of *insult* and *slander* and *libel* (all words that Calhoun and the others used repeatedly). It is not easy to live with constant moral disapproval, even if the disapproving are very careful to tell you that they disapprove only of the *system*, not of you—that while they hate the *sin*, they love the *sinner*. Somehow, if you are the alleged sinner, that does not make it any easier to take. Especially when in your own mixture of feelings, along with an angry denial at one level, there remains at another an unexpungible awareness of the moral claim you are trying to deny.

Retaliatory moralism is one response. How pure are they, after all? There is an almost overwhelming human temptation to repay one's moral accusers by accusing them *back*.

> **[Bouldin]:** [I have] no idea of imitating these petitioners, and swaggering over the North; but who first made traffic of human flesh, and made

profit by bringing the negroes here? and who expects to be paid for carrying them back?

That last was an argument one might not have heard before: that the Northerners now expected to make further money by transporting blacks *back* to Africa, profiting from the round trip. But that the first trip—the slave trade—had been perpetrated by Northern shipping interests was a recurrent theme in Southern political discourse. It overlapped with the stereotype of the money-grubbing Yankee, which prompted that parenthetical comment of Waddy Thompson's about the inappropriateness of Northerners accusing anybody *else* of avariciousness.

It was terribly important to assert that Southerners were morally as worthy a people as could be found.

[Bouldin]: Did any man ever hear or know of a nation of people on any side of Mason's and Dixon's line that stood higher for any of the cardinal virtues—honor, truth, justice, and charity—gentleness of heart, and honesty? Was it thought that we would suffer by a comparison with the petitioners?

We are at least as good and as virtuous as *they* are. (Better, actually.) Given this moral defensiveness, it did not mitigate the evil of the "incendiary" pamphlets that they were addressed to the conscience of white Americans instead of the militancy of black slaves; in a way, that magnified the evil. A straight-out call for black rebellion would have represented, to most of nineteenth-century white America, North and South, that direct threat to life and order that would justify measures of suppression. But these moral arguments against slavery, these gentle pleas to the Fathers and Rulers to end it for moral and religious reasons, addressed to the conscience of the nation, placed the Southern slaveholders in a much more difficult, an exasperating, moral position.

The moral defensiveness which is laced throughout Southerners' congressional speeches, with its resonance in the moralistic Protestant culture shared by the North and South, coincided with and reinforced the aristocratic or pseudo-aristocratic vein of *honor* and touchy pride peculiar to the South. That defensive-aggressive combination of feelings and postures added further emotional dynamite to the outright fear—how much real and how much exaggerated for polemical purposes?—of slave rebellions, and those two potent minefields of emotion heightened attachment to extreme constitutional and political positions—that it was unconstitutional for Congress even to *touch* slavery in the District of Columbia, even to *discuss* it, and therefore wrong to let those petitions get a toe in the door—those insulting, slanderous, malicious petitions.

Out of this cauldron of moral defensiveness and morbid sensitivity it finally came to pass that some Southerners argued that slavery was *not* an evil but a *good*. No, no, it wasn't evil after all. Although there had been anticipations of this stance earlier, it is exactly in the context of this fretful argument in the middle 1830s that the defiant assertion took shape and gained force that slavery was no evil but a *positive good*.

Calhoun's form of this final point, slightly more complex than that of Hammond and some Southern publicists, held it to be a positive good—given the presence of the two races in one place. In the midst of the debates of the next winter, during the short second session of the Twenty-fourth Congress, he had a revealing exchange with another Southern senator, William Rives, a Virginia Democrat, a younger friend and follower and biographer of James Madison.

Rives had said, in a debate about the petitions on February 6, 1837, that he was not in favor of slavery in the abstract. On that point he differed from the senator from South Carolina—to which point Calhoun objected.

> **Mr. Calhoun [in the Senate]** explained, and denied having expressed any opinion in regard to slavery in the abstract. He had merely stated, what was a matter of fact, that it was an inevitable law of society that one portion of the community depended upon the labor of another portion, over which it must unavoidably exercise control. He had not spoken of slavery in the abstract, but of slavery as existing where two races of men, of different color, and a thousand other particulars, were placed in immediate juxtaposition. Here the existence of slavery was a good to both. Did not the Senator from Virginia consider it as good?
>
> **Mr. Rives** said, no. He viewed it as a misfortune and an evil in all circumstances, though, in some, it might be the lesser evil.
>
> **Mr. Calhoun** insisted on the opposite opinion, and declared it as his conviction that, in point of fact, the Central African race (he did not speak of the north or the east of Africa, but of its central regions) had never existed in so comfortable, so respectable, or so civilized a condition, as that which it now enjoyed in the Southern States. . . .

This was a standard proslavery argument—how beneficent slavery was for black people (others did not bother with Calhoun's curious distinction between Central Africans on the one hand and northern and eastern Africans on the other). Furthermore, it was good for its white participants, who were in no way inferior to white people elsewhere.

> **[Calhoun]:** Both races, therefore, appeared to thrive under the practical operation of this institution. . . . The social experiment was going on both at the North and the South—in the one with almost a pure and unlimited democracy, and in the other with a mixed race. Thus far, the results of the experiment had been in favor of the South. Southern society had been far less agitated, and he would venture to predict that its condition would prove by far the most secure, and by far the most favorable to the preservation of liberty. In fact, the defence of human liberty against the aggressions of despotic power had been always the most efficient in States where domestic slavery was to prevail.

There would often be arguments, in slaveholders' speechmaking, of the sort that the twentieth century would learn to call "Orwellian": that slavery supports equality, that slavery is the best foundation of democracy, or as in this case, slavery is the best defense of *freedom.*

> He **[Calhoun]** did not admit it to be an evil. Not at all. It was a good—a great good. On that point, the Senator from Virginia and himself were directly at issue.
>
> [**Rives** spoke again. Then:]
>
> **Mr. Calhoun** complained of having been misrepresented. Again [he] denied having pronounced slavery in the abstract a good. All he had said of it referred to existing circumstances; to slavery as a practical, not as an abstract thing. It was good where a civilized race and a race of a different description were brought together. . . . He believed slavery was good, where two races coexisted. The gentleman from Virginia held it an evil. . . . Surely if it was an evil, moral, social, and political, the Senator, as a wise and virtuous man, was bound to exert himself to put it down. This position, that it was a moral evil, was the very root of the whole system of operations against it. That was the spring and wellhead from which all these streams of abolition proceeded—the effects of which so deeply agitated the honorable Senator.

In this argument between Calhoun and Rives one can see the backhanded way that an heir of Jefferson could come around to affirm that slavery was good. It was good because you could not admit it to be evil. Evil, by definition, is that which is to be shunned, avoided, terminated. A wise and virtuous man is bound to exert himself to put down that which is evil. Evil must be attacked—which is what these appalling abolitionists were doing. But we resist the idea that we should attempt to terminate slavery, and are fiercely opposed to the attempt by the abolitionists to do so. Therefore slavery must *not* be an evil. They attack *us* as responsible for the evil. Therefore we must assert more insistently that it is *not* an evil. Therefore it is a good.

ALMOST EXACTLY A YEAR before Calhoun's explorations with Rives in the Senate, James Henry Hammond in the House of Representatives had been more unequivocal than Calhoun in his endorsement of American slavery. In that full-dress speech of February 1, 1836, from which we have already quoted—this is the one in which he held up a copy of *The Slave's Friend* to shock his colleagues, and conjured up the horror of an Othello sitting someday in their midst—he had defended slavery unequivocally and superlatively as a positive good:

> **[Hammond in the House]:** Slavery is said to be an evil; that it impoverishes the people, and destroys their morals. If it be an evil, it is one to us alone, and we are contented with it—why should others interfere? But it is no evil. On the contrary, I believe it to be the greatest of all the great blessings which a kind Providence has bestowed upon our glorious region.

The society it produced, in Hammond's full-throated defense, deserved unabashed superlatives:

> **[Hammond]:** Sir, I do firmly believe that domestic slavery, regulated as ours is, produces the highest toned, the purest, best organization of society that has ever existed on the face of the earth.

He said that slavery "has rendered our southern country proverbial for its wealth, genius, and its manners." He *accepted* the charge that this virtue-laden South was in some sense aristocratic:

> **[Hammond]:** I accept the term. It is a government of the best. Combining all the advantages, and possessing but few of the disadvantages, of the aristocracy of the old world, without fostering to an unwarrantable extent the pride, the exclusiveness, the selfishness, the thirst for sway, the contempt for the rights of others, which distinguish the nobility of Europe, it gives us their education, their polish, their munificence, their

high honor, their undaunted spirit. Slavery does indeed create an aristocracy—an aristocracy of talents, of virtues, of generosity and courage. In a slave country every freeman is an aristocrat. Be he rich or poor, if he does not possess a single slave, he has been born to all the natural advantages of the society in which he is placed, and all its honors lie open before him, inviting his genius and industry.

Apologists for slavery in the American South obviously had a considerable problem on this score, in this new republic, with its strong antiaristocratic commitment to liberty and equality and the rights of man. How could slavery—a particularly blunt and absolute form of slavery, based on race and reducing people to property—be reconciled with American ideals? With Liberty? With Equality? With the Rights of Man? It was a problem—not only a moral one, but an intellectual one and a rhetorical one. This slave-based Southern society seemed at first glance—to European observers, say—to be much more easily assimilated to the hierarchical, hereditary, and antirepublican order that the Americans repudiated than to the republican ideals they affirmed. Some commanded, and others obeyed; the division between them was absolute, and was handed down from generation to generation; there was no appeal from it. That certainly looked like aristocracy—squared.

But despite appearances, American defenders of slavery were not, generally speaking, believers in a hereditary aristocracy. Calhoun, in his youth a disciple of Jefferson, in the Senate vigorously rejected the suggestion that his views accorded with those of Robert Filmer, the defender of monarchy, aristocracy, hierarchy, and hereditary society against whose work the great John Locke had written one of his treatises on government. Locke's libertarian and egalitarian and majoritarian views in those treatises had often been said to be a foundation, or even *the* foundation, of American republican idealism; Filmer was the visible spokesman for the other side. But Calhoun insisted that he abhorred the aristocratic tenets of Filmer: "So far from holding the dogmas of that writer, he had been a known and open advocate of freedom from the beginning." Only not for slaves.

But sometimes some defenders of slavery were willing to accept a certain amount of aristocratic theory after all, as Hammond did in the quotation above. Slavery makes for a wonderful society, loaded with virtue and high culture. A cult of Greece and Rome, and also of Romance, developed in the South in the decades following this winter of 1835–36. Slavery was good, because it supported such a scintillating civilization.

Other Southern members of the House and Senate made a great point of the danger of slave insurrection and the fear that their wives and daughters would get their throats cut at midnight. Hammond disdained that argument:

> **[Hammond]:** As to our fears, I know it has been said by a distinguished Virginian, and quoted on this floor, "that the fire bell in Richmond never rings at night, but the mother presses her infant more closely to her breast, in dread of servile insurrection." Sir, it is all a flourish. There may be nervous men and timid women, whose imaginations are haunted with unwonted fears, among us, as there are in all communities on earth; but in no part of the world have men of ordinary firmness less fear of danger from their operatives than we have. . . . [D]uring the two hundred years that slavery has existed in this country, there has, I believe, been but one insurrection, and that one very limited in its extent.

Elsewhere, after descanting upon the contentment and loyalty of "our slaves" ("a peaceful, kind-hearted, and affectionate race; satisfied with their lot, happy in their comforts, and devoted to their masters. It will be no easy thing to seduce them from their fidelity . . . "), he made this dismissive comment on the much-bruited subject of slave rebellions:

> **[Hammond]:** Every insurrection which has yet been meditated—and there have been but very few—when not discovered by some faithful slave, has been soon discovered by the whites, the unfortunate occurrence at Southampton [i.e., Nat Turner's rebellion] only excepted—if that can be called an insurrection which was the bloody outbreaking of six drunken wretches.

As you read Hammond's long speech—defensive, defiant, surveying the appalling rise of abolitionism, celebrating the virtue of the South, insisting that Southern slave society is the best there ever was, and that slavery can, and will, never be abolished—you realize from the emotional overflow how much there is a *personal* identity at stake. That stake is apparent also in the speeches of the austere intellectual John Calhoun, and perhaps even more so in the spontaneous utterances of the excitable and articulate younger men, Waddy Thompson and Francis Pickens of South Carolina and the Virginia hotspur Henry A. Wise. When you attack slavery, you attack the *South*. And when you attack the South, you attack—me.

JAMES HENRY HAMMOND, TWENTY-NINE years old, was just starting on a career that would soon make him a considerable figure in South

Carolina politics: governor of the state in the early 1840s and a member of the United States Senate in the last few years before secession. He was the one who would give to the world, in a famous senatorial speech, the concept that "cotton is king." But he was not a product of old South Carolina. He was instead "the son of a Massachusetts adventurer" who had moved to South Carolina and tried to break into its aristocracy but failed. The son inherited his father's ambitions and, thanks to a shrewd marriage to the heiress of a Charleston family and a thoroughgoing ideological education under the arch-Carolinian Thomas Cooper at Carolina College, had succeeded. James Henry Hammond became an instant aristocrat, with a luxurious plantation, racehorses, paintings, and condescension for the ill-bred. He was a colorful and terrible scoundrel, but his story intersects our story only at the beginning, when he sets it off. In the manner of the convert and the newly arrived, he became more Catholic than the pope. A modern editor of the famous diaries that Hammond was to keep throughout his lurid life remarked of him that he "seems to have succumbed to the myth of the Old South even before the South was old and before there was a myth."

Hammond's speech on February 1, 1836, was intended to justify the startling motion he had made on the House floor the previous December, which could be said to have been the first bomb in the Pearl Harbor of the Civil War: his motion that the abolitionist petition be *rejected* by the House. To that end, in what would prove to be his farewell to the House, he spelled out in full analytical detail this defiant claim: slavery, this great good, can *never* be abolished.

Hammond made a systematic analysis of ways in which theoretically slavery might be abolished, in order to prove that it could not in fact be done. It certainly was not going to be abolished by any of the appeals to the slaveholders themselves, which the moralistic preachers and reformers of the North thought might have some effect. Not by appeal to the *consciences* of the slaveholders—Hammond gave that possibility short shrift indeed. Not by appeal to the *hopes* of the slaveholder—"I believe I can say we are perfectly satisfied. We have been born and bred in a slave country . . . we see everything to induce us to prefer it to all others." Not by appeal to the *fears* of slaveholders—unlike other spokesmen for the slaveholding South, Hammond dismissed the threat of any servile revolt.

And not by appeal to the *interests* of slaveholders, either. Hammond, a relentless realist who placed a premium on the power of self-interest, said that that was the only consideration that could possibly budge American slaveholders, claiming that this had been the reason for the ending of serfdom in Europe and slavery in the American free states (conscience had nothing to do with that, either—only interest). But even that appeal won't work in the Southern states:

> **[Hammond]:** . . . in Southern latitudes, where great agricultural staples are produced, and where not only a large combination of labor under the direction of one head is required, but it is also necessary that the connexion between the operatives and that head should be absolute and indissoluble, domestic slavery is indispensable.

He then favored the House with a display of that high literary culture that a slave-based society, as he formulated it, would support.

> **[Hammond]:** To such a country it is as natural as the climate itself—as the birds and beasts to which that climate is congenial. The camel loves the desert; the reindeer seeks everlasting snows; the wild fowl gather to the waters; and the eagle wings his flight above the mountains. It is equally the order of Providence that slavery should exist among a planting people, beneath a southern sun. . . . Sir, it is not the interest of the planters of the South to emancipate their slaves, and it never can be shown to be so.

So slavery, as natural among a planting people beneath a southern sun as is the camel's preference for the desert, cannot be ended by any appeal to the slaveholder.

It cannot be ended by any action of government, either. Compensated emancipation would be impossibly expensive, and in any case, even to discuss such a scheme would immediately end the Union and precipitate a bloody war.

There remained only the effort to end slavery by appeal to the slaves themselves, and that won't work, either, because the slaves are loyal and happy and because the white people, not out of fear but just in case, are very watchful. Ending slavery by fomenting a slave rebellion is what these agitators have in mind, said Hammond, even though they deny it—but it won't work. Nothing will work, to the end of emancipation—not in this country.

> **[Hammond]:** In our country, where the two classes of population are so nearly equal, such a thing as now exists in Jamaica would not last a day, an hour. Sir, any species of emancipation with us would be followed instantly by civil war between the whites and blacks. A bloody, exterminating war, the result of which could not be doubtful, although it would be accompanied with horrors such as history has not recorded.

The black people would be either annihilated or once more subjugated in slavery. The upshot of this long and carefully written speech was that emancipation is forever impossible.

> **[Hammond]:** I feel firmly convinced that, under any circumstances, and by any means, emancipation, gradual or immediate, is impossible. . . . [S]lavery can never be abolished.

In addition to all the empirical reasons why slavery could not be abolished—reasons evident in the factual situation, of which he gave a thorough analysis—there was also the reason upheld in the Bible, and by God's intention. People who look the way the Africans look must always be slaves.

> **[Hammond]:** The doom of Ham has been branded on the form and features of his African descendants. The hand of fate has united his color and destiny. Man cannot separate what God hath joined.

Given that slavery could never be abolished, he warned that the effort by the abolitionists—"ignorant, infatuated barbarians"—to do so could have catastrophic effects, notice of which was sprinkled throughout his speech. And he warned his fellow legislators against daring even to touch the subject.

> **[Hammond]:** . . . the moment this House undertakes to legislate upon this subject, it dissolves the Union. Should it be my fortune to have a seat upon this floor, I will abandon it the instant the first decisive step is taken looking towards legislation of this subject. I will go home to preach, and if I can, to practice, disunion, and civil war, if needs be. A revolution must ensue, and this republic sink in blood.

12 / AM I GAGGED OR NOT?

A FEW DAYS AFTER Hammond finished his long speech and sat down, the House was favored by yet another speech by yet another South Carolinian, but this one included a proposal rather different from anything being offered by Hammond, Waddy Thompson, or Francis Pickens in the House or John C. Calhoun in the Senate.

It would be going much too far to say that this speech, and its proposal, were "moderate" or a "compromise." From the point of view of Massachusetts or Vermont, not to mention of our own time, the South Carolinian leaders of that time did not include within the options at their disposal any such position as "moderate," or a "compromise." What Garland of Virginia had proudly pronounced in his answer to Slade—"We do not supplicate; supplication is a plant that does not flourish in the South"—applied double-strength to South Carolina, and to wishy-washy concepts like moderation and compromise. The available positions in that setting may be said to have ranged from fanatical and extreme to *very* fanatical and extreme. But the standards of extremism set by Hammond and Calhoun were so high that this other South Carolinian's proposals became, for a moment, by comparison, the mainstream of congressional opinion.

This congressman bore the familiar South Carolina name of Pinckney, and was the son of the Charles Pinckney—"Constitution Charlie"—who had actively participated in the Federal Convention of 1787. In other words, he was the son of a framer of the United States Constitution. The father, in fact, claimed to have presented a proto-constitution more important even than James Madison's Virginia Plan, and there are historians to this day who give him some support. It was he, along with his cousin Charles Cotesworth Pinckney, known as "General" Pinckney, who had represented the intransigent slave-state position that led to the Constitution's compromises on slavery. The governor of the state at that time had been yet another Pinckney, General Pinckney's brother Thomas Pinckney, who would figure later in American diplomatic history as the negotiator of the Pinckney Treaty with Spain, second in importance only to the Jay Treaty in the new nation's early dealings with the Old World. So the Pinckneys were a distinguished family of many branches.

But the Pinckney who took the floor of the House on February 4, 1836, had ancestral distinction above and beyond Pinckneyhood. His full name was *Henry Laurens* Pinckney. He was descended from another revered family, and had been given the name of another South Carolina hero from the founding days, Henry Laurens. Laurens, the congressman's maternal grandfather, had been captured by the British on his way to Europe to negotiate for the American patriots, and had been locked up for a time in the Tower in London. Henry Laurens Pinckney was therefore quite a glorious mouthful of South Carolina history and American history.

He was, moreover, a rising figure in South Carolina politics in his own right. He had inherited from those distinguished ancestors a fortune in rice plantations, but had gone on to make his own way and to help found the *Charleston Mercury*, the paper that spoke for Charleston's elite in the battles of the time. He had supported Calhoun and the Nullifiers in the tremendous excitement of the Nullification Convention of 1832—challenging all the forces of the North, of the whole country if need be, and the President of the United States, asserting a state's right to "nullify" an obnoxious federal law. So Pinckney had been no maverick and no moderate, either by heritage or by his own previous actions.

But now in Congress he proposed a different course from Hammond and Pickens and Thompson and Wise—only slightly different, as it appears to us today, but different enough to elicit fury and retaliation at the time. It was not in line with what Senator Calhoun was recommending, or what Hammond had proposed in the House, and it *was* in line with what Vice-President Martin Van Buren and the Democrats wanted.

Among those who found these weeks of turmoil in the House over petitions and slavery particularly disturbing was Martin Van Buren, who had already, in May of 1835, been named by Andrew Jackson as the Democratic Party's nominee to be his successor. Van Buren, a lawyer and politician from the state of New York, had the disadvantage of being a Northerner; if elected, he would be the first president in American history who was not at the time of his inauguration either a slaveholder or a member of the Adams family. He was "the Little Magician," "the Red Fox of Kinderhook," who could be classified as one of the nation's first professional politicians. It was essential for his election to hold together the coalition that he himself had engineered for Jackson—Southern planters and Northern common folk. To keep them under the Democratic umbrella it was important to keep the issue of slavery off the floor of the House and out of national politics, and it was particularly important for this non-slaveholding Northerner to show suspicious slave-state voters—including his own party's Southern wing—that he was sufficiently fierce against the abolitionists and sufficiently strong for states' rights. At the same time he had to avoid doing these things in a way that would rile his Northern constituency. If we assume that Calhoun at this time had the objective of unifying the South around a heightened and radicalized sectional consciousness, then we can say that Van Buren had a quite different political problem: how to hold together large segments of the North and the South.

Henry Laurens Pinckney did not join his fellow South Carolinians at Mrs. Lindenberger's. He lodged, instead, at Mrs. Ballard's, on Pennsylvania Avenue, with two representatives from Pennsylvania and one from Ohio. Had he skipped mess one night to eat at the President's House? Scholars debate whether Vice-President Van Buren played a role in Pinckney's proposal; in any case, it represented the line Van Buren wanted to take.

What Pinckney proposed, in the interest of harmony and union, was that all of these petitions, piled together, should be referred to a select committee (just as some congressmen, as noted above, had been recommending), which committee should be instructed to report, first (of course), that Congress had no constitutional power to interfere with slavery in the states, and, second, that for Congress to interfere with slavery in the District of Columbia would be "impolitic," and a breach of trust, and dangerous to the Union. (But *not* unconstitutional. That, for Calhoun's followers, was the rub.) Thus all of these petitions could be disposed of in a lump—all of these, and presumably all to come on these subjects—and the whole topic excised from the House and from national politics, as had been done with other controversies.

The trick was—for Van Buren, and presumably for Pinckney—how to accomplish the end of sweeping those petitions, and the subject of slavery, out of national politics, without provoking a negative reaction in parts of the North. Why insist that Congress has no constitutional authority over slavery in the District, when nobody in power proposed to exercise it anyway? So the Democrats, eager to hold on to the presidency, and any shrewd politician, would argue. Put the quiet machinery of "respectful" reception of petitions back in place once more, and "respectfully" reject their prayers all at once.

But the times were not congenial to cool political strategy. The Southern Democrats and much of the Northern and Southern Democratic press supported Pinckney, but the fire-eaters among the Southern Whigs and all of the South Carolina Nullifiers denounced him. John C. Calhoun across the way in the Senate was taking his more extreme position in speeches and committee reports at exactly the time that Pinckney was making this proposal in the House. On January 7, Calhoun had made his first remarks on abolition petitions, from which we have quoted; on January 19, more remarks on that subject; on February 12, still more remarks urging the Senate to stop them at the threshold! On the very day that Pinckney made his proposal—February 4—Calhoun brought in his committee's report, and a bill, dealing with the "incendiary" pamphlets, and proceeded to expound his theory of slavery as (under the specific conditions of the American Union) a positive good. So while Pinckney headed back to Mrs. Ballard's after his speech, his fellow congressmen Thompson and Pickens walked over to Mrs. Lindenberger's to have supper with Senator Calhoun, presumably to tell him about Pinckney's shockingly soft, and contrasting, proposal.

Although in the histories Pinckney appears as the South Carolina Nullifier who introduced the notorious gag rule, at Mrs. Lindenberger's in early February of 1836 he was considered a traitor to South Carolina. An apostate. Those petitions should be stomped on, not sent to a select committee; the notion that Congress might have power over slavery in the

District should be flatly and instantly repudiated on *constitutional* grounds, not (merely) characterized as impolitic and inexpedient.

Although his South Carolina colleagues and their allies railed at him, Pinckney stuck to his position and defended it on the floor. When his resolutions—setting up the committee and giving it instructions—were brought to a vote, they passed easily. The Democrats had a majority in the House, and Democrats, North and South, supported Pinckney's resolution, and many Whigs did, too. William Slade voted for it. At this point one was voting only to set up Pinckney's committee and to give it the stated instructions; when the committee would *report,* the voting might be different.

The staunchly Democratic Speaker of the House, Tennessee slaveholder and future president James K. Polk, appointed to the committee eight supporters of the Jackson–Van Buren administration and one lone Whig, a colorful and important congressman named Ben Hardin from Kentucky, who would explain when the committee reported that he thought he had been appointed just to make the round number nine and had never attended a meeting. Henry Pinckney, as is the way in these matters, was the committee's chairman.

Pinckney's apostasy provoked quick and strong reactions. He was blasted in Washington by Calhoun's friend Duff Green, editor of the *United States Telegraph*, and by Calhounites back home in Charleston. He was read out of the States Rights (Nullifier) Party. He had support, too—a lot of support. But the attack by the purest of the pure was brutal. In March, Calhoun registered his disapproval of the kind of contaminated thing Pinckney was proposing when he marched out of the Senate rather than vote either for or against Buchanan's motion, which had the same premise as Pinckney's: that you could allow those awful petitions just barely to come through the door of the House, in order then to stamp a severe negative answer upon them.

Meanwhile, Pinckney was meeting with his committee, in late February through March and April and into May of 1836. On May 18, the committee made its much-anticipated report—unanimously, although Hardin asserted that he had had nothing to do with it. Of course, the report scathingly denounced abolition; there may have been a certain tendency for Van Burenites and Democrats, Northern and Southern, to heighten their denunciation of abolition as a kind of compensation for not going to the ultra-extreme lengths of the Calhounites and some Southern Whigs with respect to the petitions and the constitutional powers of Congress in the District. Almost everybody denounced the abolitionists; it was a politically safe position.

The committee then proposed not just the original two but now *three* resolutions, with corresponding paragraphs of explanation and defense. The first two resolutions were those that the House, following Pinckney's original motion, had instructed them to report. First, of course, they denied that Congress had any power to interfere with slavery in the states. Second—and this was the tough one, in South Carolinian political circles and elsewhere in the South—they went to great lengths to say that it would be "unwise" and "impolitic" for Congress to interfere with slavery in the District of Columbia. For the Calhounites these were weasel words; the committee had declined to say that it was *unconstitutional* for Congress to interfere with slavery in the District. That defect led to severe condemnations of Pinckney for having utterly departed from proper "Southern feeling."

But then there came the third resolution, a new addition, which had not been included in the committee's instructions. Where did it come from? Presumably from the pressure of the negative response to the second in South Carolina, and from Southern Whigs and fire-eaters elsewhere. But the Democratic administration supported it, too; it appeared to be another way, in this more obstreperous branch of Congress, to get the petitions and the subject of slavery out of the public eye, for the purpose of politics, and off the House floor, for the purpose of governing. Instead of sending all the petitions to a select committee, the committee now proposed the following:

> **[The Pinckney committee]:** And whereas it is extremely important and desirable, that the agitation of this subject should be finally arrested, for the purpose of restoring tranquillity to the public mind, your committee respectfully recommend the adoption of the following additional resolution, viz:
>
> All petitions, memorials, resolutions, propositions, or papers, relating in any way, or to any extent whatsoever, to the subject of slavery or the abolition of slavery, shall, without being either printed or referred, be laid on the table and that no further action whatever shall be had thereon.

Instead of sending all such petitions to a select committee, and instead of borrowing the Senate's device of receiving each petition but immediately answering it in the negative, and instead of the response favored by the Calhoun-Hammond coalition, indignantly to refuse to receive any such petition on grounds that it prayed for something unconstitutional, there was proposed an automatic tabling *a priori,* as it were, and *en bloc,* of all petitions on this subject.

Although the proposal was not quite the most extreme—Calhoun and

Hammond, as we said, had set very high standards for extremism—it was severe. The petitions would be automatically tabled, without any reference to committee, without any printing, without any member's having to make a tabling motion, and without any response to the prayer. To anyone living in a different world from Charleston in the 1830s, that would surely seem severe enough. The intensity of feeling on that committee—Northerners who devoutly wished the subject would go away, proslavery Southerners, and Democrats who wanted to prove that they could be as fierce against those petitions as their rivals—is reflected in the repetitious emphasis of the word "whatever," used twice, and in the phrases "in any way" and "to any extent," and in the specific provisions that the offensive matter should not be printed and should not be referred to committee. This proposal was to carve a place in American history as the famous gag rule.

But as the House began its consideration of the Pinckney Committee's report, it did not focus on the gag rule. Pinckney's fellow South Carolinians, and a few others like Henry Wise, ignored the gag and gave voice to their outrage on point two, that the report had not declared congressional interference with slavery in the District to be unconstitutional. Here are the remarks of Waddy Thompson, the South Carolina Whig whom we have met before, as reported not in the *Congressional Globe* but in the competing congressional journal, the *Register of Debates*, for May 26, 1836:

> **Mr. Thompson, of South Carolina,** would not allow for one moment to pass without his unmeasured denunciation of the report just read. He felt called upon to do so, that it should not go to the world with the authority of the name (not of the individual who had presented it, but) of the State from which he came. He had listened in vain for one South Carolina argument, or one honest bursting out of the feelings of a South Carolinian; not of a South Carolinian from geography only, but one who has a head to see the dangers that await us, and a heart that does not shrink from meeting them. Instead of a cool, firm, and fixed purpose to stand upon the rights, the chartered rights, of the South, what have we? an abandonment of those rights; stale homilies about union and fanaticism; puerile rhetoric, and jesuitical sophistry.

That was one South Carolinian admonishing another for being so pusillanimous as to say only that Congress *ought* not to touch slavery in the District, rather than that it was absolutely *forbidden* to do so.

Thompson also made a claim about promises Pinckney had made.

> **[Thompson]:** [Pinckney] assured me and my friend from Virginia, [Mr. Wise] and others . . . that he would not report at all unless with the distinct assertion of the principle that Congress had no constitutional power to legislate upon slavery in this District. And how had this pledge been redeemed? Puling declaration of "violation of the public faith"; Mr. T. desired to hear less of the public faith from one so regardless of private faith. Mr. T. would not, if he could fairly avoid it, send the report to the printer; he would rather commit it to the flames or to the hangman.

So although for the purposes of the large sweep of American history Henry Pinckney is the author of the notorious gag rule, which led to a nine-year battle in the House and in the nation, and which is a prime example in American political history of the suppression of civil liberty at the center of the national government itself, from Waddy Thompson's point of view Pinckney's proposal was far too mild.

And the Calhounites had their revenge. When Pinckney announced in August—to look ahead—that he was a candidate for reelection, Calhoun's surrogates executed a purge. They joined with the old Unionists—that is, those who had *not* joined Calhoun (and Pinckney!) on the pro-nullification side in 1832—and substituted the interesting scholarly figure Hugh Legaré, a Unionist, for Pinckney in the Charleston seat in the United States House of Representatives. Pinckney was thus to be drummed out of office for not quite coming up to the mark of Carolina feelings.

Mr. Thompson's thoroughly South Carolinian remarks, which indicated why Pinckney had to be chastised and replaced, were followed by long speeches from other Southern members, often in this same not-so-gentle mode, denouncing the report's implication that Congress might have the power to abolish slavery in the District. This scolding continued for a week with nothing said about the third proposal, the gag rule.

Then, on May 25, 1836, as one such speech wound to its close, the congressman who was, by a very wide margin, the most distinguished member of that House, who had not yet responded to the Pinckney Committee report, rose in his place to get the Chair's attention. Presumably he would now at last speak, from a radically different perspective, about that third aspect of the report, the gag rule. But Speaker Polk did not call on him. He recognized instead a Georgia Democrat, and member of the Pinckney Committee, George Owens, and Owens moved the previous question, which is not debatable, and which, if approved, stops debate. The House would then take the vote, with no further discussion—no discussion at all of the third resolution, the gag rule.

Mr. Adams expressed his desire to say a few words on the subject of the report and the resolutions. If the House wished to proceed to the orders of the day, he would be willing to postpone his remarks to to-morrow; but he hoped the previous question would not be pressed. . . .

Henry Wise inquired whether Owens's motion was in or out of order; to which Speaker Polk replied that it was in order.

Mr. Adams requested the gentleman from Georgia to withdraw the motion, and not call for the previous question without giving any one an opportunity to discuss the question.

Mr. Owens said he had made the motion after much deliberation, and would not withdraw it.

Mr. Adams was about to make some remarks, but was interrupted by

The Chair, stating that the question was not debatable.

Mr. Adams appealed from the decision of the Chair that the motion was in order, on the ground that the gentleman from Georgia, at the time he made the motion, was not competent to make it.

The Chair called upon Mr. Adams to reduce his appeal to writing.

Mr. Adams, after a moment, said he perceived that a majority of the House was determined to stifle discussion, and he would withdraw his appeal, and consent that the vote should be taken.

The motion for the previous question was then seconded, but the parliamentary situation left some doubt about just what the previous question *was*.

The Chair, in reply to an inquiry, said the previous question would be on concurring in the [Pinckney Committee's three] resolutions, and not on the motion to recommit or print the report.

Mr. Adams appealed from that decision.

The Chair said it was what he would decide if the main question should be ordered.

Mr. Adams said, then I will appeal when the decision is made. I am aware that there is a slaveholder in the chair. . . .

The Speaker, Mr. Polk, was perhaps not thrilled by this remark.

Mr. Adams asked if there was then time to ascertain what the decision of the Chair will be upon what is the main question?

The Chair said he had stated, for the information of the House, what the decision would be; but the time to make a decision had not arrived.

Mr. Adams demanded that it should be decided what was the main question, that the House might know upon what they were voting, and that it might be entered on the journals.

The Chair said he had not decided what the main question was, and could not, because the House might negative the demand for the main question. The gentleman from Massachusetts could attain his object as well after the House had decided whether the main question should be then put.

Mr. Adams said he could not, and was proceeding to show the difference in the points of time, when

Mr. Boon [of Indiana] called him to order.

Mr. Adams said he was speaking to order. He would ask the Chair to decide what the main question is, in order that the House might have an opportunity to decide, before they were obliged to vote for the putting of the main question, whether the decision of the Speaker was correct or not. . . .

The Chair then decided that the main question would be on the [Pinckney Committee] resolutions, and would cut off all other questions or motions to amend or commit . . . and he announced the question then pending to be, "Shall the decision of the Chair stand as the judgment of the House?"

Mr. Adams said he understood that question to be debatable.

The Chair said it had been decided that an appeal, while the previous question was pending, was not debatable, by an express vote by the House.

Mr. Williams [of Kentucky] moved the previous question on the appeal, and said he was sure that would stop debate. . . .

As **the Chair** was stating the question that would arise,

Mr. Williams withdrew the motion.

Mr. Adams asked if he was gagged or not.

The Chair said he had decided, according to a previous decision of the House, that the motion was not debatable.

Mr. Adams was going on with some remarks, but was interrupted by loud calls to order. He stated that he wanted the decision of the Chair in writing, that it might be entered on the journal.

The Chair said he had no right to make such a demand.

Mr. Adams appealed from that decision.

The Chair decided the appeal to be out of order. He said one appeal was then pending, and another appeal could not be piled upon it.

The question was then taken, and the decision of the Chair was sustained by the House.

The answer to John Quincy Adams's question, in the short term, was yes. He was "gagged." But in the longer term, the opponents of the petitions would find that they had a fight on their hands.

PART V

THE FIRST SON OF THE REPUBLIC

13 / HOW SLEEP THE BRAVE?

JOHN QUINCY ADAMS WAS not just another congressman. He had been, among many other distinctions, president of the United States, the sixth president, and the second of his family to serve in that office. But beyond that he was a living link to the nation's founders.

Washington had no children; Jefferson had no sons who survived; Madison had no children of his own, although by marrying Dolley he acquired stepchildren. Hamilton was survived by seven children, none of whom reflected the brilliance of their father; Franklin's only son went over to the other side in the Revolution. Were there no politically active, able, republican direct male descendants of the great founders of the late eighteenth century? There was John Quincy Adams.

Very few human beings can have had an upbringing in a nation's ideals comparable to his. He had spent his boyhood imbibing the meaning of the American Revolution from his extraordinary parents, at the center of the action. He had spent his adult career defining the role of the new American republic on the world scene.

He had been born in July of 1767, not too long after the repeal of the Stamp Act. Surely in his parents' homes in Boston and in Braintree he heard from his first breath discussions about the contest with Great Britain, and about the republican ideals of the United States, even before there was a United States.

His father had set out for Philadelphia in September of 1774, in John Hancock's coach, with the others in the Massachusetts delegation, to attend what would come to be called the First Continental Congress—the older Adams's first trip outside New England. Johnny, the oldest son, who stayed home with his mama, was then seven years old. For the remainder of his youth he would rarely be with both parents at the same time, because they were kept apart by the events of the nation's founding. Much of John Quincy's childhood was spent with his mother, often in some danger, in Boston and Braintree, surrounded by key events of the American Revolution. Much of his later youth he would spend with his father, who was representing the fledgling republic in the capitals of Europe. Always he would be the object of the intense desire of both his energetic, intelligent, virtuous, republican parents that he be educated to the full extent of his considerable talents to carry on what they had begun.

In one of the first of her famous letters to her husband in Philadelphia, Abigail Adams wrote: "I have taken a very great fondness to reading Rollin's ancient History since you left me . . . and I have perswaded Johnny to read me a page or two every day, and hope he will from his desire to oblige me entertain a fondness for it." (Her spelling, like everything else about her, had a vigorous individuality.) So there was the mother and her seven-year-old son, with Papa out of town, during the British threat to Boston, curled up on the eighteenth-century equivalent of a sofa, reading about the heroes of the Roman Republic to whom they would all soon be endlessly comparing themselves.

John Quincy's father was a major figure at that Continental Congress for two months in the fall of 1774, and at the Second Congress that began the following May—one "theater of action," as Abigail, writing to her husband, said. But she and her children were meanwhile living in another theater of action. Massachusetts was the most radical of colonies; Boston was the most radical part of Massachusetts. The "Intolerable Acts," as the American patriots called them, enacted in angry response to the episode of the tea, had been directed primarily at Boston: the Boston Port Bill had closed the port, and two other acts had effectively taken government and the administration of justice out of local hands. British power occupied the city. "Suffering Boston" was the focus of patriots' anger in all of the colonies, and the primary occasion for the coming together of the Congress. As John Quincy's father traveled by coach to Philadelphia in the fall of 1774 he reported by letter to John Quincy's mother the heartwarming support for beleaguered Massachusetts that he encountered along his route.

In the spring of 1775, at just the moment when John Adams was to return for what came to be called the Second Continental Congress, there occurred in the family's own neighborhood events that would electrify the colonies and serve forever after as national myths. A lifetime later, John Quincy would write a letter, or a draft of a letter, according to a footnote in *The Adams Family Correspondence*, "in a faltering hand to an English Quaker" that told from the perspective of many years about the happenings back in the famous month of April 1775.

> *The year 1775 was the eighth year of my age. Among the first fruits of the War, was the expulsion of my father's family from their peaceful abode in Boston, to take refuge in his and my native town of Braintree. . . . For the*

> *space of twelve months my mother with her infant children dwelt, liable every hour of the day and of the night to be butchered in cold blood, or taken and carried into Boston as hostages, by any foraging or marauding detachment of men, like that actually sent forth on the 19th. of April to capture John Hancock and Samuel Adams on their way to attend the continental Congress at Philadelphia.**

This marauding detachment of British power had been sent forth by the usually somewhat lethargic but now exasperated general commanding the forces around Boston, Thomas Gage, under pressure from London, to try, as John Quincy in his old age recalled and as every American used to know, to snatch two of the ringleaders of the seditionists, Sam Adams and John Hancock, and while they were at it to destroy rebel military supplies they thought were stored in Concord. Gage was rewarded for his pains by "a hurry of hoofs in a village street, a shape in the moonlight, a bulk in the dark"; by a sleepy gathering of local militia lined up on Lexington Green in the early morning, into which, after a confused beginning, the British regulars fired their muskets, killing eight; by an aroused collection of "embattled farmers" who then after Gage's troops had made a futile visit to Concord met them at the "rude bridge that arched the flood" and fired "the shot heard 'round the world"; by Middlesex farmers who "gave them ball for ball, from behind each fence and farmyard wall, chasing the redcoats down the lane, then crossing the fields to emerge again, under the trees at the turn of the road, and only pausing to fire and load"; by a disorder in the ranks of his own frustrated troops, as they pillaged and looted and attacked civilians on their way back to Cambridge and Charleston; by a disproportionate loss in this curious battle or sequence of battles of 273 casualties to only 95 for the Americans; and, eventually, by not one but two of the best-known poems in the American language, one by Ralph Waldo Emerson and one by Henry Wadsworth Longfellow. All in all, it was not one of the better days for General Gage, or for the glory of Britain.

For the British, to be sure, the whole episode was just a hiccup in the mighty history of Empire; but for the Americans, and especially for Adamses, it was to be something else.

> And yet, through the gloom and the light,
> The fate of a nation was riding that night,

*Extracts from the journals of John Quincy Adams, and from communications to his constituents and from long letters like this one, in which Adams's own voice from the time is heard at length, will be printed in italics, as here.

And the spark struck out by that steed, in his flight,
Kindled the land into flame with its heat.

IF JOHN QUINCY'S MOTHER imparted to him an ineradicable memory of the nineteenth of April in " 'Seventy-five,"* she imparted an even stronger impression of the next legendary event of that legendary year, when in June she took him to the top of Penn's Hill to watch the battle at Bunker Hill and the fires of Charlestown. Many years later, after the United States of America had settled into nationhood, some citizens placed a marker on the spot where they thought Abigail Adams and her son Johnny had stood to watch these events.

John Quincy's reminiscence, in the letter drafted as an old man, continued:

> *My father was separated from his family, on his way to attend the same continental Congress, and there* [in Braintree] *my mother, with her children lived in unintermitted danger of being consumed with them all in a conflagration kindled by a torch in the same hands which on the 17th. of June lighted the fires in Charlestown. I saw with my own eyes those fires, and heard Britannia's thunders in the Battle of Bunker's hill and witnessed the tears of my mother and mingled with them my own, at the fall of Warren a dear friend of my father, and a beloved Physician to me. He had been our family physician and surgeon, and had saved my fore finger from amputation under a very bad fracture.*

Joseph Warren—friend and collaborator of Samuel Adams, chief author of the "Suffolk Resolves," calling for independence, that arrived at an opportune moment for the Continental Congress—was a name that once would have been familiar to every American patriot. For young Johnny, however, and old John Quincy as well, Warren was more than a name at the head of a list of patriotic heroes; he was a man he knew. He was the family physician who had saved the boy's forefinger—presumably the same forefinger that he would one day point not only at a long series of

*She sometimes got even this famous date wrong, by the way. In her letter to her husband from Weymouth on June 16(?) she refers to the "never to be forgotten 14 of April." The editors of *The Adams Family Correspondence* put an affectionate but exasperated footnote to that "14": "Thus clearly in MS, but meant of course for '19'—an example of AA's habitual and extreme unreliability in dating anything whatever" (Vol. 1, p. 219). In Longfellow's poem, starting with Paul Revere's ride the night before the events in Lexington and Concord, it is "the eighteenth of April in 'Seventy-Five."

European diplomats but also, as we shall see, at a generation of Southern leaders in the U.S. House of Representatives.

The seventy-nine-year-old John Quincy's memories of his youth, put down in the draft letter discussing war and pacifism with his Quaker correspondent, continued:

> *My mother was the daughter of a Christian Clergyman and therefore bred in the faith of deliberate detestation of War. . . . Yet in the same Spring and Summer of 1775 she taught me to repeat daily after the Lord's prayer, before rising from bed the Ode of Collins, on the patriot warriors who fell in the War to subdue the Jacobite rebellion of 1745.*

Abigail Adams herself quoted this poem, William Collins's "Ode Written in the Beginning of the year 1746," in its entirety, presumably from memory, in the letter she wrote to her husband immediately after the Battle of Bunker Hill. "Those favorite lines of Collin[s] continually Sound in my Ears," she wrote. The Adams Papers editors remark of her quoting: "Except for bad spelling and punctuation this is an accurate rendering."

> How sleep the Brave who sink to rest,
> By all their Countrys wishes blest?
> When Spring with dew'ey fingers cold
> Returns to deck their Hallowed mould
> She there shall dress a sweeter Sod
> Than fancy's feet has ever trod.
> By fairy hands their knell is rung
> By forms unseen their Dirge is sung
> There Honour comes a pilgrim grey
> To Bless the turf that wraps their Clay
> And freedom shall a while repair
> To Dwell a weeping Hermit there.

John Quincy in his seventy-ninth year, recalling across the years these events of his boyhood, continued:

> *Of the impression made upon my heart by the sentiments inculcated in these beautiful effusions of patriotism and poetry, you may form an estimate by the fact that now, seventy one years after they were thus taught me, I repeat them from memory without reference to the book.*

And the old man John Quincy did repeat them, missing only one word. Hearing as a boy the sounds of the battle of Bunker Hill and seeing the fires of the destruction of Charlestown and observing his mother's response to the news of Warren's death, and reciting Collins's poem every day, clearly made an impression upon the eight-year-old boy that lasted his whole life.

The anniversary of the battle of Bunker Hill, June 17, would all his life be a doubly important day for Adams. It was a day that evoked in him the most exalted patriotic memory and emotion. But it was also, partly for that reason, a day that regularly provoked his disapproval of the way the new democracy would celebrate it.

In 1786, for example, as a nineteen-year-old student at Harvard, he wrote in his journal:

> *This day, the Bridge over Charlestown Ferry was compleated, and as the same day 11 years agone, was marked with dreadful Scenes, of Slaughter and Destruction, the managers, and directors of the Bridge, determined, that this day should be mark'd with Pleasure and festivity. I do not think however that the scheme was good. A Dinner provided for 600 people, on Bunker's hill: the havoc of oxen, sheep, and fowls of all kinds, was I suppose as great today, as that of men upon the former occasion and I dare say, there was as much wine drank now, as there was blood spilt then, and to crown the whole, the head of the table, was I hear placed on the very spot where the immortal Warren fell. I think however, that the ground which had been the scene, of such an awful Day, should [not] be made a scene of revels, and feasting. What must be the feelings of a man of Sensibility, who, would naturally say to himself "perhaps, I am now seated on the grave of my dearest friend. Perhaps this is the Spot where he drew his last gasp; and I may now be treading down his bones."*

This disapproval continued, and grew, throughout his life, and included—again to jump far ahead in our story for a moment—the occasion of the dedication of the Bunker Hill monument when Adams was in his late seventies.

> *June 17 [1843].—This was the day of the great celebration of the completion of the monument of Bunker Hill. . . . What a name in the annals of mankind of Bunker Hill! what a day was the 17th of June, 1775! and what a burlesque upon them both is an oration upon them by Daniel Webster, and a pilgrimage by [President] John Tyler and his Cabinet of slave-drivers, to desecrate the solemnity by their presence! And then a dinner at Faneuil Hall in honor of a President of the United States, hated and despised by those who invited him to it, themselves as cordially hated and despised by him.*

John Tyler, obviously no favorite of Adams's, has appeared already and will appear again later in this story. Adams, writing in his journal in 1843, continued:

> *I was a student at Cambridge when, on the 17th of June, 1786, Charles River Bridge was opened. I passed the day in the solitude of my study, and dined almost alone in the hall. But now, with the ideal associations of the thundering cannon, which I heard, and the smoke of burning Charlestown, which I saw, on that awful day, combined with this pyramid of Quincy granite, and Daniel Webster spouting, (with a Negro holding an umbrella over his head) and John Tyler's nose, with a shadow outstretching that of the monumental column—how could I have witnessed all this at once, without an unbecoming burst of indignation, or of laughter? Daniel Webster is a heartless traitor to the cause of human freedom; John Tyler is a slave-monger. What have these to do with the Quincy granite pyramid on the brow of Bunker Hill? What have these to do with a dinner in Faneuil Hall, but to swill like swine, and grunt about the rights of man? I stayed at home, and visited my seedling trees. . . .*

The parenthetical phrase about the Negro holding the umbrella over Webster's head while he spouts about human rights, which neatly captures Adams's indignation, was stricken by Charles Francis Adams in his edition of his father's diaries, and therefore does not appear in the most accessible one-volume edition, which was taken from Charles Francis. But now the editors of the thorough modern edition of the Adams Papers, in another of their many services to truth, will restore it.

JOHN QUINCY HAD NOT one but two extraordinary parents, and the relationship between the two of them was extraordinary as well, as the world has learned from their letters. John Adams and the others among the greatest American founders—Jefferson, Madison, Washington, Hamilton, Franklin—would each reveal on paper a mind of distinction, and a worthy devotion to the republican cause, as the lengthening shelves of the volumes of the papers of each of them attest. But Adams, uniquely, had a moral companion and intellectual equal at home, a dearest friend who shared to the full those characteristics—intellectual distinction and moral commitment to republicanism—with some added sparks of her own. There is no equivalent to Abigail Adams in the households of the other great American founders. And fortunately for the country and the world, she revealed her distinction and her devotion to republican government, all unself-consciously, in "papers" of her own. When you read those letters, to her husband first of all but to other people as well, you come to realize what an extraordinary person she was, and you may then infer what an extraordinary upbringing John Quincy had.

In them she reported, of course, on many family doings, but these would be mingled with reports and discussions of great events in the Revolution like the never-to-be-forgotten whatever-it-was of April in 'Seventy-five; she may not have got the dates right every time, but she caught the spirit and the meaning. And mixed them with the details of daily life. The letters about the Declaration of Independence, life being what it is, also contained discussions of inoculations for smallpox. She dealt, of course, with many items of household management; her competent managing of the farm kept the family afloat while her husband was off making a new country.

But mingled with mundane matters of health and family and household management, in the letters of both—of the mother at least as much as the father—there were reflections on politics, morals, religion, and life, often with an appropriate quotation from *Paradise Lost*, Dryden, James Thomson's *The Seasons*, or Shakespeare. And an important part of those reflections dealt with the leading issues of the time, independence and the making of republican states. John Quincy had not one but two republican political thinkers as parents.

JOHN QUINCY'S FATHER PLAYED a larger role in the making of the new nation than its citizens two hundred years later realize, and he corresponded with, and received pungent comment from, John Quincy's mother all the time he was doing it. The senior Adams was the leader in the Continental Congress for the radical side, the "Atlas of Independence," who with his cousin Sam made the decisive alliance with the radicals from Virginia, and finally won out over the conciliators from the middle states. He cut through the palaver over the several state favorites for the general of the continental forces by nominating—Massachusetts nominating Virginia—the famous colonel from the French and Indian Wars, sitting there in his uniform silently among them, Colonel George Washington. When Abigail received the "brave and amiable" General Washington in Braintree, on his way to the troops in Cambridge—that would be young John Quincy's first meeting with Washington, too—she found the new commander even better than her husband's description, and was so carried away in her enthusiasm as to break into a quotation from John Dryden.

John Quincy's father made the speeches and sponsored the resolution (the body on May 10, 1776; the more radical preamble on May 15) urging the states to declare independence and to set up their own new governments, which for him, not without reason, would be the key moment of American independence.

In response to requests from several states, John Adams wrote an influential document (a letter originally, which when published came to be titled "Thoughts on Government") that anticipated much of the form of the state and federal governments of the United States. His wife, John Quincy's mother, wrote her famous plea on behalf of "the ladies," at this time when her husband was discussing the "new modelling" of the states. "I desire you would remember the ladies and be more generous and favorable to them than your ancestors," she wrote in March of 1776, in a letter that would be widely circulated two hundred years later in the time of a renewed feminist movement. She was thinking about the enormous but particular matter of the treatment of women as a part of a still larger matter: the overall shape of new governments—the new societies—that would be brought into being in this new world, and the principles upon which they would rest.

Her husband would write, in words that would acquire their own modest fame, in his letter ("Thoughts on Government") to a fellow state maker: "You and I, my dear friend, have been sent into life at a time when the greatest lawgivers of antiquity would have wished to live. How few of the human race have ever enjoyed an opportunity of making an election of government for themselves or their children! When . . . had three millions of people full power and a fair opportunity to form and establish the wisest and happiest government that human wisdom can contrive?"

The world would forget, but the Adamses would not, that John Adams then played an important role in the making of the document that, as fortune would have it, came to be more famous than any of his, or her, own words or deeds. As he had nominated George Washington, so as a member of the five-man committee to write a Declaration of Independence he nominated another Virginian, his new young friend Thomas Jefferson, to draft that document, admitting, among the reasons Jefferson should do it, that Jefferson wrote better than he did; another reason was that Jefferson had not been a part of the fights over independence in the Continental Congress and so had not made the enemies that Adams had made.

When the draft produced by Jefferson (and amended by the committee, including Adams) was presented to the Congress on July 2–4, 1776, it was John Quincy's father who defended it on the floor of Congress for two and a half days. Jefferson was generally disinclined to speak in such meetings, and would write many years later that as the principal drafter he "thought it his duty to be a passive auditor of the opinions of others," some of which opinions, he said, "made him writhe a little." Congress went through the document line by line, and Adams, as Jefferson later gratefully wrote, defended it line by line, "fighting fearlessly for every word of it."

When Adams sent a copy of the new Declaration to Abigail, probably copied in his own hand, she may have mistakenly thought for a time that he was the drafter. In any case, when interpreting John Quincy Adams one should remind oneself that when he was nine years old his mother had, there on the table in their rooms, one of the original copies of the Declaration of Independence, handwritten by his father, who had fought for it on the floor of Congress.

It is significant to note, for the purposes of the story to be told in these pages, that opposition to slavery was one of the larger topics that John Quincy's mother brought up in her letters, including her response to the Declaration. On July 14 she wrote that she regretted that "some of the most Manly Sentiments in the Declaration are Expunged from the printed copy." It may surely be inferred that among these "Manly Sentiments" the expunging of which she regretted, the most important was the biggest cut that the Congress made, the long passage attacking slavery ("cruel war against human nature"), and blaming it, of course, on King George, that Jefferson had drafted, and that the committee including John Adams had retained, and that Adams presumably had defended in the Continental Congress.

That was not Abigail Adams's first reference to race and slavery. Very early, in one of her first letters to her husband after he had gone to Philadelphia, writing from "Boston Garrison" (as she herself signed her dateline), she reported a rumor that a "conspiracy of the negroes" had been quietly suppressed—we know nothing about this event, if it was one, except her report—and then added the remark: "I wish most sincerely that there was not a slave in the province. It always seemed a most iniquitous scheme to me—to fight ourselves for what we are daily robbing and plundering from those who have as good a right to freedom as we have. You know my mind on this subject."

Later, in 1776, raising questions about the effect of the social system of Virginia on the mind of Massachusetts's Virginia allies, she linked her apprehensions to the slave system, and her rejection of that system to elementary Christian ethics:

"I have sometimes been ready to think that the passion for liberty cannot be equally strong in the breasts of those who have been accustomed to deprive their fellow-creatures of theirs. Of this I am certain, that it is not founded upon that generous and Christian principle of doing to others as we would that others should do unto us."

. . .

THE ADAMS FAMILY WAS intimately linked not only to the making of the constitutional forms of the new nation and to the expression of its ideals, but also to the grim realities of the actual fighting in the Revolution itself. If the American Revolution is a pageant to us, centuries later, it was not a pageant but a genuine war to many then, much including the Adamses. As we have seen, they lost already in 1775, at Bunker Hill, their doctor, Joseph Warren, and John Quincy and his mother had seen Charleston in ashes (Abigail's father came from Charleston). They lost Abigail's mother and John's brother to the debilitating diseases caused in part by the British occupation, and they suffered in other ways.

But in addition, in June of 1776 John Adams was appointed the head of another committee—more important in his mind probably than the committee to produce the Declaration—on the conduct of the war. This committee was given the formidable name Board of War and Ordnance, and Adams was called its "president." He was thus the equivalent, while continuing to serve as delegate to Congress, of what later generations would call secretary of war, and still later, secretary of defense.

Adams served as "president" of this board, an enormous chore, from its inception on June 12, 1776, until he left Congress late in 1777, throughout the early stages of the Revolutionary War. Its work included all that a war department would do: raising, fitting, dispatching, and keeping track of the troops and their officers and all weaponry, and the care of all prisoners of war, and the carrying on of all official correspondence about the war. So John Quincy's father had knowledge not only of his own war experiences in a Congress being chased about the countryside by British forces (Philadelphia to Baltimore to Philadelphia to Yorktown and back once again to Philadelphia) and the experiences of his wife and children in the hotbed of eastern Massachusetts, and the experiences of friends and of the common knowledge in those two centers, but also the special knowledge that came to him in this official post.

He served in that role, agonizing about the miseries of war, and excoriating the British, through the defeat of Washington's new troops on the first battles on Long Island; the retreat of the Americans across the Delaware River; Washington's famous crossing and the victories at Princeton and Trenton; General Burgoyne's incursion from Canada through the Hudson Valley, which might have cut off New England from the rest of the colonies and therefore divided Abigail and the children from John; General Howe's baffling strategy of heading not up from New York to meet Burgoyne but out across the farms of Pennsylvania (making patriots along the way, Adams would say, out of Germans and Quakers through whose property his troops passed) to march triumphantly into Philadelphia, and to cause the Congress (including Adams, of course) to scurry to Yorktown. All of those events and more can be followed in the letters of John Quincy's parents, and as a modern reader follows them that reader might picture the intelligent boy of eight, nine, ten years old who surely is living through all those events as intensely as his parents. Abigail—generally speaking, a fiercer partisan than her husband—contributed her own reports of events and her own condemnations of the British and the Tories.

The formal surrender of Burgoyne on October 17, 1777, celebrated fiercely in Abigail's letters, satisfied European powers, particularly France, that the American cause had the possibility of victory, and brought a new chapter in the lives of the Adams family. John Adams was chosen by Congress to be one of the three American ministers to cross the water and negotiate with the French. He came home to Braintree in late December of 1777 to get ready to sail to France, and to provide yet another phase in the education of John Quincy.

HIS PARENTS DECIDED THAT, dangerous though it was, nevertheless Johnny, now eleven years of age, could accompany his father on the latter's very first trip abroad to perform this diplomatic service for the embattled, newly independent country—independent, that is, if it won. John Adams wrote to his wife as they set out, by sail, on the hazardous wartime voyage: "Johnny sends his duty to his mama and his love to his sister and brothers. He behaves like a man."

Johnny had further occasion to "behave like a man" when their ship, six days out to sea, was chased by a British man-of-war. John Adams recounted this event, and the storm that followed, twice: once in the journal he kept, or tried to keep, at the time ("I was constantly so wett, and every Place and thing was so wett, and every Table and Chair so wrecked, that it was impossible to touch a Pen or Paper") and then twenty-eight years later, when he was presumably dry, in an effort to write his autobiography. For this part of it he consulted his journal, taking over much of it word for word, so the two accounts are very much alike. And yet the old man's memory expands on the journal entry and adds some touches. He left his native shore in a sailing ship (the *Boston*) and went out onto the dangerous Atlantic, and his son went with him. It was dangerous not only because of storms and the frailty of the craft but also because the nation or colonies that Adams was commissioned to represent were at war with the mightiest naval power in the world. John Adams and his papers would have been a considerable prize for the British.

On February 19, 1778, the *Boston* sighted three large ships. At first the crew wanted to sail toward them, thinking they might be British merchant vessels that could be captured for profit. But the captain was fairly sure that they were frigates, and he proved correct: "We were near enough to see they were Frigates and count their Guns, to the Full Satisfaction of every man on Board. No man had an Appetite for fighting three Frigates at once in our feeble state." So they sailed away as fast as the wind allowed, losing two of the British men-of-war, but not the third, which gave chase throughout that day and the next.

"When night approached"—this is from John Adams's autobiography—"The Wind died away and We were left rolling and pitching in a Calm, with our Guns all out . . . all drawn up and every Way prepared for battle." Adams, the primary passenger, offered his opinion about what they should do. "I said and did all in my power to encourage the Officers and men to fight them to the last Extremity. My motives were more urgent than theirs, for it will easily be believed that it would have been more eligible for me to be killed on board the Boston or sunk to the bottom in her, than to be taken Prisoner." And if he had been killed on board or sunk to the bottom or taken prisoner, something like these fates would, presumably, have been shared by his young son.

The father sat in his cabin and saw "the Ennemy" gaining on them: "Our Powder, Cartridges, and Balls were placed by the Guns and every thing ready to begin the Action." But black clouds had gathered, and the wind sprang up, and their ship began to move, and night fell, and they lost sight of the enemy—and as that threat faded, a great storm took over as a greater threat. In his entries—autobiography adapted from journal—for February 20, 21, 22, 23, and again for 24, 25, and 26, Adams managed a vigorous description of a little sailing ship in a harrowing storm out on the open ocean, with some "particulars," as his wife might have put it ("such was the Agitation of the Vessel that instead of sleeping it was with the utmost difficulty that my little son and I could hold ourselves in bed with both our hands, and bracing our selves against the boards, planks, and timbers with our feet"). Early in the storm there suddenly came a "tremendous Report," which at first they thought might be a shot issuing after all from the British frigate, or from the *Boston*'s own artillery, but it turned out to have been a thunderclap; a stroke of lightning had hit the ship and knocked down four men, one of whom died three days later.

Adams was proud of his own self-possession during these harrowing "Chases and tempests." In a pinch he was still a son of the Puritans; he thought himself "in the Way of Duty" and did not "repent of [his] voyage." But he was also a husband and father, and he had his eleven-year-old son with him, and that was something else again. "I confess I often regretted that I had brought my son. I was not so clear that it was my Duty to expose him . . . but I had been led to it by the Childs Inclination and by the Advice of all my Friends."

The boy's behavior was all that his parents could have asked. "Mr. Johnnys Behavior gave me a satisfaction that I cannot express," the proud father wrote in his journal, "fully sensible of our Danger, he was constantly endeavouring to bear it with a manly Patience, very attentive to me and his thoughts constantly running in a serious strain."

Safely landed on the opposite shore, John Quincy was placed by his father in one of the best Parisian schools, took French lessons, met diplomats; he returned to Europe with his father again in 1779, this time with his younger brother, and attended good schools again, both in Paris and in Amsterdam and Leyden. He became proficient in French and knowledgeable in other languages, and was a good student. A Massachusetts friend of the Adamses, Francis Dana, chosen by Congress as the new republic's minister to Russia, then invited young John Quincy to accompany him to St. Petersburg as his secretary.

What was John Quincy Adams doing when he was fifteen years old? He was not practicing his jump shot every afternoon in the junior high school gym, or hanging around the drive-in hamburger joint every evening; he was not going out to the barn every morning to milk the cows and do the chores; he was not practicing the hup-hup drill with the militia on the village common; he was not covering himself with ink as an apprentice in a print shop; he was not reading college catalogs, wondering which he wanted to attend, or which he could get into; he was not attending his first proms. Lives differ. What John Quincy Adams was doing at age fifteen, in the prime of his adolescence, was translating diplomatic conversations between the American minister to Russia, who had no French, and the French minister to Russia, who had no English, in service of their joint endeavor (not successful) to obtain support from Empress Catherine for the newly independent United States.

While he was a teenager in Europe, John Quincy started his journal. He was an Adams, so he kept a journal. He *really* kept a journal. At the end of his life he observed that had he been a great writer or thinker it would have been a great work. As it stands it is not insignificant. He kept it up for well over half a century. By the end of his life it would fill a long, long shelf of volumes.

The conscientious John Quincy was given an angle of vision on the United States that no one else has ever had. He spent his childhood imbibing the ideals of the American Revolution—not secondhand, superficially, and afterward, but from principal participants, directly, and at the time those ideals were being shaped and tested. Then he was taken to the Old World, and had an education in European politics and diplomacy at the highest level, in Paris, Amsterdam, Leyden, St. Petersburg, The Hague, London, and other places, before he was twenty-one, that very few Americans have had in a lifetime.

14 / DUTY. DUTY? DUTY.

JOHN QUINCY ADAMS'S LONG life story, after that beginning, was a story of Duty, multiplied. Again and again, Duty called. Duty was always calling, and if Duty didn't call, Adams called *her*, and reversed the charges. It was a quite specific duty, a duty to republicanism and to this republic. When after many years he died, in the Capitol itself, Senator Thomas Hart Benton, for most of their careers an adversary, said in his eulogy: "Death found him at the post of duty; and where else could it have found him?"

Because of his father's appointments abroad, John Quincy spent most of his teen years in Europe, but he returned to the United States, by himself, and by his own decision, in 1785, to attend Harvard, and was graduated from Harvard in the important summer of 1787. He received his degree on July 16, which happened to be quite a memorable day at the Federal Convention down in Philadelphia—the day the Convention almost fell apart in the dispute between the small and the large states.

John Quincy had come home from Europe in part for this revealing reason: to avoid becoming too completely European. To recover his New England self toward serving his New England destiny. While on July 16 James Madison in Philadelphia was almost despairing of forming a lasting union, the twenty-year-old John Quincy was delivering the senior oration in Cambridge on the subject "The Importance and Necessity of Public Faith to the Well being of a Nation."

At the time when the conventions in the states were considering the ratification of the proposed Constitution, in the following winter, 1787–88, John Quincy Adams was studying law in Newburyport, Massachusetts, in the law offices of a family friend and distinguished lawyer, Theophilus Parsons. But no one with the load of Duty that John Quincy was carrying would be content being just another lawyer. He started out in American politics the way his father had done, by writing political pamphlets; among these was one defending President George Washington's neutral foreign policy with respect to France and England. A grateful President Washington thereupon gave him his first appointment, as minister to the Netherlands. Later he was to be sent to Portugal, but when his father succeeded Washington as president, the father shifted the son's appointment from Portugal to Berlin. Both Adams men, father and son, of course were careful to justify these appointments on merit, not connections. When Jefferson defeated Adams in the presidential election of 1800, Adams, before leaving office, recalled his son, and in the tense atmosphere between the Adams family and Jefferson following that election, John Quincy declined the appointment the family's former friend Jefferson would have offered him.

Before too long the Massachusetts Federalists chose him to serve in the Massachusetts Senate, although they knew that like his father he marched to the sound of Duty's different drummer, which meant he was very far from being a party man. Within forty-eight hours of his taking his seat he justified their fears, outraging his own party leaders by proposing that the Jeffersonian minority be given seats in proportional representation in the council or upper house. It was not long thereafter that those same party leaders chose him for the United States Senate—in part just to get him out of the state and out of their hair.

During his term in the United States Senate, his most important service to Public Faith rather than party or home constituency was the support he offered to President Jefferson's side in the matter of the Louisiana Purchase. As a Massachusetts Federalist he was supposed to oppose the infidel Jefferson and all his works, and specifically to oppose this New England–diluting addition of an unimaginably huge new continent of land. But despite his own personal and family disillusionment with Jefferson, and despite the strong objection by his party and his region, he supported it. When many years and many changes later another young U.S. senator from Massachusetts would write a book called *Profiles in Courage*, featuring independent "courageous" decisions by U.S. senators, the very first chapter would be on John Quincy Adams in the Senate defying Massachusetts Federalists and supporting President Jefferson's Louisiana Purchase.

Senator Adams further offended his fellow Federalists toward the end of his term by supporting a vigorous response to the aggressive acts on the seas by the belligerents in the Napoleonic Wars—particularly the British. The British stopped and searched American ships at sea, and even "impressed"—forced into service on their ships—American sailors. After a particularly outrageous example of this British conduct, the *Chesapeake* affair, President Jefferson proposed an embargo that prohibited American ships from sailing to foreign ports and foreign ships from taking on cargo in American ports, an action that essentially shut down foreign trade. The Federalists of New England were outraged, because they had commercial interests that would suffer, because they were pro-British (and anti-French), and because they were opposed to Jefferson. And what did their man the Massachusetts senator do? He stood by the president both in committee and on the floor.

With Adams's support of Jefferson and of aggressive measures against the British, the Massachusetts Federalist leaders in 1808–09 had had about all the service to Higher Duty from their senator that they could take. The Massachusetts legislature, dominated by Federalists, took the extraordinary step of electing a successor to Adams nine months before his term was up. Adams thereupon dutifully, and perhaps haughtily as well, resigned his Senate seat.

Jefferson's successor as president, James Madison, appointed John Quincy Adams minister to Russia, lifting him out of range of the revenge of the New England Federalists and setting in motion again his diplomatic career, which would take him to a string of major European capitals. He subsequently supported President Madison, even though Madison came from that other party—the Adamses never believed much in parties, and this was a period when the nation's first set of parties were fading—and he supported President Monroe, whom he served as secretary of state. Later, nearer the time of our story, he would on some matters even support President Jackson, who had defeated him in a bitter contest for reelection and whom by that time he did not like and who certainly came from what would prove in the new dispensation to be another party from that of the Adamses. And he supported subsequent presidents, none of whom he respected, on union-preserving issues, as well. He did so in part because he was an early believer that politics stops at the water's edge and partly because he was an experienced and well-read diplomat with a knowledge of European politics vastly superior to that of his colleagues. And, of course, from Duty. He would be a main figure in the early development of America's understanding of her place in the world; some would say even yet that he is the nation's greatest diplomatist.

After he had served, with great distinction, for eight years as secretary of state under President Monroe, there lay before him the prospect of the great office his father once had held, and that his parents had trained him from his earliest years to expect that he would one day hold. He was by far the most qualified aspirant; no one could match the positions he had held or the training in world politics he had undergone. Virginia had held the presidency year after year after year—all of the years since the beginning except for his father's four; surely it was time for Massachusetts (and the

North) again. Nevertheless, unfortunately, the office did not come begging to his door, eagerly seeking him. There was a spate of candidates. So he had to make some choices. What was Duty's message now?

THE PRESIDENTIAL ELECTION OF 1824 was unique in our history. In the aftermath of President Monroe's "Era of Good Feeling," there were, effectively, no political parties; the contest for the presidency was highly personal, and somewhat sectional, with no sharply defined issues. When the states had finished selecting their presidential electors late in 1824, the electoral votes were spread across several candidates, with none having a majority. Secretary of State John Quincy Adams was not first but *second*. He got all of the electoral votes of New England and a large majority of those from New York, which were split, but in the South, the border states, and the West, he received only a very light sprinkling (one of three from Delaware, two of five from Louisiana, three of eleven from Maryland, one of three from Illinois, none from any other state).

General Andrew Jackson, the hero of the Battle of New Orleans, by contrast, did well in all the states to the West and South, and in Pennsylvania and New Jersey as well, and had the largest number of electoral votes. But *not* a majority, as the Constitution requires. The candidate of much of the deep South was a man named William Crawford, the secretary of the treasury, whose constant maneuvering for advantage in the coming presidential contest had provoked Adams to many disgusted outbursts in his journal. Three of the original candidates sat together in President Monroe's cabinet: Crawford; Adams; and John C. Calhoun, the secretary of war, who settled in the end for the vice-presidency, in the separated balloting for that office. In addition, "Prince Hal," the able and popular rogue Henry Clay, then Speaker of the House, made one of his many attempts at the presidency.

When the tallies had rolled in from all the states the electoral vote was Jackson 99, Adams 84, Crawford 41, Clay 37. Because no one had a majority, the election was, as the Constitution provides, "thrown into the House," where the vote is to be taken among the top *three* candidates. Clay, who finished fourth, was thus eliminated, and the votes that would have gone to him were available for redistribution. The Constitution also specifies—a very important provision, cleverly inserted in 1787 by the small states led by Roger Sherman of Connecticut—that the voting in the House shall be by *states*; thus Delaware and the new states of Mississippi, Missouri, and Illinois, with only one congressman apiece, had a vote equal to that of New York, with its thirty-four, and Pennsylvania with its twenty-six. The congressmen from those one-congressman states thus suddenly became very important fellows.

In the weeks between the tally of electoral votes in December of 1824 and the vote in the House in the first week of February of 1825 there was, as the reader can imagine, a frenzy of one-on-one politics in Washington, with the presidency of the United States as the stake.

One course of action for a dutiful First Son of the Republic, theoretically, might have been to retire gracefully from the contest, advising his supporters to cast their votes in the House of Representatives for the winner of the electoral plurality, Andrew Jackson. But duty told him that Andrew Jackson was not a desirable leader for the nation, either personally or on the issues.

Another course of action, more plausible perhaps and certainly consistent with what he had done to that point, was to continue to take no steps whatever to influence the outcome, letting the choice come to him, or to another, as the citizens, the electors, and now the House members should choose. But that, too, would probably have led to a Jackson presidency (Crawford had suffered a stroke and was out of the picture). Adams pursued neither of these courses of action. Even the instructions of so stern a mistress as Duty can sometimes be ambiguous. Had he not been imbued by his mother, from his first days, not only with the *ideals* of the republic, but with the understanding that *he* should serve the ideals of the republic—supremely? Perhaps, even in an Adams, the voice of Ambition could subtly blend with the voice of Duty. Or, on the other hand, perhaps what he did can be interpreted as a quite impressive exercise in close-order politics, not at all objectionable, a response to Duty calling on another line.

Hitherto rather unsocial, Adams now made calls at boardinghouses, visited hotels, received delegations of House members in his office in the Department of State. There were conversations, assurances, subtle exchanges, perhaps even something approaching negotiations. The secretary of state in those days determined which printer in each state had the federal government's business—a valuable plum—and there were some shifts in that regard. There were careful discussions with friends of John C. Calhoun. There were careful discussions with friends of William Crawford. There were extremely careful conversations with the congressmen from Illinois and Missouri, each of whom would cast a vote that all by itself would determine the stand of his state. And above all there were conversations with representatives of Henry Clay—and with Clay himself. Adams wrote in his journal—in Latin—that he was treading coals of fire.

It was his dealing with Clay that would raise the most eyebrows, then and across the years. Adams's account in his journal of his famous, or notorious, meeting with Clay has frustrated generations of researchers. Here was a son of the Puritans who wrote down *everything* about his life, recording and examining it in detail almost daily for sixty-five years, telling what he did and what he thought, where he went and whom he met, giving the text of almost every sermon he ever heard, who when he came to what may have been the most important interview in his life, the interview that may have won for him the presidency—left a *blank*!

Adams's journal does describe their conversation—*partly*. He did record Clay's opening remarks, in which Clay indicated that he had been "much urged and solicited" by many partisans of the three candidates (yes, including supporters of Adams "disclaiming any authority" from Adams himself). "Not five minutes after I had landed at my lodgings a friend of Mr. Crawford applied to me in a manner so gross that it disgusted me." But now he wanted just to discuss with Adams "some principles of great public importance, but without any personal considerations for myself." And Adams did record Clay saying, then, in this very-high-level discussion devoid of any personal considerations for Clay himself, that "in the question to come before the House between General Jackson, Mr. Crawford, and yourself, I have no hesitation in saying that my preference would be you."

That was not the end of the conversation, however. They kept on talking—but Adams recorded nothing more. In fact, he actually left the famous, or notorious, blank space to be filled in later—but he never did fill it in. That blank space was to become the occasion, of course, for many exclamations by biographers and historians, condemnations by critics and opponents, and embarrassed explanations by family and friends. Charles Francis Adams, the son who edited his father's journal, explained that the pressure of visits and conversations at this time was extreme, which is certainly true. Still, John Quincy Adams kept his journal going through many other episodes of pressure.

The blankness of the space in the great journal-keeper's journal allows us to speculate. One guess would be that although there was no explicit quid pro quo (it is to be doubted that Adams's rectitude would have permitted that), Adams and Clay understood each other in something of the way that, for an example from another time, Lyndon Baines Johnson and his old friend from the Senate, Republican Everett Dirksen, understood each other: Johnson would talk for a time about a vote he wanted and Dirksen would mention a deserving candidate for a judgeship and the pleasant conversation would end with no explicit link and no promises, but both the vote and the judgeship would follow. Or perhaps it is not right to surmise even such a subtle implicit bargain. Still, Adams did receive Clay's support, and when Adams became president, Clay was promptly appointed secretary of state.

ON FEBRUARY 9, 1825, the House of Representatives, meeting in the same chamber in the Capitol in which much of the drama to be recorded in these pages was to be played out—Statuary Hall—for the second of only two times in American history, voting by states, chose a president of the United States. The first time, in 1800, when Jefferson and Burr were tied, was the result not of a real contest for the presidency but of a constitutional mistake, subsequently rectified by the Twelfth Amendment, requiring separate votes for president and vice-president. This time, in 1824, for the only time in American history, the House, voting by states, really did choose the president of the United States.

Daniel Webster and John Randolph were the tellers who announced the result: thirteen states for Adams, seven for Jackson, four for Crawford. Adams had, barely, the majority required. His thirteen included the six New England states and New York, whose electors had favored Adams in the first place, but then also Ohio, Kentucky, and one-congressman Illinois, which states had favored Clay, and Maryland, Louisiana, and one-congressman Missouri, which states had favored Jackson. It was an extremely close call. In five of Adams's states a change of one vote would have altered the outcome. The fierce and close contest in the big New York delegation in the House was settled, so the story goes, when devout Dutch general Stephen Van Rensselaer, praying for guidance as the vote approached, opened his eyes to see on the floor in front of him a ticket with Adams's name on it—Divine Guidance, by which one vote New York went for Adams. There have been several very thin margins in the history of American presidential elections, and some minority presidents, but never anything else quite like this.

The widespread American cynicism about politics tends to reduce everything in which power-seeking and self-advancement play a part to *nothing but* power-seeking and self-advancement, and does not allow for the mixtures of real life. In the real world these are mixed with other motives, including "higher" ones, including even "duty," if you will. Political leaders, despite the popular denigration, often *believe* in the direction of policy their career seeks to serve, so that winning an election and serving the "Well being of a Nation" are not at odds but go together. Certainly that would be true in Adams's case. So perhaps you can view his maneuvering to get the presidency (all within the frame of constitutional arrangements, after all) not as something corrupt but as quite an accomplishment.

John Quincy's destiny was fulfilled. Or was it? Life, or history, or duty, or perhaps human ambition, always adds to any accomplishment something more, not yet achieved. One would want not only to be president, but also a president who served the "Well being of a Nation" with outstanding accomplishment. Did Adams do that?

He presented in his messages to Congress, particularly the first one, which became a rather notable state paper, an unusually ambitious "National" program (he capitalized the N in that way) for which a reader 170 years later might be surprised to have, except for the endorsement of the protective tariff, a certain amount of belated enthusiasm. Adams recommended a National program of "internal improvement" (a key term, and a better one than "infrastructure"), which meant roads and canals and bridges, but more than that; a National university; government support for science and for learning as well as for commerce and industry (Adams would later be the key figure in realizing the possibilities of the bequest that became the Smithsonian Institution); a particular personal goal of Adams, a national observatory; federally supported exploration of the West; a uniform standard of weights and measures (Adams as secretary of state had written an important paper on this matter); a patent law to encourage invention; a naval academy; and the use of the great bounty of the public lands to help, along with the tariff, to support these undertakings. In sum, Adams had a vision of a qualitatively "improved" nation—"improvement" was a theme—using the federal government as the "National" instrument.

The attack on this ambitious program was severe, and often had a Southern accent. The "strict construction" of the Constitution was the argument: Adams was said to have proposed a raft of federal actions for which the Constitution provided no authority. He got very little passed. The midterm congressional elections of 1826 returned a heavy majority of Adams's opponents, creating American politics' first experience of "gridlock." The deep South strict constructionists who had supported Crawford were joining the Jackson forces in opposing Adams, and the construction of a new political party was under way.

Adams did not do much to help his program along. That was a different time, with different expectations. It was not yet expected that the president would be a legislative leader, sending up to "the hill" truckloads of "administration" proposals which he would then twist congressional arms to get passed. Adams, in particular, with his antiparty outlook, was not going to do that. He refused, as president, to remove from office officials who had opposed his candidacy for president, or to appoint those who had supported him—admirable, perhaps, by some antique standard, but the despair of real politicians like his chief cabinet member Secretary of State Henry Clay. And made anachronistic on his defeat by the Jacksonian spoils system.

Hanging over Adams's other limitations and difficulties as president there was the charge that he and Clay had entered into a "corrupt bargain." That charge did not die down or fade away. Supporters of Jackson had said there would be a fierce opposition, especially in the West and South, if Adams inveigled the presidency away from their hero, and they proved to be right. In the presidential election of 1828 they had their revenge. Two Southern slaveholders—Jackson and, again, Calhoun—defeated the two nonslaveholding Northerners—Adams and his Pennsylvania friend Richard Rush—by 178 electoral votes to 83. As Adams had followed his father into the presidential office, so he followed him also in staying there only one term.

Three points about the Adams presidency bear on the story in these pages. First, the latent issue of slavery ran silently—usually silently—underneath almost everything about it. It is very important that Adams himself was, from a slaveholder's perspective, not sound on that question; he was only the second president in American history not to be personally a slaveholder, the other one being his father. The "National" program that he proposed would have enlarged federal powers in a way that might one day threaten slavery. The "strict construction" of the Constitution and states' rights that his opponents insisted upon were, in addition to whatever other foundations in sentiment and philosophy they had, barriers of protection against interference with slavery. Both sides felt that his energetic program of federally aided "improvement," commercial, intellectual, industrial, scientific, moral, implied a culture at odds with the culture of a slave society (which Adams and his supporters did not believe to be "the highest toned, the purest, best organization of society that has ever existed on the face of the earth"). President Adams's policy toward the Creek nation in Georgia, and other Indians, more nearly just than that of his successor (which was brutal in the extreme), implied a dangerous touch of humanity that might apply to blacks as well. And when, early in his presidential term, he proposed sending U.S. delegates to a Panama conference of newly independent Latin American republics, a conference that might very well discuss such forbidden topics as slavery and the slave trade, and—worst—relations with the newly independent black nation of "Hayti," Southern leaders exploded.

His defeat in 1828 had a sharp regional cast. Leonard L. Richards worked out the percentages of the popular vote for Adams and Jackson: Adams swept New England; the North as a whole was close, with Jackson winning 50.3 percent of the vote; but Jackson walloped Adams in the

South, receiving 72.6 percent of the vote. In the deep South the margin was even greater. Richards says that the figures for the Jackson landslides were over 80 percent in Alabama and Mississippi and that in Georgia, "where the Indian haters were after Adams's scalp," the figure was virtually 100 percent. The three-fifths rule augmenting the electoral votes of the slave states figured importantly in his defeat, as it had in his father's. Richards wrote in summary: ". . . the election returns clearly indicated that Jackson was far more popular in 'aristocratic' Virginia than he was in 'democratic' Vermont and that he ran much better in the slave states of the South than the free states of the North."

Which leads to the second point: the historical placement of his presidency accidentally cast Adams as an opponent of "democracy" in a way that is overdone. The election of Andrew Jackson in 1828 by new men from the West and South, and by a new alliance of Southern planters with Northern common folk, is a convenient point to make one of the pivots of American history, and "Jacksonian" is a convenient modifier for the broader, more popular democracy developing in the period. Adams was twice the opponent of Andrew Jackson, so Adams must be placed on the other side as the symbol of an opposition that, of course, is supposed to be defeated, like the hooded wrestler in black the audience is supposed to boo at the professional wrestling match, or like the Washington Generals basketball team of puffy white guys the Harlem Globetrotters took around with them to provide opposition and be defeated at every stop.

But isn't this contrast much too sharply drawn? Is there not some element of historical accident, not only on Adams's side but Jackson's as well? Some new developments—the ending of property requirements for voting and the broadening of the suffrage—took place to an extent before, and independent of, Jackson's administration, and others—the "reform," including the public school movement—came at least as much from Adams's constituency as from Jackson's. Adams, like his father, did have a complex view of the ingredients of republican government that did not reduce it simply to popular majorities. But was he therefore so much less in tune with the norms for American democracy, which is institutionally complex, after all, than Jackson? At least the contrast between them should not be made as sweeping as has been done.

It is true that Adams had cultural standards and a sharp tongue. Here is an excerpt from his journal, from a much later time, that may suggest why he would not make a good popular hero by the standards of the newer democracy. He wrote this at home in Quincy (Braintree became a part of Quincy) while he was ex-president and President Jackson was just into his second term, on June 18, 1833:

> *Called from my nursery and garden by a visit from Mr. Quincy, President of Harvard University. He told me that as President Jackson is . . . visiting Boston, the corporation of the university had thought it necessary to invite him to visit the colleges; that he (Mr. Quincy) should address him in a Latin discourse, and confer upon him the degree of Doctor of Laws; and he intimated that I should receive an invitation to be present at these ceremonies.*
>
> *I said that the personal relations in which President Jackson had chosen to place himself with me were such that I could hold no intercourse of a friendly character with him. I could therefore not accept an invitation to attend upon this occasion. And, independent of that, as myself an affectionate child of our Alma Mater, I would not be present to witness her disgrace in conferring her highest literary honors upon a barbarian who could not write a sentence of grammar and hardly could spell his own name. Mr. Quincy said he was sensible how utterly unworthy of literary honors Jackson was, but the Corporation thought it was necessary to follow the precedent. As the people of the United States had seen fit to make him President, the Corporation thought the honors which they conferred upon him were compliments due to the station, by whomsoever it was occupied. I adhered to my determination to stay at home.*

It is nevertheless not true that Adams or his parents were, in the thoughtless jargon of a later time, "elitists." It is ridiculous indeed to celebrate wealthy Virginia plantation owners and slaveholders—practicing members of a very hierarchical Virginia society, not all that eager when push came to shove to abolish the slavery and class privilege they rejected in the abstract—as champions of the common man, while disdaining as "elitists" the hardworking middle-class Adamses, who strained their modest family resources by whole lives devoted to nothing but republican government. Perhaps, by some criteria, the wealthy and high-handed frontier land speculator, Indian fighter, and conservative cotton planter Andrew Jackson, another slaveholder on a large scale, deserved even less to be preferred as a republican to Adamses.

That leads to the third point. In all the events surrounding his presidency, Adams took a terrible beating in what would later come to be called public relations—a beating that has to some extent been continued in history-writing since then. The "corrupt bargain" charge was hammered constantly by the new Jackson press, and by supporters of Jackson and opponents of Adams throughout Adams's presidency. His proposals were mocked. For example, he had in discussing his proposed national observatory, its counterparts in Europe, and its progeny in this country used the phrase "lighthouses of the sky." In the ridicule of the nineteenth-century equivalent of late-night television and radio talk shows this was changed to "lighthouses *in* the sky": our president wants to use federal tax dollars to build lighthouses in the sky!

His political defeat was followed by nasty political attacks, and then by a personal blow. His oldest son, George—named for George Washington—after a troubled youth, either fell or, probably, jumped from a steamboat traveling from Providence to New York, and drowned. After a short stay in Washington, Adams and his wife, Louisa Catherine, returned to the old Adams house in Quincy, itself now run-down, to a despondent retirement. Or so it seemed.

WHEN ADAMS LEFT THE President's House in 1829 he had already served in about as many high public offices as any other person before or since. He had a résumé that no American has ever been able to match. He had not only been president of the United States; he had also been secretary of state, a Massachusetts senator, a United States senator, ambassador to Great Britain, and minister to the courts of Russia, Prussia, Holland, Sweden, Portugal, and France, and he had negotiated the Treaty of Ghent after the War of 1812. He was named (by President Madison), and confirmed, as a justice of the United States Supreme Court, but he declined the position. He had been appointed to high office by every one of the presidents, starting with George Washington, until he himself was elected president—every one, that is, except one, and Jefferson would have appointed him if the Adamses had been in a mood to accept. He served in more of his nation's highest positions than any other American has ever done, more even than Jefferson if you count it right, and more than any other American is ever likely to do. He had also been the first Boylston Professor of Rhetoric at Harvard, and the author of important pamphlets on public issues in the earliest days of the republic. He was the architect, as secretary of state, of the Monroe Doctrine, and a major shaper of the world role of the new United States.

After he had served in all of those positions, and done all those deeds, and been president of the United States, he might have been expected to subside into retirement. All of his predecessors—four Virginians and his own father—on leaving the president's office had retired to their big (or medium-sized) houses to be sages and exemplars, outside and above the battle, with at most occasional forays into current affairs. But John Quincy Adams, at age sixty-three (much older then than now), battered by the fierce attacks of his presidential years, apparently swept aside by the currents of the new politics represented by Andrew Jackson, apparently a rejected relic of a departed past, on being offered a chance to go back into current politics at a lowly level—accepted!

The story is often told—a heartwarming American story perhaps—about how when a friend proposed that he run for Congress, and suggested deferentially that it would not be demeaning for the ex-president to do so, Adams responded that an ex-president would not be degraded "by serving as selectman of his town, if the people elected him."

In a postpresidential role unique in American history, ex-president John Quincy Adams ran for and was elected to Congress, in fitting symbolism, from the Plymouth district in Massachusetts. He proceeded to serve in the House of Representatives, arguing energetically all the while, for seventeen years. That long service furnished a kind of a redemption after his presidential defeats. He liked to quote, in the original Latin, a saying of Cicero's: "The Republic I served in my youth, I will not desert in my old age."

15 / SEIZED WITH CRAMPS

IT IS NOT TO the purpose of this book to recall in further detail any of John Quincy Adams's many adventures before he reached the age of sixty-eight, and asked Speaker Polk upon the House floor whether or not he was gagged. There is, however, one string of episodes while he was secretary of state in the administration of President James Monroe that should be mentioned, because it adds to the story told here.

In his journal entry for February 11, 1820, Secretary of State John Quincy Adams wrote about hearing Rufus King, senator from New York, speak on the Senate floor "upon what is called the Missouri Question."* "He laid down the position of the natural liberty of man," Adams wrote, "and its incompatibility with slavery in any shape. He spoke with great power, and the great slave-holders . . . gnawed their lips and clenched their

*This was the Rufus King who, as a young delegate from Massachusetts to the Federal Convention of 1787, had made one of the few arguably anti-slavery presentations during the proceedings that framed the nation's Constitution. King, a follower of Alexander Hamilton, corresponded with James Madison and the federalist brain trust (that is, the pro-Constitution people) in New York during the fight over ratification, and was a leader of the federalist forces at the Massachusetts ratifying convention. Later he moved to New York, served in many high posts, became a leader of the Federalist Party (he was thus one of those who could be called both a federalist and a Federalist), and was now for the second stretch of time representing the state of New York in the United States Senate.

fists as they heard him. We attended an evening party at Mr. Calhoun's and heard of nothing but the Missouri Question and Mr. King's speeches. . . . The slave-holders cannot hear of him without being seized with cramps."

At that same historical moment a different figure of speech was furnished by the retired statesman at Monticello, who looked at the matter from a different, Southern, slaveholding angle—increasingly as he grew older Jefferson looked at these matters from a Southern, slaveholding angle. His memorable simile regarding the "Missouri Question" would be repeated thereafter in every textbook of American history: "This momentous question, like a firebell in the night, awakened and filled me with terror. I considered it at once as the knell of the Union." Jefferson would experience the same sense of foreboding when the university he had founded in Charlottesville was delayed in opening, so that young men had still to be sent North by their good Southern parents to receive an education from "those who are against us in position and principle." That these young men would not be indoctrinated on Southern soil, and what they might encounter in the north, drove Jefferson to discern "the speck in our horizon which is to burst on us as a tornado, sooner or later."

John Quincy Adams, considering not just the effect on Southern slaveholders, whether awakened by firebells or seized with cramps or assailed by tornadoes, but contemplating both sides and the entire drama, wrote in his journal, "I take it for granted that the present [Missouri] question is mere preamble—a title page to a great, tragic volume." The twentieth-century historian Samuel Eliot Morison, also surveying the entire drama, and with the additional advantage of hindsight, wrote that "for a moment the veil had been lifted, and some saw the bloody prospect ahead."

What was it that inspired this shower of metaphors? The Missouri Question is the short answer. Slavery in the territories is the longer answer. The contradiction between slavery and America's meaning is the still longer and more fundamental answer. For the first three decades, or four and a half decades, of the nation's life it had been kept offstage—more or less. Decisions had been made on this subject—important decisions, both to restrict, and to preserve and advance slavery—but they had not had the full focus of the nation's attention. Now suddenly the dread topic did have the center of the stage.

Why did the bells first toll over Missouri? Over a *territory*? Because in the territories the question was still open: which way would they go? Because in the territories the responsibility of the free states could not be evaded. So long as slavery was confined to the states of the original compact, the rationalizations built around the founding could endure. But when new land was to be added to the Union, those rationalizations no longer applied. Before that situation arose you could say, living in New York or Connecticut, that what went on in South Carolina and Georgia was deplorable, but that it was not part of your public responsibility; it was almost as remote as what went on in the bazaars and harems of the exotic countries described in those lectures at the lyceum. Moreover, we had had to forge a bond with those folks down there, understanding that they condoned and practiced slavery, so we were stuck with the bargain we had made.

But not with respect to territories and new states; they were every American's responsibility. Whether the new state of Missouri would be slave or free in 1820, whether Texas would be admitted as a slave state in 1837, and whether Kansas would be slave or free in 1854–56 were the common problems of the whole nation, as much the responsibility of New York and Connecticut as of South Carolina and Georgia. Moreover, the territories and new states were the *future*. They were the counters in the contest over what the United States would become.

As new states were added to the Union, political leaders were careful to maintain a balance between slave and free. With the addition of Alabama in 1819 there were eleven of each kind. But there were clearly more to come.

In 1803, President Jefferson, with young Senator John Quincy Adams's support, had taken the very bold step of purchasing an enormous tract of western land, the Louisiana Territory, from Napoleon. Slavery had existed, under French law, in large portions of that territory, particularly in the sugar plantation country around New Orleans, where slaves constituted a majority of the population. In 1804, in the first muffled peal of the distant bell, a young congressman from Connecticut named James Hillhouse proposed for this new American territory what a young congressman from Virginia named Thomas Jefferson had proposed, in 1784, for all new American territory: that slavery be excluded. Now in 1804 the democratic poet Joel Barlow, and Tom Paine, urged President Jefferson, not so young anymore, to support the Hillhouse measure, but President Jefferson did not do it. Jefferson did propose that Louisiana be closed to the foreign slave trade, which proposal did pass, out of that radically diverse confluence of motives already mentioned: morality and the protection of the home market. But as for excluding slavery—no.

Of course it would not have been easy. Slavery was already entrenched, and the sugar business depended on it. And Napoleon had insisted that inhabitants of Louisiana be assured all the rights of American citizens—which included, in the states in which it was not prohibited, the right to own slaves. The deep ambiguity, the doubleness, of American commitments is revealed again by the fact that that right could claim constitutional protection, not to be overcome by the guarantees to every state of a "republican form of government" or any of the other rights and liberties. And the inhabitants of Louisiana protested even against the prohibition of the foreign slave trade—on solid "American" principles!

In 1812 the settled portion of Jefferson's purchase at the mouth of the Mississippi River, "Orleans territory," was admitted to the Union as the slave state of Louisiana, and the immense reach of land to the north and west became known as "Missouri territory." Congress took no action applying to that territory the exclusion of slavery that was part of the Northwest Ordinance. So slavery was not excluded, and in the westward movement after the War of 1812, many slaveowners moved into upper Louisiana—Missouri territory—taking their slaves with them, and establishing plantations on the land around the two great rivers and the old trading town of St. Louis.

Then the settlers of Missouri applied for admission as a slave state. This development was distressing on two counts: Missouri territory extended north of the line that had implicitly been accepted as a boundary between slave and free states, and its admission would upset the numerical balance between them. It looked like an aggressive, expansionist move on the part of the slave states. A congressman from New York proposed an amendment to the bill for admitting Missouri that would have prohibited the importation of new slaves and freed at age twenty-one all children of slaves currently residing there—and the firebell sounded. In the debates on the Missouri Question there were speeches in Congress explicitly challenging, at root, the institution of slavery—including the speech by Senator Rufus King that Secretary of State John Quincy Adams remarked upon in his journal.

FROM ADAMS'S JOURNAL ENTRY we learn that the response to King's speech already included what would come to be a constant feature in the developing national debate on race and slavery: an insistent derogation of the motives of those who challenged the received racial pattern. In mid-twentieth-century America, white proponents of civil rights would be regularly accused of, among many other things, taking the stands that they did in order to win "the Negro vote." Certainly the abolitionists after 1831 would be subjected to the most severe and insistent and constant derogation, of every kind, which to some extent continued into history-writing in the twentieth century. And back in 1820, when slavery sprang from the closet for its first major appearance in American politics, Adams found Senator Rufus King of New York distressed at the motives opponents imputed to him.

Adams's journal for February 27, 1820, reported that "the partisans of slavery have spread abroad the idea that he [King] has been actuated in this affair by motives of personal ambition—that he is making an effort to get up a new division of parties and to put himself at the head of half of the Union." Adams returned to the subject on March 4: "He [King] . . . very naturally feels resentful at the imputations of the slaveholders, that his motives on this occasion have been merely of personal aggrandizement—'Close ambition varnished o'er with zeal.' This imputation of bad motives is one of the most venomous weapons of political and indeed of every sort of controversy. It originated with the devil: Doth Job fear God for nought?"

Did the leaders of the antislavery movement, of which this debate was a harbinger, fear God for naught? Were they motivated by close ambition varnished over with zeal? Or, to put the attack in more modern terms, what was "in it" for them?

As Adams wrote, such an imputation of bad motives was a venomous weapon in controversies of all kinds. There were passions and imputations, to be sure, in the contests over the bank and the tariff and the "internal improvements," and their subsequent equivalents. But such issues do not ordinarily entail explicit moral assertion to the same depth and prominence as do the issues of race and slavery. They have their patterns of "interest," which each side can understand, more or less, and while opposing nevertheless accept the opponent's purposes. You have your reasons for supporting a high tariff; I have mine for opposing it; we understand each other, and in the calm between our fights we need not be morally defensive or morally aggressive. Neither one of us needs to say or imply that the other is in some deep way "wrong." The position of neither one of us offends that "natural liberty" upon which the nation is founded and indeed upon which all nations ought to be founded. Therefore I need not be seized with cramps, clenching my fists, gnawing my lips in response to your arguments; I am not put on the moral defensive, in a way that raises the question of my self-worth.

But when the big guns of argument are wheeled into place on the issues of slavery and race, such questions *are* raised. I *am* put on the moral defensive, in a fundamental and not just a derivative and partial way. These issues are not, and cannot be, regarded simply from the aspect of a calculation of respective advantages. Discussion of them raises to public view our most basic understanding of the great concerns of justice and injustice, right and wrong, in human life. They include the possibility of human action for another's good, for the social good, without clear advantage to the actor. They imply at least—and often explicitly assert—that the actions and life patterns of others are unjust and wrong.

So on this topic there is a more insistent effort to discredit the bearers of such deeply unwelcome moral messages—to bring them into the more manageable and common political world of a calculation of self-interest. What is in it for them? Out of the passions of my response I strike back at you, to take you down from the moral high ground. And, to be sure, all political actors, being human, do have their vulnerable points, their multiple motives.

Whatever may be the truth about the motives of Job, of Rufus King, of John Quincy Adams, or of any of the rest of us—they will be mixed, and only God will know—it is nevertheless important to preserve some distinction between actions for interest and actions for justice and the social good. Cynics to the contrary notwithstanding, the latter are one part of our human experience. The kind of *republican* government that the Adams family worked for on this new continent is not possible unless there is some room in our understanding for the fact that citizens may not altogether neglect the *res publicae*.

If very few if any actions are ever motivated by the pure altruism of sermon endings, not so many on the other hand reflect only the narrowest, most tangible, and most selfishly personal interest. We act fairly often for the protection and advancement of large collective interests in which our personal share is negligible, or nonexistent. We are capable of recognizing the just claims of others, even though we have no share in them, sometimes even at some cost to ourselves, and sometimes we act on that recognition.

It is true that these actions partly for the social good are not without their *interested* offshoots, as in the egotism of reformers and the self-promotion of heroes. And disinterested actions for an alleged social good may not serve what God or any human actor would consider truly good at all: we dispute about that, and indeed have some of our worst disputes about it. The Civil War, after the slavery *interest* had transmuted into the glorious Southern *cause*, was such a dispute. Among other things. Under certain circumstances, with respect to certain questions, one would rather, as the sophisticated representatives of "policy" recommend, attend simply to our *interests*.

Nevertheless, one would urge that the complexity of motive not be simplified, or the possibility of action from "higher" motives foreclosed. Whatever else you may say about them, the Americans who had a deep revulsion at human slavery were certainly not an interest group in the same sense as the cattlemen's association seeking higher prices for beef.

In his journal back in 1820, Adams indignantly testified to the essential integrity and worthiness—the *dis*interested service of worthy ideals—of Rufus King. That is interesting to read, because the issue some years later would come to be, not the motives of Rufus King, who fades from the stage, but those of Adams himself. It would be asked, in effect, does John Quincy Adams serve God for naught?

While Congress held its debates on the Missouri Question, President Monroe's cabinet held its own discussions on that topic. And Monroe's secretary of state, John Quincy Adams, recorded his reactions in his voluminous journal.

It is remarkable how far-reaching, at this early date, are Adams's speculations on, and evaluations of, slavery. To the end of the passage in his journal about Rufus King's speech that gave slaveholders the cramps he affixed this comment, and then an eloquent apostrophe:

> *Never since human sentiments and human conduct were influenced by human speech was there a theme for eloquence like the free side of this question now before Congress of this Union. By what fatality does it happen that all the most eloquent orators of the body are on its slavish side? There is a great mass of cool judgment and plain sense on the side of freedom and humanity, but the ardent spirits and passions are on the side of oppression. Oh, if but one man could arise with a genius capable of comprehending, a heart capable of supporting, and an utterance capable of communicating those eternal truths that belong to this question, to lay bare in all its nakedness that outrage upon the goodness of God, human slavery, now is the time, and this is the occasion, upon which such a man would perform the duties of an angel upon earth!*

Adams himself was not to be that angel upon earth, though he was to play an important role. But not yet.

Monroe's secretary of war, the cabinet member Adams worked most closely with and was probably closest to personally, was his host on the night of the clenched fists, gnawed lips, and seizures of cramps—John C. Calhoun of South Carolina. At the time, Adams respected Calhoun, and in his journal praised him on foreign and military policy and in his role as a public servant: "Calhoun thinks for himself, independently of all the rest, with sound judgment, quick discrimination, and keen observation" (January 6, 1818). "Calhoun is a man of fair and candid mind, of honorable principles, of clear and quick understanding, of cool self-possession, of enlarged philosophical views, and of ardent patriotism" (October 15, 1821). Both of these accolades were written in the context of foreign policy and military issues which Adams and Calhoun agreed upon—the secretary of state agreeing with the secretary of war—but they are nonetheless significant; Adams in the privacy of his journal had a sharp pen, quick to etch a portrait in acid, and he did not bestow praise lightly. In the second entry, moreover, he goes on to say—perhaps this ought to be highlighted, as a surprising comment, given the career, and perhaps our stereotype, of John C. Calhoun—"He is above all sectional and factional prejudices more than any statesman of this Union with whom I have ever acted." John C. Calhoun! Above all sectional prejudices! Again, that was written in the context of a question involving the barracks at St. Augustine, Florida, not of the presence of slavery in the territories; but it is still astonishing.

On that larger question, Adams and Calhoun had conversations which as Adams recorded them in his diaries, particularly in 1820–21, are among the most remarkable of all the entries and will remain so even when the entire bulk of his journal is eventually published in thirty volumes or so. The New Englander and the South Carolinian, both highly intelligent and conscientious statesmen, a Harvard man and a Yale man, discussed race and slavery with a revealing frankness, and part of what was revealed was how far apart they were, and how completely Calhoun was a defender of a slave society and of racial prejudice.

On the question behind the Missouri Question they disagreed; and Calhoun's speculations were far-reaching, too.

> *I had some conversation with Calhoun on the slave question pending in Congress. He said he did not think it would produce a dissolution of the Union, but, if it should, the South would be from necessity compelled to form an alliance, offensive and defensive, with Great Britain. I said that would be returning to the colonial state. He said, yes, pretty much, but it would be forced upon them.*

So there would be the South, in Calhoun's perhaps minatory speculations, now independent of the North but in alliance, offensively and defensively, with Great Britain—returning almost to the pre-Revolutionary state. And what would then happen to the *North*, when the Southern colonies with whom she had formerly been united broke away and joined with England—the mistress of the seas? (This was really quite a remarkable conversation between the secretaries of state and war of the United States!)

> *I asked him whether he thought, if by the effect of this alliance, offensive and defensive, the population of the North should be cut off from its natural outlet upon the ocean, it would fall back upon its rocks bound*

> *hand and foot, to starve, or whether it would not retain its powers of locomotion to move southward by land. Then, he said, they would find it necessary to make their communities all military.*

So there it would be: the South would be allied with the naval power of Great Britain, thus cutting the North off from its natural outlet upon the ocean; when the North then moved on land against the South, Calhoun's region (now nation) would turn itself into a kind of Sparta after all. It would be dominated by military considerations, so presumably not a republic. Quite a picture. Remember that this comes straight from Adams's journal at the time, and is therefore not colored by later opinions of, or actions by, Calhoun.

Stimulated by this extraordinary exchange, Adams then confided to his journal further speculations of his own. He wrote these sentences, to be sure, for himself and not for public consumption at the time—as Calhoun's speculations were certainly not intended for the public either. Adams explored what the alternatives might be.

> *I pressed the conversation no further: but if the dissolution of the Union should result from the slave question, it is as obvious as anything that can be foreseen of futurity, that it must shortly afterwards be followed by the universal emancipation of the slaves* [presumably because of the military action that would follow]. *A more remote but perhaps not less certain consequence would be the extirpation of the African race on this continent, by the gradually bleaching process of intermixture, where the white portion is already so predominant, and by the destructive progress of emancipation, which, like all great religious and political reformations, is terrible in its means though happy and glorious in its end.*

A twentieth-century reader of these journal entries must remind herself or himself that the diarist did not know, then, what would happen—secession and confederacy; civil war; Union victory; emancipation; multiracial society. Because, living up here in "futurity," we know what happened in the decades following Adams's speculations, it is difficult to think our way back into the situation of someone who did not know, and who was trying, under the conditions of 1820, to imagine what the bell-ringing might foretell.

Adams's position on slavery is, in his journal though not yet in public, explicit:

> *Slavery is the great and foul stain upon the North American Union, and it is a contemplation worthy of the most exalted soul whether its total aboli-*

tion is or is not practicable: if practicable, by what it may be effected, and if a choice of means be within the scope of the object, what means would accomplish it at the smallest cost of human suffering. A dissolution, at least temporary, of the Union, as now constituted, would be certainly necessary. . . . The Union might then be reorganized on the fundamental principle of emancipation. This objective is vast in its compass, awful in its prospects, sublime and beautiful in its issue.

We do not now ordinarily think of the accomplishment of the American nation with respect to slavery and race as "sublime and beautiful," and perhaps it is just as well that we do not, given the grievous faults that remain. Nevertheless it is worth noting that this very thoughtful and intelligent man—a good man, who had rooted in him what the United States is all about, reflecting on these matters, trying to think how the tragic tangle could possibly be remedied, how the "great and foul stain" could be removed—would use such a phrase to describe an outcome not much different from what would happen in fact.

❧

CALHOUN AND ADAMS HAD another conversation on March 3, after a cabinet meeting at which the Missouri Question had been discussed and Adams had defended the right of Congress, under the Constitution, to exclude slavery from the territories: "What can be more needful for the establishment of justice than the interdiction of slavery where it does not exist?"

After this meeting, I walked home with Calhoun, who said that the principles which I had avowed were just and noble: but that in the Southern country, whenever they were mentioned, they were always understood as applying only to white men.

The tragedy of the inheritance of African slavery in the British colonies of North America was not only the injustice of slavery itself but the deep-seated racism on which it rested, and which it reinforced: the "noble principles" of the preamble to the United States Constitution, which Adams had been citing, were "always understood as applying only to white men."

The two philosophically inclined cabinet members then had an exchange about slavery and labor. Calhoun, by Adams's report, continued thus:

Domestic labor was confined to the blacks, and such was the prejudice, that if he, who was the most popular man in his district, were to keep a white servant in his house, his character and reputation would be irretrievably ruined. I said that this confounding of the ideas of servitude and labor was one of the bad effects of slavery: but he thought it attended with many excellent consequences. It did not apply to all kinds of labor—not, for example, to farming. He himself had often held the plough: so had his father. Manufacturing and mechanical labor was not degrading. It was only manual labor—the proper work of slaves. No white person could descend to that.

Calhoun then offered that Orwellian defense of slavery—inequality means equality, slavery means freedom—that we have noticed before.

And it was the best guarantee to equality among the whites. It produced an unvarying level among them. It did not excite, but did not even admit of inequalities, by which one white man could domineer over another.

Adams gave this report of his response:

I told Calhoun I could not see things in the same light. It is, in truth, all perverted sentiment—mistaking labor for slavery and dominion for freedom.

Then Adams, leaving Calhoun behind, as it were, in the privacy of his early morning communion with his journal, set down what he thought:

The discussion of this Missouri question has betrayed the secret of their souls. In the abstract they admit that slavery is an evil, they disclaim all participation in the introduction of it, and cast it all upon the shoulders of our old Grandam Britain. But when probed to the quick upon it, they show at the bottom of their souls pride and vainglory in their condition of masterdom. They fancy themselves more generous and noble-hearted than the plain freemen who labor for subsistence. They look down upon the simplicity of a Yankee's manners, because he has no habits of overbearing like theirs and cannot treat negroes like dogs. It is among the evils of slavery that it taints the very sources of moral principle. It establishes false estimates of virtue and vice: for what can be more false and heartless than this doctrine which makes the first and holiest rights of humanity to depend upon the color of the skin?

Although many of his contemporaries deplored slavery, not as many also condemned racial prejudice, and saw, as Adams did, how deep the evil penetrated—that it "taints the very sources of moral principle," establishing "false estimates of virtue and vice."

. . .

THE MISSOURI COMPROMISE, PUT together in the Senate, excised the prohibition on slavery in Missouri that had passed the House. Returned to the House in this altered form it finally passed 90 to 87 "after successive days and almost nights," as Adams wrote, "of stormy debate." Adams, reluctantly, supported the compromise in cabinet sessions; so did Calhoun. In his journal, together with the pragmatic accommodation, Adams included another far-reaching speculation:

> *I have favored this Missouri compromise, believing it to be all that could be effected under the present Constitution, and from extreme unwillingness to put the Union at hazard. But perhaps it would have been a wiser as well as a bolder course to have persisted in the restriction upon Missouri, till it should have terminated in a convention of the States to revise and amend the Constitution. This would have produced a new Union of thirteen or fourteen states unpolluted with slavery, with a great and glorious object to effect, namely, that of rallying to their standard the other States by the universal emancipation of their slaves. If the Union must be dissolved, slavery is precisely the question upon which it ought to break. For the present, however, this contest is laid asleep.*

Though the veil had been lifted and the bells been rung and the tornado sighted on the horizon, it was not yet possible to confront what they portended. The "Missouri Question" resulted in the "Missouri Compromise" of the history textbook: Maine was admitted as a free state in 1820, and Missouri as a slave state in 1821, and a line was drawn through the rest of the Louisiana Purchase at latitude 36°30′. Except for Missouri, which extended above that line: above it, free; below it, slave. Real issues postponed. There was a tremendous public desire and psychological pressure to postpone and evade. Of course, there would have been. Think of the matter in the terms of the people living then, confronted with the frightening possibilities Adams and Calhoun discussed. Compromise was one of the devices of evasion and postponement available to a people caught in a threatening logjam of values. It is the kind of thing that happens again and again in international affairs: not a resolution on principle, not a decision on what is right or exactly what the law is, not a clear conclusion free of ambiguity settling matters, but a temporary accommodation to the realities, a line drawn by power, an East Germany and a West Germany and a divided Berlin, which just recognizes realities without blessing them at all. So it was with the Missouri Compromise. And it did "settle" these matters, in its way, for a quarter of a century—a long time in modern history.

THE GENERAL RETIREMENT OF the question did not, however, close down Adams's reflections. Not very many white Americans at this early date deplored the evils of racial discrimination, and the plight of the free black person, as distinguished from those of slavery. Adams, however, did take some further notes on the "false and heartless doctrine" which makes "the first and holiest rights of humanity depend upon the color of the skin." On October 22, for example, he reported, from a diplomat's appeal to him, this story:

> *A colored woman, who lives with Roth* [the French chargé d'affaires] *as his cook, has been taken up on suspicion of receiving stolen money and committed to prison. . . . A shopkeeper by the name of Holmead dropped yesterday from his pocket, in the street, a cheque upon one of the banks for a hundred dollars, and a hundred and fifty dollars in bank-bills. A mulatto boy of fourteen or fifteen years of age found the cheque, and not knowing how to read, took it to a shop to enquire what it was. He was then called upon for the bank-bills, and, denying that he had found them, was tortured, thumb-screwed, and hung by the neck (so this man says) to extort confession from him. He finally named several persons to whom he said he gave the bills, and among the rest the father of Roth's cook. He denied having received the bills, but his daughter was imprisoned on suspicion of having received them from him. This is a sample of the treatment of colored people under criminal charges or suspicions here.*

In the following November, Adams set down in his journal another remarkable passage of speculation and testimony on this subject. The provocation, this time, was a long conversation with a Mr. Baldwin about Missouri's new state constitution confining citizenship to whites.

> *I told him if I were a member of the Legislature of one of the free States, I would move for a declaratory act, that so long as the article in the Constitution of Missouri deprived the colored citizens of the State, say of Massachusetts, of their rights as citizens of the United States within the State of Missouri, should subsist, so long the white citizens of the State of Missouri should be held as aliens within the Commonwealth of Massachusetts, not entitled to claim or enjoy within the same any right or privilege of a citizen of the United States.*

Tit for tat. The free black person, in those days, was a much neglected and abused person, and his or her protection rarely figured in debates over policy. Here was Adams, though, proposing to balance the deprivation of free black citizens of Massachusetts in Missouri with a corresponding deprivation of white Missourians in Massachusetts.

> *And I would go further, and declare that Congress having given sanction to the Missouri Constitution, by admitting that State into the Union without excepting against that article which disenfranchised a portion of the citizens of Massachusetts, had violated the Constitution of the United States; wherefore, until that portion of the citizens of Massachusetts whose rights are violated by the article of the Missouri Constitution should be re-integrated in the full enjoyment and possession of those rights, no clause or article of the Constitution of the United States should, within the Commonwealth of Massachusetts, be so construed as to authorize any person whomsoever to claim the property or possession of a human being as a slave. And I would prohibit by the law the delivery of any fugitive slave upon the claim of his master. All which I would do, not to violate but to redeem from violation, the Constitution of the United States.*

Not to violate, but to redeem from violation, the Constitution of the United States. A harbinger of constitutional arguments to come.

This recounting of his exchange with Baldwin in his journal for November 29, 1820, was really one of the most remarkable of all the notable entries on this subject, and worth quoting at length, to get a sense of Adams's passion on this subject. It is important for a reader more than a century and a half later, to whom this may seem commonplace or even patronizing, to remember the date, and the conditions at that date, and the attitudes of others at that date, of which this book provides some record. There were not many white folks saying, in 1820, what Adams said here. Adams recorded his having said to Baldwin about the provision in Missouri's new constitution explicitly denying citizenship to black persons:

> *If acquiesced in, it would change the terms of the federal compact—change its terms by robbing thousands of citizens of their rights. And what citizens? The poor, the unfortunate, the helpless. Already cursed by the mere color of their skin, already doomed by their complexion to drudge in the lowest offices of society, excluded by their color from all the refined enjoyments of life accessible to others, excluded from the benefits of a liberal education, from the bed, from the table, and from all the social comforts of domestic life, this barbarous article deprives them of the little*

*remnant of right yet left them—their rights as citizens and as men. Weak and defenceless as they are, so much the more sacred is the obligation of the Legislature of the States to which they belong to defend their lawful rights; and I would defend them should the dissolution of the Union be the consequence.**

Adams conscientiously records the response of Baldwin, who did not agree, which response included among other familiar items a claim that nine-tenths of the petty thievery is committed by blacks.

Going beyond this particular exchange, Adams produced a larger passage about slavery and union and the essence of the American nation, Abigail Adams's son thinking boldly, and not without point, as to what actually would happen:

If slavery be the destined sword of the hand of the destroying angel which is to sever the ties of this union, the same sword will cut in sunder the bonds of slavery itself. A dissolution of the Union for the cause of slavery would be followed by a servile war in the slave-holding States, combined with a war between the two severed portions of the Union. It seems to me that its result might be the extirpation of slavery from this whole continent; and, calamitous and desolating as this course of events in its progress must be, so glorious would be its final issue, that, as God shall judge me, I dare not say that it is not to be desired.

In time there would come yet another metaphor, perhaps the most powerful, originally from the Bible, now applied to the new American republic: a House divided against itself cannot stand.

*This passage is not included in the Nevins one-volume edition, but can be found in Charles Francis's twelve-volume edition.

PART VI

THE TEDIUM AND SUBLIMITY OF REPUBLICAN GOVERNMENT

16 / A DIRECT VIOLATION OF THE CONSTITUTION

WE LEFT SIXTY-EIGHT-YEAR-OLD Congressman John Quincy Adams protesting, in May of 1836, when debate was stifled on the third of the Pinckney Committee's proposals—the gag rule. We now go back to the beginning of that session in the House and ask what Adams had been doing.

He had refrained from comment, for the most part, during the early stages of the petition controversy in the agitated session of the United States House of Representatives that began in December of 1835; but he must have listened with growing discomfiture both to the Southerners contending with each other about the best way to stifle petitions and to their defenses, on the floor of this republican body, of human slavery as a positive good.

He had spoken once, on December 21, in the debate over the Briggs petition, to explain his view of the proper treatment of these earnest prayers. He had reminded the House that he himself had introduced petitions praying for the abolition of slavery in the District of Columbia as long ago as his first service, at the Twenty-second Congress, in 1831. Those had been petitions from "certain citizens of the Commonwealth of Pennsylvania." He had presented them, he said, "in homage to the sacred right of petition, a right which in whatever manner it might be treated by others, should never be treated by him with anything but respect." Perhaps the South Carolinians and Virginians and their friends should have heard in that last remark a hint of reproof, an admonitory anticipation of what was to come, but otherwise Adams was as sweetly conciliatory as could be.

Or almost. He was simply being the elder statesman, explaining how the petitions ought to be treated, never broaching upon their subject. Almost never. He explained that back in 1831, and again in 1834, on presenting such petitions he himself had given notice to the House and to the country that he did not support their prayer, and for the same reason that many members were now trying to prevent discussion of the petitions' subject: because it would be unprofitable to the House and to the country. But he had treated the petitions respectfully. He had moved that they be referred to the Committee on the District of Columbia; they had been duly referred; the committee had reported to the House (negatively, of course); and the House had adopted their report *sub silentio* (that is, by silent acquiescence), and that was it. Adams was recommending this course of action now, both for reasons of principle (respect for the right of petition) and for reasons of strategy (to keep their subject from fruitlessly inflaming the House and the public). On those earlier occasions, he and his future opponents seemed to share this strategic objective.

But something in what the ex-president said should have intimated to his fellow members how far he was from sharing their view on slavery itself, should the subject be opened, and on matters of republican propriety as well. He had warned them that clamping down on the petitions would have the paradoxical result of opening the discussion they wanted to close, as well as undercutting core values of the country. At the end of his speech on December 21, he had said:

> **[Adams]:** You suppress the right of petition; you suppress the freedom of the press; you suppress the freedom of religion; for in the sentiments of many respectable men, fanatics if you please to call them, they are found to act under a sense of duty to their God. Mr. A. said it was not for him to judge them, nor was it for this House to judge them. Therefore, sir, in deference to what has been heretofore the usage of this House, in deference to the right of petition, of freedom of speech, of freedom of the press, and freedom of religion, I hope, sir, that this petition [i.e., Mr. Briggs's] will be left in the possession of the Committee on the District of Columbia, and that we will hear no more about this exciting subject.

At about the time he was making this speech (before William Slade of Vermont held forth), Adams wrote to his son Charles Francis that "the voice of Freedom has not yet been heard." Undoubtedly the excited young firebrands from the South (most of them were young—certainly they were younger than the sixty-eight-year-old Adams) were looking out of the corners of their eyes at the old ex-president from Massachusetts, laden with honors and distinctions and links to the nation's glorious past, and not at all bashful about participating in the give-and-take of parliamentary activity.

The acute sensitivity of the Southern spokesmen to what Adams might say was reflected in the way they picked up on a couple of phrases he had used in his incidental contributions to the discussion. He had said that petitions respectfully received and respectfully referred to committee would thus be consigned to the tomb of the Capulets. Congressmen thereafter kept referring to this literary touch of Adams's—not only Slade, to regret his using it, but Southerners to join wholeheartedly in its application. On the other hand, Adams had, in passing, referred to "the sublime benefit of slavery" in a way that troubled the Southern spokesmen, for they detected in the remark, as well they might, a touch of sarcasm.

William Slade in the House, and the abolition leaders in New York and Boston, were disappointed in him because he explicitly dissociated himself from the prayer that slavery be ended in the District, and because he was, or seemed to be, willing to cooperate with the House leaders in muting the issue of slavery—so long as the right of petition was respected. The procedure he recommended preserved that respect, he said, but also prevented the subject from exploding into a full debate.

The Southern leaders, however, certainly had cause to worry. He talked about that full-fledged debate on slavery—which of course they were not going to have—in a way that suggested he was holding back a great deal. Oh, what he would say, if they were to have such a debate! Which of course they were not having. Then he might enlarge upon "the sublime benefits of slavery." There were in his speech little flashes of electricity that would not have reassured you if you had been a supporter of slavery.

On January 4, 1836, a petition day,* Adams wrote in his journal that he "attended the House with no small feelings of anxiety." Charles Francis, editing his father's journal many years later, remarked in a footnote that "[f]rom this day dates the great struggle which J. Q. Adams waged to maintain the right of petition in the House of Representatives."

That petitions and petition day meant something to Adams, quite apart from their relation to slavery, is evident in his journal. Back on February 20 of 1832, for example, very early in his service in the House, he had written:

> *Being Monday, the states were successively called for presentation of petitions; a most tedious operation in practice, though to a reflective mind a very striking exemplification of the magnificent grandeur of our nation and of the sublime principles upon which our government is founded.*

*The reader is reminded that according to the House rules, renewed customarily at the start of each session, on each of the first thirty days of a session there would be an hour devoted to calling the roll of the states for the purpose of offering petitions; once those thirty days had elapsed, unless there was a suspension of the rules, every other Monday was petition day.

The Tedium and the Sublimity of republican government.

The beginning of Adams's fight for those sublime principles in January of 1836 was not particularly auspicious. When Massachusetts was called, Adams rose to present first a petition on some relatively innocuous subject and moved that it be referred to the appropriate committee, as Adams thought all petitions should be, in this case the Committee on Foreign Affairs. Then, in the same business-as-usual mode, he began to present a petition from 153 inhabitants of Millbury, in "the County of Worcester and the Commonwealth of Massachusetts," praying for the abolition of slavery and the slave trade in the District of Columbia.

> *I was instantly interrupted by my next neighbor, John M. Patton* [of Virginia] *who enquired whether the petition had been received; to which the speaker* [James Polk of Tennessee] *answered that it had not; whereupon Thomas Glascock, a new member from Georgia, moved that it not be received, and was proceeding to make a speech, when I called him to order.*

There was a House rule that petitions could not be discussed on the day of their presentation, in order to save time for others to present petitions; but Speaker Polk ruled that this provision did not apply in the present case, because the petition had not been received and was not "in the possession of the House." Adams appealed the Chair's decision, and the House collapsed into one of those intricate parliamentary tangles into which parliamentary bodies are wont to collapse. On the next petition day, January 18 (according to Charles Francis's note), Adams "renewed the struggle over abolition petitions," presenting among others one signed by 148 ladies.

This is the way the people's representatives went at it on January 18, 1836, according to the *Congressional Globe*.

> **Mr. Adams** presented the petition of certain inhabitants of the State of Massachusetts, praying the abolition of slavery in the District of Columbia.
>
> **Mr. Hammond** regretted that the gentleman had thought proper to present this memorial. He felt constrained to move the question of consideration.
>
> **Mr. Adams** said he presumed that the question was subject to the decision upon the appeal taken by him on a former occasion, from the decision of the Chair.

Mr. Pinckney wished, in order that the gentlemen might have an opportunity of presenting their petitions, to make the motion that the preliminary question be laid on the table.

Mr. Adams said, the appeal which he had taken from the decision of the Chair, on a former occasion, was founded on a desire, on his part, that the subject should not be discussed so as to consume the whole of the day set apart for the presentation of petitions. With this view, he was willing to allow the gentleman from South Carolina to make the motion that the subject be laid on the table, to be taken up and decided on at the same time with the other petitions.

Mr. Pinckney then moved to lay the motion on the table.

Mr. Hammond inquired whether the motion of his colleague was in order. The petition not having been received, there was nothing to lay on the table.

The Chair said that the motion was in order. The gentleman from Massachusetts had moved that the petition be received. It was competent to lay that motion on the table.

Mr. Adams presented a similar petition to the foregoing, for the abolition of slavery in the District of Columbia.

Mr. Hammond again moved the question of consideration. He gave notice that he would make the same motion in every similar case, until he could procure a direct vote on the subject.

Of course there were a few petitions on mundane subjects, but before long:

Mr. Slade presented memorials praying for the abolition of slavery and the slave trade in the District of Columbia, of one hundred females of Cornwall in the State of Vermont; of four hundred and twenty-six females in the county of Madison in said State; of three hundred and thirty-six male citizens of McConnellsville in the State of New York, and of the officers and students of Oneida Institute, in said State, which he moved should be referred to a select committee.

Mr. Glascock [of Georgia] moved that they be not received.

Mr. Gideon Lee [of New York] moved to lay the motion on the table, which was agreed to.

Mr. Janes [of Vermont] presented a petition for the abolition of slavery in the District of Columbia.

Mr. Hammond demanded the preliminary question of reception, which motion was laid on the table.

It will be noted that some of the congressmen had discovered that double-barreled and conveniently ambiguous method for disposing of these petitions that the Senate had happened onto. After Hammond or Glascock or Pickens or Wise moved, as was now usual, that a petition not be received (or "moved the question of consideration"), then someone moved that that motion *itself* be laid on the table. There was the new wrinkle. They could combine in one parliamentary club sandwich the two leading devices for getting rid of the petitions—and arranging, as congressmen then and now like to do, a convenient ambiguity about what they were voting for. A Northern Democrat, for example, who supported Van Buren could vote to lay the motion on the table, ending debate, without committing himself one way or the other on the underlying motion itself, not to receive the petitions. A Calhounite or Southern Whig, on the other hand, could insist that the petition had never been received, because the motion not to receive it had been laid on the table. And both parties could rejoice that the petition had been swiftly tumbled out of the House and would be kept out by two barriers of parliamentary procedure.

But the House did not keep on using that new gear in the parliamentary machinery, as the Senate was to do. On this occasion the House left the matter in a limbo of parliamentary indecision until the next petition day, January 25. On that day Maine was called, and some routine petitions were presented; New Hampshire was called, with the same result; and then Massachusetts was called.

Mr. Adams presented the petition of 107 females, residing in his Congressional district, praying the abolition of slavery and the slave trade in the District of Columbia.

Hammond was instantly on his feet asking to be recognized, certainly to move that the petition not be received. But Adams was ready, too.

Mr. Adams. I claim the floor, and shall not yield it. I move that the petition be referred to a select committee, with instructions—

Mr. Glascock hoped that the gentleman would not—

Mr. Adams. I call to order.

The Chair said that the gentleman from Massachusetts was entitled to the floor. The petition which the gentleman proposed to present was still in his possession.

Here Adams abruptly switched tactics.

Mr. Adams moved that the petition be received; and was proceeding to discuss the propriety of its reception, when

Mr. Hardin rose to a question of order. It was not in order, in his estimation, to discuss the motion of the gentleman at this time.

But the Chair ruled that it *was* in order for Adams to discuss his motion that the petition be received. Adams had beaten Hammond and Glascock and Wise to the punch by moving that the petition *be* received, before they could move that it *not be* received—so that he could discuss not the substance of the petition itself, of course, but the question of its reception. The House voted to sustain the Chair's ruling.

Mr. Adams said he was glad the question had been at last decided. By the decision every member of the House having a petition to present, is authorized to debate, as long as he shall think proper, the question of reception, whether on slavery or any other subject.

Dangerous ground. If a member could discuss the merits of receiving a petition, in so doing might he not accomplish some discussion of the actual topic of the petition?

In defending the petitioners' right to be heard, Adams echoed and paraphrased Thomas Jefferson, who in his turn had echoed John Locke, who in his turn had echoed John Milton.

[Adams] believed it to be the true course to let error be tolerated, to grant freedom of speech, and freedom of the press, and apply reason to put it down. He had no sort of doubt but that a committee of the House could furnish reasons why the prayer of these petitions should not be granted, which would satisfy every reasonable and humane individual in the country.

Or if you cannot give satisfactory reasons, then something is wrong. Later that same day, Adams presented a petition from "160 or 170 citizens of Western Pennsylvania" against slavery in the District. Then Caleb Cushing, the learned new congressman from Massachusetts, presented another petition "of a similar character" from citizens of Massachusetts. When Mr. Hammond objected to receiving the petition, Mr. Cushing proceeded to give a speech whose learning and complexity and length taxed the poor *Globe* reporter into desperate summary. (This is the speech, referred to in an earlier chapter, in which Cushing took the topic all the way back to the Magna Carta.) He argued "at length," the reporter wrote, in support of the right of petition, tracing its existence "from the time of the Saxons" and pointing out that the right "was brought over by the first pilgrims to this country." Cushing also quoted "various extracts from the debates and proceedings on the adoption of the Constitution." Mr. Cushing was in favor of referring all petitions to a committee.

> **Mr. Garland** replied to Mr. Cushing, and maintained that the right of petition to Congress was limited only to a redress of grievances: and of such grievances as were within the constitutional authority of Congress. Could the people of Massachusetts petition for a change in the domestic government or institutions of Virginia? Certainly not, no more than France or England could. These petitioners from Massachusetts had no grievances from slavery, for theirs was a free State. . . .

By late January, the House was overflowing with unresolved motions and appeals on this subject, and wallowing in unanswered petitions, stacked on its tables in various stages of parliamentary undress.

And so, then, on February 1, James Henry Hammond gave the speech we have already quoted—"slavery can never be abolished." On February 4, Henry Laurens Pinckney introduced his proposal (the Jackson–Van Buren Democrats' proposal) that a committee be appointed to draw up a set of resolutions for the House. He proposed for that committee, as we have seen, the specific instructions that were, in the context of the excitement of that time and place, a compromise of comparative moderation. And though, as we have also seen, Pinckney was excoriated by his fellow South Carolinians and by some Southern Whigs for being so soft on abolitionist petitions as to allow them to be received, and so soft on the District question as to allow the implication that Congress might have some constitutional power over slavery there, his proposals nevertheless passed the House handily, with solid Democratic support in the North and with a majority of Southern Democrats, and some Northern Whigs, voting for them. John Quincy Adams voted for these original Pinckney proposals, and so did William Slade. At that stage the House members were voting simply to set up the committee with the instructions Pinckney proposed; what would happen when the committee reported might be another story.

If Pinckney's committee had followed the instructions the House had given them and the House had acted favorably on the committee report, the petitions would have been respectfully received and respectfully referred, as before, and then respectfully forgotten, as before. Moreover, the committee to which they had been referred would already have worked out a respectful answer (no—for the following reasons) to all the petitions on that subject. If the fiercest Southern spokesmen could have put up with that, the ensuing battle would not have taken place in the House, at least not on the petition issue.

This is one of those cases, not so rare, in which the ferocity and unwisdom of one side in a political contest are of immense service to the other. It is often said, in textbooks and elsewhere, that the leading abolitionists were shrill, self-righteous, and fanatical. It is sometimes even suggested that their "fanaticism" was an important cause of the Civil War. Before consenting to that one should peruse the speeches and appraise the actions of the defenders-of-the-furthest-outpost among the slave-state politicians in this gag rule controversy. After three months of meetings the Pinckney Committee, reporting to the House on May 18, 1836, brought in, as we have seen, not just the two resolutions the House had expected but a third as well. The third was to become the notorious gag rule. A point of order was raised not only about the committee's having exceeded its instructions, but also about the proposed gagging not only of citizens but of House members:

> **Mr. Phillips** [of Massachusetts] then sent to the Chair the following point of order: "Can a committee, especially instructed to report two resolutions, the form of which was given by the House, report another resolution changing the rules and orders of the House in regard to the management of its business, and depriving citizens of the privilege of obtaining the usual consideration of petitions on subjects other than these referred to the committee?"

James Polk ruled, in the wonderful stuffy language of a parliamentary body, that "it was not within the competency of the Speaker to draw within the vortex of order the question raised by the gentleman from Massachusetts." In other words, in the cliché of a later day, he would not touch it with a ten-foot pole.

The proposed gag rule markedly altered what supporters of Pinckney's original resolutions, like Adams, thought they had been voting for:

sending the petitions to a select committee. Instead, petitions were to be treated more nearly in the way that the fiercest Southern opponents wanted them treated: all petitions on the subject of slavery were now to be laid on the table *automatically* without being printed or referred, and without having any other action taken upon them. What had been accomplished by an individual member jumping to his feet on the appearance of any such petition and immediately moving that it be tabled was now to be accomplished ahead of time, as it were, by a resolution of the House. In the view of John Quincy Adams and others, that was not the respectful treatment to which the petitioners were entitled.

But, as we have seen, he was not allowed to say so. After a week of fire-eating denunciations of Pinckney for betraying the South with his committee report (because that report did not deny all congressional power over slavery), Adams at last stood to get the Speaker's attention, presumably to address the gag rule. But Polk did not call on Adams; instead, he recognized George Owens of Georgia, who promptly moved the previous question. The Democrats—Jackson, Van Buren, Polk, the House majority, and the Pinckney Committee—clearly had their ducks in a row. As we have seen, Adams requested that Owens withdraw his motion; Owens declined. The motion for the previous question was carried by a vote of 109 to 89, with Adams calling out, "Am I gagged or not?" Later, when Adams would describe these events, he would say that the gag rule had been adopted "under the screw of the previous question."

AND SO WE LEFT Adams and the other distinguished gentlemen back in Chapter 12, ready to vote, in six exciting days of May (18–26) 1836, on the items in the report of the Pinckney Committee. The main question was divided, as they say in parliamentary bodies—each of Pinckney's resolutions was submitted to a separate vote. All Adams and the others were supposed to do now was vote, but the House was in for a surprise.

The clerk read the first resolution, which went as follows:

> *Resolved*, That Congress possesses no constitutional authority to interfere in any way with the institution of slavery in any of the States of this Confederacy.

And then the clerk called the roll, for the yeas and nays, beginning with Adams of Massachusetts.

> **Mr. Adams** said, if the House would allow him five minutes' time, he pledged himself to prove that resolution false and utterly untrue.

> Mr. A. was here called to order in different parts of the House, and resumed his seat. [He had been called upon only to cast his vote, not to make a speech.]

Adams's claim that this first resolution was "false and utterly untrue" surely sent a shiver down the spines of Southern members, and not just Southern members, because this one had not been thought to be controversial. The most vociferous Southerners objected, as we have seen, to the weakness as they saw it of the second proposal about the District, and they surely expected, from more than one quarter, objections to the third, the gag rule, which had not been included, as the other two had, in the Pinckney Committee's instructions. But the first point, that Congress lacked the constitutional authority to deal with slavery in the *states* where it existed—that was bedrock. Even the antislavery people conceded this; the fierce abolitionist declaration from the Adelphi had conceded it; in the past, Adams himself had conceded it; twenty-four years later, when an antislavery party would elect a president, Abraham Lincoln, he too would concede it. So what in the world did the old man mean? The Southern contingent did not want to hear, and managed to shut him up temporarily, but eventually they would hear despite themselves.

When the House dropped the Pinckney proposals for a while in order to resume the business of the day, it took up a resolution to provide relief for refugees from Seminole hostilities in Georgia and Alabama, and it considered that matter in the Committee of the Whole, in which parliamentary situation—being technically a committee meeting—the device of calling the previous question to close off debate does not apply. Adams got the floor, and expanded his discussion of the Seminole War to the constitutional question of the war powers of Congress, and to other possible wartime situations beyond the Indian wars—in particular to the warfare that would come from the Southern and Western members' efforts to add Texas to the Union as a slave state, and to restore slavery there where it had been abolished. In 1829 the Mexican government had abolished slavery in Texas; would England or France stand for its reinstatement? He filled in the picture, and then came to a stunning point:

> [**Adams**]: Mr. Chairman, are you ready for all these wars? A Mexican war? A war with Great Britain, if not with France? A general Indian war? A servile war? And, as an inevitable consequence of them all, a civil war? . . . Do you imagine that while, in the very nature of things, your own Southern and Southwestern States must be the Flanders of these complicated wars, the battlefield upon which the last great conflict must be fought between slavery and emancipation; do you imagine that your Con-

gress will have no constitutional authority to interfere with the institution of slavery in any way in the States of this confederation? . . . From the instant that your slaveholding states become the theatre of war, civil, servile, or foreign, from that instant the war powers of Congress extend to interference with the institution of slavery in every way by which it can be interfered with. . . .

There it was: under the war power, slavery *could* be constitutionally interfered with, even in the original slave states. Twenty-seven years later, with the Emancipation Proclamation, this theory would be vindicated.* In 1836, however, it was outrageous beyond the reach of rational discussion; pandemonium greeted Adams's words, and shouts of vituperation.

One scenario that Adams suggested might bring about a constitutional emancipation under the war power was the coming of a "servile war"—a large-scale slave insurrection—in which the Southern states would call upon the federal government, or the North, for help. To look ahead and follow this point, five years after his first articulation of the theory, on June 9, 1841, Adams's reiteration of it before the House would bring forth this exchange, as recorded in the *Congressional Globe*:

Mr. I[ngersoll of Pennsylvania, in 1841] went on to express his astonishment and horror at what had fallen from the gentleman from Massachusetts [Mr. Adams] the other day when speaking on this subject. He understood the gentleman as saying that, in the event of a servile war breaking out in the South, there would be an end of the Constitution. He would be glad to know whether he (Mr. I.) had understood him.

Mr. Adams rose and said: If the gentleman wished him to repeat what he had said, he had no hesitation in saying that he had said no such thing as that in that event there would be an end to the Constitution of the United States.

Actually what Adams was thinking out was the reverse of what Ingersoll had heard: how the continuity of the United States Constitution could be *preserved*, while slavery was abolished.

What he [**Adams**] had said was, that in the event of a servile war, his own opinion would be that if the free portion of this Union were called upon to

*There had also already been, by the time of that proclamation, attempts at least to apply this theory on the part of Union generals Frémont, Hunter, and Butler, and by the wartime Congress in the Confiscatory Acts of 1861 and 1862.

> support the institutions of the South by suppressing the slaves, and a servile war in consequence of it, in that case he would not say that Congress had no right to interfere with the institutions of the South . . . there would be no longer any pretension that Congress had not the right to interfere with the institutions of the South, inasmuch as the very fact of the people of a free portion of the Union marching to the support of the masters would be an interference with those institutions; and that, in the event of a war, the result of which no man could tell, the treaty-making power would come to be equivalent to universal emancipation.

John Quincy Adams, at the end of his life, was one of the mentors of an intense young orator and reformer who would be elected to the United States Senate from Massachusetts, Charles Sumner. On the inauguration of the new Republican president in March of 1861, Senator Sumner paid him a visit, and presented to him the idea he had got from Adams: that under the war power there could be a *constitutional* emancipation of slaves in the slave states.

❧

BUT IT WOULD BE a long time before that staggering idea would gain any currency, in Congress or anywhere else. The vote on Pinckney's first resolution was overwhelming, 182–9. The nine Northerners who voted against the resolution included three from the Green Mountain State—Horace Everett and Henry F. Janes along with William Slade—and three from Massachusetts, including Adams.

A squabble about some Southern members declining to vote because of "constitutional scruples" took up the rest of that legislative day.

On the next the House finally allowed the clerk to announce the vote on the first resolution and to read, and call the roll on, the second. This was the one that had so inflamed the Southern faction, the one that said that Congress, for reasons of the national well-being (but, implicitly, not of constitutional prohibition), ought not to interfere with slavery in the District of Columbia. Adams, for reasons of the alphabet, was again the first name to be called by the clerk; and now *he* asked to be excused from voting! Speaker Polk, no doubt with a sigh, said that they would pass his name for the present. A New York member, and then Henry Wise, also declined to vote, for whatever reasons. The resolution, in spite of all the furious attacks by the firebrands on Pinckney for proposing it, was passed rather handily, 132–45.

But the big item in practical terms was the third resolution, the gag rule. The clerk read it aloud, with its preamble about "restoring tranquillity to the public mind," and again, started the roll call with Adams. What would he do this time? Of course, all he was supposed to do was cast his vote, yea or nay.

> When the name of **Mr. Adams** was called, that gentleman rose and said:
>
> "I hold the resolution to be a direct violation of the constitution of the United States, the rules of this House, and the rights of my constituents."
>
> Mr. A. resumed his seat amid loud cries of "Order," from all parts of the Hall.

Some reconstructions of this moment have Adams calling out each of these phrases over the punctuating clamor of the calls for order, interrupting but failing to arrest him. The gag rule, nevertheless, passed easily, 117–68, with the votes of Northern and Southern Democrats and many Whigs from the South, and this extraordinary resolution governed the House for the rest of that session. No more petitions on the subject of slavery! No more scuffles over the petitions! So they thought.

AS IF THESE EVENTS weren't enough, this session had in early June yet another spectacular but tightly constrained fracas about slavery, at the most basic and consequential level of power politics: the admission of new states. Arkansas had applied for admission as a slave state, with a proposed provision in its *constitution* denying the state the power to emancipate slaves; as Caleb Cushing said in a long, critical middle-of-the-night speech, the object of the provision was "in effect, to render slavery perpetual in the new state of Arkansas," a provision which Adams gave early notice he would oppose.

No new states had been admitted since the firebells, cramps, and clenched fists over Missouri, and the Jackson–Van Buren Democrats surely wanted, particularly in an election year, to avoid a repetition of the eruption and sectional rancor that had marked that earlier occasion. They had already, during the Senate's consideration of the issue in April, arranged the kind of pairing—this for you, that for me—that had finally come out of that other occasion: as the free states had then got Maine, in return for the admission of the slave state Missouri, so they now were to get Michigan in return for the slave state Arkansas. To a degree, as a congressman said, the admission of each state was held hostage to the admission of the other; but really, as another congressman observed, it was more one-sided than that: the admission of the free state of Michigan, about which there was no serious problem, was held hostage to the admission of Arkansas, with its provision for perpetual slavery. The two were joined so that finally, after the votes were taken, a congressman remarked that "as the House had been delivered of twins, he thought that after the operation they might adjourn."

But before that exhausted postpartum moment could be reached, the controlling Democratic majority, after a preliminary eight-hour bout on Wednesday June 8, put the House through an extraordinary twenty-five-hour all-night session in the Committee of the Whole, beginning on Thursday, June 9, and continuing without a break into the weary morning of Friday, June 10, beating back repeated attempts to adjourn and rousing sleepy quorums when they needed to. Michigan was taken up first, and there were some matters to be discussed—one about its boundaries with Ohio—that took time and long speeches, and so whether by accident or by design the twin bill for the admission of Arkansas, joined at the hip to Michigan, was not taken up until after midnight, in the early hours of June 10 in real time but still by the legislative calendar June 9. In the weary morning of Friday a congressman asked one of those truly bedrock questions: Were they going to be paid for only one day?

As the Arkansas bill was finally taken up, after midnight, Phillips of Massachusetts, "exhausted in body and mind," objected to "the precipitate action by which it was evidently intended to force through the committee two bills of the importance of those under consideration," but his effort to call a halt was beaten back by a heavy and apparently well-disciplined Democratic majority. Adams requested that the hour (by then nearly one o'clock in the morning) be noted in the journal (presumably to show the public what the majority was doing), but Speaker Polk said that was not in order. Twice, in the wee hours of the morning, the "committee" (the whole House meeting as a Committee of the Whole) was discovered not to have a quorum, and had to "rise" and so report to the House (to the same people in the same room in their different parliamentary identity, with the Speaker back in the chair), but then when in the House it was moved to adjourn, a loyal Democrat would insist that the yeas and nays be called, and by the time the call was completed it would be discovered that enough members had been routed out of the taverns and lodging houses to make a quorum, and the adjournment would be defeated, and the House would then vote to go back into the Committee of the Whole and keep going. When the sixty-eight-year-old Adams, who stayed in the House throughout this entire night-long episode, was finally recognized to offer the amendment that everyone knew he was going to offer, it was about five o'clock in the morning. Adams's daybreak amendment said "nothing in this act shall be construed as assent by the Congress" to the anti-emancipation article in the proposed Arkansas constitution.

Cushing, following Adams in defense of the amendment, began by saying: "Mr. Chairman, the House has now continued in session for the space of eighteen or nineteen hours, without any interval of refreshment or rest. It is impossible to mistake the intentions of the ruling majority" to keep the Committee of the Whole continuously in session until the bills admitting the two states were reported. Praising Adams, Cushing used a figure of speech, understandable under the circumstances, referring to "my colleague [Mr. Adams] the vigilant eye of whose unsleeping mind there is nothing which escapes."

Not all the references to Adams that followed were as favorable or as sober. In the hours of debate he was attacked by (as Adams put it in his journal) George Dromgoole of Virginia "drunk with whiskey" and Jesse Bynum of North Carolina "drunk with slavery." In some weary early-morning hour a vote was taken on Adams's amendment and it was defeated 98–32, and Adams promptly moved to adjourn, but the majority again refused.

As this none too inspiring sample of that mutual deliberation by which republics are governed wound on through the early-morning hours, William Slade, at "about 7 o'clock," made another futile attempt to persuade the House to reject the slavery provision in the Arkansas constitution. Henry Wise—a vocal participant, of course, opposing the Democratic steam-roller for different reasons from Adams and Slade, said the House was "too sleepy, too tired, and too drunk" to do business, and as the session neared ten o'clock Friday morning, when another legislative day was supposed to begin, said he would talk, in a kind of House filibuster, until that time. But after a dispute about the rules the majority did finally manage to extract the committee vote reporting the two bills, and on the following Monday, after Adams made yet one more effort to block the proslavery provision in the Arkansas constitution, the vote was taken and the twins were finally born, one of them, as speakers had said in the middle of the night, malformed. There was now in the Union another slave state, with two senators and a House delegation that would be augmented by the three-fifths clause. Let it be recorded, for whatever interest it may have in 1996, that John Quincy Adams voted *against* the admission of Arkansas to the Union.*

*So did William Slade, Caleb Cushing, George Briggs, and forty-six others, including a smattering of border-state Whigs. The primary reason for that vote, of course, had nothing

THE FIRST SESSION OF the Twenty-fourth Congress, destined for fame not only for that action but even more for having enacted the gag rule in a nominally free republic, finally adjourned on July 4, 1836. Those who were chosen to run faced the elections that would choose the Twenty-fifth Congress and, through the cumbersome method of the electoral college, a new president and a new vice-president.

The Whig opposition to the Democratic candidate for president, Martin Van Buren, was not a single national candidate but a cluster of candidates nominated by state legislatures in different sections of the country: Hugh White in the South, William Henry Harrison in the border states and the West, Daniel Webster in New England. This had come about partly from necessity (the Whig Party, in existence only since the fall of 1834, was just beginning to become a national institution), partly from principle (the Whigs were not yet sure they believed in national party conventions), and partly from strategy: The scatter of opponents might deny Van Buren a majority in the electoral college and pitch the election into the House, where the Whigs might do some business. But it didn't work. Andrew Jackson threw his popularity behind Van Buren, and Van Buren, although encountering strong resistance in the South, won enough electoral votes to achieve the presidency.* The Whigs made headway, however, in what would be the House, in the Twenty-fifth Congress.

None of the newly elected officials, of course, took office right away. In early December of 1836 the lame ducks of the Twenty-fourth Congress, who had flailed at each other so energetically the previous winter and spring, made their way to the muddy capital city to go at it one more time.

---

to do with later aspersions and prejudices, but was rather the slavery provision in the Arkansas constitution.

*In his journal for April 13, 1836, John Quincy Adams compared Martin Van Buren to James Madison (although he revered Madison and almost disdained Van Buren) in that they both were "remarkable in their extreme caution in avoiding and averting personal collisions." Van Buren, he said, "like the Sosie of Moliere's Amphitryon, is 'l'ami de tout le monde.' "

17 / IT THRIVES AND FATTENS ON THE DISTRESSES OF THE COUNTRY

THE HOUSE CONVENED PRECISELY at noon, according to Adams's journal, on Monday, December 5, 1836, for the short session, the second session, the final session, of the Twenty-fourth Congress. The congressmen found rooms in lodging houses—not necessarily the same ones as the previous session (Mrs. Lindenberger's was no more)—and reclaimed their seats and desks on the House floor. James Polk, the Speaker of the House, resumed his chair. Some members had prospectively lost their seats in the 1836 elections—Henry Laurens Pinckney among them—but here they were again anyway, lame ducks, still empowered to legislate for this last session. Some members had resigned. Waddy Thompson, a veteran now, with one congressional session under his belt, and perhaps trying to start off on an amiable note, came over to Adams's seat to introduce Franklin Elmore, who had taken James Henry Hammond's place. Hammond was out of commission, suffering from intestinal pain and then traveling in Europe, but his spirit lived on.

The disposition, at first, was to avoid fights. There is often a certain irenic temper to the beginning of a legislative session, as the members gather again and meet old friends and acquaintances and adversaries, and make a fresh start. Harsh words have lost their sting, sharp disagreements have faded; the ceremonial reassembling reminds one of the larger purpose of republican government, shared by all. The previous session, coming on the heels of pamphlet-burning in the Charleston post office, introduced by President Jackson's attack on the incendiary publications, torn asunder by the proliferating petitions and the new Calhoun-Hammond response to them, plagued with two months of speeches on slavery, culminating finally in the doubly controversial gag rule and the fight over Arkansas—all during a presidential election year—must have frayed the nerves of even the sturdiest polemicists. So by contrast Adams noted that, with the election over, this new session began in relative calm and amity.

At an earlier point in his service in the House, one day back in February of 1832, Adams had risen almost to a certain poetry of his own,* in

*Adams actually did write poetry, in addition to everything else he did; he, and everyone else, specifically including his son Charles Francis, agreed that it was not very good.

suggesting that somebody else might write a poem about the ritual of the House's procedure:

> *The forms and proceedings of the House, this calling over of States for petitions, the colossal emblem of the union over the Speaker's chair, the historic Muse at the clock, the echoing pillars of the hall, the tripping Mercuries who bear the resolutions and amendments between the members and the chair, the calls of ayes and noes, with the different intonations of the answers from the different voices, the gobbling manner of the clerk in the reading over the names, the tone of the Speaker in announcing the vote, and the varied shades of pleasure and pain in the countenances of the members on hearing it, would form a fine subject for a descriptive poem.*

This lame duck session of the Twenty-fourth Congress had another ritual to perform: although everyone already knew the results, and Van Buren would not take office as the new president until March, the formal counting of the votes of the states in the electoral college was a responsibility of the House, as John Quincy Adams had reason to remember.

The roll of the states was called, presumably by the clerk "in his gobbling manner," for petitions and resolutions, "multitudes of which were offered," according to Adams in his journal, "some wise, some foolish," without provoking any heavy combat. Many thought that the petition fever might drop, in this new session. The factor of partisan presidential politics, insofar as it had figured in the struggle over the petitions and the gag rule, ought now to be eliminated, or at least diminished. If to any degree the extreme High Carolinian position had been a ploy to unite the South behind a bid by John C. Calhoun for the presidency, then its application to that election, at least, was past. If the gag resolution had been a temporary Democratic Party device, to hold the South and keep a lid on it until Van Buren was elected, then it, too, was no longer necessary.

Adams may have believed that the House would not again try to interfere with the sacred right of petition. And many other members of Congress may have believed that the petitioners would cease petitioning, and congressmen would stop introducing the petitions. But neither of these expectations was to be fulfilled.

The supporters of the gag may have expected that resolution to fulfill the purpose given in its preamble: ". . . it is extremely important and desirable that the agitation of this subject should be finally arrested, for the purpose of restoring tranquillity to the public mind." And was agitation arrested? No, it was not arrested. Did the issue go to sleep? No, it did not go to sleep. What effect had the "tranquillizing resolution," as Adams sardonically called it, had? Adams wrote, "[S]o conspicuous were its sedative properties, that at the ensuing session (1836–37) it multiplied fivefold the anti-slavery petitions."

Thus the irenic spirit at the start of the session did not last very long. On December 26, the clerk having started to call the roll of states again and the roll having reached Massachusetts, John Quincy Adams arose to present a petition praying for the abolition of slavery and the slave trade in the District of Columbia. And Francis Pickens of South Carolina raised the question of its reception—that furthest outpost of opposition, the spirit of Hammond (and Calhoun) marching on. But Pickens also appealed, as a kind of second line of defense, to the gag resolution of the last session, which at the time it had been enacted he himself had vehemently spoken against and voted against, on the High Carolinian ground that the petitions did not deserve even that much acknowledgment of their existence.

And on the subject of that gag resolution, Speaker Polk made a significant ruling.

> The Speaker said . . . he considered the resolutions of the last session as expired with the session itself.

This meant that in this new session the opponents of the petitions would have to start over, and would have to be on their toes every petition day; they no longer had the automatic protection the gag rule had provided.

The House managed to get that first petition of Adams's out of the way, not by refusing to receive it, as Pickens wanted as his first choice, and not by the mechanical disposal of the gag rule, which the Speaker ruled to have expired, and not by referring it to committee, as Adams thought they ought to do, but by voting to lay it on the table.

But of course there were more petitions where that one came from. And so when Massachusetts' turn came around again, on January 9, 1837:

> **Mr. Adams** presented a petition from one hundred and fifty women, wives and daughters of his immediate constituents, praying for the abolition of slavery in the District of Columbia.

Then the Calhounite assault on the petitions—now spearheaded by Thomas Glascock of Georgia, a onetime general in the Seminole War—resumed. There was an exchange about the propriety of the role of women, of which more in a later chapter. On the treatment of the petition itself:

Mr. Glascock objected to the reception of this petition [in effect, a motion not to receive].

Mr. Adams did not expect that any objection would have been made to the reception of this petition. . . . It appeared to him that the decision of the House at the last session went quite far enough to suppress the right of petition of the citizens of this country, and quite far enough to suppress the freedom of speech; but this motion went one step further. It went to settle the principle that petitions . . . should not even be received; and that, too, directly in the face of the Constitution itself. He hoped the people of this country would not tamely submit to the injustice and wrong which would be inflicted upon them by their immediate representatives, in deciding that their petitions should not be received. He lamented deeply the decision and determination of the House at the last session, so far as it went; but this motion went one step further; and he hoped it would not be sanctioned by the House. . . .

But Glascock would not withdraw his objection to the reception of the petition.

The gentleman [i.e., Adams] had . . . thought proper to advise Mr. **G[lascock]**, for the honor of his character as a man and a citizen, to withdraw his objection to the reception of the petition. Were Mr. G. to [do so, however], he would prove recreant to his own feelings, and to the known will of the thousands who had sent him there. It was a position he had assumed last session—a position which had received the almost unanimous approbation of his constituents; and God forbid that he should be found, at this time, abandoning it.

So if Adams was going to stand by his position, Glascock was going to stand by his, too; and if Adams could appeal to Glascock and the Calhounites to stop what they were doing, then Glascock in his turn could appeal to Adams to stop what he was doing.

[Mr. Glascock] appealed to the gentleman himself that, if he wished to allay excitement, and not produce further agitation in that House, and throughout the country, to present no such petitions here. There was no necessity for it, when no good could possibly result. . . .

But neither appeal was successful. The trenches of the previous winter would serve quite well, it appeared, as the battle was renewed one year later. This time Glascock's motion not to receive the petition, rather than the petition itself, was laid on the table. After that motion had passed,

Mr. Adams [in whose hands the petition had been, according to the Chair, "arrested"] then rose and said, that as he understood, by the decision of the Speaker, the petition itself was not laid on the table, but only the motion to receive it, in order to save the time of the House, he gave notice that he should call up the motion for decision [on whether to receive the petition] every day, as long as he should be permitted to do so by the House.

Adams would fight it out on that line if it took all winter.

[Adams] felt himself impelled to this course, because he should not have performed his duty to his constituents so long as the House had not decided they would not receive it. Mr. A. was proceeding further, when

Mr. Pinckney [here he is still, a lame duck in his last session] rose to a question of order.

The Chair decided that under the rules, the notice of motion [that was what Adams was doing: giving notice about motions he was going to make] could not be debated.

Mr. Adams reiterated his notice, and declared his intention to renew it, from day to day, until it was decided.

Mr. A. then presented another memorial, signed by two hundred and twenty-eight women of South Weymouth, the wives and daughters, he said, of his immediate constituents, praying for the abolition of slavery and the slave trade in the District of Columbia.

Adams was underlining the fact that this petition came from his own constituents, and from women to whom a particular courtesy was due. Abigail Smith Adams had come from Weymouth.

Mr. A. said, as a part of his speech, he should read the memorial itself, which was very short, and would not consume much time. He was proceeding therein, when

Mr. Pinckney inquired if the doing so was in order.

The Chair said the gentleman had a right, under the rule, to make a brief statement of its contents, but nothing more. It was not for the Chair to decide whether the gentleman should make the statement in his own language, or in that of the paper itself.

Mr. Adams said he read it as a part of his speech, and was proceeding again to do so, when

Mr. Chambers [of Kentucky] renewed the point of order made by Mr. Pinckney.

The Chair then decided, that as the 45th rule declared that a member presenting a petition should confine himself to a brief verbal statement of its contents, and that . . . Jefferson's Manual, laid it down that no member could read any paper to the House without leave, not even his own speech, therefore . . . he decided that the gentleman from Massachusetts could not insist upon reading this memorial.

But if Adams was not to be allowed to read the petition, neither could Glascock, Wise, Pickens, Thompson, and the other nonreceivers at this stage command a majority of the House for their position. So Haynes of Georgia moved to lay the petition on the table, which eventually was done. Before the day was over, Adams presented yet another petition, and Joab Lawler of Alabama objected to its reception, but the House adjourned before it could repeat the pattern once more.

At this session of Congress—their second major engagement on this front—the Southerners and their Northern allies found out that the flow of petitions had by no means dried up, and that Adams would not consent to stop presenting them. Adams and his supporters found out, for their part, that the several species of petition-stiflers had not given up either. The Calhounites would keep on trying for their most extreme position, absolutely to reject the petitions at the threshold—not even to "receive" them; and then when it was shown that they did not have the votes for that, a member would move immediately to the next line of defense, instantly to lay the petition on the table, without debate, printing, or referral to committee. And that would pass.

There would be plenty of approval for that action—backhandedly to admit the petitions (by voting against outright rejection, thus in a very modest double negative way respecting the "sacred right of petition"), and then promptly to lay them on the table ("and nail them there"). Northerners could join in it. Southerners of various geographies and ideologies could either endorse it as their own or settle for it as the best they could get. Van Burenites were eager to join in it. A Democratic doughface (a "Northern man with Southern principles") like Aaron Vanderpoel from New York, who would proudly say that if his constituents sent no abolitionist petitions to him it must be because they knew he would not present them, could explicitly state that it was his position.

But tabling each petition individually was a little dangerous; somebody had to be awake to make the motion, and it was now clear that they would have to keep doing it over and over as Adams and a few others tromped in every petition day with their inexhaustible supply of petitions from the women of Marblehead and the women of Millbury and the women of Weymouth and so on and so on. There was the terrible lesson from the last session of Briggs's petition, which had "inadvertently" slipped by and been referred to a committee (Adams with characteristic sarcasm would say that the House had "inadvertently" granted citizens their constitutional right to petition). So—perhaps it was after all necessary once more to enact a gag that would automatically lay on the table all petitions on that one subject, without printing, referral, or consideration, in the way that a sorting machine on an assembly line automatically spits out misshapen parts. Were there enough votes to support that? Yes, there were.

On January 18, after skirmishing over more petitions, while Pinckney was waiting out a parliamentary development before making his own "more comprehensive" motion, a Democrat from Kentucky named Albert G. Hawes beat him to the mark and introduced exactly the gag resolution of the previous session.

> **Mr. Hawes** said, he thought it was time the House should adopt a resolution of this kind, after the time which had been lost by discussions on abolition petitions. He wished to raise no debate, because he thought they had had enough on this subject; and therefore, to test the sense of the House, he moved the previous question.

In other words, after he reintroduced the Pinckney gag he immediately moved to shut off debate on his motion. Adams, who objected to all these devices to shut off the petitions, objected also to the way the "screw of the previous question" was used to prevent the House from debating them. He tried to turn one of his opponent's own weapons against them—he raised the question of the consideration of Hawes's resolution—but the House voted 115–57 to consider it and then promptly passed it by a very comfortable margin. Although a majority of the Northern Whigs opposed it, Democrats North and South, and now almost all of the Southern Whigs and (perhaps reluctantly) Calhounite Nullifiers, supported it.

All parties were discovering that this was where the mainstream of congressional opinion could be tapped: not flatly to reject the petitions, but after an implied and very theoretical reception by the House (thus allowing those who needed to to say that they had respected the "sacred right of petition") not only instantly but—by prior specific resolution—without a new vote, to lay them on the table, without any consideration.

Adams said many times that he thought this was unconstitutional and violated fundamental freedoms of the new republic, but he did not have the votes for his position to prevail. An amoral vote-counter could view Adams's position as one "extreme," with a dozen or two votes, depending upon the precise issue, and the Hammond-Glascock-Wise position (*reject* these petitions at the threshold) as the other "extreme," with more votes than Adams's but no majority, and the gag rule as the "compromise" position that could gain comfortable majority support. It had the support not only of the retiring Jackson but of the incoming Van Buren administration, and of their party. So if you did not care about the issue, but wished only to see it vanish, that was the solution for you. After January 18 of this second session, the gag rule was in effect again.

Did this second try now halt the petitioning? Pinckney in a speech that was essentially his swan song, defending his position of the previous session, now vindicated, said that it would:

> **[Pinckney]:** . . . it is because the spirit of abolition is thus repressed and kept down by the resolutions of this House that it struggles and screams as it does with demoniac rage. Its element is agitation, its life-blood is excitement. Give it the question of reception [i.e., by following the mistaken Calhounite course]—give it a daily contest on the right of petition [by not enacting his gag]—produce constant confusion and turmoil here—produce a corresponding spirit in every section of the Union—and this is all it wants and all it asks.

The "it" in this colorful passage is the abolitionist beast.

> **[Pinckney]:** Like the abhorrent animal that preys on corpses, it thrives and fattens on the distresses of the country . . .

But of course we ultimately return to the figure of flame.

> **[Pinckney]:** All that it asks is to kindle a flame at the Capitol that may consume the Union. Allow it to do that, and its work is done. Allow it to do that, and it will soon "Cry Hecate [*sic*], and Let slip the dogs of war."

That terrible picture is what will become of a world deprived of his gag; with it, however, the picture will be different:

> **[Pinckney]:** But repress agitation—give no scope for turmoil—nail the memorials to the table—allow no discussion or action on them—and having nothing to go on, no flame to fan, no strife to stir, it must necessarily droop and die, and soon cease to infect us with its pestiferous breath.

As the reader may guess, Pinckney was wrong. "The tranquillizing effect of this [reenactment of the gag resolution]," Adams would report, "was not only to swell the flood of anti-slavery petitions, but to open a new and abundant stream of remonstrances against the [gag] resolution itself."

PART VII

THE MOST IMPORTANT QUESTION EVER TO COME BEFORE THE HOUSE

18 / THE STRANGE CASE OF THE NINE LADIES FROM FREDERICKSBURG

ADAMS WASTED NO TIME in showing that he was determined to test, defy, oppose, and evade this new gag, as he had its predecessor. On January 23, the first petition day after the enactment of the Hawes gag, he interrupted the proceedings to force the Speaker, and the House, to consider this question, which they had no inclination to consider: what happened now to the petitions that he had presented *before* the enactment of the gag, to the reception of which a member had objected, but about which there had been no decision as yet? Was it not the unfinished business of the House to vote now on whether to receive them? Surely, Adams maintained, the Hawes gag could not be applied *retroactively* to petitions introduced before it existed. Oh my. The Chair—sustained by a large majority of the House—ruled that it *did* apply. So those petitions were left forever in limbo. The Chair and the House, in order to prevent the kind of headache Adams was inviting, were willing to cut a few parliamentary corners.

But Adams was not an adversary who gave up easily. On the petition day two weeks later, February 6, Massachusetts's turn came around again, and soon Adams was on his legs, and before the House adjourned that Monday he had initiated one of the most extraordinary weeks in the history of the House. Because our purpose in these pages is not only to tell this ancient tale but also to exhume the clash of ideas, we will pause to examine that one instructive week with some thoroughness, in this chapter and several to follow.

Massachusetts was called. What must the sentiment have been, elsewhere in the hall, when Massachusetts was called? First up, though, was the representative from Newburyport, Caleb Cushing, who had delivered at the last session that long, learned history of the right of petition going back to the Magna Carta.

Cushing started by pointing out the unusual feminization of his district, almost as an excuse for what he felt he now had to do: "It happened that in his district the fair sex greatly outnumbered the other . . . so that he was probably the immediate representative of more ladies than any other member of the House." It was in obedience to 3,824 of "his fair constituents" (whom it was at all times his pleasure to serve) that he presented petitions praying for the abolition of slavery and the slave trade in the District of Columbia from the city of Lowell and the towns of Amesbury, Andover, Haverhill, Newburyport, Reading, and Salisbury.

The gag machine promptly did its work: kerchunk-wham. All gone.

Cushing then begged the pardon of his nearest neighbor from home, the gentleman from New Hampshire, Mr. Cushman, for appearing to interfere in any way with his concerns, but some ladies from his (Cushman's) district across the Massachusetts–New Hampshire state line had distinguished him with their preference as the organ for their communications to the House (New Hampshire's solidly Democratic delegation was not sympathetic to abolitionists; that delegation had voted in concert for the gag resolutions).

Cushman having responded with the 1830s equivalent of "Be my guest," Cushing then presented petitions praying for the abolition of slavery and the slave trade in the District of Columbia from the ladies of Alstead, Bedford, Boscawen, Canaan, Concord, Durham, Franconia, and twenty other New Hampshire towns down through the alphabet to Salisbury.

Kerchunk-wham. The gag machine once more did its work.

When Cushing sat down, Adams popped up, the ex-president on his legs again. What would it be? More of the same? At first, yes. Adams, warming up as it were, introduced some petitions of the same kind, also from states other than Massachusetts.

The opposing battalions, catching on that this second gag was not going to bring peace, and perhaps not even an armistice, kept their artillery in shape by firing a few desultory shots. They raised the question whether a member could present petitions from states other than his own. After the Chair had given the long-established answer—yes, he could—they appealed that decision, and debated the appeal, after which debate the House predictably voted overwhelmingly to sustain the Chair.

Then Adams—firing a shot neatly back—observed that that unnecessary skirmish had taken three times as long as it would have taken for him simply to present the petitions.

But this was all small-arms fire; the petitions, like their predecessors, were promptly vaporized by the newly installed gag machine. Clearly the same thing would happen to all the others in the stack Adams no doubt had with him there on his desk. So what was the old man going to do now?

What he was going to do now was raise some questions about some doubtful petitions he had in his collection. Now here was one that was bothering him. He presented it, but explained in doing so that he was not sure it was genuine. It purported to come from nine ladies of Fredericksburg, Virginia, and it prayed for the ending of the slave trade in the District of Columbia. He would not *name* the ladies, because "he did not know what would happen to them if he did name them" (because of the present mood in the state of Virginia, he implied, these ladies could get into trouble). The petition was, like the others, promptly shunted onto the table, and Adams calmly moved on to an even more upsetting petition—a bombshell—of which more in a moment. But that did not bring to a close the Case of the Nine Ladies from Fredericksburg.

While Adams and the rest of the House pursued those even more exciting matters, a Virginia representative, Adams's immediate neighbor at his left hand on the House floor, John Patton, who had made the first objection to the reception of a petition back in the first session, did a little investigating. Patton now represented Richmond, but he had grown up in Fredericksburg, and he could not resist the temptation to come forward to inspect this petition of the nine ladies as it literally lay there on the clerk's table, and to read the names of these audacious petitioners from his hometown. Later in the day, in the midst of very unsettling events, he got the floor:

> He (**Mr. P**) would state in his place, and on his responsibility, that the name of no lady was attached to that paper. He did not believe there was a single one of them of decent respectability. He believed the signatures to be genuine, and he recognized only one name which he had known before, and that was the name of a free mulatto woman of the worst fame and reputation. He had been raised in Fredericksburg, and believed he was acquainted with all persons of respectability residing there, and he could say there was not one respectable name attached to this paper.

The petitioners weren't "ladies"; they were not "respectable." Patton said ruefully that he wanted to pursue as "kind and respectful" a course toward the gentleman from Massachusetts as was possible but—pouting a little—he did think that Mr. Adams, sitting right there next to him, might have shown the petition to him, coming as he did from that town and knowing its citizens, so that he could have told him at the outset that it did not bear "the signatures of any decently respectable individual in Fredericksburg." The only name he recognized, to repeat, was that of a "mulatto free woman of infamous character"; the others, Patton believed, "were the names of free negroes, all of whom he believed to be bad." Surely—*surely*—if the gentleman from Massachusetts had known that, if he had shown the paper to his friend from Virginia and been told that, he would have desisted. He would not knowingly, as Patton's colleague from Virginia Congressman Bouldin would soon put it, "throw disgrace and contempt on the proceedings of the House" by introducing such a paper. Patton asked the House to recover the vile paper from the table, and to thrust it back into the hands of the member who had had the effrontery to introduce it.

But that was not the end of the Case of the Nine (Alleged) Ladies from Fredericksburg. In the course of a long speech—partly a self-defense—he gave later on that turbulent legislative day (February 6, 1837), Adams turned to Patton and took up this subject again:

> **[Adams]:** The honorable gentleman makes it a crime because I presented a petition which he affirms to be from colored women, which women were of infamous character, as the honorable gentleman says—prostitutes, I think the gentleman said.

Patton begged to differ. He had not said they were prostitutes; the objection he made was that the petition came from free mulattoes.

> **[Patton]:** As to the infamous character of the women in question, he mentioned that, not as if he deemed it a reason for refusing the right to petition, but because he wished to wipe away the stain from the ladies of Fredericksburg, as these women had been called "ladies of Fredericksburg" by the honorable gentleman [Mr. Adams]. He (Mr. P.) was sure that no ladies from Fredericksburg had sent such a petition to this House.

So the immediate issue, as far as Patton and some of the other Southern gentlemen were concerned, seemed simply to be whether these petitioners should be identified by the word "ladies." After Adams had shrugged off that verbal matter, Thomas Glascock procured from the clerk's table the original of the petition, and triumphantly pointed out that it was endorsed, in Adams's own hand, "from nine *ladies* of Fredericksburg" (my emphasis—presumably Glascock's, too, as he was speaking).

Adams once again said he did not care about that: "woman" was as good a term as "lady" to him. He was concerned about other matters altogether. But Patton and Glascock and other Southerners *did* care about that; as on so many matters, there was a clash of cultures between republican New England and the chivalric plantation South. In the latter environment one did not use the word "lady" for a prostitute, or a woman who was "infamous"; and, by clear implication, one did not use it for a woman who was black or mulatto, whether "infamous" or not. One is reminded of the passage in James Baldwin's *The Fire Next Time* which evokes what it felt like, a full century later, to return as a black American soldier from fighting a war for democracy against the racial doctrines of Nazi Germany, to discover, among many other insults, still hanging on the doors of rest rooms in Southern railroad stations, confronting one's mother and sisters, signs distinguishing white *ladies* from colored *women*.

But Adams almost did not seem to fathom that point. He asked himself another question: whether either their color or their character deprived these people of the right of petition. His answer, more shocking even than his loose use of the word "ladies," was no.

And as for the Case of the Nine *Women* from Fredericksburg, he had another point to make that really did stir the juices of the House. What follows, first, is the *Congressional Globe* reporter's effort to capture this exchange.

> **[Adams]:** The gentleman from Virginia (Mr. Patton) says he knows these women, and that they are infamous. *How* does the gentleman know it? [A laugh.]
>
> **Mr. Patton:** I did not say that I knew the woman personally. I knew from others that the character of one of them was notoriously bad.
>
> **Mr. Adams:** I am glad the gentleman now says he does not know these women, for if he had not disclaimed that knowledge, I might have asked *who* it was that made these women infamous—whether it was those of their own color or their masters. I have understood that there are those among the coloured population of slave-holding States, who bear the image of their masters. [Great sensation.]

The reporter for the rival congressional record, the *Register of Debates*, devoted a few more lines to this last speech of Adams, rendering it all the more pointed:

> **Mr. Adams** continued. He was glad to hear the honorable gentleman [Patton] disclaim any knowledge of them [the Fredericksburg Nine]; for he had been going to ask, if they were infamous women, then who was it that had made them infamous? Not, he believed, their own color, but their masters; and he had heard it said, in proof of this fact, and he was inclined to believe it was the case, that there existed great resemblances in the South between the progeny of the colored people and the white men

who claimed the possession of them. Thus, perhaps, the charge of being infamous might be retorted upon those who made it, as originating from themselves. [Great Agitation in the House.]

But the Fredericksburg petition was not Adams's only contribution to great sensation and great agitation in the House on that day; he had already introduced another topic that tended even further in that direction.

19 / AN OUTRAGE THAT HAS NO PARALLEL IN PARLIAMENTARY HISTORY

IMMEDIATELY AFTER INTRODUCING THE Fredericksburg petition on February 6, 1837, Adams asked the Speaker—one imagines him doing it quietly, as though in all innocence—about another petition.

> **Mr. Adams** said he held in his hand a paper on which, before it was presented, he desired to have the decision of the Speaker. It was a petition from twenty-two persons, declaring themselves to be slaves. He wished to know whether the Speaker considered such a petition as coming within the order of the House. Now, he (Mr. A) wished to do nothing except in submission to the rules of the House. This paper purported to come from slaves, and it was one of those petitions which had occurred to his mind as not being what it purported to be. It was signed partly by persons who could not write, by making their marks, and partly by persons whose handwriting would manifest that they received the education of slaves; and the petition declared itself to be from slaves; and he was requested to present it. He would send it to the Chair.

The Speaker pronounced himself baffled by this "extraordinary" case; he could not remember there ever having been presented a petition from "persons not free." But before he could get the House to tell him what to do, various Southern members, with escalating passion, intervened. The record seethes with their mounting anger.

Joab Lawler, a tough guy from Alabama, insisted that it appear in the journal (to be read back home) that he objected to the paper's even being sent to the Chair. Mr. Haynes of Georgia found himself making a speech to say that he was speechless. The course pursued by the gentleman from Massachusetts on every petition day astonished him; but "his astonishment reached a height which he felt it impossible to express" when such a paper as this one was offered. Adams (calmly, one surmises) called the member to order for making personal remarks. Haynes, in response, avowed his respect for the rules of the House, but-but-but—"but he would not trust his feelings to pursue the subject further" and moved that the petition be *rejected*, if it was not withdrawn.

But that extreme method of previous battles—rejecting a petition at the threshold—was not strong enough in this case. Dixon Lewis, a four-hundred-pound Cooperite from the raw new cotton state of Alabama, got Haynes to withdraw his motion, and then suggested something that more nearly approached the slaveholders' outraged feelings: *punish* the perpetrator of this evil deed.

> **Mr. Lewis** . . . believed that the House should punish severely such an infraction of its decorum and its rules . . . if the House would inflict no punishment for such flagrant violations of its dignity as this, it would be better for the Representatives from the slaveholding States to go home at once.

That was the *Register*. The *Globe* has Lewis phrasing this last point as follows:

> **[Lewis]:** If this is not done, and that promptly, every member from the slave States should immediately, *in a body*, *quit this House*, and go home to their constituents. We have no longer any business here.

Punishing an ex-president of the United States, a venerable and distinguished statesman with years of the highest service, would be no small step; nevertheless, according to the *Globe*, the proposal to punish Adams met with an enthusiastic second from Mr. Grantland (of Georgia)—"I will second the motion for punishment, and go all lengths for it," which was followed by "Loud cries of 'he ought to be expelled,' " and "Cries of 'no!' 'no!' 'Expel him!' 'Expel the mover!' "

As to the unspeakable petition which had provoked these proposals to punish, or even expel, a former president of the United States, a congressman from Georgia, Julius Alford, had a striking proposal.

> **[Alford]:** said that . . . as an act of justice to the South . . . [the petition should] be taken from the House and burnt. The moment any man should disgrace the Government under which he lived, by presenting a petition

> from slaves praying for emancipation, he hoped the petition would, by order of the House, be committed to the flames.

That would have been quite a moment in the history of civil liberty—the ritual burning of a petition by the House of Representatives of the United States of America.

While these speeches were being made, and Congressman Patton was interrupting to defend the good name of the ladies of Fredericksburg, Waddy Thompson must have been scribbling at his desk, because he was soon ready with a motion to censure Adams for "gross disrespect for the House" on account of which he should be "instantly brought to the bar to receive the severe censure of the Speaker."

None of the Southern backbenchers who were calling out "Expel him! Expel him!" quite had the guts actually to offer a motion to that effect, but Thompson's proposal was the next-best thing—not merely to censure Adams (it was expected that any congressman subjected to censure would resign) but to bring the miscreant to the bar of the House for a reprimand from the Speaker. It was proposed that the old man (now sixty-nine) who had been the sixth president of the United States (and ambassador to England under the fourth president, and secretary of state under the fifth president, and who was the son of the second president) be escorted to the front of the House and be read his reprimand and censured, rapped over the knuckles and told how bad he was, by Speaker James K. Polk.

Passions did not altogether abate for a whole week—indeed, they were revived somewhat toward the end of it, and perhaps for some members they never did abate—but cooler heads proposed a revision that reduced Thompson's proposal to a censure by the House, without the feature of being brought to the bar for the Speaker's reprimand. This slightly softened version was greeted, according to the *Globe*, with cries of "No! No! Let him be brought to the Bar!"

While some tried to tone down the proposal, others found a way to strengthen it. Thompson, presumably from habit, had referred, according to the custom of congressional courtesy, to "the honorable" John Quincy Adams. Subsequent angrily amended versions of the motion for censure got that "honorable" out of there.

The most complete version of the censure proposal, before Adams launched into his response, was the following:

> *Resolved*, that J. Q. Adams, a member from the State of Massachusetts, by his attempt to introduce into this House a petition of slaves for the abolition of slavery in the District of Columbia, committed an outrage on the rights and feelings of a large portion of the people of this Union, a

flagrant contempt on the dignity of this House; and by extending to slaves a privilege only belonging to freemen, directly incites the slave population to insurrection; and that the said member be forthwith called to the bar of the House, and censured by the Speaker.

Adams let the course of events develop to the fullest before he finally rose to respond—addressing the motion of censure brought upon him for the outrage of asking a question about a petition from slaves. He submitted—one imagines him again doing it with exaggerated innocent helpfulness—that he had felt it his duty to remain silent while these high charges against him were pending, but now before they actually brought him to the bar he felt he should correct an erroneous statement or two in the resolution for his censure.

The resolution charged him with attempting to present a petition from slaves asking for the abolition of slavery in the District of Columbia. In the first place, he would remind the House that he had not attempted to present the petition; he had simply asked for a *ruling* by the Speaker about the status of such a petition under the Hawes resolution. In the second place—and here he dropped the bomb—the gentlemen ought not to jump to conclusions about the *content* of the petition:

[**Adams**]: As to the fact in relation to the prayer of the petition, he would simply state to the gentleman from Alabama, [Mr. Lewis,] who had assumed, and sent to the Clerk's table a resolution importing that the petition was for the abolition of slavery, that the gentleman was mistaken, because it was the very reverse of this.

In fact, Adams now divulged, the petitioners were on the same side as Mr. Lewis (and Mr. Thompson and Mr. Alford and Mr. Haynes and the others who wanted to expel him). The slaves had signed—or been induced to sign—a petition praying not for the abolition of slavery but for something in the opposite direction!

Great sensation again. Furious red-faced members protested strenuously against Adams now on a new count:

Resolved, That the member from Massachusetts, above named, by creating the impression, and leaving the House under such impression, that said petition was for the abolition of slavery when he knew it was not, has trifled with the House.

Indignant members refined, and added to, and subtracted from, the motion to censure Adams, with the added impetus that he had tricked them, played a "hoax" on them, "trifled" with the House. They went on amending, revising, and expanding each other's motions for four days, trying to chastise Adams for his multiple sins as thoroughly as possible. Although "trifling" with the House was a stimulating new charge, it was still most important to express how shocked they were by the idea that a petition from slaves could be presented to the House. To the most enraged fire-eaters the authenticity of the petition no longer mattered; what did matter was that the idea had flashed through the mind of the House, and of the country, that slaves might have the right to petition. One version of the resolution of censure condemned Adams for "giving color to the idea" that slaves had the right to petition, which wording led to a few puns and some mockery. The core group of Southerners were deadly serious, however, and said that they had to stick together on this one. Franklin Elmore (Hammond's successor from South Carolina) "trusted . . . that the South would present united action, and an undivided front, and suffer all minor differences of opinion to subside"; Francis Pickens (Calhoun's South Carolina cousin) "hoped and trusted that . . . the South . . . would present but one embodied, single, unbroken phalanx."

The South Carolina extremists could not usually bring all the representatives of the vast and variegated region of the South into line with their position, however much they might exert themselves, but in this case the Southern members did respond to the summons to the barricades in condemnation of what Adams had done, and certainly did hold forth on the issue of the right of slaves to petition. On the next day—Tuesday, February 7—there were six speakers from slaveholding states in a row before one (Cambreling of New York) from a free state got the floor, five more from slave states before another from a free state (Levi Lincoln of Massachusetts), and then four more from slave states before another from a free state (Cushing of Massachusetts). Pinckney having closed out the festivities on Monday, the ratio was sixteen speakers to three by adjournment time (at six o'clock) on Tuesday. The ratio was almost as high for the rest of the week. If you subtract highly placed New Yorkers (Cambreling, Mann, Granger, Vanderpoel) and Massachusetts members including Adams himself, the proportion of slave- to free-state members who spoke that week would be overwhelming—almost a shutout. And on the basic point there was no disagreement at all. Adams had done something "wanton" (Robertson of Virginia and Pickens of South Carolina); "wrong" (French of Maryland); "absurd and offensive" (Robertson again); "odious and indefensible" (Hopkins Horsley of Georgia); "unquestionably reprehensible" (Pinckney under one interpretation of what Adams had done) or "still more unjustifiable" (Pinckney under another interpretation); "disgraceful and unpardonable" (Claiborne of Mississippi). He had committed "an outrage upon the genius and spirit of the constitution, and aimed a deadly blow at the state I have the honor to represent" (Horsley). Later it was seen as a much worse outrage than that—"an outrage that has no parallel in parliamentary history" (Claiborne again). The passions of the hour drew out, in condemnation of Adams, the full spectrum of Southern oratory: "With a parricidal and sacrilegious hand he has attempted to sap the foundations of the temple reared by our ancestors as the abode of fraternal peace and the guarantee of international liberty. . . . The people whom I represent will deny it with the sword in one hand and the constitution in the other. . . . He has concentrated in his bureau all the combustible elements of the republic, and week after week presented them to this House, under circumstances so marked and aggravated, as to leave no room to mistake his intentions" (Horsley). Not only that—he enjoyed it. Adams was one who "rejoiced in the alarm and excitement he occasions, like the midnight incendiary who fires the dwelling of his enemy, and listens with pleasure to the screams of his burning victims" (Claiborne of Mississippi, who on Friday retired the cup in the Southern Regional Competition for the Fiercest Denunciation of Adams).

When Alford of Georgia, Monday's petition-burner, finally after some difficulty regained the floor on Tuesday, he gave this account of the scene, in his vicinity and from his point of view, when Adams had brought forward that shocking petition: "When the member from Massachusetts announced his course, I looked around me and saw, or thought I saw, but one sentiment, and that was of universal disgust. . . . "

Although it did seem that something like disgust was almost universal, the willingness to carry that feeling to the point of formal censure of Adams was not quite universal, even among slave-state congressmen. During the cavalcade of Southern speakers, one, Robertson of Virginia, had already notified the House, before Alford spoke, that he would not vote to censure Adams; and another, Graves of Kentucky, was soon to do so. Although these two yielded to no one, as legislators in every century always seem to say, in their disapproval of what Adams had done, nevertheless they could not vote to censure him without compromising the liberty of speech guaranteed to every member in the hall. Robertson called Adams's affirmation of the right of slaves to petition "preposterous" and his application of it "wanton"; nevertheless, despite Adams's abominable deeds, he would defend whatever idiocy any member might utter and would not join the Southern phalanx to censure Adams.

Graves of Kentucky said much the same thing. He was a slaveholder himself, and disapproved most heartily of the course the gentleman from Massachusetts was following, and contributed further adjectives to its reprobation; but he could not bring himself to vote to censure him for asking his question, as it seemed the House was at the point of doing, "almost by acclamation." He (Graves), even if he stood alone in doing it, would not so endanger liberty of speech in the House. (Waddy Thompson, who spoke more often than any other member during this turbulent week, when he got the floor again would turn his guns against Graves: Imagine! A slaveholder taking a position like that!)

Although their unbroken Southern phalanx was thus dented slightly when it came to the formal censure of Adams, there was no disagreement whatever, anywhere in the slave-state representation, that what he had done in this instance, and what he had been doing with these petitions since the Twenty-fourth Congress began, was deeply objectionable—so objectionable that words could scarcely express it.

Many Southern speakers, in the swaggering oratorical style of the time, and particularly of the region, would congratulate themselves for their willingness to stand absolutely alone if need be; in one of his flights, Waddy Thompson, who had in fact considerable support, would quote Shakespeare's Henry at Agincourt: "The fewer the men, the greater the share of glory." But Thompson was in much larger company than Graves was. And the member most nearly alone in the chamber that week was the cantankerous old man sitting there listening to them compete in condemning him, and collaborate in refining ways to show their intense disapproval of what he had done.

20 / THE UTTERMOST EDGE OF THE SHADOW OF INDIGNITY

While the Southerners were exercising their lungs in excoriations of Adams, what were the congressmen from the free states doing? Did none of them spring to Adams's defense? As suggested by the count of speakers in the last chapter, there was not much springing, and not much defending.

Of course, in order to defend Adams, you had to get the floor, and there is plenty of evidence in the speeches that this was not easy to do. Members would complain that they had been trying to get the floor for some time, or explain that their point applied to some matter swept by long ago in the oratorical flow, or apologize for taking time when so many wanted to speak. William Slade, we know from a letter he sent to the *National Intelligencer*, tried to get the floor toward the end of the week, if not earlier, but was never called upon. We may be sure that each time a congressman appeared to wind down on the floor, there would be a multitude calling out "Mr. Speaker! Mr. Speaker!" and Polk would then have the opportunity and the necessity to choose whom to recognize.

The Northerners whom he did recognize were for the most part established figures in the House. The state which was about to furnish the nation its first New Yorker in the President's House was called on more often than any other free state; Abijah Mann early in the week, and Aaron Vanderpoel late in the week, both Van Buren men, provided two doughy slices of Northern caution to contain the hot Southern barbecue in between. Two other congressmen from New York, Churchill Cambreleng and Francis Granger—both "distinguished" House leaders, a leading Democrat and a leading Whig, respectively—made what one may guess both they and their supporters would regard as "statesmanlike" interventions, a word which once again requires quotation marks.

The flavor of the Northern support for Adams, as we may very loosely call it, can be conveyed by quotations from Abijah Mann, the first free-state member, after the Southern outburst and proposals of censure from Lewis and Thompson, to obtain the floor. Mann was a defender of Adams only in this extremely limited sense: he said he would not vote to censure him. Alford of Georgia was later to deplore what Mann had said, because his speech was the first indication that the "universal disgust" with Adams would not lead, as Alford had expected, to a virtually unanimous vote to censure him—to his censure, as Graves of Kentucky would put it, "almost by acclamation." So Abijah Mann of New York did break the spell of disapproval, somewhat. Alford asked: What else could you expect, from a state so far gone in wickedness as to allow free Negroes to vote?

But Mann's defense of Adams, if you can call it that, was hardly one to warm Adams's heart; it was more offensive to him, one might guess, than tons of Southern vituperation. Mann said that the House should excuse the "deplorable spectacle" Adams presented on every petition day on account of his age: "It would be unjust to believe that, in the prime and vigor of manhood, the honorable member would have adopted the course of action which, at this late period of his life, seems to control him. The high noontide of that life has long since passed with him, and its wane is no doubt upon him, before he is either aware or sensible of it." (Adams was sitting there—he was very regular in attendance—listening to this.) Mann, "with the aid of a liberal charity," found both the cause and the apology for Adams's conduct in that he was "far advanced in the autumn of his career." And so, disapproving though he was, Mann nevertheless could not support, as it stood, the resolution to censure Adams.

One may safely guess that the Van Buren crowd, about to take over the executive office and counting on Northern as well as Southern support, did not want to be caught in the position of providing votes for so extreme an action as the formal censure of the distinguished ex-president of the United States. But at the same time, they wanted very badly to set themselves at a great distance from what he was doing, and from anything else that smacked of abolitionism. Hence this spectacularly backhanded defense of Adams against censure.

The Van Buren Democrats would want more explicitly to reassure the Southerners, whose support they needed, that they were untainted by the heresies of Adams and the abolitionists. Of course, in a sense, it had nothing to do with the matter on the floor—whether or not to censure Adams—but Mann went out of his way to repeat the pledge to the Southern members (what they wanted to hear, and hear again, from Northern members, and especially from representatives of the administration that would in a month assume power) that they would adhere to the original compact, and not interfere in the "domestic institutions" of other states. The Southern members should "give themselves no uneasiness" on account of "these ill-advised proceedings." We Northerners will keep our side of the constitutional agreement.

As to the petition that had provoked all this: Mann said that he had already known, before the honorable gentleman revealed it, the prayer of the petition, and he had already suspected that it was a hoax. (Cambreleng later said he had known and suspected these things as well; how had these well-placed New Yorkers known and why had they suspected these things?) It appeared that "some mischievous persons" had trifled with the honorable gentleman and "he, in turn, seeks to trifle with the House and country, by treating with seriousness that which was probably, in its origin, levity." In a later speech the anonymous originator of the offending petition was called a "wag." After the revelation that the petition had been intended as a kind of a joke on Adams, Waddy Thompson would protest: No, no, we cannot regard this as mere levity. "Is it a light thing, for the amusement of others, to irritate, almost to madness, the whole delegation from the slave states?" Regardless of the content, and regardless of the origin, of the petition, Thompson wanted Adams censured.

Churchill Cambreleng, after an intervening dose of Southern vitriol, reinforced the Democrats' position. He was an experienced Jacksonian from New York City and chairman of the Committee on Ways and Means, then as now one of the House's most important committees; Churchill Cambreleng would not have any trouble getting the floor when he wanted it. In the first onslaught of Southern fury he had explained in a calming, above-the-battle, avoid-both-extremes manner that the republic would survive, and that though he had at first been inclined to vote to censure Adams, he had changed his mind when he learned from conversation around his desk that the petition was a hoax, coming from "a slaveholding quarter," designed to insult Adams himself for presenting so many abolition petitions. The scheme had been, said the knowledgeable Cambreleng, to make Adams appear ridiculous by presenting a petition from slaves asking for his own expulsion! (So that was what the phony petition prayed for! Adams had not exactly said that it was in favor of slavery—just that it was not in favor of abolition, but in the other direction.)

So now Cambreleng could not attach to this topic the same solemnity as did the gentlemen from South Carolina. That was one reason he could not endorse the motion for censure: it was "too trifling" a matter on which to bring an ex-president of the United States to the bar. The other reason was that Adams had said from the start that he did not endorse the prayers of the antislavery petitions; by this avowal of his "hostility" to abolition in the District, said Cambreleng, Adams made some "atonement" for the "disorder he had occasioned from week to week in presenting these petitions." (Adams himself did not think he needed to make any "atonement" for presenting the petitions, and would not have described his position as "hostile" to abolition in the District, although he was for his own reasons, and for the time being, opposed to bringing the issue to the floor.) Such was the Northern Democratic establishment's defense of Adams against censure.

And what did the Whig establishment say—Adams's own party, insofar as he had one? Francis Granger, the other New Yorker to be called on fairly early, a leading Whig, twice the nominee for governor and in the complicated election just past for vice-president, was a tad closer to the petitioners than the Democrats Cambreleng or Vanderpoel or Mann or Ward would be. Later Granger would cautiously introduce petitions that were friendly to the antislavery cause, and still later in life he would hold high office under the Whigs. Adams was his friend, at least in the way that friendship is rather loosely defined in legislative bodies. But on this occasion Granger had to speak, more in sorrow than in anger, full of regret, in opposition to the course his good friend from Massachusetts had taken. It was the first time they had disagreed. He was afraid that Adams had cheapened the right of petition, to which they were both categorically committed in their opposition to the gag rule, by using it indiscriminately and irresponsibly—by failing to remedy his ignorance of the names, condition, and character of the supplicants. With Adams as its custodian, the right of petition was rendered "a mere bauble, to be played with." But, Granger conceded, Adams should not be censured until his intentions and the Chair's opinion were known more fully.

There were in those four days of much speechmaking only two Northern members who supported Adams on the floor (one could hardly count Congressman Mann, who excused him on the basis of his decrepitude, as supportive). Both of these speeches were made by colleagues of Adams from Massachusetts: Levi Lincoln and Caleb Cushing. Levi Lincoln was a politician of some distinction, a former governor of Massachusetts, a relative of other Massachusetts Lincolns active in politics. Years later, in 1856, when a Lincoln out of Illinois received about one hundred votes for the vice-presidential nomination of the brand-new Republican Party, he modestly and humorously remarked that there was a famous politician named Lincoln in Massachusetts, and the delegates must have thought they were voting for that man. Eight years after that, the Lincoln out of Massachusetts would serve as a Republican elector and cast his vote for the reelection to the presidency of the now much better-known Lincoln out of Illinois.

Back in the House, in 1837, Levi Lincoln spoke boldly about his Massachusetts colleague, both on the issue and as a person:

> **[Levi Lincoln]:** Mr. Speaker, it has fallen to the lot of my venerable colleague to have been charged with more of these petitions than all of his associates in the delegation together. His age, his character, the stations he has held, and his standing before the world, have brought upon him responsibilities which others might not have borne. The people have thrown upon the shoulders of Ajax the weight which no common man could have sustained. They trusted his talents, his learning, and his great experience, to secure to him the deference of respect due to these qualifications in the duties he was called upon to discharge.

He made his support for Adams into a dramatic personal testimony:

> **[Lincoln]:** . . . whether I stand alone or whether I am supported, I can never consent that my venerable colleague shall be brought to your bar, to be censured for a conscientious discharge of duty. What he has done he has manfully, rightfully, nobly done, in defense of the inestimable right of petition and the freedom of speech in this House.

But the larger part of Lincoln's speech dealt not with the right of slaves to petition, or the worthiness of Adams in insisting on that issue, but rather with the much broader matter of the petitioners in general, and with the benign influence, in general, of Massachusetts and of New England.

THE OTHER MAN TO speak up for Adams on the House floor in early February of 1837 was a man whom we have already met, of whom we should now take particular notice. He will play a curious role not only in this story but in the events leading up to the Civil War and beyond.

This is Caleb Cushing, the second-term representative from Newburyport who had started the week's fireworks with a petition from 3,824 ladies in assorted towns in his home state of Massachusetts, and many more from ladies in New Hampshire towns, and who had in his first appearance in the House, in the previous session, stunned the members with his learning and oratorical powers when he gave them a lecture on the history of the right of petition, and again in the early-morning hours had given a thorough criticism, supporting Adams, of the slavery-perpetuating provision in the Arkansas constitution.

Cushing was thirty-six years old at the time of these events, in the early stages of what would be if not a great career at least a fascinating one. He was one of the Newburyport Three, as we may call them for the purposes of this story, the other two being William Lloyd Garrison and John Greenleaf Whittier, both of whom he knew. He was very proud of his descent, as he put it in the House during this debate, "from the king-killing Roundheads of the reign of Charles the First"—in other words, from the heritage of the great English Puritan struggle for liberty out of which the United States was born. He was a Puritan by heritage, although like some other Puritans he had pretty thoroughly turned into a Yankee.

He was, like Adams, a learned man—another Harvard man, and had in fact entered Harvard at thirteen. He had received a Harvard law degree and had taught mathematics at the college for a year; it was said that he could have gone on to a brilliant teaching career. He wrote learned articles, gave public addresses, traveled widely in Europe. He mastered, we are told, at least four modern languages. He was to become a master of international law. With his erudition he was a very unusual item in the politics of the raw democracy of the Jackson era. If as a European observer, say, you had been told in the 1830s that the greatest leader of American public life in the nineteenth century would prove to be, not the distinguished old man Adams, nor the distinguished young man Cushing, but an obscure self-taught lawyer out in the rough settlements of Illinois, whose formal schooling amounted to about a year, who knew no modern languages except English and who could not be counted on to spell words correctly in that language, who had no ancestral lines in any direction, and certainly no fortune ("the short and simple annals of the poor" about covers it, he would say), you would not have believed it.

The well-connected Cushing had come into politics as a supporter, against Andrew Jackson, of John Quincy Adams: one Massachusetts egghead endorsing another. That was in 1824, when Adams was—eventually—chosen president in the unique and controversial election that we have described.

In 1826, while Adams was serving as president, Cushing ran for Congress, but lost. He persisted, however. He wanted a public career, not simply a legal or academic one, and with the help of the Quaker poet John Greenleaf Whittier, who brought abolitionist votes to his support, he did take his seat in this Twenty-fourth Congress. He thus had first arrived in Congress just in time to hear Fairfield present his petition, and Hammond his motion—just as the legislative battles described in these pages began.

In the midst of that excitement, as we have seen, Cushing had himself presented abolitionist petitions, first along with other Massachusetts congressmen on January 18, 1836, and then on his own on January 25, when he traced the right of petition back to the Magna Carta, insisting that the House was *bound* by the Constitution to receive petitions. So Cushing did support civil liberty; he knew its history, and all its arguments, and he could bring a powerful mind and elegant training to its defense. He also knew he was supposed to disapprove of slavery. Many in his Massachusetts district told him that; Whittier certainly did. And Cushing did disapprove of slavery—up to a point.

But there was some chemistry in Cushing working in another direction. He was no Quaker, and although he had all that old Puritan blood, he had newer Yankee blood, too. He was the well-fixed heir to a shipping fortune in the bustling port city of Newburyport, a wealthy lawyer tied in with New England shipping interests. Maritime law was one of his specialties. He was by temperament as well as inheritance a supporter of the existing order. So we may infer that there was taking place at this time a certain contest for Cushing's soul, symbolic perhaps of what was happening in one strand of Northern opinion. Caleb Cushing will turn up later in some spots in American history that will surprise you.

Now he had come on his second trip to Washington for a congressional session—the second, lame duck session, of the Twenty-fourth Congress. Since his first trip he had had to face the voters for reelection, in the elections of 1836; he had won again, and Whittier had supported him again, and brought along the Essex County Anti-Slavery Society—and promised to plague him with petitions. Perhaps that gave Cushing a little extra incentive to do what he had done to start this week—to offer all those petitions from the feminine element in his district and in New Hampshire. Now, a few days later, he had to deal not only with the recurring issue of the petitions but also with the quite extraordinary actions of his venerable colleague from Massachusetts.

AMONG CUSHING'S OTHER DISTINCTIONS was audibility. The acoustics in the old House chamber were not good (Charles Dickens wrote that it was "an elegant chamber to look at, but a singularly bad one for all purposes of hearing"), and many members had trouble on that score—but not when Cushing was speaking. He had a strong voice and was an accomplished orator, combining old-fashioned orotund purple rhetoric in presentation with an astonishing range of knowledge. It was sometimes lamented—by Adams in his diary, among others—that the slaveholding side commanded all the orators; but Cushing was an exception. Now imagine Cushing booming out this personal pledge, in defense of his venerable friend:

> **[Cushing]:** [T]o no resolution of censure, based on the matters now before us, to no rebuke, express or implied, to no action of the House that shall touch that individual [Mr. Adams] with so much as the uttermost edge of the shadow of indignity, will I give my assent. If, in the present contingency, any thing had transpired of itself tending to justify the resolution of censure, I could not fail to remember that he, who is the object of it, has presided over the destinies of my country; that he is at this moment a representative, in common with myself, of the State of Massachusetts; that eminent as he is by reason of his long public services, and the exalted stations he has held, he is yet more eminent for his intellectual superiority; that his character no longer belongs to his State or his country, but to the history of civilizations and of liberty, and I would have members ponder well the case, before they proceed, whether to gratify friends or appease foes, to record their votes in censure of such a man.

He would not vote for any motion that would touch Adams with "the uttermost edge of the shadow of indignity"! Adams belonged "not just to his State or his country but to the history of civilizations and of liberty"! That would certainly seem to be handsome enough. But if you read the passage carefully you will note that one reason Adams is not to be censured is that he comes from the same state as Cushing himself. You will also notice an "if" at the beginning of a sentence that suggests that Cushing's superlative praise is intended not for what Adams may have done in the present instance, but for Adams in general—perhaps even *in spite of* what he is now doing. And that was almost all Cushing had to say directly about Adams.

He went on to develop his theory of the right of petition, to which we will refer in a later chapter, comparing it to Adams's. And then he spent a great deal of his time defending not Adams but the *North*, and especially New England, and especially Massachusetts. Defending the abstract—very abstract—right of petition called upon his lawyer's learning, and he gave a lecture on the subject. Defending his venerable colleague Adams was his duty, and he did it briefly, in boilerplate superlatives of the highest order (with a little "if" slipped in to protect him in the present case). But defending New England! Defending Massachusetts! That he did with his heart's blood.

The provocation came from the irrepressible Waddy Thompson in a speech on the second exciting day, Tuesday, February 7, of the fracas over petitions from slaves. He had spoken in response in particular to Levi Lincoln, who in the course of his mild defense of Adams had defended the right of the people of the North (i.e., the petitioners), however misguided, to "sympathize with human suffering—with the oppressed—with those improperly held in bondage."

> **[Thompson]:** Now, sir, what does all this mean, when translated? It means this: that we of the South are oppressors; holding men in bondage so cruel and unlawful as to enlist the sympathies of the generous, the warm-hearted people of the North—sympathies of which we must be destitute, or we would cease from such wickedness. Now, sir, gentlemen must expect these charges to be repelled.

And Thompson had set about to repel them. He repelled them in small part by a short restatement of the new and extreme slave-state doctrine—just becoming current in the mid-1830s—that slavery was no evil at all but a positive good: "I regard African slavery, in all its bearings, as a blessing." So Thompson said. It is a blessing to the slave himself (" . . . nowhere on the earth, in his native land or any other, is the African so elevated in the scale of being . . . "), but much more: "I am satisfied that in no country where domestic slavery does not exist has the character of man ever been, or ever will be, found in its highest development. I believe [the Orwellian note again] it essential to the maintenance of liberty."

But not content with that, Thompson next launched a full counter-attack against the alleged "goodness" of the North, citing the banishings, whippings, ear-croppings, imprisonments, hangings, and perhaps even the boring of tongues with a hot iron, mostly against Quakers and Anabaptists, that had once taken place in Massachusetts, thus to challenge New England's reputation for philanthropy and for devotion to the freedom of opinion and of speech. That, and sympathies with the Indian and the African, Thompson said, were the "three great topics of New England cant":

> **[Thompson]:** When the gentleman (Mr. Lincoln) speaks of the sympathies of the North for human suffering, for the oppressed and those held in unlawful bondage, I cannot forbear to congratulate him upon the return of those feelings—for it was not always so . . . even now it seems to be a most modified benevolence, a most restricted philanthropy, which demands, as indispensable, that their objects should have a red or a black skin; for their own color and race, their hearts are as cold as they ever were. . . .

The coldness of New England hearts was, along with New England money-grubbing and avarice, a particular charge of Southern orators when sufficiently annoyed. Such philanthropy as these cold and avaricious Northerners may seem to exhibit is recent indeed.

> **[Thompson]:** [A]s long as the slave trade was profitable and tolerated, it had no horrors in their sight. . . . they had no sympathies with the poor Indians until they had literally exterminated all the tribes by whom their fathers, flying from another land, were kindly and hospitably received. . . . Now, when they are no longer incommoded by the vicinity of the savage, their sympathies are not with their brethren, circumstanced as their fathers were. Their philanthropy and their selfish interests are never opposed. . . . I like not your courtesan turned prude, after ability to be vicious has ceased. . . .

All of this was too much for New England's champion. He pointedly described the proper New England way (in implicit contrast to that of other regions) to deal with such matters:

> **[Cushing]:** Bred in the perpetual inculcation of habits of order and self-control, we are accustomed to think that, in questions like the present, involving the first principles of civil liberty and the dearest rights of mankind, passionate invective, rash menace, and random exclamation, are poor substitutes for reason and argument.

He did not say, but one could certainly guess, whom he was implicitly accusing of "passionate invective, rash menace, and random exclamation."

> **[Cushing]:** [I]n the stormy progress of this question a multitude of strange things have been thrown upon the troubled surface of controversy, and made to assume the form of menace, defiance, and crimination, towards the people of the North. Observations have fallen from the lips of one gentleman, especially, reflecting somewhat gratuitously on the character of New England in such terms that . . . I should feel I was a recreant craven . . . if I failed to counter them with the prompt, honest indignation they deserve.

No recreant craven, Cushing countered them at length. Thompson had attacked New England's treatment of the Indians; he responded:

> **[Cushing]:** . . . the gentleman undertakes to show that "the blackest and bloodiest pages in the history of this country, or of man, are to be found in the treatment of the aborigines by New England." Ay, indeed? All that is most atrocious in the history of man, outblackened by the bloody annals of those quiet little colonies of New England? Upon what facts is this monstrous accusation based?

Thompson's research—his swift thumbing of the history books—had been a little faulty, as Cushing was willing scornfully to point out.

> **[Cushing]:** The gentleman has given us an original idea on the history of those old times. Philip of Mount Hope exhibited, like a caged tiger, a spectacle for gaping multitudes? Never! Philip's forces were shattered in battle; he himself was hunted to his lair by Captain Benjamin Church, and brought to bay there, and shot to the heart by a private soldier under that brave man's command. Events as familiar in the mouth of every child in New England as household words.
>
> Mr. **Thompson** rose and said: It was not Philip, then, but some other chief.
>
> Name him! **(said Mr. C.)** Sir, the gentleman is silent. . . .

See! He does not know! He does not know facts that are household words to every New England child! Thompson had got that one wrong.

Cushing went on to answer him on the weightier issue that lay behind this display of mutual regional aggression: which region was the true home of American Liberty?

> **[Cushing]:** [T]he gentleman from South Carolina proceeds to demand, in a tone of triumph, "where, when the liberties and honour of this country

have been assailed by enemies, foreign or domestic, have they flown for refuge?"—alluding, if I understood his language aright, to the conduct of the North and of the South, respectively, in the last war [the War of 1812, which major leaders in New England opposed].

Mr. Thompson rose and said: Yes, and to the alien and sedition laws.

The gentleman tells me (**continued Mr. C.**) that he does refer to the conduct of New England in that war, and also to the alien and sedition laws. As to the latter, they were the acts of the Congress of the United States, not of the States of New England.

That was not a strong answer. The Alien and Sedition Acts, enacted in 1798 during the excitements of the spillover of the French Revolution into American politics, had been, as we have already said and as the reader knows, the first great test of the nation's commitment to the civil liberties that the Bill of Rights had guaranteed. These laws had been enacted indeed by Congress, but they had been supported most strongly by New England Federalists. Jefferson and Madison had led the opposition, drafting resolutions opposing them that were passed by the legislatures of the states of Virginia and Kentucky. Of course, this invidious regional distribution of credit and blame omits much and distorts much, but Waddy Thompson could claim, in a debater's way, that it had been the *South* (Virginia, Kentucky, Jefferson, Madison) that had defended the liberty that the North—New England—was willing to assail.

Cushing, however, had another argument, of a kind that human beings almost always have, in disputes ranging from the playground to the clash of nations: You're Another. *Tu Quoque*. So's your old man. You did it, too.

[Cushing]: And are they [the Alien and Sedition Acts] not precisely the things which South Carolina herself, in common with other States of the South, has recently called on the States of the North to do? That is, to extend the law of seditious libel, and to punish aliens who intermeddle with our domestic institutions?

Spokesmen for slaveholding states—in this House as well as elsewhere—had called on the North to enact laws against another Thompson, very different from Waddy, the notorious Thompson, the miscreant Thompson—the English abolitionist George Thompson, who, as we have noted, toured the states in 1833—and other English abolitionists. They had also called upon the North, in the first summer's shock at the "incendiary" pamphlets, to pass laws to suppress this material. That had been a common theme in Southern speeches on the House floor. You Northerners want to know what you can do to help us? Please pass laws to stop this outpouring at its source! Were they not calling for exactly what Waddy Thompson deprecates in the Alien and Sedition Acts? Those laws had allowed "Jacobins" to be expelled, for their ideas; the slaveholders now asked that abolitionists be expelled, for their ideas. Those laws had allowed suppression of papers for infidel subversive ideas; these appeals wanted suppression of papers for "incendiary" ideas.

As to the issue of the conduct of New England in the War of 1812 (the "late war")—threatening disunion: Cushing did not have much trouble, just four years after the performance of Thompson's home state in the Nullification Crisis, pointedly countering that one in the same debater's way:

> **[Cushing]:** Does the gentleman from South Carolina know of no other state which has ever placed herself in like wrongful position?

Thompson's attack on New England that had the nearest bearing on the current question, next after the discussion of civil liberty, was this charge:

> **[Thompson]:** Are the gentlemen ignorant that mainly on New England rests the responsibility of the great importation of slaves to this country? That the colonial legislature of Virginia passed twenty-two acts against it? And that it was through the power and influence of the New England colonies that the trade was not stopped? It was a business in which they could turn a penny, and their humanity slept. . . .

Those efforts by colonial Virginia to end the slave trade, and the unwillingness of the English authorities to allow it, figured in the polemics of other Southerners, too, notably Thomas Jefferson, notably in the excised part of the Declaration of Independence, but elsewhere, too—in his Summary View two years before the great Declaration. It was to say, it is the fault of the British that the slave trade continued; Jefferson even said it was the British that fastened the institution of slavery upon us. Now here decades later another Southern slaveholder referred again to those efforts by colonial Virginia to end the slave trade, and blamed New England's influence with the imperial government for preventing it.

But there is this difference in the moral setting of the argument: Jefferson throughout his life held slavery to be an evil—a great evil. But now Waddy Thompson, like Hammond and Pickens and Calhoun, and a growing number of Southern apologists, was saying that it was not an evil but a great good—a blessing, making a better life for the African, furnishing the base for the highest development of humankind, supporting Liberty. So why was anyone to be blamed? The slave traders should be thanked, for bringing to the South, to the slave, and to the world so great a benefit.

Cushing did not turn that point against Thompson, and he did not get a chance to state on the floor any substantial response to his charges about New England's role in the slave trade, because the members were becoming restive at this digression into reciprocal regional defensiveness and aggression. But he did have brief notes for a response that he was able to give to the *Register*. Expanding a little on the brief paragraph in that note, we may discern that he would have given the kind of fallback defense about which there is a standard joke, particularly in law schools (my client was nowhere near the murder scene; the victim was already dead when my client got there; the victim struck the first blow so that my client struck in self-defense; my client had to strike him first in order to prevent his blow). Thus it seems that Cushing was planning to have said: (1) Nobody in Massachusetts ever traded in slaves, (2) Those in Massachusetts who carried on the trade did so "in defiance of the good opinion of their countrymen," (3) Slave trading in Massachusetts stopped with the first line of the state's constitution, (4) At least the new state of Massachusetts never furnished a *market* for the slaves its traders brought over.

But Cushing did not have the opportunity to say those things, because members, eager to speak, had interrupted to ask what all this had to do with the question before the House (on the censure of Adams for presenting a petition from slaves).

Cushing answered, in effect—*he* started it. "Who introduced these foreign matters into the debate?" Thompson did, said Cushing. Lincoln did, said Thompson. Thompson did, in his first speech on Monday, Lincoln might have said. Adams did, Thompson might have responded.

But Adams didn't. What Adams, who took no part in this exercise in regional attack and counterattack, had started was something bigger—started with ammunition supplied inadvertently by the opposition. The House got these two strutting regional champions stopped—Thompson only for the moment—and went back to its curious business, disposing at last of the attempts to censure Adams.

21 / HE MISTOOK HIS MAN

SO ADAMS'S DEFENSE FELL mostly to himself—the defense, that is, not of his region, or of his own large role in American history, but of his action in this particular instance. He had indicated, as the great waves of molten rhetoric rolled over him, that he would like a chance to defend himself before a vote was taken, and at last, after four days of speechmaking by others, he obtained the floor to respond to their attack.

He had spoken briefly a couple of times in the early going, and some of the things he had said then could have been taken, by those who did not want to vote to censure him, as reassurances or even concessions. For one thing, he insisted that he had meant no disrespect to the House. On the contrary: he had asked his question about the status of this petition under the Hawes resolution out of deep respect for the House. His record as an utterly conscientious member made that claim convincing in general, if not absolutely in the present case. He twisted the knife a little by insinuating that it was exactly the existence of that gag rule that had required him to ask his question; he had needed to know whether this paper fell under it.

He had also said that he now believed the paper to be "a forgery by a slaveholding master, for the purpose of daring him to present a petition purporting to be from slaves," and so, because it was not genuine, whatever happened to the current motions for censure, he would not try to present it. It was therefore hinted in one of the motions that he had apologized, or changed his position, but Adams scotched that notion: he had not apologized; he had nothing to apologize for; and, as for ideas, he withdrew nothing.

Nevertheless, the words of Adams and his few defenders, and perhaps the setting of some suns and the coming of some second thoughts, were persuasive enough to shift the formal indignation slightly; some proposals thereafter were impersonal, directed not specifically at Adams by name but to *anyone* who would presume to offer petitions from slaves.

At the end of the session on Thursday (February 9, 1837) of this noteworthy and revealing week, during the second round of censure proposals, Adams finally did defend himself. He summarized, not without a certain amount of sarcasm, the efforts to find the right language with which to censure him. He dealt painstakingly with his theory of the right of petition, of which he had an exalted notion. He made the right of petition a symbol of the most fundamental of all human rights.

But he also made arguments that struck directly not only at the clearest principles but also at the self-interest of the members of this (or any other) parliamentary body: next time it might be your speech, your petition, your conscience.

When Waddy Thompson first proposed censure, in his shock and fury he had likened Adams's outrageous act to the inciting of a slave rebellion:

> **[Thompson]:** Does the gentleman know that there are laws in all the slave states and here, for the punishment of those who incite insurrection?

Thompson then made further pointed reference—and this is the moment at which one might have heard a sharp intake of breath—to the grand juries of the District of Columbia before which incendiaries might be tried:

> **[Thompson]:** I can tell him [Adams] that there are such things as grand juries, and if, sir, the juries of this District have, as I doubt not they have, proper intelligence and spirit, he may yet be made amenable to another tribunal, and we may yet see an incendiary brought to condign punishment.

Adams had not missed the implication of that remark. In the midst of a later rhetorical flight of Thompson's he had interrupted to quote him on the point and ask him whether he stood by what he said. Thompson did not deny it—affirmed in fact that if the petition had been as he first thought, he would stand by his position.

So there it was on the record—twice! Adams, in his long speech of rejoinder, had that exchange read, to bring the point home to the members of Congress:

> **[Adams]:** There, sir, stands the sentiment; there is the written record, in which the gentleman has threatened me with an indictment before the grand jury of the District of Columbia as a felon and an incendiary, for words spoken in this House! And now the gentleman has again avowed the sentiment, and declares that, if the petition had been such as he imagined, he would still not only call me to the bar of this House to be reprimanded by the Speaker, but, in addition to this, he would invoke the vengeance of a grand jury upon my head! Yes, sir, he would make a member of this House amenable to a grand jury! . . . I would beg to invite that

gentleman, when he goes home, to study a little the first principles of civil liberty. . . .

The first principles of civil liberty included near the top the freedom of debate in the people's legislature. That principle went back to the beginning, and straight to the core, of republican government. Citizens of the American republic may already then, and certainly have now, grown away from the memory, but the principle of free speech was derived in the first place from the principle of free debate in governing assemblies.

Thompson had cited the slave code of his home state as the standard by which to judge these matters. Adams was not reluctant to turn "the first principles of civil liberty" sharply against any such appeal as that:

> **[Adams]:** If the law of South Carolina is a good argument to the gentleman from South Carolina, and if a member of that Legislature is made amenable for words spoken in debate, not only to the Legislature, but also to the grand and petit juries—if that, sir, is the law of South Carolina, I thank God I am not a citizen of South Carolina! (Great agitation.)

Adams was willing to provide Thompson, and such other members as might need it, with the lesson:

> **[Adams]:** In the kingdom of Great Britain . . . the first thing the Speaker addresses to the King, after his election, is a demand of freedom of speech in the House; and the King never sends him, sir, to the grand or petit jury, to know how far the House is under liability for words spoken in debate. . . .

Such a threat as Thompson held out to a fellow representative, when published to the world, "cannot fail to excite contempt and amazement." Indeed, why did not the Speaker rebuke such an utterance? What *really* deserved censure?

> **[Adams]:** If, sir, a resolution of censure was ever called for, I know not what could more imperatively demand it than such a declaration made in this House. I know not what it could be possible to utter more proper to subject any member to be called to answer for as a gross contempt upon this House!

Adams elucidated Thompson's threat for the benefit of his colleagues from the North:

> **[Adams]:** What, sir! We, the representatives of the nation, are all of us subject to the grand jury of the District of Columbia for words here spoken? We from the Northern and Eastern States are liable, sir, to be indicted as felons and incendiaries for presenting petitions not exactly agreeable to some members from the South? Is that the tenure on which we hold our seats?

But then he swung it around to Thompson himself, and to every member, wherever he might hail from:

> **[Adams]:** How long will it be before the gentleman from South Carolina himself (Mr. Waddy Thompson) will have to answer before a grand and petit jury of the District, as an incendiary for words spoken here against the Executive? . . . Let that gentleman, let every member of this House, ask his own heart with what confidence, with what boldness, with what freedom, with what firmness, he would give utterance to his opinions on this floor, if, for every word, for a mere question asked of the Speaker, involving a question belonging to human freedom, to the rights of man, he was liable to be tried as a felon or an incendiary, and sent to the penitentiary!

Thompson's ideological companion Henry Wise, who was also an opponent of the Democrats and their leader "King Andrew" and derisive of "executive tyranny," had had wits enough to anticipate one of the responses that Adams would make to Thompson—that these grand juries before which congressmen might be brought were under the control of the executive branch. Wise interrupted Adams to dissociate himself from Thompson on that one point. But Adams now pressed it to Thompson, and to any member who had missed it before. Maybe not everyone in the House could grasp the first principles of civil liberty, but every congressman could understand the threat posed to himself by a rival branch. Certainly every Whig should be able to do so, because a sense of the danger of Jackson's executive legacy had been the primary occasion for that party's birth.

> **[Adams]:** And this jury, selected by an officer of the President, are to be the supreme judges of the sovereign American people, in the person of their representatives! Such is the avowed doctrine of the gentleman from South Carolina—such are his notions of freedom of speech and of civil liberty!

As we have already noted, there was in this loquacious House of the People a great deal of strutting and posturing, of striking dramatic poses about standing firm and alone though every other member should desert. In February of 1837, John Quincy Adams could say that sort of thing with more reason than was usually the case. He had been flailed at and attacked for four days of long speeches. The House was trying to censure him, and he was very nearly alone, among the vocal members, on the fundamental issue. He certainly was not going to be deterred by reference to the repressive laws of the slaveholding states.

> **[Adams]:** Did the gentleman think he could frighten me from my purpose by the threat of a Grand Jury? If that was his object, let me tell him *he mistook his man*. I am not to be frightened from the discharge of a duty by the indignation of the gentleman from South Carolina, nor by all the Grand Juries in the universe.

Reading these speeches, one must remember that they were not private or obscure. They were disseminated throughout the land by the newly efficient press (yes, sir, powered by steam!), and they were the material for public debate at a time when there were fewer distractions than later ages would provide, and perhaps a more innocent, uncynical appreciation of the role of Congress. The citizens of the republic would read about, and maybe even read, these speeches.

> **[Adams]:** The right by which the national representative holds his seat here, is of vital importance; and that it may be understood, I hope that this debate will go forth and be read by the whole people, and that, among other remarkable things, they will *mark* this *threat* of the gentleman from South Carolina.

Adams pointed out that this was a threat to bring punishment outside the House for debate inside the House—against all the traditions of parliamentary freedom. He turned the recurrent Southern celebration of unalloyed Anglo-Saxon blood and heritage against Southern failure to understand Anglo-Saxon *institutions*:

> **[Adams]:** Sir, we have heard much of the great superiority of Anglo-Saxon blood. Is there a man living, with a drop of that blood in his veins, who will subscribe to this doctrine of the member from South Carolina? Are these the principles of freedom by which to regulate the deliberations of a Legislative Assembly? I ask any member of this House what he thinks would be the issue, if a member of the British House of Commons should rise in his place, and tell another member that for words spoken there he should be held amenable to a Grand Jury of Westminster? Sir, it would be

considered too ridiculous for indignation; it would be received with one universal shout of laughter. . . .

Waddy Thompson tried to defend himself by saying that he had meant that if a member should introduce a petition from slaves, that would indicate that he had had contact with slaves *before* and *outside* a meeting of the legislative body, and that the congressman would therefore be liable for *that* crime—dealing with slaves, which would have taken place outside the House, not for what he said or did inside it. Thompson was not the only one to notice that there were in the slave states laws against such behavior.

In one of his interventions, Francis Pickens said that Adams's "wanton" attempt to introduce the paper from slaves indicated that Adams had had communication with slaves, which "was evidence, in law, of collusion."

But that was not a very effective argument. The law that Pickens and Thompson were referring to was South Carolina slave-state law, startling to free-state citizens. You mean any talk whatever with slaves, any "fraternization" whatever (to use a word from a later time), was "evidence of collusion," and therefore illegal? And were they proposing now to try to apply such a law to congressmen from Massachusetts? Adams shamed his listeners into disavowing any intention of taking him to court, their own self-interest perhaps as well as a modicum of principle recoiling from the prospect.

An editor of the *Boston Daily Advertiser*, an orthodox Whig paper, at the end of a long report of these events made this comment about Adams's performance:

> The effect of this speech on the House has been rarely if ever exceeded by the influence of any speech on any assembly. It was delivered after the opponents of Mr. A. had inflamed themselves to the highest exacerbation, by most vehement harangues for four days. [Adams] had to address a majority strongly prejudiced against him, and eager to seize any tolerable ground of censure for his previous course in presenting abolition petitions. And yet the result of this speech, under all these disadvantages was, that but twenty-two members could be found to vote even indirectly and remotely to censure. All the resolutions were rejected.

❧

ALL RESOLUTIONS PERSONALLY BEARING on Adams were indeed rejected. Some historical and biographical writing, focusing on Adams personally, leaves it at that, as the *Advertiser* did—Adams made a powerful speech, bowled over his colleagues, and won. And the episode of the petition purporting to come from slaves, which instigated the effort to censure him, is treated as a minor matter, a joke, or, to borrow a word bandied about the House floor, a "farce," and is consigned to a brief reference or a footnote.

But one can find in that episode more than the amusing strategic element of Adams pseudo-innocently setting the trap (with bait someone in the opposing camp had provided him), and the Southerners plunging through it in full cry, and more also than the drama of Adams's spectacular self-defense and victory. The question of the right of slaves to petition, however whimsically it got there, was still before the House.

22 / THEY ARE RIGHTS OF HEAVEN'S OWN GIVING TO (ALMOST) EVERY HUMAN BEING

THE SOUTHERN SPOKESMEN DID want to get the larger question of a petition from slaves, now that it had unfortunately been raised, clearly settled. They had often in this tumultuous week made plain how appalling they found the whole discussion to be—even the mere discussion, let alone the preposterous, insolent, and monstrous position put forward by Adams. Francis Wilkinson Pickens (lodging with his friend and cousin Senator Calhoun again in this session, this time in the mess at Miss Corcoran's, at the corner of Pennsylvania Avenue and Four and One-Half Street) stated the core principle most succinctly: the very idea of a slaves' petition "broke down the principle that the slave could only be known through his master." It did not matter upon which side, or upon which topic, the petition's prayer was to be found; Adams's trick—if it was a trick—of holding back what the petition prayed for did not matter in the slightest. The offense was in presenting a petition, on any side whatever of any issue whatever, that came from slaves. As that other veteran of Mrs. Lindenberger's, the irrepressible Waddy Thompson, said (as reported in the *Register of Debate* for February 6):

> **[Thompson]:** It makes not the slightest difference; it is the attempt to introduce a petition from slaves for any object; as insolent if it be for one

purpose as for another. It is the naked fact of the presentation of a petition from slaves.

He went on to give the bluntest expanded expression of this idea, including a doctrine about slaves in the Constitution that even many slaveholders would find extreme:

> [**Thompson**]: Slaves have no right to petition. They are property, not persons; they have no political rights, and even their civil rights must be claimed through their masters. Having no political rights, Congress has no power in relation to them, and therefore no right to receive their petition. They are property, not persons, under the constitution. The constitution is the paramount rule of the House; and any attempt, however made, to present petitions from them is a violation of that constitution and a flagrant disrespect and insult to a portion of its members.

Even the most vigorous champions of slavery usually did not deny that the slaves were persons, both in fact and under the U.S. Constitution, which in its tortured sentences on the subject used specifically the word "persons." But Thompson was greatly provoked, as was further revealed in a personal reference:

> [**Thompson**]: Does any man dare to claim that the House of which I am a member is a tribunal to which appeals from my slaves are to be addressed, and in which their denunciations of me are to be received? This is a question I will not argue.

In this session and on this point, South Carolina stood together. The lame duck Henry Laurens Pinckney, who had broken with his colleagues in the previous session, and lost his seat as a result, now in his final session stated the doctrine about slaves petitioning as brusquely as anyone in Charleston could ask (how absurd to suppose that they can petition here!) and made a particularly demeaning analogy, to which later Adams would respond:

> **Mr. P.** said he would just as soon have supposed that the gentleman from Massachusetts would have offered a memorial from a cow or horse—for he might as well be the organ of one species of property as another. Slaves were property.

Not all of the instruction about the nonrights of slaves came from South Carolinians. Robertson of Virginia, a messmate this session of Calhoun and Francis Pickens, whom he was to disappoint by his unwillingness to vote to censure Adams, nevertheless made a contribution on this subject:

> **[Robertson]:** That gentleman [Adams] is too intelligent to assert, in his calmer moments the preposterous position, that those who under the constitution are recognized as property, who constitute no part of the body politic, can exercise political rights.

In fact there occasionally appeared the suggestion that free blacks, like slaves, were also, to use a term from another time and setting, nonpersons. Thus Jesse ("drunk with slavery") Bynum of North Carolina, a particularly blunt exponent of an extreme slaveholders' view, presented as one of the proposed resolutions the proposition that it was contempt of the House, worthy of censure, to introduce a memorial or petition not only from a slave but also from a free Negro. And Henry Laurens Pinckney, no doubt anticipating his return to Charleston, went out of his way to show that he could be as fierce not only against abolitionists and slaves but also against Negroes as anyone else. He insisted that his resolution of the previous session (the gag rule) could not at all be blamed for Mr. Adams's conduct. That resolution had applied *only* to those who were constitutionally entitled to address the House. And who might they be?

> **[Pinckney]:** It relates exclusively to the free *white* citizens [my emphasis] of the United States. Who ever dreamt that any member of this House would so far forget its dignity as to attempt to evade the resolution . . . by attempting to introduce a memorial from Negroes!

As we have said, it was not easy to get the floor in these moments of high excitement; the Speaker tended to call upon the established figures. The speeches by New Yorkers Mann, Cambreleng, and Vanderpoel, who did not have trouble being called upon, made clear what the leading Democrats and the incoming Van Buren administration wanted to do with this week's hot potato: they wanted to head off any censure of ex-president Adams—that would be a sensational event that would cause trouble in Northern opinion—but at the same time they wanted to make very clear especially to their Southern brethren, but to everyone else, too, in the House and in the country, that they had no sympathy whatever with Adams's preposterous, insolent, and monstrous suggestion that slaves had a right to petition. Aaron Vanderpoel (who came not only from New York

State and the Democratic Party but from Van Buren's home town) himself supplied the last of these epithets:

> **[Vanderpoel]:** The idea that slaves had a right to petition the American Congress is indeed too monstrous to justify any labored attempt at refutation. . . . Had anyone, before today, ever dreamed that the appellation of "the people" embraced slaves?

In sum: once the sensitive matter of the censure, direct or indirect, of ex-president Adams had been satisfactorily sifted out of the resolutions, many Northern Democrats, and many Northern Whigs, too, had no trouble joining their brethren from the South in repudiating the idea that slaves had any right to petition. That was a nice safe question. Needless to say, there were no slaves in the House; there were no blacks in the House; there were no slaves in your Northern district, and precious few if any of your constituents were free blacks and fewer still of those, and only in a few places, could vote. Now here was a chance to vote with the Southerners, and to restore some amity and fellow-feeling—and to give reassurance that the House was not going to upset the applecart of Union by supporting the preposterous notion that slaves could petition.

And so on Saturday, the House, having been frustrated in its effort to censure Adams directly, got a chance at least to consider the monstrous suggestion implied by his action and explicitly defended in his speeches.

❧

THERE WAS, TO BE sure, a certain philosophical hurdle on the question of slaves' right to petition. English and American forebears of the new republic had said repeatedly, with a now embarrassing universalism, that the rights for which they contended belonged to *every* human being; it was a little awkward now to propose an implicit amendment saying, "except American slaves."

The issue, although "abstract" in the sense that nothing immediately practical was going to come from its consideration, nevertheless went to the heart of the new American republic. On the one hand, as Southern spokesmen, and Northerners, too, kept explaining all week, the slave was (by law) altogether shut out of the body politic—no vote (certainly not), no civil rights, not even any independent will, so far as the government was concerned. Therefore to imply that slaves had any right of petition would undercut the whole system; it was—to repeat words that congressmen used—"preposterous"; "insolent"; "monstrous." On the other hand, the right of petition—the "sacred" right—had an uncomfortably exalted place and wide definition in the new republic's memory.

Slaves were property, said the slaveholders. Slaves were also persons, the slaveholders usually admitted (the outbursts quoted above, in a moment of passion, notwithstanding). Indeed, when it had been to their advantage, as in the shaping by the framers of the power base in the Constitution, they had *insisted* that slaves were persons—so that they were able to justify counting a state's slave population (as we have noted, they had to compromise at the fraction three-fifths of that population) in the allocation of House seats to states. If the slaves were only property, the delegates from Northern states had exclaimed, why not count all the cows in Vermont?

Back in 1788, when it fell to him to argue (in a quite peculiar *Federalist* paper, number 54) in behalf of this weird three-fifths arrangement, James Madison had almost given himself an intellectual double hernia trying to defend the mixed person-property nature of slaves that was alleged to justify it. Behind two veils of anonymity (all the papers were signed "Publius"; in this one Madison in addition further distanced himself from his argument by putting it into the mouth of "one of our Southern brethren") he argued that in addition to being property the slaves were also—sort of—persons.

Fifty-five years after that effort, and six years and two Congresses after the events we are here describing, in 1843, John Quincy's son Charles Francis Adams would draft, and the Massachusetts legislature would pass, and John Quincy would introduce in the House, a resolution proposing that the Constitution be amended to eliminate the three-fifths ratio. The House (skewed by the feature the proposed amendment would abolish) would defeat that attempt overwhelmingly—156 to 13—and would turn back three more such efforts in the following year. The three-fifths provision would continue to tilt the foundation of power in the House until the force of arms and the post–Civil War amendments made it moot.

THOSE BATTLES DEALT WITH the distribution of power. In this other moment, in February of 1837, the House dealt with related questions more philosophically, more abstractly, in a way that went all the way to first principles. And the issue they dealt with—the right of slaves to petition—was, according to Adams, "the most important question that ever came before the House since its first origin."

Adams was joined, up to a point, in making his argument on this most important question by Caleb Cushing. But only up to a point. Comparing the remarks of these two Harvard men provides an instructive contrast in the application of the new republic's original ideals to the actual American state, a contrast not without its point even yet.

Adams gave his view several times during the week—first, in the midst of the spontaneous excitements of Monday; again, in the early going of Tuesday, before members started on the speeches they had prepared overnight; and then again on Thursday, as a part of his bowled-them-over speech in his own defense.

The younger and less spontaneous Cushing—who, as a much less senior and less distinguished member, probably had a harder time getting the floor—made only one major intervention. This came at the end of the day on Tuesday, when he delivered the full-dress speech to which we have already referred—the one in which he defended Adams, briefly, in the most superlative terms, for his lifelong work, without overdoing his defense of Adams's activity the previous day, and in which he took on Waddy Thompson for his slanders of New England. Cushing spent another large part of this speech giving his own view of the right of petition. He gave it the full force of his booming voice, his learned allusions, and his intricate but well-formed sentences.

Up to a point, as I have said, the two men agreed. In fact, on Thursday, when he gave his wind-up speech, and had the benefit of Cushing's address, Adams associated himself—as legislators say—with an aspect of his remarks:

> **[Adams]:** My colleague [Mr. Cushing] has, more forcibly than I can do, already discussed the proposition of the freedom of petition. He has shown that it is a right not derived from the constitution, not given by Parliament, but prior to the constitution; given, by the God of Nature, to every man when he created him. . . .

And indeed Cushing had said that, with eloquence and sweep—a greater eloquence than Adams's:

> **[Cushing]:** They are rights of Heaven's own giving . . . the free donation of the eternal God, when he made us to be men.

Both men affirmed, then, that these rights, including the right of petition, are more fundamental even than "republican" governmental forms, or legally protected civil liberties:

> **[Cushing]:** We did not constitute this Government as the means of acquiring new rights, but for the protection of old ones, which nature had

conferred upon us; which the constitution rightly regards as pre-existing rights.

[Adams]: Sir, the framers of the Constitution would have repudiated the idea, that they were giving to the people the right of petition. No, sir. That right God gave to the whole human race, when he made them men—the right of prayer, by asking a favor of another.

Both men said, too, that these rights could not *properly* be limited.

[Cushing]: It [the right of petition] is a liberty, native, inborn, original, underived, improscriptible. . . . [A]ll the constitution does is to provide that these rights neither you, nor any power on earth, shall alter, abrogate, or abridge.

[Adams]: Yes, sir. . . . They [the framers] recognized no limitation of any kind on this sacred right.

But as these large abstract agreements approached their concrete application, a certain divergence appeared. Adams said explicitly what one would think that Cushing's sweeping statements implied—that this unabridgeable and unlimitable God-given right is possessed by every human being:

[Adams]: That right [to petition] God gave to the whole human race. . . . My doctrine is, that this right belongs to humanity. . . .

Moreover, as in the moral order, so too in American law:

[Adams]: Does [your law] say that, before presenting a petition, you shall look into it, and see whether it comes from the virtuous, and the great and the mighty? No, sir, it says no such thing; the right of petition belongs to all.

Adams said specifically and repeatedly, moreover, that this right was possessed in particular by the humblest, without regard to their worth or merit:

[Adams on Monday and slightly differently on Thursday]: The Sultan of Turkey cannot walk the streets of Constantinople and refuse to receive a petition from the meanest and vilest in the land.

> **[Adams on Monday]:** Where is your law which says that the mean, and the low, and degraded, shall be deprived of the right of petition . . .?
>
> **[Adams on Tuesday]:** What was a petition? It was prayer, a supplication to a superior being—that which we offer up to our God; and if the Creator of the universe did not deny to the lowest, the humblest, and the meanest, the right of petition and supplication, were they to say they would not hear the prayer of these petitioners because they were slaves?
>
> **[Adams on Monday]:** . . . so far from refusing to present a petition because it might come from those low in the estimation of the world, it would be an added incentive.

Cushing, for all the grand sweep of his ideas, did not draw implications like those of Adams—*all* humankind, *especially* the humblest—perhaps because he could see where they were tending; his affirmation of the universality of these rights remained safely confined to some combination of heaven and Massachusetts. Congress, in Cushing's view, not only had no obligation to receive the petitions of slaves; it had a positive obligation *not* to receive them. "Heaven's own giving"—Cushing's fine phrase—apparently somehow passed by the African slaves in America.

Cushing, caught in a tight place by his larger principles, straining a little, and regretting that the great matter of civil liberty had come to be mixed with this unpleasant issue of slavery, did grant a carefully controlled, minimal—one might say irrelevant—right of petition for slaves, but he put that forward in a most gingerly way. "Common sense," he said—no longer the great decrees of heaven, now cautious common sense—will tell us that there are some very carefully limited circumstances in which one might properly receive the request—that is, the petition—of a slave:

> **[Cushing]:** If I see him drowning in the canal, or about to be struck down by a stranger, and he cries to me for succor, may I not listen to him? Suppose a memorial to come to me from a slave, setting forth . . . that he is in a foreign land, oppressed and wronged, and his master . . . does not know it, or cannot be found; may I not bring the matter before the Government, whether it be Congress or the Executive, whichever has the power to afford redress?

In such circumstances, said Cushing, it might be "proper and reasonable" to "lend an ear" to the petition of a slave—but not on anything having to do with abolition, or with slavery in this country, or with his treatment by his "master." If he were drowning on his own, so to speak, maybe it would be "proper and reasonable" to hear his cry; if he were being drowned by his "master"—then no one could properly interfere. If a stranger beat the slave—maybe one could hear his plea; but if his master beat him—tough luck. In some foreign country one might "lend an ear"—but not in the United States. Against some stranger or foreigner—but not against his "master." Out from under this Constitution, perhaps. But not under the sway of this Constitution.

In his wrap-up for the Democratic administration on Saturday, Aaron Vanderpoel mocked these cases put forward by Cushing: "I had supposed that the gentleman was too sound a logician," said the well-educated Vanderpoel, who supplied a Latin maxim, *Exceptio probat regulam,* "to suppose that such extreme and far-fetched cases against a proposition prove its unsoundness." A slave with no master and some problem in a foreign country ought to go to the U.S. consul—through channels, and leave it to proper authorities to do any petitioning.

But Cushing in any case was not going anywhere with his examples; he was just filling in the points in his lecture. So far as the present issue was concerned—American slaves petitioning Congress on matters having to do with slavery—Cushing was altogether on Vanderpoel's side.

Cushing's eloquent gestures in the direction of a universal right of petition for all human beings, combined with his careful lawyer's restrictions of that right for slaves under this Constitution, put him in the position in effect of saying: this Constitution *withdraws* from certain "persons" (slaves are persons—the Constitution does say that) the universal human rights *they otherwise possess*. It was a curious mirror of the view taken by his Newburyport acquaintance William Lloyd Garrison, who also held that the Constitution denied to American slaves the human rights that are the gift of heaven to all human beings. But Garrison made a quite contrary practical application of this view: he therefore condemned the Constitution. Cushing therefore denied any practical rights of American slaves.

Cushing was, as we have said, exceedingly proud of his Puritan and his New England heritage; his ancestors were a "race of men . . . never backward in the struggles of liberty." He matched the swaggering personal posturing of others with some of his own:

> **[Cushing]:** I am ready to do as they did—to abandon all the advantages of country, home, fortune, station—to fly to some western wilderness—and to live upon a handful of parched corn and a cup of cold water, with God's blessing on honest independence—sooner than I will surrender one

> jot or tittle of those great principles of liberty which I have sucked in with my mother's milk.

It is not recorded, however, that in the ensuing quarter of a century of struggle on behalf of the most fundamental principles of liberty, Caleb Cushing fled anywhere or abandoned anything or did anything remotely resembling living on parched corn. Already in other parts of his speech it was apparent, despite that swagger about his king-killing ancestors, how careful Cushing would be never in his own generation to be forward in the struggle for liberty.

Caleb Cushing, the younger Whiggish above-the-battle middler, condemned the "extremes" and congratulated himself on his superior middleness:

> **[Cushing]:** Gentlemen at each end of these remotest extremes of opinions are to be seen, cutting loose from practical facts to bewilder themselves in the mazy subtleties of mere abstraction. And thus I find myself in the singular predicament of addressing to the ultra friends of liberty at home, and the ultra friends of slavery here, the same arguments of moderation.

As to slavery itself, Cushing for all his learning and intelligence confessed he had not yet arrived at a position, and would not want to do so without a careful survey of the facts:

> **[Cushing]:** [W]ise legislation, like sound philosophy, was the result of induction. [On the matter of slavery] he would not be the fool to rush in where angels fear to tread. He had no formed opinions, no convictions, no settled judgment, as to the future of this momentous question.

Here is one of the most learned men in the House, or in the nation for that matter, fully articulate and loaded with opinions on all subjects of the day, who has not been able to form an opinion about slavery. Despite his "moderation" and middleness and not rushing in where angels fear to tread, though, Cushing had nevertheless managed to reach conclusions on the key questions for the week, not about slavery in general—that one was too tough—but about whether slaves had a right to petition. And his conclusion was that they did not.

Cushing's sweeping principles made the House leaders nervous, and his far-fetched examples made them snort, but when he reached the points that had immediate practical significance he turned out to be perfectly sound.

Would he present to this House a petition from slaves?

> **[Cushing]:** I would no more present a petition from slaves, in derogation of any of the constitutional rights of the South, than I would offer a deliberate insult to the Chair or to the House.

Is it proper for anyone to present such a petition?

> **[Cushing]:** I cannot infringe the legal rights of the master without becoming amenable to the law of the land; nay, to a higher forum, since I should be doing an act immoral and dishonorable as well as illegal.

But John Quincy Adams, now seventy-one years old, and by superficial measures about as complete a member of what a later century would call the "establishment" as one could find, did not arrive at the same cautious, conservative, and thoroughly acceptable conclusions as did his thirty-six-year-old colleague from Newburyport. The old ex-president shocked the establishment of the time to a degree that it is difficult for later generations, after all the dust has settled, to appreciate. Perhaps the speeches and proposals and votes cited here will give some sense of it. An outburst of John M. Claiborne of Mississippi comparing Adams to "the midnight incendiary who fires the dwellings of his enemy, and listens with pleasure to his burning victims," suggests, as do many other passages, the fervor of the response to Adams's actions and arguments.

There would be, as readers of these pages will discover, a later and more concerted effort to censure Adams on the House floor, one which is more often written about and which got more public attention at the time. But that attempt would be planned. It would be a calculated act of political infighting. This effort in February of 1837, by contrast, was *spontaneous*—a genuine outpouring of shock and anger.

Adams did have a very broad doctrine of the nature of petitioning, which in the context of this discussion—no purely academic seminar, after all—was menacing.

> **[Adams on Tuesday]:** Petition is supplication—it is entreaty—it is prayer.

> **[Adams on Thursday]:** What was a petition? It was a prayer, a supplication to a superior being; that which we offer up to our God.

He maintained, with an explicitness that would make Cushing and many others uneasy, that the right "does not depend upon the condition of the petitioner, and . . . cannot be denied to a man in any condition."

Not in *any* condition? Although Adams and Cushing both insisted that heaven and God and nature had given this right to every human being, when the time came to be more specific, Cushing underlined its particular meaning for his forebears and his fellow citizens of Massachusetts, while Adams underlined its particular meaning for the humblest and the least powerful. Adams called it "this first and humblest right given from God to every human being," adding, "The right of petition contests no power. It admits the power. . . . It is the cry of distress, asking for relief."

How can such a right—the right to cry out in distress, to pray for relief from the powers that be—be limited, or denied to anyone?

> **[Adams]:** When you begin to limit the right, where shall it stop? . . . [I]f you attempt to fix any limit to it, you lay the foundation for restriction to any extent that the madness of party spirit may carry it.

We have noted that Henry Laurens Pinckney, making amends perhaps for his sins against Carolina in the previous session, had used a particularly unedifying figure of speech—that memorials might as well have been accepted from a cow or a horse as from a slave. Both Aaron Vanderpoel and John Quincy Adams were to respond to that figure.

Vanderpoel, mending fences not, as Pinckney was, in South Carolina, but in New York and in the North and, on behalf of the incoming Van Buren administration, in the nation, recommended that Southern gentlemen "temper their valor with a little discretion":

> **[Vanderpoel]:** An honorable gentleman from South Carolina [Mr. Pinckney] in the ardor of debate, had resorted to a simile which, if true, might rather have been waived. He told us that he would as soon believe that a cow or a horse, a dog or a cat, had a right to petition, as that a negro slave had a right to petition this House. Speeches like that, and measures, that are akin to them, furnish texts from which abolitionists will write and preach whole volumes.

Avoid such statements not because they are wrong or demeaning or outrageous, but because abolitionists will make use of them.

Adams had in the meantime made his own response to Pinckney's figure of speech. Twenty-two years later, Abraham Lincoln, in response to a repeated passage from his chief adversary, Stephen Douglas, in which Douglas made an implicit comparison of Negroes with crocodiles, would point out the moral degradation of that kind of speech. Adams, with his eye on his very broad theory of petition, took a different tack:

> **[Adams on Tuesday]:** A gentleman had said on yesterday that he would as soon receive a petition from a horse or a dog as from slaves. Sir, said Mr. A., if a horse or a dog had the power of speech and of writing, and he should send him a petition, he would present it to the House; ay, if it were a famished horse or dog, he would present it.

Adams had certainly answered the questions of the week, and he had answered them in the opposite way from his colleague Caleb Cushing: yes, he would introduce a petition from slaves; yes, slaves had a right of petition; no, the Constitution did not deny it to them. On the contrary, Adams repeatedly affirmed, the Constitution guaranteed it.

> **[Adams on Tuesday]:** . . . if the Creator of the Universe did not deny to the lowest, the humblest and the meanest the right of petition and supplication, were they to say they would not hear the prayer of these petitioners because they were slaves?

> **[Adams on Thursday]:** If this House decides that it will not receive petitions from slaves, under any circumstances, it will cause the name of this country to be enrolled among the first of the barbarous nations.

Congressman Jenifer of Maryland asked Adams, one imagines with a suggestion of a sneer, why, if he held to such an exalted view of the right of petition, he did not simply introduce this one, instead of asking his question of the Speaker. Because of his deep respect for the House and its rules, Adams replied; the House, against his strong protest, had passed the resolution of January 18 (the Hawes gag), so he had to inquire whether or not this particular petition fell under its ban.

Adams described petitions from slaves that he would introduce if the rules of the House allowed it:

> **[Adams on Tuesday]:** If slaves sent to him a petition for any thing unjust or improper, or any thing which the House ought not to hear, he would pause at least before he asked the Speaker the same question which he asked on yesterday. If, however, on the contrary, he should receive a petition from slaves, saying that they were perfectly satisfied with their situation; and that they would rather be slaves than freemen; that their masters were kind to them, and that when they were reduced to infirmity by old age, their masters would take care of them, and praying that they might be left in this situation, he would, if the House would permit him, present it.

Adams did not go on to say what his logic plainly implied, that he would equally present a petition from slaves (respectful and proper in tone, and the like) which asked an end to slavery or the slave trade, or redress from grievances under slavery. That such petitions might be received was a terrifying idea to a slaveholder, but from Adams's premises hard to argue against. Once again Adams took a position that combined principle with strategy in a way that caught his opponents in an uncomfortable bind. On the large issue, as we have seen, he kept emphasizing the hallowed right to petition, as part of the core of the Bill of Rights. He pushed the understanding of that right deep into the moral grounding of the nation, and even of human life; the right to cry for mercy to the possessors of power was "the first and humblest right given from God to every human being." He insisted, just as all the congressmen did, as all Americans did, that it was a *sacred* right. He separated the right, as they all would in theory, from the content, the prayer, of the petition; he would introduce respectful petitions on both sides, or all sides, including those with which he personally disagreed. So would other congressmen, to be sure, in theory and within limits. In fact, Adams emphasized repeatedly—to the discomfiture and confusion of some abolitionists—that he did not personally support the prayer of the petitions asking the end of slavery in the District. He underlined that point again this week. He did not publicly state his reasons for that nonsupport; when he stated his reasons privately, in a letter several years earlier to a leading Rhode Island Quaker, they were prudential only, not very satisfying to those who read the letter. But for the purposes of his actions on the House floor, that nonsupport was quite important; it isolated and underlined his defense of the right of petition. He was certainly not supporting abolition in general. He was not even supporting abolition in the District. All he was doing was defending the sacred right of petition. And to do that he introduced abolitionist petitions—by the dozens.

So also on the narrower issue of the gag rule he combined strategy with principle. He respected the rules of the House. No one respected the rules of the House more than he. Therefore he had to abide by the gag rule, when the House had voted it, even though he had fought against it and regarded it as unconstitutional and wrong. And in order to abide by the gag rule he had had not to introduce this petition—although he did hold that slaves had a right to petition—but just to ask his question of the Speaker. Did a petition purporting to come from slaves fall under the ban against all petitions dealing with the subject of slavery? And so the gag rule itself had precipitated this whole exploration.

Adams ground on the nerve of the universality of the right of petition, available to all:

> **[Adams on Thursday]:** What, sir, places the right of petition on the character and condition of the petitioner, or bases it upon a mere political privilege? . . . When you establish the doctrine that a slave shall not petition because he is a slave, that he shall not be permitted to raise the cry for mercy, you let in a principle subversive of every foundation of liberty, and you cannot tell where it will stop. The next step will be that the character and not the claims of petitions will be the matter to be discussed on this floor, and whenever, as in the case of the gentleman from Virginia (Mr. Patton) any member finds a name on a petition which belongs to a person whom he says he knows to be of bad character, a motion will be made not to receive the petition, or to return it to the member who offered it. . . . [S]ir, sad will be the day when it is entered on the Journal of this House, that we will, under no circumstances, receive the petition of slaves.

As to the nine ladies of Fredericksburg—Adams had not known they were "colored," but it would not have mattered if he had.

> **[Adams]:** Here then is another limitation to the right of petition. First it is denied to slaves, then to free persons of color, and then to persons of notorious bad character. Now, sir, if you begin by limiting this right as to slaves, you next limit it as to all persons of color, and then you go into inquiries as to the character of petitioners before you will receive petitions. There is but one step more, and that is to inquire into the political faith of petitioners. Each side will represent their opponents as being infamous, and what becomes of the right of petition?

Cushing and Adams had started at the same place, with the same general moral ideal: universal human rights, the gift of heaven to all mankind, existing in a moral order prior to legal systems including the American Constitution, which rights cannot justly be limited or abridged by any human agency. But the starting points are one thing; ending points another.

No one else defended Adams's sweeping doctrine of the universal natural right to petition as a plea from every kind of weakness to every kind of power, available to American slaves as to the humblest and least powerful and most aggrieved anywhere. William Slade would have done so, and Slade tried to get the floor, but the Speaker did not call upon him. Slade did not ordinarily speak much in the daily rough-and-tumble with the oratorical quick-bloomers from farther south than Middlebury, Vermont, and the Speaker may not have been particularly eager to call upon him.* But he was not able to speak, and no one else spoke on that side either.

The first resolution voted on in this conclusion of the "exciting" week still trailed a hint of the origins of the controversy:

> *Resolved*, That this House cannot receive the said petition without disregarding its own dignity, the rights of a large class of citizens of the South and West, and the constitution of the United States.

This one, essentially rejected two days before in the aftermath of Adams's speech, but now reconsidered, was passed by a very large majority—160 to 35. But some of Adams's supporters apparently still felt that in its reference to a specific petition it did touch Adams, to borrow from Caleb Cushing, with the "uttermost edge of the shadow of indignity." Cushing and Levi Lincoln voted with the thirty-three others against it.

But then came a second resolution that had meanwhile been cast up in the discussion as a clearer way to express the opinion of the House. It was pure—an abstract statement of principle, as it were, without referring to anything or reflecting on anybody. It was short, and certainly forthright enough. This is the whole thing:

> *Resolved,* That slaves do not possess the right of petition secured to the people of the United States by the constitution.

By what margin would that resolution pass, in the House of Representatives of the United States of America, in 1837?

It differed from its predecessor in that even the faintest reference to Adams and the current petition was removed, and all reference to sections of the country was removed, and all connection explicit or implicit to the fracas of the week had been removed. The question was now confronted, unadorned. Do slaves have the right of petition? In this country? Under this Constitution? The right secured to "the people"? The House answered no, by the thundering margin of 162 to 18.

Among the Northerners who voted in favor of this resolution as well as its predecessor were not only Franklin Pierce and Aaron Vanderpoel and Abijah Mann and Churchill Cambreleng—a string of Northern Democrats, as might be expected—but also both of Adams's chief defenders in the debate about his censure. The distinguished former governor of Massachusetts Levi Lincoln voted that slaves have no right of petition, and so

*Slade did put a statement of his views into the *National Intelligencer*.

did the eloquent and learned quintessential Puritan-Yankee with the blood of four generations of liberty-loving roundheads flowing in his veins, Caleb Cushing.

Only eighteen votes out of 242 members of the U.S. House of Representatives sustained the right of slaves to petition. Besides Adams, the eighteen included William Slade, as was to be expected, and two others from the state of Vermont, one of whom, Henry F. Janes, had introduced abolitionist petitions before and would again; three representatives, in addition to Adams, from Massachusetts; five representatives from the large and diverse state of Pennsylvania, from which once had come the first abolitionist petitions; three representatives from the almost equally diversified state of New York; and one each from Ohio, Connecticut, and New Jersey. Five of the eighteen, including William Slade, were messmates at the lodging house kept by Mr. Fletcher, on E Street near the General Post Office—the mess at which Caleb Cushing had stayed during the previous session, but from which he now had moved.*

Many of the eighteen were names one had seen, and would see again, introducing abolitionist petitions, but they were not names to be found in the major speechmaking or the leadership positions. Almost none of them were among the vocal and the powerful in the House—the ones who were called on often, and who had power and influence.† The only chairman of a major committee who voted against the resolution, and the only member who spoke often who voted against it, was the chairman of the Committee on Manufactures, John Quincy Adams.

The main bulk of free-state congressmen, having declined to join the fire-eaters in their desire to censure Adams, had now gone along with the earnest pleas and arguments and threats of the slaveholding states on this one, and quite probably with their own convictions as well: there is no right of petition for slaves.

To be sure, the resolution said "secured . . . by the constitution,"

*During the first session of the Twenty-fourth Congress, Cushing had stayed at Fletcher's lodging house with a passel of New Englanders including three congressmen and a senator from Vermont—the most antislavery state—and two others from Massachusetts, one of whom was George Briggs, who had introduced the "inadvertent" petition. In other words, he had taken his meals in a mess that would have been sympathetic to the petitions, maybe even somewhat to abolition. But in this second session he lodged not with Mr. Fletcher but instead with a Mr. Clubb, on Capitol Hill, where he had companions who were in no danger of sympathy to the abolition cause.

†There were in this second session of the Twenty-fourth Congress thirty standing committees in the House; the chairmen of only three, two of them minor ones, voted against the resolution—the latter two being Heman Allen of Vermont, who was chairman of the Committee on Expenditures in the Department of the Treasury, and Edward Darlington of Pennsylvania, who was chairman of the Committee on Expenditures on the Public Buildings.

which might allow a Northern casuist to say that although petitioning was a natural right of all human beings it was nevertheless not a legal or political right secured to slaves by the U.S. Constitution. Francis Pickens, the South Carolina fire-eater, angrily pointed out this possible interpretation in a speech he made on Saturday not long before the voting, and he wanted to close the last moral loophole by insisting that the notion that slaves had a purely *natural* right be rejected, too. He wanted it to be affirmed that slaves had no right to petition anywhere, ever. Indeed, he wanted the whole subject dismissed out of hand. Henry A. Wise declined to vote on the matter, and explained his unwillingness to do so by claiming that "Congress had no power to interfere, in any way, with the subject of slavery." The issue should never have come before the House.

The position that must be assigned to Cushing—natural right, yes; constitutional right, no—put the congressmen holding that view in the awkward position of saying that there were great rights of humankind that were not protected—that were even *violated*—by the revered instrument of the nation founded on the premise of human rights, the United States Constitution. A very awkward position indeed, if you thought about it. On the one hand, to allow slaves to petition was a terrifying idea. And the slaveholders said that it placed in jeopardy not only the whole structure of chattel slavery but the Union as well.

Nevertheless, to have claimed for yourself the great universal rights of humankind, given by heaven to every human being, in particular the humblest, as English and American partisans of liberty across three centuries had done, and then to turn around and to deny those rights to others—outsiders, as you once had been, seeking natural human rights—was a little embarrassing. Some might even say it was preposterous, insolent, and monstrous.

PART VIII

WELCOME TO THE TWENTY-FIFTH CONGRESS OF THE UNITED STATES

23 / SECESSION

SO THAT OLD TWENTY-FOURTH Congress, having in its day enacted both the Pinckney gag and its successor, and having admitted a new slave state to the Union, and having at the end said with almost one voice that slaves have no right to petition, expired, and in March of 1837 a new Congress nominally, and a new presidency actually, began. Martin Van Buren was inaugurated president on March 4, 1837, succeeding the ailing old man Andrew Jackson.*

The new president, with other things on his mind, tried to make a preemptive strike, as it were, against those pesky petitions, and against the extremely disturbing topic of slavery. He announced—in advance, in his very Inaugural Address—that he would *veto* any bill touching slavery in the District or the slave states.

Did that stop the flow of petitions? No, of course it did not. Just two months later, in May of 1837, the American Anti-Slavery Society meeting in New York decided to *concentrate* its efforts on petitions, making the petition effort vigorous, systematic, national, the primary activity of the society.

The flow of abolitionist petitions and memorials had been, in the earliest years of the republic, a tiny sprinkle, with an occasional drizzle, as in 1828. After 1834 this became the steady stream that so agitated the messmates at Mrs. Lindenberger's. In 1837 and afterward it was to become a flood. Petitions in much larger numbers with much longer lists of names were now sent to state legislatures and to the Senate, but above all to those immediate representatives, the fathers and rulers in the U. S. House of Representatives.

As the procedure was rationalized, so were the petitions themselves. Although the Fathers and Rulers petition kept on being used by women

*That was the last time a sitting vice-president would succeed to the presidency by election until George Bush succeeded Ronald Reagan in 1989.

petitioners, most petitions now were shorter than that one—short enough that even under the gag, a congressman who wanted to could get most of the petition out just while stating its subject, before the Speaker could rule it out of order or a member object. In addition to those that prayed for an end to slavery in the District of Columbia, there were now also petitions against the annexation of Texas, against the interstate slave trade, against slavery in the territories, and against statehood for Florida so long as slavery was permitted within its borders. Adams spent many evenings dutifully recording and cataloguing these petitions: who sent them, how many signatures, what their prayer was.

And now there were petitions against the gag rule itself. The Pinckney gag had been enacted in May of 1836, and, as Adams predicted, had proved to be not a sedative or tranquilizer but a stimulant. The Hawes gag had been enacted in the second session of that Twenty-fourth Congress, in January of 1837, and that renewed gag was followed by a yet again augmented supply of petitions. It will not surprise the reader to learn, in anticipation, that there were to be further extensions of the gag, and that they would have similar results.

MEANWHILE, HOWEVER, THE FATHERS and rulers in the House, and the new president of the United States, were worried about other matters. A reader of these pages should not infer that the events recounted here were the center of the politics of the time; for most politicians then, and for some historians now, these episodes were on the periphery. They were, after all, not something a practical man could do anything about.

This was particularly true in the spring of 1837. No sooner had the little magician from Kinderhook, Martin Van Buren, been inaugurated as Andrew Jackson's successor than his magical powers evaporated and the economy collapsed. Banks failed, prices plunged, bankruptcies multiplied, unemployment grew, cotton could not be sold, debts could not be paid. The nation suffered its most serious economic downturn in its short history—the "Panic," as it came to be called, of 1837. It was followed by a depression, from the political effects of which the Van Buren administration would never fully recover. Even in those olden times, citizens of this republic tended to give to the sitting president the credit and the blame, and particularly the blame, for the condition of the economy. The Whigs, the reader will not be surprised to learn, pinned all the blame for the Panic on the policies, and nonpolicies, of the Jackson–Van Buren Democratic regimes.

Van Buren called a special session of Congress in September of 1837 to try to cope with the Panic, so the members of the new Twenty-fifth

Congress met for the first time not, as normally under the leisurely old schedule, in December of 1837, but three months earlier. Many new men filled the desks and listened to the gobble of the clerks and saw the Mercuries carry the messages when this new Congress assembled. Although the Democrats still controlled the House, and elected Polk again as Speaker, their margin was reduced. The Jackson era would soon be over.

That short special session, called for the first Monday of September, lasted into the middle of October of 1837, and was devoted exclusively to issues cast up by the Panic. The members passed a resolution "discarding from consideration" all other subjects, so an immense and growing pile of petitions would be there, backed up and waiting, for the regular session in December. "At that session the anti-slavery petitioners and remonstrants were increased to a number exceeding two hundred thousand," according to Adams. And John Greenleaf Whittier, at work on Nassau Street drumming up petitions, wrote to his sister in anticipation: "By the time Congress meets there will be petitions enough to break all the tables in the Capitol, ready for delivery."

WHEN THIS CONGRESS REASSEMBLED, after a short six-week hiatus, at its regular meeting time in early December, it had a major item left over from its wrangle over economic matters in the special session—the Independent Treasury bill supported by Van Buren—but it also had that stack of petitions. And no gag. And the first thirty days from the beginning of the session were, as always, petition days.

So, sure enough, on December 20, 1837, up rose Congressman Slade from Vermont, holding in his hand a petition, this time from upward of five hundred citizens of his state.

Slade seems to have made it his practice to write out for the beginning of each Congress one full-dress speech on the subject of slavery; he had done so in 1835–36; he did so now, at the moment to which we have come, in December of 1837; and he would do so again, as we shall see, in 1839–40. Each speech went further than the last, and each one went further than any congressman had gone before.

This time Slade made a breathtaking motion: that this petition should be referred to an extraordinary select committee with instructions to report a bill providing for the *abolition* of slavery and the slave trade in the District of Columbia. Slade's motion, according to one historian, threw the "entire representation of the South into a paroxysm of rage." In fact, he never got through his speech. He was interrupted by one call to order after another, one objection on technical grounds after another. The petition and the motion applied only to the District and the present; therefore the protesting members shouted their cries of order and objection and irrelevancy of debate against any reference to slavery at any other place in any other time. He was not permitted to read a judicial decision; he was not permitted to quote Benjamin Franklin; it was out of order to refer to what Virginians had said fifty years before; it was out of order to recollect what the Continental Congress had done. Slade had trouble even completing a sentence. Speaker Polk enforced rules against Slade that ordinarily were not enforced and, by what Adams called an arbitrary decision, finally made him sit down.

This turbulent scene was obviously difficult for the *Globe* reporter to record, and for participants later to reconstruct; Adams notes in his journal that the record is not accurate. The effort to record some of this turmoil goes like this:

> **The Speaker** declared that he had done all he could to prevent the gentleman from Vermont from debating the subject, and said if it were possible he would allay the excitement.
>
> **Mr. Turney, of Tennessee.** I rise to a question of order.
>
> **Mr. Slade.** I ask leave to read a paper.
>
> **Mr. Garland.** I object to the reading.
>
> **The Speaker.** The gentleman will take his seat.
>
> **Mr. McKay, of North Carolina.** Has not the gentleman been declared *out of order*?
>
> **The Speaker.** He has.
>
> **Mr. McKay.** Then has he the right to proceed?
>
> **Mr. Slade.** I propose to read a paper.
>
> **Mr. Turney.** I object.

One account says that "[a]fter a sturdy, manful resistance, Slade was obliged to sit down without having completed even the interrupted sentence."

At some point in these exchanges, Henry Wise had called upon all members from Virginia to retire from the hall; Halsey of Georgia had done the same for that state; and Rhett of South Carolina had announced "in a stentorian voice" that the members from South Carolina had *already* left the hall. Fifty or sixty members *did* leave. None of these interjections provoked a call to order, or was declared out of order.

A North Carolina member moved to adjourn, but Adams and his supporters, "determined to proceed in the business before the House as though nothing unusual had happened," opposed adjournment. If those slaveholding congressmen wanted to desert the House and leave it to those who remained to conduct the nation's business, so be it. The result was that there were not enough members to carry a vote to adjourn unless the "recusant members" returned to their seats, which enough of them did, one imagines a mite sheepishly, and the boiling House did then vote to adjourn. As they were preparing to leave, a South Carolina member shouted an invitation to all the delegates from the slaveholding states to meet in a committee room.

For the first time in the history of this republic, the word "abolition" had been uttered, as a serious proposal to be acted upon, in the formal proceedings of the legislative halls, and the response was not only the word "secession" but in a sense an *act* of secession. Congressman R. Barnwell Rhett, of South Carolina, in a letter to his constituents, specifically used that word; he called their leaving the hall "a memorable *secession* of Southern members," and explained further that he had prepared an amendment to Slade's motion, which in the excitement he did not get to introduce, that would have (1) declared it expedient that the Union be dissolved; and (2) proposed a committee to explore the best means of dissolving it.

Adams meanwhile focused his indignation on that extraordinary meeting of Southern members that followed the "secession." In a report to his constituents written and published later he wrote:

> *This meeting, in which no member from a non-slaveholding State was admitted to participate, but in which the members of the slave representation in the Senate took part in common with those of the House, prepared and adopted a gag-resolution, in substance the same with that of the two preceding annual sessions; and they appointed Mr. Patton, a member of the House from Virginia, to present it to the House, and at the same time to move the previous question upon its adoption. It was accordingly presented to the House the next day, admitted by a suspension of the rules, debarred from all deliberation by the previous question, and carried by yeas and nays, 122 to 74; of which majority 51 members were from non-slaveholding States, who received and voted for this resolution, as dictated by the Southern conventicle of Senators and Representatives,*

*without having been permitted to share in the deliberations of the meeting by which it had been prescribed.**

Adams had a particular scorn for those fifty-one Northerners.

This new gag resolution, the product of the secession caucus of Southern members from both parties, including senators as well as House members, introduced by that same Virginia doctor-congressman Patton who knew who was respectable and who was not in Fredericksburg, provided for the laying on the table, without their being debated, printed, read, or referred, of "all petitions, memorials, and papers, relating to the abolition of slavery or the slave trade" not only in the District and the states but also—this was new—in the territories. "Under that order," Adams wrote, "about two hundred thousand petitioners were refused a hearing by the House."

THE TWENTY-FIFTH CONGRESS, more closely divided between the parties than its predecessor, convened in an economic panic, inundated with abolitionist petitions, its regular session begun with a walkout of Southern members, and accompanied by the usual clashes of personality and faction, was to be even more turbulent and fractious than the Twenty-fourth. Like all the American Congresses, it was supposed to represent that replacement of physical force and violence by institutions of reasoning and arguing, of representative government, of formal and civil discourse and mutual deliberation, which is the very core of the "republican" and the American political accomplishment.

But that mutual deliberation is a very fragile construct. There was in 1837–38, and for many years thereafter, an ominous cloud of potential violence surrounding the congressional deliberations. There were threats; there were altercations; there were already some who carried bowie knives into the House chamber itself. In early November of 1837, between the special and the regular sessions of this Congress, the abolitionist Elijah Lovejoy had been killed by a mob while defending his printing press in Alton, Illinois, "fallen victim," Adams wrote in his journal, "to the cause of human freedom." And the following February, while the regular session was meeting, the House itself would furnish from its own membership an egregious sample of mindless violence, when one young first-term member, a Kentucky Whig, Congressman William Graves (the same Graves who had so shocked Waddy Thompson because though a slave-

*Adams is quoted here from the introduction to the printed version of his Texas speech.

holder he had not been willing to vote to censure Adams), had in a duel shot and killed another, a Maine Democrat, Jonathan Cilley, leaving Cilley's young wife and three children as survivors.

Public indignation at the Graves-Cilley affair was widespread, and was directed not so much at the principals as at the seconds, who had egged them on, and in particular at the swashbuckling Henry A. Wise, a noted duelist and—one might borrow a twentieth-century term to say—"consultant" on dueling. Wise, it was charged, had deliberately provoked the challenge in the first place, and, serving as Graves's second, had urged a second try, after both men (who were said to have liked each other) had emerged unharmed from the first exchange, and then even to have suggested when they escaped the second, that they shorten the distance, after which Cilley was killed.

Adams abominated the barbarous practice of dueling, and was quite willing as an ex-president in his seventies to say things that younger, less securely placed free-state congressmen would not risk, for fear of offending the prickly "honor" of swaggering Southerners. He was quite capable of facing them down, and speaking very plainly in his own right, as these pages have shown. Listening to the insistent defenses of dueling by Southern slaveholders, he came to regard the practice as an "appendage to slavery." When after the shock of young Cilley's death Senator Prentiss of Vermont introduced a bill forbidding dueling in the District, Adams became its sponsor in the House and guided it through to eventual passage: the Prentiss-Adams Act.

In the immediate aftermath of the killing there had been a movement in the House itself to try Wise or Graves for a capital crime. Adams, the dutiful republican, had opposed this trial, for a criminal offense committed outside the House, he said, should be conducted not by the legislative body but by the courts.

No threats of violence, however, no "secession," and no gag rules could now keep the subject of slavery out of the nation's councils. In this Twenty-fifth Congress the issue of Texas, in its first round, was to raise that subject in a particularly insistent way.

24 / SULPHURIC ACID IN HIS TEA

EARLIER EFFORTS TO PURCHASE Texas from Mexico, in which John Quincy Adams, when he was president, had been a leader, were part of the expansionist impulse without overt reference to the issue of slavery. But the significance of acquiring Texas—"annexing" it, now—became quite different after the Mexican government abolished slavery in 1829. Now for the first time there would be a step backward—the United States, "the Empire of Liberty" in Jefferson's fine phrase, would now serve as the agent of the empire of slavery.

The Americans, many of them from Southern states, who had moved into Texas, often taking their slaves with them, and who had fought for the independence of Texas, wanted to bring Texas into the United States. Remembering the massacre at the Alamo in March of 1836, they had defeated the Mexican forces in the Battle of San Jacinto late in April—shortly before the first gag resolution had been passed, in May of 1836. From that date forward there were efforts to annex independent Texas as a slave state, or possibly as a collection of several slave states, and another outpouring of petitions from the antislavery forces opposing this annexation.

The annexation of Texas as a slave state would have a decided effect on the balance of power in the United States government, adding two senators from one slave state (or more!) to the evenly balanced Senate (Arkansas's two, newly present in this Congress, had been balanced by Michigan's) and, because of the three-fifths rule, more representatives than the voting population justified to the House and to the picking of presidents. So the contest over the annexation of Texas was now seen to be—by the antislavery forces, almost exclusively—a struggle for power over the future of American freedom.

Certainly it was seen that way by John Quincy Adams. Beginning in 1836, Adams had had correspondence about Texas and slavery with Quaker abolitionist Benjamin Lundy, the founder of the early abolitionist paper on which young William Lloyd Garrison had got his start in the journalism of abolition. The saintly Lundy—a man Adams much admired—was in a quiet way a leading opponent of slavery in the 1820s, before abolition exploded onto public consciousness in the 1830s, and Lundy focused on Texas. He had twice journeyed to Texas to explore the possibility of producing plantation crops without slavery. He was forestalled by the Texas Revolution, but became convinced by his experience that the "domineering tyrants of the South" would use the annexation of Texas to expand their power.

John Quincy Adams read a tract by Lundy on the subject of Texas at about the time the gag rule controversy started. "People of the North!" wrote Lundy. "Will you permit it?" The "abominable outrage" of the annexing of Texas? "The establishment of slavery in a land of freedom?" The placing of the necks of the American people under the feet of those domineering tyrants? Adams was persuaded by Lundy's polemics and made his first speech against the annexing of Texas, using Lundy's arguments, on May 25, 1836—the day before the Pinckney gag passed the House.

NOW, TWO YEARS LATER, many of the petitions about Texas did mention slavery and the slave trade, but many of them did not. So why should the petitions that said nothing on that subject be excluded under the gag? Yet if a petition against the annexation of Texas were to be discussed on the House floor it would certainly lead to a discussion of slavery—exactly the discussion the slaveholding congressmen wanted to avoid. Adams wrote,

> *This resolution* [the reinstituted gag] *was understood, not to include the petitions, remonstrances, and memorials, against the annexation of Texas to the Union; but as most of these did touch the abolition of slavery, and the buying, selling, and transferring of slaves, whenever any such paper was presented, some slave Representatives moved it should be laid on the table, which motion the standing majority of the House always sustained; and thus summarily were the prayers of about one hundred thousand more petitioners disposed of.*

And not only the petitions of individual citizens. There had already been, under the first two gags, instances of resolutions by state legislatures that were also summarily dismissed, and, on the subject of Texas, these increased. Adams's account continued:

> *Resolutions of the Legislature of the State of Rhode Island, remonstrating against the annexation of Texas, were presented on the 29th of December, and laid on the table. They were not printed on the Journal of the House, as by a practice without exception till then had always been done.*

Vermont prided itself upon being the first state to have abolished slavery, in its constitution. A resolution adopted by an overwhelming bipartisan vote in the Vermont legislature was not permitted to be read, and was laid on the table, but by some slip was printed. It joined the issue of civil liberty—that is, the gag rule—with that of the annexation of Texas:

> Against every form of oppression the people of Vermont have, at all times, borne honorable testimony. In their Constitution they have published to the world their everlasting opposition to all slavery—even down to the minutest and least revolting of its modifications. . . . [There have been] fearful sacrifices of important interests by the North, demanded by the South to be offered up for the security of her peculiar institution—the surrender that she asks from us of the freedom of speech—liberty of the press—the right of petition—All these united inspire your Committee with a well founded apprehension that the additional weight which the annexation of Texas would give to the slaveholding interest in our political organization, would, in all probability, soon lead either to a dissolution of the Union or to the political degradation of the Free States and eventually to the entire overthrow of their common liberties.

When the Vermont resolutions were presented by that state's Senator Swift in the United States Senate—to shift over to that side of the Capitol for a moment—Senator Calhoun was confronted with acute ideological indigestion. On the one hand, he persisted in his view that all petitions on these subjects must be suppressed; that he and his cohorts must not "yield an inch to the increasing spirit of fanaticism." On the other hand, for him states' rights were fundamental; he had come to insist, in the Nullification Controversy and afterward, on the original and unmitigated rights of the *sovereign* states.

Now here was a sovereign state—Vermont—most soberly and earnestly addressing the federal legislature in a formal document, and instructing its representatives to pursue its expressed will. Was Vermont any less "sovereign" than South Carolina? This was the prayer not of a little band of private citizens (all too readily dismissed as "fanatics"), but of a state's legislators. Were they, too, to have the door slammed in their face?

At first Senator Calhoun, taken by surprise, did not know quite how to respond, and asked for time. The other senator from Vermont, Senator Prentiss, explained that to the common sense of the people of Vermont, who were not abolitionists, the procedures in Congress were nothing less than a refusal to receive petitions; the purpose of the signers was to maintain the right of petition, and they would keep sending them until that right was recognized on this subject as on any other. Eventually the Senate, like the House, laid the Vermont resolutions on the table.

But, again, the logic of a free, or a half-free, society and the depth of the passions on their own side worked to defeat the purposes of the petition-stiflers. In this case their purposes were further damaged by their hunger for territorial expansion. Although there were prominent Whigs who were in the forefront of the cry for expansion, and some Northerners, the greater concentration of those who eagerly supported Western expansion was among the Democrats, and, by region, in the South and the West, so that to a certain extent the body of opinion favoring expansion and that defending slavery overlapped. But pressing for new territory and new states regularly exacerbated the tension over slavery and brought that subject to the center of national politics.

Legislatures in Southern states, not to be outdone by their Northern counterparts, sent memorials to Congress *favoring* the annexation of Texas. On March 5, 1838, for example, there were presented to the House a matching set of resolutions by state legislatures on the subject: Ohio, against; Alabama, in favor. The Ohio resolutions had directed the governor of that state to accompany the transmission of the resolution with a statement of the votes by which it had passed (unanimously in one branch, without opposition in the other), but—as Adams put it, with icy disdain, when he recounted these events—

> *To such straits were the party of suppression reduced to sustain their system, that they refused permission to the member from Ohio, who presented the resolutions, to read to the House this letter from the Governor.*

But denying such a reading of a letter, even from a governor, was one thing, and stonewalling a resolution of a state legislature another—especially when there were resolutions from other state legislatures on the opposite side. The congressional majority could scarcely keep its face straight as a free parliamentary body if it received the one set of resolutions while turning aside the other.

The wall of silence began to crumble. On a subsequent remonstrance against the annexation of Texas "the vigilance of the dark spirit of slavery was at fault" (as Adams pungently put it) and the remonstrance, instead of being laid on the table, was referred to the Committee on Foreign Affairs. Resolutions from the state of Tennessee were presented in *favor* of the annexation of Texas, together with a motion that the whole subject be referred to a select committee; that proposal was greeted with a motion to lay on the table, and the motion did carry by a wide margin, almost exactly the same as the almost two-to-one margin for the Patton gag resolution. But the composition of the vote differed from that of the gag resolution. Nineteen free-state opponents of the gag resolution switched in the other direction and voted to lay the motion on the table, presumably because they did not trust a select committee appointed by Speaker Polk. And—this was the news—several members from Tennessee, Alabama, and South Carolina, whose legislatures had passed resolutions favoring the annexation of Texas, and a scattering of other Southern congressmen, who had voted for the gag resolution, now voted with the majority—*not* to lay on the table the state legislature petitions about Texas. Adams wrote about this development:

> *[H]ere was the dawn of a new day. It was evident that henceforth the members from the States whose Legislatures have adopted resolutions favoring the annexation would vote for opening the discussion, and it was equally clear that the Texas question once opened, the gag upon the slavery topics could no longer be effectively maintained.*

Further resolutions on Texas were presented, in the spring of 1838, and finally there came a motion to refer the entire collection of resolutions and petitions, now including seven from state legislatures, to the Committee on Foreign Affairs, which motion passed. The collection of resolutions and petitions was, so to speak, inside the door of the House.

But not very far inside. That committee (on which sat five members from slaveholding states, and only four from nonslaveholding states, and six or seven supporters of the Van Buren Democratic administration to two or at most three opponents) made a rather prompt report, on June 13, 1838, that recommended no action on the subject of Texas. It said—despite the petitions—that that subject was not before the House, and the committee further recommended that all of this pile of petitions and resolutions be laid on the table, and that the committee be discharged!

Among other exchanges in response to this peremptory and dismissive report there was this one:

> **Mr. Adams** asked if the numerous legislative resolutions, and the memorials of thousands and tens of thousands of the citizens of this country, in relation to this subject, had ever received five minutes' consideration in the Committee on Foreign Affairs.
>
> **Mr. Dromgoole** [of Virginia, spokesman for the committee] said he had but one answer to make to this question; which was, to deny explicitly any right of that member, or any other member, to catechise the committee as to its action.

Mr. Adams immediately rose, (amidst varied cries of "order!" "go on!" &c.) and said: That is enough, sir! That, sir, is enough for this House, and for the country. The committee refuse to answer. [Much confusion.]

The implication that the committee had dismissed all of these resolutions and petitions without any reading, or a moment's consideration, rather got under the committee members' skin, and Adams did all he could to keep it there. On many later occasions he returned to the subject.

Mr. Adams had a word to say. On a former day he had asked a question of the member of the Committee on Foreign Affairs who reported this resolution, as to the length of time and the degree of attention bestowed by that committee upon the subject-matter of the large number of resolutions of State Legislatures, and of petitions of the People, referred thereto. This question had been met with a denial of the right of a member of that House to ask it. At the time he (Mr. A.) had said that the country, as well as himself, would draw its own conclusions from this reply. His present purpose was to ask the chairman of that committee if he and the rest of that committee held the doctrine that a member of that House, in the discharge of his public duties, had no right to make inquiries of a committee as to the mode in which they had discharged their duties? Does the chairman take that ground?

Mr. Dromgoole here rose, and wished to ask a question of the Chair. Had a member of this House a right, under the rules, to propound such inquiries to a committee thereof?

Mr. Shields here asked if the hour for going to the orders of the day had not arrived?

Mr. Adams renewed his inquiries of the chairman and the other members of the Committee on Foreign Affairs.

Mr. Howard [from Maryland, the chairman of the committee] rose to reply.

The Chair announced the orders of the day.

Mr. Howard would prefer to reply at that time. There being no objection, he proceeded to say that, in making the report they had, the committee had acted under a sense of their duty to the House; and it was for the latter, as a body, to decide whether or not they had acted regularly in so doing. In reply to the gentleman from Massachusetts, he would say that he did go the whole length of the ground taken by his colleague of the committee, [Mr. Dromgoole,] who had brought in the report under consideration. He thought it disrespectful to a committee of that House for a member to catechise its members as to the precise time spent in the discharge of its duties, and the mode in which those duties were discharged. He stood by the gentleman from Virginia [Mr. Dromgoole] on this point.

Mr. Adams rose amidst much confusion, occasioned by calls for the orders of the day, and other cries, from various parts of the Hall, and said that the gentleman from Maryland [Mr. Howard] had not chosen to meet the issue tendered him. He was interrupted by the Chair, who again announced the orders of the day.

Later, in a long speech at the end of the session, Adams returned to this embarrassing question of whether the committee had bothered even to look at the petitions, and, if not, whether that was proper.

[Mr. Adams]: When the subject first came up, I rose in my place and inquired of the Speaker, not of the gentleman from Virginia, whether the committee had given as much as five minutes' consideration to the several resolutions of the Legislatures of sovereign States of this Union, and the very numerous memorials and petitions of individual citizens which had been, by order of this House, referred to their consideration? When I put that question to the Chair, the gentleman from Virginia rose, and denied my right to do so, and declared that he would not be catechised by me. I said, at the time, that the reluctance of the committee to answer that question was, of itself, sufficient for me, and that I trusted it would be sufficient for this House and for the American People. It was a concession that the committee never had taken these papers into consideration at all. That, I trust, will be the deliberate conviction of the People of the United States.

. . . My question was not personal to the gentleman from Virginia. I did not ask what consideration *he* had given to these documents; I asked whether the *committee* had considered the memorials of the thousands and hundreds of thousands of American citizens, and the solemn resolutions of the Legislatures of not a few of the States of this Union, which had been sent to them that they might be considered. The only answer is that of an individual, that "*he* will not be catechised." This is not the answer to which I was entitled; and I demand an answer yet. Until I get it, my inference will be that those documents never were considered by the committee.

Adams added that he had thought to ask each of its members whether the committee had considered the resolutions for even five minutes, but then had thought better of it.

Mr. Legaré [Hugh Legaré, Pinckney's scholarly successor from Charleston] said that, for one, he was prepared to answer the gentleman's question, though he protested against his right to catechise the committee; and as soon as he could obtain the floor he should give the reasons why the committee declined being more explicit in their report, or entering on the merits of the general question. They were under no obligation to do so; and that for the reason stated in their report. He was fully aware of the importance and novelty of the general principle to which the gentleman was now speaking, and would give his views of it as soon as an opportunity should be allowed him to get the floor.

Mr. Adams. I did not distinctly hear the gentleman. I now understand him to decline answering my question.

Mr. Legaré. What I said related to the committee. For myself, I have no hesitation in admitting that I have not read the papers, or looked into them, nor was I bound to do so.

Mr. Adams. I understand the gentleman from South Carolina now formally to admit that he has never looked into the documents referred to the committee on the subject of Texas at all.

Mr. Legaré. Not one of them.

Mr. Adams. Into not one of them?

Mr. Legaré. Not one.

Mr. Adams. I beg leave, now, to read the 76th standing rule of this House.

"It shall be the duty of the Committee on Foreign Affairs to take into consideration all matters which concern the relations of the United States with foreign nations, and which shall be referred to them by the House, and to report their opinion on the same."

There is the letter of the law. (**Mr. A.** here read the rule, very slowly, a second time.) The gentleman from South Carolina says that he is aware the question is one of immense importance.

Mr. Legaré said he had done nothing incompatible with that rule. He had fully *considered* the *subject* on which the committee reported, and as far as the report went. It was by no means necessary to look into the arguments for or against admitting Texas, when the committee concluded that no question as to the admission of Texas had yet arisen in the House, and did not choose themselves to become the authors of any proposition, without the express order of the House.

Mr. Adams. The gentleman has taken into consideration the resolutions of sovereign States, and of a vast body of memorials and petitions, and has never looked into one of them. [A laugh.]

The resolutions of Vermont and the others had been referred to the Committee on Foreign Affairs, and that committee, after the cursory treatment that Adams exposed, brought in its dismissive report proposing that it be discharged from the responsibility of responding, and proposing further that all such petitions and resolutions be laid on the table. There was no minority report from the committee, but when, in the person of the wonderfully named Congressman Dromgoole, the committee made its report on the floor, Adams's Massachusetts colleague Caleb Cushing, who was also a member, explained that he dissented from the report entirely, but had had no opportunity to present a minority report. He therefore moved that the whole matter be sent back to the committee for the purpose of having the subject "more deliberately and argumentively presented to the House." (This time, somebody at least should read the resolutions.) So that was the main motion, on the House floor: to recommit.

Waddy Thompson, Jr., who could be counted on to do something to harm his own side, moved an *amendment* to Cushing's main motion, which amendment would give the committee specific instructions to report a joint resolution directing the president to take the proper steps to annex Texas. That had the effect of bringing the nest of questions surrounding the annexation of Texas directly to the House floor. On the next day (June 15), Adams moved an amendment to Thompson's amendment, instructing the committee to report resolutions *denying* that Congress, or any part of the government, had the constitutional power to annex any independent foreign state, which power is reserved solely to the people, and also resolving that any attempt by Congress to annex Texas would be "a usurpation of power, unlawful and void."

Adams's motion was an amendment to the amendment proposed by Waddy Thompson to the motion offered by Caleb Cushing, and because it was an amendment to an amendment—which is the end of the line in the House's parliamentary procedure—no further amendments could be proposed. (This parliamentary procedure, although tedious to recount—tedious probably even if you had been there—was nevertheless important, a curious formalized kind of battle in a civilized republic, a ritual with its rules like sumo wrestling or the chest-pounding duels of the Yanamamo, but with words and ideas and public proposals instead of physical force.)

So Adams, having filled in the last slot in the parliamentary board game, had the floor, on the subject of the instructions to give the committee if the collection of petitions and resolutions should be recommitted, which also meant the subject of annexing Texas, which also meant the subject of the gag rule, which created the situation out of which the treatment of those resolutions and petitions arose, which also meant—or did it?—the root subject which all those gagging maneuvers were trying to keep from the floor, and which gave fire to all the petition-writing about Texas: slavery.

Adams in the long speech that followed would skate close to the subject of slavery, and then skate away, and then sometimes dart into it suddenly, and out again, and sometimes Southern members would call "Order! Order!" and sometimes Speaker Polk would interpose. The Speaker had immense power in those days to enforce the rules of the House. Polk must have been listening to Adams intently, and watching him, the two men eyeing each other like Western gunslingers at high noon in a showdown, with parliamentary procedure as the instrument of their contest.

Not all the Speaker's interpositions had to do with the more or less forbidden subject of slavery. Here is one sample, in a passage in which Adams was claiming that the performance (or nonperformance) by the Committee on Foreign Affairs and the committee's defense (or nondefense) of it was a yet more execrable example in microcosm of the larger wickedness of the gag rule:

> **Mr. Adams.** [T]his committee have gone further in trampling upon the right of petition, of which the House has given them an example. The House has not gone the length of refusing to receive petitions, but with a distinction, which I am ashamed to mention in the face of this nation, they have resolved, with great solemnity, to receive memorials and then not to consider them. That principle has been extended by this committee. Sir, if a Yankee was ever charged with manufacturing wooden nutmegs, that was the man to advance such a principle. [A laugh.] Is this principle the

wooden nutmeg of the House? It is that, or it is nothing. I say this for the benefit of such members of this House as are willing to take shelter from the indignation of their constituents under such a distinction.

The Chair here interposed, and reminded the gentleman from Massachusetts that it was not in order to speak disrespectfully of the action of the House.

Mr. Adams. I am much obliged to the Speaker for not having stopped me before. [A laugh.] I assume it as a principle that it is the duty of this House to receive the petitions of all the citizens of the United States, if couched in respectful language; and I further assert it as a principle, that it is our duty not only to receive, but to consider them; and I say that if we receive and refuse to consider, we shelter ourselves under a distinction unworthy of this House—a distinction that would be unworthy of any man in private life, and much more of the highest legislative body in the country.

The Speaker here interposed, and observed that he could not perceive how these remarks were connected with the subject before the House.

Mr. Adams. That I will endeavor to show. I will endeavor to make it very clear to the Speaker. I say that the principle avowed by the gentleman from South Carolina [Mr. Legaré] is but a carrying further of a principle which I reprobate, though it has been three times sanctioned by a vote of this House. The gentleman extends the principle by carrying it into the doings of a committee. In this case, the House, after receiving and slumbering over multitudes of petitions and memorials, and after treating, in various methods, the solemn resolutions of State Legislatures, after laying them on the table time after time, did finally condescend to refer one to the Committee on Foreign Affairs. That was a reversal, so far as it went, of the doctrine and practice which had prevailed. The House, in that case, treated a memorial with so much respect as to refer it to a committee.

. . . One petition was referred to that committee; I understood the chairman to say it was done through inadvertence. Happy inadvertence! it has given us one step in advance of that system of treatment by which the People of the United States have been governed for years. But what a strange thing it is for the chairman of a standing committee of this House to say that a petition on a most important subject, a subject involving the very existence of the Union, has, through the inadvertence of the House, been suffered to be referred to a committee! What is this inadvertence? Why, sir, it is the inadvertence of our not having been sufficiently cautious in suppressing the right of petition. [A laugh.] Yes, sir, in an unguarded moment we opened the doors of this House for the People to petition it; we opened the door to the Legislatures of the States to commune with the Legislature of the Union on a subject of the most vital importance.

On another occasion the intervention of the Speaker did have to do with Adams's having broached the forbidden topic, and even with his having uttered the forbidden word, as in the television quiz show in which a duck drops into view when a particular word is uttered. Adams (on June 23) was recounting the story of the gaggings, and began to recall the action of the previous Congress that we have described here—the denial to slaves of any right to petition, and the attempt to censure him for asking the Speaker about the petition apparently from slaves. A parliamentary altercation ensued.

> . . . From the interdict of *subjects of petition* from the consideration of the House, **Mr. Adams** passed to that of *classes of petitioners*; and here it was impossible for him to pass over the formal resolution of the House of Representatives of the 12th of February, 1837, "*That slaves do not possess the right of petition secured to the People of the United States by the Constitution.*" In adverting to this resolution, he observed that it excluded one sixth part of the People of the United States from the mere naked right of petition; that it denied them the right of prayer—the right which is not denied to the meanest and vilest of the human race by his Maker. He proceeded to say that it was the last of a series of resolutions offered to the House, with the avowed object of invoking a sentence of severe censure upon him, by the House, for simply asking the question of the Speaker, whether a petition purporting to be from slaves came within the resolution of the 19th of January, 1837, the gag-law of that session. He said the members of the present House, who had been present on that occasion, would recollect that he had then explicitly avowed the opinion that slaves were not excluded by the Constitution of the United States from exercising the right of petition; and that—
>
> Here **the Speaker** interrupted Mr. Adams, and declared him out of order.
>
> **Mr. Adams** insisted that he was not out of order; that he was adducing, by way of illustration to his argument, an historical fact. That he had declared, at the time, that if a petition from slaves, complaining of any grievance or distress, to which all mankind might be liable, and which it would be in the power of the House to relieve, should be sent to him, and the House would receive it, he would present it; and that since that time—

> Here **Mr. Legaré,** of South Carolina, rose and called Mr. Adams to order. Calls of order! order! were repeated by sundry other members: there was much confusion in the House, and the Speaker ordered Mr. Adams to take his seat.
>
> **Mr. Adams** persisted in holding the floor, and in affirming that he was not out of order. He demanded that, conformably to the 23d rule of the House, the words which he had spoken, and alleged to be disorderly, should be taken down in writing; and said that he would then appeal from the decision of the Speaker of the House.
>
> **The Speaker** refused to have the words alleged to be disorderly taken down in writing; said that the Speaker was not, in calling a member to order, bound by that rule. That he called Mr. Adams to order for "irrelevancy in debate"; and read the rule that a member shall confine himself to the question under debate; a rule so perfectly vague and indefinite, that the Speaker never resorts to it, unless when sure of being sustained by a majority of the House.
>
> **Mr. Adams** said that this was not a fair statement of the question. That he would not appeal from the decision of the Speaker as so stated; but he still insisted that the words spoken by him, and alleged to be disorderly, should be taken down in writing, and said he would then appeal from the decision.
>
> **The Speaker**, nevertheless, took the question of the appeal, by yeas and nays, upon his own statement, and his decision was sustained by a vote of 115 yeas to 36 nays.

But Adams still had the floor. He had taken it, under the parliamentary situation already described, on Saturday, June 6, 1838. The session was committed to an adjournment in early July. Adams filled the "morning hour" for committee business—the hour not under other orders of business—on that Saturday, and the Tuesday following (Monday being reserved), and on Wednesday, and Thursday, and kept on going. He was then seventy-one years old, and he had a tremor in his hands, but he still took his daily exercise (in warm weather, his famous early-morning skinny-dips in the Potomac), and he was there every day to hold the floor and keep going through all the rest of the morning hours of June, and on into July, including the Fourth, until the last morning hour scheduled for the session, Saturday, July 7, when he was still not through, and held the floor, and technically was entitled to take up again when the House would reconvene in its next session in December.

This and other performances by the old man call to mind a pungent appraisal by Ralph Waldo Emerson: "Mr. Adams chose wisely and according to his constitution, when, on leaving the presidency, he went into Congress. He is no literary old gentleman, but a bruiser, and loves the melee. When they talk about his age and venerableness and nearness to the grave, he knows better. He is like one of those old cardinals, who, as quick as he is chosen Pope, throws away his crutches and his crookedness, and is as straight as a boy. He is an old roué who cannot live on slops, but must have sulphuric acid in his tea."

During these three weeks, Adams went over the issue of the annexation of Texas in relentless detail, charging that the Jackson administration had secretly sought to annex Texas and was still doing so, charging that the administration had withheld documents that would prove that point, defending his own record with respect to Texas when he had been secretary of state and president (had not Adams also sought to add Texas to the Union? Yes, but under quite different circumstances at an earlier and different time, with different methods). Adams recapitulated, also in thoroughgoing detail, the controversy over the gag resolutions, and defined at length, colorfully and repeatedly, his own conception of the right of petition, which those resolutions violated. He read, or caused the clerk to read, the full text of the resolutions passed by the state legislatures on the subject of Texas—both those that favored annexation (Alabama and Tennessee—the resolution by South Carolina had not been transmitted to the House) and those that opposed it (Vermont, Rhode Island, Ohio, Michigan, and—saved until last—Massachusetts) that had been so swiftly dismissed, and casually treated, by the Committee on Foreign Affairs. Now the whole House had to hear them, and Adams's comment on them. He caused to be read a second time, and suggested that the delegate from the Territory of Florida might want to comment on, the section of the memorial from the legislature of Alabama which referred disdainfully to "the unappropriated portions of Florida, consisting mainly of barren sands and poisonous everglades." How do you like that, Florida? Alabama says you consist of "barren sands and poisonous everglades"!

Adams, as we said, could have had the floor to continue when the next session convened in December of 1838, and Southern spokesmen promised to reply to him then, but in the interim between the two sessions the ostensible reason for that discussion vanished. Adams and the anti-Texas resolutions had unsettled the administration sufficiently for it to call off any schemes to annex Texas, and had unsettled the Texas government sufficiently for it to withdraw its proposal and its negotiation in Washington, for the time being. It was a kind of victory, although a temporary one, for the opponents of annexation, and therefore also for the opponents of slavery.

Benjamin Lundy did not live to see what would happen in the longer run—six years later—about Texas, but John Quincy Adams did. Most of our victories, in politics and in history, are for the short run; perhaps one could say all of them are, because, as John Maynard Keynes's best-known line put it, in the long run we are all dead. In another battle six years later, Texas, to the dismay of Adams and other opponents of slavery, would be annexed to the United States. But there are long runs and still longer runs. A little over twenty years after that event there would come a time when slavery would be abolished everywhere in this empire of liberty, which now included Texas.

PART IX

THE GREAT MORAL MONUMENT

25 / THE POOR CLERK WAS NEARLY FRIGHTENED OUT OF HIS WITS

WHILE THE H.R.U.S.—AS Adams called it in his journal—was tying itself in various kinds of knots over the abolitionist petitions, the instigator of many of those petitions, Theodore Weld, had talked and talked and talked, and argued, and orated, and persuaded, and debated, as an agent of the Anti-Slavery Society, across Ohio, and western Pennsylvania, and then across upstate New York, in a year-and-eight-months tour in 1835–36 that became an abolitionist legend—and then had lost his voice.

This last misfortune, obviously fraught with symbolic possibilities, had happened late in 1836. Just before, he had suffered a rare defeat: Troy, New York, had resisted his repeated efforts at persuasion. It had not been converted in the way that Circleville, Ohio, and many other tough places, had been. Even Utica, the scene of that riot led by Congressman Beardsley in the fall of 1835, had been transformed by Weld's sixteen lectures in February of 1836. Hundreds now attended Weld's lectures; hundreds more had to be turned away; and large numbers came forward for the abolitionist altar call. In fact, Utica had become the headquarters of the New York Anti-Slavery Society. Such success was the usual experience for Weld, who by all accounts and evidence was an enormously persuasive speaker.

But it did not work in Troy. The mobs were supported by the mayor of the city, and they did not let up. They drove him from one church, would not let him speak in another, surrounded his place of residence at night; forced the sponsors to end his meetings before they started; threw stones, hitting him twice; persisted. Weld persisted, too. Garrison wrote to invite him to speak at the state convention in the tough state of Rhode Island—let Troy go, and come to Newport. Weld declined, and wrote an "I'll be a martyr" letter. But the mobs, with official blessing, kept preventing him from speaking. Finally the mayor offered him the choice of leaving on his own or being ridden out of town, and at last he did leave.

The A-S Society (as Elizur Wright would abbreviate it, in his letters from Nassau Street) had meanwhile acceded to Weld's pleas that more agents be put into the field, and had insisted that Weld himself recruit them, which, with help, Weld did. (This augmented band, as we have noted before, would be celebrated in abolitionist history as the legendary seventy, loaded with former Lane rebels.) In addition, the society insisted that Weld come to the first gathering of these new agents in New York, in November of 1836, to serve as their chief trainer. That was not the kind of thing Weld, a loner and perhaps a little ostentatiously the humble small-town Western man, liked to do—coming to a big city and dropping both his solitary itinerant evangelism for abolition and his comparative anonymity. But he agreed to come.

There were meetings in the morning, meetings in the afternoon, meetings in the evening, with Weld at the center, talking, staying up late despite a cold to prepare to talk some more the next day. Biographer Robert Abzug, in *Passionate Liberator*, dramatized the result: "By the final day of the convention, Weld, the master orator training those who would follow, could not speak above a whisper. . . . Their agents' convention was his swan song as an orator. After his final whispered phrases at New York, he rarely ascended the speaker's platform for the fifty-seven remaining years of his life."

He also, without intending to do so, gave up the "West"—which then meant Ohio and western New York and Pennsylvania; being a Western man had been part of his persona, but now, able only to whisper on the platform, he stayed in New York, and he would remain for the rest of his life in the East. And so in the winter of 1836–37, while Congress in Washington was having its second round of battles over the gag, Weld was living in a room in Manhattan with a black couple and making his way each day to Nassau Street. There he found Elizur Wright, the Damascus-blade intellect in charge of the office; and Joshua Leavitt, the husky Puritan, the editor of the *Emancipator*.

After the Anti-Slavery Society's decision in May of 1837 to step up the petition drive, the voiceless Weld went to work on it, and was joined by two other noted young agitators: John Greenleaf Whittier was called to New York specifically to help with the escalated petition drive, and he and Weld were joined by Henry B. Stanton, whom we know as another Lane rebel, and the second most effective abolitionist orator after Weld. Stanton had had his triumphs, too, and his mob scenes, in Rhode Island—notably in Newport—and then in New England more broadly. Here now in New York City was a troika of big guns of abolition, with a cause, talking, arguing, abolitionizing, devoting their considerable energies to the rousing of the citizenry to sign petitions against slavery.

Those local and state antislavery societies that the Southern congressmen would mention with such deep foreboding were growing in number. A thousand of them, many planted by the lectures of Weld and the other itinerants, were now spread across New York and Ohio and Massachusetts and Pennsylvania and Vermont and Rhode Island and Connecticut, with sprinklings out in new places like Indiana. There were over 100,000 members. That was a frightening host, if you were a South Carolina congressman, but from Nassau Street's point of view, these members represented a challenge to organizational skill. The association in New York would say to the local societies:

"The success which has attended the exercise of the right of petition thus far, in producing discussion in legislative bodies, in arousing the people to a defence of this right and to a contemplation of the character of slavery, and in the passage of the noble resolutions in the legislatures of Vermont and Massachusetts has shown, that it is one of the most efficient instrumentalities which the friends of the slave can employ. The voice of the people, thus expressed, can arouse the nation. This voice has not yet begun to be heard."

Let the local associates be joined in county associations. Let each county send the names of two persons who will in turn send the names of two persons in each township, with whom Nassau Street—Elizur Wright—can correspond, and to whom—if they prove to be "thorough and efficient abolitionists"—the association can send bundles of petitions with detailed instructions for their circulation. Let the signed petitions then be sent, not directly to the congressmen, but to the county officers, who will check the names and send them to the congressman from the district, if he be one who will introduce them, or, if not, to New York, where the national organizers will decide to which trusted congressman to send them—to John Quincy Adams or another.

The lively instructions by the New York staff—quoted first by Gilbert Barnes in 1933, and since then by Weld's biographer Benjamin Thomas and by abolitionist historian Merton Dillon and by the more quantitative abolitionist historian/social scientist Edward Magdol, and by various scholars in articles, and now by me—create a picture of their work that helps one both to imagine what these volunteers were doing, and to sense the organizational verve of the leaders. "Let petitions be circulated wherever signers can be got," these instructions said. "Neglect no one. Follow the farmer to his field, the wood-chopper to the forest. Hail the shopkeeper behind his counter; call the clerk from his desk; stop the waggoner with his team; forget not the matron, ask for her daughter. Let no frown deter, no repulses baffle. Explain, discuss, argue, persuade."

Gilbert Barnes wrote: "Petitions were placed in stores, banks and barber shops; they were passed around at the hustings, at church fairs, at log-rollings and camp meetings. But most of them were carried from door to door and from farm to farm by devoted volunteers."

The result of all this activity was the avalanche of petitions to the Twenty-fifth Congress that Whittier told his sister would break all their tables. Abolitionist historians report that the time of several clerks of the House was occupied entirely with them; they were shoved away in the antechambers "by the waggon loads." There were enough of them, according to a sympathetic account, to fill a room twenty by thirty by fourteen feet, "close packed to the ceiling." When Adams moved that they be printed, together with all the names, there was—understandably—consternation in the printing department. Gilbert Barnes reported in a footnote (his footnotes are often better than his text) a conversation between a New York reporter and the clerk in charge of the petition file. "At the very thought of printing them," the reporter said, "the poor clerk was nearly frightened out of his wits."

The results in Washington, in the number of petitions lining the halls and filling the chambers, was impressive, but the results in Livingston County, New York, and in Cummington, Massachusetts, and in Conway, Massachusetts, and in Windham, Vermont ("38 females of Windham"), and in Waterville, Maine, and in Harrison County, Ohio ("Male subscribers" in one column, "female subscribers" in a parallel column—many from Ohio in this format), and in Providence, Rhode Island, and vicinity (526 signatures plus 68 from Compton, 37 from Smithfield and Coventry, and 56 from Pawtucket, equaling 687 in all)—the results in these and in hundreds of other communities named on the crumbling papers in the boxes in the National Archives, we may surmise, would be at least as important in the long run. Explain, discuss, argue, persuade.

These were your neighbors who sought you out in your home or field or forest, behind your counter, at your desk, with your team—in a time more innocent than ours, before such canvassing was commonplace and at a time when a petition meant something. There were no telephones, cars, television sets, or radios, and you were not drowned in stimuli. You did not have the variety of distractions and entertainments that a commercial popular culture, just beginning in that decade with the penny press, would come one day munificently to provide. When you went to church on Sunday morning, or on Wednesday evening to the prayer meeting, in the Congregational church in Franklin, Vermont, or the Presbyterian church in Batavia, New York, or the Methodist church in Clermont,

Ohio, there was a chance that you might hear an abolition sermon. A major part of discussion, debate, argument, persuasion took place within churches, and a considerable part among clergymen. The great Protestant denominations were being altered in mind and conscience in the North such that very soon the Methodists and the Presbyterians would split apart into Northern and Southern branches, largely over slavery, not to be reunited for more than a century. The woman who approached you with her petition in hand, at Wednesday-night prayer meeting, or in your barbershop or at your door, would probably be somebody you knew, or somebody who knew somebody you knew.

Some of the petitions showed the local initiative, idiosyncrasies, and spelling: Eight "legal voters" of Massachusetts, "beleaving" that the trade in "rational and immortal men, which is now carried on between the several states of this union, is impolitic, disgraceful, and cruel"—made their handwritten petition to "abolish such trade without delay." But though the language of most was no longer of this locally produced kind—many were just the short statements produced in New York, and sometimes there would be long rows of signatures in the same hand, pasted on—and though opposing Congressmen would sometimes complain about this mass production (new in those days), the campaign was nevertheless still profoundly local in that the bearers of the petitions were volunteers from your neighborhood. The signings proceeded by "neighborhood influence." The circulation of the petitions, we certainly may infer, "raised the consciousness," as a later generation would put it, of neighborhood after neighborhood.

GETTING SOBER NUMBERS ABOUT those "waggon loads" of petitions is a little hard, through the encircling fog of the passage of years, the enthusiasm of advocates, and the reliance of scholars on each other. It appears that at one point someone was carried away, and the number of *signers* was taken to be the number of *petitions*, and that this inflated number slipped out into the bloodstream of scholarship: one may read that there were sent to the House in that one year, 1837–38, 130,000 petitions against slavery in the District of Columbia and 32,000 petitions for the repeal of the gag rule. But if you will stop and look at those numbers and think about it, you will see that they are impossibly high for the number of *petitions*. James G. Birney, who became the American Anti-Slavery Society's secretary, reported to the society that during the period January 1837–March 1838 the society had collected petitions with half a million signatures, equally divided between men and women; that 130,246 of those signatures had appeared on the old standby, petitions praying for the end of slavery in the District (hence, presumably, the number above, assigned to petitions instead of signatures); that an even larger number of signatures, 182,392, had appeared on petitions against the annexation of Texas; 31,836 for the repeal of the gag rule (hence the other number above); and numbers in the twenty thousands for petitions against the admission of more slave states, for abolition of the slave trade, and for abolition in the territories.

To look further ahead, the historian of abolition Dwight Dumond made a close study of the next session, the third session, the short session, of the Twenty-fifth Congress, which would meet from December 1838 to March 1839, and found, by counting what was there in the archives of the House in the 1960s, that there were 1,496 antislavery petitions presented in the House. Some of them tied together more than one of the five subjects on the association's list; if you separate them into single prayers, there were 3,335 petitions. They bore 163,845 signatures from—subtracting duplications—101,850 people. Abolition in the District garnered the largest number of signatures—80,755—with the abolition of the interstate slave trade second—54,547; the others—exclusion of slavery from the territories, and from new states, and opposition to the annexation of Texas, each had some forty thousand signatures. The two states supplying the largest numbers of petitions were New York (362) and Massachusetts (346); the next two highest were little Vermont (177) and hotly contested Ohio (171); Pennsylvania and Maine each sent more than one hundred, and four other states more than twenty.

The member introducing, or trying to introduce, the largest number of antislavery petitions, the reader of this book will not be surprised to know, was John Quincy Adams, who brought forward in that session 693. William Slade, as will also not surprise the reader, was next with 430. Joshua Giddings, a new member of whom more in a moment, presented forty-two, and eleven others presented fifteen or more. In later sessions the circle would grow larger.

A recent thorough petition-counting student of these matters, Edward Magdol, wrote that "the 1838–39 petition campaign exceeded even the well organized one of a year earlier. Extending beyond the ranks of the abolition societies, it garnered 2 million signatures on various antislavery issues. . . . Half a million signatures . . . were gathered specifically for the abolition of slavery in the District of Columbia." There may be some inflation in that number, two million signatures on all the antislavery petitions, which Magdol cited more than once; it appears that it was taken from Russell Nye's book *Fettered Freedom*, and by Nye in turn from an estimate that Henry Stanton made, not for the one year, but for the years of the concentrated petition drive, and for petitions to state legislatures as well as Congress. Thus the nineteenth-century abolitionist and abolitionist historian Henry Wilson wrote that ". . . it was estimated by Mr. Stanton that there were sent, under the auspices of the executive committee at New York, during the years 1837–39, more than two million signatures to Congress and the State legislatures." No doubt that number would include many duplications of names, and it does include several different abolitionist petitions, to several different legislative bodies. Nevertheless, if after we have deflated it properly we take it as having some accuracy, it is a very impressive number indeed, in a nation that in the 1830 census had a grand total, including the South and the border states and including all who would not sign petitions for anything and all who were hostile or indifferent to the abolitionists, only thirteen million persons. In 1840, the total American population, including slaves, would be seventeen million.

Gilbert Barnes—to continue for a moment reporting these efforts at counting—worked out, and Magdol in the 1980s twice repeated, an interesting count of the average number of signatures per petition in the yearly campaigns, showing a steady and marked increase: 32 signatures per petition in 1836–37; 59 in 1837–38; 91 in 1838–39; and 107 in 1839–40. Presumably—my presumption—the more there were per petition, the more efficient was the campaign's organization. More certainly, the more signatures per petition, the more widely accepted the prayer of the petition in the relevant community. Presumably, again, there is in these matters a kind of tipping point, at which the opinion in that relevant social unit becomes widespread enough to bring along the waverers, the followers, the uncertain—so you can *average* 107 names per petition.

Gilbert Barnes, who looked at these already ancient petitions back in the early 1930s, and had studied with scholars who dealt with them still earlier in the twentieth century, reported that even though petitions after the 1838–39 session had not been kept systematically, there had been nevertheless, early in the twentieth century, several truckloads of them "stored here and there about the Capitol." Barnes also reported in another of his footnotes—whether it is believable or not, it ought to be repeated—that a professor at the University of Michigan would tell his classes that "when he was making his *Guide to the Archives*, he found a caretaker in the Capitol keeping his stove hot with bundles of antislavery petitions. There were so many of them, the caretaker said, that those he used would never be missed."

With the renewal and alteration of scholarship about the abolitionists after the 1960s there has come a renewed interest in such of those petitions as remained unburned, boxed away now in the National Archives. Although for reading purposes they are impossibly repetitious, for counting purposes they must be wonderful. Those multiples of boxes of multiples of petitions with multiples of signers are a potential gold mine for the scholarship that builds on counting and correlating and using a computer, and some such studies have been done, drawing occupational and social and political and religious and, as we now say, "gender" profiles of the signers, and examining the signers in particular counties and cities. Who were the women who signed petitions in Sandwich, New Hampshire? From which occupational groups did they come in Fall River, Massachusetts? These studies are more careful than those of Barnes and his teachers and predecessors, but they usually are not accompanied by such colorful footnotes as Barnes's.

Among such close studies are those of Edward Magdol, of the petitioners from eight medium-sized cities "in the early stages of industrialization" in Massachusetts and upstate New York, including Schenectady, Fall River, Lynn, and that scene of many events in this story, Utica. His results reveal a more variegated group of people than one might have guessed. Although the signers were, as would be expected, virtually all Protestants, and most often from the freer, more pietistic denominations, they were not as exclusively "middle-class" as had been hitherto thought, and not as exclusively Whig in party politics. In those eight places at least there were, alongside the professional and commercial groups, large numbers of "mechanics," workingmen, artisans—"cordwainers" in the shoemaking business in Lynn, armorers in Springfield, machinists in Worcester, tailors in Utica—and, despite the program of the national party, a considerable number of Democrats. Mr. Magdol wrote, in summary: "The people who signed antislavery petitions made up a grand coalition of social groups for reform. The men and women in the antislavery campaign lived in all parts of the cities and in the nearby countrysides. They came from all walks of life. Their varied occupations, from 'agent' to 'wool grader,' were listed under at least 120 out of a possible 212 classifications used in this study."

The women in Magdol's cities were not simply the middle-class housewives that may be evoked by my phrase in an earlier chapter, "churchwomen." There were working women too: "Most of them were operatives—weavers, spinners, dyers, and others in woollen and cotton mills. Some were sewing girls in merchant tailor shops." Magdol could identify 242 of the signatures on an 1836 petition in Lowell, Massachusetts, which had 1,409 signatures in all, as coming from women who worked in Lowell's plants and mills—16.8 percent of those who signed, and "significant evidence," Magdol wrote, "of working class participation" in the petition movement. These working women would often make a connection, in song and slogan and argument, between their situation as working people—their own "slavery"—and the slaves of the South.

One might extrapolate from Magdol's studies and infer from the large numbers cited above that the petition drive cut a wider swath across the population than the stereotype of the abolitionist as a middle-class professional, and the concentration on the movement's leaders, would lead one to believe. One value of the work of scholars poring over those names on the petitions, and correlating this way and that with town records and the like, is that even in their dry numbers and charts and sociological preoccupations they bring home to the imagination the larger social dimension of this movement: the multitudes of folk whose names we do not know, except that we can find them on the petitions, who were local leaders, or local followers, in great numbers and of many kinds.

The petitioning kept going. Looking still further ahead, we may notice that 1839–40 was to be a time of change for the abolitionist movement, as to some degree for the country: the abolitionist organizations argued and split and changed. One part of the abolition impulse went into political party work; there would be an abolitionist third party, the Liberty Party, both in 1840 and 1844. The big issue of Texas, on its first round, would occupy some of the space that had been taken up by abolition. And the economic downturn that began with the 1837 Panic and colored all politics cut sharply into the profits of A. Tappan & Co., and therefore into the resources of Nassau Street. But the volunteers and the local societies kept going, and the petitions kept on arriving on the desks of congressmen until the last days of 1845, and the looming contest with Mexico over Texas.

Gilbert Barnes wrote of this petition campaign of 1837–45 that "outside of politics, it was the greatest project in propaganda that had ever been conceived in our history."

WHILE WE ARE LOOKING at the impressive numbers of those petitions, let us go back to the destination of the larger number, the House of Representatives in Washington, on petition day in the regular session of the Twenty-fifth Congress, in February of 1838, after the Anti-Slavery Society's decision of the previous May had set in motion the great table-breaking, poor-clerk-frightening campaign, and after the "secession" and the Patton gag of the previous December had tried to shut the gate. On this February petition day:

> **Mr. John Q. Adams** then rose and stated that he had before him about three hundred and fifty petitions, signed by between thirty-four and thirty-five thousand names, which he had been requested to present to this House.

Three hundred and fifty is a lot of petitions for one member on one occasion, and 35,000 a lot of signatures. Not long before that, the reader will remember, Adams had been presenting individual petitions with fifty or a hundred signers. Obviously numbers of this new magnitude required some innovations in management.

> **Adams** wished to present these 350 petitions with as little consumption of the time of the House as possible. He had, therefore, been obliged to alter the manner pursued heretofore in presenting petitions separately, one by one, announcing the place from which the petitions came, the name of the first petitioner, and the number of names signed to such petitions; instead of which he proposed now to offer them by classes, stating the number of petitions in each class, and, as well as he could, the number of petitioners included in each.

But, he insisted, rubbing it in, this simplifying, time-saving task was made difficult by the gag rule.

> [**Adams**] had a considerable number of petitions in relation to which he himself entertained doubts as to whether they came under the general order of the House, which prescribed that petitions of a certain description should be laid upon the table without reading, or any other action of the House being taken upon them.

He also made clear to the House once more that the effect of its effort to shut off petitions had been the opposite of its intention.

> [**Adams**]: It has happened, that in consequence of the decision of this and [the] former House of Congress in relation to the right of petition [i.e., the gag rules], a great degree of excitement has been produced in a certain portion of the country, and the effect of this proceeding, on the part of the House, and of the excitement occasioned by them, had tended very much to multiply these petitions, which the House appears to be so little disposed to receive and to treat in the manner in which, in his opinion, all respectful and decent petitions ought to be treated.

So, it served them right that they were inundated with petitions. Adams then reiterated that he had about 350 to present; and that he had this statement to make, giving his reasons for presenting them by class "in order that the time of the House might not be consumed." He was about to proceed with his statement when the Chair called him to order.

Mr. Adams then said if he was not permitted to make the statement to the House, he should be compelled to present his petitions separately, which would take up the whole day, and perhaps another day.

Adams recorded in his journal the careful classification and count he had intended to use of the topics of those 350 petitions: 158 "for the rescinding of the Patton gag, or the resolution of December 21"; 65 for the abolition of slavery and the slave trade in the District; 4 in the Territories; 17 for the prohibition of the internal slave trade; 2 against the admission of any new state whose constitution tolerates slavery; and 54 against the annexation of Texas.

And there was one "praying that Congress would take measures to protect citizens of the North going to the South from danger to their lives." Adams's journal of February 14, 1838, told the story of that one:

> *When the motion to lay that on the table was made, I said that "in another part of the Capitol it had been threatened* [by Senator Preston, he later notes in the journal] *that if a Northern abolitionist should go to North Carolina and utter a principle of the Declaration of Independence—" Here a loud cry of "Order! Order!" burst forth, in which the Speaker yelled among the loudest. I waited till it subsided, and then resumed, "that if they could catch him they would hang him." I said this so as to be distinctly heard throughout the hall; the renewed deafening shout of "Order! Order!" notwithstanding. The Speaker then said, "The gentleman from Massachusetts will take his seat;" which I did, and immediately rose again, and presented another petition.*

26 / ADDING ONE INJUSTICE TO ANOTHER

TO RAISE DEEP QUESTIONS about one part of the settled social world is often to encourage raising such questions also about another. If it was wrong that the slave—a human being—had no civic existence except through his master, was it not also wrong that women—also human beings—had no civic existence except through husbands, fathers, brothers?

From the point of view of the Southern and Northern resistance, that sort of question was yet another count against this fanaticism. Where would it end? It was particularly galling to the congressional opponents of the petitions that so many of them were signed by women. Worse: they were initiated and circulated by women. Worse: women stood right up in front of audiences and made speeches encouraging abolitionist ideas, and the signing of these petitions. Still worse: they spoke not just to other women, but sometimes even to "promiscuous assemblies"—men and women sitting right there together, listening to a female. And worst of all: some of one's colleagues—not many, but some—right here in the bastion of lawmaking, the House of Representatives, took these female productions so seriously as to introduce them into the public's business.

No doubt, for all the flavoring of chivalry, the female origin of many of the petitions made it easier to reject them. The debates in the House, in these years, were loaded with heavy-handed comments like this one from Congressman James Garland of Virginia in that first petition debate, in December 1835, about Francis Granger of New York, who had introduced one of the petitions:

> **[Garland]:** Sir, I was very much interested and amused at the sublime and beautiful description of the character and virtue, of these ladies, with which the gentleman [Granger] entertained the House. They are all gentleness, all kindness, all benevolence. Oh, yes, sir, and their objects are all designed for good; and so absorbed are they, in their benevolent designs, that they have not brought themselves to contemplate the awful consequences of their rash proceedings.—Now, sir, I have one single recommendation for the gentleman. It would seem from his remarks, that one of the peculiar virtues of these females is, to disturb his slumbers, and as I understand the gentleman is a bachelor, and these female petitioners are, I do not doubt, old maids, not exceeding twenty five, for they never get beyond that age, I would recommend him to take one of these interesting, charming ladies for his wife, and, in doing so, I have no doubt he would lessen the ranks of the abolitionists by one, at least, and secure himself against any further disturbance of his midnight slumbers. . . .

Marry one of these old maids and that will take care of her excitement. There are many other examples of that kind of thing. And also of the kind of thing that Thomas Glascock, the Indian killer from Georgia, said later in response to Adams early in January of 1837, before the Hawes gag was enacted:

> **Mr. Adams** presented a petition from one hundred and fifty women, wives and daughters of his immediate constituents, praying for the abolition of slavery in the District of Columbia.

Mr. Glascock objected to the reception of this petition.

Mr. Adams did not expect that any objection would have been made to the reception of this petition. The petition was entirely respectful in terms, and came from women, mothers and daughters of his immediate constituents. . . . He put the case to the gentlemen: suppose the petitions to be from their own mothers, would they treat it with contempt or disrespect? He trusted not. . . . He did not consider that the House had anything to fear from this petition of females, certainly not insurrection and blood and slaughter.

Glascock undertook to answer, reassuring the gentleman from Massachusetts that the gentlemen of the South were fully respectful to their mothers and daughters: "No man had, or could have, a higher regard for petitions emanating from such a quarter, if upon proper subjects, than himself." On proper subjects! But on *this* subject we have heard all we need to hear. Furthermore, it is doubtful that these women have in fact done the work themselves:

It was true that this petition emanated from females; but **Mr. G.** must be permitted to remark, that he had great doubts whether all these petitions were not got up for effect of some kind or other, and that an improper influence had been exercised over them by mischievous and designing men.

And as to the question the gentleman from Massachusetts had raised: how could one reject petitions from one's own mothers and daughters? Glascock had an answer on behalf of the chivalrous gentlemen of the South:

[Glascock]: He would have told them something to this effect: Your prayers, though they may be just according to the views of those who surround you, and in your immediate section of the country, yet it is impossible they can be heard at this time: and as the subject is one calculated to renew a great excitement in the country which it is desirable should be allayed, let me, as a son, advise you, at least, to withhold them.

And the gentleman from Georgia turned the appeal around:

[Glascock]: Need he tell the gentleman [Adams] that they of the South had mothers and daughters? Need he appeal to the mothers and daughters of the North that, if they would spare many a bitter pang, and many

> an anxious feeling, they would withhold these petitions? He would beseech them to do so. This is the kind of language he would hold out, not only to the mothers and daughters of the East, but to every person in this country. Why should these memorials be introduced here, when no possible good could result, and much evil was to be apprehended?

THERE HAD BEEN FOUR women at that 1833 founding meeting of the American Anti-Slavery Society, at the Adelphi in Philadelphia, and one of them, the distinguished Quaker Lucretia Mott, was invited to speak. At the end of that event the delegates, who were all males, passed a resolution that thanked the women *as the outsiders* in attendance "for the deep interest they have manifested in the cause of antislavery, during the long and fatiguing sessions of the convention." Perhaps indeed it was fatiguing, sitting there "as the outsiders," listening to the men doing the talking.

Later, Lucretia Mott, Lydia Maria Child, Sarah Grimké, Angelina Grimké, and Elizabeth Cady—who would be important names in nineteenth-century feminism—would all be petition-circulators, and organizers of the circulating of petitions by others. Young Susan B. Anthony (sixteen years old in 1836) would garner signatures for so many petitions that once, we are told by Gilbert Barnes, they filled two boxes in the archives of the House. After looking at them, Barnes called her "indefatigable." The petition drive drew upon a great reserve of frustrated public spirit, shut out of public affairs otherwise by the barriers of the time.

The Grimké sisters were a particularly difficult case for those on the other side, because they had impeccable South Carolina credentials. They had never approved of slavery, even as little girls growing up in a slaveholding family in Charleston, but they had been vaguely colonizers until they came under the influence of the new currents of thought in Philadelphia. Like other able and serious people of their generation—like Whittier, Garrison, Weld, and Leavitt—they experienced a kind of moral conversion and found in opposition to slavery the cause worthy of their life's devotion.

When in 1835 Angelina read about Garrison's frightening experience with the Boston mob—his being paraded through the streets with a rope around his neck—and also about the mobs' threats to the Boston Female Anti-Slavery Society, she wrote a letter to Garrison that expressed her radical commitment: "It is my deep, solemn, deliberate conviction that this is a cause worth dying for." Garrison published the letter in the *Liberator*, to the sisters' initial consternation. That started their career as public advocates of abolition. Theodore Weld, who had not then met the Grimkés, read that letter, and felt vibrations.

Angelina and Sarah wrote pamphlets urging Southern women, and the "clergy of the South," to work against slavery by moral suasion—documents which made the sisters famous in the abolition world, and notorious back home in South Carolina. As they had done with the "incendiary pamphlets" of the previous summer, postmasters burned the pamphlets publicly. And "the Charleston authorities instructed the police, if [Angelina] returned to that city, to prevent her landing while the steamer remained in port and to see to it that she should not communicate with any person in the city, and, further, that if she should elude their vigilance and go on shore she should be arrested and imprisoned until the return of the vessel."

On moving to Philadelphia, the Grimké sisters had left the Episcopal Church and become Quakers. The Quakers, unlike the other communions, allowed women to speak in their religious assemblies, and the sisters began to believe that they had an aptitude and a vocation to give antislavery lectures. To get more training they turned up at that agents' convention in New York in November and December of 1836, two ladies in Quaker bonnets, sitting there in the audience of Lane rebels and male reformers as Theodore Weld held forth about how to be an agent. As Weld was later to say, he had already felt a bond when he read Angelina's letter in the *Liberator* the year before, so Angelina later said that in the intervening year she in her turn had felt a bond when she read Weld's letter about Circleville, published by Elizur Wright without Weld's approval in the *Emancipator*. It must be one of the more unusual instances of a couple finding each other through the columns of newspapers.

Weld served as coach for the two sisters in antislavery orating. The sisters attended black Sunday schools and prayer meetings in New York, and spoke to small gatherings of women, but found commercial New York, with its many ties to the slaveholding South, hard going. The abolitionist leaders recognized, of course, that these sisters from South Carolina had distinctive value as authentic converts from a slaveholding family, and they invited them to tour New England. One history of these matters says: "From then until Angelina's marriage to Weld in May 1838, she blazed a trail of oratory from New York to Boston and Providence which Wendell Phillips said doubled the hold of the antislavery cause in Massachusetts."

Their sensational whirlwind tour of Massachusetts made them heroines to Weldites (and quite specifically to Weld) but an abomination to conservatives; the attack on them, as attacks often do, helped to bring them fame. Some opponents called Angelina "Devilina." One of the biographies claims that "at the time of their New England tour in 1837 Angelina Grimké was the best known woman in America."

Angelina, like others, came to see a link between the plight of slaves and of women: "The investigation of the rights of the slave has led me to a better understanding of my own." And she dealt specifically with the use by women of the constitutionally protected right of petition: "The right of petition is the only political right that women have," she said. "If, then, we are taxed without being represented, [she underlined the analogy to the Revolutionary ideology] and governed by laws we have no voice in framing, then, surely, we ought to be permitted at least to remonstrate. . . . The very least that can be done is to give [women] the right of petition in all cases whatsoever [another phrase from the Revolutionary era]; and without any abridgement. If not, they are mere slaves, known only through their masters."

Garrison and his group sponsored the sisters' tour of New England, and while they were in his territory, to Weld's consternation, they came under the influence of Garrison's perfectionist and anarchical ideas. The disputes that would later lead to a split in the abolition movement were beginning to show. They centered around these points: the sweeping attacks of Garrison and some of his followers on the churches and the clergy, as hopelessly corrupted; a little later, and perhaps the key point, a disagreement about whether abolition should stick absolutely to moral suasion, as Garrisonians argued, or whether it should engage in politics, as Stanton and some others were beginning to say; closely connected with the argument about politics, a disagreement about Garrison's "no government" views—his anarchism, to use a word he did not use; and, not altogether separated from these other matters, the disagreement about whether to add women's rights to the abolition agenda.

Some of the opposition on this last point was substantive—abolition males sharing the conventional attitude on women's place—but some part of it was strategic—a belief that the pursuit of rights for women would divert energies, split the movement, and compound difficulties of persuasion. Some abolitionists who resisted adding women's rights to the cause may be compared to the participants in the civil rights movement in the middle 1960s who believed it was a mistake for Martin Luther King to become a leader in the opposition to the war in Vietnam, not because they supported that war, but because they believed as a matter of strategy that King's leadership was capital in the civil rights movement that should be conserved.

The high point of Angelina Grimké's brief public career would come in February 1838, when she testified before a committee of the Massachusetts legislature on behalf of the abolition of slavery—the first woman in American history to appear before a legislative body. She brought with her an antislavery petition with the signatures of twenty thousand women.

In her appeal by "ethos," as the students of rhetoric call it (by the character of the speaker), she cited her background and multiple identities and obligations (it is a little startling to hear her anticipating Winston Churchill):

> As a Southerner, as a repentant slaveholder, and a moral being I feel I owe it to the suffering slave, and to the deluded master, to my country and to the world to do all that I can to overturn a system of complicated crimes, built upon the broken hearts and prostrate bodies of my countrymen in chains and cemented by the blood and sweat and tears of my sisters in bonds.

A reporter for the Boston *Mercantile Journal*, quoted in the *Liberator* (and in scholarly books since), wrote about her testimony: "It was a noble day when for the first time in civilized America, a Woman stood up in a Legislative Hall, vindicating the rights of women."

NO WOMEN STOOD UP in that bastion of male chauvinism, the United States House of Representatives. There was, however, one long—very long—attack on the prevailing attitude, on the antique point that the social order then had reached: whether it was proper and desirable for women to participate actively in public affairs. This was to come in the midst of the argument about the Texas petitions and memorials in the regular session of the Twenty-fifth Congress in 1838. In the course of the report from the Committee on Foreign Relations, the committee's chairman, Benjamin C. Howard of Maryland, had made this (very typical) comment:

> **[Howard]:** Many of these petitions [against the annexation of Texas] were signed by women. He always felt regret when petitions thus signed were presented to the House relating to political matters. He thought that these females could have a sufficient field for the exercise of their influence in the discharge of their duties to their fathers, their husbands, or their children, cheering the domestic circle, and shedding over it the mild radiance of the social virtues, instead of rushing into the fierce struggles of political life. He felt sorrow at this departure from their proper sphere, in which there was abundant room for the practice of the most extensive benevolence and philanthropy, because he considered it discreditable, not only to their own particular section of the country, but also to the national character, and thus giving him a right to express this opinion.

In his long speech dealing with the report of that committee and with the report's subject—Texas; but Texas meant also petitions and slavery—in June–July 1838, the member from Plymouth, Abigail Adams's son, gave a full-dress answer to Howard and to all those who held the view that women should confine themselves to "cheering the domestic circle," should avoid the "fierce struggles of political life." In this exchange he progressed from appeals to chivalry to appeals to human rights.

He cited "sacred history," to start with, with many examples and quotations: Miriam, the prophetess, the sister of Aaron ("and all the *women* went out after her"); Deborah, the prophetess ("she *judged* Israel at that time"); Jael, who slew the dreaded enemy of her country; Abigail; Huldah; Judith, the beautiful widow of Bethulia; and Esther, who by a PETITION saved her people and her country ("then said the King unto her, what is thy *petition*, Queen Esther?"). One might suspect that Adams had used as a source for his examples the publications of Angelina Grimké, in which all of these heroines, and particularly Queen Esther, appear.

He noted that he had heard a sermon since he had begun speaking which reminded him that Lazarus was raised from the dead—here he was stretching things a little—on the petition of a woman.

From classical history there was a long list of public-minded heroines, and then from British history (Boadicea and Elizabeth) and from the Continent an assortment of queens (did Isabella of Castile, in supporting Columbus, bring discredit on her sex by mingling in politics?). Turning to the history of the United States itself, Adams read long passages from two books dealing with the American Revolution, both, he noted, written by distinguished citizens of South Carolina, that extolled the role of women in the Revolution ("And from whence did relief arrive at last? From the heart where patriotism erects her favorite shrine . . . the ladies of Philadelphia immortalized themselves . . ."; " . . . the ladies of South Carolina conducted themselves with more than Spartan magnanimity . . ."). He then exclaimed:

> **[Adams]:** Politics, sir! rushing into the vortex of politics! glorying in being called Rebel ladies! refusing to attend balls and entertainments, but crowding to the prison-ships! mark this; and remember that it was done with no small danger to their own persons, and to the safety of their families. But it manifested the spirit by which they were animated. And, sir, is that spirit to be charged, here, in this hall, where we are sitting, as being discreditable to the country's name? Are we to be told this? Shall it be said here that such conduct was a national reproach, because it was the conduct of women, who left their "domestic concerns," and "rushed into

the vortex of politics"? Sir, these women did more; they *petitioned;* yes, they petitioned—and that in a matter of politics.

Another of Adams's instructive instances was the performance during the Revolution (rendering themselves glorious) of the women of Baltimore (given his opposition, Adams specialized in references to South Carolina and Maryland). Howard responded that there was not the slightest resemblance between those heroic women and the petitioners about Texas. Perhaps he should have left it at that. Having the floor, however, he went on to suggest "that the gentleman from Massachusetts might find more appropriate models to hold up for imitation to the modest and virtuous girls of New England than the two which he had selected from ancient and modern history—one of whom, Aspasia, was notorious for the profligacy of her life; and the other a woman who had usurped the habiliments of the other sex, and, in man's dress, associated with men for years together. He believed that the females of New England would not relish either of these examples."

Adams was not quite sure whether he wanted to spring to Aspasia's defense or—historians differ—drop her overboard; but he managed to turn the argument and to take a roundhouse swing back at Howard: "The character of Aspasia was to be viewed in connexion with the opinions of the age and the country in which she lived. Those opinions, with regard to women, were not unlike those still entertained by the Turks, that women have no souls; opinions, he would say, which differed but little from what seemed to be those of the gentleman from Maryland, as declared upon a former day."

On a later day Adams adduced, without mentioning the Grimké sisters by name, the two sisters from "a state very deeply concerned in this question," South Carolina:

> **[Adams]:** Sir, I said that with this hand [the hand upon which Joseph Warren saved the forefinger] I have had the honor to present the memorials, petitions, and remonstrances, of more than fifty thousand women, in this House. . . . I do believe, in my conscience, that four fifths, at least, have been obtained by the influence of two women of South Carolina, natives of that State; from their position, well acquainted with the practical operation of the system; intelligent, well educated, highly accomplished, and bearing a name which South Carolina will not disown. . . . Their own names are attached to one of these petitions; and they are almost the only ones with which I have the honor to be personally acquainted. I say I have that honor; for I deem it an honor.

And yet their right to petition has been openly denied.

> **[Adams]:** If there is a gentleman from South Carolina here who is anxious for a correspondence with those ladies for the purpose of a discussion of either or of all those points, I can answer for those ladies that it will be in his power to obtain what he wishes. And if he does enter on the discussion, all I shall say is that I wish him well out of it. [A laugh].
>
> **[Mr. Pickens, of South Carolina, rose to explain.]** The gentleman from Massachusetts has alluded to two ladies of my own State, and, as I understand, to certain statements of theirs which have appeared in the papers, and has spoken of their character in very exalted terms, and I do not in the least dispute what he has said; but I take this occasion to say that I have read the statements alluded to; and, though I know nothing personally respecting the ladies who have put them forth, I must say that I never saw such a tissue of prejudice and misrepresentation as is now going the rounds of the public papers under their names. . . .

Adams picked up on this reference to a "tissue of prejudice and misrepresentation" to contradict it, both with respect to the Grimkés and generally:

> **[Adams]:** I wish, if the gentleman pleases, that he will be so good as to specify the particular misrepresentations with which he charges these ladies, and each of them. He admits that their characters are of an exalted description; yet what they have given to the world is, it seems, a tissue of misrepresentation. Sir, the gentleman himself is in the case of many and many a slaveholder; he knows nothing of the real operation of the system.

In Adams's view the ladies knew what they were talking about, and Pickens did not. He cited a specific case that he knew about: a mother taken with her four children from her husband, a free Negro, who in a dungeon in Alexandria killed with her own hand two of her children and would have killed the other two had she not been restrained. "The woman was asked how she could perpetrate such an act"—Adams is telling this story on the floor of the House of Representatives, with, presumably, the slaveholding members being seized with acute cramps—"for she had been a woman of unblemished character and of pious sentiments. She replied, that wrong had been done to her and to them; that she was entitled to her freedom, though she had been sold to go to Georgia; and that she had sent her children to a better world."

Mr. Legaré, of South Carolina, here rose and called Mr. A. to order. What he was talking about had nothing to do with the question before the House. . . .

Mr. Elmore [of South Carolina—Charleston, in fact] requested his colleague to let the gentleman go on with his insane ravings.

The Chair urged Adams to stick to the point.

Mr. Adams: Here is a single incident in the history of slavery in the District of Columbia, of which I speak, because I was a witness to it. And now, sir, if this debate shall be properly reported, (as I have no doubt it will be) and shall go throughout this country, I do not doubt but through the whole Southern portion of the Union there will be raised one universal shout, that the whole statement is "a tissue of prejudice and misrepresentation!"

I have stated all this in reply to the gentleman from South Carolina, who has told us that similar statements made by those two distinguished ladies of South Carolina whom I have referred to are one tissue of misrepresentation and prejudice. I, for one, believe in the whole "tissue" of facts stated by those ladies in communications addressed to their sisters in a different part of the Union. They are precisely that kind of misrepresentation a sample of which I have now given to this House in the facts I have stated. This I say, calling on that gentleman, or any other gentleman from that State, in answer to these insane ravings of mine, to state facts, and bring the proof that what I have stated is "a tissue of misrepresentation." I say that this story is but one of multitudes of the same kind, not perhaps equally horrible, but all of the same moral complexion. . . .

Adams's defense of women's participation in politics made concessions to the traditional opinion of the day (which he to some extent shared) specifying a "proper" sphere for women, and a certain special virtue in them, but he then expanded, and turned around, that traditional opinion:

Why does it follow **[said Abigail Adams's son]** that women are fitted for nothing but the cares of domestic life? for bearing children, and cooking the food of a family? devoting all their time to the domestic circle—to promoting the immediate personal comfort of their husbands, brothers, and sons? Observe, sir, the point of departure between the chairman of the committee and myself. I admit that it is their duty to attend to these

> things. I subscribe, fully, to the elegant compliment passed by him upon those members of the female sex who devote their time to these duties. But I say that the correct principle is, that women are not only justified, but exhibit the most exalted virtue when they do depart from the domestic circle, and enter on the concerns of their country, of humanity, and of their God. The mere departure of woman from the duties of the domestic circle, far from being a reproach to her, is a virtue of the highest order, when it is done from purity of motive, by appropriate means, and towards a virtuous purpose.

One point in the exchange suggested that Adams might even consider breaking new ground. When his mother had written her now-famous paragraph asking his father to "remember the ladies," back in the heady days of fundamental thinking about the nature of society and government in 1776, John Adams had responded rather badly, passing off her remarks with jocular references to the true power that the petticoat brigade possesses behind the scenes; in correspondence with her friend Mercy Otis Warren, Abigail observed that he did not do so well when he was called upon to apply his principles at a point (women's rights) that might go against his own interest. But perhaps she had more of an effect than she realized. In other correspondence, about the philosophy underlying the shaping of state constitutions, John Adams then himself raised the question—Abigail we may infer had planted the seed—now, just why is it that we say women should not be granted the vote?

Now sixty-two years later the son of Abigail and John Adams is answering the more than heavy-handed remarks of Colonel Howard of Maryland, chairman of the Committee on Foreign Relations of the House, who had suggested that because they could not vote, therefore it might be that women should not be allowed to sign petitions.

> And the right to petition, according to the gentleman, (**said Mr. A.,**) is to be denied to women because they have no right to vote!

Now, John Quincy at that point *might* have argued, as his theory of petitions certainly allowed, that even the weakest, etc., etc., deserve the right to petition. But he did not. He argued otherwise:

> **[Adams]:** Is it so clear that they have no such right as this last [i.e. the right to vote]? And if not, who shall say that this argument of the gentleman's is not adding one injustice to another?

. . .

THE NINETEENTH-CENTURY AMERICAN feminist movement would arise out of abolition in something like the way that a renewed late-twentieth-century feminist movement arose out of, or at least was much stimulated by, the civil rights movement. As Weld wrote to Angelina Grimké, "Mind gravitates from a general principle to its collaterals. It begins with a case self evidently clear and strong, and then takes up its ramifications." Human rights established through the one case find expanded application in the other.

In both cases there was both a positive and a negative connection: positive, in that the awakening to combat social evil in the one regard encouraged it also, by analogy and extension, in the other; negative in that the conventional barriers encountered even in this environment of humane reform sharpened awareness of another injustice. Why is it that the men ride around in command cars and converse on walkie-talkies and hold press conferences while the women do the work? In the earlier movement the question came at an earlier stage: why should not women, as well as men, sign petitions? Surely, they can sign petitions. Why not address public meetings? More radical: why should they not address public meetings at which men were present? Why should they sit in the balcony as spectators at the world convention of abolitionists in London in 1840? And from the operational questions on the one side, and the theoretical/moral ones on the other, the much larger questions, and then affirmations, would arise: were not women, as well as slaves, unjustly subordinated? Were they not "free moral agents," as much as the black persons for whom they were speaking? Were they not also "created equal"?

27 / GOOD BAD BOOKS

SO THERE WAS WELD in the New York headquarters of the Anti-Slavery Society, training the new agents and then, along with Whittier and Stanton, overseeing the tremendous petition campaign of 1837–38. At the same time, staff assignments in small reform organizations being what they are, Weld was made head of the nonperiodical publications department, and, for the same reason, wrote most of the nonperiodicals himself.

The first of these was *The Bible Against Slavery*, a long pamphlet putting on paper a speech he had often used on his tours, especially on Sunday. Of course, one of the arguments you encountered, as you took your petitions to the farmer in his field, the woodchopper in the forest, the shopkeeper behind his counter, was that the Bible endorsed slavery. Many preachers said so, citing biblical passages. Weld cited other passages, and made contrary arguments. To describe American slavery he used a phrase that anticipates the outlook of twentieth-century religious writers, like Martin Buber, Paul Tillich, and Nicholas Berdyaev: THE REDUCTION OF PERSONS TO THINGS. That is Weld's phrase, and those are his capital letters. Slavery in the Bible, he argued, was not like that—not as bad as American slavery.

Another set of objections you would encounter, as you were carrying one of the petitions to the clerk at his desk and the wagoner with his team—not forgetting the matron and her daughter—were horror stories about what had happened after emancipation in the British West Indies. Weld persuaded the executive committee of the society to provide the money to send his old comrade in arms from Lane Seminary, James A. Thome, who was worn out and ill from his own traveling as an agent, to the West Indies for six months, together with an abolitionist editor, to study the differing results of differing kinds of abolition in three islands. They produced a manuscript of eleven hundred pages, which Weld, in his function now as editor, said was too long, and then after cuts still too long. He changed the manuscript and sharpened the argument, in the way editors do, and Thome, in the way writers do, felt pain, but acquiesced. The result, *Emancipation in the West Indies*, showed—at least to those predisposed to believe it—that the more unqualifiedly immediate the emancipation, as in Antigua, the better the results for everybody. The more gradual apprenticeship system, in Barbados, had not worked so well.

But the argument you would hear most directly addressed to the primary petition you were carrying, as you came around, letting no frown deter, no repulses baffle, to Explain, Discuss, Argue, and Persuade, had to do with the constitutional power of Congress over slavery in the District of Columbia. Those senators and congressmen you read about in the newspapers—Calhoun and Hammond and Waddy Thompson and Henry Wise and Francis Pickens—were insisting vehemently, with the threat of disunion behind the insistence, that Congress had no such power. Many Northerners were willing to accept at least some version of their arguments, convenient as it was to their desire to evade the topic. So Weld wrote a series of articles in the *New York Post* on "The Power of Congress over the District of Columbia," which was brought together as a pamphlet and made available to you in your local antislavery society.

Weld in this pamphlet made an important argument that would go on to a long history. Slavery, he said, was the product of (only) local "positive" law, which could be repealed by local law; wherever there was no such "municipal" law on the books, the more fundamental legal and moral commitment of the nation—that is, freedom—prevailed.

By far the most widely read of Weld's publications, however, was intended to respond to a larger and even more potent kind of resistance in your Northern friends to all of your petitions about slavery: their refusal to admit, or face up to, what slavery in fact was like. As the twentieth century would put it, their "denial." The neighbors whom you asked to sign the petition did not believe, or did not want to let themselves believe, that slavery was in fact as bad as the abolitionists claimed it was. Surely not. Here are these gracious and polite white Southern folks we meet when they come North, or Southern friends, or relatives, whom we visit in the South; surely they are not the sort of people who would be associated with a monstrous evil. The stories we hear about slavery must be false, or at least much exaggerated.

When Weld began to put together a book that would respond to that "denial" he had the help of the Grimké sisters. He and Angelina had been married, after their mostly epistolary courtship during the sisters' New England tour, in Philadelphia on May 14, 1838, and Sarah moved in with them in the place they found in Fort Lee, New Jersey. The three of them worked together on the book that would show what American slavery was really like.

Although this book was loaded with, and shaped by, a quite explicit moral outlook and conclusion—no book was ever more so—its essence was something else: a careful assembling of attested *facts*, to make its point. It might be said to have in it an anticipation of the muckraking and investigative journalism, and even of the social science in the service of reform, that would develop in the late nineteenth and early twentieth centuries. To be sure, it includes much explicit and hortatory moral argument of a sort that progressive journalists and social scientists of a later day would eschew. The authors or compilers did not simply tell you the facts and let the facts speak for themselves; they told you, repeatedly, what to think of these facts. Nevertheless, the resulting production has its resemblance to these later efforts in this regard: that it tried to persuade you by assembling overwhelming piles of undeniable specifics.

The title of the book tells you its composers' intention; it is called *American Slavery As It Is: Testimony of a Thousand Witnesses*. Underline the phrase "as it is": you have beliefs and you have heard fictions about American slavery, and your Southern friends and their Northern apologists tell you reassuring tales, but in this publication we will tell you what it really *is*. We will tell you so in the voices of a thousand witnesses—named, attested, undeniable. The publication, aimed at persuasion of a known audience with a known resistance and known attitudes, exhibits a conscious and explicit desire both to be scrupulously accurate and to let the reader know that it is scrupulously accurate. American slavery as it *is*. "Great care," Weld says in his note asking for further testimonies, "should be observed in the statement of facts."

And much is made not only in that subtitle but in the conception of the book, and again and again throughout as well, of the reliance on those witnesses. That American slavery is a moral abomination will be shown by their testimony. What they give you is not simply moral reasoning by which American slavery is declared to be an abomination, although there is plenty of that, too; what they give you also are the facts, so that you can decide for yourself. The book will tell you what these witnesses saw and heard and observed themselves: what slaves ate and wore and how they were housed, and how they worked, and—not a small point—how they were punished and controlled. By all of that concreteness you may be persuaded more effectively than by a thousand rhetorical flights and denunciations.

Much is made of the trustworthiness of the witnesses: in the language of a later century, these are credible witnesses, witnesses you must believe. When Weld asks readers in his note for further testimonies ("Who that can give it and has a heart of flesh, will refuse to the slave so small a boon?"), he is careful to request that those who were not personally known to any of the leaders of the Anti-Slavery Society should furnish references from some person or persons "of respectability." In the book the names and residences of the witnesses are generally given, wrote Weld, except where they still reside in a slave state, and so publishing their names would be "to make them victims of the popular fury."

These witnesses all have some personal and direct experience with slavery in the American South, which experience is specified. The Grimké sisters themselves are quite valuable witnesses for that reason. Whereas Weld knew slavery only as a Northerner who took it upon himself to oppose it, and learned about it in the course of doing so, the Grimkés had been born and had grown to adulthood in a slaveholding family in the heart of the slaveholding culture of Charleston, where their relatives still lived. Angelina wrote, early in her testimony, explaining why she was doing it:

> But it is not alone for the sake of my poor brothers and sisters in bonds, or for the cause of truth and righteousness, and humanity, that I testify; the deep yearnings of affection for the mother that bore me, who is still a slaveholder, both in fact and in heart; for my brothers and sisters, (a large family circle,) and for my numerous other slaveholding kindred in South Carolina, constrain me to speak; for even were slavery no curse to its

victims, the exercise of arbitrary power works such fearful ruin upon the hearts of *slaveholders*, that I should feel impelled to labor and pray for its overthrow with my last energies and latest breath.

In the quest for the facts, Weld had prepared a form letter that asked for such personal letters and documents from those who had lived in the South. That was one component. For the other large component of the book he and the Grimkés consulted Southern newspapers—advertisements for runaway slaves, accounts of court cases, unwary quotations (slaveholders speaking, little realizing that some earnest researchers up in New York would copy their words). Newspapers then, just at the beginning of the days of the steam press, just before the first wire service and just before the telegraph, were much more provincially local than they would later be. In the argument with which Weld surrounded this material he would insist, again and again, that in this part of the testimony, as well as in the speeches and documents, the slaveholders inadvertently pronounced their own condemnation. "As slaveholders and their apologists . . . are flooding the world with testimony that their slaves are kindly treated; that they are well fed, well clothed, well housed, well lodged, moderately worked, and bountifully provided with all things needful for their comfort," Weld wrote in his introduction, "we propose—first, to disprove their assertions by the testimony of a multitude of impartial witnesses, and then to put slaveholders themselves through a course of cross-questioning which shall draw their condemnation out of their own mouths."

The three authors began in 1838 to obtain all of the Southern newspapers at a New York library as these papers were to be discarded, and they clipped and they clipped and they clipped (or perhaps to save the papers they copied and copied rather than clipped). They worked at this project, along with their other antislavery work, for many months. They claimed that they consulted more than twenty thousand copies of Southern newspapers. Although the book has thousands of facts about slavery, Weld wrote, it "contained but a tiny fraction of the nameless atrocities gathered from the newspapers examined." When the book that resulted from their labors was published, Weld, in an "advertisement to the reader" at the front—in another effort to close every loophole for disbelief—invited those who found it incredible to come to 143 Nassau Street in New York City, where almost all of the papers quoted were available for inspection. (It is further typical of the ostentatious scrupulosity of this project that Weld is careful to say that *almost* all of the papers are there, and to express regret that a few are not. "The idea of preserving them on file for the inspection of the incredulous, and the curious, did not occur to us until after the preparation of the work was in a state of forwardness," he explained, but nearly all the papers are there, and for those that are not the *name* of the paper is given, and "with very few exceptions, the place and time . . . of publication." He goes on to say—this meticulous and explicit precision is essential to his purpose—that in a few cases—probably not a thirtieth of the whole—extracts taken early in the project are without date.)

For still more material the book's producers gathered remarks in the records of congressional debates, in other government documents, in memoirs—in any unimpeachable source. "[W]e will establish all these facts," Weld wrote in the introduction, "by the testimony of scores and hundreds of eye witnesses, by the testimony of slaveholders in all parts of the slave states, by slaveholding members of Congress and of state legislatures, by ambassadors to foreign courts, by judges, by doctors of divinity, and clergymen of all denominations, by merchants, mechanics, lawyers and physicians, by presidents and professors in colleges and professional seminaries, by planters, overseers and drivers. We shall show, not merely that such deeds are commited, but that they are frequent; not done in corners, but before the sun; not in one of the slave states, but in all of them; not perpetrated by brutal overseers and drivers, merely, but by magistrates, by legislators, by professors of religion, by preachers of the gospel, by governors of states, by 'gentlemen of property and standing,' and by delicate females moving in the 'highest circles of society.' "

Weld and the two sisters then sat with this immense collection of items—I don't know where or how they did it, but I picture them at a table at 143 Nassau Street, or the dining-room table at their new home in Fort Lee, Bergen County, New Jersey—surrounded (as it may be) by their immense collection of letters of testimony and their copyings from newspapers and books—and they arranged them in piles. They organized them this way, and they organized them that way.

One way was to present a complete "testimony" from a witness uncut and consecutively: "Testimony of the Late Rev. John Graham"; "Testimony of Mr. William Poe"; "Narrative and Testimony of Sarah M. Grimké"; "Narrative and Testimony of Rev. Horace Moulton."

Mr. Moulton—for example—was at the time of his testimony "an esteemed minister," as the text says, of the Methodist Church in Marlborough, Massachusetts, but he had spent five years, between 1817 and 1824, near Savannah, making and burning brick, and overseeing slaves making and hauling brick; sometimes he was overseer for slaves in both the field and the brickyard. He explains that he will not cite particular cases of cruelty, "though I might a great number," but will tell in detail the life of the slaves in the brick-making near Savannah that as a young man he had witnessed.

"Testimony of Mr. William Poe": "Mr. Poe is a native of Richmond, Virginia, and was formerly a slaveholder. He was for several years a merchant in Richmond, and subsequently in Lynchburg, Virginia. A few years since, he emancipated his slaves, and removed to Hamilton County, Ohio, near Cincinnati; where he is a highly respected ruling elder in the Presbyterian church." (The "respectability"—hence presumably trustworthiness—of the witnesses is emphasized throughout.)

The testimony, characteristically a string of observations of slave life including atrocities the witnesses had seen, accompanied by exclamations, would then be printed, as the witness had written it, in full and in the first person. Thus Mr. Poe, the reformed Richmond merchant and Presbyterian Elder, began this way:

"I am pained exceedingly, and nothing but my duty to God, to the oppressors, and to the poor downtrodden slaves, who go mourning all their days, could move me to say a word. I will state to you a few cases of the abuse of the slaves, but time would fail, if I had language to tell how many and great are the inflictions of slavery, even in its mildest form."

Then he launches into the first of the atrocities he remembers:

"Benjamin James Harris, a wealthy tobacconist of Richmond, Virginia, whipped a slave girl fifteen years old to death. While he was whipping her his wife heated a smoothing iron, put it on her body in various places, and burned her severely. The verdict of the coroner's inquest was "Died of excessive whipping."

Early in Sarah Grimké's testimony she strikes a note that recurs in this volume. The perpetrators of cruelties to slaves included those who were, and remained, "in the highest circles of society," fully accepted and respected:

"And here I may premise that all the actors in these tragedics were all men and women of the highest respectability, and of the first families in South Carolina, and, with one exception, citizens of Charleston; and that their cruelties did not in the slightest degree affect their standing in society."

One of the "tragedics" to which she testifies, for example, was a particularly cruel punishment invented by "a female acquaintance in Charleston," whom Sarah heard claiming her invention "with much satisfaction." The punishment was standing on one foot with the other held in the hand, which was later "improved" by a strap around the ankle and the neck, so that "the least weight of the foot resting on the strap would choke the person—a punishment dreaded more by the slaves than whipping." Sarah gives further testimony about the particular cruelties of this female acquaintance, tells the reader that the woman's husband was somewhat less cruel than his wife but was urged on by her, and describes his conscience-stricken death at which she—Sarah—was present.

Another way the composers of *American Slavery As It Is* organized their material was by categories of slave life—food (amount of food; quality of food), clothing, shelter, conditions of work, punishments, and the like—explicitly described to counteract common comforting beliefs about slavery. You believe—as dozens of apologists for slavery have told you—that the African slave is well fed and well housed, living in much better conditions than he would have in Africa, and better than many Northern white working people? The authors printed item after item about the neglect and exposure and malnutrition of slaves—not in those general terms, but in the specifics of dozens of concrete reports. You have been told that punishment of slaves was mild and rare? The book-makers assembled a particularly gruesome collection of dozens of reports about beatings, mutilations, and deaths, all witnessed, from Southern sources. Apologists tell you that the breakup of families is rare? (Hammond argued on the House floor that no more black families were separated under slavery than white families were broken by separation and divorce—so, therefore, apparently, the forcible breakup by someone else's power, under slavery, was to be excused.) The book, again, answers with pages of specific instances of the breakup of families. Weld and the Grimkés thus shaped their presentation quite specifically to the rhetorical situation of the time: to answer the notion that these cruelties to slaves did not happen, or—the next line of defense—that they were rare and not typical. "It is no marvel," Weld wrote,

> . . . that slaveholders are always talking of their kind treatment of their slaves. The only marvel is, that men of sense can be guiled by such professions. Despots always insist that they are merciful. The greatest tyrants that ever dripped with blood have assumed the titles of "most gracious," "most clement," "most merciful," &c, and have ordered their crouching vassals to accost them thus. When did not vice lay claim to those virtues which are the opposites of its habitual crimes? The guilty, according to their own showing, are always innocent, and cowards brave, and drunkards sober, and harlots chaste, and pickpockets honest to a fault. Every body understands this. When a man's tongue grows thick, and he begins to hiccough and walk cross-legged, we expect him, as a matter of course, to protest that he is not drunk; so when a man is always singing the praises of his own honesty, we instinctively watch his movements and look out for our pocket-books. Whoever is simple enough to be hoaxed

> by such professions, should never be trusted in the streets without somebody to take care of him. Human nature works out in slaveholders just as it does in other men, and in American slaveholders just as in English, French, Turkish, Algerine, Roman, and Grecian. The Spartans boasted of their kindness to their slaves, while they whipped them to death by the thousands at the altar of their gods.

WELD AND THE GRIMKÉS were engaging in an attempt at moral persuasion, as they always were; but in this book they—and their witnesses—were carrying on the moral argument at a different stage: not to dispute your premises and values, but to alter your understanding of actual conditions. This peculiar publication cries out on every page against the complacency and avoidance the composers obviously had encountered repeatedly in the white public.

Still another way they organized their material was explicitly shaped to answer specific arguments; the second half of the book is called "Objections Considered." You find the claimed cruelties incredible? Here is testimony after testimony after testimony, much of it from slaveholders themselves. You say, "Slaveholders are proverbial for their Kindness, Hospitality, Benevolence, and Generosity"? Here is instance after instance after instance to the contrary.

One cannot say that *American Slavery As It Is* is a good book by our usual criteria. It was not *written*, exactly, but rather pasted together, with hortatory material introducing each section. The organization is a mess. The index is one of the more spectacularly amateur indexes one is likely ever to encounter, with items of every kind and degree of importance jumbled together; it would be amusing if the subject were not so grim. From this index you learn that you can find "knocking out of teeth" on pages 13, 20, and 83 (one learns from this book that there was a practice of knocking out front teeth of slaves as a means of identification); "Pregnant slaves whipped" on pages 20, 90, and 106; "Pig-sties more comfortable than slave huts" on page 101; "Phillip II and the Moors" on page 8; and a reference to the church father Ignatius on page 10 (Weld called on his seminary learning in his introductory material). The table of contents has something of the same hopelessly mixed-up quality, with an effort to be hyperorganized, on several different and conflicting principles, resulting in chaos. The text itself is such that today no publisher would publish it, no magazine or newspaper editor would serialize it, no faculty could pass it for any degree. Nevertheless, it has a greater merit in its own way than most productions that fulfill the criteria for acceptance under those headings. Why do we write our books anyway? Weld and the Grimkés certainly knew why they were putting this book together, and the earnest passion in their relentless accumulation and repetition-with-variations has a powerful effect, even now, when the issues it dealt with are settled. What must it have been in 1839, and the years of the 1840s, when it was not!

Although the project was begun as part of the publication effort to support the petition drive that had moved up to a faster gear in 1837, *American Slavery As It Is* was not published until 1839. The authors worked at the thing, while Weld was joining with Stanton and Whittier in directing the intensified petition drive, and the Welds were enjoying the first period of their marriage, for two years. The result of their labors was published by the Anti-Slavery Society itself, with no name of an author, but with this line at the bottom of the note asking for further testimonies: "Communications may be addressed to Theodore D. Weld, 143 Nassau Street, New York." It became thereafter the most widely used American antislavery publication. It was part of the "antislavery library" that Nassau Street helped to provide for you, to answer your questions, and to give you ammunition as you carried your petitions door to door. All the publications put together by Weld sold well, but this one outdid the others. It is said to have sold 100,000 copies in its first year.

The immense circulation of *American Slavery As It Is* indicates again the difficulty under which the defenders of slavery labored in a nation that had a commitment to civil liberty. It is impossible to imagine, but for contrast one might imagine anyway, that such a book had been composed, published, and circulated in Nazi Germany, describing from all the sources some brave souls could find multitudes of specific instances of the torment of Jews and others, and specific details of the operation of the death camps, and Nazi experiments on human subjects and the like—not in general terms but in specifics, with names and dates and instance after instance. Suppose it had been circulated as widely in Hitler's Germany as Weld's book was in the United States in 1839 and afterward—100,000 is a lot of copies in a nation of seventeen million, and that was one year only; the book kept on selling, and copies were part of an antislavery library to be read by many. If such an unimaginable thing had happened in Hitler's Germany, the psychology of avoidance and denial in the German population would have been put under a powerful counterpressure.

But to make the suggestion of such a thing in a twentieth-century totalitarian state immediately makes the point. Such a thing was altogether impossible in Nazi Germany, for a long string of reasons: anyone attempting it would have been liquidated; you couldn't get the sources—the testimonies and the newspaper clippings; you would not have had the press to publish it; if such a book had been produced it could not have been openly circulated in Germany. The American slavery system operated with a double disadvantage, by that comparison: it tried to maintain itself in a nation that had civil liberty built into its original institutions, and also into the minds of its citizens—including the minds of its citizens in the slaveholding South. Although the slaveholders could attempt, and to some degree obtain, an "intellectual blockade" within their own states—censoring mail, blocking the circulation of offensive materials, keeping out objectionable speakers—they could not do that with anything like the efficiency of a twentieth-century totalitarian state. There would be seepage, because the blockade could not be complete, the boundaries could not be closed, the Northern citizens of the one nation could not be persuaded to suppress publications (in 1835 at the time of the pamphlet war there had been, as we said, Southern requests to Northern governors to use the full force of government to stamp out the offensive publications, but to no avail). Despite the opposition to its composers and its themes, *American Slavery As It Is* sold and sold, and became a kind of handbook of the antislavery cause.

FROM THE POINT OF view of the defenders of slavery, however, there was worse to come. One of those who read Weld's *American Slavery As It Is*—read it, and kept it with her—was Harriet Beecher Stowe, who had been in the audience, as a young woman of twenty-three and the daughter of the great seminary president Lyman Beecher, at the Lane debates in 1834. Weld, of course, had played the leading role in those debates. After about fifteen years of turbulent history on America's part, and of practice in writing on Harriet Beecher's part, there would come to her as from the hand of God a story about a slave girl's attempt to save her son from sale down the river, which story would become one of the most astonishing phenomena in the history of the printing press and of advocacy.

Harriet Beecher had been surrounded all her life, through her father and brothers and sisters, with the debate over slavery. In 1836, after she married the professor of biblical literature at Lane Seminary, Calvin Stowe, she began to write stories, mostly for religious magazines, and in 1845 she produced an essay defending "Immediate Emancipation" for the Congregational paper the *Evangelist*. The passage of the fugitive slave law as part of the Compromise of 1850 was a major stimulus for her taking the larger step of writing a novel. Published in 1851 in installments in the abolitionist journal *National Era*, and in 1852 as a book, *Uncle Tom's Cabin* was to have an astonishing sale, becoming in the years leading up to the Civil War the most widely sold book in the nation, second only to the

Bible. It may even be true, and not just legend, that when President Lincoln met Harriet Beecher Stowe he said, "So this is the little woman who made this great war."

While she was writing it, she kept Weld's *American Slavery As It Is* with her, carrying it in her purse and even sleeping with it under her pillow. All of those terrible truths Weld and the Grimkés had assembled seeped through the pillow in the night into her head, and came out the next morning in the gripping story that the whole country read. Much of the world, too—the book and its author were honored in England and elsewhere, and the book was translated, according to the Library of America, into "22 different languages ranging from Armenian to Welsh." But the important point was its inescapable ubiquity in its home country.

What the slaveholding world did in response to *Uncle Tom's Cabin* was to produce several counter-novels and other publications—which is quite Jeffersonian, quite the way a civil-libertarian society is supposed to work. The defenders of slavery could not suppress the book, at least in the North, and the barriers between North and South could not be made absolute, and in this relatively free society in the age of many printing presses, Truth and Error, as Milton and Locke and Jefferson recommended, could openly contend the ground. In the book's last chapter, "Concluding Remarks," Harriet Beecher Stowe stepped out from behind her story and defended its authenticity by citing witnesses and attested examples, exactly in the manner of Weld's book. In 1853 she published a "key" to *Uncle Tom's Cabin*—a defense of its authenticity, an answer to those who said such things do not happen, or are rare—which drew heavily and explicitly upon *American Slavery As It Is*.

And when you read *Uncle Tom's Cabin* you are reminded of the atmosphere of *American Slavery As It Is*—and vice versa. Both books have a mingling of a romantic nineteenth-century American Protestant Christianity, including its sentimentality and "moralism," with a perhaps surprisingly resolute attitude toward a very big social and moral topic indeed. Neither book has the discipline or the rigor or the restraint or the discriminations of the intellect encouraged in writers both by the more classical attitude that preceded and the scientific attitude that followed their world. But vulnerable as they may be on many counts to a more recent sensibility, they have a human power not many more sophisticated productions attain. As a sample of what I mean I will quote one more extract from *American Slavery As It Is*, from the very end of the testimony of Sarah Grimké herself (apparently she saved it for the climax). I suggest that as you read this you hear the rumblings of Uncle Tom, if you know the moral atmosphere of that story at all. Uncle Tom, of course, shows to the white characters in the book a heroic devotion to the religion they all supposedly adhere to. Here is Sarah Grimké's testimony:

> A beloved friend in South Carolina, the wife of a slaveholder, with whom I often mingled my tears, when helpless and hopeless we deplored together the horrors of slavery, related to me some years since the following circumstance.
>
> On the plantation adjoining her husband's there was a slave of preeminent piety. His master was not a professor of religion, but the superior excellence of this disciple of Christ was not unmarked by him, and I believe he was so sensible of the good influence of his piety that he did not deprive him of the few religious privileges within his reach. A planter was one day dining with the owner of this slave, and in the course of conversation observed, that all profession of religion among slaves was mere hypocrisy. The other asserted a contrary opinion, adding, I have a slave who I believe would rather die than deny his Saviour. This was ridiculed, and the master urged to prove the assertion. He accordingly sent for this man of God, and peremptorily ordered him to deny his belief in the Lord Jesus Christ. The slave pleaded to be excused, constantly affirming that he would rather die than deny the Redeemer, whose blood was shed for him. His master, after vainly trying to induce obedience by threats, had him terribly whipped. The fortitude of the sufferer was not to be shaken; he nobly rejected the offer of exemption from further chastisement at the expense of destroying his soul, and this blessed martyr *died in consequence of this severe infliction.*

Whether or not you believe this story—it is thirdhand, to be sure, not directly witnessed by Sarah, and may to some readers have a suspiciously predictable neatness (but was it invented out of whole cloth?)—if you know *Uncle Tom's Cabin*, I believe you can recognize the emotional atmosphere and ingredients. It is almost as if this memory of Sarah Grimké's seeping through Harriet Beecher Stowe's pillow at night had furnished the kernel from which the powerfully imagined Christlike Uncle Tom would grow. Sarah adds, ending her testimony:

> Oh! how bright a gem will this victim of irresponsible power be, in the crown which sparkles on the Redeemer's brow; and that many such will cluster there, I have not the shadow of a doubt.

In the twentieth century, George Orwell cited *Uncle Tom's Cabin* as one example of a "good bad book"—"bad" (sentimental and inartistic) by literary criteria (Edmund Wilson, with a slight nod of surprise, noted that it was not as bad by those criteria as one had been led to expect) but good by some other, nonliterary criteria. The phrase "good bad book" had originally been Chesterton's, and had originally meant a book that lasts, and that the public likes, and that has some kind of thumping unabashed merit—like a good music hall song—even though one would be embarrassed to place it in the higher reaches of art. Most of Orwell's examples are like that, too—not political or moral at all, just worthy popular stuff. But then he particularly cited *Uncle Tom's Cabin,* and for the moment, perhaps without quite realizing it, he introduced a new meaning into the word "good" in the phrase "good bad book."

It may be possible—although not desirable—to teach the history of American public life without mentioning any of the novels of Nathaniel Hawthorne, or essays by Ralph Waldo Emerson, or even poems by Walt Whitman, but it is not possible properly to teach the history of American democracy without reference to this book. *Uncle Tom's Cabin* was to be a kind of apex to the Great Moral Monument of the petitions.

PART X

THE TRIBULATION OF THE WHIGS

28 / HISSES AND MURMURS; OR, THE LION OF ASHTABULA

So far in this story, through the adjournment of the second session of the Twenty-fifth Congress in July of 1838, with Adams going full whistle against the annexation of Texas, he had been almost the only articulate antislavery leader in the House. William Slade was almost the only other member to take initiatives, and the taciturn New Englander, although stalwart, was not made for the fast footwork of parliamentary brawling. But when the House reconvened in December of 1838, this pair of leaders were joined by a third. The new man, arriving for the short last session of the Twenty-fifth Congress in December 1838, was a big, stocky, and vocal Midwesterner named Joshua Giddings. He came from Jefferson City in Ashtabula County in the Western Reserve of Ohio, and before his service was done he would earn the title "the Lion of Ashtabula."

This lion-to-be had been elected to fill the term of a member who had resigned. He would thereafter be elected and reelected for nine consecutive terms, roaring on through twenty-one years, up through the birth of the Republican Party to the brink of civil war.

Giddings kept a journal during his first session in Congress. Later, as happens with most journals, he neglected it; only John Quincy Adams could keep a journal going through a very active political life, for sixty-five years. But Giddings did keep his going long enough to record the difficulty a new member, especially one from an opposition party and with an unpopular stance, would have in getting the floor, and getting his topic onto the floor.

He also recorded in his journal the diffidence and nervousness a new member feels on first entering such a body, even though he is on his way to becoming a lion. There comes a moment when he does get the floor, and for the first time gets up on his legs and makes a speech, with these two hundred pairs of eyes watching and ears listening, with all the electricity of cultural difference and political and historical significance in the air. Like all the Phineas Finns in the history of parliamentary government, he had that first moment when he wondered about his voice:

> [Giddings's journal, December 29, 1838] The subject of granting pensions came up in debate; it being a subject upon which I thought myself possessed of tolerable information, and the House being thin, I ventured for the first time to address the House. I expected to be greatly embarrassed and to have my voice tremble, but was surprised to find my voice full and to be able to make myself heard through the whole hall. I spoke but a moment, not intending to occupy time, but wishing to try my voice.

After a month, Giddings had begun to emerge from the pack:

> [January 7, 1839] I have now fairly made my debut and to-day I fancied myself, on entering the hall, greeted more warmly than heretofore; members who had previously barely paid the passing salutation, now came to my seat, with great politeness inquired after my health, and many of them congratulated me upon the favorable reception of my speech. . . .

Meanwhile in those early days while he was getting his voice he was noticing the contrast in the representatives of the sections:

> [December 14, 1838] It is a fact, which every man of observation must see, by spending a few days in the Representatives' hall, that there is a vast difference in the character of the members from the North and South. . . . [E]very person present must have witnessed the high and important bearing of the Southern men; their self-important airs, their overbearing manners, while the Northern men, even on the subject of slavery, are diffident and forbearing. I have myself come to the honest conclusion that our Northern friends are, in fact, afraid of these Southern bullies.

For himself Giddings was determined not to be afraid of the Southern bullies: "This kind of fear I never experienced, nor will I submit to it now." In his very first days he prepared the boldest of resolutions:

> [December 14, continuing] I have drawn up a resolution calling for information as to the slave trade in the District of Columbia, which, among other things, calls for a statement of the number of slaves who have murdered themselves within that District during the last five years, after being sold for foreign markets, and the number of children who have been murdered by their parents during said time, under the apprehension of imme-

diate separation for sale at a foreign market, and the amount of revenue collected on sale of licences to deal in human flesh and blood.

But, after all, even a young lion had to develop some prudence:

> [December 14, continuing] I showed the resolutions to several friends, who advise me not to present them on two accounts: first, that it will enrage Southern members; secondly, that it will injure me at home. . . .

Giddings noticed the atmosphere of suppressed and threatened violence that underlay the motions and procedure and speechmaking in the House. He made this report, in his first long speech:

> **[Giddings]:** Sir [addressing the Speaker, as is the form], upon this floor I have heard gentlemen—honorable gentlemen—say that those citizens who had . . . petitioned the House [against slavery and the slave trade] should be hanged if found in Southern states.

To be sure, Giddings was to learn that the "slaveholders, slavedrivers, slavebreeders" of the South, whom one treated as one monolithic horrendous stereotype in the discussions of the Ashtabula County Anti-Slavery Society, were not all of a piece. There was some graciousness and civility, even to him, along with contrasting responses, and there was among them a wide variety of ability and even of position. As it happened, Giddings, coming in the middle of a Congress, drew a seat in the hall alongside a congressman named Isaac Holmes, who had succeeded Legaré, who in his turn had succeeded Pinckney, from—Charleston! They managed.

But for twenty-one years, whenever Giddings got up to speak much of the South would find it very hard to take.

GIDDINGS WAS STILL CONSCIENTIOUSLY keeping his journal in the early days of his first session of Congress, when the House dealt once again with the gag.

> [Giddings's journal, December 11] The rules were then suspended and Mr. Atherton arose to sustain his resolutions by a written speech, at the close of which he called for the previous question. Excitement now arose, . . . hisses and murmurs of contempt for the *man* and *the act* became audible. . . .

The notable fact about this event, and a reason for the hisses and murmurs, was that Atherton was a *Northerner*. The italics are Giddings's own, and the hisses and murmurs of contempt reflect, we may surely surmise, the response by other free-state congressmen—Whigs in particular—to the introduction of a gag for the first time by a free-state congressman (Pinckney, Hawes, and Patton had all come from slave states; Atherton came from New Hampshire).* By this act Atherton's name was to be enrolled, in the growing community of opponents of slavery and defenders of civil liberty, on the list of particular villains. The late-nineteenth-century German historian von Holst, not constrained unduly by claims of objectivity, wrote of him: "This gag earned a peculiarly sad celebrity, because a northern representative turned Judas. To this one deed, Atherton of New Hampshire owes it that his name shall always assert for itself a place in the history of the United States."

It has a place—or two places—also in the antislavery poetry of John Greenleaf Whittier. In a poem greeting the New Year of 1839, Whittier deplored Northern congressmen's subservience, in the year past, to their Southern colleagues:

> Yet, shame upon them! there they sit,
> Men of the North, subdued and still;
> Meek, pliant poltroons, only fit
> To work a master's will.
>
> Sold, bargained off for Southern votes,
> A passive herd of northern mules,
> Just braying through their purchased throats
> Whate'er their owner rules.

Whittier then singled out, in this passive herd of northern mules, a particularly meek and pliant poltroon and identified him in a footnote:

> And he,* the basest of the base,
> The vilest of the vile, whose name,
> Embalmed in infinite disgrace,
> Is deathless in its shame?
>
> A tool, to bolt the people's door
> Against the people clamoring there,

*Charles G. Atherton of New Hampshire lodged during this third session of the Twenty-fifth Congress in a lodging house kept by a Mrs. S. A. Hill, "nearly opposite Gadsby's," with ten representatives every one of whom came from a slave state.

An ass, to trample on their floor
A people's right of prayer!

The asterisk indicated Whittier's own footnote of identification of this "vilest of the vile": "The Northern author of the Congressional rule against receiving petitions of the people on the subject of slavery," in other words, Charles G. Atherton of New Hampshire.

A few years later, in 1846, there would occur in New Hampshire, which had up to that point been the New England state that most solidly supported the Democrats and the alliance with the South, a political upset, and the opponents of slavery would win some startling victories. Whittier (anonymously, and of course ironically) greeted the victory for his side with a retrospective mock lament in the voice of a defeated Democrat:

Was it for such a sad reverse
Our mobs became peacemakers,
And kept their tar and wooden horse
For Englishmen and Quakers?

For this did shifty Atherton
Make gag rules for the Great House?
Wiped we for this our feet upon
Petitions in our State House?

Shifty Atherton, back in 1838, was subject to hisses and murmurs also for giving a "written speech" (!) and then moving the previous question, which if voted would end, or in this case prevent, any discussion. But presumably the hisses and murmurs were directed finally at the evidence of a Van Buren–Democratic steamroller. What Giddings presumably did not know was that the motion Atherton made, with a states'-rights preamble, had been written by the Democratic leadership in Speaker Polk's apartment.

The Van Buren–Democratic–Polk leadership was determined *not* to allow another speech like the one that Slade had attempted to make at the start of the previous session, which led to the "secession" by Southern members. The gag was now introduced smack at the beginning of the session, without the usual period of trial and testing, during which Slade, Adams, and others could slip in some petitions and some speeches on slavery. And as soon as it was introduced, the previous question was called and passed, preventing all debate. For four regular sessions in a row the gag resolution had been enacted at progressively earlier stages: May 26, 1836; January 19, 1837; December 21, 1837; December 11, 1838.

On the night that Atherton's motion passed, Adams wrote in his journal one of his more sweeping predictions, with a Puritan-Calvinist tinge, about the ultimate outcome:

The conflict between the principle of liberty and the fact of slavery is coming gradually to an issue. Slavery has now the power, and falls into convulsions at the approach of freedom. That the fall of slavery is predetermined in the counsels of Omnipotence I cannot doubt; it is a part of the great moral improvement in the condition of man, attested by all the records of history. But the conflict will be terrible, and the progress of improvement perhaps retrograde before its final progress to consummation.

Atherton's resolution, an example perhaps of that retrograde movement, denied Congress not only the right to touch slavery in the states, the District, or the territories but also the right to "prevent the removal of slaves from one state to another" (not just from one *slave* state to another), and also moreover and most broadly the right "to discriminate between the institutions of one portion of the states and another." Atherton's philosophical prelude put the gag on the foundation of a rigid states'-rights restriction on the power of the national government.

The parts of his proposal were voted on separately, and his preliminary states'-rights constitutional statement received an even larger majority (146 to 52) than the gag resolution itself (126 to 78). We may interpret this to mean that a great many Northerners, Northern Democrats particularly, supporters of the Van Buren administration, *wanted* it to be affirmed that they had *no* power over slavery—that this matter was entirely to be left to the control of the Southern states. It would be a relief to believe that. It would be a political advantage to believe that (holding together the Democratic Party, and the support for Van Buren's administration in the South and North). And the Democrats had a states'-rights heritage. A journal that supported the Democratic Party—the *Democratic Review*—made this smug comment, in its April issue of 1839, about the passage of the Atherton resolutions:

By one of the most skillful, prompt and energetic parliamentary movements that we have ever witnessed, the Democratic party in the house blighted in the bud every hope that might have been cherished of weakening the daily growing strength of the [Van Buren Democratic] administration at the south, by the agitation of this [the slavery] question. By the famous "Atherton resolutions," not only was this long-vexed question, as a political one, placed at last, fully and distinctly, on its true ground of the state-rights principle, so as to be able to combine the free support of all

> the democracy of the north, of which many had before had but an imperfect understanding of it, but, moreover, a sudden and total extinguisher was put upon the very possibility of making it a means of party agitation within the halls of congress. This movement set the matter at rest. . . .

But of course it did not set the matter at rest. Upon the passage of each of these gag resolutions there would be such editorials of rejoicing, gloating, and relief in Southern papers, and in Democratic Party papers, but each time the rejoicing would prove to be misplaced. So it would prove with Atherton's "sudden and total extinguisher"; although it may have damped the fires in the House, it fanned them in the Northern public.

And it did not altogether put out the flames in the House. It is very hard to keep a particular subject from being discussed in a free society's parliamentary body, if there are those, in the public and in the body itself, who want to discuss it. The very attempt to stifle the discussion heightens the significance of every approach or approximation to it, every hint of it. And the suppression in the legislature stimulates opposition in the public, even among those who had no sympathy with the stifled subject. Civil liberty becomes the issue, joined to, or superseding, the issue the stiflers intend to squelch.

IN GIDDINGS'S FIRST WEEK on the floor, on December 11 and 12, Atherton and the Democrats had put forward their prompt and philosophically justified (states'-rights) gag rule. Giddings, of course, voted against every part of it, but otherwise played no role in the matter.

Soon, however, after some preliminary efforts at direct assault with petitions were thrown back by the gag, Giddings joined Slade and Adams in flank attacks, making his first important speech in the House not on petition day but during regular business, on February 12, 1839, in response to a report from the Committee on the District of Columbia. That committee proposed a bill providing $30,000 to build a free bridge across the eastern branch of the Potomac River—the Anacostia River of today—and to purchase the stock of one of the existing toll bridges. Perhaps it was a useful example of those "internal improvements" that Whigs generally favored. But Giddings rose to move to strike out the enacting clause, a device congressmen use to kill a bill, and he gave as his reason—the slave trade. And he explained why at length.* He said that the tax money of

*The *Congressional Globe* reporter for that day was either unsympathetic or not very competent, because he gave only a short botched summary of Giddings's carefully worked-out speech, but it was printed in a local newspaper and distributed through antislavery circles.

free-state citizens should not be used for improvements in the District so long as it remained a slave market:

> **[Giddings]:** It is known, sir, that the slave trade, in its worst and most abhorrent forms, is being carried on here to an alarming extent. (Here Mr. Giddings was called to order, but the chair decided him in order.) We are told by some honorable gentlemen, that the subject of its continuance cannot be discussed in the House; that a dissolution of the Union would follow as the inevitable consequence of any interference with the traffic on the part of Congress.

But Giddings was not going to let that threat carry the day; there were strong feelings, more worthily based, after all, on the other side.

> **[Giddings]:** On the other hand, I have come to the conclusion that Northern men, who have from their infancy been bred up in the love of liberty, where every precept impressed upon their youthful minds, every principle of their matured years, has habituated them to think of the slave trade with disgust and abhorrence, to contemplate it as only existing among barbarians and uncivilized nations, to look upon it with horror; I say, sir, that it is my opinion that such men can never consent to continue the seat of government in the midst of a magnificent slave market. I say it distinctly to the committee, to the Nation, and to the world, that Northern men will not consent to the continuance of our National councils where their ears are assailed, while coming to the capitol, by the voice of the auctioneer publicly proclaiming the sale of human, of intelligent beings.

The Speaker had to decide whether this discussion fell under the ban of the gag rule. Giddings kept going, despite the rumbles of disapproval, and gave his reasons, and described what it felt like to be gagged.

> **[Giddings]:** I have been induced to embrace the present opportunity by a deep and solemn sense of justice, which I think is due to the district which I represent, and to a large part of the Northern States. They, sir, feeling an honest abhorrence of the slave trade, have sent in their petitions against it. I have myself presented the petitions of many thousands of Northern freemen on the subject, but their petitions have been disregarded, and the voice of American freemen, in favor of liberty, has been silenced. Their representative sent here with authority to act for them, to speak their views, to express their wishes, has been bound, hand and foot, with a sort of legislative straight-jacket, so far as the subject of this slave trade is concerned, and his lips have been hermetically sealed, to prevent him from a declaration of their views, and from demanding their rights. . . .

And now he made that new argument about the free citizen's taxes, and joined that to the rejecting of the petitions and memorials in a pattern of injustice:

> **[Giddings]:** But, sir, while the voices of Northern freemen are silenced upon this floor, and their Representatives here are not permitted to declare the sentiments of those who sent them, we are called on to make heavy appropriations of their money for the benefit of this District. Many thousands of our people have endeavored to express to this House their views of the slave trade as carried on here. We refuse to hear them; we treat their petitions with contempt, but, in answer, say "Your money shall be taken for the improvement of this city, although it be a slave market; we will not hear your objections to the slave trade, but we will tax you to build a slave market."

We reject their petitions, Congressman Giddings said, but we take their tax money to support (indirectly at least) what they are petitioning against.

> **[Giddings]:** This, sir, is wrong; it is palpably wrong. . . . The language of the people of this District is expressed in their memorials, lately presented to both houses of Congress. In those memorials the free and independent citizens who petition us in regard to the slave trade of this District are termed "a band of fanatics;" their petitions are termed "seditious memorials;" their efforts to stop the inhuman and barbarous practice of selling men, women, and children, are termed "foul and unnatural." Sir, under all this abuse, I am asked now to contribute from the funds of the people thus abused, to the improvement of this city and for the benefit of those who thus assail their motives and stigmatize their acts. I object to the appropriation, under these circumstances. I protest against it and I repeat, that while this state of things remains, I shall be opposed to all appropriations in this District, not necessary for the convenience of Government.

Later Giddings, who after all was no "meek, pliant poltroon," gave a description, like those of Slade, of the slave trade in front of the Capitol itself:

> **[Giddings]:** I, sir, have alluded to the fact that, on the beautiful avenue in front of the capitol, members of Congress, during this session, have heard the harsh voice of the inhuman auctioneer, publicly selling human beings, while they were on their way to the capitol. They have also been com-

pelled to turn aside from their path, to permit a coffle of slaves, males and females, chained to each other by their necks, to pass on their way to this National slave market.

That was too much, and brought another interruption, and a wrangle and excitement the *Globe* reporter tried to write down. Both Slade and Adams came to Giddings's aid, and Giddings, just getting to know the ex-president, had an encounter with him on the House floor that he described in this way:

[Giddings's journal]: . . . the House became a scene of perfect confusion and uproar. Some appeared to enjoy this very much; among these the venerable ex-President [who] laughed most heartily, and coming to my seat, advised me to insist upon my rights; not be intimidated by the course taken by the Southern men.

When the confusion got straightened out enough to take a vote, Giddings won a victory, of a sort. Although it was a thin House—presumably many Southerners had decamped during Giddings's obnoxious speech—and although it is always easy to vote against spending money, not necessarily for fancy reasons like Giddings's, still his motion to strike the enacting clause carried by a vote of 76 to 56. That free bridge across the Anacostia, caught in the high winds of larger issues, would have to wait for calmer times.

29 / ENDING SLAVERY WITHIN THE CONSTITUTION

SHIFTY ATHERTON'S EARLY AND peremptory gag, of course, did not stop Adams and Slade and the petitioners from evading it in ingenious ways. Immediately after its enactment in December of 1838, Adams introduced a resolution stating that "the powers of Congress, being conferred by the Constitution of the United States, no resolution of this House can add to or deduct from them." That's it. That's the whole resolution. Adams, of course, meant to imply that the gag rules could not take away the powers of Congress; that in spite of the rule, Congress got its powers from the Constitution and could not be impeded; that the gag rule was unconstitutional. But members could make their own contrary interpretation of the resolution's general statement, so after at first denying a suspension of the rules to pass this very general resolution right away, the congressmen looked at it again—and passed it! No harm in that one. It was certainly the only one of these provocative resolutions that passed; it was too subtle, or too unspecific, to have any result.

Adams would make lists of topics that would certainly bring slavery onto the House floor gag rule or no, and high among them would be the new nation's foreign relations, and the efforts to cope with the now illegal slave trade, and more specifically questions concerning the newly independent nation of "Hayti." When, in this third session of the Twenty-fifth Congress he offered a petition urging the opening of negotiations and international intercourse with Hayti, Henry Wise protested that this would represent "wholesale amalgamation, incorporating a black Republic with a white one."

A bit later in that same session, Adams presented a memorial from "sundry inhabitants of Boston" asking Congress to remove the seat of government from the District of Columbia to some point farther north, where the principles of the Declaration of Independence are "not treated as a mere rhetorical flourish." Needless to say, that one did *not* pass. Adams apparently discussed it with a straight face, referring to a memorial he had presented at the previous session, never acted upon, from residents of the District, proposing the return—"retrocession"—of the District to Maryland and Virginia. Now, said Adams, apparently in all seriousness, we can treat *this* new memorial as a *compromise*, and he moved its reference to a select committee to consider how to give the District back to the states. A new member from Maryland who would play an important role in sessions to come, William Cost Johnson, did what he would often do: he moved to lay the motion on the table, which was voted 108–53.

But Adams promptly introduced another memorial, which won the prize for audacity in this session. This one, in its ironical way, attacked not slavery but what in the late twentieth century would come to be called racism. Imagine the early-nineteenth-century slaveholding Southerners listening to this. It is the *Congressional Globe*'s reporter who editorially characterizes the memorial as humorous:

> **Mr. Adams** presented another memorial of a humorous character, asking the appointment of a "committee on color" to whom should be referred all office holders and members of Congress, for the examination of their respective pedigrees; said committee to report on the same, and in all cases where the parties shall be found to have the least drop of colored blood in their veins, they shall be expelled from office and their places filled by persons of pure Anglo Saxon blood.

Mr. Adams was about to make some remarks on the subject, when

Mr. Dromgoole rose to ask if the memorial had been received, as, if not, he would raise the question of reception. He considered the memorial as an evident ridicule of the House.

The Speaker stating that it had not as yet been received—

Mr. Dromgoole raised the question of reception.

Mr. Adams denied that the memorial was in the least disrespectful to the House, and demanded the yeas and nays on the question of reception; which, being ordered, were—yeas 24, nays 117.

So the House refused to receive Adams's memorial proposing a committee to look into the members' own racial purity.

Mr. Adams inquired, as the House had refused to receive, whether the motion to refer would be entered on the journal?

The Speaker replied that it would not, the memorial being in the possession of the member.

Mr. Adams said, if it was in order, he would move the printing of the memorial, that the House might see what it was they had refused to receive.

The Speaker said that such a motion was not in order.

Mr. Adams then made a request that it be entered upon the journal that he had made the motion to print.

The Speaker decided the motion to be out of order.

William Slade offered, in addition to a straightforward resolution attacking the slave trade in the District ("trade in human beings . . . outrageous violation of human rights . . . disgrace to the country") and another proposing to rescind as much of the Atherton gag as applied to the slave trade in the District, which, needless to say, were laid on the table by an overwhelming vote, another resolution, which might have taken the prize for ingenuity, under conditions in which the gag rule excluded resolutions on slavery. It did not mention that subject by name:

Whereas, on the 30th day of January, in the year of our Lord one thousand eight hundred and thirty-nine, there were driven by the doors of the Capitol of the United States in view of members of both Houses of Congress, thirty men chained and handcuffed, together with twenty women and children; and whereas there are circumstances which justify a strong suspicion that it was for no offence against the laws of the United States, or of any of the States, that said men, women and children were chained, handcuffed and driven as aforesaid: Therefore,

Resolved, That a committee of seven members of the House be forthwith appointed to inquire and report:

1. The authority under which the said men, women and children were thus chained, handcuffed, and driven as aforesaid . . .

And so on. What had these men, women, and children done, that they were thus chained, handcuffed, and driven? What crime had they committed? Congress should investigate.

Adams and Slade and Giddings were not the only congressmen presenting petitions that challenged, evaded, or mocked the gag rules. Congressman Granger of New York presented a petition from sundry citizens of Hopewell, New York, praying for protection of the constitutional right to the use of the post office, and for adequate security for their persons in all states of this union—and Henry Wise objected to its reception. Congressman Francis James of Pennsylvania introduced a petition praying Congress to look into the laws of the District and the territories, and to repeal everything therein that was inconsistent with the Declaration of Independence and with the principle of doing to others as we would have others do to us. Henry Wise promptly moved that that one be rejected, too. Of course, everyone understood that the petitioners meant to imply that slavery and the slave trade violated the Declaration of Independence and the Golden Rule—but the resolution did not say so. Wise and the gaggers, by rejecting and killing the petition, in effect accepted that implication, as by moving to reject it they accepted the implication in Granger's petition that they did not support freedom of the mails and personal movement. They were limning a portrait of themselves that would make larger and larger sections of free-state opinion more and more distressed.

ADAMS'S PRACTICE THROUGHOUT this long battle was to subordinate—or to appear to subordinate—the antislavery cause to the issue of civil liberty. He made his fight for the "four freedoms," as he would call them, anticipating FDR's twentieth-century phrase for a different list. Adams's four did not include freedom from want or freedom from fear, but did include the civil-libertarian heart of the republican government for which his father and mother, and the founding generation, had fought: freedom of speech, freedom of petition, freedom of debate in Congress, freedom of the press.

The abolitionists, although applauding his fight against the gag rule, and although grateful to him for introducing, or rather trying to introduce, their petitions, were nevertheless not in accord with him on this subordination. Certainly they did not understand his position on slavery in the District. Why when he would introduce whole carloads of their petitions asking its abolition would he then state that he himself was not in agreement with the prayer of the petitioners? Why in his private letters to them would he then suggest that they desist from focusing on this point, that they focus instead on the issues in the West—the annexation of Texas or of other new slave states?

On the one hand the "venerable ex-President," as Giddings called him, gave to the fight against the gag rule and the other slaveholder repressions a voice and a visibility incomparably greater than there would have been without him. He was not a fringe figure, as were the abolitionist leaders, but a central figure to the history of the nation. And the old man certainly gave the fight for the right of petition, the fight for his four freedoms, everything he had. His was no perfunctory or part-time support, but unremitting, constant, forceful, and intelligent.

On the other hand, he kept saying he did not support the prayer of the petitions he was presenting and so energetically defending. Thus on January 21, 1839, during what we may call the first Giddings session (the third, lame duck session of the Twenty-fifth Congress), he made a long speech in which he asked personal privilege, and then explained again where he stood:

> **[Adams]:** . . . I wish distinctly to aver that though I have earnestly advocated the right of persons to petition for the abolition of slavery in the District of Columbia, I myself am not prepared to grant their prayer. On the contrary, if the question were presented at once, I should vote against it. What change a fair and full discussion might make upon my mind I do not know, but so far I see no reason to change my opinion, though I have read all that the abolitionists themselves have written and published on the subject.

Notice that he suggests that if there were a "fair and full discussion" (implication: which the gag rule prevents) he might change his mind. Nevertheless his avowal once again of his position was distressing to his antislavery allies.

William Slade gave voice to this distress to his new colleague Giddings. Giddings wrote in his journal: "This day Mr. Slade, of Vermont, came to me with an expression of great anxiety in regard to the exposition which Mr. Adams had made of his views concerning slavery. He appears to apprehend great results from these disclosures. Not feeling any very serious apprehensions on the subject, I told him that the opinions of Mr. Adams would pass off like the opinions of any other man. That I intended to give my own opinion as a counterbalance to that of Mr. Adams." Rather audacious for a freshman congressman! This was two weeks before the episode of the Anacostia bridge.

Slade meanwhile had written to Adams respectfully suggesting that a fuller explanation was due to all the faithful who had been sending him their petitions against slavery in the District, and looking up to him. "Must we wait until the 'Northern man with Southern principle' [President Van Buren, who Slade, with good reason, implied was behind the Atherton gag] shall consent to *un*gag us, for an exposition of [your] reasons?" Adams replied that he would try to say something more at this session, and on February 25 he asked the Speaker's leave to present a resolution, which he managed to have read, and entered in the *Globe*, for information. The resolution consisted of this proposed amendment to the Constitution of the United States:

> 1st. From and after the 4th day of July, 1842, there shall be, throughout the United States, no hereditary slavery; but on and after that day every child born within the United States, their Territories or jurisdiction, shall be born free.
>
> 2d. With the exception of the Territory of Florida, there shall henceforth never be admitted into this Union any State, the constitution of which shall tolerate within the same the existence of slavery.
>
> 3d. From and after the 4th of July, 1845, there shall be neither slavery nor slave trade at the seat of Government of the United States.

There were, as one would expect, immediate objections to Adams's resolution, and to his attempt to present a petition supporting it from William Jay (son of the founding father John Jay) and "43 most respectable citizens of New York." The proposed constitutional amendment was never even considered by the House.

Adams candidly admitted that it was addressed, really, to the abolitionist petitioners, to show them the only way in his opinion that the abolition of slavery could be brought about peaceably, justly, and constitutionally. The petitioners might well respond to Adams: and you call *us* impractical! The notion that this amendment, that you could not even arrange to have discussed on the House floor, would somehow someday manage to pass over the two high hurdles of the relevant constitutional method to amend the Constitution—a two-thirds vote in both houses, and ratification by three-fourths of the states (a significant number therefore necessarily of slave states)—that really was "impractical"! So the abolitionists might say to Adams. And must the enslaved black population wait for liberation until the day when that amendment somehow passed? (On the other hand, just how was it, as a practical matter, that the abolitionists were proposing to end slavery? By the moral conversion of slaveholders?)

There was criticism of Adams in the antislavery press in those months. Adams was enough separated from the purer abolitionists for there to have been opposition to him, with some strength, in the election just before this session, the election of 1838. No one had been formally nominated to oppose him, so, presumably, many of his own supporters would not bother to vote. In the peculiar atmosphere of eastern Massachusetts, Democrats took advantage of this situation, and of the discomfiture of the purer abolitionists with the impurity of Adams's position, to run a thoroughgoing abolitionist against him as a write-in candidate, and Adams had retained his congressional seat by a margin of only a few hundred votes.

In the contending great values in this period of American history—ending slavery, preserving the Constitution, preserving the union—Adams held firmly to all three. The ending of slavery must happen—however it would—within the Constitution and the preservation of the Union. The two proposals that he made were both within the Constitution: this amendment, and his earlier radical and shocking point that the war power allowed emancipation.

In this regard he differed from at least the radical wing of the abolitionists, and perhaps in degree from the moderate wing as well. William Lloyd Garrison had not yet performed his most memorable symbolic act—burning a copy of the U.S. Constitution—or put as a slogan on the masthead of the *Liberator* "No Union with Slaveholders," or declared the Constitution to be "a covenant with death and an agreement with hell," but he and his followers had already decided that the Constitution and the

Union were hopelessly compromised by their acceptance of slavery. That was not John Quincy Adams's opinion of the United States Constitution or of the Union.

The continuity of the United States of America under that Constitution stood at the core of his values. He had in addition to the motives of other patriots the awareness that his parents had played a central role in bringing this Union into being, and that they had imposed on him the heavy duty of contributing to its continuation. Although one could find in the privacy of his journal speculations that it might one day be necessary for the nation to break apart, and that if it did slavery was the issue on which it ought to do so, that was not a suggestion that John Quincy Adams would make lightly. He was in the decades of his service in American politics a dedicated and thoroughgoing unionist, opposed to the states'-rights people of every stripe, including those of his native New England in the episode of the Hartford Convention during the War of 1812. The Union and the Constitution were values to him as vital as opposition to slavery, and he had an awareness of the fragility of the order created in the late eighteenth century in the time of his father that the abolitionist leaders, with their much less profound political experience, did not have. For them, coming out of a revival meeting convinced that slavery was a sin and a stench in the nostrils of God, the Constitution and the union ("Union with slaveholders") might be dismissed rather easily. But not for Adams.

The reasons Adams gave for opposing the prayer of the primary petitions, going back to the first petitions he presented in 1831, and to a letter in answer to a query from a Philadelphia Quaker, featured various points of practicality, prudence, and strategy. Not enough Northerners, not enough originally of his own constituents, supported such an action; the votes in the House for such a bill would be embarrassingly few, and it could not be passed; if passed, it would be very difficult to administer, given the continuing existence of slavery in the surrounding states. At the same time, his comments on slavery do have a tendency to jump to the issue of slavery overall, in an apocalyptic and/or utopian mode—his comments in his journal at the time of the Missouri Question that we have quoted, for example. Regularly in his speeches when he used the rhetorical device of saying what he was not talking about—that he was not talking about slavery—he suggested that it was such an immense topic that were he to take it up—which to be sure he was not doing—what he would say would be so much more sweeping and fundamental than anything that anybody else had said as to go far beyond this little particular question (slavery merely in the District). The abolitionists are accused, in their own time and ours, of being utopian, impractical, and anti-incremental; but it may nevertheless be the case that their proposed chipping away at particular pieces of the structure of slavery was more "incrementalist" than the outlook of their great ally, John Quincy Adams.

It wasn't just that Adams, in introducing the petitions, would say he did not support their prayer; he also wrote to abolitionist leaders discouraging the sending of further petitions on that topic. On others of the shared topics his position was different. There is no doubt that he supported the prayer of petitions against the annexing of Texas; he was in the lead on that matter, which was still an open question. He explicitly supported all efforts to prevent the *expansion* of slavery. He would say to his abolitionist correspondents: put your energies *there*.

And, then, to return to the point of beginning, Adams was a stalwart beyond all others on the subject that was not concerned directly with slavery at all: the civil liberties that the slaveholders' program violated, in particular the right of petition. The fact that John Quincy Adams on the one hand said he rejected the prayer of these petitions about the District, and on the other hand fought indefatigably to keep on presenting them, dramatized the independent value of the right of petition itself, and thereby of civil liberty itself—including the liberties of Northerners and whites and citizens quite outside the circle of sympathizers with the abolitionists.

Civil liberty was, of course, a great substantive value for Adams—a value in its own right. But he was fully aware, at the same time, of the strategic service its defense could render in unsettling the slave power. The clearest testimony to his awareness of this point comes from a surprising source—his leading adversary in the gag rule fights, the volatile Virginian Henry A. Wise. Sometimes our adversaries see what we are doing more clearly than do our allies.

Wise went on, after this great gag rule episode, to a long political career, including service as Virginia's governor just before the Civil War. In his campaigns he would tell stories about his famous exchanges in the House with ex-president John Quincy Adams—in fact, he seemed rather proud of the linkage, to have something of a love-hate relationship with his great adversary, from whom, by opposing him, he borrowed prestige. Campaigning for governor of Virginia in 1855, he said:

> I have had a very severe training in collision with the acutest, the astutest, the archest enemy of Southern slavery that ever existed. I mean the "Old Man Eloquent," John Quincy Adams. I must have been a dull boy indeed if I had not learned my lessons thoroughly on that subject.

And he mentioned the lesson he claimed to have learned from his great adversary in a way that mingled a touch of admiration with his opposition, and also stated flatly his memory of Adams's reason for not supporting the prayer of the petitions:

> And let me tell you that again and again I had reason to know and to feel the wisdom and sagacity of that departed man. Again and again, in the lobby, on the floor, he told me vauntingly that the pulpit would preach, and the school would teach, and the press would print, among the people who had no tie and no association with slavery, until, would not only be reached the slave-trade between the States, the slave-trade in the District of Columbia, slavery in the Territories, but slavery in the States. Again and again he said that he would not abolish slavery in the District of Columbia if he could; for he would retain it as a bone of contention—a fulcrum of the lever for agitation, agitation, agitation, until slavery in the States was shaken from its base. And his prophecies have been fulfilled. . . .

What did happen, in the end? Adams insisted that antislavery efforts should concentrate on preventing the expansion of slavery, and, after the Mexican War, that is what happened. He believed that antislavery efforts should focus on the Slave Power's violation of our shared civil liberty, and, in the 1850s, that is what happened. He shocked everyone by arguing that slavery, even in the states, could constitutionally be ended, under the war power, and, in the actions of Union generals and the confiscatory acts of Congress and supremely in the presidential Emancipation Proclamation, that is what happened. And he argued that American slavery could be ended categorically, under the Constitution, with the Union intact, only by a constitutional amendment, and, twenty-six years later, after the terrible scourge of war, that also is what happened.

30/THE RULE OF THE HOUSE

THE EVENTS SO FAR recounted in these pages have covered the time of two United States Congresses, the Twenty-fourth (December 1835–March 1837) and the Twenty-fifth (December 1837–March 1839), in both of which the Jackson Democrats had a majority and elected James K. Polk as Speaker. But the new Twenty-sixth Congress that assembled on December 2, 1839, would be different. It had been chosen in the congressional elections of 1838, after the Panic of 1837 and the ensuing hard times, some of the blame for which had spilled onto the incumbents, the Van Buren Democrats. In those elections the Whigs made gains, and came close enough to electing a majority of House members almost to be able to organize the new Congress.

But only *almost*. When the newly elected "immediate representatives" convened to make a new House of Representatives in December of 1839, the balance of forces—partisan, and also sectional—was such as to occasion the first of the four fierce battles over the speakership that would foreshadow the Civil War. In this one Adams would play an interesting role.

A new Congress forms itself when the clerk, left over from the previous session, calls the names of the states in order, so that each state's delegation may be duly certified. In December of 1839 the clerk of the previous session was a Van Buren Democrat, and, as was his duty, he did start to call the states in order, but when he reached New Jersey he refused to call that state. New Jersey had had disputed elections, and on the outcome of the settlement of that dispute would turn the control of the House.

The Whig disputants had been certified, but the Democrats had an alternative delegation. If the Whigs were seated, the Whig Party would organize the House. If the Democrats, or neither, were seated, the Democrats would organize the House. The clerk, Adams wrote in his journal, "had his lesson prepared for him"; he was to exclude both sets of New Jersey delegates until the House was safely organized by the Democrats, after which the House could decide about New Jersey. Predictably, however, there was objection, and chaos ensued—"party speeches, frothy with the rights of the people, technicalities, and fraud," wrote Adams, with members seizing the floor and with no way even to vote to adjourn properly. As the members tumbled out of the hall following one such session, Henry Wise commented, "Now we are a mob."

After four days of this the venerable ex-president, who had so far remained silent at his desk, rose and addressed the "members-elect" directly (in an organized House one does not address the members but rather the Speaker). In this parliamentary equivalent of the state of nature, Adams berated them: "[W]e degrade and disgrace our constituents and the country." He turned upon them the fire of his own mixture of eloquence and sarcasm:

> **[Adams]:** We do not, and cannot organize; and why? Because the Clerk of this House, the mere Clerk, whom we create, whom we employ, and whose existence depends upon our will, usurps the *throne*, and sets us, the Representatives, the vicegerents of the whole American people, at defiance, and holds us in contempt! And what is this Clerk of yours? Is he to

> control the destinies of sixteen millions of freemen? Is he to suspend, by his mere negative, the functions of Government, and put an end to this Congress? He refuses to call the roll! It is in your power to compel him to call it, if he will not do it voluntarily.

Here he was interrupted by a member, who said that he was authorized to say that compulsion could not reach the Clerk, who had avowed that he would resign, rather than call the State of New Jersey.

> **[Adams]:** Well, sir, then let him resign, and we may possibly discover some way by which we can get along, without the aid of his all-powerful talent, learning and genius. If we cannot organize in any other way—if this Clerk of yours will not consent to our discharging the trusts confided to us by our constituents, then let us imitate the example of the Virginia House of Burgesses, which, when the colonial Governor Dinwiddie ordered it to disperse, refused to obey the imperious and insulting mandate, and, *like men*—

At this point "the multitude could not contain or repress their enthusiasm any longer, but saluted the eloquent and indignant speaker, and intercepted him with loud and deafening cheers, which seemed to shake the capitol to its centre." So one account says.

When Adams submitted a motion requiring the clerk to proceed in calling the roll, a member asked, "Who will put the Question?" Adams called out, "*I* intend to put the Question!"

That sentence, we are told, rang with rare authority over the chaotic House. Robert Barnwell Rhett, a relatively new member from South Carolina, who would soon be a chief among the Southern hotheads and one of Adams's most implacable foes on the gag rule, mounted a desk—so the story goes—and proposed first that the one member even older than Adams, Lewis Williams of North Carolina, be temporary speaker, and, when Williams declined, that Adams fill that role; when Rhett called for a vote, the cheers and yeas of the relieved members drowned out any nays. So with the House returned to a presocial state, as it were, Adams temporarily took the Speaker's chair, and conducted the sessions during which, after many votes, the representatives, excluding the New Jersey members, finally constituted the House, but chose as Speaker not a Democrat and not a Whig but a Whig-leaning independent (a states'-rights friend of Calhoun), Robert T. M. Hunter of Virginia, who managed to unite all the Whigs with (according to Adams's journal) some "malcontents of the [Van Buren] administration."

Adams left the chair with relief. The significance of this episode was not only the sharp, close partisan division to which the House had now come, but also the evidence it offers of the prestige of Adams, and, despite everything, the high regard in which he was held, for a purpose like this, even by his severest opponents. When it was all over, none other than Henry A. Wise offered him congratulations. He said this was Adams's proudest hour, and that if he (Wise) were to select the words "that would give the character of the man, to be placed on his tomb," he would choose "*I* will put the Question!"

But such fundamental respect, exhibited in a moment of organizational breakdown, did not carry over to the House's business when it came to the petitions and slavery. On the contrary; many members who were glad for the leadership of Adams in that moment—including Rhett and Wise—would in another moment try to deny him a chairmanship, to censure him, and somehow to "stop" him. And certainly to stop those petitions, of which he was such an indefatigable and perverse champion.

In fact, exactly this same Twenty-sixth Congress, almost controlled by the Whigs, enacted the most extreme of all the gags. That ill-fated party, just learning how to do these political things, and eagerly expecting a big Whig victory in 1840, held its first national party convention almost a full year before the election, in Harrisburg, in December 1839—that is, just as this Congress was starting to organize itself. The members of this Congress, therefore, knew who the Whig candidate for president would be as they began to do their congressional business.

But the Whigs could not win a national victory if they were perceived to be, to borrow the idiom of a later politics, soft on abolitionism. Jesse Bynum, a fierce slaveholding Democrat from North Carolina ("drunk on slavery" when Dromgoole had been "drunk on whiskey," according to Adams, in the Arkansas all-nighter), would in this Congress, for one example of the problem of the Whigs, specifically claim that as many as seventy-five members of that party were really abolitionists at heart: the Whig Party, therefore, was the party of *abolition*. Terrible words. The party's situation under those charges in an overheated political year must have been something like that of the Democrats more than a century later, in the days of Joseph McCarthy, when they were charged with having "lost" China and being soft on communism and even being the party of *treason*. The response of some Whigs may resemble the response in this later case of the battered lifelong anticommunist liberal Democrat Hubert Humphrey, proposing in anticipation of a hazardous campaign in 1954 that the Communist Party be *outlawed*, thus to show, by the simple economy of the most drastic proposal, the fierce sincerity of his anticommunism, and thus to put those charges to rest. Charges like those of Bynum, in this political year, must have made even more excited than they usually were the excitable Southern Whigs Henry Wise and Waddy Thompson and the important new member from the border slave state of Maryland, William Cost Johnson. Their proposal dramatized their opposition to abolition by carrying the gag to its furthest extreme.

And so it was the irrepressible Henry Wise himself, at this point still a Whig,* shortly after the Harrisburg convention and the ragged beginning of this Congress, who on December 30, 1839, moved a suspension of the rules in order to allow him to propose a *permanent* rule of the House. That was the new, and more extreme, feature: to make the gag rule a permanent rule, like the rule on amending motions or appointing committees, that did not need to be passed anew each year. On failing, Wise tried again the next day, and on failing again announced that he would keep making the same effort every day.

Changing the standing rules of the House was a good deal harder than passing a resolution. And so the proponents of the change were not able to enact a gag immediately upon the organization of the House, as had been done with the Atherton gag. By striving for this more extreme exclusion of the subject of slavery, and by failing to achieve it right away, paradoxically they left a period at the beginning of the session when that forbidden subject *could* be discussed.

And it was. 1839 turned into the election year 1840, and the legislative days of January went by, and no gag having been enacted, there were speeches. One of them was that of Jesse Bynum, already mentioned. But another was very different: that by William Slade.

No quick-talking debater like his Southern opponents, the Vermonter seems to have prepared, as we noted before, one carefully written speech on slavery for the beginning of each Congress. He had given the first clear-cut speech in favor of the right of petitioning for the end of slavery and the slave trade in the District, in December of 1835, at the very outset of the whole controversy, and the first clear-cut call for the *abolition* of slavery in the District, in December of 1837. Both of these speeches had led to expressions of outrage and to "secessions," as we might say, of Southern members, and fairly directly to the gag resolutions of their respective sessions. Now on January 18 and 20, 1840, he "delivered himself of the burden that has been four years swelling in his bosom," as Adams wrote in his journal, and urged immediate abolition of slavery throughout the United States. It was the most advanced antislavery speech made in the House so far, and from the point of view of South Carolina and Georgia and most of Virginia, and of slave states generally—indeed, from the point

*Not many years later he would turn into a Democrat.

of view of most of the North as well—it was an unbelievable and unconstitutional affront. (From our perspective, looking back, it is a point of honor. One hopes that someone up in Vermont has made sure Slade's name is spelled right on his tombstone.)

But Slade's speech, frightening and infuriating though it no doubt was to most of his fellow Whigs, and particularly to those from the South—he was saying things that confirmed the worst charges against their party—nevertheless gave its support to the party's nominee in the forthcoming election. In the very same speech in which he made the first call for abolition on the floor of the House, he also spoke in support of "General Harrison." He supported him not because he claimed Harrison was an abolitionist (he was a "colonizer") but because Harrison and the Whigs would be better for other, largely economic, reasons.

> **[Slade]:** [Abolition] is not and cannot be, the great practical question at the approaching Presidential election. The public mind is not prepared to have an abolition candidate for the Presidency; nor to have an abolition President.
>
> I cannot act in obedience to blind impulse. I must see that some good is to be attained. What possible good can come to abolition, or to any other interest, by now bringing the question into the Presidential election? I have never been able to see any. On the contrary, it seems to me the cause of abolition would be deeply injured by it.

Slade at this point was one of those abolitionists who argued for their staying within, and supporting, the Whig Party. Although in the eyes of his House colleagues from South Carolina, Virginia, Georgia, and elsewhere in the South, Slade was the rankest of the fiends of hell, from the radically different perspective of abolitionist politics, he had now been made into a "moderate," with two layers to his left: the new abolitionist Liberty party, which would run a pure abolitionist third-party candidate (James Birney, as it turned out) in this election of 1840; and, still further out, the even purer moralistic antipolitics of the Garrisonians.

Presidential politics aside, however, the effort to enact the more stringent gag had led to almost a month of the kinds of speeches the gaggers wanted to avoid, of which Slade's was the worst. But at last Waddy Thompson finally did manage to get onto the floor the motion that Henry Wise had wanted to make; to amend the *permanent House rules* to dispose summarily of abolitionist petitions, and to keep the subject forever—*forever*—off the House floor. The way Thompson proposed to do it, however, was cumbersome. It was that two-step method that his House colleagues had sometimes used, and that the Senate used regularly: upon the presentation of any abolitionist petition it should "be considered as objected to"—and the question of its reception laid on the table. He proposed that this double-barreled action be carried out automatically: no actual congressman would need to be there in the House, with his eyes open, in order to make the two motions (not to receive the petition; then to lay that motion on the table); both of them would be considered to have been made, on any such petition, by the instruction of a standing rule. But Thompson's particular motion was not to pass.

Adams arose and proposed an amendment to Thompson's proposal—an amendment that would have turned it around completely, and altered everything that Waddy Thompson and Henry Wise were trying to do. Adams accepted (and tried to steal from his adversaries) the new inclination on the part of the House to enact a standing rule dealing with the avalanche of petitions, and accepted (and tried to deflect) the judgment that there might be petitions which, for a specific reason, the House would decide not to receive—but he insisted that the House would have to make that decision on each petition, and specify the reason. "Every petition presented by the Speaker, or by any member, with a brief verbal statement of its contents, shall be received," his proposal said, "unless objection be made to its reception for special reason; and whenever objection shall be made to the reception of a petition, the name of the member objecting, and the reason of the objection, shall be entered upon the journal. The question in every such case shall be, *shall the petition be rejected?* and no petition shall be rejected but by a majority of the members present." That's the whole thing.

This proposal has sometimes been called the "Adams gag," but it was no "gag." His amendment to Thompson's gag would have eviscerated it—taken away its reason for being. Adams's proposal would not have excluded a specific group of petitions by *topic*—which of course is what Thompson, Wise, and company wanted to do, and was their only reason for undertaking the project. They were not interested in the general theory, or practice, of the right of petition, but only in keeping the one specific topic of slavery off the floor, and putting the severest possible stamp of disapproval and rejection and exclusion on that one *kind* of petition. Adams's proposal—unlike all the gags—contains no mention of slavery, or the abolition of slavery in the District, as a peculiar topic; his proposal would have applied to petitions on any subject whatever. Moreover, no petition would be whisked into oblivion by the automatic working of this standing rule; a member presenting a petition would make a brief verbal statement of its contents, and if some member *then* wanted to object to its reception that member would have to be present and awake and listening and stand on his legs and object *and give reasons*, and then the House would vote *on each petition*, whether to "receive" it or not. You might almost say that Adams's proposal would have required the House to *consider* a petition—in order to determine whether to consider it or not.

Adams accompanied his proposed amendment with a speech—not, as he once again explained, on the subject of slavery, but rather on the subject of petitions in the House. He said at the opening that he would not talk about slavery and the slave trade; he said at the end that he had not talked about slavery and the slave trade; and he explained, at greater length, in the middle that he was not talking about slavery and the slave trade.

> **[Mr. Adams]:** . . . I shall not now enter on the great and wide question of slavery or the slave trade in any State, District, Territory, dominion, or nation on the face of the globe. The subject is too large. I hope the day will come when I shall have an opportunity of delivering my opinions on that whole subject, but I assure gentleman that I shall not attempt it on a little petty resolution about the reception of petitions.

This was another sample of the moral and rhetorical strategy that we noted in the last chapter: slavery is much too big a subject; I have not discussed it; I am not talking about it now. One should not be quick or glib or superficial about such a subject. Adams kept insisting that the cause of freedom, the attack on slavery, had barely begun. There is always so much—so much *more*—to be said.

> **[Adams]:** We have listened to speeches of great ability on both sides; we have heard slavery defended by all that can be said in its defence, and the cause of freedom advocated—I will not say by all that can be said in its behalf—but at least by something. The reserve has been all on that side. Indeed, I do not think that any gentleman has attempted formally to contend for it, but my friend from Vermont (Mr. Slade). All the speeches I have heard, save one by the gentleman behind me (Mr. Granger) have been on the other side. Gentlemen from the North have shown us how far they can go in supporting the rights of the South. That has been the subject; that has been the argument. They have been arguing the cause of slavery, although they are the Representatives only of free men. The cause of freedom, in all its power, has not even been touched, save by the gentleman from Vermont; and even by him rather in the way of apology for the unfortunate abolitionists, than in appeals to the laws of God, the laws of Nature, and the Declaration of Independence made by the original thir-

teen States of this Union. . . . That is the ground that will be taken by the defenders of freedom. But I will not now enter into that question.

No, we certainly won't enter into that question. All we are talking about here is a little tinkering with the rules of the House.

Adams plied sweet reason with his Southern colleagues. Why not let these matters be discussed? If you let a proposal to abolish slavery in the District come to a vote on the House floor, it would not obtain ten votes out of 240. Adams himself, at least until he heard arguments to change his mind, would not vote for it. So what were they afraid of? Adams appealed to these Southern "Jeffersonians" to practice a little of the freedom of the mind, the freedom of debate, that their hero endorsed:

[Adams:] Gentlemen of the South . . . [w]hy will you not discuss this question? Do you fear the argument? If not, why do you refuse to enter into it? If you are so firm, so confident, so immovably resolute, why will you not speak? I call upon you to speak; explain this subject to us who do not understand it. Show us the "blessings" of this institution. Let us look at them. I believe some of you think that slavery is a blessing which we ought to take to ourselves. If so, give us your reasons; show us how it will be for our interest, and how it can be made to conform to our sense of duty. Perhaps we shall come round; who knows but you may convert us? [A laugh.] I do not resist; I am open to conviction. Suppose you try it.

Did they try it? No. The answer to Adams's speech, and to his proposal for a different kind of a standing rule, was another steamroller. Not long after Adams was seated, William Cost Johnson, the Whig from Maryland mentioned above, obtained the floor, and, working up to a decisive motion to do what Wise and Thompson had started out to do, held the floor for parts of three days.

Mr. Johnson, of Maryland . . . argued the impropriety and unconstitutionality of the people of the North attempting to deprive the people of the South of their slave property, which was valued at twelve hundred millions of dollars. This was the capital, the most available, in fact, upon which the South [had] done all its business; and he considered that it would be equally constitutional and proper for this section of country to make movements in that Hall and elsewhere, to deprive the North of all her manufacturing and other capital, the great sources of its wealth, as for the North to conspire, for the purpose of depriving the South of her slave property. It would be equally a violation of the Constitution, and justice, and right, in one case as in the other.

Johnson was different from the other proponents of gags. He came from a district only 10 percent black, was soon to be Whig nominee for governor of Maryland, and was the first Whig to offer a gag rule successfully. The earlier makers of the successful motions—Pinckney, Hawes, Patton, and Atherton—had been either Democrats or, in Pinckney's case, collaborators with Democrats. Johnson's Whiggery was not of the states'-rights/oppositionist sort of strong proponents of gags from the deeper South—Hammond, Wise, and Thomas Gilmer (an important Virginia politician, now entering the story), all of whom would soon leave the Whig Party, or of Waddy Thompson; Johnson was a nationalist, a Unionist. He was a "diffusionist," and proud of Maryland's record in persuading freed slaves to settle in colonies elsewhere. The leading historian of these matters, William Freehling, looking at this story from the point of view of the inner politics of the South heading for secession, sees in Johnson's action not only Whig politics—an effort to establish the Whig Party's anti-abolitionist credentials, and to put the squeeze on the Northern Democrats (the Southern Democrats would have to support his proposal, and would press their Northern party members to join them)—but also border-state politics, to show that under assault from Northern moralists a Maryland Unionist could resist as strenuously as a South Carolina Nullifier. More so, indeed, since Johnson's proposal took the cake for extremity. A Maryland unionist Whig could make the arguments, too, as bluntly as anyone from further South:

> **Mr. J.** argued that it had been a blessing to the colored race to keep them in slavery, and drew a comparison of their condition in Africa and this country. In the former, they were little more intelligent than the ourang outang species; but now they had become a civilized and Christianized people, and would, under the dispensations of Providence, contribute to the spread of Christianity throughout the benighted regions of their native country.

In his journal for the day (January 28, 1840), Adams describes Cost Johnson (as they called him) as having been "about half-tipsy, and in his merriest and wittiest mood." At this distance one cannot determine whether the following double entendre, mixing petitions with women petitioners, is inadvertent, or whether it belongs to Mr. Johnson in his tipsy merriment, or to the limitations of the *Congressional Globe* reporter:

> **Mr. Johnson** . . . thought the Representatives of the North had better tell their women petitioners to attend to knitting their own hose and darning

their stockings, rather than come here and unsex themselves, be laid on the table, and sent to a committee to be reported on.

Mr. Johnson also said that he considered abolition but one degree in the rear of amalgamation, and that the people of Maryland would not submit to have their property (meaning slaves) severed from them except by the sword. And in the midst of all this tipsy merriment he eulogized General Harrison, and gave reasons why the South should support Harrison. One is accustomed to the strange bedfellows that politics makes, but even so it is striking that in this discussion in the House in the winter of 1839–40 the speeches both of William Slade and of William Cost Johnson recommended William Henry Harrison for president.

Johnson ended his long speech by proposing, as an amendment to Adams's amendment, the successful version of this most extreme gag yet offered. Cutting through the complexity of the efforts by Waddy Thompson and Henry Wise, it just flatly stated, as a standing rule, "[t]hat no petition, memorial, resolution, or other paper praying the abolition of slavery in the District of Columbia, or any State or Territory, or the slave trade between the States . . . shall be received by this House, or entertained in any way whatever." That was all there was to it—simple, and extreme. Johnson said his proposed amendment would "kill the hydra, Abolition, in an instant, in such manner that it could not germinate its species again."

It was clear that the supporters of this new gag, now led by these Southern Whigs but joined to Southern and some Northern Democrats, had laid their plans together. Adams wrote in his journal that "Linn Banks . . . had been put by the Speaker into his chair expressly for the occasion." Banks was a leading Virginia Democrat who now held the seat that Patton had occupied, and was clearly, to Adams's mind, part of a bipartisan plan to pass this rule.

Immediately after Johnson sat down, Aaron Vanderpoel, the Democrat from Van Buren's hometown in Kinderhook, New York, was promptly called upon, although several others sought the Speaker's eye, and made a Democratic Party contribution to this particular chapter in the effort to stifle free discussion. The *Congressional Globe* described the scene thus: "Mr. Vanderpoel rose, and several gentlemen rising nearly at the same time, and claiming the floor, the Chair awarded it to Mr. V." Mr. V. said he would move the previous question.

Reading between the lines one infers that Giddings and Adams, and perhaps everybody else, sensed what was going to happen—a motion for the previous question, closing off all debate, and bringing Johnson's proposal, undiscussed, to a vote—and that Giddings and Adams tried to stop it. Giddings, still a new congressman not well acquainted with the parliamentary rules and practices, raised a point of order when the Chair awarded the floor to Mr. V., because, said Giddings, a member in order to be called upon was supposed to rise in his place, and Vanderpoel had not risen from his seat. The Chair said he had never heard that one before; several experienced members gently explained to Giddings that addressing the Chair out of one's seat was common practice. Other members tried another point of order: the Chair hadn't stated the question that Mr. V. called for the previous question on; but the Chair then did state the question, and allowed V. to retain the floor.

As Vanderpoel started to speak, Adams raised *this* point of order: Vanderpoel had said he would move the previous question, which was not debatable, so he could not make a speech. Vanderpoel replied that he had only remarked that he would *probably* move the previous question, and went on speaking. He deplored the "interminable and unprofitable" debate; he said that although he was a Northerner with abolitionists in his district he had never wooed them and he deplored their petitions, which he had never been asked to present; a colleague had been asked to present them instead. He found them mischievous, incendiary, and insulting to our Southern brethren. He had always voted to receive these petitions, but the moment they were presented he had voted, and would always vote, for the strongest possible rejection of their prayer, to "nail them to the table, mingle them with the rubbish of your garret, and in the strongest mode mark our disapprobation of the subject." This was to be the only speech disagreeing with Johnson's motion—from a member who after receiving the petitions would mingle them with the garbage. He did, however, vote with Adams against Johnson's rule. Given that position (possibly, given Mr. Vanderpoel's New York Democratic connections, the position of the embattled Van Buren administration), it was especially important for him to make clear how strongly Northern Democrats, too, abominated the abolitionist petitions. The *Globe* rises to capital letters in reporting the end of Vanderpoel's speech:

> **[Vanderpoel]:** As I once before remarked on this floor, I tell you, my Southern brethren, that great mass of the North will fulfill the compact of the letter and spirit. We recognized your property in slaves when we entered into solemn convention and union with you. We solemnly agreed that they should form part of the basis of representation on this floor; and UNTIL WE BECOME WRETCHES, AND WHOLLY INSENSIBLE TO THE OBLIGATIONS OF COVENANT AND DUTY, WE WILL FAITHFULLY FULFILL THE COMPACT.

After making his speech, the Democrat Vanderpoel then *did* move the previous question on the Whig Johnson's amendment. The House voted to close debate, and began voting on the three layers of motions.* Johnson's amendment to Adams's amendment was carried, and Adams's was therefore thrown on the ashcan of history. There now was no discussion as the body rolled on through the parliamentary layers—the train was moving. The reader will remember how it is in formal deliberative bodies—how they will spend hours and days and many speeches on precise points, and tie themselves in procedural knots, and then suddenly in a rush of collective impatience decide all sorts of very big matters in a hasty half hour. Perhaps that is the way it was in the U.S. House of Representatives on January 28, 1840—or perhaps the whole affair had been greased by a bipartisan gaggers' caucus. In any case, after a month of elaborate considerations of the proposals by Wise and Thompson and Adams, the most extreme proposal—indeed, the most extreme proposal in the whole history of this matter going clear back to James Henry Hammond—now sailed through in an afternoon, with only the speeches by Vanderpoel and Cost Johnson himself as discussion—and with Mr. V., with his very qualified opposition, as the only opposing speech (an opposing speech that—suspiciously—ended by closing the door to any *other* opposing speeches).

Adams tried in one more way to stop the train, by moving that the question be postponed until the whole House was constituted—that is, until the state of New Jersey was represented—but the Chair ruled that motion out of order.

The House now came, without further discussion, and with another call for the previous question, to the main motion as amended—one hopes all the congressmen knew what they were voting on†—which was to amend the *permanent* rules as *Johnson's* amendment stated. The vote

*Adams said in his journal that his own amendment had been an amendment to an amendment (Thompson's) and therefore the end of the parliamentary line, and he raised a point of order against Johnson's motion, but that Thompson forestalled him by accepting Johnson's motion as his own. Maybe so, but that is not quite the way the *Congressional Globe* reads. The *Globe* indicates that no motion prior to Thompson's was on the floor—Wise had not been able to obtain the requisite suspension of the rules—and that therefore Thompson's was the main motion, Adams's an amendment, and Johnson's an amendment to an amendment, stopping the process in the way that Adams's had done in the previous session. Thompson did rise to accept Johnson's amendment in place of his own, but was told that under the circumstances that was out of order.

†It is not clear from the *Globe* that the House took the *two* further votes required to work its way through the parliamentary situation they had created; parliamentary bodies can lose track of what they are voting on, and skip a step, in these situations, and perhaps that could have happened in 1840 even in the U.S. Capitol. Or perhaps it was too complicated for the *Globe* reporter, or the present author, to follow.

was closer than the vote on any gag had been, but the motion carried 114–108, with almost all congressmen from the slave states, and twenty-four Northern Democrats, supporting it. "And thus it was made a rule of the House," wrote Adams in his journal, "that no abolition petition shall be received."

❧

WHETHER THE HOUSE MEMBERS quite comprehended what they were doing or not, it really was a remarkable action, in the history of free republics. You can find in libraries a copy of the House rules for the early 1840s, in which the new rule is printed, Rule 21 (later 23 and then 25), right alongside the rules of parliamentary procedure. It is particularly startling, when one reads through and finds this rule, to see Thomas Jefferson's name on the cover. Jefferson had written "A Manual of Parliamentary Practice composed originally for the use of the Senate of the United States by Thomas Jefferson" back in 1797, when he was vice-president; the cover of the rules goes on, "with reference to the practice and rules of the House of Representatives"; and then—in smaller print—"the whole brought down to the practice of the present time," and so on. The version here quoted is dated 1843.

On reading through it one finds what one expects to find in a Manual of Parliamentary Practice: procedures for making motions and seconding them, the proper sequence of amendments, points of order, points of personal privilege, which motions are debatable and which are not—all the sorts of things that generations of free peoples have been bored by under the heading "parliamentary procedure." One finds also the role of the Speaker (very powerful) and of committees and of the clerk and the printer and the sergeant-at-arms, and the order of business in the day and in the week, and the order in which committees are to be called, and the "morning hour" and the "orders of the day" and the receiving of messages, and the rules of decorum and debate (Rule 28: "When any member is about to speak in debate, or deliver any matter to the House, he shall rise from his seat, and respectfully address himself to 'Mr. Speaker,' and shall confine himself to the question under debate, and avoid personality"). In other words, you find what you would expect to find, the formal rules of orderly procedure, the neutral ground rules of order and civility, by which the House is to conduct its business, without reference to the content or substance of its work.

But there is this one exception, which jumps off the page—the new Rule 21, which enters into the *substance* of policy to say that there is one matter the House cannot talk about:

> 21. No petition, memorial, resolution, or other paper praying the abolition of slavery in the District of Columbia, or any State or Territory, or the slave trade between the States or Territories of the United States, in which it now exists, shall be received by this House, or entertained in any way whatever.

There it is, as William Cost Johnson in tipsy merriment at the end of his three-day speech had proposed it, and as it zipped through the amending process in one afternoon. You cannot talk about this topic. If you try, a member will shout "Order! Order!" (Rule 29) and the Speaker will sustain him, or the Speaker himself will call you to order and make you sit down.

The gag thus entered into the House rules went much further than the previous gag resolutions, in two ways. It represented—at last, one might say—the most extreme form of the gag, as it had been proposed by James Hammond in the House, and by John C. Calhoun in the Senate, back when the controversy began in 1835–36, and defended thereafter by Henry A. Wise, Waddy Thompson, and others: no petition or memorial praying for abolition "shall be *received* by the House, or entertained in any way whatever." The door is slammed shut in their face.

Not only that. The Johnson (Thompson-Wise) gag of 1840 really was a gag *rule*, where the others had been gag resolutions. Its being planted in the House rules made it much harder to uproot. The resolutions expired with each session, and had to be reenacted at each new session; the period before they were enacted, and the parliamentary ducking and weaving to get them enacted, had allowed, as we have seen, much discussion of slavery to spill out upon the House floor. Now the *rule*, once adopted by a Congress, would apply to both (or all) sessions of that Congress, and would ordinarily be adopted routinely, along with all the other rules about clerks and amendments and points of order, all in one routine bundle, at the beginning of each new Congress: "Mr. Speaker, I move the adoption of the rules as they existed at the end of the last Congress"; "Second the motion"; "As many in favor"; so ordered. The burden or onus would now be on Adams and his group to try to exclude that one rule from adoption, in the bundle of rather routinely adopted rules of the previous Congress, at the start of a Congress. If they missed their chance, they would have to try to rescind an already adopted rule at the start of a later session—uphill work. Adams said the earlier gags to this one were as petty larceny to highway robbery. The forces of the gag had won a great victory.

They had won a great victory—and thereby hurt themselves all the more. They had shot themselves in one foot, and then they shot themselves in the other foot, and now they were starting to work on their ankles.

Their margin of victory had shrunk to the point that future victories became problematical. The supporters in the North were peeling off. The vote by which the abolitionist petitions introduced by Congressman Fairfield had been laid on the table without discussion, back in December of 1835, was 180–31, a whopping 149-vote margin. The next spring, the first Pinckney gag, a weightier matter with a distinguished ex-president arguing full whistle against it, nevertheless had still passed 117–68, a 49-vote margin. The Patton and Atherton gags had each passed with a 48-vote margin. But now the Johnson permanent gag rule passed by only a 6-vote margin.

The number of free-state congressmen who voted for the gag—a number that Adams would record and comment upon, as being particularly contemptible—declined precipitously. Sixty-four had voted for Pinckney's gag, fifty-one for Patton's, forty-nine for Atherton's, and now only twenty-eight for Johnson's permanent rule. During the days of debate on the rule a few *Southern* congressmen had disclaimed all attempts at gagging. Although large majorities of Northern Democrats had voted for all the previous gags—the gag resolutions, proposed by members of their party, with the support of their party's administration—now while twenty-six Northern Democrats voted for this most extreme of all gags, a larger number, thirty-six, voted *against* it. Despite the role of Southern Whigs in proposing it, *all* of the free-state Whigs voted against it. So now, in part as a cost of ratcheting the gag rule up to highest notches of severity, the proponents of the gag had drastically shrunk their support. And had sharpened the divisions along sectional, rather than party, lines.

And as the gag was squeezed to its tightest, the objection to it spread to its widest in the public, as well as in Congress. Adams's role, in particular, made the opposition to the gag newsworthy; his speech on Texas, with its long acid summary of the history of the gags, had been widely circulated. The resentment of the outlook that Southern leaders expressed, and their violation of the shared tradition of civil liberty, grew. Now that violation had reached, as it seemed to many in the free states, its most arrogant extreme: telling free people what they could petition for, and doing so in the most presumptuous way, in the very rules of the legislature of the republic.

Here are verses John Greenleaf Whittier wrote early in the petition controversy, published in the *Boston Courier* and elsewhere, that gave expression to the resentment that was now growing. The poet is referring in the first line—"his slaves"—to the "haughty neighbor" to the south.

> Must fetters which his slaves have worn
> Clank round the Yankee farmer's door?

Must *he* be told, beside his plow,
What he must speak, and *when* and *how?*

Must he be told his freedom stands
On slavery's dark foundations strong—
On breaking hearts and fettered hands,
On robbery and crime and wrong?
That all his fathers taught is vain—
That freedom's emblem is the chain?

Rail on then, "brethren of the south"—
Ye shall not hear the truth the less—
No seal is on the Yankee's mouth,
No fetter on the Yankee's press!
From our Green mountains to the sea,
One voice shall thunder—*we are free!*

31 / AN ASSORTMENT OF WHIGS

THERE ONCE WAS A practice, in some American schools, a long time ago, of requiring a young scholar, even as early as the second grade, to give in chronological sequence the name of the American president that fell to his or her turn, before that scholar could leave the room for recess. If you had to do that, you would wish that American history had skipped over the period in which this story is set. If you were chosen by the teacher to begin the game—as you never were—you could just name George Washington and scramble out to the playground. If you sat next in the row, you could name John Adams, and go join your chums. You would have found it fairly easy to give the name that fell to you all the way up through Andrew Jackson, if you were careful to remember (as you sometimes didn't) that John Quincy Adams follows the helpfully euphonious "M's" of his predecessors. But after Jackson there would be a great dark hole, and if it fell to you to give names in there you would have to go to the end of the class. If someone would just lift you across that abyss of the forgotten to *Tyler*, you could then swing confidently into the easy sailing of Tyler-Polk-Taylor, which sequence by its sound gave you solid mnemonic support, and might enable you to go on out to play with the lucky stiff who had drawn George Washington, perhaps in time to join a game of marbles with the big kids from the fourth grade. If someone else could then make the very difficult link to *Fillmore*, you could then breeze into another such sequence, almost as easy for some reason, Fillmore-Pierce-Buchanan, before you reached the great home base of Abraham Lincoln. (As a second-grader, of course, you half-thought that Tyler was enjoined to poke Taylor, a memorable scene, and Fillmore to pierce Buchanan. By the fourth grade you made them mentally into a double-play combination, like Tinker to Evers to Chance: Fillmore to Pierce to Buchanan.) But back there after Jackson, all was dark. Nothing to remember.

It is a little that way still when one becomes an adult, although for different reasons. Perhaps that is unfair to Martin Van Buren, the little magician from Kinderhook. But he was less memorable than any of his predecessors at least for these two quite objective reasons: he served only one term, and his last name was not Adams. He was the first American president of whom those two things could both be said. Up until he took office, every American president, except the Adamses, had served two terms; beginning with him every American president, until Abraham Lincoln, served only one term, *at most*. All the presidents up through John Quincy had been founding fathers themselves, or closely connected with the founding. With Jackson that link was broken, but he nevertheless was a figure of stature, certainly in the eyes of the public; he gave his name to a distinctive new departure in American political history. Van Buren was an epigone. And who was elected after Martin Van Buren? The failure to remember that name has cost many a youngster half of recess.

It is necessary also to mention, as one certainly did not do in the lower grades, political parties. The founders did not intend or anticipate parties, but, as we also know, parties developed anyway in the 1790s, around the issue of the American response to the French Revolution and for other reasons. Jefferson and Madison were the leaders and founders, as we know, of the one party, the Democratic-Republican Party, which although undergoing a marked alteration—or revival—under Andrew Jackson (with Martin Van Buren pulling the strings) may nevertheless be seen to be continuous with the Democratic Party as we have it today in the late twentieth century. (The party, which has, or used to have, its Jefferson-Jackson Day dinners, sometimes describes itself, with that generosity to itself to which such organizations are prone, as the longest continuously existing political party in the world.)

The United States, in its two centuries plus, has had only four such major parties. Although one couldn't do it in the lower grades, an adult citizen can, of course, name all four—the Democrats, and then the three different major opponents the Democrats successively have faced. The Republicans, now. The Federalists, back at the beginning. And . . . would the reader have known the name of the fourth major party if it had not been named in previous chapters and in the title to this one?

In this book we are concerned not with the opposition to the Democrats in what political scientists call the first party system, when the opposition was the Federalists, nor yet the opposition which came into being in the 1850s and has lasted through the vicissitudes of almost a century and a half, down to the present day, when the opposition to the Democrats is the Republicans, in the so-called third party system, but rather with the Democrats' opposition in that important interlude between these two systems, about 1834–54, the Whigs. The eminently forgettable president who was elected after Van Buren, William Henry Harrison, would be the first to serve the nation in its highest post from that short-lived and eminently forgettable party.

The American Whig Party has the disadvantage not only of sharing a slightly silly name with a more famous English cousin, and of lasting only twenty years, but also of having disappeared. It has the further disadvantage of having elected, in twenty years of existence, only two of the dimmer names for second-graders to try to remember when they name the presidents. And although the Whigs did elect those two presidents, both of them promptly died.

Or fairly promptly: after one month in William Henry Harrison's case, after sixteen months in Zachary Taylor's case. Both of these forgettable presidents were succeeded by vice-presidents who were not only forgettable but also markedly altered the direction of policy: John Tyler, who turned out not even to be a Whig, and Millard Fillmore, who changed the course apparently taken by his predecessor, Zachary Taylor, with respect to the fugitive slave law of 1850, in a way that may have helped to kill off his party.

The reasons for remembering the forgotten and unlucky Whigs in these pages are that in 1841 they would for the first time take over the government and that, to a considerable extent, our battle over American slavery and American civil liberty was being fought out among them.

In an excellent book called *The Political Culture of the American Whigs* the author, historian Daniel Walker Howe, observed that "there was more debate over slavery within the Whig party than within the Democratic party, just as, in the 1960s, there was more debate over the Vietnamese war within the Democratic party than within the Republican party." The Democrats of that later time had vocal doves and resistant hawks (and/or vice versa). The Whigs of the 1840s had opponents of slavery—and the strongest of the strong opponents of abolition.

The Whig Party had all the characteristics associated with opposition to slavery. It was strongest in New England and the New England diaspora out in the upper Midwest. It had a closer, and a more exclusive, connection to American Protestant Christianity (both old Puritan and new Evangelical) than any other of America's major parties. It was far closer than the Democrats to "Reform" and the reformers: to education reform (Horace Mann was a Whig); to prison reform; to temperance (a new movement of the time). The Whigs in general were somewhat less inhumane toward the American Indian than the party led by the old Indian fighter Andrew Jackson. The Whigs in general were somewhat less expansionist than the Democrats, although there were exceptions (expansionism, as we said before, tended to be associated with the South and West and support of slavery). The handful of congressmen so far expressing some opposition to slavery—Adams, Slade, Giddings, and a few others—were all Whigs. The elections of 1838 had brought a few more abolitionists into the House to join Giddings and Slade—especially Sherlock J. Andrews of Ohio and Seth M. Gates of New York, whom Theodore Weld had converted to abolitionism—and they were all Whigs. The very few free blacks who were allowed to vote, in only six states, overwhelmingly voted Whig.

So Bynum was right? The Whig Party was the party of abolition? No, there is another side, or several other sides, to the story. The Whigs reflected, one might say, the two faces (or the several faces) of "the Protestant Ethic," as it developed in the American setting: the moralistic face, but also the economic face, the self-improving (and success-achieving) face. Reading Professor Howe's discussion of individual Whigs, one can pick out two words to describe them, using these words in all of their meanings: Industry, and Improvement. Self-improvement, social improvement, economic improvement. The Whigs were the party that, in contrast to the laissez-faire Democrats, wanted to use the central government to "grow" (as the 1990s phrase insists on putting it) the economy. Their program was: "internal improvements" (federally supported roads and canals to make the movement of goods and services easier); a national bank (fights over the bank with Jackson brought the party into existence); a uniform national currency; the positive use of public lands for public revenue (in contrast to the give-aways to individuals supported by the Jacksonians); the protective tariff (to build up home industry and provide revenue—in contrast to the free trade favored by the Southern Democrats in particular).

And there was another side of the Whigs, related to both of these others: their republican respectability. The Whig Party was not only the ghost of Puritanism; it was also the political ghost of the "civic humanism" and "republicanism" of America's English past. It produced orators who quoted Burke and Cicero and lawyers who had studied the Scottish moralists. One did not use the term "Wasp" in the 1830s and 1840s because there were not enough non-Wasps around, in sufficiently visible positions, to require that "Wasps" be separated and labeled, but the Whigs were certainly, overwhelmingly, Wasps. One did not, for a similar reason, speak then of "ethnics," but insofar as the Whigs had an ethnic identity it was the ethnic identity that did not notice that it had one, derived from the older and the more recent crossings of the water by Englishmen. To use a word from a different world, which Whigs certainly would reject, they were perhaps America's, and therefore perhaps almost the world's, premier "bourgeois" party.

Therefore the Whigs believed in harmony. To Whigs, talking about "social class" in the way we have learned to do since Karl Marx and the other tough guys of the modern world infused into the term an invidious and combative aspect—class *conflict*—would seem distastefully "factional." Whigs would rather look to the whole nation's good than fan the flames of group conflict among the several parts into which conniving (Jacksonian) politicians could break the nation apart. Caution. Moderation. Respectability. Michael Holt, the leading scholar of American Whigs, in an article on the demise of that party, quotes (and rather tends to vindicate) the flippant, or pungent, comment of a Mississippi editor: "[T]he Whigs died of too much respectability and too few people." (The Democrats had neither of these problems.)

It is important not to try to fit the parties of that time into the categories of this one. The Whigs were not premature New Dealers, but they were not premature Reagan Republicans either. They represented a different combination of the elements of morals and politics, in a different era. They were the party of commerce and industry (more than of agriculture); they were also the party more amenable to social and moral reform. They believed—more than their opponents—in the Union (as against the Democrats' greater emphasis on states' rights; Daniel Webster, the great orator of Union, was of course a Whig); they believed in the *nation*, in the *federal* power, in positive national government (in contrast to the antigovernmental, localistic tendency of the Democrats, with that slogan attributed to Jefferson, and carried on the masthead of a Democratic Party organ, about the best government being the least government). But they did *not* believe in "strong" presidents. They came into being in 1834 by the drawing together of opponents of what they saw to be an excessively powerful president, a "usurping" president, "King Andrew" Jackson.

The reasons for opposing King Andrew's "usurpation" reflected the civic-minded moralistic republicanism to which those who became Whigs were prone. One reason for opposing Jackson was his novel institution of the "spoils system," more delicately described as "rotation in office"; it meant that Jackson replaced government workers with his own people (William Slade was let go by the State Department when Jackson took office; Martin Van Buren was the new Secretary of State who did the letting go). Another reason for opposing Jackson was his "high-handed" removal of government deposits from the National Bank, and his high-handed un-Whig behavior in general about banks.

Given that ethos, and the American nonparty beginnings, and the antecedent nonparty Era of Good Feelings out of which this party division arose, the Whigs did not at first think of themselves exactly as a *party*. Partyhood had some of the "corrupt" and unrepublican faults they associated with Jackson: factionalism, contention, the seeking of group advantage instead of the common good. They used the word "faction" as a pejorative, in the way that it came down out of the English past into the *Federalist*. They disapproved of the "caucus," another conniving, self-interested, conflict-driven instrument the Jacksonians used. And at first—in 1836, their first run at the presidency—they did not have a convention, or even—as we have seen—a national presidential candidate. But the Whigs, with a bit of distaste, because they had to do so to combat the Jacksonians, became a party and came to use the new party tools, and held their own first national convention late in 1839—as we said, way ahead of time for the 1840 election—and nominated the forgettable Harrison.

Two test questions on this section: Why did free blacks vote overwhelmingly for the Whigs? (That one is easy.) And, slightly harder, given his geographical, class, and religious connections, why was young Abraham Lincoln, out in Democrat-dominated Illinois, a convinced and active Whig?

❧

IF YOU HAD BEEN a Northern conscience Whig in late 1839 you might have entertained (although cautiously of course) high hopes for a victory and a great improvement in the nation's leadership and condition. Van Buren and the Democrats (and the country) had not yet fully recovered from the financial panic of 1837. Andrew Jackson, the popular hero, was out of the picture, and Jackson's handpicked successor, Martin Van Buren, never remotely as popular, was beatable. Time appeared to be running out for the Jacksonians. In response to the economic conditions the political parties were shaping up, offering alternatives, and the more activist Whig alternatives looked promising. You could imagine that—say—the unusually able politician, and popular figure, Henry Clay would be nominated, and elected, and reelected in 1844, and there would be solid Whig majorities in Congress, and a Whig program would be enacted.

And on slavery? At least there ought to be an end to that ridiculous and offensive gag rule. The Northern and Eastern Whigs—and the Whigs were strongest in the North and East—had furnished virtually all of the votes against the gags from the start, and when it became a permanent House rule, Northern Whigs had voted *unanimously* against it. (It is true that it had been introduced by Whigs—Wise, Thompson, and Cost Johnson—but they were all slave-state Whigs, and presumably a big Whig victory would bring in a preponderance of the Northern stripe.) Opposing the gag rule was a vote on which Northern Whigs of varying sorts could unite; it could be seen as a strong antislavery vote, but it need not be that—one could vote against the gag on the basis of the proper conduct of republican institutions, of ancient civic liberties, of which Whigs regarded themselves as better guardians than the Democrats. Henry Clay, in the Senate, had typically had a both/and position about disposing of the petitions, but he made clear that he would not do anything to interfere with the "sacred right."

And on other slavery-related issues, the Whig administration of President Henry Clay would do much better than any Democratic administration. Although Clay's positions straddled an immense ideological gulf—that was a talent of his—he had said many times that slavery was an evil, and he was a founder of the Colonization Society, which could be presented as a kind of gradual emancipation. He could be persuaded, with Whig majorities, to stand against the annexation of Texas. There would not be any war with Mexico, in these eight years of President Henry Clay.

And what happened to that hope, or that expectation? Time and chance happen to all political parties, and they happen with special force to the Northern Whigs. Even before the convention in Harrisburg the Whig Party effectively set aside Daniel Webster; at Harrisburg itself it set aside Henry Clay, who must be the unluckiest figure among major presidential candidates in American history. Eager to win, the Whigs nominated instead of either of these major figures a minor one, a candidate usefully free of too visible a record, who had done rather well as one of the Whig sectional candidates in the complex election of 1836, and who, like Andrew Jackson, could be presented as a victor in a famous battle.

It used to be said that the party in 1840 then solved the problem of its platform—by not having one. Of the candidate's speeches—by his not giving any. Of arguments on the hustings—by passing the hard cider. The answer to the issues of the day was—Van Buren in the President's House eats off golden plates, and Harrison was born in a log cabin. Tippecanoe and Tyler, too!

But scholars now assure us that the election of 1840 was not as empty-headed as the old textbook picture; on the contrary, they say, there were rather clear-cut differences in policy, rather clearly presented over time and at other levels, if not in the presidential campaign itself. One of those scholars, Michael Holt, has suggested that if the Whigs had waited until later—even the spring of 1840—to nominate their presidential candidate, they could have had their heart's desire, their true leader, Henry Clay, because by that time it would have been clearer from economic conditions and public response that they could win without the glamor and ballyhoo of the Harrison campaign. But they did not do that.

Nevertheless, as noted, the Whigs did win in 1840—gaining the presidency and majorities in both houses of Congress. But, as also noted, time and chance happen to us all.

Before the new Whig administration could get going, there had to be, under that leisurely old original lame duck constitutional arrangement, another session of the *old* Congress. It was a kind of a gone-today-here-tomorrow arrangement; congressmen who had been defeated (like Henry Laurens Pinckney back in 1836) nevertheless showed up again in Washington, enacting laws, for one more session. In the winter of 1840–41, while Harrison and Tyler and newly elected Whig congressmen waited to take office, the ghostly lame ducks of the Twenty-sixth Congress gathered in December, and met until March 3, 1841, with the anticipation—the hope or dread as the case might be—of the new Whig administration that would start on March 4.

While that lame duck session was meeting, Adams, as we shall see in a later chapter, had some other business elsewhere in the Capitol building; nevertheless he did his duty, of course, in the "H.R.U.S." At the earliest opportunity—on December 9—he moved to rescind Rule 21, though now that it was a permanent rule, already adopted for this Congress, inertia aided his opponents.

> **Mr. Adams,** after stating his reasons for offering the resolution at so early a period of the session observed that he was not willing the rule in question should remain in force for a single hour longer, as, in his opinion, it was a direct violation of the Constitution of the United States.

Opponents moved to lay his motion on the table; momentarily withdrew the motion; considered whether to wait for a fuller house, when William Cost Johnson would be present to defend the rule he had introduced; decided to go ahead with the vote to table even with a skimpy house; and voted to table 82–58, with accompanying regrets that the gentleman from Massachusetts had even thought it proper to offer such a motion, after the previous session had disposed of the subject by "a resolution solemnly ratified by the House."

That was it for that session, and for that Congress, but there was no doubt that the old man, despite their regrets, would raise the matter again in the next, which would then be a new Congress, under Whig control, and free to adopt its own rules.

The anticipation of the coming Whig ascendency added spice to a conflict later in that short session between two vocal Whigs, Waddy Thompson and Joshua Giddings.

Late in February, Thompson proposed an appropriation to support the war against the Seminoles in Florida. Giddings, well prepared, responded with a three-hour speech attacking that "war" as an exercise in the reenslavement of escaped slaves who had hidden out with that Indian tribe. He had done a lot of research for this speech, and filled it with quotations and references to governmental documents. His theme was that the U.S. Army was being used for the purposes of the slaveholders—the "negro-catchers." If the federal government—as the slaveholders maintained—should have nothing to do with slavery, then why were the federal forces in Florida doing the slaveholders' ugly business? Giddings argued that "the hard earnings of free whites" were supporting, by their taxes, this work of the "man-stealers." He maintained, as the terse summary of his long speech in the *Globe* put it, that "the kidnapping of Negroes" had "a powerful agency in the cause of the hostilities in Florida." He presented detailed evidence that in those hostilities the federal government—and therefore the Northern taxpayer—was subsidizing the recapture of escaped human beings, whose right to freedom, according to America's founding, was guaranteed "by the laws of Nature and Nature's God." The great nation whose watchword had been "liberty or death" was now using its armed forces for the purpose of slavery—of reenslavement. (It was parliamentarily possible for Giddings to talk about these matters, including what the *Globe* reporter called "the Abolition Question," without having the Speaker silence him under the gag rule because the House had gone into the Committee of the Whole, to consider Waddy Thompson's proposal of money for the Seminole War.)

Giddings's remarks, as you might guess, did not sit well, to put the matter altogether too mildly, with the slaveholders in Congress. Those particularly outraged included the one congressman from Florida, Charles Downing, and the congressmen from Georgia—nearest to the "war" and most involved—named Edward Black, Mark Cooper, and (a man we have met before) Julius Alford. Not to mention Waddy Thompson himself.

Uproar in the House. Joshua Leavitt, who was there in Washington for a purpose we will describe in the next chapter, wrote in the *Emancipator* that "the House was nearly all the time agitated like the waves of the sea." Giddings himself described it as a "peaceful riot." When he was finished, Black made pointed mention of the *lynch* law, and made remarks intended to be insulting by the duelist's code. Cooper, "in a very agitated manner, defended his constituents from the charge brought against them by Mr. Giddings of stealing Negroes from Indians, etc." And this uproar, among Whigs or with Democrats making charges against Whigs, took place just as the Whig president-elect Harrison and his entourage were arriving in the city for the inauguration.

The Whig Downing of Florida observed that if the Whigs of the South imagined that Harrison sanctioned the "ground taken by Mr. Giddings on the Abolition question" they would have said to him "begone forever." Downing wanted the country to know that Giddings was not the mouthpiece of the great man (Harrison) who came from the same state (Ohio); there were men of the Whig Party acting with him on other subjects who "in this matter would not touch him with a pair of tongs."

But the big gun opposing Giddings was Waddy Thompson. First he objected to remarks by some Georgia Democrats; as usual, he insisted that the South should stick together, as reported in the *National Intelligencer*:

> **Mr. Thompson** of South Carolina would appeal to the honorable member from Georgia to say whether it was prudent or proper, in this discussion of a topic (however improperly dragged into this debate) upon which every Southern man should only feel as a Southern man, to be provoking this family quarrel between Southern Whigs and Southern Democrats. . . .

Notice that it is the *South* that is the family, more than the United States or the Whigs or the Democrats. The Georgia Democrats had suggested that the outrages of Giddings had something to do with his being a Whig; Thompson wanted that idea to be stamped out entirely. He asked (the italics are in the original)

> **[Thompson]:** . . . whether it is just to regard the *very obscurest of the obscure* members of the Whig party as an exponent of the feelings and opinions of that party on this subject. Would it not be better, more fair and more just, to wait one short month and hear the distinguished head of that party speak for himself?

The Whig Waddy Thompson was very sure that when the Whig William Henry Harrison took the office of president he would not speak of abolition in the way the obscurest of the obscure Whigs, Joshua Giddings, had done.

On the next day, Giddings asked for the consent of the House to respond to this "matter personal to himself"—Thompson's remarks as printed in the *Intelligencer*. "The words (said Mr. G.) to which I allude, are printed in italics, and I suppose they are intended as a direct personal insult."

It is reported (although not in the *Congressional Globe)* that Julius Alford, the Georgia Whig, muttered that he would sooner spit on Giddings than listen to more of his abolitionist insults, which explains what the *Globe* reports Giddings saying next:

> **Mr. G.** said that it was related of a veteran marshal, who had grown old in the service of his country, and who had fought a hundred battles, that he happened to offend a young and fiery officer, who spat in his face for the purpose of insulting him. The General, taking his handkerchief from his pocket, and wiping his face, remarked: "If I could wash your blood from my soul as easily as I can this spittle from my face, you should not live another day."

At this point—so the reports have it, though again not in the *Globe* (what does a congressional reporter do with this kind of thing?)—Alford sprang from his seat "with profane and menacing language," as Henry Wilson put it, and rushed toward Giddings. However, Mr. Briggs (of Massachusetts and the inadvertent petition two Congresses before) intercepted Alford and "persuaded him to return to his seat." Then, Giddings, who was a big man—six feet two inches, 225 pounds—specifically stated that he would not respond to these insults after the manner of the South. As to his alleged obscurity:

> I will (remarked **Mr. G.**) say to the member from South Carolina (Mr. Thompson) that I claim no station superior to the most humble, nor inferior to the most exalted. . . . [T]he gentleman from South Carolina took it upon himself publicly to assign me a station "*the very obscurest of the obscure members of the Whig party*." I say to the member, that at the North we have a different mode of punishing insults from what exists at the South. With us, the man who wantonly assails another is punished by public sentiment.

The Whig president-elect Harrison, arriving in town just as these fireworks among Whigs took place, soon proved Downing of Florida correct in this regard, that indeed he would not touch Giddings's position on slavery "with a pair of tongs." In fact, when Giddings called on him the day after these events, Harrison "gave him such unmistakable indications of his displeasure that he [Giddings] never called upon him again."

What was the position of the Whig Party to be, on the subject of slavery, in this first moment of its national power? Harrison and multitudes of Congressional Whigs made it clear: certainly *not* the position of Giddings and Adams.

In 1872, Henry Wilson, the abolitionist historian, interpreted Thompson's slur on Giddings and the relationship of Harrison to the two of them in this way:

> Mr. Giddings was from the same State [as Harrison—Ohio], had served with him in the war of 1812, and had toiled for his election; but true to his convictions, he maintained the freedom of debate, and exposed the crimes of the Florida war. Mr. Thompson was from a state that had given General Harrison no vote, and had insulted an honest and God-fearing man because of his stalwart defense of right and outraged humanity. The former was rewarded by a Northern president with the mission to Mexico [President Harrison would appoint Waddy Thompson American minister to Mexico], the latter [Giddings] with coldness and manifest tokens of displeasure.

Mirror, mirror, on the wall; who is the obscurest Whig of all? Henry Wilson, writing during Reconstruction, before the backlash against it, had no trouble answering:

> But Mr. Thompson, though the recipient of executive favor, is forgotten, or scarcely remembered; while Mr. Giddings, whom he insolently characterized as "the very obscurest of the obscure individuals belonging to the Whig party," left a national reputation which his countrymen cherish with increasing regard, a name which they "will not willingly let die."

32 / FOR SUCH CONDUCT WHAT LANGUAGE OF EXECRATION CAN BE TOO STRONG?

On March 4, 1841, the government changed hands. The president-elect, William Henry Harrison, who had been supported by all of these quarreling Whigs—by Joshua Giddings as well as by Waddy Thompson, by William Cost Johnson as well as by William Slade—was inaugurated.

Since the Whigs made the primacy of the *legislature* a central tenet, this new and first Whig president filled his inaugural address with promises of executive restraint and deference to the legislature. He would use the veto rarely, defer to Congress, poll his cabinet on important decisions, eschew the spoils system, and retire after one term. Dying in office just a month later was, perhaps, carrying executive restraint a step too far.

He was succeeded by the Tyler of "Tyler, too." Who was Tyler? He was the Virginian who had been attached to the ticket by the Harrisburg convention to attract Southern states'-rights voters, a man whose views were sharply at odds, as events would prove, with the Whiggery of the free states. He was the Virginia states'-rights advocate who in the Senate had almost matched Calhoun in the clashing antlers of absurdly high principles.

Was Tyler really *president*? Up to the point of Harrison's death in April of 1841 the nation had had no experience with the death of presidents and the succession of vice-presidents. Many, including John Quincy Adams and Henry Clay, thought that John Tyler was the *acting* president, the vice-president acting as president, not the pure article like George Washington. They called Tyler "His Accidency." Adams wrote in his journal for June 4, 1841, "I paid a visit to the Acting President John Tyler" (about the Smithson bequest), using the capital letters as though that were his formal title. But Tyler took the undiluted full title and full powers of the office, setting a precedent that was thereafter to be followed, up to the time of this writing, by Millard Fillmore, Andrew Johnson, Chester A. Arthur, Theodore Roosevelt, Calvin Coolidge, Harry S. Truman, Lyndon Baines Johnson, and Gerald Ford.

Adams's journal for June 4 goes on to say: "When I went into the room where Mr. Tyler received me, I saw H. A. Wise in the back portico facing the Potomac." From the point of view of our story it says a great deal to note that Henry A. Wise was a close friend and adviser, and was to be a biographer, of John Tyler. The ambiguities of Harrison on the slavery issue were succeeded abruptly by the unambiguities of Tyler—no hope, to put it mildly, for any antislavery impulse.

So much, as far as the presidency was concerned, for the hopes that might have been entertained, less than a year before, by a Northern Conscience Whig. Clay was replaced by Harrison; Harrison died and was succeeded by Tyler. Tyler not only was adamant against abolition but was opposed to most of the Whig program.

But Whigs, anyway, believed more in legislatures than in presidents. President William Henry Harrison, in his brief tenure, had had time not only to snub Giddings and appoint Waddy Thompson as minister to Mexico but also to call a special session of Congress for the summer of 1841. He did the last of these at the urging of the great Whig leader, the almost-but-not-quite-president Henry Clay, now in the Senate, who was exuberant about the Whig victory, "a great social revolution" ending the Jackson era, and wanted to get going with his Whig program.

In the normal course, the new Congress, on that old leisurely, contrapuntal schedule, would not have assembled until December—thirteen months after the November in which most of the members were elected* and (imagine this!) nine months after the new president had been inaugurated. That was much too slow-moving for an activist Whig like Clay, who rather proposed to be a prime minister of sorts—leading Congress, which would lead the government, which would enact a Whig program. President Harrison, like many other Whigs, had long been an admirer of Clay, and had made all those promises of executive restraint; now he had a chance to practice what he had stood there in the rain and preached. He balked a little, but then did accede to Clay's urging and called the special session.

It was to be devoted to the economic difficulties that had helped persuade Harrison to call it, and to Clay's Whig program. So what then about petitions, the gag rule, and slavery? Were such issues to be postponed, in the excitement and promise of the great social revolution? Or were they to be a central part of that revolution? The little band of antislavery Whigs were in a situation they had not been in before; their party now had power, and a program to enact.

The antislavery Whigs certainly did not have the votes to affect the important choice of Speaker. Adams recorded in his journal a visit on that

*The dates for the election of congressmen were not yet the same in all the states.

issue from Slade, Giddings, and Gates, but in the event the Whigs—the House—chose a man named John White of Kentucky, another of the border state compromisers the Whigs, particularly, produced; Slade disappointed his abolitionist admirers considerably by voting for this slaveholder. Adams did not; he voted for a Pennsylvanian named Joseph Lawrence, who got only five votes. On the other end of the Whig spectrum, Wise got eight votes; William Cost Johnson got one—Wise's.

Slade once more disappointed his abolitionist admirers by recommending that they hold off on their petitions to this first special summer session of the Congress, postponing them until the regular session in December.

But still, the new Whig Congress had to adopt *rules*. And in this first Whig House in American history the Whigs had a comfortable majority of more than forty votes. So surely the story of the gag would now be different—would it not?

In the beginning it was. On the very first day of the Twenty-seventh Congress, meeting in special session, May 31, Henry Wise moved that the old rules be provisionally adopted for a period of ten days, while a committee examined possible changes. Underwood of Kentucky moved an amendment proposing that the old House rules prevail, instead of for the limited number of days, *until* a committee's proposed revisions be adopted. (A small change? A big change.) And John Quincy Adams then moved the decisive and controversial point, an amendment to the amendment: " . . . except for the 21st rule, which is hereby rescinded." With the accession of Whig members, would there be enough votes to knock down that obnoxious rule? The first answer is yes. The second answer is no.

The vote on Adams's amendment to Underwood's amendment was very close, but for the first time in the long sequence since the first gag resolution, the opponents of a gag *won*. This was a shocking turn of events: Adams's amendment *carried* by eight votes, 112–104. The division, Adams said in his journal, was "almost exclusively bond and free."

But then there had to be a vote on Underwood's amendment, now stripped of Rule 21 by Adams's successful amendment, and then on the main motion, as perhaps amended. Those close votes had a shocking result, too. The House members, no doubt eager to organize, and perhaps not quite realizing what they were doing—these were the very first days for many new members—defeated two attempts to adjourn and then voted, still on June 7, by a vote of 125 to 94 to adopt Wise's original motion as amended not only by Underwood but—the important point—by Adams. They adopted the rules *without* Rule 21. Adams's journal goes on, "After much struggling, the question was carried to adopt the rules with the exception."

So there it is—victory? The rules were adopted without the gag? The gag rule is dead? Here, in its very first meeting, the new Whig regime removes the loathsome rule? Our story is over? Then why are there so many more pages in this book?

BEFORE ANSWERING THOSE QUESTIONS, let us pause to introduce, and to notice the joy expressed on this occasion by, an important new Whig voice, the *New York Tribune*. The *Tribune* was a paper of the sort that had come into being with the steam press in the previous decade, the penny press, intended to appeal to a much wider readership than the old six-cent papers for the gentry and commercial people. Most of this new popular penny press had up to now been Democratic/Jacksonian; President John Quincy Adams had taken a beating in those papers. But the *Tribune* was different. In his first editorial, "A Plain Talk to Whigs," the editor promised that his newspaper would be "devoted to Literature, Intelligence, and the open and fearless advocacy of Whig Principles and Measures."

This fearless Whig advocacy had commenced, by perhaps ominous coincidence, exactly on April 10, the day of the funeral of the new Whig president, who had been succeeded by a vice-president who turned out not to be an adherent of "Whig Principles and Measures" at all, and who would veto key measures passed by the Whig Congress.

But, again, Whigs believed in the legislature, and in June of 1841 one did not know those Tyler vetoes were coming. The editor of the *Tribune*, full of hope for this Congress, was Horace Greeley, an earnest young native of New England, loaded with the Protestant Ethic. His place in America's collective memory has been unfairly reduced to one probably apocryphal piece of directional advice to young men and one town in Colorado; there was more to Greeley than that. On June 10, 1841, this serious and interesting new Whig spokesman rejoiced editorially about the "Repeal of the Gag Law":

> We rejoice that one of the first decisive acts of the new Congress has been the rescinding by the House of Representatives of the rule of 1839 [actually passed in early 1840] by which petitions and memorials addressed by the People to that branch of government which may be related to Slavery were to be unceremoniously *rejected*, without consideration, hearing or even *reading*.—This arbitrary and extraordinary provision—expressly contravening that clause of the Constitution which declares that the right of Petition shall not be impaired, and eminently calculated to foster and

inflame the spirit which threatens the dissolution of the Union—has been stricken from the Rules of Congress.

The *Tribune* then proceeded joyfully to give the vote "on this important question" thoroughly and in big readable type, yeas, by states, and then nays, by states, with Democrats (always called Loco-Focos* in this relentlessly Whig paper) in italics. No newspaper today presents congressional votes as thoroughly and as clearly as the *Tribune* did.

But the rejoicing, alas, was premature. The "victory" was like a long kickoff return for a touchdown that then is called back by a referee's flag—except that the calling back was not done by neutral referees. And it was done in torturing stages. Greeley's *Tribune* in its assessment after the deed was done put the blame on "a skilful commingling of Treachery, Sectional Feeling, and unprincipled partisanship." Under this last heading Greeley put a cadre of Northern Democrats—in particular from New York and Pennsylvania—who had voted *for* Adams's amendment eliminating the gag, and *for* the adoption of the rules without the gag—but who then moved to *reconsider* these votes!

Had they planned to do that all along? (In the rules of parliamentary procedure, you can only move to reconsider a vote you have *supported*—for obvious reasons.) Had they voted to repeal, thinking that their vote would look good to their constituents, but that the repeal would fail? Were they motivated, as Greeley charged, just to make "mischief"—to impede the business of this Whig Congress?

The semiorganized House (what rules were they operating under, before they adopted the rules?) did a few other preliminaries, including arranging for memorial ceremonies for the deceased President Harrison (House chairman on the ceremonies: John Quincy Adams), but then, the next day after the touchdown, in the midst of routine but contested House business—the election of a sergeant-at-arms—two Pennsylvania Democrats (Loco-Focos to the *Tribune*) interrupted, one after the other, bang-bang, to move reconsideration of previous votes: C. J. Ingersoll, reconsideration of the passage of Adams's amendment, and Joseph Fornance, reconsideration of the adoption of the rules as amended by it.

Adams wrote in his journal: "Everett opposed consideration of Inger-

*"Loco-Foco" was a term of mockery and abuse originally applied to the "barnburners," or radicals among the Democrats, particularly in New York; the term derived from a kind of match used to start fires. As a political pejorative it implied dizzy, irresponsible radicalism. Greeley, a partisan Whig, applied it to the entire Democratic Party.

soll's motion as out of order—as it certainly was. But a slave-holding speaker [the newly chosen John White of Kentucky] could not reject this new convert to the servile cause; and Wise, Cost Johnson, and King of Georgia were all clamorous for hearing Ingersoll."

Ingersoll was a "high-toned" Democrat from Philadelphia whom a twentieth-century historian and biographer of Polk, Charles Sellers, described as a "vain, erratic, intellectual snob."* Up in New York Horace Greeley had the following further unkind words about him:

> Our readers will have observed by our Washington advices that Mr. Charles Jared Ingersoll—the gentleman who once publicly declared "if I had lived in the days of the Revolution, I would have been a Tory"—after first voting with the Free States to rescind the Gag Law, has moved a reconsideration of the decision, and thereupon threw the House into confusion and convulsion, wasted one day, and then commenced an endless speech about Abolition, Whiggery, British philanthropy, and the like, which was just in its opening, having scarcely reached nineteenthly when the House adjourned.
>
> Let the people mark the men who are wasting their time and money in desperate attempts to exasperate local jealousies, create heart-burnings, and obstruct the progress of public business. Brand them.

It was during this long Ingersoll speech in favor of reconsidering the vote that struck the gag, perhaps before he reached nineteenthly, that Ingersoll and Adams had the exchange, reported in an earlier chapter, elaborating Adams's contention that slavery could be constitutionally abolished under the war power—a shocking idea to Ingersoll and to almost everybody, North and South. Ingersoll expressed his horror, and said that for his part he stood ready to march to suppress an insurrection of slaves.

Nevertheless, when the vote was taken on Ingersoll's motion to reconsider the vote that adopted Adams's amendment "except for Rule 21"—Ingersoll lost. Adams, as it were, won again, by another of these close votes, 107–113. "A second deliverance as by fire," he wrote in his journal.

But still more deliverances were needed, and they were not to be forthcoming. The other Pennsylvania Democrat, Joseph Fornance, had already in that bang-bang intervention on the earlier day placed into the parliamentary backlog a motion to reconsider even the vote to adopt the rules

*Sellers quotes an observer of the time as saying of Ingersoll that he "looks upon common people through gold specs and ornaments his fingers with costly diamonds."

(without 21) themselves. But, Greeley's rigorously partisan interpretation notwithstanding, it was not the Democrat Fornance who picked up on this waiting motion, but the ubiquitous Whig Henry Wise.

Wise had made the original motion to adopt the old rules in the first place, but of course voted against his own motion once it carried Adams's amendment. Wise now called up Fornance's motion, and held forth, with interruptions, and postponements, including a dramatic fainting spell that Adams describes in his journal, for the better part of four days. "The real object of these postponements," Adams wrote, on June 12, "is to give time for the five members from Alabama to come in." He added: "They are all, of course, slave-dealers." Apparently by June 14 enough members had arrived, because the vote was then taken on Fornance's motion, and it *carried*, 106–104. The adoption of the rules, except for Rule 21, was *reconsidered*. The touchdown was called back. Adams wrote, "[T]he House again was left without rules."

Observers began to be disgusted. The Whigs had an ambitious program to enact, after all; this was the first Congress they had ever controlled, and this was a *special* session called by their newly elected Whig president William Henry Harrison, just before he died, at the behest of their great Whig leader Senator Henry Clay. So—could not the Whigs, with a forty-vote margin in the House, get their act together sufficiently, after *two weeks*, even to organize the House?

After several abortive efforts to make changes and substitutions the House came back, on the evening of June 15, to the original bare motion, now reconsidered, to adopt the old rules minus 21—and now rejected it. Apparently Alabama had showed up. Apparently a significant number of congressmen were willing to say, in effect, we won't have *any* rules, if we can't have Rule 21 blocking abolitionist petitions. Adams observed in his journal that there were "several members on both sides [I take this to mean from both parties] changing their votes to make up a majority."

The *Tribune* gave its own particular report—in which there appeared an old family name later to be famous in New York and national politics—of the vote-switching to which Adams had referred. The italics are Greeley's:

> So recklessly is this game played that on the last important vote on Tuesday evening there was first a clear majority in favor of adopting the Rules of the last Session, the XXIst excepted, when several Loco-Focos, alarmed that the reign of Mischief was thereby overthrown, rose and *changed their votes from the affirmative to the negative! Mr. Jas. J. Roosevelt* of this City came in after the vote had been taken, asked and was granted leave to have his name recorded, and in direct defiance of his own former

vote, *now voted in the negative!* In this manner the proposition was defeated—110 to 106—and the House adjourned without organization! For such conduct what language of execration can be too strong?

But if Democrats were switching, and manipulating, whether because they were really in favor of the gag or just to block business in the House—Whig business they weren't in favor of, and didn't mind blocking—the Whigs still had their forty-vote margin. Those close votes, and those defeats, could not have happened had not the *Southern* Whigs—all but four out of forty-five—joined in voting down any rules that did not include 21.

Adams had argued for the dropping of Rule 21, to some degree in party terms. He said the gag had been "a Democratic measure, a measure of Northern men with Southern principles, a sectional measure." It had been adopted, said he, when "a majority of the House was anxious above all things not to be thought abolitionist"—implying that the situation, now that Whigs were the majority, might be different. He depicted the gag as a measure instigated by the Van Buren administration and the Democrats, and indicated that the Whigs should now undo it; he once even seemed to hint that undoing the gag was an administration measure. Henry Wise, who was a great deal closer to "the administration" as it now was (Tyler having succeeded Harrison), objected to these efforts of his great adversary:

> **Wise:** We have been told by the gentleman [Adams] that the 21st rule was an administration measure—a measure of the last administration—that it was a proposition which the Whigs of this House would never have attempted to carry through; and the gentleman from Massachusetts has made a covert appeal to the Whigs of this House to reverse that measure. And if he (Mr. W.) had rightly understood the gentleman [Adams] he intended to say that it would be the policy of the present Administration to reverse that rule. He (Mr. W.) did not know what the gentleman defined to be the Administration; if, by the Administration, he meant the Executive now in power, he (Mr. W.) undertook to say that the Executive would never countenance the introduction of the topic of abolition into these halls.

As far as the nominally Whig executive was concerned, now that John Tyler sat in the President's house: Wise rightly felt he knew more about that than Adams did.

SO AFTER THIS SERIES of up-the-hill, down-the-hill close votes, and after two weeks, the House was still not organized. What was to be done? The *Tribune*'s advice was to let go of the effort to kill the gag, and to organize the House with the gag still in the rules. And that is approximately what happened.

On June 16, Virginia congressman A.H.H. Stuart, one of the four Southern Whigs who *had* voted for the rules without the gag, proposed a compromise of sorts. The *special* quality of the special session figured into the compromise: the House resolved to confine itself at this session to a bankruptcy law (an important and successful Whig project; there were many editorials in Greeley's paper on that matter) and only such other topics as appeared in the president's message. Petitions on *all* other subjects (not just abolition) could for this session be excluded, and the Committee on Rules could be authorized to continue its work.

That could be interpreted as a postponement, rather than a resolution, of the fight over the gag. The House would, as Adams put it in his journal, "hang up all petitions for this session, and put off the debate on the rule to the winter session." Clearly the Whigs wanted to get on to business: the previous question carried; Stuart's motion carried; a deliberate preemptive strike motion to reconsider failed. And though the margins were slim, with a hundred plus on each side, the door was shut. The House was organized, and could get on with its business, but the gag was still (or rather—*again*) in the rules, even in this Whig Congress.

Adams, pointedly summarizing in the December regular session the efforts in the special session in June to excise Rule 21 from the House rules, said that the House had voted to rescind the rule *three times*, and in a sense it had:

—On June 7, 112–104, to adopt Adams's amendment;

—also on June 7, to adopt the rules without 21, 125–94;

—and on June 10, to reject Ingersoll's motion to reconsider that vote, 107–113.

But all that came to naught when the House, after Wise's long delaying speech, voted just barely, 106–104, for Fornance's motion to reconsider the adoption of the rules with the Adams exception, and then 106–110 to decline to adopt them with that exception, and finally after all that on June 16 to compromise by provisionally adopting the rules with 21; omitting all petitions except on specified topics in this session; and awaiting a report of a committee on rules.

These last thrashings produced at the end a split among those who usually stood together. Which was more important: to keep fighting *now* until you got rid of the gag? Or to let that go for now so you could get on to the House's business, the Whig program?

The *Tribune*, which we take as a representative Northern Whig voice, had been very favorable to Adams's apparently successful move against the gag at the start, and critical of the pro-gag forces for not accepting gracefully their defeat. But once that victory was taken away, and the fight nevertheless went on, the editorials began to turn negative—critical of *both* sides of the fight. By June 14, for example, Mr. Greeley's paper was saying: "It is not to be disguised that the Abolition discussion in the House has somewhat disorganized the Whig majority, which the ill-considered remarks of Mr. ADAMS (not his motion, which was right and necessary) were eminently calculated to do. Mr. WISE, on the other hand, has been equally unwise and intemperate, and a few other members were disposed to follow these bad examples."

This plague-on-both-their-houses linking of Adams and Wise was repeated in the final editorial: "Messrs. Adams and Wise have done their worst by including speeches and criminations to shiver the Whig party and break up the Extra session without effecting anything for the country."

But, happily from the *Tribune*'s point of view, these shiverers of the Whig Party did not succeed. When, in spite of Adams and Wise, the "compromise" passed, Greeley gave his editorial the very Whig title "FACTION VANQUISHED!" "[T]he better genius of the Country has triumphed," he wrote, "and a compromise of the vexed question has been effected."

It was a "compromise" in that a select committee was directed to proceed with a revision of the rules, which might mean that Rule 21 would then be challenged, which presumably was the reason diehard defenders of the gag (including key Southern Whigs) voted against it, and one could perhaps say it was a compromise also in that abolition petitions were not the only ones excluded in this Extra Session. But Rule 21 was (however apparently "provisionally") readopted. Adams would vote against the "compromise" for that reason, and because he did not believe in excluding other petitions, either.

When it gave its list of the strange-bedfellow votes for Stuart's successful "compromise," the *Tribune* gave the reader quite explicit instruction as to what to think of each side of the vote. Thus it printed first the yes votes, under the heading:

YEAS—[*in favor of organization*]

These included:

Vermont . . . Slade

and

Ohio . . . S. J. Andrews . . . Giddings

But the next list was headed:

NAYS—[*in favor of perpetual anarchy*]

and included not only:

Maryland . . . W. Cost Johnson

and

South Carolina . . . Pickens

and

Virginia . . . Wise

but also

Massachusetts . . . Adams.

PART XI

THE TRIALS

33/I KNOW YOU WELL, SIR, BY YOUR WRITINGS

IN THE WINTER BEFORE his summer contribution to perpetual anarchy, Adams had been growing closer to some of the abolitionists. Although he had been a founder of the Whig Party, he did not speak on Whig candidate William Henry Harrison's behalf in the campaign of 1840. When Harrison marched to his rainy inauguration in March of 1841 a place had been reserved for ex-presidents in the parade, but ex-president John Quincy Adams did not march in that place. He was, instead, closeted at home with a new friend working on a new project.

The new friend was Joshua Leavitt, the abolitionist from Nassau Street, editor of the *Emancipator*. The project was the defense before the United States Supreme Court of the freedom of a group of Africans in the famous case of the *Amistad* mutiny.

The case had begun in 1839. The Africans, who had taken control of the slave ship on which they were being transported, ordered the crew to take them to Africa, but instead they sailed, by night, west toward the United States, presumably in hopes of landing at some Southern port where the claims of slave owners would be properly respected. But in a nice irony the *Amistad* had missed the slave half of the United States and hit the free part instead. So the mutineers were now being held in Connecticut jails, and were claimed by Cuban "owners" as slaves, and by the Spanish government both as "pirates" for taking over the ship and as murderers because in their shipboard revolt they had killed the ship's captain and cook.

The Africans were passionately defended by abolitionists, especially Lewis Tappan and Leavitt, and by various Yale people (they were jailed in New Haven) as free human beings who had been illegally captured by clandestine slave traders (illegally because all the relevant nations had now, by law and treaty, abolished the slave *trade*, although slavery itself was still legal in Cuba as well as the southern half of the United States).

Spanish officials in Havana had winked at a kind of African-laundering operation in Cuba, by which newly captured Africans could be registered and passed off as longtime (therefore legal) slaves; that is what had happened to the *Amistad* captives. To their defenders these Africans, fresh from the Mendi tribe in Nigeria, were obviously too young (the treaty abolishing the slave trade had been signed in 1817) and too ignorant of Spanish or any other Western language to have been what their captors claimed them to be, slaves for some years, who were being transported on the *Amistad* by their Spanish owners.

The Van Buren administration, approaching the presidential election of 1840, had responded to the double pressure of its political need to hold the slaveholding South and its diplomatic need to honor the claims of a sister nation, Spain, by arguing through its lawyers for the "return" of the captives to Spain and to Cuba for trial and slavery.

For Leavitt and Tappan and the Yale Divinity School students and the abolitionists, given their convictions and their limited experience with, or sympathies for, the great world of power, this position was outrageous. For John Quincy Adams, the matter might not have been so simple, however. He knew from a lifetime of diplomacy the sometimes grim necessities of relationships among sovereign nations. In one episode, for example, in the aftermath of the War of 1812, he had had to negotiate with Great Britain the return to their rightful American owners of slaves captured and set free by the British forces. That kind of distasteful conduct was a realistic necessity in the great world of politics among nations. No American had more experience with those realities than Adams. Experienced and "realistic" diplomatic hands would argue, in the *Amistad* case, that the United States, like any other nation, could not "look behind" the claims of another nation at peace (in this case Spain) to see whether they were valid in our eyes; those claims should be honored.

So which of the contrasting interpretations of the *Amistad* case did Adams accept? As noted before, people do not in all cases become more "conservative" as they grow older. Adams flatly accepted the interpretation that saw the *Amistad* group as free persons, unjustly captured, who should not be turned over to a "trial" by slave smugglers.

He had read about the case in the *Emancipator*, which carried an indignant letter about it from William Jay, a prominent abolitionist, son of the founder John Jay. Adams wrote a letter expressing his own indignation to Jay, and so it became known in abolitionist circles that Adams was in full sympathy with their view of the matter.

The case worked its way from the trial in the district court in New Haven, where the *Amistad* Africans won a slightly qualified victory, through the appeal of the decision by the Van Buren administration to the circuit court, which affirmed the judgment of the district court, to the United States Supreme Court. These decisions and their surrounding advocacies had taken place in 1840, during the first session of the Twenty-sixth Congress, and under the shadow of the presidential election, in November—one reason, as noted, for the Van Buren administration's earnest efforts to have the group categorized as slaves and turned over to Spain.

Adams, in the House, during the winter of 1840, put through a resolution calling upon the president to make available the official papers on the case, and, discovering in the English mistranslation of a Spanish word what he thought to be evidence of a "cover-up" (as a later politics would put it) of the slave-laundering in Cuba, called for, and became chairman of, a committee investigation, which kept the issue before the public.

The slaveholding forces, becoming nervous, responded. Calhoun in the Senate introduced resolutions that affirmed that ships on the high seas were strictly under the jurisdiction of the nations whose flag they flew, and that when forced by events into the port of any other nation, such ships should have their cargo and property "and all the rights belonging to their personal relations" as established by those states protected by the friendly power into whose port they had been forced. These resolutions made no mention of Spain, Cuba, slavery, or the *Amistad*—but everyone knew these were the true subjects.

Adams countered with proposed resolutions in the House—which did not succeed—specifically denouncing the unlawful detention and imprisonment of the Africans of the *Amistad*. Here were the old colleagues from Monroe's cabinet going at each other again on the subject of slavery, now indirectly with resolutions about the *Amistad* case in the two legislative houses: Calhoun's resolution in the Senate, Adams's answering resolution in the House.

The case came to the United States Supreme Court in January of 1841, after the elections in the previous November but before the inauguration of the new administration in March, while the lame duck last session of the Twenty-sixth Congress was meeting. This was the business Adams was attending to while Giddings and Thompson went at each other about the Seminole War and who was more obscure than whom. Up to that point the abolitionists, with Lewis Tappan playing the main role, had not formally availed themselves of Adams's services. But the lawyers they had hired had begun to leave the case, in some instances—lawyers even then mostly being lawyers—because Tappan and Leavitt and company were having trouble coming up with the fees (as we have noted before, the Panic of 1837 and the ensuing recession had hit the Tappan brothers' dry goods enterprise, and the businesses of other benefactors as well, so the abolitionist movement was having a harder time finding funds). Other lawyers whom Tappan approached turned him down, for reasons of fees or lack of sympathy with the cause or both. Finally he did turn to Adams.

Adams had not expected, when he volunteered his services, that he would be asked actually to appear before the Supreme Court. He was seventy-four years old. Doing other things, he had not appeared as an advocate before any court for thirty-one years, and even in the brief periods when he had been active as a lawyer in those earlier years he had not done so often. Moreover, he was preoccupied with the battles in the House.

But now Tappan and company wanted him to appear himself as an advocate before the highest Court, and told him the very lives of the *Amistad* group were at stake. With misgivings, he accepted. And so on some days in late February of 1841, while Washington and the country waited for the inauguration in March of the new Whig administration, and while the lame duck session of the House in the Twenty-sixth Congress was meeting in one side of the Capitol, congressman and ex-president John Quincy Adams was making an argument for the Africans of the *Amistad* in the Supreme Court chambers on the other side of the Capitol.

The Supreme Court then met in the basement, or lowest floor, of the Capitol, underneath the Senate chambers. Adams and the Court heard the government's case (the case of the outgoing Van Buren administration), which cited, among much else, his old adversary Calhoun's resolutions in the Senate. Then Adams was first up for the defense. He held forth for four and a half hours before the Court adjourned that day, and then for three hours more when the Court reconvened. These were free men by Spain's own laws! Victims of the outlawed transatlantic slave trade! He carried the argument to the fundamental principles of human morality—as he must have heard his father say that James Otis had done in that Boston courtroom in 1761 on the day—his father had written—that American independence was born, and the elder Adams's career as the Atlas of Independence had begun.

Between the arguments and the Court's announcing of its verdict came the inauguration of President William Henry Harrison and the Whigs; that is why Adams and Joshua Leavitt, collaborators now, were closeted at Adams's house as the inaugural festivities took place. On March 9, the senior justice, the famous Justice Joseph Story, announced the verdict: as Adams wrote to Tappan, "The captives are free!" Leading abolitionists, including Whittier, wrote thanks and praise to Adams; Leavitt wrote "Praise be the God of Justice!" Although Tappan waited nervously for a bill for Adams's services, Adams never sent one.

. . .

JOSHUA LEAVITT WAS IN Washington not only for the *Amistad* case but also as editor/journalist for the *Emancipator*, and, less openly, as a forerunner of an abolitionist presence in the nation's capital. There Leavitt, Yale Divinity School graduate, minister, journalist, and reformer, met Giddings—two Joshuas joining in this modern battle of Jericho—and stayed on after the *Amistad* case into the early days of the new Whig administration, and of the special session of the new Twenty-seventh Congress. Leavitt heard the speeches of Adams, and Giddings, and watched the disappointing but stimulating touchdown-called-back votes on Rule 21 in that session, and saw the stacks of petitions in the corridors, and realized, with anticipatory verve, that Washington was, or could be, in the idiom of young folks a century and a half later, where the action was.

Leavitt was a pure reformer who had never met the elected representative's equivalent of a payroll. He did not know the political realities and rules of the House, and he urged congressmen to take actions—about the election of a Speaker, and about the organization of the House and Rule 21 and the petitions—that he thought he would have taken in their place. But the experienced politicians Slade and Giddings responded to the abstract idealism of Leavitt's urging as politicians of all ages do: you don't know what is possible and impossible; you don't know what you are talking about.

Slade had been disappointed in Adams, and Giddings had been disappointed in Slade, and Leavitt was disappointed in Giddings, and William Lloyd Garrison was disappointed in Leavitt, and a still more thoroughgoing remaker of the world named Henry C. Wright may even have been disappointed in Garrison: they were reformers.

Giddings had been disappointed in Slade because Slade, who had been a government servant and a politician—in the odd proto-Whig Anti-Masonic Party—before organized abolition became a force, had become a loyal Whig, and in the prospect and reality of a Whig victory had been willing to subordinate abolition to Whig policy more than Giddings, who was also a loyal Whig, but of a younger generation, would do—for example in the choice of "slaveholder" John White of Kentucky as Speaker.

Garrison was disappointed in—or in disagreement with—Leavitt for even as much commitment to political action as he made; Garrison was a "no government" man, rejecting the compromises of politics and parties altogether for moral purity. This last division—between the Garrisonians and the other wings and parts and leaders of the antislavery movement—was a lasting and important one, never healed.

The domain of American antislavery was, like other movements to change the world on the basis of a moral ideal, prone to internal disputes and divisions over the nature and purity of the ideal, and over acceptable and effective strategy. One may make the analogy to governments in exile: there is in such reform and radical movements a hothouse flowering of a luxuriant variety of ideas about possible actions, possible leaders, possible decisions, of what-ought-to-bes and why-nots, that have not had to try to grow and survive in the dirt and the snow and the wind of the real outer world. The moral convictions of the abolitionists had not as yet—despite the mobs and burnings and outraged resolutions—had to face the very big guns of the very big facts of American society at that time. But now in the Whig Congress of 1841–42 they were to come much closer to doing so.

Leavitt, the less politically experienced, purer reformer, argued vigorously with the handful of abolitionist congressmen about the priorities for the coming December session of the Twenty-seventh Congress, in which the Whigs would have control, now no longer in a special session but in a long regular session: don't subordinate the antislavery cause to the economic and other issues of the Whig Party, or to party unity. Writing to Giddings in October, Leavitt gave this summary of the differences between the two Joshuas:

> In some respects we differ—you thinking it is better to aim first at specific points of policy which you deem beneficial to free labor or rather to the North . . . while I look upon all reforms as uncertain and unavailing which involve the continued toleration of slavery. . . . [I]t is the greatest of evils and the prime cause of other evils.

These differences, however, were not deep, and the two men were collaborators, discussing tactics for a common objective.

The congressmen gathered in the late fall, and the key figures—Giddings, Slade, and their newer abolitionist colleague Seth Gates—took their winter lodgings at Mrs. Sprigg's, getting ready now for the regular session of the Twenty-seventh Congress. Hitherto the antislavery forces, such as they were, had been merely responsive; now they were to take the initiative and carry the battle to the "enemy"—to seek, and to make, occasions to take up the issue of slavery openly. Hitherto the handful of congressmen inclined to some sympathy for the abolitionist cause had functioned independently; now there was to be an explicit and continuing collaboration. Hitherto antislavery had ranked below other issues in the priorities even of its adherents in the House; now for this small group it was to have the highest place.

They formed themselves—the key congressmen, plus Leavitt—into what Giddings dubbed a "Select Committee on Slavery." They *planned* their program for the session: bills and resolutions that would open the discussion of slavery upon the House floor, in spite of the gag rule. And then after Giddings, Slade, Gates, Andrews of Ohio, or Francis James of Pennsylvania, had managed to make the speech on the floor with the slaveholders' interruptions and objections, the speeches would be polished by the speaker, printed in official records, and circulated to the country. Officially printed, they would be far more valuable than abolitionist tracts and pamphlets.

But the "select committee" needed help in order to do these things. A congressman in those days had no staff, so how, and when, could the abolitionist congressmen do the research to give facts and strength to their speeches?

Giddings's "select committee," forming itself into what is sometimes called a "lobby" (although it was a curious kind of a lobby—composed of congressmen themselves), not only rented rooms but decided to hire a research assistant. How did they pay for that? They were paid $8 a day per diem and mileage, grand total, for their service, and they reached into their pockets to pay for the lobby rooms and the researcher.

The man they hired brings the threads of the story together. They hired Theodore Weld. In addition to his powers of persuasion—Giddings, Gates, and Andrews were among Weld's many converts to abolitionism—he was the leading researcher of the antislavery movement, as *American Slavery As It Is* and the other books had proved.

Weld was a family man now, living in New Jersey with his wife, Angelina Grimké Weld, and their two children, and his sister-in-law Sarah Grimké, on a fifty-acre farm, slightly run-down, that they had purchased with all their ready cash at a sheriff's sale. The Anti-Slavery Society could no longer afford to pay him. Lewis Tappan did lend them enough money for cows, chickens, and farm supplies; the sisters' eventual inheritance, and the back pay owed to Weld, were the prospective sources of the funds to pay him back. Weld did the farming and repair work on the property (memories of the manual labor institutes!); sheltered runaway slaves; worked gratis for the remnant of the society; and stayed out of the internal battles within abolitionism.

When in December of 1841 he received from Leavitt the invitation to come to Washington on behalf of the little band of abolitionist congressmen, he wrote to Lewis Tappan:

> Dear brother Tappan:
> The last mail brought me a letter from brother Leavitt at Washington, written at the request of a number of the Abolition members of Congress;

> he mentions Giddings and Andrews of Ohio (in both of whose families I spent some time when lecturing on slavery in that state) James and Mattocks of Pennsylvania, Gates N.Y., Slade, Vt. and Borden, Mass. He says that since the passage of the new gag and, under the circumstances of aggravation attending it, these members are thoroughly roused and are determined to carry the war in upon the enemy, to shift the plan of the campaign and attack slavery at every point.

Weld described to Tappan the "select committee's strategy and intention":

> . . . during the session they have resolved to bring in bills and introduce resolutions of inquiry, etc.,which will open the whole field for discussion in a shape in which the gag or any gag which it is possible for Congress to pass cannot touch them. These speeches they propose to distribute at convenient distances through the winter months, perhaps through the session. The subjects named in the letter upon which a speech is to be made by some of them are District [of] Columbia, Territory [of] Florida, Internal Slave trade, Constitutional rights of Colored citizens, Texas, Hayti, Colonization, etc., etc.
>
> As they are pressed with multiplied duties in the House on Committees, etc., etc., and have little leisure for gathering materials they request me to spend the winter there and aid them in the matter.

Weld gave the argument that had been presented to him, about the particular value of work done in Congress.

> That these men are in a position to do for the A-S cause by a single speech more than our best lecturers can do in a year, we all know. The fact that these speeches, prepared for the press by the speakers themselves after the delivery, will be published in the *National Intelligencer* or the *Globe* and thus scattered over the South as well as the North settles the point.

So Weld agreed to come to Washington to join this "lobby," which we might call the greatest of Washington lobbies, in late December of 1841. Giddings got a room for him—where would you expect? In Mrs. Sprigg's boardinghouse.

On New Year's Day, a Saturday in 1842, Weld wrote to his wife describing his arrival, and his fellow lodgers:

> My dearest love,
>
> I am arrived here Thursday evening at six o'clock well, came at once

> to Mrs. Sprigg's, and found Leavitt, Giddings, and Gates expecting me, and received a hearty welcome. Giddings and Gates both seem hearty in the cause. . . . Giddings is fearless, self possessed, and not to be put down by threats or bluster. Gates is a man of mind and moral courage, but no *speaker*—is as timid about speaking in public as J. G. Whittier—but really a courageous man in the utterance of his conscientious convictions. Andrews called here last night, was very cordial. . . . The abolition members are I think determined to do something this winter and three or four of them will make vigorous onsets upon slavery. . . . We have about twenty boarders, mostly members of Congress, 8 of them from Pennsylvania and the rest from the free states. Only Gates and Giddings [are] abolitionists, but *all* the others are *favorable*. They treat brother Leavitt and myself exactly as though we were not fan[a]tics, and we talk over with them at the table and elsewhere abolition just as we should at home.

In the long history of this nation, it was going to be very important that in the end the boarders at Mrs. Sprigg's in 1842 would win out over those who had boarded at Mrs. Lindenberger's seven years earlier.

In the letter he wrote to his wife the next day, Weld explained that in this rather special setting he could observe his diet without censure: his eating no meat, no butter, no tea, no coffee, "etc." (one wonders what all would be included, or excluded, in Weld's "etc.") "excites of course some attention but no sneers."

And then he told about two adventures on New Year's Day. First at the president's:

> Yesterday (New Year's Day) President Tyler held a Levee. The doors of the palace were thrown open at 11 o'clock and whoever pleased whether in silks or sackcloth, frocks or robes of office, went to *shake hands* with him. Leavitt, Giddings and I went, but took care *not* to shake hands with him. An introduction to him was offered me but I refused it. The crowd of persons of both sexes was immense.

Then Weld and his companions went on to a more congenial social setting:

> After staying at the President 15 minutes, looking with sadness and pity at the pomp and tinsel and fashion and display of magnificence, we went to pay our respects to John Quincy Adams. Found him and his wife living in a plain house, plainly furnished, and themselves plainly dressed—the old gentleman very plainly. When Mr. Leavitt introduced me, Mr. A. asked "is it Mr. Theodore D. Weld?" Yes. "I know you well sir by your writings."

So Weld and Adams had now met: an important moment for the story told in this book. We know from his journal that Adams read, and admired, the Quaker abolitionist of the older generation Benjamin Lundy. We infer from his long speech about women in politics that he had read Angelina and perhaps Sarah Grimké. We learn from his journal that he came to admire Giddings as much as any fellow congressman, and to befriend the younger man. He even wrote a bad poem celebrating his friendship with Giddings. And, as Weld wrote his wife, Adams was familiar with him from reading him. "I know you well, sir, by your writings."

Weld told Angelina that Adams inquired after her, and then "at once began to talk with us on slavery, the case of the *Creole* [another high-seas slavery case, of which more in a moment], the abolition by the Bey of Tunis, and the prospect of abolition in Cuba." The Adamses' rooms were full of visitors, Weld wrote, "who had come to pay their respects to the Old Nestor; among the rest I was glad to see some slaveholders."

In the early days of January of 1842, Weld went to work in an alcove in the Library of Congress that was provided to him, on his introduction by a member, Giddings. "From nine in the morning till three in the afternoon," he wrote his wife and sister-in-law, "I spend in the Library of Congress *generally*, with the exception of about an hour from one to two o'clock when I run into the Senate or the House of Representatives for relaxation." He was putting together the materials for the assault by the "select committee"—Abolition House, as Mrs. Sprigg's came to be called—on slavery.

Weld was invited to dinner by J. Q. and Mrs. Adams on January 8. "It was a genuine abolition gathering," the abolitionist Weld wrote to the abolitionist Grimkés, "and the old patriarch talked with as much energy and zeal as a Methodist at a camp meeting. Remarkable man!"

The "Select Committee on Slavery," with Weld as staff and John Quincy Adams as either a member or close collaborator, was ready now in the winter of 1842 to do more than anyone had done before in the U.S. Congress on the issue of slavery: to go beyond sporadic individual effort, responding to initiatives from the other side. They were ready now to take the initiative themselves, in a concerted effort.

But in the meantime their opponents, far more powerful, were to make their concerted effort to end this obnoxious movement by chopping off its head.

34 / THE VEXED QUESTION STILL VEXED

WOULD ADAMS AND ABOLITION HOUSE be able to win, on the great matter of Rule 21, in the first regular session of Congress ever controlled by Whigs?

Let the eager Whig Horace Greeley, in his *Tribune* for November 30, 1841, set the stage:

> The Second Session of the Twenty-seventh Congress commences on Monday next. There being no Speaker or other officers to be chosen [because they were already chosen at the Extra Session], and a moral certainty of a quorum at the outset, we look with confidence for the delivery of the President's Message at 12 o'clock on Tuesday next. The only conceivable obstacle is the raising the question of the reception of Anti-Slavery Petitions; and this, we earnestly trust, will be postponed until the two Houses shall have been fully organized and the Message delivered.

Notice that even for the knowledgeable antislavery Northern Whig Horace Greeley the matter of the rule against antislavery petitions is seen more as an obstacle to the organizing of the House than as an abomination to be got rid of at the start. Dealing with that matter should in Greeley's view be postponed.

> As soon as this [the President's message to Congress] is apportioned to the several Committees, and preliminary investigations and deliberations commenced, let the subject of the Right of Petition come up and be thoroughly adjusted.

So Greeley wrote. The flaw in that view was that organizing so as to distribute the president's message, and to get those other matters started, would *already* have determined a position on the petitions and Rule 21 that would be difficult—probably impossible—to dislodge. Greeley's *Tribune* went on, demonstrating further his misunderstanding of the *timing* of the battle:

> There will be exhibitions of passion, violence and disorder; but let them come. The evil passions exist now; let them have vent, and the perturbed

breast will eventually work clearer and calmer. Very little is usually accomplished on the floor of either House in December; and if that month shall be successfully devoted to the settlement of the "vexed question" on a just and enduring basis, it will have been most profitably employed.

But the "vexed question" could not be postponed for the leisurely December consideration *after* the House was organized that Greeley wanted; it had to be confronted immediately in the organizing of the House itself. If even Horace Greeley did not quite understand that, how many new, young Whigs could be expected to? But William Cost Johnson *did* understand.

The rules, including Rule 21, it will be remembered, had been adopted supposedly only provisionally for the one session, after that called-back touchdown in the Extra Session, with a committee appointed to consider changes. That committee had reported, but on the very last day of the session, so nothing could then be done.

Now on the very first day* of the regular session William Cost Johnson, while up for other purposes (to request that he not be appointed to the committee on Land Claims, and to announce that he would propose a National Foundry), apparently almost casually made a pseudo-innocent proposal:

> While up, **Mr. J.** said, he would make an effort, he knew not whether it would be successful or not, but he would at all events make the effort, to enable the House at once to proceed to an organization, and the transaction of the public business. For which purpose he would offer a resolution providing that the rules and orders of the 26th Congress be adopted and be the rules and order of this Congress till otherwise altered or changed by the House. He made this motion in order to suit the various interests in the House, and he hoped there would be no opposition to its adoption.

This was deceptively simple-sounding and low-key: by the way, let's just adopt the old rules now to get started; we can change them later if we want to. Johnson said he knew there were some members very much opposed to the one-hour rule, and to some other rules. (The one-hour rule! Johnson of course knew there was a weightier objection to "some other rule.")

*The *Globe* gives this date as "Monday, December 7, 1841," which then is followed by Tuesday, December 7, 1841. If one regarded it as highly improbable that there were two December 7ths in 1841, then one's faith in the accuracy of the *Globe*, if one had had any in the first place, would have been shaken.

Adams immediately—but in the same calm beginning-of-the-session agreeable mode—said he had an amendment which if adopted would enable him to vote for the resolution of the gentleman from Maryland. And what was it? "Except for the 21st Rule." Adams noted that that rule had been "disclaimed by three distinct votes of the House" at the Extra Session.

Johnson—still in a no-big-deal mode—answered that the practical effect at that session nevertheless had been the same as before: that no abolition petitions were received.

Adams answered that, no, it was not exactly the same, because the Extra Session had extended the rule to "all petitions whatever, as well as to Abolition petitions; except for petitions bearing on the bankruptcy law and matters in the President's message." And Adams noted again—he wanted to make sure they got this point—that this House in its previous session had three times distinctly disclaimed the 21st Rule. Let's now finish it off.

But before Adams's amendment could be voted on, another amendment, proposing a limit of the period during which the old rules would apply to fifteen days, and making that report of the Committee on Rules—left dangling by the Extra Session—the order of business on the next day, and the day after that, and so on until it was acted upon, was proposed, and then just barely defeated. Maybe it left a confusing residue in the chamber.

One infers that Johnson and Adams, focused, from opposite sides, on the gag rule almost exclusively, were probably neither one particularly eager to take up that leftover report of the Committee on Rules, Adams because a conservative committee had included a gag in its report, and Johnson because this Whig Congress, confronted head-on with a chance to consider an extreme and complicated gag, might very well defeat it. Both of these adversaries ignored the pending report of the Committee on Rules and struck straight for their objective on the first day.

Adams tried to move the previous question on his amendment, but what rules were they operating under, since no rules had been adopted? As you can imagine, that topic generated plentiful, and complicated, discussion, and when, finally, the House did vote on Adams's amendment it just barely, 84–87, defeated it. Did the new Whigs comprehend that this would really be their only chance to rescind the gag rule in this session? A reader of the *Globe*'s account, a reader 153 years later, has the distinct impression that they did not.

That all happened right away, on the very first day of the session, on the December 6 that the *Globe* thought was December 7.

On the real December 7 the smooth Mr. Johnson called up his own motion again, as the pending unfinished business. Millard Fillmore, the moderate Whig from upstate New York who would one day be president, asked Johnson to modify his resolution to limit the number of days the adopted rules would apply, and to make the report of the Committee on Rules the order of the day until disposed of. "Unless this were done," Fillmore—quite rightly—observed, "he saw no prospect of getting at an amendment of the rules after the adoption of the resolution." The experienced Fillmore knew how that worked; many of his colleagues, we may surmise, did not.

The *Globe* reporter then collapsed the responses to Fillmore into the following: "After some remarks from Messrs. JOHNSON, ADAMS, AND PROFFIT . . ." and followed with Johnson's accommodation, or pseudo-accommodation:

> **Mr. Johnson** modified his resolution, by adding the provision making the report of the Committee on the Rules the order of the day for Thursday next, and for every day thereafter till disposed.

That was, as stated, on Tuesday the real December 7, so Thursday was the day after tomorrow, and the resolution adopting the old rules, including, of course, Rule 21, might therefore sound reassuring to the uninitiated: in just two days we can reconsider the gag, when the Rules Committee report is taken up.

And so they voted, and this alongside the defeat of Adams's amendment was the only vote that really counted, and again by a very close vote this Whig Congress adopted Johnson's resolution, which meant adopting the gag again, 97–95.

But what about Thursday? When Thursday came, the House was, of course, deep in other business and also adjourned early out of respect to a member who had died, so the report of the Committee on Rules was bumped to Friday, and when Friday came, this is what happened:

> **Mr. Cave Johnson** inquired if the first business in order was not the report of the Committee on the Rules and Order of the House. That subject had been made the special order for yesterday (Thursday) and for every succeeding day till disposed of. He should think that this report was the first business in order.
>
> **Mr. Johnson of Maryland** said that as many gentlemen were anxious to proceed with other business, he would move the postponement of the special order.

The Speaker asked the gentleman if his motion contemplated a fixed day to postpone the special order to.

Several gentlemen named Monday next.

Mr. Johnson of Maryland said that he should not fix on any day. If the postponement should be carried, the House could take the report up any day it pleased.

Mr. Williams of North Carolina moved to amend the gentleman's motion so as to postpone the order to Monday next.

Mr. Johnson of Maryland then said that he should vary his motion so as to move to lay the report on the table. The House could then take it up when it pleased.

Mr. Fillmore asked, if the report was laid on the table, if it would not require a vote of two-thirds to take it up again.

The Speaker replied in the affirmative.

Mr. Arnold called for the yeas and nays on Mr. Johnson's motion; which, having been ordered, the question was taken, and decided in the affirmative—yeas 96, nays 88. . . .

Notice how Johnson—Wm. Cost Johnson, of Maryland—keeps calmly moving the actual consideration of the report of the Committee on Rules just out of reach, calmly proposing that it be postponed, calmly avoiding the first call to name a fixed day, calmly upstaging a motion to name Monday, calmly, suddenly, coming in with a death blow that the novices in the room may not recognize as a death blow—a motion to lay the matter on the table, calmly explaining that "the House could then take it up when it pleased"; and then when Fillmore, to his credit may we say across the years (Millard Fillmore does not get, or perhaps deserve, much credit in American history), reminds the House that it takes a two-thirds vote to take something off the table (that is why it is a death blow), a colleague, Arnold of Tennessee, jumps in and calls for a vote. The vote is taken—do they understand what they are voting?—and Johnson's motion to lay on the table the report of the Committee on Rules is passed 96–88, and the last faint chance to rescind Rule 21 in this Whig session of Congress is dead.

❧

WHAT HAD HAPPENED? Johnson apparently knew about the squatter's-rights, or posssession-is-nine-tenths-of-the-law, aspect of this rules fight, and had skillfully got the old rules including his Rule 21 planted right away. Then he and his cohort used the desire of the members to get organized and get going, and their sense derived from the surrounding discussion that they were adopting the rules only provisionally and would have second chances—both the mention of the fifteen-day limit and the continually pending discussion of the committee report were symbols of that—to keep kiting away any change in the now adopted old rules.

The *Tribune* correspondent in Washington that evening, December 9, sent the following dispatch:

> The advocates of the Right of Petition were completely outgeneraled in the House this morning—regularly floored.

The *Tribune* went on to tell what the Committee on Rules would have proposed, had its report been taken up:

> You are aware that the famous Committee on Rules had reported an addition or amendment to the last Rule of the House to cover this subject—an amendment substantially re-enacting the Gag Resolutions of Pinckney and Atherton. It provides that on the presentation of any Petition, Memorial, or other paper touching the existence of Slavery in the United States, District, or Territories, the question of reception shall be regarded as raised, and that question shall be laid on the table—and so the Petition not received.

The committee would have proposed the old Waddy Thompson two-stage version of the gag rule.

> This is to make the Rule more stringent than it now is [said the *Tribune*; but would it have?], and is just such a proposition as could never be carried in a full vote of the present House.

This last might have been the important point, if the report of the committee had been allowed to come before the House: given a clear consideration on the merits, the Whig Congress might have rejected such a rule. And might it then have had done with all such rules? William Cost Johnson did not want them to have a chance to find out.

The *Tribune* went on:

This morning, however, as soon as it could be reached, Mr. WM. COST JOHNSON of Md. called the Report up and moved that it *do lie on the table*. Mr. STANLY of N.C. [the *Globe* says Arnold of Tennessee] promptly moved the Previous Question, which was ordered; and the Report was laid on the table: Yeas 96; Nays 88: nearly every Loco-Foco and most of the Southern Whigs (there were some noble exceptions) voting Yea. The effect of this vote is to put the whole subject to rest, and leave the XXIst Rule in full operation; for a question so laid upon the table can only be taken up again by a two-thirds vote, unless it is reached in the order of business, which never occurs. It looks, therefore, as though the Anti-Gag Members were "headed;" but if there be a way to evade it, Mr. Adams will find it.

Adams would indeed find it, but he would not for this session have the chance again to get Rule 21 rescinded.

Not that he wouldn't try. On the next calling of petitions he was back at the old stand, as the *Tribune*'s Washington correspondent would report on December 14:

Mr. Adams presented . . . [a petition] for the abolition of slavery in Florida. Being informed by the Speaker that this was not receivable, he requested the Clerk to file on the petition "not received under the rules of the House," that it might appear to the petitioners why their petition was not received. The Speaker replied that there was no rule requiring this.—Mr. A. said by the rule, nine-tenths of the petitions of his constituents were rejected from this House, while *all* petitions coming from south of the line—that ill-fated line—(Mason & Dixon's)—were received. He came from that portion of the country whose rights were suppressed by the rejection of petitions. He did hope, after three decisions of the House against the 21st rule . . .

The *Tribune* writer left this an incomplete sentence because Adams was not allowed to finish it.

He was here called to order by the Speaker.

He next presented a petition praying that Abolition petitions should be received equally with others; the reference of which petition he moved to a Select Committee of nine members to be instructed to report a resolution rescinding the 21st rule.

This was a step beyond the endurance of the anti-Abolitionists. . . .

Adams was trying to reopen the issue of Rule 21. His opponents moved to lay Adams's petition on that much-overburdened table, failed at first by five votes, and had to scramble; they rallied their troops and finally defeated the motion, which would have opened again the Rule 21 can of worms.

The *Tribune* correspondent, in his dispatch on December 14, corrected himself in a way that suggests how the Slick Willie of 1841, William Cost Johnson, had accomplished his purpose:

> The rules of the last Session of the 26th Congress were adopted some days since, until displaced by others, and not, as stated, for fifteen days only.

So the *Tribune* correspondent had once been confused on that point. If he was, then why not also young unpracticed congressmen?

> The resolution making the report of the Committee on Rules the special order for Thursday last has since been laid on the table, by which the subject of their permanent adoption is postponed for a time, during which Mr. A. will be obliged to submit to this "infamous" rule.

OBLIGED TO SUBMIT OR not, outgeneraled or not, Adams nevertheless would introduce in this Whig Congress, one after another, a particularly provocative series of petitions and memorials.

One was a petition from "a number of citizens of Massachusetts, stating that the Constitution of the United States guaranties to each State in the Union a Republican form of Government, and that there are thirteen states [naming the slaveholding States] whose governments are absolutely despotic, onerous, and oppressive in its exactions on a great number of its citizens." The petitioners prayed that Congress adopt "some feasible measures by which this alarming evil may be remedied, and a Republican form of Government guarantied to such of the States as are now without it."

Immediately after that one was stifled, in late January of 1842, Adams brought forward an even more provocative resolution, this one from the Anti-Slavery Society of Pennsylvania:

> **[Adams reading the Pennsylvania petition]:** "Whereas it is proposed that this country shall go to war with England, for the purpose of obliging the British Government to assist in holding natives of the United States in slavery. . . ."

There was some truth, now largely forgotten, in this assertion about international affairs at that moment. Samuel Flagg Bemis was to write, in the middle of the twentieth century, "It is difficult for the twentieth-century historian to realize that the United States and Great Britain were on the verge of a third war in 1841." Although there were other points at issue—over the boundaries, east and west, with Canada—those rooted in slavery and the slave trade were important. One American complaint, for example, objected to British vessels, trying to suppress the illegal slave trade, searching suspected slavers flying the American flag. The Pennsylvania petition Adams introduced went on:

> [**Adams continuing the reading of the Pennsylvania petition**]: Therefore resolved, That such war would as much exceed in unrighteousness that which was waged against this country by England in 1776, as the wrongs and privations inflicted on the slaves in some of the States in this Union exceed in magnitude the wrongs which led to the Declaration of Independence.

> The *Globe* reporter added this parenthetical paragraph:

> [During the reading of this preamble and resolution, **Mr. Adams** was frequently called to order by **Mr. Wise,** and decided to be out of order by **the Speaker;** but after each interruption, he continued reading additional portions of the paper, until, by this means, he had contrived to get through with the whole of it—much noise and excitement prevailing at the time.]

> **The Chair** said the question had been raised before, and decided that it was not in order for a member of Congress to read the contents of a petition, without the permission of the House. He must give a brief statement of its contents.

> **Mr. Adams.** Well, sir, I am giving a brief statement of its contents.

> **Mr. Wise.** The question is, whether the petition is presentable at all.

> **Mr. Adams,** [his face flushed, and much excited.] Ah! The gentleman comes to the *"presentable,"* does he?

> **The Speaker.** The gentleman from Massachusetts is out of order, and will take his seat.

> **Mr. Wise** said that his point of order was this: The paper presented by the gentleman from Massachusetts was not a petition, and was nothing more

than a series of resolutions, with which the House had nothing to do on petition day.

Mr. Adams. It is not a series of resolutions. It is a single resolution, with a preamble, which states that it is to be presented to Congress.

Not only was the petition objected to, and the question laid on the table, but also Adams's request that it be printed was denied—because the petition, not having been received, "was not in possession of the House."

[Adams]: Well, sir, I will submit if I must; but you may hear more of this subject before the session is over.

And then he promptly proceeded to present two more petitions.

Mr. Adams presented a remonstrance from a number of citizens of Massachusetts, concluding with the declaration that they cannot conscientiously obey the provisions of the Constitution so far as to take up arms for the protection of slaveholders.

The question of the reception of this paper was raised, and that question was laid on the table.

One consequence of the nation's being half slave and half free, bound in a federal union, was that the free part might be called upon to fight the slave part's battles, in a slave rebellion, for example. It was not a small matter, to segments of Northern opinion, that their states, their resources, their men might be called upon to fight, for the federal forces, to defend the Southerners' slavery.

It was also not a small matter that slavery violated defining principles of republican government—like habeas corpus.

Mr. Adams presented the petition of (as he said) 41 citizens, colored seamen of the United States, stating that on visiting . . . some of the Southern ports of the United States they are, in violation of the Constitution, and without being accused of any crime but their color, subjected to grievous and unjust restrictions, and praying redress.

Mr. Weller raised the question of reception of this petition, and that question was laid on the table.

The denial of rights to, and mistreatment of, free black sailors who came off ship in Charleston had been a scandal for some years. In 1822, on the theory that such free black sailors had infiltrated the city's black community with ideas of freedom, the South Carolina legislature had enacted a law *jailing* black sailors while their ship was docked. England protested. The American secretary of state at the time was John Quincy Adams himself, and he protested to South Carolina's governor, and a federal circuit court decision, not surprisingly, declared South Carolina's law unconstitutional. But in an early sample of nullification, South Carolina kept on doing it anyway. The state legislature declared that the "duty to guard against insubordination or insurrection" (notice that even "insubordination" was included) is "paramount to all laws, all treaties, all constitutions." The federals let this remarkable challenge go by, so the scandal was still there to be petitioned against in 1842.

Of course, the proponents of gagging and the defenders of slavery could not, in response to this barrage, resist the temptation to return fire with resolutions and petitions of their own. Thus—to go back to earlier Congresses—even in the session in which the Atherton gag clamped the lid on right at the start, Congressman Stanly of North Carolina had introduced (on December 31, 1838) a complex four-part resolution arguing that Congress had no power over slavery anywhere, and in its last part setting forth succinctly a common Southern argument directly on the point of the right of petition.

> **[Stanly]:** Resolved, That "the right of the people peaceably to assemble and to petition the Government for a redress of grievances," as secured by the first article of the amendments of the Constitution, does not give to citizens of non-slaveholding States the right to petition Congress to interfere with or abolish slavery, either in the District of Columbia, or in the Territories, or in the States, inasmuch as slavery is denied by the citizens of the slaveholding States to be a "grievance," and was not so considered at the time of the formation of the Constitution.

There were a number of other such resolutions and petitions from the pro-slavery, or the pro-gag, side. Henry A. Wise had many. Here is just one other example, from another congressman:

> **[John P. Kennedy of Maryland]:** Resolved, That the Constitution rests on the broad principle of equality among the members of this Confederacy; and that Congress, in the exercise of its alleged powers, has no right to discriminate between one portion of the States and another, with a view of abolishing the institutions of the one, or promoting those of the other.

Other efforts came from outside the House, from wits in the slaveholding states who made use of Adams's defense of the right of petition to generate petitions of their own, sending them not to their own partisans but to Adams, testing him. They sent a petition praying that all free Negroes be reduced to slavery. He presented it. They sent a petition asking that he himself be expelled as a public enemy. He presented it. They sent a petition praying that he be demoted from the chairmanship of the Committee on Foreign Affairs on the ground that he was crazy. He presented it, and soberly asked for time to be heard in opposition to it. And on January 21, 1842, just after he presented the petitions quoted above, he brought forward another petition, this one from some citizens of Georgia, that dealt again with his fitness to be chairman of the Committee on Foreign Affairs. This one was to furnish the first scene of the final act of the drama.

35 / MONOMANIA

If Abolition House was a new platoon, now ready to take initiatives, the army on the other side, which had been taking initiatives all along, was preparing to escalate its efforts, too. The proslavery army upon this Gettysburg of parliamentary conflict, much more formidable than the little band from Abolition House, had not with all their victories in specific battles (the Pinckney-Hawes-Patton-Atherton-Johnson gags, among others) been able to win the larger war. They had not won decisively either in parliamentary procedure or in public opinion. So now they tried what we might call, for its passionate recklessness, and to keep the Gettysburg metaphor for the moment, Pickett's charge. They now moved to their utmost strategy: a headlong attack on the only great leader of their opponents.

The House members, the press, and the public could not ignore or dismiss Adams as they might any of the abolitionist congressmen. Some of the young evangelical reformers from the antislavery societies of Ohio and New York were shy and tongue-tied, and might be reluctant to tangle on the House floor, in front of two hundred colleagues and the press, with the practiced Southern talkers, spellbinders like Henry A. Wise and Waddy Thompson and John Henry Hammond and William Cost Johnson and (an important new member from Virginia, a former governor of that state) Thomas Gilmer. But not Adams. Adams gave as good as he got, and then some. And he was a skillful and knowledgeable parliamentarian and parliamentary battler. He maneuvered and made motions and raised points of order and came right back in their exchanges at least as skillfully as his opponents. And, his age and palsied hands notwithstanding, he could keep at it as long as they—longer.

Adams's journal abounds with injunctions to himself to be restrained and controlled and civil, but on the floor he often did not abide by the injunctions. John Quincy did not have the "little capillary vein of satire" that marked his more peppery, colorful, original, and humorous father. The son's style ran, rather, to earnestness, and to sarcasm—the sarcasm of felt superiority. If his Southern opponents indulged in florid personal attacks and invective, John Quincy, venerable statesman or not, was not above retaliation, or initiating such attacks in his own style. The reader may remember how a stinging reference to Speaker James K. Polk—I know there is a slaveholder in the Chair—seemed to pop out of him in the midst of House business. In the showdown to come, Adams would make a reference to his having opposed the clamor in the House for formal action against Henry Wise after Wise's role in the Cilley/Graves duel even though Wise had come into the House *with blood on his hands.* (Here one may imagine a sharp intake of breath through the House.) Adams said that young Thomas Marshall of Kentucky—who will appear on the scene in a moment, and who was a nephew of the great Chief Justice John Marshall—had a long way to go in the study of the law before he deserved that last name.

So now the opponents of Abolition House clarified to themselves the new objective on the seven-year battleground of the House of Representatives: silence John Quincy Adams. As Thomas Gilmer of Virginia, whom we have just mentioned, was to put it: "Stop the music" of John Quincy Adams.

That way of putting the point had come into the chamber after Adams referred in passing to Gilmer ("the gentleman from Albemarle") as having decided to play the second fiddle to his colleague from Accomac (Wise). Responding to which,

> **Mr. Gilmer** amid repeated and deafening shouts of order, order, said that he played second fiddle to no man; but that he had been endeavoring to prevent the music of one,
>
> Who, in the course of one revolving moon,
> was poet, fiddler, statesman, and buffoon.

Adams was now receiving an immense outpouring of abusive and threatening mail. He would later bring before the House—to show Gilmer some of his "auxiliaries"—two of the many assassination threats. From

Jackson, North Carolina: ". . . unless you very soon change your course death will be your portion. Prepare, prepare, for by the —— of ——, you will unexpectedly be hurried into eternity, where you ought to have been long since." Another came from Gilmer's own state.

> He had here [said **Adams**] a picturesque representation [which he exhibited to the House] of himself, with the mark of what appeared [to be] a rifle ball, "at the shortest distance," on the head, and the word "abolition" written over. On the sides were the words "mene tekel upharsin." He presumed that members of this House knew where it came from. Underneath were the words, "Stop the music (precisely the words the gentleman from Albemarle had used) of John Quincy Adams, the sixth President of the United States, who,
>
> In one revolving moon,
> Is statesman, poet, babbler, and buffoon.

Adams noted the correspondent's change of one word.

> **[Adams]:** The gentleman from Albemarle had used the word fiddler, which was here supplied by babbler. That he was a babbler he could not deny, but that he was a fiddler was a new discovery. [A laugh.]

The threats of assassination with real bullets, Adams suggested, were encouraged by the language of his opponents on the House floor, in their efforts now to stop the music of John Quincy Adams. One campaign was the attempt, to be described in this chapter, to dislodge him from his chairmanship of the Committee on Foreign Affairs. Adams was certainly convinced, and at pains to show, that this effort was deliberate, the product of secret caucusing. So was the other, larger, almost simultaneous attack, aimed at persuading the whole House to *censure* him, which will be described in the next chapter.

As a result of the new Whig power in the House, Adams had at last been given the appointment that his long service in diplomacy made obvious—chairman of the House Committee on Foreign Affairs. But that appointment now became the occasion of a direct assault, beginning with a petition from Georgia—from Clarksville, in Habersham County, which was represented in the House by a Colonel Habersham—that Adams himself introduced on a busy petition day.

The petition was quite respectful in tone, and paid tribute to Adams's many qualifications for the foreign affairs post. But it nevertheless asked that he be demoted from the chairmanship for this curious and revealing reason: that he was "possessed of a species of monomania on all subjects connected with people as dark as a Mexican," and therefore could not be trusted to deal with important policy issues touching on Mexico.

Adams conscientiously presented this petition, as he had many others of its ilk, and promptly claimed the floor as a matter of personal privilege to defend himself against it. That was the catch, for the defenders of slavery in a free, or partially free, society: their efforts, serious or farcical, to promote their point of view kept exploding in their hands. They repeatedly gave their opponents a parliamentary opening and platform. Indeed, Adams seems to have used this perhaps mocking or fraudulent petition from his enemies to smoke out and thwart an actual plot, as well as to give himself a chance to make freewheeling speeches against slavery.

Adams was careful to make clear that the charge—that his racial views, too favorable to black persons, disqualified him from this responsible position—was not unique to this perhaps whimsical petition, but was to be found elsewhere as well. He insisted that Wise himself had made essentially the same charge against him, and had made a similar charge against Giddings as chairman of the Committee on Claims. Or rather—he had made his complaints against the Speaker for appointing such chairmen.

Where had Wise made this charge? In a letter to his constituents, which eventually, after much resistance from Wise and William Cost Johnson and their allies, Adams managed to read to the House. Wise's letter complained that the Speaker had appointed a majority of *non-slaveholders* to the committee that was to deal with the question of the recognition of "the negro Government of Hayti." Adams said that such a view reflected "a slaveholding, a slavetrading and a slavebreeding feeling"; that the Georgia petition reflected the same feeling; and that it was yet another way the slave power sought to disenfranchise all the representatives of freedom:

> **[Adams]:** I am adducing evidence that the same spirit in this same section of the Union, that would disfranchise all the members of the House from the North, who were opposed to slave trading—that that same spirit . . . characterized this petition. [Calls to order.]

Perhaps the Georgia petition was another hoax. Early in the discussion the member from the district in Georgia from which it purported to come made a statement.

> **Mr. Habersham** . . . was ready to give testimony on this subject. The gentleman from Massachusetts [Mr. Adams] had submitted this petition to him (Mr. H.) a week ago. He had told the gentleman, after a careful examination, all the names having been in the same handwriting as the petition, that he had no knowledge of one of the persons as residing in that county. There were some of the surnames of persons residing there, but none having the same Christian names attached to the surnames, so far as he knew. He had told the gentleman from Massachusetts that he believed the petition to be a hoax.

Some of his opponents even suggested that Adams himself was the source of the hoax. When it appeared that the House might give Adams the privilege of the floor to respond to the charge in the petition, Mr. Sprigg of Kentucky said what some others were thinking:

> **Mr. Sprigg:** I am required to yield to the gentleman from Massachusetts the privilege of addressing this Hall, and of interfering with its appropriate business, when, in fact, by the rules of the House, he has no right whatever to do so, there being no question before it. I could as well as he present a fabricated petition—[here Mr. S. was called to order.]

Adams defended his belief in the petition's genuineness.

> **Mr. Adams:** And, by the way, he had had further light thrown on that petition by the declaration of the gentleman from Maryland, [Mr. Johnson,] that it was written upon Congressional paper, from which he (Mr. A.) believed it had been commenced in this House. And he now called upon whoever might have originated that petition to stand up and avow it like a man. He believed it had been sent to Georgia, and that every means had been resorted to deceive him into the belief that it was a genuine paper, that he might present it as such. He did so because it was couched in respectful language, and because, from the character of the petition, expressing as it did express what he knew to be the opinion of a large portion of the people of that section of the country and of the members of this House, he believed it to be a genuine paper. He would not have presented it had he believed it to be a fabrication.

Adams pressed William Cost Johnson to disavow any knowledge of the petition but found Johnson's disavowal ("very imperfectly heard . . . by reason of a sore throat under which he was laboring") to be unsatisfactory. So perhaps this petition was another product of Johnson's tipsy merriment.

Whether or not this particular petition was a joke, Adams used it to claim the privilege (or, some insisted, the "courtesy," not the obligatory privilege) of defending himself against the charges in it, and to expose to view an undertaking that was not a hoax: slaveholder efforts to prevent nonslaveholders from holding key committee positions.

Mr. Adams: The charge itself was no hoax. It was that upon questions connected with persons of a color as dark as a Mexican, he was utterly unfit to act. Such questions, for instance, as whether we shall go to war with England to prevent the suppression of the slave trade or whether we shall go to war with England on the question whether infamous slave traders shall be indemnified for their abominable traffic.

Messrs. Wise and Wm. Cost Johnson called Mr. A. to order, and demanded that he take his seat.

Mr. Adams: Well, sir, if the Speaker requires me to take my seat, I shall do so—not otherwise.

The Speaker having called **Mr. A.** to order, he was proceeding with his remarks, amid loud calls to order, when

Mr. Johnson insisted that he had no right to proceed, till permitted to do so by the House.

Mr. Adams still continuing his remarks,

Mr. William Cost Johnson insisted on the rules of the House being observed.

Mr. Adams, (with much acrimony) I see where the shoe pinches, Mr. Speaker.

The Speaker: The gentleman from Massachusetts is clearly out of order, and must take his seat.

Mr. Adams: I am in my seat.

When Adams read—or tried to read—a letter from a Democratic senator from Alabama showing, by reverse English, what he, Adams, claimed, that there was an alliance between the Southern slave traders (Democrat and Whig) and Northern Democrats—there were protests.

Wasn't he supposed to be defending himself against a charge of monomania? Of unfitness to be chairman? Adams claimed that what he was saying was relevant because that alliance, using charges like that, had determined to unseat him from the chairmanship.

AFTER MUCH PARLIAMENTARY MANEUVERING, Adams finally got his opportunity to defend himself, and unleashed another of his speeches, and Abolition House had its first real chance to get some of its material into the record of the House. Theodore Weld was there in the House chamber, listening, and enjoying himself, and brought an English abolitionist with him. On Sunday, January 22, 1842, Weld wrote to his wife and sister-in-law an account suggesting that from Weld's point of view it had been an afternoon well spent.

> Saturday Mr. Adams presented a petition from Habersham County, Georgia, praying Congress to remove him (Mr. A.) from the office of chairman of the committee on Foreign Affairs on account of his abolitionism, saying that he had on the subject of color a perfect monomania, etc., etc. The slaveholders instantly pounced upon it, as upon every thing likely to lead to discussion of slavery, and moved to lay it on the table; but Mr. A. started the question of *privilege,* demanding to be heard in his own defence against an attack upon him as a member of the house and the head of one of its committees. The speaker decided that he was in order, as "the question of privilege" as it is called rides over every other. So the Old Nestor lifted up his voice like a trumpet; till slaveholding, slave trading, and slave breeding absolutely quailed and howled under his dissecting knife. Mr. A. had said the day before that he should present some petitions that would set them in a blaze, so I took care to be in the house at the time, and such a scene I never witnessed. Lord Morpeth, the English abolitionist of whom you have heard, was present and sat within a few feet of Mr. A., his fine intelligent face beaming with delight as the old man breasted the storm and dealt his blows upon the head of the monster. Wise of Va., Raynor of N.C., W.C. Johnson of Md., and scores more of slaveholders, striving constantly to stop him by starting question of order and by every now and then screaming at the top of their voices: "That is false". "I *demand* Mr. Speaker that you *put him down*". "What are we to sit here and endure such insults". "I demand that you shut the mouth of that old harlequin". A perfect uproar like Babel would burst forth every two or three minutes as Mr. A. with his bold surgery would smite his cleaver into the very bones. At least half of the slaveholding members of

the house left their seats and gathered in the quarter of the Hall where Mr. A. stood. Whenever any of them broke out upon him, Mr. A. would say "I see where the shoe pinches, Mr. Speaker, it will pinch *more* yet". "I'll deal out to the gentlemen a diet that they'll find it hard to digest". "If before I get through every slaveholder, slavetrader and slavebreeder on this floor does not get materials for bitter reflection it shall be no fault of mine."

At the end of his speech Adams moved—as he had said from the start he would do—that the Habersham County petition be referred to the Committee on Foreign Affairs, with instructions to choose a new chairman if the members of that committee should think proper. That was what they had been fighting about, at one level: what person (with what racial views) should be chairman of the Committee on Foreign Affairs. In fact, Adams said, he was willing to put the motion in the form suggested by Mr. Hopkins the other day. On Friday just at the close, George Washington Hopkins of Virginia, a member of the committee, had made his views clear:

Mr. Hopkins . . . moved its reception, with instructions to the committee to report a resolution in conformity with the prayer of the petitioners.

Now on Monday, in response to Adams, Hopkins reiterated his desire to change chairmen:

Mr. Hopkins said, yes, sir, my opinion is made up fully, and I most heartily concur with the petitioners in the propriety of removing the gentleman from the station of Chairman of the Committee on Foreign Affairs, and am ready to give that vote whenever it may be my privilege to do so.

And he was not alone. Adams's charge that there had been a plan afoot to remove him as chairman certainly appeared, from the readiness of these colleagues to commit themselves, to have the color of truth to it. Thomas Gilmer of Virginia, the "stop the music" man, who was an ally of Wise and Tyler, was willing to fight it out in committee.

. . . **Mr. Gilmer** rose and desired to be informed by the Speaker whether the Committee on Foreign Affairs had not the power to proceed to appoint another chairman, without instructions from the House?

The Speaker said that he could not take official cognizance of anything of the kind. The committee, when they assembled in their room, could look to their own rules, and see what was the extent of the power they possessed.

Mr. Gilmer: I presume they have the power, and may exercise it, without instructions from the House.

Mr. Adams: Leave that to the Committee on Foreign Affairs.

Mr. Gilmer said he, for one, was willing to meet the responsibility.

And so they all did meet the responsibility, whether they wanted to or not, in committee.

The end of this concerted effort to remove Adams from the chairmanship would be mingled with the working out of the other, larger effort to squelch him, to be discussed in the next chapter. In the midst of that bigger battle, on the floor, Adams smoked out a touch of "tampering" (his word and their word) that had been revealed in a remark by a Southern member of the committee. Someone—Adams thought it was Gilmer but it later proved to be, by his own confession, Robert Barnwell Rhett of South Carolina—had dropped hints to Caleb Cushing, who was not only Adams's colleague from Massachusetts but his colleague on the committee, and himself a former chairman of the Committee on Foreign Affairs, that if Adams was removed, then Cushing would replace him: "to propitiate Yankees by putting another Yankee in my place." Cushing indignantly denied the report at first. But then it came out that something had been said, after all. One may surmise that Adams combated this effort by seizing on the Habersham petition and bringing it out in the open on the House floor—as Gilmer and company had not intended. At the same time he exposed material like Wise's letter, showing a more general Southern disposition, and perhaps even plan, to tilt the key committees of the House toward slaveholders.

Adams had taken the fight to them and exposed their plan before they were ready. So after this open debate, or quasi-debate, could Adams's opponents win in committee? Committees met in the morning before the House assembled at noon. Adams as chairman put the matter to Gilmer directly: Gilmer had said he would move that a new chairman be chosen, so move it. Gilmer, proceeding not perhaps in the way he had hoped or intended but under Adams's gun, did so:

Mr. Gilmer says, that the chairman having brought this subject to the consideration, first of the House and now of the committee, this respondent feels relieved from whatever of personal delicacy he might have felt in originating such an inquiry, and that for one he is prepared to vote against the honorable member from Massachusetts, Mr. Adams, as chairman of this committee.

There were nine members present, so the matter became one of those samples of the small, closet politics among a handful through which the great politics of nations sometimes pass, and by which they can be much affected. We do not know precisely what happened behind the doors of the committee, but the record does show that twice on efforts to postpone or evade the issue Adams voted *with* the Southern contingent, against his fellow Northerners (Cushing, Everett, Granger); various Northerners wanted the issue to go away, but Adams wanted to face it.

The members went in the afternoon to the heated sessions of the whole House, also largely devoted to attacks on Adams, in which he extracted Rhett's admission that he had tampered, and the admission that the Southerners had met to concert an attack on him; he also held forth at length on the larger questions, including slavery.

When the smoke had cleared within the little world of the committee, it was not Adams who resigned from the committee, but Thomas W. Gilmer of Virginia, R.T.M. Hunter of Virginia, Robert Barnwell Rhett of South Carolina, William Cost Johnson of Maryland, and George H. Proffit of Indiana (Proffit was originally from Louisiana, and, on issues touching slavery, voted more consistently than any other Northern Whig with the Southern Whigs). In other words, unable to supplant Adams as chairman, the Southern members, plus one, themselves quit the field.

When the Speaker made appointments to replace this group, three more Southerners he named—from Alabama, South Carolina, and Virginia—asked to be excused from serving, and in turn had to be replaced. The late-nineteenth-century German historian Dr. Hermann Eduard von Holst, a scholar not reluctant to state his own opinion, remarked about this episode: "The fact that six slaveholders and one knight of the slaveocracy [i.e., Proffit] declared it irreconcilable with their honor to sit in the same committee with Adams could not grieve him, but only add to his triumph."

36/THE TRIAL OF MR. ADAMS

ADAMS'S OPPONENTS HAD A larger plan. They were looking for the right occasion for their most audacious move: to induce the whole House to vote to *censure* him.

They had found what they thought they needed in a petition Adams offered not long after the floor business on the monomania resolution. This apparently vulnerable petition was brought forward on the same busy afternoon during which Adams offered the particularly provocative series of petitions described in an earlier chapter: the petition asking that all states have a "republican government," naming the states the petitioners thought did not have one; the petition insisting that as citizens of Massachusetts the signers could not "conscientiously obey the provisions of the Constitution so far as to take up arms for the protection of slaveholders"; the petition protesting the treatment of colored sailors in Southern ports "subjected to grievous and unjust restrictions, in violation of the Constitution," and "without being accused of any crime but their color"; the petition arguing that a war to make the British government "assist in holding natives of the United States in slavery" would be a "war that would as much exceed in unrighteousness that which was waged against this country by England in 1776, as the wrongs and privations inflicted on the slaves in some of the States in this Union exceed in magnitude the wrongs which led to the Declaration of Independence." None of those, deeply offensive to the South and many in the North though they no doubt were, was quite right for the purpose of Adams's opponents. They wanted something not so closely tied to sectional interests or to the peculiar institution.

And directly after that stirring list of prayers from the citizenry, Adams presented a memorial from a group of his constituents in Haverhill, Massachusetts, which his opponents thought served their purpose. This petition had a prayer by which they could take it upon themselves to be truly shocked—*shocked*—quite independently of questions about slavery. In not many years their seizing on this particular petition would be covered with historical ironies: the prayer of the petition of the good citizens of Haverhill was that the union be dissolved.

The reason the Haverhill petitioners so proposed was, of course, tied to slavery ("Because a vast proportion of the resources of one section of the Union is annually drained to sustain the views and course of another section . . ."), but slavery was not mentioned. The staunch and lifelong Unionist Adams could be attacked for daring to present—disagreeing with it, of course—a petition asking that the Union be dissolved—by Southern leaders, who, nineteen years later, would actually take their states out of the Union. Adams himself, even at this earlier moment, commented wryly on the objections coming from a quarter "in which there have been so many calculations of the value of the union."

To be sure, the real reason the opposing forces sought Adams's censure was not this petition but his course of action across nine years. For their purpose, though, they had to be *shocked:*

> **Mr. Holmes** [of Charleston, SC—incredulously?]. This is a petition for the dissolution of the Union.

Mr. Adams: I move its reference to a select committee, with instructions to report an answer to the petitioners, showing the reasons why the prayer of it ought not to be granted.

Mr. Hopkins [of Goochland County, Virginia]. Is it in order to move to burn the petition in the presence of the House?

Mr. T. L. Turney [of Winchester, Tennessee] moved that the petition be laid on the table and printed, that the country might understand what its character was.

But the Southern Whig leaders had a more immediate objective.

Mr. Wise, (addressed the Speaker.) Is it in order to move to censure any member presenting such a petition, and to move that the House do now proceed to inquire whether a member has offered such a petition to this body, and to proceed accordingly?

Mr. Adams: Good!

As with the effort to depose him from the Foreign Relations Committee chairmanship, so with this movement to censure: the combative Adams welcomed the attempt. A little later on that Monday afternoon, Wise's collaborator Thomas Walker Gilmer of Albemarle County formally offered the resolution that Wise's question had suggested (it was here that Adams said Gilmer was playing second fiddle to Wise), a motion that declared that the gentleman from Massachusetts had "justly incurred the censure of the House."

There it was, a formal motion to *censure* the ex-president of the United States: not something to be taken lightly. As the afternoon wound to its close there were several efforts to put aside this hazardous escapade—by laying it on the table, by declaring it out of order, by prematurely adjourning—but Adams did not join in them. On the contrary: he welcomed and encouraged his "trial."

Giddings gave this report of the actions and the mood in the House after adjournment on that Monday when the motion to censure Adams was made:

Most of the members showed no anxiety to leave the hall. Many remained, and gathered into small coteries, earnestly engaged in conversation upon the extraordinary events of the day. Many appeared deeply indignant, and with knitted brows, compressed lips, and clinched fists, uttered imprecations against all "agitators" and abolitionists; others exultingly declared Mr. Adams to be in the power of the democratic party, as all southern Whigs would act with them, and they declared it necessary to make an example of him.

These portents during the day on this Monday led to a busy Monday evening. According to Giddings, there were separate preparatory gatherings of the two sides, like the Blue and the Gray in camp before the great Civil War battles to come, to prepare for the encounter on the morrow:

Public notice was given that a meeting of members from the slave States would be held that evening in the room of the "Committee on Foreign Affairs," to make proper arrangements for the trial. . . .

Forty or fifty "members from the slave states" attended this gathering, according to the admission Adams was able, later in the week, on February 4, 1842, to extract on the House floor:

Mr. Adams next complained that the proceedings against him were the result of a caucus. This brought up

Mr. Triplett, who declared that the resolution [the revised resolution to censure Adams, of which more in a moment], of the gentleman from Kentucky [Marshall] though it was read to a meeting of members of Congress, was not a part of their proceedings, and was neither considered nor voted on. The meeting was one of members of Congress, called from the Southern States, to consider what course they ought to take in regard to Abolition petitions, and had nothing to do with the subject under consideration.

Mr. Marshall confirmed the statement of Mr. Triplett and said that he attended the meeting spoken of [some forty or fifty members], and at that meeting had read the resolution.

Giddings reported that at the meeting the Kentucky Whig Thomas Marshall was chosen to be the group's spokesman because the chief actor Thomas Gilmer (like Wise, a friend, and soon to be an appointee, of President Tyler) was regarded now as a Democrat or anti-Whig; the aim was to avoid the appearance of a *partisan* persecution.

It was therefore proposed [Giddings wrote] that some slaveholding Whig should appear as prosecutor; and Hon. Thomas F. Marshall was nominated and appointed to that duty. He was comparatively a young man, a nephew of the late John Marshall, Chief Justice of the United States Supreme Court. He seemed to have inherited the genius and ability of his ancestors, had already distinguished himself in the Legislature of his own State, and had now come to Congress under more favorable auspices than any other member west of the Allegheny Mountains. He was anxious to distinguish himself upon the new theatre on which he had but just entered.

The opposing camp—"members willing to stand by and assist Mr. Adams in meeting the persecutions and dangers surrounding him"—on that same Monday night before the battle, was not as large. Most Northern Whigs said no to a proposed pro-Adams gathering because it would make the matter look like a sectional quarrel; apparently they did not hear, or want to hear, in the chambers of the House on this Monday in 1842, the distant drumbeat and the faint anticipatory music of "The Battle Hymn of the Republic."

But the Abolition House congressmen and some few others, not so unwilling, if it came to that, to have a sectional quarrel, *did* meet, along with Weld and Leavitt. These last two non-congressmen "were appointed a committee to wait on Mr. Adams and inform him that they and the members convened tendered him any assistance in their power."

Here is Giddings's report of the visit that Weld and Leavitt paid on John Quincy Adams:

> They [Weld and Leavitt] immediately repaired to the residence of Mr. Adams, though the hour was late. They found him in his parlor, and without delay stated the object of their visit. The aged statesman listened attentively, but for a time was unable to reply, laboring under great apparent feeling. At length he stated that the voice of friendship was so unusual to his ears, that he could not express his gratitude; that he would feel thankful if they would examine certain points to be found in the authors of which he gave them a list, and have the books placed on his desk at the hour of meeting the next day, and then dismissed them, and turned his own thoughts to a preparation for the contest.

Weld's report of the meeting with Adams, in a letter to his wife a few days later, appeared in the context of a report of his own activities as a research assistant to Adams:

> I[n] defending himself he [Adams] will take up nearly all the relations of *slavery* to this government. Since his case came on I have been incessantly

> occupied and expect to be equally till its conclusion. At its commencement I at once offered him my services to relieve him from the drudgery of gathering the requisite materials for his defence. He replied "I thank you. I accept your offer gratefully."

So the stage was set for the events of Tuesday, the anticipation of which drew a crowd. Giddings described the scene:

> On the following morning, long before the hour for the house to convene, the spacious galleries were filled to their utmost capacity, and all approaches to the hall were crowded with anxious men and women, endeavoring to get where they could hear the proceedings. Foreign ministers, *"attachés"* and privileged persons filled the lobbies and the outer space within the hall and outside the bar.

The first business on the floor, however, was a motion, left over from the previous day, to lay Gilmer's censure motion on the table. Had that motion carried there would presumably have been much disappointment in the spacious galleries.

All the lodgers at Mrs. Sprigg's, and the other antislavery congressmen—Slade, Giddings, Sherlock Andrews, Seth Gates, Francis James, Francis Granger, Briggs of Massachusetts—voted to lay on the table the motion to censure John Quincy Adams.

Many well-disposed Northerners and some Southern Whigs (Underwood of Kentucky; Botts of Virginia) voted to lay the censure motion on the table either for that same reason—that censuring Adams was not a proposal worthy of consideration—or because they wanted to avoid discussing the matter and wanted to get on with other business. New York congressman and future president Millard Fillmore, who throughout his congressional career (at least if you read the record with attention to issues about slavery) kept trying to change the subject and to get on to other matters, voted to lay this disturbing matter on the table.

But—Adams himself voted on the other side! He voted on the same side as Henry Wise, Thomas Gilmer, Colonel Habersham of Georgia, Robert Barnwell Rhett of South Carolina, Holmes and Campbell of South Carolina, and the Southern fire-eaters: *not* to lay the censure motion on the table! Let's have it out. Let's *see* if you can censure me. (And—if you try, you will have to let me defend myself. Have you considered what that means?) The nays had it 112–94. Gilmer's motion to censure Adams was not laid on the table, and the show did go on after all.

Young Thomas Marshall, the "prosecutor" chosen the night before, his moment in the sun having arrived, arose immediately after the motion to table had been defeated and offered a motion to improve upon Gilmer's rather too brief and spontaneous motion to censure—the improved resolution that had been read the previous evening in the Southern camp. It was full of whereases and aforesaids and resolveds, and resolved therefores, and resolved furthers, and of "the deepest indignity," and "insult," and "outrage," and it concluded that though this "insult" and "wound" (presenting the Haverhill resolution) might well be held to merit *expulsion,* the House members, out of their grace and mercy, and in consideration of his past services, would inflict on Adams only censure—their "severest" censure—for conduct so utterly unworthy of his past relations to the state, and to his present position. This they hereby did for the maintenance of their own purity and dignity; for the rest, they turned him over to his own conscience and the indignation of all true *American* citizens. (The emphatic underlining of the word "American" is not mine but appears in the resolution itself; these fervent young Southern congressmen were ready to instruct the son of John and Abigail Adams about what it means to be an American.)

Marshall's long speech included disclaimers of any sectional bias, or any personal animosity. Marshall insisted that he had hitherto been an admirer of John Quincy Adams. "His name," said Mr. M., "and the name of his family, had been connected in years gone by, with my name and the name of my family." Marshall's hearers would know what that meant: it had been John Quincy's father who had appointed Marshall's uncle to his great role as chief justice of the United States Supreme Court, and to other important positions before that. And Thomas Marshall himself had his ties to John Quincy: "I devoted the first years of my life in aiding to elevate him to the first office in the gift of this great people. . . ." But when a proposition so *monstrous* (Marshall's word, and emphasis) as this Haverhill petition was brought before the House—*then* (sorrowfully) it was necessary to offer this rebuke:

> **[Marshall]:** [The member from Massachusetts had] gravely submit[ted] to the House a proposition calling upon its members to betray the trusts solemnly confided to them by the people, violate their oaths, and destroy a Constitution which they are bound by every consideration of honor and of conscience to support and defend.

Shocking! Shocking! Mr. Marshall's rather synthetic indignation did not have much to work with; he even had to pretend to deplore Adams's routine proposal that the petition be referred to committee:

And that was not all; it was coupled with a motion to refer a proposition of this kind to a committee of that House to take it into serious consideration, and to report upon it. It struck him, **Mr. M.** said, with horror; it stupefied him. He had not believed it possible that there could be men wild enough in the country—though the result had proved otherwise—men wild enough, and mad enough, to make a proposition that the Government of the United States should terminate its own existence, and then to submit it to the members of that House, inviting them to commit perjury and moral treason. There might have been men wild enough and mad enough to do this out of that House; but that there was a member of that House that could be willing to assume the responsibility, through all coming time, of presenting such a proposition to that House, he had not believed. He had heard whispers, it was true, that such a petition would be presented, but he had rejected the idea with utter incredulity and perfect scorn.

He certainly did pretend to regard this petition with the utmost horror:

[Marshall]: Had such a proposition been made by his own father, and had he, in addition to the ties that bound him to him as a son, all the ties that bound him to [the] member from Massachusetts—if he knew his own soul—he should have pursued the same course that he now did.

Marshall ended with the charge that by introducing such a petition Adams had invited the members of the House to commit *high treason* against the United States.

Giddings dramatized what happened next:

Mr. Adams was expected to state the grounds of his own vindication before any friend could venture to speak in his defence; accordingly, when Marshall closed, he rose to address the House, and as that gentleman had charged him with high treason, and represented him as seeking to overthrow the Government, it was supposed he would now reply with that overwhelming severity for which he was distinguished; but he exhibited no such desire. When the Speaker announced that he was in possession of the floor, all eyes were instantly upon him. His appearance was venerable; he was dignified in his bearing. He looked around upon his peers, who sat before him as judges, with a countenance beaming with kindness: he had long served his country, had filled the highest office on earth with honor to himself and friends; and now, at the age of seventy-five years, he stood arraigned on a charge of treason to that country to which he had so

> long devoted his labors, to that people whose rights he was seeking to maintain.
>
> At length, turning to the Speaker, he said; "It is no part of my intention to reply to the gentleman from Kentucky at this time. I prefer to wait until I learn whether the House will retain these resolutions for discussion. I call for the reading of the first paragraph in the Declaration of Independence."

So picture now this scene, in the U.S. Capitol on January 25, 1842. The son of John Adams, the chief defender of the proposed Declaration of Independence in the Continental Congress on July 4, 1776, is sitting there in a U.S. Capitol that had not then existed, in the federal city of Washington which had not then existed, about to be put on "trial" for inviting high treason against the Union, calling upon the clerk to read to this people's house in the government of the new nation the document that had declared to a candid world its independence.

> **[The Clerk]:** When in the course of human events, it becomes necessary for one people to dissolve the political bonds which have connected them with another . . .

The clerk read on through the decent respect for the opinions of mankind, and at Adams's insistence, through the inalienable rights to life, liberty, and the pursuit of happiness, and through this part:

> **[The Clerk]:** . . . that to secure these rights, governments are instituted among men, deriving their just powers from the consent of the governed; that whenever any form of government becomes destructive of those ends, it is the right of the people to alter or to abolish it. . . .

And the clerk continued, at Adams's insistence ("Proceed! Proceed! Down to the 'right and duty'!"), to the action that must be taken when an evil trend goes too far:

> **[The Clerk]:** But when a long train of abuses and usurpations, pursuing invariably the same object, evinces a design to reduce them under absolute despotism, it is their right, it is their duty, to throw off such government. . . .

Adams rested his defense of the propriety of the petition on the Declaration of Independence. The Haverhill petitioners had the same right as their forefathers to petition for the redress of grievances, and the same right and duty to propose to throw off such government as did not respect their fundamental rights.

Adams kept tying the current battle to the deepest principles of republican government—to the Declaration of Independence, as here in this extraordinary episode; to the ancient right of petition, antecedent to the American government and even to republican government; and to a cluster of other civil liberties fundamental to the form of government to which they were all devoted. Thus he said, about the Haverhill petition:

> **[Adams]:** If the right of habeas corpus, and the right of trial by jury are to be taken away by this coalition of Southern slaveholders and Northern Democracy, it is time for the Northern people to see if they cannot shake it off, and it is time to present petitions such as this. I can say it is not yet time to *do* this—

. . . that is, actually to proceed to the disunion the Haverhill people proposed. But almost. In any case, one could certainly present the petition of those who believed it *was* time.

Henry Wise, of course, was soon upon his legs, and started off by sending to the clerk a volume of George Washington's speeches: his Washington to trump Adams's Jefferson, as it were. Wise had marked for the clerk's reading passages of the Farewell Address, warning against disunity:

> **[Wise]:** He tells you to frown upon the first dawn of every attempt to dissolve this Union. He points you to the cause—the most fearful cause—that may bring about that event. That cause is foreign influence. That influence is at work in this very question—in this nation—at this day.

The foreign influence against which Wise warned was the same power against which Washington had fought—Britain. It was a theme of Wise's and of anti-abolitionist argumentation that abolition was yet another scheme of *English* power—not only English but English *Tory* power!

There is some indication that even some of Wise's ideological party had reservations about this theme. Wise had risen after Marshall had finished, and Adams had asked that Marshall's resolution be printed and he be given time to prepare his answer, and the distinguished congressman from Vermont Horace Everett had reminded the House what weighty issues were before them in that resolution—revolution, disunion, radical sectional disagreement—and had moved to postpone debate and print the resolution in preparation for it. Wise, eager to get going, had ascertained that that motion was debatable, and plunged in with his quotation from the Father of the Country and his theory about the British.

[Wise]: Sir, there are some who are moving on the subject of the dissolution of the Union from religious fanaticism . . . honest and fanatical, and religiously sincere. For these he entertained nothing but feelings of pity; but he believed there were political parties, who took root at the very commencement of the Government, which had exited from that time, exhibiting by the tendencies of their measures a deliberate design to break up this Union. At the very foundation of the Government, there was an English party, and a Tory party in the country. . . .

No man knew better than the gentleman from Massachusetts the past history, the political party history, to which I refer. Yes, sir, this antipathy to the slaveholding section of the country, and to the Democratic portion of it, not only in the South, but in the North, wherever it might be located, had grown up with the English Tory party that denounced the apostle of liberty [Mr. Jefferson] in 1801, as the red waistcoated representative of Jacobinism, and roused the jealousies of the Democratic party, by upbraiding them with a French alliance.

Sometimes the volatile Wise could be carried away by the helium of his own oratory, and this first afternoon of the attempt to censure Adams may have been one of the times. According to the *Globe,*

[Wise] went on to say that the nation had evidence of the hatred of this English party to Mr. Jefferson, and its antipathy to slaveholders, in doggerel rhymes aimed at his domestic relations. No one better knew to what poetry he alluded than the gentleman from Massachusetts. . . .

Here **Mr. Everett** again interposed, and called Mr. Wise to order for irrelevancy. The question was on printing and postponement.

The Chair's reply was in a great measure lost to the Reporter, but he was understood to decide that, though this latitude of remark would not be in order on a motion to print, it was less out of order on a motion to postpone.

Mr. Adams: I hope he will be permitted to go on.

In the course of two days of attacking Adams and defending slavery, Wise also made one of the more egregious statements of what we have called the Orwellian defense of slavery:

[Wise]: The principle of slavery is a leveling principle; it is friendly to equality. Break down slavery and you would with the same blow break down the great democratic principle of equality among men.

The *Congressional Globe* reporter noted that this remark brought laughter from "one portion of the House."

THE "TRIAL"—THE DEBATE on the censure motion against Adams in the House—went on for two weeks in January and February of 1842, and drew a new level of attention from the press and the public. One of the strategic disadvantages under which his opponents labored, defending slavery in a society with free institutions, was that when they attacked Adams and heaped their scorn upon him and tried to deny him his chairmanship and now actually proposed to censure him—tried to discredit him and shut him up—they handed him the opportunity to reply. They thus inevitably brought to the floor of a representative body with parliamentary traditions exactly the subject they were trying to exclude.

After the severe and long and personal attacks upon him by Marshall, Wise, and the other Southern spokesmen, Adams on February 2, 1842, gained the floor to present his own defense against what they had said—and there he was. He was seventy-five years old, but he held the floor for a week, and showed no signs of weakening, pounding away day after day against slavery, with materials that Theodore Weld had helped him prepare.

And he answered to the full the attacks his opponents had made. Marshall had ended his first long speech defending his resolution with an apostrophe—Oh! what a falling off is there!—to Massachusetts and the name of Adams.

> **[Marshall]:** What, Massachusetts! of all the lands on which Heaven's bright sun beams its radiant smiles—Massachusetts to come forward, and through a man bearing the name which the gentleman did, make a proposition to dissolve this Union! If she had done this, let the severest censures of that House fall upon the man through whom this proposition came.

When, later, Adams was engaged in his defense, he, for his part, noted (with sadness, too) the role in the present episode of *Virginia*—Wise and Gilmer, and Marshall, the nephew of a great Virginian, who now lived in that extension of Virginia which became Kentucky:

> **[Adams]:** It grieved him from the very soul to see these propositions come from Virginia. If there was a State in this Union for which even now he felt an attachment greater than to any other except his native State, it was to Virginia. In his early years, it was from Virginia that he was introduced

into the service of this nation—first by George Washington, whose warning voice had been repeated here to operate against him; and which voice had been to him, from the time it was delivered down to this moment, next to the Holy Scriptures, on his heart and mind.

The *Globe* reporter went into his summary-with-comment-in-brackets mode for part of Adams's speech:

> **Mr. A.** here went at some length into the history of his past life, his intercourse and friendship with, and the confidence he had enjoyed of Washington, Jefferson, Madison, and Monroe, during their successive Presidential terms, as manifested by the various important offices conferred upon him—alluding to historical facts in this connection. Which was listened to with much interest, and a report of which the limited time prevents us from giving.

Later the harried reporter moved to third-person indirect discourse:

> **[Adams]:** had spoken of the confidence, the friendship, and the esteem of those great children of Virginia, and his affection and gratitude to them and their memory. It would be impossible for him to extinguish the affection for that State which he had held from a boy. This was the experience he had had during the course of a long life with the most distinguished sons of Virginia; and what a heart could he possess if it were possible for him not to feel, as he did, to its deepest and inmost fibres, a feeling of gratitude towards them, and affection for their memory and the State whence they came! But when he saw the treatment he was receiving from the children of that State, who now represented it—a part of them at least—what could be his feelings? What must they have been to find himself charged here with such a violation of public duties as a member of this House, as that the censure of this House was invoked on him? And with respect to one resolution, to find charges of such infamous crimes as subornation, of perjury and high treason, attempted to be fastened on him and his good name to the end of time? There must be a great change in the feelings of Virginia.

Adams could speak with a kind of authority about the founding fathers that nobody else could begin to match: the chief founders had all been his friends; one of them had been his father; he had been appointed to high office by almost all—it could have been all—of the early presidents before he served as president. Now he invoked this unique authority, with respect to the Virginia founders, on the matter that lay behind this dramatic encounter on the House floor: human slavery.

> **[Adams]:** In all his intercourse he had had with these men, from Washington down to Monroe, never, in the course of his life, was there a question between them and him on the subject of slavery. He knew that they all abhorred slavery, and he could prove it, if it was denied now, from the testimony of Jefferson, of Madison, and of Washington themselves. There was not an Abolitionist of the wildest character in the Northern States but might find in the writings of Jefferson, at the time of the Declaration of Independence, and during his whole life down to its very last year, a justification for every thing they say on the subject of slavery, and a description of the horrors of slavery greater than he had the power to express.

Perhaps Adams permitted himself a little license on that score. He dwelt on his personal relations with the great Virginia founders, but a reader examining this scene a century and a half later may sense the larger Massachusetts-Virginia backdrop in the making of the republic. One might almost say that this country came into being when Massachusetts met Virginia and the two formed an alliance. One might almost specify further: this republic was born in the autumn of 1774 when John Quincy's father and cousin, the brace of Adamses John and Samuel, went to the Congress in Philadelphia and there met, and allied themselves with, Virginia radicals Richard Henry Lee and Patrick Henry and others, and then when they returned to Philadelphia in the spring of 1775 John Quincy's father, in particular, befriended the new addition to the group of Virginia radicals, the younger man replacing Peyton Randolph, Thomas Jefferson, and the friendship and collaboration of Adams and Jefferson continued on through the subsequent sessions of the Congress and the enormous events of '75 and the even more enormous events of '76. Massachusetts joining Virginia: that was close to the core of the beginning of America.

And now, seventy years later, here was Virginia attacking Massachusetts, over the issue of slavery, and Massachusetts returning some blows. The events on the floor of the U.S. House of Representatives, on this day of Adams's reference to the Founders—Thursday, February 3, 1842—ended in this way:

> **[Adams]:** . . . it was unexpected, most perfectly unexpected to him, when he knew what these great men of the Revolutionary times, who were Virginians, thought of slavery—of the institution to which now every thing was to be sacrificed—when he now saw members from that State, endeavoring to destroy him and his character, for the sole cause of presenting a petition. He should have hoped better things of Virginians, and that the representation of that State upon this floor would have felt something of—

That holy shame which ne'er forgets
What clear renown it used to wear,
Whose blush remains when virtue sets,
To show her sunshine has been there.

Mr. A. here yielded the floor.
And on motion of **Mr. Thompson** of Indiana,
The House adjourned.

Adams wrote that night in his journal of his performance in the House:

> *I reviewed my relations with the Virginian Presidents of the United States heretofore—Washington, Jefferson, Madison, Monroe—and contrasted them with this base conspiracy of three Virginians, banded here, together with numerous accomplices in and out of the House, for my destruction. Near four o'clock I closed for the day, with an apt quotation from Moore's* Loves of the Angels, *and came home very much exhausted.*

Adams had received many threats on his life throughout the contest over the gag rule. Of course, he conscientiously filed them all, and biographers can quote whole pages of invective and vituperation and personal threat—and now these reached a crescendo. But at the same time there was mounting support in the North, in the press and in the public, and petitions of another sort poured into the House—petitions against the attempt to censure Adams. The Northern allies of the Southerners began to fall away, and even some Southerners weakened. They began to see that their Pickett's charge, their reckless frontal attack against the strongest point of the enemy, had not been wise.

Finally the proposer of the first short resolution of censure, Thomas Gilmer of Virginia, said he would withdraw his resolution (still on the floor, not displaced by Marshall's) if Adams would withdraw the petition that started it all. But Adams disdainfully declined to do that. To do that would be to give up the principle which he had been defending—the right of petition for the whole people of the United States. "If I withdrew the petition I would consider myself as having sacrificed the right of petition; as having sacrificed the right of habeas corpus; as having sacrificed trial by jury; as having sacrificed the sacred confidence of the post office; as having sacrificed freedom of the press; as having sacrificed every element of liberty that was enjoyed by my fellow citizens. . . ." In other words, no. Adams not only declined to withdraw the offending petition, he insisted that all these rights were bound up with the right to petition.

Adams kept talking. Petitions supporting him kept pouring in. The press in the North now widely supported him. The opposition to him within the House began to crumble, and the slaveholders knew it—wished they had not got into this whole thing. On February 5, in the midst of his defense, there was an objection that he was discussing the forbidden subject of slavery, but the Speaker ruled against the objection and on appeal to the House that ruling was sustained 97 to 25, the first clear-cut victory in the American House of Representatives against the forces of the slaveholding South. Adams wrote in his journal: "I saw my cause was gained. . . . I came home barely able to crawl up to my chamber, but with the sound of 'IO TRIUMPHE' ringing in my ear."

After a Sunday interlude, on Monday, February 7, Adams, still going strong after a week of his defense, with Theodore Weld feeding him materials, announced that he would need yet another week for his defense—but that if anyone wished to move to table the whole affair, he would be satisfied. A Virginia Whig did move to table the resolutions to censure him, and the House, probably with a sigh of relief, voted to lay the whole matter on the table 106 to 93. Adams had won. The forces of the "slave power," as he increasingly called it, had failed.

And with his victory, and "Io Triumphe" ringing in his ear, what did he do? He promptly set about introducing more petitions—nearly two hundred of them that very day before adjournment.

37/FREEDOM IS THE PREMISE

THEY COULD NOT CENSURE Adams. Frustrated, they tried to censure Giddings. And succeeded. For the moment.

On March 21, 1842, six weeks after the effort to censure Adams had collapsed, Giddings managed at last to put before the House the resolutions about the *Creole* case that Abolition House had developed.

The *Creole* case was another in the line of the *Amistad,* but in this case the freedom fighters had certainly been slaves. They had mutinied, in November of 1841, while being transported from Newport News to New Orleans by a coastal vessel. They had killed one of the owners and forced the crew to take them to Nassau, where the British authorities had tried and hanged those identified as the murderers, but freed the rest. (Freeing those slaves from the *Creole* was one of the complaints of the slaveholding South against Great Britain, in the background of a possible Anglo-American war in 1841.) The owners of the freed slaves demanded compensation. Congressman Holmes from Charleston had his resolutions about the *Creole* in his desk, and sitting right next to him Joshua Giddings had his radically contrasting resolutions in his.

The collaborators in Abolition House had thought that that case, and the resolutions in Giddings's desk drawn up with the assistance of Weld, would be the occasion for a showdown in this Congress. But those resolutions had been for the moment put aside because the slaveholders had attacked first, with their effort to censure Adams. Now the *Creole* case came to the floor.

Giddings's resolutions represented an important chapter in the intellectual and doctrinal opposition to slavery. Adams and Giddings and the members of Abolition House, in contrast to Garrison and others, wanted to maintain a Union with slaveholders, while seeking to find a way to stop them from holding slaves. They wanted to sustain, and not to destroy, the Constitution, and the Union, while finding a way, under it, to end slavery.

To end slavery under the Constitution there had to be a giant political transformation, but there also had to be, alongside the great boom-boom of mass politics, the quieter and more serious voice of developing constitutional doctrine that delegitimated slavery. There had to be doctrine that would change the formal American understanding of the nation-making instrument from one that sanctioned slavery to one that only reluctantly acquiesced in it as a fact, on the way to its being a document that explicitly forbade it.

This development began to appear in theories that found slavery prohibited by the underlying premises of the moral order on which the Constitution rested. That meant that slavery would bear the burden of justification. Slavery could exist, in this view, only where it had been specifically established by "positive law"—by explicit laws written on the books. Being a violation of the moral order on which the nation stood and out of which the Constitution arose, slavery was legitimate only where a state specifically by explicit law sanctioned it. That meant that, as the slogan summarized it, freedom was national, slavery local. It was merely "municipal." Whenever one was out from under such a state's jurisdiction—in the territories, in the District, on the high seas—freedom instantly broke out. Or rather, the underlying and fundamental freedom of all persons, which was there all the time, was once again in force.

Theodore Weld, working away at his desk at Nassau Street after his voice broke, had developed such a theory, as we noted, in the pamphlet he wrote, as part of the petition campaign, called *The Power of Congress over the District of Columbia.* Henry B. Stanton had presented such a theory in testimony to the Massachusetts General Court, on behalf of the Massachusetts Anti-Slavery Society, in February of 1837, in the same session at which Angelina Grimké made her famous appearance. And now Joshua Giddings presented such a theory, out of the conversations in Abolition House, in his resolutions on the *Creole* affair on the floor of the national legislature itself.

Giddings took the Southerners' constant claim that slavery was strictly a *state* matter, and applied it double-strength—in a more thoroughgoing way than they intended. They say it is strictly a *state* matter—all right then, it is *strictly* a state matter. Since slavery was a matter of "municipal" (i.e., state) law, then the minute a ship left the territorial waters of a slave state (e.g., Virginia) the laws of slavery no longer applied. "[B]y the 8th section of the 1st article of the Constitution, each of the several States surrendered to the Federal Government all jurisdiction over the subjects of commerce and navigation upon the high seas." And out on those high seas, where no state law applied, the laws of the moral order did.

> **[Giddings]:** . . . slavery being an abridgement of the natural rights of man, can exist only by force of positive municipal law, and is necessarily confined to the territorial jurisdiction of the power creating it. . . . [W]hen a ship belonging to the citizens of any State of this Union leaves the waters and territory of such State and enters upon the high seas, the persons on board cease to be subject to the slave laws of such State. . . .

So the slaves on board the *Creole,* after she left Virginia waters on her way to New Orleans, were freed by the change of jurisdictions; when they revolted to achieve their freedom they were defending a freedom already granted by natural right, and now restored by their having left the boundaries of Virginia. They were not felons; they were, in the idiom of a later time, freedom fighters.

Southern slaveholders, Democrat and Whig, were horrified at Giddings's proposals and at his and Weld's municipal theory of slavery. Under that theory there would be no protection whatever of slave "property" outside the boundaries of the slave states: no protection on shipboard on the high seas, on which the "property," as in this *Creole* case, could suddenly become *men,* and strike for freedom; no protection if the "property" escaped across the Ohio River and became men instead of runaway slaves (therefore no fugitive slave law, such as had been passed in 1793, and would be made much stronger in 1850); no protection if an owner took his property into a territory or free state, whereupon the property could become a human being and turn around and say goodbye (therefore certainly no Dred Scott decision). It was to defenders of slavery a horrifying and repugnant argument, and their first response to it was not to argue against it but to expel the congressman who presented it.

Giddings's nine resolutions setting forth this view provoked much hemming and hawing of a parliamentary sort, but no consideration on the merits. A motion to refer his resolutions to the Committee on Foreign Affairs was laughed aside. The House clearly was not going to consider his proposals seriously—they were too far outside the body's mainstream thought. The previous question silencing debate was quickly moved, and carried easily, 122–61.

A number of Northern congressmen—many of them Whigs—asked to be *excused* from voting on Giddings's resolutions (a congressman who is present must request permission of the House not to vote). These I-don't-want-to-vote-on-it congressmen included some who were among the most distinguished, and, significantly, our friend Caleb Cushing of Massachusetts. They pled the complexity of the issue; one may surmise also that, after the manner of politicians in all times and places, they had friends on both sides. They were, however, not excused.

It was moved to lay the resolutions on the table, but before that was done—

> **Mr. Fillmore** [of New York; the future president] rose and said he had never asked to be excused from voting, and he never would. But he wished to inquire whether it was in order for him to ask the gentleman from Ohio [Mr. Giddings] to withdraw the resolutions? [Cries of "No, no."]
>
> **Mr. Giddings** inquired of the Speaker whether or not the resolutions were within the control of the mover?
>
> **The Speaker** read the 40th rule, and decided that the resolutions *were* within the control of the mover. . . .
>
> **Mr. Giddings** said that when he had risen to offer his resolutions he had distinctly stated that they were important, and that he merely laid them before the House.
>
> [Cries of "not in order—sit down," &c.]
>
> **The Speaker.** The gentleman will either withdraw his resolutions or not.
>
> **Mr. Giddings.** I was merely stating why I was about to—

The Speaker. It is not in order. The gentleman will either withdraw his resolutions or not.

Mr. Giddings withdrew the resolutions.

One can infer that Giddings, having got his resolutions before the House and therefore in some sense before the country, saw that they would be overwhelmingly defeated, and therefore withdrew them.

ALTHOUGH, LIKE ADAMS'S VENTURES in constitutional construction and amendment, Giddings's resolutions were swept aside in the Congress as it was then, the doctrine they reflected was to have an important subsequent history. In the 1850s the Free Soil and Republican parties would continue to make the argument that freedom was national, slavery local—which is to say that there was a moral premise underlying the Constitution and the nation that made slavery fundamentally, morally illegitimate. That doctrinal position would run through the politics of the 1850s, be articulated supremely by Abraham Lincoln as a politician and a president, and finally be made explicit in constitutional law in post–Civil War amendments to the Constitution.

What was the grounding, in the shared constitutional heritage, of a moral order that made the rejecting of slavery the universal *a priori?* One such ground was the ancient doctrine of natural law, from the Stoics and the Christian past; that doctrine was by no means unknown in American jurisprudence and its English and other European sources. Another such ground was the somewhat more empirical and specifically English concept of the common law. There was a great case, called *Somerset* in the shorthand of lawyers, and there was case law developed from it, in England and America, to which appeal could be made. Henry B. Stanton argued before the Massachusetts General Court that "on the principles of the common law, slavery is everywhere null and void. Common law operates as an abolition act whenever it comes in contact with slavery. By it, every slave is free." Similarly Weld, in his pamphlet, wrote that the common law was a "universal, unconditional abolition act."

But in the distinctively American setting there was another grounding for the principle that freedom was the universal premise and norm, and this ground had the solidity of a specific and honored American document: the Declaration of Independence, with its sweeping statement of truths we hold to be self-evident. John Quincy Adams argued that the Declaration, with its claim of universal human equality, was not simply a hortatory statement of ideals, without effect in law, but was rather as much a part of the public law of the land as the Constitution itself; it had preceded the Constitution, and preceded also the Articles of Confederation. From 1776 to 1781 it was our Constitution.

These advanced ideas would take no root and yield no result without an enormous change in the political atmosphere. But that change would come—and the beginnings of it were the events recounted here.

Meanwhile, back in the House in 1842, Giddings's opponents were not satisfied simply to allow him to withdraw his outrageous resolutions. John M. Botts, the Virginia Whig, got the floor and offered a resolution, already prepared, to censure Giddings for conduct "altogether unwarranted, and unwarrantable, and deserving the severe condemnation of the people of this country, and of this body in particular." The resolution had a long "whereas" preamble attempting to justify the censure, holding that "it is the duty of every good citizen, and particularly every selected agent and representative of the people to discountenance all efforts to create excitement, dissatisfaction, and division among the people of the United States" while the United States and Great Britain were involved in negotiations "of a most delicate nature" on this subject (the *Creole* matter) that might result in war.

The content of the resolutions and their timing were sufficiently offensive to explain the action the House would take, but there was in addition to those considerations a partisan element—intrapartisan. The Whig Party leadership had its own reasons for taking Giddings's measure. They wanted to put down this insurgency by abolitionist Whigs who now put their antislavery projects ahead of the party's program. Botts was a leading Whig. And the frustration at not having been able to get the big game—Adams—must have increased the desire to get the more vulnerable prey, Giddings.

The disputes that followed Botts's resolution (which became, for complicated parliamentary reasons, the resolution of Mr. Weller from Ohio) did not at all concern its merits—whether or not it was a censurable offense to offer such resolutions at such a time—but dealt almost exclusively with another matter: whether Giddings should be allowed, as a matter of privilege, to speak in his own defense. The answer was no.

Then the dispute shifted to this issue: was the answer really no?

And this issue: did the journal accurately reflect what had happened?

There was much amending and correcting of the journal. The frustrated Whig majority was angry at Giddings as the leader of an insurgent Whig group whose proposals threatened the delicate threads holding together the Northern and Southern wings of the party, and hence impeded the party program. But on the other hand they did not want the record to show them being disrespectful of Giddings's rights or of parliamentary propriety—or too unequivocally siding with the slaveholders.

There was a widespread desire to censure Giddings. There was a widespread desire to put a stop to his long, shocking antislavery speeches. But—oops!—*not* to have it appear in the journal that he had not been allowed to speak in his own defense. That he had been condemned without a hearing. That would not do.

The slavery and gag rule forces were caught again by the civil liberties nemesis that followed them all the time. They did not want to allow Giddings actually to *speak*. They knew what he would do; he would use the occasion for another of his antislavery harangues, like the one that he had given on the Anacostia River bridge and that other one on the Seminole War. But on the other hand, they did not want it to *appear* that he had not been allowed to speak in his own defense.

Botts and others did manage to show up in the *Globe* asking that he be granted the privilege of the floor. But Giddings wanted two weeks to prepare. Some congressmen are shown in the *Globe* as having been willing to grant that. But Mr. Weller of Ohio, adopting Botts's motion as his own, had immediately moved the previous question—closing debate, if passed. And although the Speaker had ruled that Giddings's request for privilege took precedence, the House voted to overrule the Speaker, and after that rebuke the Speaker enforced the House's decision strictly. So Giddings could not speak—not after two weeks, and not right away, either.

Weller at one point tried to recoup civil liberty's appearances, while still keeping Giddings restricted.

> **Mr. Weller** said he had no disposition to prevent his colleague [Mr. Giddings] from defending himself against the resolutions he had submitted on yesterday. His object in moving the previous question had been to prevent a general debate, which might lead to the obstruction of other more important business. If his colleague would now declare that he desired to be heard in his defence, he would take pleasure in withdrawing the previous question, and thus give him an opportunity of doing so, with the understanding that after that defence was closed, the vote should be immediately taken without further debate.
>
> [Cries of "No understandings—we will have no understandings."]
>
> **The Speaker.** The gentleman will either withdraw the demand or not.
>
> **Mr. Weller.** I will withdraw it on that condition.

The Speaker. The Chair cannot entertain any conditions.

Mr. Weller not withdrawing, unconditionally, the demand for the previous question—

Mr. Giddings rose and addressed the Chair—

The Speaker said the gentleman was not in order, the House having reversed the decision of the Chair, and decided that the rules in relation to the previous question should be rigidly enforced.

The let-him-speak situation (or rather the shut-him-up situation) having slipped out of control, various members tried to recover and save face, but Giddings declined to speak impromptu, or as courtesy merely, or under limitation. If he was going to be allowed to speak, then he wanted really to speak—to have time to prepare, and no conditions. His opponents knew what that meant.

Mr. Brown hoped, then, that the gentleman would rise and say whether he wished to address the House.

Mr. Giddings declined to rise. . . .

Mr. Charles Brown asked that the gentleman from Ohio [Mr. Giddings] be now heard, by general consent, in his own defence.

Mr. Giddings still declined to rise.

Adams, aiding his new friend Giddings, moved after this last exchange to lay the whole subject on the table, but the House by a sizable margin (125–70) declined to do that. They *wanted* to censure Giddings.

As the vote on the censure itself approached:

Mr. Giddings then rose and said, I stand before the House in a peculiar situation—

Mr. Mark A. Cooper objected to Mr. G.'s proceeding; but, at the request of colleagues, Mr. C. withdrew his objections.

But Mr. **Giddings** did not resume the floor.

Giddings sent to the reporter for the *Intelligencer* a copy of what he would have said:

[Giddings in the *Intelligencer*] When I rose so often during the confusion of the proceedings of the House this day, and was so often called to order, the last time by Mr. Cooper of Georgia, I had written, and desired to have stated to the House, what follows:

Mr. Speaker, I stand before the House in a peculiar situation. It is proposed to pass a vote of censure upon me, substantially for the reason that I differ in opinion from a majority of the members. The vote is about to be taken without giving me time to be heard. It would be idle for me to say that I am ignorant of the disposition of a majority to pass the resolution. I have been violently assailed in a personal manner, but have had no opportunity of being heard in reply. I do not now stand here to ask for any favor or to crave any mercy at the hands of the members. But in the name of an insulted constituency—in behalf of one of the sovereign States of this Union—in behalf of the people of these States and the Federal Constitution—I demand a hearing, agreeably to the rights guarantied to me, and in the ordinary mode of proceeding. I accept of no other privilege—I will receive no other courtesy.

Then came the vote on the resolution of censure itself (the preamble, giving reasons, would be voted on separately), and it carried by a vote of 125–69, with not only—of course—Northern Democrats like shifty Atherton and the entire New Hampshire delegation, and Charles Jared ("brand him") Ingersoll and his colleagues from Pennsylvania, and Giddings's colleagues Weller and Goode from the other part of Ohio, joining all Southern Democrats and virtually all Southern Whigs, but also almost half of the Northern Whigs who were present, in voting in the affirmative. When the time came for the vote on the preamble, a few members appear to have gone on to their lodging houses for mess: it was adopted 119–66.

On the next day the House fought over printing multiple copies of the proceedings on Giddings:

Mr. Everett rose and moved a suspension of the rules to enable him to offer the resolution which follows. . . .

Resolved, That five thousand copies of so much of the journal of yesterday as relates to the action of the House on the resolution in relations to the Hon. Joshua R. Giddings, be printed for the use of the House.

Mr. Stanly. Include the resolutions which the said Joshua R. Giddings offered to the House, and I will vote for 20,000 copies.

Mr. Everett. I accept the modification.

Mr. Adams. Fifty thousand copies.

Mr. Botts. I shall not vote for the expenditure of the public money for any such purpose. . . .

Mr. Stanly inquired of the Speaker whether the Journal proposed to be published would include the remarks made by the gentleman from Vermont, [Mr. Everett,] protesting against the incendiary course of the gentleman from Ohio, [Mr. Giddings.]

The Speaker. The Chair cannot state what the Journal will or will not contain.

The public and the press were not unaware of these proceedings, though; this was a well-publicized afterpiece to the sensation of the Adams trial.

LATER THE SPEAKER "laid before the House" this letter:

Washington City, March 22, 1842

Sir: I hereby resign my office of Representative in the Congress of the United States from the sixteenth Congressional district of Ohio.

With great respect, your obedient servant,

J. R. Giddings

Adams, who liked Giddings as well as, or better than, any other of his colleagues in the House, wrote in his journal after the vote to censure him:

I can find no language to express my feelings at the consummation of this act. Immediately after the second vote, Giddings rose from his seat, came over to mine, shook cordially my hand, and took leave. I had a voice only to say, "I hope we shall soon have you back again." He made no reply, but passed to the seats of other members, his friends, and took leave of them as he had done of me. I saw him shake hands with Arnold, who had voted against him. He then left the House, and this evening the city.

But Giddings did come back. William Cullen Bryant, the poet and newspaper editor in New York, although a Democrat, wrote that he wished he lived in Giddings's district so he could vote to return him. Many other Northerners, not necessarily Whigs, shared that view. Giddings's district in the old Western Reserve voted overwhelmingly to send Giddings back to Washington again in the seat his own resignation had left vacant.

That the voters in Ashtabula and the surrounding congressional district in Ohio defiantly returned the censured congressman, and that many voices elsewhere in the North passionately supported their doing so, was another step in the long, slow undoing of American slavery. The peculiar institution had once looked, on the surface, impregnable. But it rested on an unsteady foundation.

The reason for that unsteadiness was, of course, the nation's original ideal of human rights. That ideal, flatly contradictory to slavery, made the efforts to say that slavery was essential to freedom (laughter from one part of the House), and a support for equality (laughter again from one part of the House), and overall a *positive good* (more laughter and sarcasm), such sweaty, uphill work. In their anxious efforts to tamp down their own uneasiness the defenders of slavery ran into some others among the nation's original ideals, closely related to human rights but sometimes with a differently shaped constituency: civil liberties; representative government.

The accumulating offenses against civil liberty not only by the mobs and vigilantes but by local officials and leaders had reached a new level with the formally enacted gag resolutions, building into the law of the land a prohibition against the discussion of one specific topic, by citizens and their representatives, North or South, in the people's national legislature itself. That wound to republican liberty had been made deeper by the fastening of the gag into the very rules of the House itself, and then had been dramatized to the nation's whole public by the effort to censure an ex-president. When that failed, the gaggers had proposed a censure of another colleague in the people's house—and they had succeeded. A duly elected representative had been censured, and had resigned. Not only were you restricted as to the grievances for which you could ask redress, in a formal petition; now, it seemed, you might even find your duly elected representative censured, and sent home. And what had been his offense? Had he done anything more than to propose something, with which the majority disagreed?

What he had proposed, which the whole people would one day affirm, was that freedom was the nation's moral premise.

PART XII

ENDINGS

38 / SOME MUSICK IN CANANDAIGUA

THE MALE MEMBERS OF the Adams family did not receive much popular acclaim in their own day, and they haven't received much popular acclaim in these later days, either. They were not very popular during their political careers, and they have not been very popular since then. If it weren't for Abigail, the Adams family would be pretty much out of luck in the popularity department.

John Quincy's father had been the "Atlas of Independence," leading the battle in the crucial place in the crucial time, in 1774 and 1775 and 1776 in the Continental Congress. As we have noted in an earlier chapter, he had written the "Thoughts on Government" that had helped to set in motion the American constitutions. He had made the arguments that persuaded the delegates to support independence, and had proposed the decisive May 10 and May 15 resolutions that, if you know your history from an Adams point of view, were more important than anything that happened on July Fourth. As we said, he had been the one who had broken the deadlock of states and regions and nominated Colonel George Washington—Massachusetts endorsing Virginia—to be head of the new union's army, and as we also said, he had been the chairman of the five-man committee to write a Declaration of Independence, and had nominated young Jefferson to compose the draft, and had been the one (while his new friend Jefferson squirmed in silence) who had defended every line of it for two and a half days in the Continental Congress. He had been the chairman of the Board on War and Ordnance—a one-man Pentagon—making the decisions about prisoners and provisions in the Revolutionary War. He had served on an unbelievable ninety-five committees in the Continental Congress—maybe more—doing the arduous work of republican government.

And yet who would know any of that? George Washington would be steeped in honors, called the "Father of his Country." Jefferson would come to be celebrated around the world. Even the shy young Madison would be called the "Father of the Constitution." Hamilton would be honored as Jefferson's great counterweight in the nation's ideological balance. Ben Franklin would be the world's EveryAmerican. Subsequent generations, Adams would write, would think that Benjamin Franklin just struck the earth with his lightning rod, and out sprang George Washington and the United States was born. But what about John Adams? Where is the Adams monument?

When George Washington and the other generals that Congress had chosen (Lee and Schuyler) marched out of Philadelphia "on their way to the American Camp before Boston," as John Adams had written to his wife, Abigail, on June 23, 1775, the three generals had all been on horseback, and many delegates from the Continental Congress, including Adams himself, had gone in their carriages to see them off, and many officers of the militia and of the Troop of the Light Horse in their uniforms were there. John Adams, describing the scene in the privacy of a letter to Abigail (little guessing how many strangers would be reading it two hundred years later), indulged himself for a moment in a little pout of jealousy. "Musick playing &&& Such is the Pride and Pomp of War," he wrote. "I, poor Creature, worn out with scribbling, for my Bread and my Liberty, low in Spirits and weak in Health, must leave others to wear the Lawrells which I have sown; others, to eat the Bread which I have earned." Why am I not on horseback? Why isn't the Musick playing for me?

Adams sensed that the glory would go to Colonel, now General, George Washington, who would lead the troops in battle, not to him, John Adams, who would fight those other battles in the committees of Congress. In his letter to Abigail he had caught himself, after this revealing little outburst of self-sympathy, with the awareness that he was not the only victim of the uneven distribution of the world's "Lawrells." He added the phrase: "A common case."

As for John Quincy, his career was magnificent—as long as it was appointive. He spent twenty-eight years abroad, serving his country in all those European capitals. The presidents who appointed him valued his qualities. When he had to win votes from the public, though, or even from legislators who had to face the public, he, too, would not do well. He could scarcely claim to have been a popularly elected president. And as the father was swept out by a Jefferson tide, so the son was absolutely drowned by a Jackson flood. Very honorable indeed of him to pick himself up and run for Congress, and to serve there year after year. But "Jacksonian democracy" had carried the day.

To look ahead for a moment, the time would come, although his opponents in the House may have thought it never would, when John Quincy Adams would die. On a Monday in 1848 he would vote no on a motion to honor Mexican War generals, and soon thereafter collapse at his desk; on Tuesday, according to the *Globe,* the congressional chaplain would "tenderly and delicately" allude "to the venerable sage who [lies] in an adjoining room, unconscious of all earthly concerns, on the verge of eternity"; on Wednesday he would die; and on Thursday the House orators would have their speeches ready.

Would those speeches, here in this room and in this legislative body in which he had served for seventeen years, capture his contribution to the republic? The speeches would certainly be full of exclamation points ("My late venerable colleague is no more! A great and good man has fallen!") and of elaborate summaries of Adams's career and of purple nineteenth-century oratorical prose, but to one reading through them (not an easy thing to do) the answer is no.

The first two would come from Massachusetts congressmen, one of them, as chance would have it, the Speaker at that time, Robert C. Winthrop, a man with whom, and with whose distinguished family, Adams had had many dealings. Winthrop, however, was thoroughly a Cotton Whig, and John Quincy's Conscience Whig son Charles Francis and—especially—Joshua Giddings had had sharp disagreements with him. Winthrop now, on this solemn occasion, did his dutiful best by his distinguished former colleague, as did the other Massachusetts spokesman, the senior member of the state's delegation. Although the second New England eulogist would suggest silence as a most appropriate response, and would move that the House adjourn until the funeral services on Saturday noon, there would be, before a vote to adjourn could be taken, another member asking for the floor, ready, with his speech in hand, to offer something other than silence to honor the fallen colleague.

And who might that be? It was Isaac Holmes, from Charleston, South Carolina, the holder of the seat once held by Henry Laurens Pinckney, and later by Hugh Legaré, the South Carolinian seatmate of Giddings, who had strongly opposed Adams on the gag rule and much else, and who had his resolutions in his desk, contradicting those of Giddings on the *Creole* matter. Holmes apparently did not want the day to go by without showing these tongue-tied Yankees what a memorial speech should be.

Remember the acid comments in Adams's journal, like those on the ceremony at the dedication of the Bunker Hill monument, where Daniel Webster spouted about the rights of man while a Negro held an umbrella over his head, and imagine the acerbic Adams, like Tom Sawyer, returning to witness his own funeral, and listening to the following:

> **Mr. Holmes, of South Carolina,** rose and said: Mr. Speaker, the mingled tones of sorrow, like the voice of many waters, has come unto us from a

sister State—Massachusetts weeping her honored son. The State I have the honor in part to represent, once endured, with yours, a common suffering, battled for a common cause, and rejoiced in a common triumph. Surely, then, it is meet that in this the day of your affliction we should mingle our griefs.

When a great man falls, the nation mourns; when a patriarch is removed, the people weep. Ours, my associates, is no common bereavement. The chain which linked our hearts with the gifted spirits of former times has been rudely snapped. The lips from which flowed those living and glorious truths that our fathers uttered are closed in death. Yes, my friends, Death has been among us! He has not entered the humble cottage of some unknown, ignoble peasant; he has knocked audibly at the palace of a nation! His footstep has been heard in the Hall of a State! He has cloven down his victim in the midst of the councils of a people! He has borne in triumph from among you the gravest, wisest, most revered head! Ah! he has taken him as a trophy who was once chief over many States, adorned with virtue, and learning, and truth; he has borne at his chariot wheels a renowned one of the earth! . . .

Now his spirit mingles with the noble army of martyrs and the just made perfect in the eternal adoration of the living God! With him "this is the end of earth" [these were said to be Adams's last words, of which Holmes here makes rhetorical use]. He sleeps the sleep that knows no waking. He is gone—and forever! The sun that ushers in the morn of that next holy day, while it gilds the lofty dome of the Capitol, shall rest with soft and mellow light upon the consecrated spot beneath whose turn forever lies the PATRIOT FATHER and the PATRIOT SAGE!

Holmes's speech, stripped of its rhetorical elegance, almost boiled down to: (1) Adams had held a number of offices; (2) he had been old; (3) he was now dead. His first paragraphs are not about Adams but about the interstate collaboration in grief and the peregrinations of Death. And the last paragraph was mostly about death's permanency. Holmes could certainly use this material in other funeral orations.

There would be two other speakers, one of them from another oratorical powerhouse, the state of Virginia, before the House would adjourn on that Thursday. Perhaps one should add that all of the speakers would make the link between Adams and his father, and the fathers and the founding, with some noting that Adams's death had almost come on George Washington's birthday, and that there would be references throughout to his presence in this House and to his desk (a motion to leave it vacant, and shrouded, for thirty days: would they remember the days it held a monster petition, sitting there in silent rebuke?). The Virginia orator said, somewhat implausibly, "No human being ever entered this Hall without turning habitually and with heartfelt deference first to him, and few ever left it without pausing as they went to pour out their blessings upon that spirit of consecration to the country which brought and which kept him here"—all very nice, but was it true? In a House that had three times tried to censure him (once before the events in this book), that mostly denied him the chairmanship of Foreign Relations, and that tried to remove him when that post was granted?

Truth is not a requirement in lapidary utterance, as Samuel Johnson said, and "controversial" matters are to be shrouded in funeral moments. Still, it bears mentioning that so far as an attempt at reading them all through can discern, there would be in those speeches no reference, even of the most indirect kind, to Adams's role in the long fight over petitions, gags, and the discussion of slavery in the nation's councils. Giddings would not be called upon by Winthrop to speak, nor would any other veteran of Abolition House. When on the Saturday there would be a great national pageant of a funeral, with the president, the Supreme Court justices, the diplomatic corps, and all the rest, the twelve pallbearers would include Hon. J. C. Calhoun, S.C., Chief Justice R. B. Taney (who would later write the Dred Scott opinion), and an assortment of bigwigs, but not Giddings, whom Winthrop, who detested him, deliberately excluded. In death we are in the midst of life.

One of the many tributes, eulogies, and appraisals that would appear in the days thereafter would be written as an anonymous newspaper article by the great poet of American democracy, Walt Whitman, then a young newspaperman working briefly in New Orleans. He wrote a piece in the *New Orleans Crescent* that has only in the twentieth century been found and identified as Whitman's. He was responding to complaints in some of the obituaries and eulogies that "the People" had not sufficiently appreciated Adams when he was alive; young Whitman's journalistic purpose was to defend the People against that charge.

Whitman conceded that Adams had been "a virtuous man"—but what did that matter to Whitman's democracy? He conceded that Adams had been a "learned man"—but that mattered even less, perhaps counted against you in a Jackson/Whitman democracy. Whitman conceded that Adams had had "a singularly enlarged diplomatic knowledge"—but, as later generations would vulgarly say, so what? Adams, Whitman would write, came from the old school, that "had its source too near monarchy and nobility to be entirely free of their influences." He was—the plenary condemnation for Whitman—"not a man of the people." "Never, at any time," Whitman would write, "did he [Adams] heartily espouse the side of any of those hot struggles of the rights of man, as opposed to wealth and conservatism. . . . Is it wonderful then, that he was never a popular man?" You are in deep democratic trouble indeed if even the great bear-hug embrace-everybody poet of democracy Walt Whitman, who would write "not till the *sun* excludes you do I exclude you"—excludes you.

Never at any time did he heartily espouse the side of any of those hot struggles for the rights of man? What about the struggle for fundamental civil liberties—the right to petition? The struggle over slavery?

Not on his death, nor later either, would John Quincy, as with the male Adamses generally, be much appreciated or favored by the great public, in other than the formal and rather empty terms required at funerals and in textbook-writings and the listing of presidents. That would be the general story.

But now we are privileged to tell about the one little moment of exception, which moment came happily while John Quincy was still living. To return now from this flash-forward to the days of Adams's own life—after his widely publicized "trial," there began to be, in some places in the North, a fairly widespread and fairly hearty appreciation for his role.

When he returned to Massachusetts from the congressional session in which he had been tried, in the summer of 1842, he was greeted with an outburst of popular enthusiasm that it had not been his lot to experience before, or perhaps not his father's either. His constituents thanked him with a grand reception. A great procession formed in Weymouth (his mother's home) and marched to Braintree, filling every niche of the old meeting house. There were large white banners surrounding the pulpit. Above it a banner read: "Let there be light!" On one side another banner read: "Welcome, defender of the right of petition." On the other side the legend left something to be desired by the criterion of brevity (never an Adams strong point), but still the citizens meant well. This certainly unedited banner read: "Shame on a nation that fosters and sustains an institution which dares assail and would destroy the sacred right of petition."

In the next summer, the summer of 1843, Adams agreed to go along on what was planned to be simply a private family trip to upstate New York, to see Niagara Falls. As the party went along by train through towns whose names he recorded, seeing sights he recorded, he began to receive invitations to come to this town and to that, and the trip, as his son wrote in a footnote in the *Memoirs,* "was converted by public feeling into an ovation." Would you please sign my daughter's album? Come to Buffalo. Come to Syracuse. Come to Utica. He was the guest of the city of Buffalo, to which his hosts took him by way of Lake Erie on a chartered steam launch; flags and buntings were flying from a multitude of masts as they entered the harbor, and he noted in his journal, "We were received by shouting multitudes at the landing." Adams "received a complimentary address from Millard Fillmore" and responded. "I rode round the city with Mr. Fillmore and the Mayor, then to the American Hotel, and shook hands with some hundreds of men and women. Firemen's torchlight procession." At Batavia "a crowd was assembled" and a "platform in front of the door broke down from the weight of the pressure upon it." At Rochester the party "found guns firing, bells ringing, and an immense crowd of people shouting." More speeches honoring him, more shaking of hands. "In the evening I received the ladies at the Eagle Hotel, and made them a short speech." Another torchlight procession. At Canandaigua "we met a cavalcade in military uniform, with a band of music"—so at last for an Adams there was "Musick playing &&& and marching and uniforms." Adams further described the event at Canandaigua:

> *. . . numerous carriages, all of which united in a procession a full mile, with bells ringing and a firing of cannon, which left me in amazement to enquire of myself what all this was for. The procession, however, led me to the Brick Church, where Mr. Francis Granger* [the Whig Congressman in the gag rule days] *introduced me to all the beauty and fashion of Canandaigua, in a highly complimentary address, which I answered as best I could, in a speech full of inanity and gratitude, shamefaced and awkward, as I must always be in answering compliments to myself. . . . At Geneva and several other places on the road crowds were collected to shake hands with me, to hear me speak a few words, and to shout me onward.*

In Utica, in addition to an episode well repeated in the biographies, in which the reading of excerpts from his mother's letters while he was being introduced at the Female Seminary caused him to weep at her memory, there was also a visit by a "committee appointed by the colored citizens of Utica to wait on me and return their thanks for my efforts in protecting the right of petition and promoting the abolition of slavery." In response he thanked them and said, according to his journal,

> *I had no claim of gratitude from them for services in which I had performed no more than my indispensable (duty)* [his son as editor supplied the obvious omitted Adams word]; *that I should still and ever be happy to serve them to the utmost extent of my power, and commend them to the protection of our common Father and Creator.*

Of course, before this trip full of plaudits and praises was over, Adams began to complain in his journal about the ceremonies with which he was "already satiated with repetitions." But it is also evident from the journal that he was touched and gratified. He kept saying how "unfit" he was for such personal celebration, and describing his own responses to the adulation as consisting of "mortifying inanity," and he kept enjoining himself to humility, but at the same time, after all the long drought of battering and neglect (so far as the large public was concerned) surely he was thirsty for a little bit of recognition. One would still have to plan its geography with care, to be sure, but in the right places, in at least the burned-over district, the Western Reserve, and New England and its diaspora, there were, at last, some Lawrells for an Adams.

There was more. One of the invitations he received while on that trip was to deliver the address at the laying of the cornerstone for a new observatory in Cincinnati. Adams, who had done the primary work through the years to bring into being the Smithsonian Institution, and who was a more scholarly president than most, had long promoted the development in this country of astronomy, of observatories—of lighthouses *of* the sky—and he was pleased to accept the invitation, even though it meant more travel, this time in November weather. And this trip, which included crossing Ohio on the Ohio Canal, also was "converted by public feeling into an ovation." Travel in those early days of the railroad was complicated, and there were hitches. First by train, eventually to Buffalo; and across Lake Erie on a steamer to Cleveland. Then by the Ohio Canal southward across the state to Cincinnati, with crowds and celebrations and praise in Newark, Hebron, Columbus in particular, Jefferson, Springfield, Dayton, Lebanon. Among the items from his journal that every biographer must include (along with his skinny dipping in the Potomac) is the episode in Akron in which a young woman, who he said was "very pretty," kissed him on the cheek, at which he "returned the salute on the lip, and kissed every woman that followed, at which some made faces, but none refused." In Cincinnati itself, where he was feted for four days and his long learned speech was a considerable success, he was greeted with a huge banner across Sixth Street which read, as though in direct anticipatory refutation of Walt Whitman, "John Quincy Adams, the Defender of the Rights of Man."

There were invitations to other cities, most of which he had to refuse; he did cross into Kentucky, where in Covington a young woman requested "the first kiss in Kentucky," and where he spoke highly of Clay, and directly denied that there had been any bargain between the two of them. More celebrations and greetings on the complicated way home, including four days in Pittsburgh where among other speeches there was one to an assembly of African-Americans (as we say now—"colored people" then) of that city, to which we will refer again. He was cheered in college towns and train stops all the way to Washington, where he arrived in late November, after an arduous month's trip and such accumulated public cheering as no Adams could expect ever to hear. He arrived just in time for the beginning of the first session of the Twenty-eighth Congress, and a new attack upon the gag rule.

Among the many expressions of support Adams received during this time was an item from a manufacturer in Meriden, Connecticut, a present if he would take it. This was a "milk-white Ivory cane, one yard long, made of one elephant's tooth"—as Adams described it in his journal—"tipped with silver and steel, with the American eagle inlaid in gold on its top, and a ring under the pommel, inscribed with my name, and the words, 'Justum et tenacem propositi virum' which is a quotation from a once familiar poem by Horace that can be translated, roughly, 'A man just and tenacious in purpose.' " The poem goes on, appropriately enough for Adams, "and is not shaken from that purpose by the objection of people around him." Later Adams recorded another line on the cane: "Right of Petition Triumphant." The letter with the gift requested that on the day the gag rule was abolished he should have the date inscribed on the ring. Adams said he could not as a matter of policy accept the cane as a personal gift, but that he would accept it as a trust to be returned when the date of the extinction of the gag rule was known.

39 / WHETHER IN PEACE OR IN BLOOD, LET IT COME

LEGISLATIVE CONTESTS DO NOT often have the tidiness that would satisfy a dramatist, or an audience in a theater. They often are settled on procedural motions, dribble away unresolved, or are upstaged by other contests and shuffled inconclusively out of sight. The decisive votes often are taken on apparently tangential matters rather than head-on, yes or no, on the central substantive issue. The gag rule fight came to its sufficiently dramatic real climax in 1842 in the failed attempt to censure Adams, with after-curtain business in the ultimately unsuccessful effort to put Giddings out of the House.

Nevertheless the gag rule itself was still on the books, a scandalous anomaly in the new American republic, and removing it was no small matter. Certainly it was important to Adams. At every session after it was first enacted he either moved that the 21st (or, by later numbering, the 25th) rule be rescinded, or, at the start of a new Congress, moved that the rules be adopted without it.

On December 5, 1842, the very first day of the lame duck session of the Twenty-seventh Congress, the Whigs' last chance, Adams gave notice (as the rules required) that on the following day he would offer a resolution rescinding the gag rule.

> **Mr. Wise** objected to the reception of the resolution.
>
> **The Speaker** said it was only offered as a notice.
>
> **Mr. Wise** inquired whether the notice took precedence of the other orders of the House.
>
> **The Speaker** replied that it did not.
>
> **Mr. William Cost Johnson** asked whether it was susceptible of amendment.
>
> **The Speaker** said that the resolution could be amended when it came properly before the House; at present it is only offered in the form of a notice.

One can be sure that on the next day, when Adams did offer his resolution, these two and many more met it with an expanded attack.

The two sides then proved to be parliamentary wrestlers of almost equal strength, each of whom could keep from being thrown, but could not throw the other. On December 6 the vote was 85–93 *against* laying Adams's resolution on the table, but 84–99 *against* putting the question (that is, bringing the matter to a vote). On December 7 it was 90–91, a real squeaker, against laying it on the table (on William Cost Johnson's motion)—and then 91–93 against putting the question. When on December 8 the House started off the same way—refusing 92–95 to lay the resolution on the table—a member understandably asked whether it was going to go on like this all the way through the session. Apparently it was; the representatives then again voted that although they would not lay the resolution on the table (which meant effectively to kill it, as Wise and Johnson wanted, and as the members now presumably realized), they also were not ready—and voted 95–100 against—having the question put (as Adams wanted).

Notice that the total number of votes was slowly growing, and that the totals on putting the question were in each case a little larger than the totals on laying on the table: the pro-gag forces presumably were stalling while their cohorts arrived, and when in danger were able to rustle up the few extra votes they needed. It would be relatively easy to persuade a colleague to vote not to put the question quite yet.

Then, because the House had to get on with its business, committees were appointed and President Tyler's message was received, and Millard Fillmore moved that the president's message now be made the order of business. Adams objected that his resolution was still before the House, and the House, with the excuse of the overriding presidential business, and with enough members now arrived to achieve the outcome the gaggers wanted, *did* turn him down and did vote, although again by a small margin, 106–102, to lay Adams's resolution on the table. That result meant that Rule 21 was still in force, and would not be rescinded by this, or any, Whig Congress. The next Congress, the Twenty-eighth, much of it already chosen, would be heavily Democratic.

Why were the Whigs, this party of Protestant "improvement," and of reform, and of republican rectitude, as well as of capitalist "industry" and commerce, unable to overturn the gag? Partly because, even in their Northern expression, they had the mixtures of purpose that that complex identity suggests.

As with slavery, so, to a degree, with the gag: in order to win victories against it there would have to be a persistent and concentrated purpose that would put the objective in the first place, and keep it there; the Whigs, even in the North, were capable of no such clarity of purpose. Generally speaking, they represented at most the mere "sentiment" of disapproval of slavery that had proved in American history thus far too weak to match the determined interest on the other side. And then the Whigs were sharply split by section, and if the Southern Whigs supported the gag, as they continued to do (all but four or five from border states), then there were no further Whig votes to be gained; the Northern Whigs had been opposing the gag overwhelmingly ever since it became a rule of the House, and a plurality had opposed the gag from the start.

The Whigs had a forty-vote margin in this House—but there were forty-five slave-state Whigs, so even if the Northern Whigs were unanimous, if the Democrats held together on the other side—if the Southern Democrats could persuade most of the Northern ones to stand with them—the pro-gag forces, aided by inertia and the harder parliamentary task of getting rid of an already adopted rule, could, with skillful generalship, just barely, win. And, just barely, they did.

The retaining of the gag, as usual, did not prevent Adams and Slade—and Abolition House, and the citizens who wrote petitions—from once more banging their heads dramatically against it, and letting the world know it. Slade moved to suspend the rule to allow him to present resolutions of the legislature of Vermont opposing slavery in the District—again it was a sovereign state's legislature, not private individuals—but, sovereign state or not, the House refused 73–109.

In February, Adams rose with a unique petition, a champion petition, from 51,863 citizens, which he asked the House to grant consent that he introduce, which consent was of course denied.

> **Mr. Adams.** Well, I hope I shall have an opportunity to present the petition in the course of the day (loud cries of "Order! Order!" from Mr. Wise and others) for I do not wish the petition to remain here as a monument (—"of infamy," some gentleman remarked).

The reporter for the *Congressional Globe,* who wrote the inserts in the above quotation, also attempted a description of this item:

> The petition to which the honorable gentleman referred was placed on his desk, on a large wooden framework, and presented the appearance of a gigantic reel, or a juvenile water-wheel, and it bore the following inscription: "Great Petition to Congress."

The prayer of the petition of the 51,863 citizens whose signatures were arranged on this wheel was that Congress enact such laws and amendments to the Constitution "as may forever separate the people of Massachusetts from all connexion with slavery." What Adams did, since the House refused to receive it, was to leave this monument on his desk for the rest of the session, as a kind of inescapable visual aid.

WOULD ADAMS LIVE LONG enough to see the end of the gag rule? Although, like his father, he took his exercise—including the famous swims in the Potomac—and although he was justly rather proud of his stamina, at the same time he had a significant and increasing supply of physical complaints, of which, because he kept so complete a journal, we have an abundant record. At the time of the *Amistad* affair, back on March 29, 1841, for just one example, he had written:

> *[T]he world, the flesh, and all the devils in hell are arrayed against any man who now in this North American Union shall dare to join the standard of Almighty God to put down the African slave-trade; and what can I, upon the verge of my seventy-fourth birthday, with a shaking hand, a darkening eye, a drowsy brain, and with all my faculties dropping from me one by one, as the teeth are dropping from my head—what can I do for the cause of God and man, for the progress of human emancipation,*

> *for the suppression of the African slave-trade? Yet my conscience presses me on; let me but die upon the breach.*

At some point in the extended struggle in the early days of the first session of the Twenty-eighth Congress, at the end of 1843 and the beginning of 1844—to be recounted in a moment—Adams, battling every morning for the repeal of Rule 21, told Giddings that "he had become nervous and unable to sleep," according to Giddings's *History of the Rebellion,* "avowed himself physically disqualified to contend longer for the floor," and asked Giddings to take over for him. "He said," Giddings reported, that "he had indulged the hope of living to see the gag rule repealed, but he now regarded it as doubtful."

Both in his journal and in his history, Giddings reports a moment during those days when Adams, depressed, said earnestly (of course it would be earnestly) to Giddings that there was "but one cause for public men," and that was to *"do their duty."*

In the same period—during the last long debate on Rule 21 going into early 1844—there came an episode that was often to be referred to thereafter. One of the many Southerners engaged in assailing Adams—as Giddings tells the story—a man from Alabama named Dellet, quoted, as part of his attack, what he took to be a shocking passage from a speech Adams had given to "the colored people of Pittsburgh, Pennsylvania":

> **[Dellet quoting Adams]:** We know that the day of your redemption must come. The time and the manner of its coming we know not: It may come in peace, or it may come in blood; but *whether in peace or in blood,* LET IT COME.

Dellet dramatized this passage, and then to underline its offensiveness, read it a second time. As he was finishing, Adams, in his seat, added, *"I say now let it come."*

Dellet, presumably shocked at this further outrage from Old Man Adams, said:

> **[Dellet]:** Yes, the gentleman now says let it come, though it *cost the blood of thousands of white men.*

> **[Adams responded]:** *Though it cost the blood of* MILLIONS OF WHITE MEN, LET IT COME. *Let justice be done, though the heavens fall.*

Never did he heartily espouse the side of any of those hot struggles of the rights of man?

TWENTY-ONE YEARS LATER THE president of the United States would make a point, in the next-to-last paragraph (not the last—the next-to-last) of his Second Inaugural Address, which, although vastly different in tone and context, in grace and in moral complexity, from this stark assertion of Adams's, was nevertheless, when one sorted out its naked meaning, not so very different from it:

> If we shall suppose that American Slavery is one of those offences which, in the providence of God, must needs come, but which, having continued through His appointed time, He now wills to remove, and that He gives to both North and South, this terrible war, as the woe due to those by whom the offence came, shall we discern therein any departure from those divine attributes which the believers in a Living God always ascribe to Him? Fondly do we hope—fervently do we pray—that this mighty scourge of war may speedily pass away.

To be sure, this paragraph of Lincoln's precedes, and provides a profound dark backdrop to, "with charity for all, with malice toward none" in the renowned last paragraph. But notice the fierce and terrible image that ends this not often closely examined penultimate paragraph:

> Yet, if God wills that it [the terrible scourge of war] continue, until all the wealth piled by the bond-man's two hundred and fifty years of unrequited toil shall be sunk, and until every drop of blood drawn with the lash, shall be paid by another drawn with the sword, as was said three thousand years ago, so still it must be said, "The judgments of the Lord, are true and righteous altogether."

Let it come. Let justice be done, though the heavens fall.

WHEN CONGRESS CONVENED IN December of 1843, with, again, the echoing pillars, the tripping Mercuries, the calling of states, the different intonations of ayes and noes, the gobbling manner of the clerk, it was a *new* Congress, the Twenty-eighth, which meant that once again it would be *adopting* its rules. And this one really was a *new* Congress.

When in the late twentieth century there would be lamentations over the power of incumbency, and the minimal turnover in the elections to the House, the elections for this Twenty-eighth Congress would be cited as a shining anti-incumbency moment from the golden past: only 24 percent of the incumbent congressmen had been returned.

The Democrats had made huge gains. The Whigs, whose whole party life seems to have been a series of near-misses, of almost ups followed by unmistakable downs, had lost all that they had gained in the period from 1837 up through the election of 1840. The prime reason appears to have been that they hadn't produced, in the Twenty-seventh Congress, the economic program they had promised, to counter the depressed conditions that had brought them to power in the first place.

The fall-off from the Whigs had started right after the Extra Session, at which, under Henry Clay, they had passed "Whig Measures," only to find them vetoed by the putatively Whig president, His Accidency John Tyler. He had vetoed more the next year, after which his cabinet had almost all resigned, and the Whigs had a ceremony reading him out of the party. What kind of a party is that? Elections then being spread across the months, the Democrats during these Whig agonies were electing state legislators, governors—and members of this Congress.

There was another reason for the abrupt Whig decline in the Twenty-eighth Congress: the reapportionment that followed the 1840 census. It is claimed that the Democratic legislatures, now in power in many states, gerrymandered relentlessly. In addition, the total number of congressional seats was *reduced,* a rare but not impossible happening in America's earlier history.* The Twenty-seventh Congress had had 242 Congressmen; the Twenty-eighth had 224, of whom 142 were Democrats and 82 Whigs. The Democrats had made a large gain, from 102 to 142 seats, with the latter number bigger than it looks because in a smaller House, and the discomfited Whigs had suffered an even more striking decline.

The Whigs' brief moment of control had passed. One might have thought that if the blockade against discussion of slavery were ever to be overturned it would be done by a Whig Congress. But although, as we have seen, the Twenty-seventh Congress had seen repeated close votes—repeated and repeated close votes, very close votes—still it did not happen on the watch of the Whigs. It might have seemed to have been even more unlikely, then, that it would happen in a Congress controlled by the Democrats, who had instituted the gag in the first place and had always been the party with the more consistent nationwide opposition to anything smacking of abolition. So there would surely be no hope now to overturn the gag.

*The total would later begin to move up again, although not in an unbroken line, until it reached our present number, 435, in the 60th Congress.

NEVERTHELESS, ONE WOULD TRY. On the first day this new Congress assembled, December 4, 1843, Democratic congressman George Dromgoole of Virginia (despite the turnover, he is still there, with his perfect congressional name—not made up by Anthony Trollope or by the present author but a real name) moved the adoption of the rules of the previous Congress. And Adams, at seventy-six, was right there to seize the moment: he promptly moved to except the gag rule. After some intervening business, Adams's motion was rejected, but by the surprisingly close vote of 91–95—surprising in this Democratic House. In fact, the margin was not much different from those in the previous Whig congress. But still Adams's motion lost.

There was more vintage Adams, including a sharp jab at the Speaker, now Democrat James Jones of Virginia, and a jab back by Speaker Jones. On December 20 there was more of the same, notable for Adams's mock submissiveness in the midst of it.

> **Mr. Adams** presented various petitions on the subject of slavery; but the chair ruled them out of order.
>
> **Mr. Adams** said he had more of the same description, with hundreds of thousands of signatures.
>
> **The Chair** remarked to the gentleman from Massachusetts, that it was not in order to debate the subject of these petitions.
>
> **Mr. Adams.** I do not debate it, sir. I submit with lamb-like patience.

The *New York Post* (on December 22) reported that "[t]he words 'lamb like' were uttered with such a shrill, sharp intonation, amounting almost to a positive scream, that the whole House roared with laughter."

All of this was as it had been in many sessions. But then came the surprise, on December 21: a sudden reversal or apparent capitulation by the volatile Henry Wise. In the midst of these standard opening fireworks, Wise called reporters to come closer to get straight what he was saying; the *Globe* reporter put in parentheses "(and he wished reporters to be particular in taking down what he said)." What he said was that he was quitting: "henceforth, and forever, he ceased to contend in the war which was being carried on in that House by certain men against the South. He would hereafter oppose nothing; but leave the gentleman from Massachusetts, and all others, to take their own course with the whole subject." There was a proposal by Adams on the floor that a committee be appointed to reconsider the rules, undoubtedly to propose dropping the gag rule. Wise now said, "He would vote, therefore, for the motion of the gentleman from Massachusetts, and let him have his committee, and disclose his designs in full, that they might know on what terms they stood in the House." There was a bit of a pout in all this, but still Wise seemed to be throwing in the towel.

Why, after nine years as a leader in the fight for gags, did he do so? Wise's friend John Tyler was now president, and three times had nominated Wise to be minister to France, but the real Whigs in the Senate, led by Henry Clay, had headed that off each time. Then Tyler had proposed Wise as minister to Brazil. Wise's biographer Craig Simpson, in the biography titled *A Good Southerner,* speculates that Wise's willingness to abandon the struggle "reflected an effort to curry favor among Northern senators whose votes could shortly aid in confirming him as minister to Brazil." Or, Simpson further speculates, he "might also have wanted to deflect Northern criticism away from such projects as the annexation of Texas, which meant far more to the South than maintenance of the gag rule." But the biographer found something more: "[T]he tone of his remarks . . . suggests a sense of relief from a burden lifted." Elsewhere Simpson says that "Wise eventually acknowledged defeat amid circumstances suggesting that perhaps he believed himself undeserving of victory."

Maybe so, but Wise's tone sounds equivocal and grudging to another reader, and there were more acts to the play. A Committee on the Rules was indeed appointed as Adams had proposed, and Wise had acquiesced to; Adams, having made the proposal, was appointed committee chairman. The rules of the past Congress were again adopted ("provisionally"?) until this committee reported.

In early January, Adams reported for the committee a revision of the rules that—of course—dropped the gag rule, and the House proceeded to its longest discussion ever of this issue. It filled a tedious two months and more with speeches, amendments, points of order—with Wise now back at the old stand, supporting the gag, making all his old arguments. His renunciation had been brief. Again we may ask, what happened? Simpson speculates, about this second turn in his double reverse, that there "must have been intense criticism, mostly in private and addressed to the legitimacy of his credentials as a Southerner."

When, exhausted, the House began to work its way back through the forest of amendments and amendments to the amendments, this was the important point: it refused, by a vote of 86 to 106, to reintroduce the gag into the gagless revised rules that Adams's committee had proposed. Notice that vote, for future reference. And then it refused, by an even larger margin, 55–116, to reconsider that vote.

So a touchdown again? No doubt this time the anti-gag forces eyed the field warily for referees' flags, and were quite tentative in celebration—and, as events then proved, rightly so. Whatever those votes portended for the future, they did not, after all, determine the outcome on this occasion. Remember how complicated parliamentary procedure can be. For when at last it was moved to adopt Adams's committee's revised rules (without the gag), there was a motion to lay *that* motion on the table—and it carried a suspiciously diminished House by the suspiciously frustrating margin of just one vote, 88–87. And a motion to reconsider *that* vote was defeated.

So all the work of Adams's committee, and the two votes refusing to insert the gag into that committee's proposals, and the two months of tedious argument, went down the drain. The old rules, including the gag, which had been provisionally in place while all this went on, became the rules of the House once again.

No doubt a certain weariness over the long battle helped the pro-gag forces finally squeak out this victory.* No doubt the way the votes went served the interests of some unbrave politicians. A Northern Democrat could have been on record voting with Adams against reinserting the gag in the new rules proposed by Adams's committee—and then could have been persuaded to stay away during the suspiciously skimpy vote to lay on the table, allowing the whole thing to be discarded.

Also, if you were young and new and inexperienced and exhausted and inattentive and eager to get on to the current business of the House, or any combination of these, then the motion to lay the matter on the table might sound to you (particularly after a two-month wrangle) vaguely, loosely, like nothing more than a convenient temporary setting aside of the matter, for the moment; but of course it was not that. It took only a majority to lay on the table, but a two-thirds vote to take it off the table, and on controversial matters like the gag, the latter vote was never possible. A vote to lay on the table was a vote to kill.

Adams was not getting any younger, as we have observed, and this had been a grueling battle; it was in the midst of these months of debate that he made his uncharacteristic call on Giddings for help. Adams had been seventy-five during the fight in the last session of the Twenty-seventh Congress, and was seventy-six at the beginning of the Twenty-eighth. He

*Scholar Robert Ludlum: "One can almost hear the official reporter's sigh of relief as he wrote, 'So the whole subject was laid on the table, leaving the rules of the [last] Congress in force, and among them the rule excluding abolition petitions.' "

had to be present every day to engage in the parliamentary fencing. Thus, for example, on January 30, 1844, in the middle of the battle we have just recorded, he described how heavy his labors were:

> *Five days in the week, the report of the Committee on the Rules is the first business in order to be transacted in the House, and if I were to be absent one day, when it would be called up, it would be laid upon the table without redemption.*

His chance to move to rescind the gag rule would be gone for that session.

> *When I call it up, scarcely a day passes but some dirty trick is devised to postpone the taking of the question.*

On the next day, January 31:

> *I hurried up to the capitol, to be there at the meeting of the House. The report on the rules was immediately taken up, and Andrew Johnson, a new member from Tennessee* [the future president—described by Adams in the previous entry as "another slaveholder"] *made an hour's speech in support of the gag rule and especially abusive upon me. So they all are.*

Nevertheless—was that earlier vote by which this Democratic House refused to put the gag into the revised rules a decisive indicator of the new strength of forces? Were Adams and company—figuratively speaking—closing in on Richmond? Was the exhausted one-vote lay-it-all-on-the-table victory of the pro-gag forces just a delaying action? Was it, to shift metaphorical wars, a Battle of the Bulge, a last stand before collapse?

After further Adams efforts to evade and mock the just barely restored gag in the Twenty-eighth Congress, the first session adjourned, and many members fell to work in the presidential election of 1844. Then they came back to go at it once more.

40/IO TRIUMPHE

WHEN THAT CONGRESS REASSEMBLED in December of 1844 for its second, lame duck session, the presidential election had intervened, but throughout this session the president would still be the very lame duck, now in his last presidential days a man without a party, John Tyler, and Congress would be the old group with a heavy Democratic majority chosen in 1842–43.

Adams gave notice on the first day of the new session that he would move to rescind the gag rule. On the second day, December 3, 1844, the earliest possible moment, he introduced his resolution to do that. And, as sometimes happens in life, the door that had been slammed shut repeatedly, and stuck shut and implacably resistant for so long—suddenly swung open.

We report what happened with the help of Horace Greeley's paper.

Congressional Proceedings
By The Reporter of the N. Y. Tribune
The Gag-Law rescinded . . .
Washington, Dec. 3, 1844

> Mr. John Quincy Adams, in pursuance of notice given yesterday, sent up the following resolution, written with his own trembling hand:
>
> RESOLVED, that the 25 Standing Rule, for conducting business in the House, in the words following [Adams with his trembling hand, and the *Tribune* with its steady print, here reproduce the rule, which is just as William Cost Johnson wrote it back in 1839–40] be, and the same is hereby, rescinded.
>
> MR. JACOB THOMPSON, of Mississippi, moved to lay this resolution on the table. The Yeas and Nays were ordered on the motion to lay on the table: Yeas 81 Nays 104. I need not send you [wrote the *Tribune* reporter, using the first person] the yeas and nays on this, as you have them on the passage of the resolution.
>
> MR. ADAMS's resolution was then put, the yeas and nays being called, when there appeared for the resolution 108 [printed in large bold numbers by the *Tribune*] against it 80. . . .

At the end the report—hard to distinguish from an editorial—once again gave credit where it was due:

So the 25th Rule is rescinded.
Perseverance has crowned the "old man eloquent" with success.

From the *Globe* and Adams's journal we may gather a couple of things the *Tribune* did not include. When Thompson made his motion to lay Adams's motion on the table, Giddings and Adams simultaneously called for the yeas and nays on that tabling motion, to get it out of the way—they must by then have known their strength—and the vote was ordered and they won, as the *Tribune* reporter noted, by almost exactly the same vote as would carry Adams's motion to victory—so the lines were already clearly drawn. And then before the roll was called on the motion itself the opposition tried yet another tactic—one used successfully before. John Tyler, Jr., his father's private secretary, appeared below the bar with the president's annual message, to hear and respond to which might be presumed to take precedence over the votes on Adams's motion. Thompson announced that he now hoped the president's message would be read. Adams for his part responded that he hoped that the calling of the yeas and nays would be proceeded with. And this time the vote was not interrupted. The yeas and nays were called, with the result that the *Tribune* reported.

Turning now to the editorial page of the same edition of the *Tribune* (December 5, 1844), we find, as the lead editorial:

> The Gag-Rule Abolished
>
> Let every lover of freedom rejoice! The absurd and tyrannical XXVth (formerly the XXIst) Rule of the House which required the rejection of all petitions relating to slavery has been *repealed* by a decisive vote! The Sage of Quincy has won a proud victory for the Rights of Humanity. May he long live to rejoice over it! Here is a motion which will not go backward. There will be no more Gag-Rules.

Why, after all the years of debate, this sudden victory? It may be that one reason was that there had been a change in the cast of characters. In a narrative that features the agency of one, or a few, individual actors on the one side it would not do to neglect individual agency on the other. The reader may have noticed that it was a new figure, someone named Jacob Thompson from Mississippi, and not any of the old familiar names, who objected to Adams's motion in this session. The old adversaries were gone. The other Thompson, Waddy Thompson of South Carolina, had been appointed by President Harrison, in his brief month of service, to be minister to Mexico, and so had departed even before the Twenty-seventh Congress. He was just now finishing his two-year stint. He would return to private life; perhaps surprisingly, he would oppose the Mexican War. A good commercial Whig, he would make a fortune from his cotton plantation in Florida; the reader will remember his proposal for more funds for the Seminole War in that state. He would lose his fortune in the Civil War—and (would it be proper to add?) would then be to historical memory one of the obscurest of the obscure Whigs. Farewell to Waddy Thompson.

William Cost Johnson of tipsy merriment and well-timed motions to lay on the table had not stood for election to the Twenty-eighth Congress. He was defeated in the debacle of the Whigs in his run for governor of Maryland, and he too then retired to private life, as—a harbinger of the postcongressional careers of thousands of deft congressional operators in years to come—a lawyer in Washington.

And now in this second session of the Twenty-eighth Congress even Henry Wise, Adams's most vocal opponent from first almost to last, was gone. On August 2, 1844, he had arrived in Rio de Janeiro to take up his duties as American minister to Brazil, which is an interesting story in itself, but which for our present purposes just meant that he was no longer in the House.*

As for Adams's other adversaries: James Henry Hammond had got a stomachache after his bold move in 1836, and had left the House right then, and had gone on a recovery trip to Europe with his wife's money, and on to a Carolina political career outside the House. He kept a remarkable series of diaries, begun in 1841, that record among much else his sexual exploitation of his female slaves. He would take as a mistress an eighteen-year-old slave with a one-year-old female child, and then when that child was twelve take her as his mistress as well. He would engage in some cuddling and fondling—at least—with four teenage daughters of his brother-in-law Wade Hampton II, which when discovered would cause a scandal that would keep him out of politics after his term as governor ended in 1844. But, astonishingly, it would not prevent the legislature from choosing him for the Senate in 1857, although perhaps not on a platform of family values. James Henry Hammond would die in 1864, three days before Sherman began his march through Georgia.

Henry Laurens Pinckney had long since been knocked out of the

*Henry A. Wise, swashbuckling defender of slavery's interests in the House for eleven years, went down to Rio—and became a swashbuckling *opponent* of the slave trade, collaborating with the *British* ambassador! Now a Democrat, he would be the governor of Virginia when John Brown made his famous raid on Harpers Ferry and a "political general" in the Confederate army. One of those present at Appomattox Court House when Lee surrendered to Grant would be the ubiquitous Henry A. Wise.

House by the indignant Calhounites, not for the gag, but for his insufficiently Carolinian fervor, and would end his public career in the ignominious position of tax collector in Charleston. Hawes, Patton, and Atherton were all gone—Atherton to the Senate, where he continued to be shifty from an abolitionist point of view. Thomas Gilmer, who had joined Wise in trying to censure Adams, had been appointed secretary of the navy, by Tyler, and then in February of 1844 had been killed, along with Secretary of State Abel Upshur and others, when one of the guns on the USS *Princeton,* a new steam-powered battleship, exploded during an excursion by a presidential party on the Potomac.

The career of young Thomas Marshall, who had been put forward by Adams's enemies to make the speech and the motion for Adams's censure, had come to an abrupt end right after that effort, partly as a result of revelations Adams made. When Adams crossed into Kentucky on his trip to dedicate the observatory in Cincinnati, he and Marshall had a little no-hard-feelings exchange.

So Old Man Adams had outlasted them all.

To be sure, there are other levels of analysis beyond the cast of individual characters. For help in analyzing the decisive vote, especially as it played out in the political parties, we call first upon Horace Greeley, whose analysis can be found in the *Tribune*'s wonderful and enviable (but *not* "objective") presentation of the vote, which we have noted before. On this important matter the vote on each side—the yeas and then the nays—is conveniently subdivided into Northern Whigs, Northern Locos, Southern Whigs, Southern Locos.*

In this *Tribune* presentation of the vote there there are two notable *zeros:* under yeas, "Southern Locos . . . 0"; under nays, "Northern Whigs . . . 0!"—this second with an exclamation point to emphasize the unblemished purity of the Northern Whigs. Not a single Democrat in the South voted with Adams to end the rule, and not a single Whig in the North voted against him.

But that wasn't new. The Northern Whigs had been the main, almost the sole, source of votes against the gag from the start, and large majorities of Northern Whigs had voted against the gag ever since it was made a rule of the House in 1839–40. And, at the opposite end of things, Southern Democrats had always solidly supported the gags: for them it had become bedrock resistance to abolitionism. The change across time, if there were to be any, had to come from the other two groups.

When the Whigs had come to have a majority in the House, at the

*Short for "Loco-Foco," the unvarying *Tribune*-speak for Democrat.

beginning of the Twenty-seventh Congress, as we have seen, Adams had briefly tried to make a partisan appeal to his fellow Whigs, labeling the gag as something that had been done by the Democratic administrations that could now be undone by Whigs—but that did not work. Although it is of some importance that a small handful of Southern Whigs, all from border states, would vote against the gags, it is also important that no more than that small handful ever did. In this decisive last vote there were only five, three from Maryland, one from North Carolina, and former Speaker White of Kentucky. No Whig from the deep South could, or did, vote against any gag. So if the gag was to be overturned, the votes of Northern Democrats had to do it.

And they did. The winning total was composed of almost equal parts from the two parties: fifty-three Whigs and fifty-five Democrats, the latter entirely from the North. Northern Democrats voted 55–16 against the gag. In his editorial, Horace Greeley made a not too grudging acknowledgment of the role, this time, of that other party: "We have given an analysis of the Vote, by which it will be seen that an unusual proportion of the Northern Loco-Focos voted on the side of freedom."

Historian William Freehling, analyzing the final vote well over a century later, gave a historical comparison, and for the last vote distinguished two parts of the North: "In 1836, [the Northern Democrats] had voted 53–14 for Pinckney's diluted gag rule; in 1840, they had split 36–26 against Johnson's undiluted gag rule." In the finale, "[I]n 1844, Upper North Democrats polished off the last potential gag, 32–5; Lower North Democrats less overwhelmingly but still decisively voted it down, 22–11."

One could also draw a West/East line. Of the sixteen Democrats from free states who still voted to retain the gag—a group covered in infamy, of course, in Adams's opinion—nine came from Ohio, Indiana, and Illinois—the Northwest Ordinance states of the West—and only three, all from New Hampshire, from New England. We might note, since Greeley editorially admonished us, across the years, to "brand him," that one of Pennsylvania's two votes to keep the gag came from the unrepentant proto-Tory C. J. Ingersoll.*

Why did a preponderance of Northern Democrats now vote to rescind the gag? Freehling's interpretation had to do with internal party and sectional pressures: "When Slavepower demands could corral only one-third of the Democrats in the most friendly half of the North, the time to cease pressing northern friends for gags had arrived."

*Ingersoll would, as the years went by, keep trying, as chairman of the Committee on Foreign Affairs, to obtain American compensation for the Spanish "owners" from the *Amistad* affair, and Adams and then Giddings would, as the years went by, keep opposing him, and winning.

And—to expand on that—sectional pressures would then outweigh party pressures in both parties, because by this time, on this issue, the overriding division in public opinion had become not partisan but sectional. When pressure from the Southern wing of the Democratic Party to hold the Northern wing in line could no longer be effective, the gag rule was killed.

Why had that not already done its work in the *first* session of this Congress, which had, after all, the same composition? One answer is that it almost did. Another answer is that something happened between the two sessions of the Twenty-eighth Congress. Now we deal in that quite particular politics that always accompanies great decisions of state: Northern Democrats had a quite specific new reason to be angry at Southern Democrats.

When the Democrats had gathered in Baltimore in the previous May to nominate their ticket for the presidential election of 1844, ex-president Martin Van Buren, that infinitely pliable favorite in particular of Northern Democrats, had the pledges of a majority of the delegates. He expected, and he was expected, to be the nominee. But before the voting took place, some Southern pro-Texas delegates (the overarching issue in that election was Texas), led by a Mississippi delegate and aided by some renegade Van Buren delegates, reinstituted (it had already been used, when it didn't matter, in the Jackson–Van Buren conventions of 1832 and 1836, but not in 1840) a dreadful requirement for convention votes for Democratic presidential nominees: the two-thirds rule, which would go on to have an extended and lamentable history in Democratic conventions long after slavery was dead, leading, for just one example, to a mind-numbing 103 ballots at the 1924 convention. The implicit point of this rule, of course, was to protect the interests of the South in that party, providing the kind of regional veto of the sort that Calhoun would recommend for the nation as a whole. Its continued use would help to produce the doughface Democratic presidents—Pierce, Buchanan—before the Civil War and an ugly fracas and a party split in 1860.

In the immediate context in 1844, what it meant was that Van Buren could not get the nomination. He received a majority on the first ballot—but not two-thirds, and his vote declined on subsequent ballots until there was deadlock and then the nomination, on the ninth ballot, of American politics' first real dark horse, James K. Polk of Tennessee, the Speaker of the House from the first days of the gag, and, as Adams had then acidly observed, a slaveholder.

So Northern Democrats, and particularly Democrats from Van Buren's home state of New York, came to the House of Representatives the next December without any great feeling of tenderness toward their

Southern party colleagues. The reader will remember how New York delegates, one of them with the later famous name of Roosevelt, had switched their votes to save the gag in the extra session of the Whig-controlled Twenty-seventh Congress. But if you are a Democrat from New York at the end of 1844, why should you do the Southern Democrats' bidding anymore? Let us look for one last time at the *Tribune*'s handy presentation of that decisive vote, and make a count. Yes. There it is: there are *seventeen* Democratic votes from New York to rescind the gag—the largest number from either party from any one state on either side of the final balloting.

So that was it? After all the nine years of high-level moral and political argument (well, some of it was high-level) about slavery and the sacred right of petition, the gag was ended because of an intramural partisan resentment? Because some Northern Democrats were angry at some Southern Democrats? On another issue altogether—the presidential nomination, the two-thirds rule?

Not exactly. Not only for that reason. While we can assume that this vote was not quite the doing of justice, though the heavens fall—that like all politicians (which is to say, like all of us in political situations), these congressmen wanted to do, at best, only as much justice as could be done without having the heavens fall—it surely would be reductionist to say it was nothing but the revenge of the New York Democrats for the defeat of Van Buren in the Baltimore convention. Like most votes, it involved a great tossed salad of motives. Among them, surely, justice was not altogether missing.

Some of the New York and other Northern Democrats may now have been freed, by a diminished obligation to the Southern Democrats, to vote in line with something that they had felt all along, or had come to feel increasingly: that the *rejection* of petitions on one specific subject, in the very rules of the House, was, as Greeley said, "absurd and tyrannical." Surely some congressmen were bothered by, among the other things, the civil liberties implications of that gag, which Adams kept hammering on. And some surely were aware, too, of the evils of slavery that Adams and Giddings and Slade kept demonstrating to them, despite the gag. And some congressmen, if not bothered so much by these matters on their own account, no doubt were by proxy: they found that increasing numbers of their constituents were, so they were, too.

The gag had almost been defeated in this Congress before there was a Baltimore convention. At the start of the *first* session, Adams's direct motion to rescind had failed, as we have noted, by only four votes, 91–95. After that vote, on December 28, 1843, Adams had insisted in a speech that the will of the people in the Northern states (implicitly: Democrats as well as Whigs), as he himself knew from his recent trip, was strongly against the gag:

> **[Adams]:** The people of the North and the Northwest—he spoke of the people of New York, Pennsylvania, and Ohio, whose opinions he had a recent opportunity to ascertain—were, as might be seen by the proportions in which their representatives had voted, against that rule. He (Mr. A.) knew it; he had been told it by themselves, and in a manner which spoke for the reality of their opinions. With one voice, on his recent visit amongst them, they treated him as if he were a child returned to his father's family; and all unanimously gave, as their reason, that he had been the champion of the right of petition.

Adams listed the votes of representatives "fresh from the people" in those states as further evidence that the people were opposed to the rule:

> . . . on the second day of the session, when he (**Mr. A**) made a motion to strike out the obnoxious rule, thirteen members from Ohio out of eighteen, fresh from the people, voted with him to rescind that rule. . . . And how was it with the State of New York? Why twenty-seven out of thirty-two voted to rescind that rule.
>
> **A Voice:** Thirty-four.
>
> **Mr. Adams:** New York had thirty-four Representatives, but there were only thirty-two that voted on that question.

So Adams had had those New York Democrats, or almost all of them, before the Baltimore convention even happened. And then, looking back further at that first session, when the non-gag rules proposed by Adams's committee were before the House, there was that vote against inserting the gag to which we called attention: 106–86, only two votes shy of the final winning vote in the next session. Two excruciating months of argument had followed, and that effort to rescind the gag had finally failed by only one vote and exhaustion and possibly some deliberate absences and the complication of parliamentary procedure (that the full committee report had still to be adopted had given the opponents, after two months of argument, another shot, and the motion to lay on the table, in a tired moment, with one more group of newcomers, once more could have sounded like a mere postponement, when in reality it was death). All such votes are complex club sandwiches of motives and reasons; there were deeper changes underway than the response of Northern Democrats to their disappointment in Baltimore; and that episode, we may surmise, was but another in a larger chain of happenings and influences tending to disengage the Northern Democrats from their Southern party colleagues.

Leonard L. Richards, who is one of the scholars calling attention to the resentment by Northern Democrats as a factor in the final vote, cites also individual examples of political difficulties these Democrats had been facing as a result of the pro-gag votes that their Southern colleagues had pressed them to cast: a Pennsylvania Democrat who said abolitionists had no clout in his district until the passage of the gag rule ("Abolitionists now called meetings to discuss the right of petition and talked about slavery for hours on end"); an Ohio Democrat who voted for the 1840 rule only to find Whigs using it against him constantly; another Ohio Democrat who said the gag would ruin the party in his district; Martin Van Buren himself, who said the party in New York was damaged "in every limb" by the support it had given to Southern men and Southern measures including the gag. The old Democratic party line, under Van Buren in his days in power, had been to keep the issue of slavery *out* of politics (that had been the point of the Van Buren/Pinckney gag); but now these expansionist pro-Texas Southern Democrats were aggressively injecting slavery *into* politics by their campaign for Texas.

Richards also says that many Northern Democrats, who might have supported the original Pinckney gag resolutions, were bothered on constitutional grounds by the Hammond/Cost Johnson further step of prohibiting *reception* of petitions. Richards names as an example, along with Hannibal Hamlin of Maine (later to be a Republican and Lincoln's first vice-president), a surprising figure: none other than Samuel Beardsley of New York, once the heroic defender of Utica against the disgrace of an abolitionist meeting.

The handful of Southern Whigs, though a small part of the total vote, were an important sign of the gag's weakness. If you were a Democrat in a Northern district, you could find it embarrassing to have to explain to your constituents why you voted for the slave power's arrogant ban on antislavery petitions when even some slave-state representatives opposed it! To be sure, what that sentiment reveals is how divided by sectional pressures the nation was becoming. If democracy works at all, underneath votes like this, in the longer term, are great tides and shifts in the people's judgment. And if civil liberty works at all, those great tides and shifts are affected by the winds of doctrine and free argument and debate. Adams had hammered away through nine years making arguments, giving reasons, dramatizing.

We can say as a kind of shorthand that the gag ended when sectional identity sliced through party identity. It had already done so among

Whigs; now it did so also among Democrats. But one should not forget that the *motive* for the vote need not have been "sectional." It may have been sectional *de facto*, so to speak, but not *de jure*. As Abraham Lincoln would explain in the debates with Douglas fourteen years later, the new party of which he was a member was not sectional by desire or design; it held to a principle that, not by the party's will but by the decisions of others, had been generally appropriated only in one section. The point is the principle, not the geography. In this anticipation of later events, as more and more of the free-state public began to recognize the principle, more and more of the free-state congressmen, of both parties, recognized it too. Adams wrote in his diary, a little too piously, the evening after the gag was beaten, "Blessed, forever Blessed, be the name of God!"

FOR ALL THE SCRAMBLE and comedy of legislative halls, there are moments that have their drama, both personal and historic, if you know what they mean. In Richmond in June of 1788, at the Virginia ratifying convention, James Madison watched the pivotal handful of wavering votes go the right way to make a vote of 88–80 for Virginia to ratify the proposed federal Constitution, which until then had hung in the balance. Without Virginia the new Constitution of the United States could not have gone into effective operation. No Virginia, no Constitution. But a few doubtful delegates from across the mountains did vote the right way, and Virginia ratified, and the Constitution did go into effect.

In Washington in June of 1964, floor leader Hubert Humphrey, in a front-row seat in the United States Senate, watched the votes fall into place for the first-ever cloture on a civil rights bill, shutting off an eighty-three-day filibuster, and he raised his hands over his head in a gesture of gratitude and triumph. Shortly thereafter the Civil Rights Act of 1964 was passed.

Most significantly for the story told here, there was to come in this very room in this very body, the House of Representatives—much transformed—on January 31, 1865, the vote on the proposed Thirteenth Amendment ending slavery, which had already received the required support in the Senate and needed a two-thirds vote now in the House. When enough Northern Democrats broke with the bulk of their party so that the amendment attained the needed margin with two votes to spare, 119–56, there was a remarkable scene in the chamber in which Adams had fought his long battle: prolonged and unprecedented cheering both on the floor and in the gallery, to which black persons had just been admitted in the previous year, with weeping and embracing and finally a vote to adjourn in honor of the deed.

And a little more than twenty years earlier in the same room, in December of 1844, ex-president John Quincy Adams had watched the House vote that prefigured that one to come. After almost ten years, the devices to shut off petitions and debate on the issue of slavery had been killed. The gag rule was dead, and never would be revived. The antislavery representatives gathered around his desk when the vote was announced. Symbolically, and to an extent really, one could no longer close the door to the discussion of slavery, to proposals about slavery, in the deliberative body composed of the people's representatives in this republic. Now that topic could be deliberated about, too.

Adams's biographer Samuel Flagg Bemis wrote that this outcome "was a turning point from slavery to freedom." Some historians would discount such a claim. The many, many events and actions necessary for the abolition of slavery, they would rightly say, were still to come, and they were loaded with contingency. Victory in the gag rule fight was no guarantee that slavery would be ended; some would add that the fight was, at least by this time, a sideshow. Economic issues had been the main focus of these panic-and-depression years, and, insofar as the issue of slavery was concerned, it was the annexation of Texas, not the gag rule, that brought it center stage. As to the development of public opinion against the "Slave Power," the issue of the right to petition and the clampdown on discussion of slavery in the House was rather "abstract," it would be said. The public would need the raw meat of personal and emotional scenes, like those that would come with the enforcement in the North of the new fugitive slave law after 1850. Then the citizens of Boston—for example—would have to watch, helpless, while federal troops sent by President Pierce at a cost of $100,000—huge, in the dollars of that time—to "insure the execution of the law," would march the escaped Virginia slave Anthony Burns to the wharf to be put on a ship and returned to his owner and to slavery in Virginia. *That's* the kind of thing that makes the public's blood boil, makes new converts, and really dramatizes the evil of the Slave Power, some would say. At least, the public needs not parliamentary arguments about the ancient right of petition but the sort of thing that would happen in 1856 when, after Charles Sumner's Senate speech on the crime against Kansas, the South Carolina congressman Preston Brooks would come over to the Senate and beat Sumner with his cane until Sumner collapsed with his head covered with blood—and all across the South citizens *rejoiced* in the beating, lionized Brooks, and sent him canes marked "Hit him again!" *That* was the sort of thing that really dramatized the evil of the Slave Power.

No doubt there is some truth in these points, putting the gag rule, and Adams's campaign against it, in perspective. But terrible and dramatic episodes of violence occur, alas, on all sides, and through all history, in all parts of the world. Both troops and mobs act for many different, and clashing, purposes. There would be terrible killings by the Confederate Quantrill gang and Missouri bushwhackers in Lawrence and elsewhere in Kansas, but there would be terrible killings by the abolitionist John Brown and Kansas jayhawkers in Pottawatomie and elsewhere, too. One still must ask about the social principles that people defend, and at the last that comes not to bullets, fists, canes, or bombs, but to arguments, convictions, and values, and to the lasting institutions built out of them. The new republic that John Quincy Adams's parents had helped to get started in the New World had extracted from the Old a principle of law, and of republicanism as the way to decide the law, that was to have its great test—testing whether this nation, or any nation so conceived, should long endure—growing out of the issue of slavery. Republicanism meant that the government should rest not on tribal emotions or arbitrary will but on law, and law on the institutions of the people's representatives, engaged in mutual deliberation, and that deliberation should rest upon the great conversation of the People, carried on in freedom. The gag rules were violations of the very principle of republican government, demonstrating the greater violation, human slavery, behind them. Adams himself, a competent if not a disinterested judge of the matter, wrote in a letter that this—the defeat of the gag rule—was the first clear victory over the Slave Power in the United States.

Adams was an old man who would not live to see the other steps taken, through all the contingencies, that would finally end American slavery within an enhanced American union. He would hand on the torch, as it were, to others—to the younger House colleague he most admired, Joshua Giddings; to his son Charles Francis Adams; to the Massachusetts senator Charles Sumner, who would come to admire and follow him in his last days; and perhaps we may say symbolically to a greater leader than these. As for now, on the elephant's tooth ivory cane there would be inscribed the date December 3, 1844. The eleven-year-old boy who heard his father tell the captain of the *Boston* to "fight them to the last extremity," now a seventy-seven-year-old man, had won at last, and the gag rule was dead.

PART XIII

EPILOGUES

41/THE GREAT SAUSAGE OF FREEDOM

OUR STORY IS ENDED, but the larger story has barely begun. During the next seventeen years of turbulent American history the lives and careers of veterans of the petition fight would be woven into the repeated political battles on the subject of slavery that, interrupted by some lulls and truces, grew larger, fiercer, and more and more central to the national drama, and ended in a conflict no longer of words and ideas but of bullets and of blood. Or rather, ended, after that war, with the amendments that abolished slavery, affirmed racial equality, restored and bolstered the Union, and completed the work of the founders.

The candidates for president of the United States in the decade and a half before the Civil War would consist almost entirely of veterans of the gag rule fight in the House and the petition fight in the Senate, flavored with a sprinkling of generals from the Mexican War. Politics through that period generated, piece by piece, the elements that would one day go into the making of the decisive agent of the resolution of the slavery controversy, the Republican Party.

The first and essential proto-Republican component might be said to have emerged within the story told in these pages, in the Whig insurgency of 1842. The two Joshuas, and the others, with John Quincy Adams as their great ally, out of their own pocket, and their own conscience, formed the select committee known as Abolition House, and, defying their own party's leaders in the Whig-controlled Twenty-seventh Congress, put opposition to slavery above all other commitments.

The battles over slavery in the new territories acquired from Mexico, and the other events of the late 1840s and the 1850s, would generate at each stage new elements of the eventual, or the actual, Republican Party. And they would push others in the opposite direction—including, as one extraordinary example, our old friend who had "the blood of the king-killing Roundheads of the reign of Charles the First flowing in his veins"; whose Puritan and New England ancestors by his own claim were "never backward in the struggles of liberty"; who swore to "live upon a handful of parched corn and a cup of cold water, with God's blessing on honest independence sooner than surrender one jot or tittle of those great principles of liberty which he had sucked in with his mother's milk": Caleb Cushing of Massachusetts. Cushing would leave the Whigs for the Democrats; would be appointed attorney general by Democratic president Franklin Pierce; and in that post would be the great national overseer of the enforcement of the fugitive slave law, and in fact would introduce procedures that made its enforcement more rigid.

How had Caleb Cushing, from Harvard, from Massachusetts, indeed from Newburyport, where in youth he had been an acquaintance of William Lloyd Garrison and a friend of John Greenleaf Whittier; Caleb Cushing, who had entered politics as a supporter of John Quincy Adams, come to this pass? How had this learned man, who had drunk deep from the wellsprings of Western learning, and had been marinated in the experience of republican New England, got himself into this position?

Cushing's career represents a development complementary to the extruding of antislavery proto-Republican elements at one end of the political squeeze: the discharge of anti-antislavery politicians at the other. When our story started, both Caleb Cushing and Joshua Giddings were Whigs; by the late 1840s, neither was. They had exited in opposite directions. Most of the anti-antislavery ex-Whigs who became Democrats—for example, Henry Wise and Frances Pickens, both of whom would go on to hold high office as Democrats—came from the South. But not Caleb Cushing.

One can see the beginnings of the later trajectory of Cushing's career in episodes in these pages. His defense of republicanism, of New England, of Massachusetts, of Adams, was in truth less a defense of the principled substance than an expression of collective egotism—of individual egotism projected onto the collective, as are so many patriotisms and tribalisms. Cushing's defense of himself projected into New England was the mirror image of Waddy Thompson's defense of himself projected into the South.

Cushing had a high intelligence, but in addition to his fine mind and excellent education, he had an enormous ego, a kind of legalistic rigidity, and a fundamental lack of sympathy with the broader reaches of humankind, especially with that portion of it that has a black face. His sympathetic biographer, Claude Fuess, had to grant that Cushing "looked upon negro servitude as an economic system which the Southern plantation owner should be allowed to maintain if he so desired; and it must be admitted that he considered black men as members of an inferior and subject race."

As attorney general, Cushing issued an opinion that the Missouri Compromise had been unconstitutional, violating the "equal treatment of states." (This is a common notion in proslavery argument, that to be antislavery is to treat the slave states unequally compared to the free states.) He also issued an opinion that free black persons, not being regarded by the federal Union as citizens, were not eligible for passports. He was still attorney general when the Dred Scott case first came to the High Court. Chief Justice Roger Taney, who would in 1857 render that notorious decision, including the dictum that under the Constitution the members of the Negro race (not just slaves—all black persons) "had no rights which the white man was bound to respect," consulted Cushing, and accepted his legal reasoning. Fuess, again, concedes: "If Taney, as seemed likely at one time, had died in 1856, and Cushing, who was the best available candidate, had been appointed Chief Justice, the 'Dred Scott decision' would have been tendered in substantially the same spirit and language."

When Taney did render the decision, Cushing was in the courtroom, and heartily and completely endorsed it. And in the furor that followed he delivered a speech in Newburyport, printed and circulated widely, in which he defended Taney as "the very incarnation of judicial purity, integrity, science, and wisdom."

As the critical 1860 election approached, Cushing, now an active Democrat, was chosen to be the presiding officer at the party's tumultuous Charleston convention. When that convention split, and the Southern wing reconvened in Richmond, Cushing of Massachusetts was again chosen to preside, and was offered, but refused, the nomination as vice-presidential candidate on its ticket, headed by John Breckinridge. Cushing was now a close associate of William Yancey, Jefferson Davis, and the group that would before many months passed lead the secession. He defended their point of view up to the point of secession. He now was even further from the position of Lincoln and the Republicans than was Lincoln's key opponent Stephen Douglas. Cushing held not that people in territories should be allowed to choose slavery or freedom (Douglas's popular sovereignty) but that slavery *could not constitutionally be excluded* from the territories.

He fought hard in the campaign of 1860 against the Republican Party, and when it nevertheless was victorious, the lame duck Democratic president James Buchanan (Pierce's successor, the veteran of the petition fight in the Senate) sent Cushing to Charleston to try to prevent the South Carolinian secession. He was in his hotel in Charleston on December 20, 1860, when he heard the shouts heralding the South Carolina convention's decision to secede. He was given a courteous invitation to attend the formal signing of the secession document—*as the emissary of a foreign state.* It was a moment of choice for him.

Up to this point the irony in Cushing's curious history had been the contrast between his background and some of his early speeches, on the one hand, and the course of his actual later politics, on the other. But now, at last, the irony runs out. Cushing indignantly refused to attend the ceremony in that role. He heard the shouts and saw the fireworks when Governor Francis Pickens (another veteran of the gag fight, Calhoun's cousin, the Pickens of Mrs. Lindenberger's mess) said, "I declare the State of South Carolina an independent commonwealth."

"Then and there," Fuess wrote, "[Cushing's] choice was made. He was with the South to the verge of rebellion—but not beyond it." He returned to Washington to tell his tale to President Buchanan and the cabinet, and thereafter supported the Union, eventually becoming a Republican after all. Legality was on that side now. Some moral victories are aided just by the modest fact that our evildoings don't go as far as they might; Cushing's iniquity had its limits. (Lincoln promptly forgave him, but some radical Republicans never did. In 1876, after much water under the bridge and the healing of many wounds, President Grant nominated him to be chief justice of the United States Supreme Court; those who had not forgotten pursued him relentlessly so that finally his name was withdrawn.)

THE OPPONENTS OF THE gag rule were not, for the most part, major participants in the later events through which the fight against slavery moved to the center of politics. The estimable William Slade became the Whig and antislavery governor of Vermont in 1844, left the Whig Party for the Free Soil Party, and then left the slow work of politics altogether to take up the even slower work of education, where, under the influence of Horace Mann, he helped to plant young Yankee schoolmarms, carriers of New England culture, in the schools of Ohio, Indiana, Wisconsin, Michigan, and Illinois. Elizur Wright, Jr., of the Adelphi and Nassau Street, when he could no longer support his family working for abolition (movements intent on saving the world often being poor employers), put his Damascus-blade intellect to work on insurance reform, and in the end achieved such eminence as sometimes to be called "the father of life insurance." His religious views changed sufficiently for a biographer to use this alliterative title: *Abolitionist, Actuary, Atheist.* About Henry Stanton it needs only to be said that, in ironic contrast to the ordering of things in his heyday, one can now read in late-twentieth-century feminist books a gentle, generous comment (in a different voice) that there once was a man named Henry Stanton who deserves to be taken seriously in his own right, as more than simply the spouse of Elizabeth Cady Stanton.

The later life of the Grimké sisters and Theodore Weld was mostly private, but it is, perhaps, worth noting their response to the Civil War. The reader will remember that the Grimkés, and particularly Sarah, had condemned even the martyred Elijah Lovejoy for raising his pistol—for threatening to use "carnal weapons." But a quarter of a century later their attitude toward the terrible scourge of war was very different. "This blessed war is working out the salvation of the Anglo-Saxon as well as of the African race," Sarah wrote in a letter to Garrison. "The war is the holiest ever waged, is emphatically God's war, and whether the nation will or not, He will carry it on to its grand consummation, until every American enjoys the rights claimed for them in our Declaration of Independence."

Weld wrote: "I profoundly believe in the righteousness of such a war as this is, on its anti-slavery side." He believed in it, he said, "notwithstanding its mixtures of motives, and base alloy and half truths, and whole lies, thrown on the surface." For, underneath all of that, "the elements of a vast moral Revolution are all aglow, in the surging mass of a national religious revival, better deserving the name than anything that has preceded it—Simple right is getting such a hearing as never before on this Continent."

And Angelina wrote to her son Thody: "You see how warlike I have become—O yes—war is better than slavery."

Avoiding liquor, coffee, meat, "etc.," eating graham crackers and milk, and exercising daily for decades, Weld would live on, an honored old man, until 1895, when he died at ninety-one. For five years the planet earth would manage simultaneously to support both Theodore Weld of the Lane debates of 1833 and Dwight Eisenhower of Normandy Beach in 1944.

As THE BATTLE OVER slavery moved to the center of Amercian politics, after 1848, the key figures came to be politicians. One might give as some obvious names the Democrat Salmon P. Chase of Ohio; and the Whigs Henry H. Wilson in Massachusetts, William Seward in New York, Charles Sumner of Massachusetts, Giddings's son-in-law George W. Julian in Indiana, and perhaps John Quincy's son Charles Francis Adams in Massachusetts, as well as Abraham Lincoln in Illinois, as representative of many others. Except for the very special case of the martyred Lincoln, they have not been given as much credit for their role in ending slavery as they deserve.

Part of the reason is exactly because they were politicians, working within the limits and mixtures and hard choices of politics in the real world. By the nature of their undertaking they could not be as "pure" as the agitating abolitionists; they had to deal with a broad electorate as it was and with existing institutions as they were.

At the core of their work was the building of a new major party. That new party, in sharp contrast to the Whig Party it replaced, would not avoid but would confront the inescapable issue of slavery, and it would make that confrontation the party's first and almost its sole defining element. But because it sought national victory as a major party, it would confront slavery only at the point and in the way that it could be resisted in the broad public of a democracy. The party would oppose the *extension* of slavery into the territories, which program could unite the high ideals of the moral rejection of slavery with other items that were not so elevated.

There is a remark of Bismarck's, quoted so often as to have become a cliché, that in order to appreciate either politics or sausages one should not inquire too closely into how they are made. The Republican Party in the 1850s was one of the great sausages of American politics. We have seen the original fixings cast up by the successive anti-gag and antislavery battles. But the ideological fixings, when the time came to put them together in 1854 and afterward, were still more diverse and gamier than the bits and pieces extruded by previous battles, and were by no means confined to the purest antislavery impulses, let alone to abolition.

Eric Foner, the historian who has done the most to analyze it, gave this summary of the ideology of the newly born Republican Party: "Resentment of southern political power, devotion to the Union, anti-slavery based upon the free labor argument, moral revulsion against the institution, racial prejudice, a commitment to the northern social order and its development and expansion—all these elements were intertwined in the Republican world-view." Notice the combination of worthy elements with much less worthy ones in that list.

The new party played upon a growing sense of sectional difference. It played upon (and added to) a growing hostility to the culture of Southern aristocrats, and it promoted a marked sectional pride: the dynamic free-labor North, in which in theory any man could make his way upward in the economic scale, was seen to be categorically superior to the slave South, with its degraded slaves, its static class of unambitious poor whites, and its tiny top layer of decadent plantation slaveholders. This stereotyped hostility and pride was accompanied by some conspiracy theory, which you can find plainly enough, for example, in Lincoln's famous debates with Douglas in 1858. Lincoln and other Republicans limned a portrait of a menacing and imperialistic Slave Power, which was seeking not only to protect slavery in the South (which the new party would not oppose), not only to extend it into the territories (which it would strongly oppose), but even to fasten slavery onto the North. "Stephen, Franklin, James, and Roger" (Douglas, Pierce, Buchanan, and Taney) must have conspired with each other; their actions are too neatly dovetailed to make the result they all want to result from the workings of chance. Are they not taking actions that, after the next step, will make it constitutionally impossible to exclude slavery from any state in the union?

To make an analogy from later history—Senator Arthur Vandenberg of Michigan in 1947 told President Truman and Secretary of State Dean Acheson that in order for Congress to be persuaded to pass the first measures of "containment" of the Soviet Union, Congress and the public would have to be frightened into it by a dramatized picture of an alarming, expansive worldwide communist power. Similarly, Republican orators in the 1850s frightened their audiences with the picture of a menacing Slave Power. The Slave Power threatened the North, threatened free white labor, threatened the common heritage of civil liberties and republican government. (Adams had long since prepared the way, especially on this last point; the fight on behalf of the right of petition and against the angry extremism of the gag, culminating in the gag *rule* in the seat of the common government itself, had shown to citizens of the free states the ugly face of an arrogant slave power corrupting the core of republican government: slavery and the right to petition, slavery and civil liberties, slavery and republican institutions, stood opposed. By the late 1850s there had been a great many more object lessons on the point.)

Although moral opposition to slavery was a potent ingredient in the Republican ideology—if you read Lincoln's speeches and letters 1854–1860 you will be impressed with his persistence in condemning the moral wrong of slavery, using the authority of the Declaration of Independence to do so—it was nevertheless not by any means the whole of it, or even a necessary item. Still less was there any required belief in racial equality. One could be quite opposed to slavery as an institution without being sympathetic to the actual human beings who suffered under it. Large numbers of Northern white citizens held such views, and the Republicans needed their votes. One could be fiercely opposed to the extension of slavery out into the Western territories without either opposing the institution as such (if they wanted it in South Carolina, okay) or sympathizing with slaves, and certainly without believing in racial equality; very large numbers of Northern white citizens held those views, and the Republicans needed their votes, too.

Notice that Foner included, side by side, in the elements of the Republican ideology "moral revulsion" against slavery and "racial prejudice." These first Republican politicians had to formulate antislavery appeals that did not depend upon any pure moral revulsion against slavery, or upon antiracism—indeed, that were entirely compatible with, and sometimes that even expressed, racism. Another theme Foner noted, "anti-slavery based upon the free labor argument," is to be distinguished, perhaps sharply, from antislavery based on moral revulsion. The Republicans could present the outrage of the expansion of slavery into the territories as primarily or exclusively the damage done thereby to white labor, free labor. This key feature—that expansion of slavery into new territory menaced the interests of free white labor—which had already been anticipated in the Free Soil Party, was a rather big chunk in the Republican sausage.

There was also, not so much in the final product as in the process of making it, nativism. The antagonism to Catholics and foreigners in the early 1850s was strong and pervasive enough as almost to have become the basis of the party that replaced the Whigs. The largely Protestant constituency for that attitude overlapped with the primary constituency of active opposition to the extension of slavery. It tells you something about this overlapping to notice that when the Know-Nothings (the nickname for the nativist party) captured control of the Massachusetts General Assembly, they passed the most forward-looking laws on race of any state. You can say, if you want to dramatize the point, that these "bigots" on one issue were strong opponents of bigotry on another. The political necessity for those composing a new major party was to separate the nativists most opposed to slavery (or the expanded territory for slavery) from the others, and to bring that part of the Know-Nothing movement into the new party.

All of this was not a work for moral purists. It was not a work for those whose main impulse is to be "right" themselves, and to keep their hands clean, and to feel their superiority to those who were not as "right" as they were. The Republican politicians had to put all the ingredients together into a political outlook that had strong appeal to the actual human beings with whom they dealt, and in very large numbers—enough to win the relevant elections, including the election for president.

Does that practical and realistic bent necessarily make these politicians less worthy than the abolitionists and reformers? Not necessarily. If the larger current of opinion, at least earlier in this century, in the textbooks and popular culture and even in scholarship, disparaged the abolitionists, and presented them as fanatics whose extremism helped to precipitate the war, a smaller countercurrent in later years, celebrating the abolitionists, has tended to put them on a higher moral plane than the political leaders who came later, because the moral commitments of abolitionists were "purer," less compromised—therefore "higher," making them better than the politicians. But, again, as Sportin' Life said in another connection, it ain't necessarily so. Politicians may get some moral credit for attending to what actually happens in the real world, and operating within its constraints in the attempt to change it. We know well enough the perils of their line of work, and the vices into which they may fall: dealing constantly with complexity and the limits of the possible, they may over time lose track of any original moral vision; dealing in the world of power, they may grow to love power, and want it for themselves, and never mind larger purposes.

But moral reformers have characteristic perils and vices, too. The vanity and egotism of humankind takes many forms. The moral reformer may deal in principles abstracted from any actual worldly effect, and sometimes even with a perverse worldly effect. The moralist's focus may be his own moral superiority for holding to such wonderful principles. It is a false morality indeed that places William Lloyd Garrison on a higher moral plane than Abraham Lincoln. In some cases the politician's work might be more commendable, although no judgment can be made in the abstract.

JOSHUA GIDDINGS'S CAREER AS one of those politicians bridged the earlier and later periods of antislavery effort. After his censure and reelection in 1842 he continued to serve the Western Reserve in Congress, and to be the most articulate antislavery member of the House—as an obstreperous Whig until the break in 1848, and after that, from 1848 to 1854, as the leader of the little band of Free Soilers. Then he would become one of the organizers of the new Republican Party, and he would serve under that banner until he had a heart attack in the hall of Congress, and in 1858 did not run for reelection.

He served in the House of Representatives for twenty-one years, under these varying party banners but always as a leader of the vigorous opponents of slavery. He participated in the great floor fights of that portentous time: the Wilmot Proviso; the elements of what became the "Compromise" of 1850—in particular whether California should be admitted as a free state and, to be sure, the fugitive slave law, of which Giddings was as would be expected an unrelenting opponent; the fight over whether "bleeding Kansas" should be slave or free; the Dred Scott decision of the Supreme Court. It fell to the House to discipline its member from South Carolina Preston Brooks, after his attack in the Senate chamber on Charles Sumner of Massachusetts, and also South Carolina congressman Lawrence Keitt, who had accompanied Brooks in the assault. Giddings's opinion is indicated by this sentence from his book, the colorful and not impartial *History of the Rebellion:* "Unfortunately, they [Brooks and Keitt] believed in the practice and habits of the South, and instead of maintaining the intellectual conflict, they had recourse to physical violence."

After the end of all gag rules in 1844, Southern representatives fought against the open discussion of the abolition of slavery at the next line of battle: the composition of committees and the organization of the House. They sought to arrange the memberships and chairmanships of committees so as to prevent the reporting of any petition or resolution on slavery. To do that they needed the office of Speaker, because the Speaker had power to appoint the committees and the chairmen. Therefore, in this period, there were three protracted and bitter battles over the speakership, with Giddings in the middle on the first two, in 1849 and 1855. The third, after his health had forced him to leave the House, was fought on the eve of the Civil War, in 1859. All three—complicated, extended, and fervent—foreshadowed in their parliamentary warfare and rhetorical bleeding the literal war with actual blood that would follow.

In 1849, Giddings and the small number of other Free Soilers in the House stunned the Whigs by not voting with them in the contest for Speaker. Too complicated to describe, the fracas went on for sixty-three ballots, and in the end had to be decided by surrendering the principle of majority rule. The House chose its Speaker, slaveowner Howell Cobb of Georgia, finally, in desperation, by *plurality*—by a majority of a *quorum* present, not of the total membership.

In 1855 there would be an even more protracted struggle—two months and 133 ballots—in which Giddings played an even more important role, and the choice this time, again in desperation by plurality, was the candidate from a free state, Nathaniel Banks of Massachusetts, who promised the Free Soil members that there would be an antislavery majority on the Committee on Kansas. This was a key moment in the emergence of the new Republican Party: the coalition in the House that supported Banks (who would be a politically appointed general in the Union army in the Civil War) was a last ingredient in the sausage.

In both of these contests the big issue was: how would the Speaker compose committees? Especially the Committee on the Territories. And a big question intertwined with that one was—respect for the right of petition. In the second contest, Giddings let it be known that his group would not support anyone who was not pledged to *sustain the constitutional right to petition.*

When Banks won, Giddings (by then the oldest member of the House) administered the oath to him, and did so in the following way, as Giddings described it, speaking of himself in the third person:

> He walked into the open air in front of the Speaker's chair, and, taking a position some thirty feet from him, desired that officer to raise his right hand, which he did, and the oath was administered in a loud voice, according to the form practiced in New England from the time of the Pilgrims.

In the aftermath of the first of the contests over the speakership, Senator Sumner wrote to Giddings: "John Q. Adams said to me that you were the most valuable member of Congress. He said the truth."

THE REPUBLICAN CONVENTION OF 1860 in Chicago, the second in that party's history and the first to nominate a winner, at first rejected Giddings's effort to restore to the platform a reference, like the one in the first party platform in 1856, to the self-evident truths of the Declaration of Independence as the foundation of the nation and of the party. Giddings, an old man now, "unwilling to sit in a convention that hesitated to reassert the cardinal truths on which the Government was founded," thereupon left the hall. A young New York delegate, George William Curtis, who later said he felt as he saw Giddings leave that "the original impulse of the party was leaving the convention in his person," urged him to stay and took the initiative to add the reference to the Declaration in another place in the platform. A speech by another delegate swept the convention, and the reference to the Declaration was restored. Giddings returned to the hall, and "ten thousand voices," according to Giddings's son-in-law George Julian, "swelled into a roar so deafening that for several minutes every effort to restore order was in vain." The new party had been reestablished, for the moment at least, on the principled foundation for its historic role.

42 / ALL THE WHILE— INDIVIDUAL CONSCIENCE AT WORK

AMERICAN SLAVERY IN 1835 was a formidable institution which appeared to be, for reasons given in the early pages of this book, invulnerable. It could never be abolished.

And yet in 1865, just thirty years later, the Thirteenth Amendment to the Constitution did abolish American slavery: "Neither slavery nor involuntary servitude . . . shall exist within the United States. . . ." The formal equality, as citizens, of black persons (or rather of all citizens, without regard to race), which would in 1835 have seemed even less likely of achievement, was affirmed by the Fourteenth Amendment in 1868. And the right to vote, which the resistant segments of the white population would have been the most reluctant to grant because it meant a shift in the foundation of power, was formally guaranteed to all citizens, regardless of race, by the Fifteenth Amendment in 1870.

In order for those amendments to be enacted a giant rebellion had to be put down by force of arms, in a grisly war that represented, on the surface, the collapse and the failure of the free republican institutions whose tortured workings have filled these pages. The republic reached a moral impasse which the peaceful institutions of republican lawmaking could not resolve. On the election of a "Black Republican" to the presidency of the United States in November of 1860, some slave-state officials—among them Francis Pickens and James Henry Hammond of South Carolina, who had shared mess at Mrs. Lindenberger's thirty years earlier, and who were now, respectively, governor of and senator from South Carolina—set about, as promised and as threatened, to take their state out of the Union. That secession and the secessions and withdrawals that followed were the culmination of the blockades, gags, "secessions," and walkings-out of earlier times; they were in a direct intellectual line from the outlook developed at mess in that shared lodging house in 1835 and the actions of the previous summer and fall and in the ensuing Congresses. If that one subject is touched upon: burn the pamphlets; stop the mails; stone the speaker; close the hall; repudiate the petition; gag the petitioners; shut the door; knock the man down; leave the chamber; secede from the Union.

The new president in his Inaugural Address in 1861 would carefully explain to his "dissatisfied countrymen" that "the government will not assail *you* . . . *you* have no oath registered in Heaven to destroy the government, while *I* shall have the most solemn one to 'preserve, protect, and defend' it." He sent provisions to Fort Sumter; the secessionists opened fire; "the government" defended the Union. As he would say after four years of war, in his Second Inaugural Address, "Both sides deprecated war; but one of them would *make* war rather than let the nation survive; and the other would *accept* war rather than let it perish."

"And the war came." The war when it "came" was far more destructive than anyone had foreseen. As Lincoln went on to say in his Second Inaugural: "Neither party anticipated for the war, the magnitude, or the duration which . . . it attained." It was a terrible war, and the measure of its destruction is not completed by the counting of the dead and wounded.

It does not, however, dishonor those who died or make light of that destruction—rather, the opposite—to insist that out of this terrible scourge of war there did come an extraordinary constructive achievement. An American in the decades before the war might have desired three great but deeply conflicting goods: to end slavery, to vindicate the Union, and to avoid a fratricidal war. Only the first two would be attained in the end, but those two, apparently irreconcilable, were attained, and gave deep meaning to the war.

The whole of the immense event of which the Civil War was a part did *not* represent, at a deeper level, a breakdown, but rather a fulfillment, and a giant advance, of the nation's free institutions. The war was part of a larger process through which those institutions were not only continued but markedly reformed.

One part of that achievement was the objective for which it was originally fought, the preservation of the Union. All of the other advances that accompanied and followed the war were brought about, the war notwithstanding, with the continuity of the constitutional union never broken. We number our presidents and our Congresses consecutively from the first ones in 1789 down through the sixteenth president, Abraham Lincoln, and the Thirty-sixth, Thirty-seventh, and Thirty-eighth Congresses (from all or part of which the gentlemen of the South had withdrawn) to the current president and the current Congress. We held elections not only in 1860—which led to the rebellion—but also in 1862 and 1864, while the troops were fighting; in 1864 we held an election for president in the midst of the warfare. Not many republics have held real elections under those conditions, and not many governmental systems of any kind have held together under the kind of ferocious bloody division the United States experienced in 1861–65. No president made himself a dictator; no military leader overthrew the government; no irreconcilable band of guerrillas took to the hills; no government in exile fled to South America. The nation did not split apart, or require constitutional reorganization as a Second Republic. Americans in the comfortable security of a prosperous and long-established republic late in the twentieth century would be reminded again, at the end of the Cold War, by the fissiparous chaos in the empire of their erstwhile adversary the Soviet Union and in many other places on the globe, how fragile those human constructs, governmental systems, really are. Any particular *form* of government is a frail and changeable product of human beings; it is not written in the necessities of nature.

In persisting through the rebellion the new nation not only preserved but also strengthened the Union, and did so not for herself alone but for the cause of republican government worldwide. Republics—governments by the people—in particular were thought to be, until the United States came along, especially vulnerable to change, chaos, division, and overthrow. A republic of continental size was thought to be impossible. It was a primary work of the founders, and particularly of James Madison, to think through how and why that presumption could be proved wrong, by the designing of republican institutions that would serve a continent-sized nation and that would last. The breakup of the formerly United States would have proved the critics right; the victory in the war not only avoided that conclusion and helped to vindicate republican institutions to the world, but also strengthened the Union. We were now unambiguously one country.

To preserve the Union, to establish against challenge its formal perpetuity, was not a small accomplishment. But there was more. During the war, in 1862–63, the objectives came to be much enlarged, from Union to Freedom and Equality. Out of that enlargement of the war's purpose would come the Emancipation Proclamation, and the Civil Rights Act of 1866 and the Reconstruction Acts of 1867, and above all the three constitutional amendments we have named, changing the nation forever.

A modern historian, David Potter, acutely sensitive to the cost of the war, argued that though the war "saved the Union and freed 4,000,000 slaves . . . it can hardly be said that these immense values were gained at a bargain. For every six slaves who were freed, approximately one soldier was killed; for every ten white Southerners held in the Union, one Yank or one Reb died." No, it was not a "bargain." One should not dismiss or underestimate the terrible destruction and killing of the war. But one should also not underestimate, or wrongly identify, the stakes in the war, or the "gain."

The "gain" was a great deal larger, and is to be measured in another way, than is suggested by Potter's sheer weighing and balancing: how many white Southerners "held in" the Union; how many slaves freed for how many soldiers killed. It was not simply that a certain large number of *that day's* slaves were freed. These slaves' children and grandchildren were freed. It was the Day of Jubilee. And the masters and mistresses were freed. The *nation* was freed. Slavery was *abolished*. The *institution* was eliminated. A utilitarian numerical computation does not get at the deeper moral issue: a great evil, intrinsically wrong, was eliminated. The whole nation and its future life was made free, and its fundamental moral meaning was clarified, redefined. The moral integrity of the nation was vindicated. There was a "new birth of freedom."

The national actions taken during and after the war not only abolished slavery; they also established the formal claim of black persons to the full rights of citizenship. And the formal recognition of the equality—of the equal protection of the laws, of the right to vote—in a setting in which its primary application was to African-Americans foreshadowed its application to every other group; it eliminated formal racial exclusiveness at the level of the whole nation's laws and ideals, and made possible a new kind of nation, in which racial tribalism is formally excluded from its self-definition. The backsliding after 1876, and the mammoth problems associated with race down to the present day, should not blind us to the extraordinary accomplishment that preceded them. Imagine what it would have meant in the 1830s to know that within three decades slavery would be abolished! That the right of blacks to vote, and the equal protection of the laws, would be affirmed in the Constitution itself! At the time of this writing there are in the House twice as many black members as there were votes, in 1837, against a resolution that denied to black slaves even the right to sign a petition.

ONE MIGHT ARGUE THAT the whole slavery-abolishing, union-enhancing, race-equalizing action is the greatest of all the achievements of this country, in its more than two centuries. We do not ordinarily think of it that way, because our common national memory is saturated with the Civil War, and to call this result a great national achievement may seem to slight the terrible destruction. But one might respond that such an assertion serves rather to underline, as people at the time certainly did, the redemptive meaning of the appalling sacrifices. Not all wars mean much in the end, after all the blood is spilled, but that one did.

The superlative—the claim that the ending of American slavery within the enhanced American union is the greatest of all the accomplishments in our national history—is not necessary to our story, but still it might be argued that the rival claimants all depend decisively upon that one.

Of course, one may say that the nation's greatest accomplishment was its beginning and original definition. But the great original accomplishments of the late eighteenth century, when some honorable and able leaders seized the "fair opportunity," as John Adams called it, to construct upon this continent a new nation with a distinctive conception and a distinctive dedication, would not have begun to fulfill its purpose had it continued to countenance an enormous and morally perverse contradiction to that conception and that dedication. You cannot be very convincing as the Land of the Free if one of your major institutions is human slavery.

And—to skip forward to our more recent past—those great deeds of the Second World War and afterward in the Cold War, vivid in the experience of citizens still alive, in the middle and the last half of the twentieth century, could not have happened had American slavery not been ended with the union enhanced. A slave power would not have made a very good "leader of the free world."

Neither would a balkanized American continent. That series of unsordid acts, beginning with the Second World War and continuing after the triumph over the Nazis with the Marshall Plan and the long costly containment of the second totalitarian empire, in which long series of events the New World came to the rescue of the Old, would not have been possible, morally or materially, had the New World's significant newness been vitiated by the continuing presence of a radically barbarous relic of "old" institutions, or by the breakup of the union into warring smaller states.

The ending of slavery, and the formal affirmation of the equal rights of all citizens without regard to race, within an unbroken continental union, was not only the necessary completion of the work of the founders in the past, but also the necessary anticipation of the world role and moral mission of the nation in the present and the future.

~

HOW DID SUCH A prodigious national accomplishment come about? We have already said that one could answer that territorial expansion, in the backhanded way that history often works, was the primary cause of the American confrontation with slavery. The territory added to the United States in the late 1840s was larger than either the thirteen original colonies or the Louisiana Purchase. This immense new stretch of land had something of the function of the District of Columbia in the petition drive, except that it was huge, and—from the point of view of the United States—new and open to formation. Throughout this vast territory the issue was pressing and unavoidable: what would these territories/states be, slave or free? There had been territorial expansion, and a consequent debate about whether new territory should be slave or free, before the 1840s, but without provocation of a lasting major political contest with issues involving slavery at the center, as did the territorial expansions of the late 1840s and the 1850s. What had intervened to make the change? The events told about in these pages had intervened. Dozens of speakers, pelted with eggs and rocks, and hundreds of pamphlets and books, and thousands of petitions with hundreds of thousands of signatures, and a passionate romantic best-seller, and eventually even a handful of congressmen in the nation's Capitol itself, had explained and explained and explained why slavery was a sin, a wrong, a moral evil, a violation of Christianity and of American ideals. They had also explained, in contrast to many of the opponents of slavery who had preceded them, that racial inequality was a violation of Christian and American ideals, and that the end of slavery should not be brought about by moving black persons somewhere else.

Of course the amendments that ended slavery were made possible by the victory of the Union armies. But the long argument over slavery and freedom in America's free institutions defined what was done with that victory.

Although the tough-minded historian or political realist in a later time might say that all that arguing and petition-signing and parliamentary maneuvering was merely verbal froth, that is not what the defenders of slavery—themselves certainly realists—thought of it. The apprehensions of John C. Calhoun, who knew his Puritan/Yankee enemies partly because he had lived among them and partly because he resembled them, were significant and revealing: if there is a constant drumbeat of moral argument, Calhoun said, eventually it begins to have its effect, even upon those who initially reject the argument. Calhoun did not say but somewhere within himself must have known that that will happen—*if* that argument is sound. If it has resonance in the makeup of the hearer, as the argument against human slavery and racial inequality did to any American republican, including Southern slaveholders. It had a resonance within the American community of which they were a part. If they were not themselves, immediately, and on the surface, affected, their neighbors would be; their wives would be; their children would be. A person can have at the same time latent in his makeup more than one response to a question—for example, more than one idea about race and slavery. A group of people, a culture, certainly has many ideas on the same topic, diverse and contradictory, simultaneously present. Argument and persuasion, and the changing of the cultural atmosphere, can elevate one idea and subordinate another. Calhoun had said to Adams, when they had their talk when they were both members of Monroe's cabinet, before Calhoun gave his dismissive answer to Adams's praise of Rufus King's attack on slavery, that those were "noble" ideas. If they were noble, might he not someday entertain them himself? If he and his colleagues did not fear that this kind of thing could happen, why did they respond so fiercely to some words on a paper, to some signatures by schoolmarms and preachers? They saw all that petitioning and arguing as a potentially dangerous enemy, and they responded. They *over*responded, and by that revealing overresponse, they inadvertently strengthened the position they opposed. They gave Adams and others the evidence and the occasion to dramatize the conflict between slavery and the core American ideals of civil liberty; they provided Adams the opportunity to show both the intransigence and the imperialism—that is, the willingness to reach an imperious hand into the core of the common life—of what a public would begin to see and fear as the slave power.

THE EVANGELICAL REFORMERS WHO were central actors in achieving the great end of abolishing slavery were often oversimple in interpreting how it would come about—at first, they thought, simply by a change of heart, in a moment, individual by individual, as at a revival, as in the debates at Lane Seminary. Convert the slaveholders. In addition there was—implied—a markedly simple and foolish picture of human action in history, vastly overestimating the control of the whole field of actors that any person or group can or should have. Acting in society is not like carpentry, in which the actor has an inert piece of wood to saw and hammer to his heart's desire. Gardening is a better metaphor, because it acknowledges active independent forces to which the gardener must respond, but it is inadequate, too. All metaphors lie, essential though they be; none reproduces the truth of history and human society. The plants and the soil and the weather, although outside the gardener's control, do not talk back to him or her. Do not have minds and wills of their own. People do; your foes, and the indifferent, and the confused, and your comrades—sometimes comrades are the most difficult—do. And as they think and talk back and act in ways you cannot control they create a new situation to which you must respond, and they to you, and then another round and another.

IN SUCH A MULTIGENERATIONAL, many-handed accomplishment it is not simply those who have the result as their conscious purpose who make a contribution; others do, too, on the side, in backhanded ways, sometimes even perversely. The indifferent, the self-occupied, the only vaguely committed, the persuaded but frightened, the conflicted, the great numbers whose attention is elsewhere, may make their contributions to the result by mitigating their resistance, by shifting slightly their responses, by some brief appearance of the better angels of their nature. They may be helped to do those things by clarity of moral definition by the reformers, by skillful redefinitions by the politicians, by the influence of a changed atmosphere. Despite all the indifference and selfishness and racism that one could find in the nineteenth-century American population (in the twentieth-century population, too, of course, and in other countries as well), there was, mixed with everything else, a little spark of the sense of justice on slavery and even on race, from the churches and from the enlightenment/founding heritage and from natural humaneness; some leaders and some events (including a war) could fan that spark for a moment into a flame. Abraham Lincoln said, according to his own notes for his speech, when he addressed the local colonization society out in Illinois, and traced the history of the attack on slavery, and celebrated the action of heroes like Wilberforce: "*All the while*—individual conscience at work."

And the "foe" is part of the field of human will that makes for the result. Defiant and romantic fire-eating was far from being the only strand in the makeup of the many-layered body of secessionists. The opposition to the eventual national achievement was by no means total. Along with all the resentments and defiance there were lasting attachments to the union even among those who had broken from it, and human attachment to its Northern citizens. Part of the American South *did* know, deep down, though rejecting it on the surface, that (as the new president said in his First Inaugural) we were not enemies but friends, that though passion might strain it should not break the bonds of affection, that the mystic chords of memory stretched from shared battlefields and shared patriot graves to living hearts and hearthstones North and South.

And in addition to the attachments to the Union and Northern brethren there was significant Southern awareness that slavery was morally indefensible. American Southerners living in the midst of the institution knew its wrongness existentially in a way the Northerners could not. Mary Chesnut, the wife of a highly placed Southern slaveholder, would write in her diary with some disdain about those Yankee churchwomen who condemned slavery out of their book-reading. What did they know, compared to the real knowledge that thousands of Southern women had, of the real horrors of the institution? As at Lane Seminary, so throughout the history of race and slavery in the United States, some of the most clearly seen and deeply felt condemnations of the wrongs came from white Southerners.

And Americans South and North shared the attachment to republicanism as the original national ideal. One reason the United States has been able to accomplish what it has is that it had as its core a sound original ideal; the nation was not built on ethnic loyalties or on sheer territoriality, or on raw tribal interest, nor even on shared history alone—all of these on their ugly side engender exclusion, irredenta, lasting hatreds—but rather on a worthy, humane, and inclusive ideal. And the Southerners, of course, shared that ideal. One of their number, a slaveholder, had given it its most potent expression. Another, a slaveholder, had been the most important single framer of its constitutional expression. Yet another, also a slaveholder, had been its indispensable original hero-president. Though on the fringes at Carolina College and in some writers and in some passages of James Henry Hammond and others there were some antirepublican aristocratic and hierarchical conceptions, those were not dominant or successful. Calhoun, in our story, indignantly rejected the imputation to him of the political philosophy of John Locke's antiliberal *opponent*. The great bulk of Americans in the Southern regions were *republicans,* not aristocrats; indeed, they would try perversely to justify their peculiar institution by reference to the superior republicanism it undergirded (for white men). Race was to be an American Dilemma, but it was a *dilemma*. There was a moral embarrassment, set up by the original American creed, shared by Northerner and Southerner alike. There were, and perhaps are, nations, lacking those ideals, in which racial exclusion and domination are no dilemmas at all, but straightforward expressions of national will. Not the United States, North or South.

The rebels in the American Civil War, who had in them along with all that made them rebel also an attachment to the Union, to their Northern brethren in the common country, and to its republican ideals, did not continue to fight or to nurse the most fundamental hatreds. The United States did not turn into the Balkans of the Western Hemisphere.

The story of the United States after the Civil War, especially with respect to the treatment of black citizens, and perhaps in the relationship of the sections, and in some other ways as well—as measured by the original

American moral project—is not a worthy one, not one of which we can be proud. We focus upon the failures, and that is as it should be. But we should not therefore deny or take for granted the great triumph that preceded those failures—that allowed us as a nation, if one may put the point a little flippantly, to fail at a higher level. Think of John Quincy Adams, an admirable though difficult and crotchety man with the root of the original American ideals in him, musing in his diary at the time of the Missouri debates in 1820, saying that a union reconstituted on the fundamental principle of emancipation would be "vast in its compass, awful in its prospects, sublime and beautiful in its issue." Here we are, living with, although we would never so describe it, that sublime and beautiful issue.

Not all of the hands that contributed to that "issue" were Northern. Bruce Catton, near the end of the third volume of his history of the Civil War, *Never Call Retreat,* tells of the graciousness both of Grant and of Lee at the time of the surrender at Appomattox, and of a trusted lieutenant who came to Lee urging him not to surrender but "simply to tell his army to disperse, each man taking to the hills with his rifle in his hand: let the Yankees handle guerrilla warfare for a while and see what they could make of that." Lee said no; Catton quotes the officer who made the suggestion as having said that Lee "showed me the situation from a plane to which I had not risen, and when he finished speaking I had not a word to say." Catton himself continued: "The unquenchable guerrilla warfare this officer had been hinting at was perhaps the one thing that would have ruined America forever . . . the long, slow-burning, formless uprising that goes on and on after the field armies have been broken up, with desperate men using violence to provoke more violence, harassing the victor and their own people with a sullen fury no dragoons can quite put down. The Civil War was not going to end that way (although it was natural to suppose that it might, because civil wars often do end so) and the conquered South was not going to become another Ireland or Poland, with generation after generation learning hatred and the arts of back-alley fighting." In the 1990s a reader could, unfortunately, name other places as examples. Catton credited Lee, and the substitution of the romanticism of the Lost Cause for the ugly reality of guerrilla warfare. We might credit as well those aspects of the South mentioned above: the better angels of our nature, in their Southern expression. Catton observed: "Civil wars have had worse endings than this."

It is true that the nation's performance on racial issues in the century after the Civil War would include an appalling retreat, a capitulation in 1876, the imposition of black codes and Jim Crow, lynchings and the Klan. It is true that there would be what historian C. Vann Woodward called a "lost hundred years"—that it would be necessary for the nation, with great strain and difficulty, to enact in 1964 a Civil Rights Act that did not do much more than repeat what had been enacted in a civil rights act almost a century earlier, and in 1965 a Voting Rights Act that did no more than to endeavor to make real what had been formally guaranteed by the Fifteenth Amendment ninety-five years earlier. It is true that the sections were scarred by the war in ways that have not vanished over a century and a quarter later. It is true that the North turned aside and went about moneymaking and (mostly) forgot the plight of freedmen, but nevertheless used the bloody shirt from the war, and the "treasury of virtue" stored up in its alleged moral superiority, to dominate. It is true that the white South, defeated, constructed a new pattern of racial domination. But for all that, the nation did not fall apart, did not abandon republicanism (democracy), did abolish slavery, and did affirm the formal equality of black persons (or rather of all persons born or nationalized in the United States, of all citizens without regard to race, color, or previous condition of servitude). It did strengthen the Union, and make itself more clearly one nation. Winning the war by itself would not have been sufficient to accomplish these things, if the opposition to them had been unconditional, unambiguous, absolute, unified, fueled by a radically contrary philosophy and a bottomless hatred. But it was not.

AFTER ALL IS SAID, the greatest credit for producing this national achievement should be granted to those who intended it. Surely there is something perverse in arguing otherwise.

The giant multitude of four million black Americans, radically shut out of the political process that has been the focus of this book, nevertheless must have been a powerful silent presence with effects that we cannot begin to measure. They have perforce not been part of our story, which has taken place within political structures from which they were almost entirely excluded. But that they were an important influence upon it, in a way that was not true, for example, with British abolitionism, we may surely infer. The moral imagination even of individuals, let alone of groups, is rarely vivid and powerful enough to enter deeply into the situation of another without any actual human encounter. The social distance that the laws of the slave states were designed to preserve did not prevail altogether in the country as a whole, as the exchange between Adams and Waddy Thompson about the laws of South Carolina reveals; we may infer many effects of the presence of slaves and ex-slaves and free black persons upon the attitudes of the citizens who could take an active part in the politics of these events. The program of "colonizing" freed African-Americans, which might have sounded plausible and acceptable in a superficial all-white setting, would be shown by any serious encounter with black Americans to be ridiculous, demeaning, and unjust. And the rejection of the program of the American Colonization Society by some vocal and energetic white Americans would be a decisive turn in American history. Garrison would learn to reject the specious appeal of colonizing by his association with free blacks in Baltimore; Weld would have his immediatism confirmed by living with black Americans in Cincinnati and in New York. The testimony of ex-slave James Bradley would be one of the potent moments in the Lane debates. The Convention of American Women Against Slavery that was held in May of 1837 in conjunction with that annual meeting of the American Anti-Slavery Society that stepped up the petition drive brought together some seventy black and white women—more black participants, it appears, than the men's meetings characteristically included, one of whom was the Grimké sisters' particular friend and correspondent Sarah Mapps Douglass. The role of black abolitionists, Frederick Douglass and others, has been outside our story and mostly outside our time period, but in the larger story, by the Civil War they would have become peculiarly potent participants in the argument of a putatively free society And in the war itself there would come the immense human fact of the slaves of the South crashing through the lines of the Union forces, presenting themselves as an unavoidable reality, the ironical "contraband" of this war, expecting freedom.

Among the white Americans to whom active politics was then confined, one must list two groups, and not just one, and add the moral stuff, fragile and limited and perhaps small but still real, in the broader American population that gave their work a certain resonance.

The first to be listed are those folk at the Adelphi and Lane Seminary in the 1830s and after—the immediatists, together with all those matrons, daughters, farmers, clerks, woodchoppers, shopkeepers, and mechanics whom they persuaded to sign petitions. They were a necessary but not a sufficient moral agency for the ending of slavery in America. They brought forward a worthy strain in American culture. For slavery to be ended there had to be some individual human beings who did what they did. However complicated we want to make our historical reflections on what did happen, in the event, thereafter, we should not lose sight of this thread: there were some people—a very small number, on the margin of society, condemned and harassed—who nevertheless made it the first order of their life's business to oppose American slavery, and to insist that it was a grotesque evil that should be eliminated, and that in a little over thirty years, it was.

But another group, harder to romanticize, was also essential to that result. These are the politicians, discussed in the previous chapter, who operated in the great main arena of politics, and amid complexities had as a primary purpose opposition to slavery for reasons of its radical injustice. Their work comes mostly in the years beyond the reach of this story, but they, too, are a key to the ending of slavery.

These politicians depended upon their predecessors, the evangelistic abolitionists, for the pressure, for the agenda-setting, for the raised consciousness that made their work possible; but the abolitionists depended in their turn on these politicians, to gear their affirmations into the machinery of the real world. Both were necessary to bring about the total result, putting the elements together—ending slavery within an enhanced constitutional Union. John Quincy Adams at the end of his life was both an agent of those abolitionists and a harbinger of those politicians.

ADAMS HAD CONTINUED TO serve in the House, fighting and grousing and arguing and doing his duty to the republic as long as he could, for more than three years after the end of the gag rule. When Texas was annexed to the Union he said it was the end of Western civilization, more or less. He was reelected, by a generous margin, in 1846, when he was seventy-nine. His handwriting got so shaky that he had to stop writing his journal, after a tidy sixty-five years. He slumped over his desk in the House on February 21, 1848, when he was eighty years old, and, as we noted in an earlier chapter, died in a committee room of the House two days later. In the Capitol in Washington one can go to see the marker on the spot in the old House chamber where Adams was working at his desk when he was stricken.

It is altogether fitting and proper, for the purposes of the inner history and collective memory of the American people, that on the day that Adams fell there was seated, in a not very good seat in the back row of the House chamber, a young Whig congressman from Illinois serving his first and only term, a messmate of Joshua Giddings at Mrs. Sprigg's lodging house, Abraham Lincoln.

Appendix

Sessions of the House of Representatives, 1835–1845

Twenty-fourth Congress

(141 Democrats, 95 Whigs)*
James K. Polk (Dem., Tenn.), Speaker

1st session: Dec. 7, 1835–July 4, 1836

Dec. 16: John Fairfield (Maine) petition to end slavery in the District of Columbia

Dec. 18: James Henry Hammond (S.C.) motion for nonreception of Fairfield petition

Dec. 18: George Briggs (Mass.) petition referred to Committee on the District of Columbia

Jan. 4: John Quincy Adams introduces petitions and enters petition fight

Feb. 1: Hammond speech: "Slavery can never be abolished"

Feb. 4: Henry Laurens Pinckney (S.C.) proposals regarding petitions about slavery

May 18: Pinckney Committee report, includes first gag resolution

May 25: Adams gagged

May 26: **Pinckney** proposals, including gag resolution (all petitions about slavery automatically laid on the table), enacted (117–68)

June 9–10: All-night meeting of the Commiteee of the Whole on the admission of Arkansas and Michigan; voted on June 13

[Nov. 1836: Martin Van Buren (Democrat) elected president]

*Counts include both members in case of a succession of a Whig by a Democrat or a Democrat by a Whig during the term, and disregard other parties than Democrat and Whig.

2nd (lame duck) session: Dec. 5, 1836–March 3, 1837

Dec. 26: Speaker Polk rules resolutions of last session (including gag) had expired

Jan. 9: Adams presents petitions

Week of the Slaves' Petition:

Feb. 6: Adams offers petitions from nine women from Fredericksburg and from slaves; Waddy Thompson (S.C.) makes motion censuring Adams

Feb. 7: Caleb Cushing (Mass.) speech defending Adams

Feb. 9: Adams defends himself in speech on right of petition

Feb. 10: Attempt to censure Adams fails; House votes not to receive slaves' petition presented by Adams

Feb. 12: House denies slaves' right of petition

[Martin Van Buren inaugurated president March 4, 1837]

Twenty-fifth Congress

(129 Democrats, 119 Whigs)
James K. Polk (Dem., Tenn.), Speaker

1st (special) session: Sept. 4–Oct. 16, 1837

(Special session called by Van Buren to deal with the panic; petitions "discarded from consideration")

2nd (long) session: Dec. 4, 1837–July 9, 1838

Dec. 20: William Slade (Vt.) moves to refer antislavery petition to select committee with instructions to bring in bill for abolition in the District; pandemonium; Southerners walk out of House, hold their own meeting.

Dec. 21: John **Patton** (Va.) **gag** resolution (similar to Pinckney and Hawes, includes territories) enacted

Mar. 5: Resolutions on annexation of Texas from Ohio and Alabama legislatures; petitions and resolutions on Texas referred to Committee on Foreign Affairs

June 13: Committee on Foreign Affairs report recommends laying all Texas resolutions on the table

June 15: Adams starts long speech about Texas

July 7: Session ends with Adams still holding floor

[Administration calls off plans to annex Texas]

3rd (lame duck) session: Dec. 3, 1838–March 3, 1839

[Giddings new member]

Dec. 12: **Atherton** gag resolution (based on states'-rights principle) enacted (126–78)
Dec. 13: attempt to suspend the rules
Feb. 12: Giddings's Anacostia bridge speech
Feb. 25: Adams proposes constitutional amendment abolishing hereditary slavery in the United States, prohibiting admission of new slave states, and abolishing slavery and the slave trade in the District of Columbia

Twenty-sixth Congress

(126 Democrats, 116 Whigs)*
Robert T. M. Hunter (Independent, Va.), Speaker

1st (long) session: Dec. 2, 1839–July 21, 1840

Dec. 2–16: Long battle over N.J. delegation and speakership. Adams: "I will put the question." R. T. M. Hunter of Virginia finally chosen speaker
Dec. 30: Henry Wise (Va.) moves to suspend rules of House to enact a permanent gag rule (almost a month of speeches on slavery and petitions follows)
Jan. 18 & 20: William Slade speech urges immediate abolition throughout United States
Jan. 22: Waddy Thompson proposes two-step gag; Adams proposes amendment radically altering Thompson's proposal
Jan. 28: William Cost Johnson (Md.) moves an amendment to Adams's amendment, a simple permanent gag, which is passed 114–108 and becomes **Rule 21**

[The Whigs win the elections of 1840–41; William Henry Harrison is elected president, John Tyler vice-president; Whigs will control both houses]

2nd (lame duck) session: Dec. 7, 1840–March 3, 1841

Dec. 9: Adams's resolution against adopting Rule 21 laid on the table
Feb. 13: Waddy Thompson proposes appropriations to support the

*Close call; NJ disputed.

Seminole War; Giddings's speech attacks Thompson's proposal as an effort to recapture escaped slaves

[Feb.–March 1841: Adams argues *Amistad* case before the Supreme Court; William Henry Harrison inaugurated President March 4, 1841]

Twenty-seventh Congress

(144 Whigs,102 Democrats)
John White (Whig, Ky.), Speaker

1st session, special: May 31, 1841–Sept. 13, 1841

(Extra Session called by President Harrison before he died in April; first time Whigs control)

May 31: Attempts to block adopting Rule 21; John White of Kentucky elected Speaker
June 3: Adams attempts to rescind Rule 21
June 7: House refuses to renew Rule 21
June 10: Ingersoll (Penn.) motion to reconsider defeated
June 14: Fornance (Penn.) motion to reconsider prevails
June 16: Stanly (N. C.) resolution to extend rules of last House (including Rule 21) adopted

2nd (first regular) session: Dec. 6, 1841–Aug. 31, 1842

Dec. 6: Adams attempts to block adoption of Rule 21
Dec. 7: Previous rules adopted pending report of committee
Dec. 10: Committee report laid on table

Trial of Adams

Jan. 21: Adams presents a petition from Habersham County, Ga., asking that he be replaced as chairman of the Committee on Foreign Affairs because he had a "monomania" on people of color.
Jan. 22: Adams uses speech in his defense to attack slavery
Jan. 24: Adams presents petition to dissolve union
Jan. 25: Gilmer (Va.) and Marshall (Ky.) present resolutions censuring Adams; Adams has clerk read first paragraph of Declaration of Independence
Jan. 26: Wise speech attacks Adams and defends slavery
Jan. 27: Adams demands right to defend himself
Feb. 1: Adams maintains chair of Committee on Foreign Affairs
Feb. 2–7: Adams's speech defending himself
Mar. 21: Giddings's resolutions regarding the *Creole*

Mar. 22: Vote in favor of censuring Giddings; Giddings resigns

[Summer 1842: grand reception for Adams in Weymouth and Braintree; July 11, 1842: Adams turns 75; Nov. 1842: Adams wins by 52 percent margin as a Whig in redrawn district; Democrats are making large gains, will control 28th Congress]

3rd (lame duck) session: Dec. 5, 1842–March 3, 1843

(Whigs' last control)

Dec. 5: Adams gives notice that he will move to rescind Rule 21

Dec. 6: Adams submits the resolution which is neither laid on table (85–93) nor put to a vote(84–99)

Dec. 7: Adams's resolution again is neither laid on table (90–91) nor put to a vote (91–93)

Dec. 8: Adams's resolution once more is neither laid on table (92–95) nor put to a vote (95–100)

Dec. 12: After the House begins to organize, Adams's resolution is finally laid on table, 106–102

[In February 1843, Adams tries to present, and, failing, leaves on his desk for the rest of the session, the waterwheel-shaped Great Petition asking that the people of Massachusetts be forever separated from all connection with slavery]

[July 11, 1843: Adams turns 76; July–Aug. 1843: Adams's trip to upstate N.Y., with celebrations; November 1843: Adams's trip to dedicate the observatory in Cincinnati, and to other points in Ohio, Kentucky, and Pennsylvania, with more celebrations, returning just in time for the new Congress]

Twenty-eighth Congress

(142 Democrats, 82 Whigs)
John W. Jones (Dem. Va.), Speaker

1st session: Dec. 4, 1843–June 17, 1844

Dec. 4: Dromgoole (Va.) moves adoption of previous rules; Adams's motion to exempt Rule 21 is rejected (95–91)

Dec. 20–21: Adams presents petitions; Adams moves that there be a committee on the revision of the rules

Dec. 21: Wise announces he will no longer participate in fight over the gag rule, and that he will vote to let Mr. Adams have his committee

[In early January 1844, Adams's committee reports a revision of the rules omitting the gag; two months of argument follow; an attempt to reintroduce the gag into the committee report is defeated 86–106, and an attempt to reconsider is defeated; but then the House declines to adopt the committee report itself 87–88, and the old gag is still in force]

[November 1844: Democrat James K. Polk wins the presidential election]

2nd (lame duck) session: Dec. 2, 1844–March 3, 1845

Dec. 2: Adams gives notice that he will submit resolution to rescind Rule 25

Dec. 3: Adams submits the resolution; a motion to lay on the table is defeated 81–104; and then Rule 25 is rescinded 108–80

[July 11, 1845: Adams turns 78]

Notes

CHAPTER ONE

A Personal Introduction

PAGE

3 "the Pearl Harbor of the slavery controversy": Freehling, *Road to Disunion*, p. 308.

6 "Antebellum specialists . . . might flunk an exam": Freehling, *Road to Disunion*, p. 308.

CHAPTER TWO

A Formal Introduction:
Completing the Work of the Founders

9 The speech by Hammond given on February 1, 1836, is reprinted not only in the *Globe* but also in Hammond, *Selections*, pp. 15–50.

The figure for the federal government's receipts in 1830 comes from *Historical Statistics of the U.S.*, Part 2, p. 1104. While the receipts were $24,800,000, the expenditures were only $15,100,000. Different times.

10 Lincoln's New Haven speech was given on March 6, 1860; the quoted passage appears in the Library of America collection, *Abraham Lincoln: Speeches and Writings 1859–1865*, p. 135.

12 "vulgarity": "The vulgarity of their tactics almost surpasses belief," McPherson, *Battle Cry*, p. 789.

16 The percentage of slaves in the Northern colonies is taken from Table 1 in the appendix to Kolchin, *American Slavery*. The cited figures are the estimates for 1750. The 1770 figures show New York at 11.5 percent, New Jersey 7 percent, Rhode Island down to 6.5 percent.

"The Contagion of Liberty" is the title of Chap. 6 in Bernard Bailyn's *Ideological Origins of the American Revolution*. The effect of the contagion on slavery is the consideration in the first part of that section.

19 Madison's letter to Jefferson about the Constitutional Convention,

including his remark about the inflexibility of South Carolina and Georgia, was dated October 24, 1787, and is printed in Rutland et al. (eds.), *Papers of Madison,* Vol. 10, pp. 206–19.

20 The historian Don Fehrenbacher . . . "diffuse, sporadic, moralistic, and tentative": Fehrenbacher, *Slavery, Law, and Politics*, p. 15.

In fact, William Freehling . . . "important American laws on any subject": Freehling, *Road to Disunion*, 136.

21 The old version of the federal ratio, with the word "white" in it, is quoted in Robinson, *Slavery in the Structure of American Politics 1765–1820*, p. 199.

I used an ancient pamphlet copy of the Constitution of the Confederate States of America, dated 1861, available still—presumably continuously since it was issued—in the University of Virginia Library.

"It is as though . . . lifted their eyes": Fehrenbacher, *Slavery, Law, and Politics*, p. 15.

CHAPTER THREE

An Indignant Rebuke to the Fanatics of the North

28 The quotations from Calhoun's reference to "Our Thermopylae" can be found in Wilson (ed.), *Papers of Calhoun*, Vol. 13, p. 105.

29 The theme of South Carolina's "morbid sensitivity" on the issue of slavery is fundamental to William Freehling's book on the Nullification Controversy, *Prelude to the Civil War.* The phrase appears first in the Preface, p. x: ". . . I hope to show that the nullification impulse was to a crucial extent a revealing expression of South Carolina's morbid sensitivity to the beginnings of the antislavery campaign. . . . I hope the following analysis of the acute anxieties surrounding the mere discussion of slavery during these years of transition will help to explain why South Carolina led the South in a suicidal assault on the federal Union a generation later."

33 Did Hammond or Calhoun initiate Hammond's motion *not to receive* the petition? Calhoun biographer Charles Wiltse, in his *John C. Calhoun Nullifier, 1829–1839*, Vol. 2, held that it was a common project of the Calhoun mess; Merrill Peterson, in *The Great Triumvirate*, p. 201, said that "[Calhoun's] young friend James H. Hammond, a freshman congressman in the South Carolina delegation, had been given charge of the campaign in the House to close the doors to the abolitionists." Charles Sellers, in his biography of Polk, says that "Calhoun decided to provoke a decisive struggle . . ." and his messmate Hammond "moved that the [first] petition not be received" (Sellers, *Polk,* Vol. 1, p. 312).William Freehling in *Prelude to Civil War,* on the other hand, felt that Hammond acted on his

own, and a claim in Hammond's own diary five years after the event that "it was a bold move made more from impulse than reflection" would tend to support the Hammond-alone view—if you believe Hammond. William Freehling's later book, *The Road to Disunion: Secessionists at Bay*, pp. 312–19, draws upon Hammond's extensive correspondence in the Library of Congress—Hammond saved everything, Freehling says, with a historian's gratitude—to discuss the much larger question of whether there was, as sometimes charged, a Great Slave Power Conspiracy already here in 1835, with Hammond's motion a deliberate act by the conspirators to provoke the North, unite the South, divide the country, and save slavery. The answer is no, not exactly. There *was* much inflammatory congratulatory correspondence to Hammond along those "conspiratorial" lines—but the letters came *after* his motion, not before it, proposing it. The source of these letters was the circle of Thomas Cooper, the radical secessionist professor at Carolina College in Columbia, who had been Hammond's professor and mentor. From a Cooper (and Hammond?) point of view, Calhoun was too timid, moderate, compromising. Presumably the motion was Hammond's own impulsive idea, but it came from a hothouse of such ideas.

34 Information about the boardinghouses comes from Young, *Washington Community 1800–1828*; from Green, *Washington: Village and Capitol, 1800–1878*; and, in particular, from Goldman and Young (eds.), *United States Congressional Directories 1789–1840*, from which comes the cast of characters in Mrs. Lindenberger's (p. 293).

CHAPTER FOUR

Here the People Rule

42 Information about the House came from Galloway, *History of the House;* Richards, *Life and Times;* Young, *Washington Community;* Alexander, *Sectional Stress;* Silbey, *Shrine;* and Green, *Washington.*

44 "Who but a slaveholder . . . in each others vicinity": Barnes and Dumond (eds.), *Letters of Weld and the Grimkés,* Vol. 2, p. 914.

Counting by James Sterling Young: Young, *Washington Community.* On p. 57 Mr. Young discusses "[t]he extraordinarily high number of resignations from the early Congress."

45 The numbers of new House members in the various Congresses appear in Richards, *Life and Times*, pp. 57–58.

49 The quotation from James Madison's jottings comes from notes he made for an article in the *National Gazette:* Rutland, *Papers of Madison*, Vol. 14. The quotation was brought to view by Drew McCoy in *The Last of the Fathers,* pp. 234–35.

CHAPTER FIVE

The Ramparts of the Green Mountains

52 William Slade made his character known by his speeches as recorded in the *Globe* and the *Register of Debates*, and sometimes more carefully printed in the *National Intelligencer*. His life and career, like those of the others in this story, are described in *Who Was Who in America* and the *Dictionary of American Biography*. And there is more about him in Crockett, *Vermont*, Vol. 3, and in Ludlum, *Social Ferment in Vermont*.

56 Henry Wise, who will appear in many other chapters, is described not only in *Who Was Who* and the *Dictionary of American Biography* but also in two biographies: Simpson, *Good Southerner;* and B. H. Wise, *Life of Henry A. Wise*. One can learn something from Henry Wise's own *Seven Decades of the Union*. He certainly made himself known in his speeches in the House.

59 "Mr. Slade . . . to a veritable fury": Burgess, *Middle Period*, p. 258.

CHAPTER SIX

Fiends of Hell, East

For the abolition movement I have consulted, in this chapter and the next and throughout this book, some of the newer books, written since the changes of the 1960s: Perry and Fellman (eds.), *Antislavery Reconsidered;* Perry, *Radical Abolitionism*; Dillon, *Abolitionists;* Stewart, *Holy Warriors;* Pease and Pease (eds.), *Antislavery Argument,* a collection of antislavery materials; and Duberman (ed.), *Anti-Slavery Vanguard*. But the purposes of this book were not served by entering into scholarly argument; I have tried to bypass those arguments, while respecting them. For my purposes these older histories and discussions of abolition were at least as useful as the new ones: Barnes, *The Antislavery Impulse;* Dumond, *Antislavery;* and Filler, *Crusade Against Slavery*.

65 I relied on two biographies of Whittier—Mordell, *Quaker Militant;* and Wagenknecht, *Whittier*—and on Whittier's own essays and reminiscences.

Bret Harte would write a parody of Whittier's "Maud Muller" in which the Judge, instead of passing by, *marries* Maud, with unhappy results; the parody's reversal of Whittier's last lines may have more inadvertent relevance than the original to many human situations, including American slavery:

> If some sad words of tongue and pen
> Are these: it might have been

Sadder by far are those we daily see;
It *is*—But hadn't Ought to Be!

66 The biographer of Whittier who quotes the lines "Forego thy dreams of lettered ease," applying them to Whittier, is Mordell, in *Quaker Militant*, p. 68.

68 Whittier's two accounts of the meeting in the Adelphi are found in *The Prose Works:* "The Anti-Slavery Convention of 1833," pp. 171–86, and "Anti-Slavery Anniversary," pp. 193–95.

70 I used an original copy of the *Declaration of the Anti-Slavery Convention* found in the Special Collections section of the University of Virginia Library.

72 Whittier, *Justice and Expediency,* in *Prose Works*, p. 25.

CHAPTER SEVEN

Fiends of Hell, West

82 There are two biographies of Theodore Weld (and nineteen—according to C. Vann Woodward—of John Brown. Can this be just?). The earlier biography is Thomas's *Theodore Weld*; the more recent biography is Abzug's *Passionate Liberator*. It is the better book, but makes too much of an effort to psychoanalyze its subject. Barnes and Dumond (eds.), *Letters of Weld and the Grimkés,* is particularly valuable.

83 Gilbert Barnes's *The Antislavery Impulse*, although sixty years old, is particularly valuable for the link between the Finney revivals and the new abolition. The abolition histories noted above provide information for this chapter, too.

86 Lane Seminary and the Lane debates are described in the biographies of Weld and in chaps. 6 and 7 of Barnes's *The Antislavery Impulse*. Lesick's *The Lane Rebels* is a short study devoted exclusively to that subject.

CHAPTER EIGHT

Yes, Sir, Worked by Steam

94 "by strewing . . . the boat dock": quoted in Barnes, *Antislavery Impulse*, p. 100.

The following quotes are all found in Wilson, *Papers of Calhoun*, Vol. 13:

98 Calhoun's response to President Jackson's message on incendiary pamphlets, pp. 7–9;

99 the report of the Calhoun committee on that exciting subject, pp. 53–67; Calhoun's proposed bill, pp. 67–69; his speech in reply to criticisms of that bill, pp. 147–65; "further remarks" on, pp. 166–69 and 234–36.

Calhoun's curious civil-libertarian argument is found in the same source, on these pages:

99 "the object of publishing," p. 56; "rests on the same principle," p. 56;

100 "a poor triumph," p. 56;

"done by the states already," p. 235.

102 The story of the pamphlet war is told briefly in Barnes, *Antislavery Impulse,* pp. 100–1, and at greater length in Nye, *Fettered Freedom*, pp. 67–85, and Eaton, *Freedom-of-Thought Struggle*, Chap. 8. I pick up the phrase "intellectual blockade" from one of Eaton's chapter titles.

CHAPTER NINE

Suffer Us We Pray You, Fathers and Rulers of Our Country

106 James Madison's original version of the clause on petitioning appears in Rutland, *Papers of Madison,* Vol. 10. A discussion of the significance of changes between his original proposal and the final form of the Bill of Rights appears in my own *Business of May Next*, Chaps. 17 and 18.

109 The story of Weld's travels is told in both biographies and in the notes and his letters in the Weld-Grimké collection.

Weld's account of his adventures in Circleville, in his letter to Elizur Wright, is taken from Barnes and Dumond, *Letters of Theodore Weld and the Grimkés*, Vol. 1, p. 207.

110 And so is the Fathers and Rulers petition, Vol. 1, p. 175.

111 The numbers of petitions and petitioners and the quotations about those numbers are taken from the *Fifth Annual Report of the Board of Managers of the Massachusetts Anti-Slavery Society.* (The meeting was held at Boston, January 25, 1837, in the loft of the stable attached to the Marlboro Hotel.)

CHAPTER TEN

I Would Have My Head Dissevered from My Body

115 "the most majestic . . . Satan": Potter, *Impending Crisis*, p. 98.

"a cast iron man . . . extinguished": Peterson, *Great Triumvirate*, p. 406. (Peterson himself says, on the next page, that "Calhoun appeared as the Calvin of American politics—a deductive reasoner to wrong conclusions.")

"Mr. Calhoun had no youth . . . any other man": Hammond, "An Oration on the Life, Character, and Services of John Caldwell Calhoun, Delivered on the 21st of November 1850, in Charleston, S. C., at the Request of the City Council," *Selections from the Letters and Speeches,* p. 244.

116 "intensely serious . . . 'whereas' ": Peterson, *Great Triumvirate*, p. 27.

The quotations from Calhoun in the Senate are taken from Wilson, *Papers of Calhoun*, Vol 13, on the days cited in the text:

117 "[T]he Senator from North Carolina . . . wait an answer," p. 27;

123 "We are here . . . distract our ranks," p. 73;

124 ". . .show these fanatics. . . . cease to agitate," p. 27;

"[T]his claim . . . commit ourselves?," p. 102;

"Under the decision . . . on such a contest," p. 111.

"profess high principles . . . absurdity": Peterson, *Great Triumvirate*, p. 302.

CHAPTER ELEVEN

The Greatest of All the Great Blessings

132 Calhoun's exchange with Senator Rives appears in Wilson, *Papers of Calhoun*, Vol. 13, pp. 389–91.

137 "seems to have succumbed . . . a myth": Bleser (ed.), *Secret and Sacred*, p. 304. Bleser also said, succinctly, that Hammond was "a tough-minded son of a bitch"; it is unlikely that any reader of his diary will disagree.

CHAPTER TWELVE

Am I Gagged or Not?

140 Henry Pinckney's background and career are described in Freehling, *Prelude to Civil War*, p. 182.

CHAPTER THIRTEEN

How Sleep the Brave?

154 "I have taken a very great fondness . . . for it": Letter dated August 19, 1774, in Butterfield (ed.), *Adams Family Correspondence*, Vol. 1, pp. 142–43.

John Quincy's faltering-hand draft letter to an English Quaker about the events of both April 19, 1775, and Bunker Hill appears as an extended footnote in Butterfield, *Adams Family Correspondence*, Vol. 1, pp. 223–24, to his mother's letter to his father, June 18, 1775, in which letter she quotes the Collins poem.

Emerson's "Concord Hymn" and Longfellow's "Paul Revere's Ride" should be found in almost any collection that includes nineteenth-century American verse.

158 John Quincy's disapprovals of the Bunker Hill celebrations are cited in the long footnote to his mother's letter of June 18, 1775, mentioned above, in the Butterfield, *Adams Family Correspondence*, Vol. 1, p. 224.

160 Information about the life of John Adams was drawn from the biography produced by John Quincy and Charles Francis and also from the modern biography by Page Smith.

161 Abigail Adams's famous letter dated March 31, 1776, with the passage "remember the ladies": Butterfield, *Adams Family Correspondence*, Vol. 1, p. 370.

164 The account of the trip across the Atlantic on the *Boston* by the Adamses, father and son, in February and March of 1778 is described in shorter pieces in J. Adams, *Diary and Autobiography,* Vol. 2, p. 271; the excitements of February 21, 22, and 23 are combined in one entry, pp. 275–77; the complaint about the general wetness is on p. 276. The story is told again in Vol. 4 of the same series, beginning with p. 6, with same adventures and excitements on pp. 13–14.

CHAPTER FOURTEEN

Duty. Duty? Duty.

167 "Death found him . . . him?": This quote appears in slightly different form in Howe, *Political Culture of the American Whigs*, p. 66; Bemis, *John Quincy Adams and the Union*, p. 538; and Clark, *John Quincy Adams*, p. 418.

Bemis's is still the leading biography of John Quincy Adams, pending a new one by Paul Nagel. Marie B. Hecht's *John Quincy Adams: A Personal History of an Independent Man*, a more recent one-volume biography, is a useful supplement to Bemis.

For this short sketch of Adams's career, and particularly for the election of 1828, I used not only the sources named above but also the older, lesser books by Morse and Seward, mentioned in the footnote in the chapter itself, and Clark, mentioned above, exactly because they reflect old advocacies rather than modern objective scholarship.

Two treatments of Adams of particular value, to supplement the biographies, are Richards's *Life and Times* and Howe's *The Political Culture of American Whigs,* Chap. 3. Adams, a "nonpartisan politician," is the first exhibit in Howe's collection of Whigs.

170 Was Jackson also the winner of a popular plurality? Insofar as there was a popular vote and count, yes. But in six states—Vermont, New York, Delaware, South Carolina, Louisiana, and Georgia—the electors were chosen by the state legislature, and there was no popular vote—zero. The Adams argument would be that since in those states taken as a group Adams did markedly better than Jackson in the choice of electors, he would

have achieved a significant popular margin as well, if there had been a vote; New York would have been particularly important. In other states the total vote was markedly lower than in the most recent state election. Two varieties of Adams's arguments can be found in older popular biographies: Morse: *John Quincy Adams*, in a Houghton Mifflin American Statesman series; first published in 1882, republished in 1910, pp. 168–73; and Seward (Lincoln's secretary-of-state-to-be, at the time of the publishing of this book governor of New York, "with the literary assistance of an able writer"), *Life of John Quincy Adams,* first published in 1849, republished by Kennikat Press in 1971, pp. 149–50. But the Jackson people certainly thought their man had received a popular, as well as an electoral plurality.
175 Leonard L. Richards's percentages of the popular vote for Adams and for Jackson in 1828, and the quotation about the "Indian haters" is on page 15 of Richards's *Life and Times of Congressman John Quincy Adams.*

CHAPTER FIFTEEN

Seized with Cramps

180 The quotation from Samuel Eliot Morison ("The veil has been lifted") is found on page 405 of his *Oxford History of the American People.*

The quotations from Adams's journal in this chapter all appear, on the date cited, in the short Nevins one-volume version, *The Diary of John Quincy Adams*:
179–80 King's speech and clenched fists, p. 226;
183 King's unhappiness at having his motives questioned, p. 229;
King's further unhappiness ("Doth Job fear God for nought?"), p. 232;
185 the praise of Calhoun on the cited dates, pp. 191 and 265;
186 the first conversation with Calhoun ("returning to the colonial state"), p. 228;
188–9 the second conversation with Calhoun ("applying only to white men") followed by Adams's extraordinary speculations ("taints the very sources of moral principle"), pp. 231–32;
191 the mulatto boy tortured, pp. 245–46.

The conversation with Baldwin of Missouri ("not violate but to redeem the Constitution") appears in Nevins, *Diary*, but in this case his editing omitted the passage I wanted to quote; the whole entry is found in C. F. Adams (ed.), *Memoirs of J. Q. Adams*, Vol. 5, pp. 209–11.

Another striking passage on race and slavery in Adams's journal can be found in the *Memoirs*, Vol. 5, pp. 4–7, a somewhat rambling but rich reflection on the Missouri Compromise, after its passage.

There are many additional comments of interest on race and slavery, and it is tempting to quote more, or to put together a little compendium. On December 27, 1819 (*Memoirs,* Vol. 4, p. 492), for just one example,

John Quincy made this prescient comment on Jefferson, the Declaration of Independence, and slavery:

> *Jefferson is one of the great men whom this country has produced, one of the men who has contributed largely to the formation of our nation's character—to much that is good and to not a little that is evil in our sentiments and manners. His Declaration of Independence is an abridged Alcoran of political doctrine, laying open the first foundations of civil society; but he does not appear to have been aware that it also laid open a precipice into which the slave-holding planters of his country sooner or later must fall. With the Declaration of Independence on their lips, and the merciless scourge of slavery in their hands, a more flagrant image of human inconsistency can scarcely be conceived than one of our Southern slave-holding republicans. Jefferson has been himself all his life a slave-holder, but he has published opinions so blasting to the very existence of slavery, that, however creditable they may be to his candor and humanity, they speak not much for his prudence or his forecast as a Virginian planter. The seeds of the Declaration of Independence are yet maturing. The harvest will be what West, the painter, calls the terrible sublime.*

One should read through all of these repeated statements in Adams's journal and speeches and letters deploring slavery, racial prejudice, and the treatment of blacks so that one does not overrespond to the mention—virtually the only such thing in the many, many volumes from Adams—remarking negatively on *Othello*. An article on this last (MacLean, "Othello Scorned: The Racial Thought of John Quincy Adams") features the latter, but in elaboration concedes the former.

CHAPTER SIXTEEN

A Direct Violation of the Constitution

199ff The quotations from Charles Francis Adams in this chapter are footnotes, on the days mentioned in the text, to his editing of his father's journal in *Memoirs of J. Q. Adams.*

210ff The quotations in the section on the admission of Arkansas all come not from the *Globe* but from the *Register of Debates*, for Wednesday and Thursday, June 8–9, 1836. Although in the real world the session continues into the morning of Friday, June 10, in legislative time, and therefore in the *Register*, it continues to be June 9. The reporter himself will occasionally note the hour—that it is 4:00 a.m., 7:00 a.m.; the congressmen in their speeches make repeated cries of weariness and complaints about the lateness of the hour. Caleb Cushing's speech in the middle of the night, arguing strongly in favor of Adams's motion to reject the provision in the Arkansas constitution "to make slavery perpetual" (as Cushing put it), is the high point of his antislavery phase; this speech would be printed and widely distributed. The conclusion of the matter is found in the *Register* for Monday, June 13.

CHAPTER SEVENTEEN

It Thrives and Fattens on the Distresses of the Country

214 Although for the most part I used either the one-volume Allan Nevins edition of Adams's journal *(Diary)* or the twelve-volume Charles Francis Adams edition *(Memoirs),* for Adams's account of the opening of the second session of the Twenty-fourth Congress I used the journal on microfilm at the Massachusetts Historical Society in Boston.

215 Adams's description of the House back in 1832—the tripping Mercuries, the gobbling manner of the clerks—can, however, be found in Nevins, *Diary of J. Q. Adams,* p. 430.

CHAPTER EIGHTEEN

The Strange Case of the Nine Ladies from Fredericksburg

CHAPTER NINETEEN

An Outrage That Has No Parallel in Parliamentary History

CHAPTER TWENTY

The Uttermost Edge of the Shadow of Indignity

CHAPTER TWENTY-ONE

He Mistook His Man

CHAPTER TWENTY-TWO

They Are Rights of Heaven's Own Giving to (Almost) Every Human Being

Chapters Eighteen through Twenty-two are taken almost entirely from the *Globe*, with supplements as noted from the *Register of Debates* and the *National Intelligencer.* They cover just one week, February 6–12, 1837, in the House proceedings. It was useful to have the two sources.

272 The standing committees and their chairmen in the second session of the Twenty-fourth Congress, which are compared, at the end of Chapter 22, to the votes for and against petitioning by slaves, are found in Goldman and Young, *United States Congressional Directories, 1789–1840*, pp. 308–15.

CHAPTER TWENTY-THREE

Secession

279 For Slade's attempt to make his speech at the start of the regular session of the Twenty-fifth Congress, and the "secession" of Southern members, and Congressman Rhett's use of that word to his constituents, I drew not only on the *Globe* but also on older histories, written back when they still told of these events: von Holst, *Constitutional History*; Wilson, *Rise and Fall*; Clark, *John Quincy Adams*. The quotations are from von Holst, Vol. 2: "paroxysm of rage," p. 263; Slade could not complete his sentence, p. 264.

CHAPTER TWENTY-FOUR

Sulphuric Acid in His Tea

284 I am grateful to Celeste Walker, of the Adams Papers project at the Massachusetts Historical Society, for, among other kindnesses, providing me with a list of the letters between Adams and Benjamin Lundy.
290 I have used a separate printing of the long speech that Adams delivered at the end of the regular session of the Twenty-fifth Congress, in fragments of the morning hour from June 16 to July 7, inclusive, printed by Gales and Seaton. I have drawn upon his introduction as well as his account.
297 "Mr. Adams . . . sulphuric acid in his tea": Emerson, *Journals*, Vol. 6, pp. 349–50.

CHAPTER TWENTY-FIVE

The Poor Clerk Was Nearly Frightened Out of His Wits

301 Weld's story can be followed not only in the two biographies already mentioned and in the abolition histories, but perhaps best of all in the two volumes of Barnes and Dumond, *Letters of Weld and the Grimkés*.
302 "By the final day . . . years of his life": Abzug, *Passionate Liberator*, p. 152.
303 "Let petitions be circulated . . . discuss, argue, persuade": Barnes, *Anti-Slavery Impulse*, p. 136. The next quotation—"Petitions were placed . . . by devoted volunteers"—follows.

The quotations from petitions are taken from petitions themselves, in Record Group 233 in the legislative branch of the National Archive.

305–6 Dumond's counting of petitions in the short session of the Twenty-fifth Congress and Birney's figures for the earlier period appear in Dumond's *Antislavery*, pp. 245–46.

306 "the 1838–39 petition campaign . . . in the District of Columbia": Magdol, *Antislavery Rank and File*, Chap. 5.

307 ". . . it was estimated . . . the State legislatures": Wilson, *Rise and Fall*, p. 273.

. . . Magdol in the 1980s . . . 107 in 1839–40: Magdol, *Antislavery Rank and File*, p. 56; and Magdol's article in Kraut (ed.), *Crusaders and Compromisers*, p. 46.

CHAPTER TWENTY-SIX

Adding One Injustice to Another

311 The story of women in the abolition movement, and specifically in the petition drive, is now the subject of scholarly, and perhaps some popular, attention. So in particular are the Grimké sisters. Wendy Venet, *Neither Ballots Nor Bullets,* gets a running start on its subject, women abolitionists and the Civil War, through dealing with the earlier period; see Chapter 1. Alma Lutz, *Crusade for Freedom*, deals with the earlier period more fully. The abolition histories and the biographies of Weld do deal with women's role, and the Grimkés. The collection of Weld-Grimké letters is particularly valuable; see the exchange between Weld and Whittier in New York, and Angelina and Sarah traveling in New England, and the Grimkés' letters to Henry Wright, on the subject of the women question, in Barnes and Dumond (eds.), *Letters of Weld and the Grimkés* (Vol. I, p. 414), noting particularly Whittier's argument to the sisters (p. 424).

318 Adams's discussion of the role of women in politics, including his exchange with Chairman Howard, on June 26–July 3, 1838, is printed not only in the *Globe* but in the separate pamphlet, referred to before, in which Adams caused his long Texas speech for that year to be printed.

CHAPTER TWENTY-SEVEN

Good Bad Books

325 *American Slavery As It Is* has been reprinted first by the Arno Press in 1968 and then by the Ayer Company of Salem, New Hampshire, in 1991. I used this last version, which copied the pages of the original 1839 edition of the American Anti-Slavery Society in all its confusing glory. Sarah Grimké's closing story appears on p. 24.

334 The Library of America edition of *Harriet Beecher Stowe: Three Novels*, in the chronology in the back (p. 1471), says that *Uncle Tom's Cabin* was reprinted in twenty-two languages.

CHAPTER TWENTY-EIGHT

Hisses and Murmurs; or, the Lion of Ashtabula

339 The most recent and valuable biography of Giddings is James Bremer Stewart, *Joshua R. Giddings and the Tactics of Radical Politics*. It supersedes the little "sketch" by Buell. But George Julian's biography still has value for its own reasons. Julian was Giddings's admirer, messmate, friend, protégé, and finally son-in-law, and was himself an active antislavery politician, as representative and then senator from Indiana. He had knowledge of his own of the politics of the time. Giddings tells the story of his first congressional days not only in his journal but also in shorter form in his *History of the Rebellion*; his son-in-law, George W. Julian, makes use of both sources, and added material of his own, in his biography, *Life of Giddings*.
342 The poems in which Whittier immortalized Atherton are found in his *Poetical Works,* Vol. 3, Anti-Slavery Poems, Songs of Labor and Reform: "The New Year," p. 67; "A Letter," p. 120.

CHAPTER TWENTY-NINE

Ending Slavery Within the Constitution

356 "I have had . . . on that subject": B. H. Wise, *Life of Henry A. Wise,* p. 61.
357 "And let me tell you . . . been fulfilled." B. H. Wise, *Life of Henry A. Wise,* pp. 61–62.

CHAPTER THIRTY

The Rule of the House

358 The story of the 1839 battle over the speakership can be followed in the *Globe*; personal accounts appear in Adams's diary and Giddings's journal. Of the secondary accounts in the biographies and histories, the most colorful is in Clark, *John Quincy Adams*, pp. 341–50, from which come the quotations in the text.
366 William Freehling describes William Cost Johnson, his place and his role, in *The Road to Disunion*, pp. 347–48.

370 I obtained a copy of "A Manual of Parliamentary Practice . . . by Thomas Jefferson" from the library of his university.

CHAPTER THIRTY-ONE

An Assortment of Whigs

375 Daniel Walker Howe's excellent *The Political Culture of the American Whigs* has been an important source for this chapter, and other parts of this book; "there was more debate . . . Republican party" is on p. 37.
377 I have also been helped by the articles collected in Michael Holt's *Political Parties and American Political Development from the Age of Jackson to the Age of Lincoln.* The Mississippi editor's breezy explanation of the demise of the Whigs is on p. 239.
384 The quotation from Henry Wilson comparing Giddings with Waddy Thompson ("from the same state . . .") appears on 534 of Volume I of Wilson's *History of the Rebellion;* the second quotation ("But Mr. Thompson . . .") is on pp. 534–35.

CHAPTER THIRTY-TWO

For Such Conduct What Language of Execration Can Be Too Strong?

The quotations from the *New York Tribune*:

388 "devoted to Literature . . . Measures": in "A Plain Talk to Whigs," Vol. 1, No. 1 (April 10, 1841), p. 2.
"We rejoice . . . the Rules of Congress.": in "Repeal of the Gag Law," Vol. 1, No. 53 (June 10, 1841), p. 2.
391 "So recklessly is this game played . . . too strong?": Vol. 1, No. 60 (June 18, 1841), p. 2.
394 "It is not to be disguised . . . these bad examples": Vol. 1, No. 57 (June 14, 1841), p. 2.
"[T]he better genius . . . has been effected," and the vote lists, including "in favor of perpetual anarchy . . .": lead editorial, "FACTION VANQUISHED!" Vol. 1, No. 61 (June 19, 1841), p. 2.
390 "vain, erratic, intellectual snob": Sellers, *Polk*, p. 54. Sellers also quotes, on the same page, an observer of the time as saying of Ingersoll that he "looks upon common people through gold specs and ornaments his fingers with costly diamonds."

CHAPTER THIRTY-THREE

I Know You Well, Sir, by Your Writings

399 The story of the *Amistad* can be traced in Adams's diary for January 30, February 20, February 24, and—particularly—March 29, 1841; in Richards, *Life and Times*, pp. 135–39; in Giddings's *History of the Rebellion* (not an unimpeachable source, but one of those lively contemporaneous works which are valuable for their revelations of the attitudes and outlook of the time, and from which one can garner valuable contemporary feeling); and especially in Bemis, *John Quincy Adams and the Union*, pp. 384–414. See also the letter from Kali (one of the *Amistad* captives) to Weld in Barnes and Dumond, *Letters of Weld and the Grimkés*, Vol. 2, p. 878, and the footnote.

Joshua Leavitt and his role are described in McPherson, "The Fight Against the Gag Rule."

405 Weld's joining the "lobby" can be followed not only in abolition histories and biographies of Adams but also in Weld's letters in the Weld-Grimké collection (Barnes and Dumond, eds.), beginning with his letter (gently asking for a little money) to Lewis Tappan (pp. 879–82), and continuing in the New Year's Day letter to his wife (p. 882), the letter about Mrs. Sprigg's and his visits to President Tyler and ex-president Adams (p. 884), and further letters to and from home (to p. 938).

CHAPTER THIRTY-FOUR

The Vexed Question Still Vexed

The quotations from the *New York Tribune* all come from Vol. 1—this was the first year of the *Tribune*'s existence—all in late 1841:

409 "The second session . . . Message delivered": lead editorial, No. 200 (November 30), p. 2.

414 "The advocates . . . completely outgeneraled . . . regularly floored": No. 211 (December 13), p. 2.

415 "Mr. Adams presented . . . against the 21st rule": No. 214 (December 16), p. 2.

416 "The rules . . . not, as stated, for fifteen days only": No. 214 (December 16), p. 2.

417 "It is difficult . . . a third war in 1841": Bemis, *John Quincy Adams and the Union*, p. 456.

CHAPTER THIRTY-FIVE

Monomania

The story of the smaller battle over Adams's chairmanship is not treated separately or as fully in most of the biographies as is his "trial," by which it was overshadowed and with which it was intertwined, but it can be sorted out in the *Globe*.

426 "Saturday Mr. Adams . . . no fault of mine": Barnes and Dumond, *Letters of Weld and the Grimkés,* Vol. 2, pp. 899–900.
429 "The fact that six . . . add to his triumph": von Holst, *Constitutional History*, Vol. 2, p. 470.

CHAPTER THIRTY-SIX

The Trial of Mr. Adams

Adams's trial is described in Bemis, *John Quincy Adams and the Union*, Chap. 20, and in the other biographies. Bennett Champ Clark's biography, although not scholarly and perhaps suspect on other grounds, gives the events the dramatic touch of one who has served in legislatures. Adams's own account in his journal begins *sotto voce* in the entry for January 24, 1842. Giddings's account in his *History of the Rebellion* has the flavor of immediacy and passion; although written almost twenty years after the event, it reflects a valuable personal knowledge. When Giddings had to resign from the House, after he had a heart attack in 1859, he supported himself in part by public lecturing, and his top set-piece lecture was "The Trial of Mr. Adams." The quotations from Giddings come from his *History of the Rebellion,* pp. 161–64.

433 "I[n] defending himself . . . 'I thank you. I accept your offer gratefully' ": Barnes and Dumond, *Letters of Weld and the Grimkés,* Vol. 2, p. 905.

CHAPTER THIRTY-SEVEN

Freedom Is the Premise

444 The *Creole* case is put in context with other like cases, and the fight summarized, by Giddings himself, in Chap. 11 of his *History of the Rebellion*—of course from his point of view. It is also described in his son-in-law's biography of him (Julian, *Life of Joshua R. Giddings*) and in Stewart's modern biography, *Joshua R. Giddings and the Tactics of Radical Politics*. All these sources and the abolition histories also tell the story of

Giddings's censure. The most important source for this chapter, in addition to the *Globe* itself, is William M. Wiecek's *The Sources of Anti-Slavery Constitutionalism in America 1760–1848*. Wiecek tells the story of the *extrajudicial* sources, the sources in politics, thought, popular argument, of the changed American constitutional doctrine about slavery, starting with the Somerset case in England, and including the work of Weld, Stanton, and Giddings. He tells the story of Giddings's House speech on the Creole case, and his censure, on pp. 214–15, in the context of the developing doctrine.

CHAPTER THIRTY-EIGHT
Some Musick in Canandaigua

457–8 The career of the senior Adams can be followed in his letters to his wife in Butterfield, *Adams Family Correspondence*; in his diary; and in Page Smith, *John Adams*. His little lament "Musick playing . . . which I have earned" is in his letter to Abigail of June 23, 1775, in the *Correspondence*, Vol. 1, p. 226.

461 The little article now known to have been written by Walt Whitman when John Quincy died was discovered, in the *New Orleans Crescent*, in this century and later printed as a tiny booklet with the title *The People and John Quincy Adams* by the Oriole Press of Berkeley Heights, New Jersey, in 1961. There is a copy in the Special Collections section of Alderman Library at the University of Virginia.

462 The reception for John Quincy Adams in the summer of 1842 is described in Bemis, *John Quincy Adams and the Union*, pp. 443–46.

The material about his trip to New York, Pennsylvania, and Ohio comes primarily from Adams's *Diary*, pp. 551–59; Canandaigua appears on pp. 553–54. There is a fuller account in C. F. Adams's *Memoirs of J. Q. Adams,* Vol. 12, pp. 388–405.

465 The story of the ivory cane appears in Bemis, pp. 447–48, and C. F. Adams's *Memoirs of J. Q. Adams*, Vol. 11, p. 543, and Vol. 12, pp. 15 and 82.

CHAPTER THIRTY-NINE
Whether in Peace or in Blood, Let It Come

The quotations from Giddings's *History of the Rebellion* are from pp. 216–18. Giddings, telling the story of Adams's exchange with Congressman Dellet, goes on to say, after Adams's stunning assertion "*Though it cost the blood of* MILLIONS OF WHITE MEN, LET IT COME: *Let justice be done though the heavens fall*": "These words rose from the lips of the aged patriot like the prayer of faith from one of heaven's anointed prophets: A sensation of horror ran through the ranks of the slaveholders: Dellet stood apparently lost in astonishment, and all were silent and solemn until the Speaker awoke members to the subject before them by declaring the *gentleman from Massachusetts was out of order.*"

The discussion of Henry Wise's sudden announced abandonment of the gag rule fight appears in Simpson, *Good Southerner*, pp. 59–60.

473 "reflected an effort to curry . . . ," Simpson, p. 59.
"might also have wanted to deflect . . . ," Simpson, p. 60.
"Wise eventually acknowledged . . . ," Simpson, p. 29.
474 Robert Ludlum's comment is from his "The Antislavery 'Gag-rule': History and Argument," *Journal of Negro History* 26 (April 1941), pp. 220–21.

CHAPTER FORTY

Io Triumphe

480 "In 1836 . . . voted it down, 21–11": Freehling, *Road to Disunion*, p. 351.
Freehling's sentence of conclusion—"when Slavepower demands . . . ," appears on p. 351 of *Road to Disunion.*
484 L. L. Richards's analysis of that vote is in his *Life and Times of J. Q. Adams,* pp. 176–79.
486 Bemis's claims that the ending of the gag rule was "a turning point . . ." appears on p. 447 of his *John Quincy Adams and the Union.*

CHAPTER FORTY-ONE

The Great Sausage of Freedom

491 The formation of the Republican Party: Eric Foner's *Free Soil, Free Labor, Free Men;* William Gienapp's *Origins of the Republican Party*; Chap. 9 of William Fogel's *Without Consent or Contract*.
495 Weld: "I profoundly believe . . . on this continent": from a letter from Weld to his old friend, now adversary, Charles Stuart, quoted in Abzug, *Passionate Liberator,* p. 276.
496 Eric Foner's summary of the ingredients in the new Republican Party—"Resentment of Southern political power . . ."—appears on p. 310 of his *Free Soil, Free Labor, Free Men.*
500 The quotation from Giddings about Brooks and Keitt is on p. 393, *History of the Rebellion.*
501 The story of Giddings and the restoration of the reference to the Declaration of Independence in the Republican party platform of 1860 is told in Julian, *Life of Giddings,* pp. 372–74.

CHAPTER FORTY-TWO

All the While—Individual Conscience at Work

504 "saved the Union . . . one Reb died": Potter, *Lincoln and His Party*, p. xx.

509 Lincoln's notes for his talk to the colonization society, on, perhaps—the editors are not sure—January 4, 1855, including the phrase "*All the while*—individual conscience at work," appear in Basler (ed.), *Collected Works of Lincoln,* Vol. 2, p. 299.

511 "simply to tell . . . make of that" and subsequent quotations: Catton, *Never Call Retreat*, pp. 430–31.

Sources

The Reporting of Congressional Debates

Because the purpose of this book is more to re-create an event for the general reader than to uncover something unknown for the specialist, the most important sources are those that attempt to supply simply a record—the daily record of congressional debates, of speeches and of parliamentary fireworks, in the houses of Congress, primarily the House of Representatives. So even with all their faults, warts, and sins the primary sources have been the *Congressional Globe*, with its appendices; the *Register of Debates*, and the journal put out by the same printing firm, the *National Intelligencer*; and the speeches sometimes separately printed by congressmen when the *Globe* or *Register* was thought not to be adequate, or for other reasons (e.g., "Speech suppressed by the Previous Question").

Our contemporary *Congressional Record*, the official reporting of debates and proceedings in Congress produced by the Government Printing Office entirely at government expense, did not yet exist at the time of this story—would not come into existence until 1873. The *Congressional Globe* and the *Register of Debates* were productions by private printers who also published political journals and other materials, who had their own political allegiances, and who competed with each other for selection as the printer to each of the houses of Congress. Sometimes the House and Senate, under different party or factional control, would have different printers.

The *Register of Debates,* although second in importance for this book, was the first in the field. It was published by the printing firm of Gales and Seaton, which also published the important journal the *National Intelligencer,* which, one might say, stretching things a little, was the *New York Times* of its era.

The *National Intelligencer*, one of the earliest newspapers published in the new capital city on the Potomac, had had as its first distinguished owner, printer, and editor Samuel Harrison Smith, friend of the new president Thomas Jefferson, onetime secretary of the American Philosophical Society, and husband of Margaret Bayard Smith, hostess and chronicler to the city in its first days. In 1810, Joseph Gales, Jr., a lively British-born journalist, bought the paper and brought his brother-in-law, the Virginian William Seaton, who would later be five times the mayor of the city, to join him in running it. So "Gales and Seaton" was an old (by this new country's standards) and well-connected printing firm, and the *Intelligencer* an old and well-connected paper, which, because the British admiral regarded Gales as a traitor, had the honor of having its offices destroyed when the British invaded Washington in the War of 1812. Gales and Seaton and their wives were important participants in the social life as well as the politics of the new capital city.

In 1824, Gales and Seaton added to their list of publishing ventures a current daily record of the speeches and debates in the two houses of Congress, to which they gave the name *Register of Debates*. If you will think about it you will recognize two things: one, the importance of such a record; and two, the difficulty of producing it.

Here was a new republic whose central institution was this debating society, or this pair of debating-and-negotiating-and-voting societies. These deliberative bodies. It was important, but difficult, to know just what congressmen and senators *said* in their arguments. Those bodies could themselves keep an official transcript of *actions*—motions made, passed, and defeated, and the votes, although even that would not be easy. But the speaking and arguing that surrounded those actions, although of the essence of republican government, were not captured in the frozen speech of print. A man named Thomas Lloyd from New York, who knew shorthand, had tried to record congressional debates in the flush of the excitement of the First Congress, in 1789–90, but from 1790 to 1825—we learn from the *Congressional Quarterly's Guide to Congress*—the debate in the House was recorded only in a haphazard way in "some of the better newspapers" and that in the Senate not at all. Gales and Seaton, as a further display both of their responsibility and of their enterprise, would later make the effort to collect such materials as there were for the First through the Twelfth Congresses; you will find the result in libraries when you want to examine something that happened in those first Congresses. But beginning with the Thirteenth Congress, in 1825, Gales and Seaton sent their own reporters to the two houses of Congress to record, as nearly verbatim as possible, the full daily record of the argument and speechmaking, and they published the result every day when Congress was in session in the *Register of Debates*.

Gales and Seaton were part of the ruling elite of early Washington. When they started the *Register of Debates,* the nation was in that period of its history, at the end of the Monroe administration, called the "Era of Good Feeling" because the old party system had disappeared with the fading away of the Federalists. Gales and Seaton and their publications were identified as "National Republican," after the dominant allegiance of that time, and then when the so-called second party system began to take shape, they were identified with the opposition both to the Jacksonians and to Calhoun. In the time of our story they were a moderate Whig printing firm.

In those days of a vigorous and rapidly changing print culture the rival factions each tried to have its journal. Calhoun was supported by the oft-quoted journalist Duff Green and his *Telegraph*. In 1831 the emerging Van Buren–Jacksonian party brought its journal into the field: the *Washington Globe*, published by the firm of Blair and Rives. John C. Rives was a printer who by 1850 would be running four steam-powered presses; the "Blair" of Blair and Rives was Francis P. Blair, a Jackson Democrat from Kentucky. The *Globe* was the publication in which Jackson announced that he would be running for a second term in 1832.

In 1833, Blair and Rives added another publication: the *Congressional Globe*, which would compete with the *Register of Debates* in giving a daily full (or more or less full) account of the speeches and debates in the two houses of Congress. The *Congressional Globe*, despite its faults, is the primary source for this book in part because it kept publishing throughout the nine years of the story it covers. Quotations in the text come from the *Globe* unless some other source is indicated. I have endeavored to give the date of the *speech* (not of the *Globe*'s publication) in the text in each case.

Although both publications would have an interest in keeping their daily record as straight and accurate as they could, the *Globe* was published by a Jackson-Democratic printer and the *Register* by a Whig printer. The partisanship of the printer may sometimes distort their accounts—certainly there were complaints—but other human frailties probably affected it more. Full speech texts submitted by congressmen would sometimes be published as an appendix.

Various Riveses would continue to be connected with the *Congressional Globe*, which was published until the *Record* came into existence in 1873.

The *Register of Debates* kept publishing only until 1837, so we have the *two* daily records only for the period 1835–37 in our story. But the *National Intelligencer*, the journal published by Gales and Seaton, kept going, and lasted indeed until 1869—an extraordinary length of time for a political journal. And the *Intelligencer* became a daily and would often carry speeches, communications from congressmen, and some debates; Whig congressmen like Adams and Giddings would use it to carry full texts, to correct the record, and to communicate to their audiences. And they would use Gales and Seaton to publish speeches as separate pamphlets.

Taking down those debates in shorthand, and then transcribing them for the printer, without the recording and transcribing devices that would come later, cannot have been easy; so have pity on those reporters. Joseph Gales either was accidentally present or had been asked by Daniel Webster to be present in the Senate when Webster gave his famous reply to Hayne, and Gales himself took down as much of it as he could in shorthand, and then got his wife's help to transcribe what he had written, and thus made available one of the most famous of American orations. One must be grateful to those reporters even with all their faults and errors.

The Adams Papers

There was another rich source for this book: John Quincy Adams's journal. It was an astonishing production, the granddaddy of all journals. I decided simply to call it his "journal" in the text, to avoid confusion over the various names that have been given to various editions of it.

Something of its sheer bulk may be suggested by the following editorial pyramid. I have most often used an edition edited by Allan Nevins and first published in 1928, republished in 1951 by Scribner's, given the title *The Diary of John Quincy Adams*. This is a hefty book, 575 large and very full printed pages. But it is only a small fraction of the work from which it was selected, Charles Francis Adams's edition of his father's journal, published between 1874 and 1877. That edition, called *Memoirs*, filled twelve large volumes, which have also been consulted for the present work at key points. And Charles Francis's edition, it turns out, was only a portion less than half of the available total, which is available on microfilm from the Adams Papers, and also has been consulted, and quoted, occasionally for the present book. The editors of the modern scholarly edition of the Adams Papers have estimated in print that their edition of John Quincy Adams's journal might run for twenty to twenty-four volumes, and now that they have worked on it further they say that it might run to thirty or more.

THE "FORMIDABLY COMPLEX," BUT ALSO altogether admirable, project of publishing the Belknap Press edition of the papers of the Adamses was a considerable resource for this book. The Adams Papers is the collective name for the entire editorial undertaking, for which the editor-in-chief was L. H. Butterfield and now is Richard Ryerson. It includes several series of books, each with its own editors, numbering, and index. The value of these volumes lies not only in the papers and letters they contain but also in the notes by the editors, which are sometimes extensive.

Bibliography of Works Consulted

Abzug, Robert H. *Passionate Liberator: Theodore Dwight Weld and the Dilemma of Reform*. New York: Oxford University Press, 1980.

Adams, Charles Francis (ed.). *Memoirs of John Quincy Adams, Comprising Portions of His Diary from 1795 to 1848*. 12 vols. Philadelphia: J. B. Lippincott.

Adams, John Quincy, and Charles Francis Adams. *The Life of John Adams*. Philadelphia: J. B. Lippincott, 1871.

Adams, John Quincy. *Speech of John Quincy Adams, of Massachusetts, Upon the Right of the People, Men and Women, to Petition; on the Freedom of Speech and of Debate in the House of Representatives of the United States; on the Resolutions of Seven State Legislatures, and the Petitions of More Than One Hundred Thousand Petitioners, Relating to the Annexation of Texas to This Union.* Washington: Gales and Seaton, 1838.

Alexander, Thomas B. *Sectional Stress and Party Strength: A Study of Roll-Call Voting Patterns in the United States House of Representatives, 1836–1860*. Nashville: Vanderbilt University Press, 1967.

American Anti-Slavery Reporter. John Greenleaf Whittier, ed. and publisher. Vol. 1, No. 6 (June 1834).

Ames, William E. *A History of the "National Intelligencer."* Chapel Hill: University of North Carolina Press, 1972.

Angle, Paul M. (ed.). *Created Equal? The Complete Lincoln-Douglas Debates of 1858*. Chicago: University of Chicago Press, 1985.

"The Anti-Slavery Record": Volumes 1–3 1835–1837. Westport: Negro Universities Press, 1970.

Bailyn, Bernard. *Ideological Origins of the American Revolution.* Cambridge: Harvard University Press, 1969.

Barnes, Gilbert Hobbs. *The Antislavery Impulse 1830–1844*. New York: D. Appleton-Century, 1933.

Barnes, Gilbert H., and Dwight L. Dumond (eds.). *Letters of Theodore Dwight Weld, Angelina Grimké Weld and Sarah Grimké, 1822–1844*. Gloucester, Mass.: Peter Smith, 1965.

Barone, Michael, and Grant Ujifusa. *The Almanac of American Politics 1990*. National Journal Inc.

Basler, Roy P. (ed.), and Marion Dolores Pratt and Lloyd A. Dunlap (asst. eds.). *The Collected Works of Abraham Lincoln*. Vols. 2–4. New Brunswick, N.J.: Rutgers University Press, 1953.

Bemis, Samuel Flagg. *John Quincy Adams and the Foundations of American Foreign Policy*. Westport, Conn.: Greenwood Press, 1981.

Bemis, Samuel Flagg. *John Quincy Adams and the Union*. New York: Alfred A. Knopf, 1965.

Birney, Catherine H. *The Grimké Sisters: Sarah and Angelina Grimké: The First American Women Advocates of Abolition and Woman's Rights*. Boston: Lee and Shepard Publishers, 1885.

Bleser, Carol (ed.). *Secret and Sacred: The Diaries of James Henry Hammond, a Southern Slaveholder*. New York: Oxford University Press, 1988.

Buell, Walter. *Joshua R. Giddings: A Sketch*. Cleveland: William W. Williams, 1882.

Burgess, John William, Ph.D., LL.D. *The Middle Period: 1817–1858*. New York: Charles Scribner's Sons, 1897.

Butterfield, L.H. (ed.). *The Adams Papers: Diary and Autobiography of John Adams. Vol. 2 (Diary 1771–1781)*. New York: Atheneum, 1964.

Butterfield, L. H. (ed.). *The Adams Family Correspondence*. Cambridge: Belknap Press of Harvard University Press, 1963.

Catton, Bruce. *Never Call Retreat*. Vol. 3. New York: Doubleday, 1965.

Channing, Steven A. *Crisis of Fear: Secession in South Carolina*. New York: W. W. Norton, 1970.

Clark, Bennett Champ. *John Quincy Adams*. Boston: Little, Brown, 1932.

Coit, Margaret L. *John C. Calhoun: American Portrait*. Boston: Houghton Mifflin, 1961.

Congress A to Z: A Ready Reference Encyclopedia. Washington, D.C.: Congressional Quarterly, 1988. 2nd ed. 1993.

Congressional Quarterly's Guide to U. S. Elections. Washington, D.C.: Congressional Quarterly, 1975.

Constitution of the Confederate States of America. Milledgeville, Ga.: Boughton, Nisbet & Barnes, State Printers, 1861.

Corwin, Edward S. *The Constitution and What It Means Today*. Rev. by Harold W. Chase and Craig R. Ducat. 14th ed. Princeton: Princeton University Press, 1978.

Crockett, Walter Hill. *History of Vermont*. Vol. 3. New York: Century History Company, 1921.

Current, Richard N. *The Lincoln Nobody Knows*. New York: McGraw-Hill, 1958.

Current, Richard N. (ed.). *The Political Thought of Abraham Lincoln.* New York: Bobbs-Merrill, 1967.

Declaration of the National Anti-Slavery Convention. American Anti-Slavery Society.

Dickens, Charles. *American Notes and Pictures from Italy.* 1842. Reprint. New York: Oxford University Press, 1957.

Dictionary of American Biography, American Council of Learned Societies. New York: Charles Scribner's Sons, 1928–58.

Dillon, Merton L. *The Abolitionists: The Growth of a Dissenting Minority.* DeKalb: Northern Illinois University Press, 1974.

Donald, David Herbert. *Charles Sumner and the Coming of the Civil War.* Chicago: University of Chicago Press, 1960.

Duberman, Martin. *The Anti-Slavery Vanguard; New Essays on the Abolitionists.* Princeton, N.J.: Princeton University Press, 1965.

Dumond, Dwight Lowell. *Antislavery; The Crusade for Freedom in America.* Ann Arbor: University of Michigan Press, 1961.

Eaton, Clement. *The Freedom-of-Thought Struggle in the Old South.* New York: Harper & Row, 1940.

Emerson, Ralph Waldo. *Journals of Ralph Waldo Emerson, 1820–1822.* Edward Waldo Emerson and Waldo Emerson Forbes, eds. Boston: Houghton Mifflin, 1911.

Faust, Drew Gilpin. *James Henry Hammond and the Old South: A Design for Mastery.* Baton Rouge: Louisiana State University Press, 1982.

Fehrenbacher, Don E. *Prelude to Greatness: Lincoln in the 1850s.* Stanford: Stanford University Press, 1962.

Fehrenbacher, Don E. *Slavery, Law, and Politics: The Dred Scott Case in Historical Perspective.* New York: Oxford University Press, 1981.

Fehrenbacher, Don E. (ed.). *Abraham Lincoln: A Documentary Portrait Through His Speeches and Writings.* New York: New American Library, 1964.

Fifth Annual Report of the Board of Managers of the Massachusetts Anti-Slavery Society with Some Account of the Annual Meeting, January 25, 1837.

Filler, Louis. *The Crusade Against Slavery: Friends, Foes, and Reforms 1820–1860.* New York: Harper & Row, 1960.

Fogel, Robert William. *Without Consent or Contract: The Rise and Fall of American Slavery.* New York: W. W. Norton, 1989.

Foner, Eric. *Free Soil, Free Labor, Free Men: The Ideology of the Republican Party Before the Civil War.* New York: Oxford University Press, 1970.

Fourth Annual Report of the Board of Managers of the Massachusetts Anti-Slavery Society with Some Account of the Annual Meeting, January 20, 1836.

Freehling, William W. "The Founding Fathers and Slavery." *American Historical Review,* Vol. 77, Nos. 1–2 (1972), pp. 81–93.

Freehling, William W. *Prelude to Civil War: The Nullification Controversy in South Carolina, 1816–1836*. New York: Harper & Row, 1965.

Freehling, William W. *Road to Disunion: Secessionists at Bay 1776–1854*. New York: Oxford University Press, 1990.

Fuess, Claude, M. *The Life of Caleb Cushing*. 2 vols. New York: Harcourt, Brace, 1923.

Galloway, George B. *History of the House of Representatives*. 2nd ed. Rev. by Sidney Wise. New York: Thomas Y. Crowell, 1976.

Genovese, Eugene D. *The Political Economy of Slavery: Studies in the Economy and Society of the Slave South*. New York: Random House, 1967.

Giddings, Joshua R. *History of the Rebellion: Its Authors and Causes*. New York: Follet, Foster, 1864.

Gienapp, William E. *The Origins of the Republican Party, 1852–1856*. New York: Oxford University Press, 1987.

Goldman, Perry M., and James S. Young (eds.). *The United States Congressional Directories, 1789–1840*. New York and London: Columbia University Press, 1973.

Goodheart, Lawrence B. *Abolitionist, Actuary, Atheist: Elizur Wright and the Reform Impulse*. Kent, Ohio: Kent State University Press, 1990.

Grayson, Benson Lee. *The Unknown President: The Administration of President Millard Filmore*. Washington, D.C.: University Press of America, 1981.

Green, Constance McLaughlin. *Washington: Village and Capital, 1800–1878*. Princeton, N.J.: Princeton University Press, 1962.

Gunderson, Gerald. "Slavery." In *Encyclopedia of American Economic History: Studies of the Principal Movements and Ideas*, Vol. 2. New York: Charles Scribner's Sons, 1980.

Hamilton, Holman. *Zachary Taylor: Soldier in the White House*. New York: Bobbs-Merrill, 1951.

Hammond, James H. *Selections from the Letters and Speeches of the Honorable James H. Hammond, of South Carolina*. Spartanburg: Reprint Company, 1978.

Haraszti, Zoltán. *John Adams and the Prophets of Progress*. Cambridge: Harvard University Press, 1952.

Harwell, Richard Barksdale. *"The Touchstone": William Lloyd Garrison and the Declaration of the Anti-Slavery Convention, Philadelphia, 1833*. Northampton, Mass.: Smith College, 1970.

Hecht, Marie B. *John Quincy Adams: A Personal History of an Independent Man*. New York: Macmillan, 1972.

Historical Statistics of the United States, Colonial Times to 1970. Washington: U. S. Govt. Printing Office, 1975.

Holt, Michael. *The Political Crisis of the 1850s*. New York: John Wiley & Sons, 1978.

Holt, Michael. *Political Parties and American Political Development from the Age of Jackson to the Age of Lincoln.* Baton Rouge: Louisiana State University Press, 1992.

Howe, Daniel Walker. *The Political Culture of the American Whigs.* Chicago: University of Chicago Press, 1979.

Jaffa, Harry V. *Crisis of the House Divided: An Interpretation of the Issues in the Lincoln-Douglas Debates.* Garden City, N.Y.: Doubleday, 1959.

Jay, William. *Inquiry into the Character and Tendency of the American Colonization and American Anti-Slavery Societies.* New York: Negro Universities Press, 1838.

Jefferson, Thomas, *A Manual of Parliamentary Practice.* Philadelphia: Hogan and Thompson, 1843.

Julian, George W. *The Life of Joshua R. Giddings.* Chicago: A. C. McClurg, 1892.

Kolchin, Peter. *American Slavery, 1619–1877.* New York: Hill & Wang, 1993.

Kraditor, Aileen S. *Means and Ends in American Abolitionism: Garrison and His Critics on Strategy and Tactics, 1834–1850.* Chicago: Ivan R. Dee, 1967.

Kraut, Alan M. (ed.). *Crusaders and Compromisers; Essays on the Relationship of the Antislavery Struggle to the Antebellum Party System.* Westport: Greenwood Press, 1983.

Lesick, Lawrence Thomas. *The Lane Rebels: Evangelicism and Antislavery in Antebellum America.* Studies in Evangelicalism No. 2. Metuchen, N.J., 1980.

Lincoln, Abraham. *Abraham Lincoln: Speeches and Writings 1859–1865.* New York: Library of America, 1989.

Lipsky, George A. *John Quincy Adams: His Theory and Ideas.* New York: Thomas Y. Crowell, 1950.

Ludlum, David McWilliams. *Social Ferment in Vermont, 1791–1850.* New York: Columbia University Press, 1939.

Ludlum, Robert P. "The Antislavery 'Gag-rule': History and Argument." *Journal of Negro History,* Vol. 26 (April 1941), pp. 203–43.

Lutz, Alma. *Crusade for Freedom: Women of the Antislavery Movement.* Boston: Beacon Press, 1968.

MacLean, William Jerry. "Othello Scorned: The Racial Thought of John Quincy Adams." *Journal of the Early Republic,* Vol. 4 (Summer 1984), pp. 143–60.

Magdol, Edward. *The Antislavery Rank and File; A Social Profile of the Abolitionists' Constituency.* New York: Greenwood Press, 1986.

McCoy, Drew. *The Last of the Fathers: James Madison and the Republican Legacy.* Cambridge: Cambridge University Press, 1989.

McPherson, James M. *Battle Cry of Freedom.* New York: Oxford University Press, 1988.

McPherson, James M. "The Fight Against the Gag Rule: Joshua Leavitt and Antislavery Insurgency in the Whig Party, 1839–1842." *Journal of Negro History*, Vol. 48 (July 1963), pp. 177–95.

Merrill, Walter M. *Against Wind and Tide: A Biography of William Lloyd Garrison.* Cambridge: Harvard University Press, 1963.

Miller, William Lee. *The Business of May Next: James Madison and the Founding.* Charlottesville: University Press of Virginia, 1992.

Mordell, Albert. *Quaker Militant John Greenleaf Whittier.* Port Washington, N.Y.: Kennikat Press, 1969.

Morgan, Edmund S. *American Slavery, American Freedom: The Ordeal of Colonial Virginia.* New York: W. W. Norton, 1975.

Morison, Samuel Eliot. The Oxford History of the American People. New York: Oxford University Press, 1965.

Morse, John T., Jr. *John Quincy Adams.* New York: Houghton Mifflin, 1910.

Nevins, Allan (ed.). *The Diary of John Quincy Adams, 1794–1845: American Diplomacy, and Political, Social, and Intellectual Life, from Washington to Polk.* New York: Charles Scribner's Sons, 1951.

Nevins, Allan (ed.). *Polk: The Diary of a President, 1845–1849, Covering the Mexican War, the Acquisition of Oregon, and the Conquest of California and the Southwest.* New York: Longmans, Green, 1952.

Niebuhr, Reinhold, *The Irony of American History.* New York: Charles Scribner's Sons, 1952.

Nye, Russel B. *Fettered Freedom: Civil Liberties and the Slavery Controversy 1830–1860.* East Lansing: Michigan State College Press, 1949.

Pease, William H., and Jane H. Pease (eds.). *The Antislavery Argument.* New York: Bobbs-Merrill, 1965.

Perry, Lewis. *Radical Abolitionism; Anarchy and the Government of God in Antislavery Thought.* Ithaca, N.Y.: Cornell University Press, 1973.

Perry, Lewis, and Michael Fellman (eds.). *Antislavery Reconsidered: New Perspectives on the Abolitionists.* Baton Rouge and London: Louisiana State University Press, 1979.

Peterson, Merrill D. *The Great Triumvirate: Webster, Clay and Calhoun.* New York: Oxford University Press, 1987.

Peterson, Svend. *A Statistical History of the American Presidential Elections.* Westport, Conn.: Greenwood Press, 1981.

Portrait and Biographical Record of the Sixth Congressional District of Maryland. New York: Chapman Publishing, 1898.

Potter, David M. *The Impending Crisis, 1848–1861.* New York: Harper & Row, 1976.

Potter, David M. *Lincoln and His Party in the Secession Crisis*. New Haven, Conn.: Yale University Press, 1962.

Rable, George C. "Slavery, Politics, and the South: The Gag Rule as a Case Study." *Capitol Studies*, Vol. 3 (Fall 1975), pp. 69–87.

The Resolutions of Virginia and Kentucky: Penned by Madison and Jefferson, In Relation to the Alien and Sedition Laws . . . Richmond, 1826.

Richards, Leonard L. *The Life and Times of Congressman John Quincy Adams*. New York: Oxford University Press, 1986.

Robinson, Donald. *Slavery in the Structure of American Politics 1765–1820*. New York: W.W. Norton, 1979.

Roseboom, Eugene H., and Alfred E. Eckes, Jr. *A History of Presidential Elections from George Washington to Jimmy Carter*. 4th ed. New York: Collier Books, 1979.

Rutland, R., et al. (eds.). *The Papers of James Madison*. Vol. 10. Chicago: University of Chicago Press, 1977:

Rutland, R., et al. (eds.) *The Papers of James Madison*. Vol. 14. Chicago: University of Chicago Press, 1983.

Schlesinger, Arthur. *History of American Presidential Elections*. New York: Chelsea House, 1971.

Sellers, Charles. *James K. Polk, Jacksonian, 1795–1843*. Princeton, N.J.: Princeton University Press, 1957.

Sellers, Charles Grier, Jr. *The Southerner as American*. Chapel Hill: University of North Carolina Press, 1960.

The Senate 1789–1989. Vol. 4, Historical Statistics 1789–1992. Bicentennial Edition. Washington, D.C.: U. S. Government Printing Office, 1993.

Seward, William H. *Life and Public Services of John Quincy Adams, Sixth President of the United States, with the Eulogy Delivered Before the Legislature of New York*. 1849. Reprint. Port Washington, N.Y.: Kennikat Press, 1971.

Silbey, Joel H. *The Partisan Imperative: The Dynamics of American Politics Before the Civil War*. New York: Oxford University Press, 1985.

Silbey, Joel H. *A Respectable Minority: The Democratic Party in the Civil War Era, 1860–1868*. New York: W. W. Norton, 1977.

Silbey, Joel H. *The Shrine of Party: Congressional Voting Behavior 1841–1852*. Pittsburgh: University of Pittsburgh Press, 1967.

Simpson, Craig M. *A Good Southerner: The Life of Henry A. Wise of Virginia*. Chapel Hill: University of North Carolina Press, 1985.

The Slave's Friend. New York: Published by R. G. Williams for the American Anti-Slavery Society, 1836–1839.

Smith, Page. *John Adams*. 2 vols. Garden City, N.Y.: Doubleday, 1962.

Smith, Robert G. *The Arguments over Abolition Petitions in the House of Representatives in December, 1835: A Toulmin Analysis*. Ph.D. Thesis, University of Minnesota, 1962. Ann Arbor, Mich.: University Microfilms, 1963.

Stampp, Kenneth M. *And the War Came: The North and the Secession Crisis, 1860–1861*. Louisiana State University Press, 1950.

Stampp, Kenneth M. *The Peculiar Institution: Slavery in the Antebellum South*. New York: Alfred A. Knopf, 1956.

Stephenson, George M. *A History of American Immigration, 1820–1924*. Boston: Ginn, 1926.

Stewart, James Brewer. *Holy Warriors: The Abolitionists and American Slavery*. New York: Hill & Wang, 1976.

Stewart, James Brewer. *Joshua R. Giddings and the Tactics of Radical Politics*. Cleveland: Press of Case Western Reserve University, 1970.

Stowe, Harriet Beecher. *Uncle Tom's Cabin*. In *Harriet Beecher Stowe: Three Novels*. New York: Library of America, 1982.

Thomas, Benjamin P. *Theodore Weld: Crusader for Freedom*. New Brunswick, N.J.: Rutgers University Press, 1950.

Thomas, John L. (ed.). *Slavery Attacked: The Abolitionist Crusade*. Englewood Cliffs, N.J.: Prentice-Hall, 1965.

Tyler, Alice Felt. *Freedom's Ferment: Phases of American Social History from the Colonial Period to the Outbreak of the Civil War*. Minneapolis: University of Minnesota Press, 1944. Reprint. New York: Harper & Row/Harper Torchbooks/The Academy Library, 1962.

Venet, Wendy Hamand. *Neither Ballots nor Bullets; Women Abolitionists and the Civil War*. Charlottesville and London: University Press of Virginia, 1991.

von Holst, Dr. Hermann Eduard. *The Constitutional History and Political History of the United States, 1828–1846: Jackson's Administration—Annexation of Texas* (John Joseph Lalor, A.M., trans.). Vol. 2. Chicago: Callaghan, 1879.

Wagenknecht, Edward. *John Greenleaf Whittier: A Portrait in Paradox*. New York: Oxford University Press, 1967.

Weld, Theodore Dwight. *American Slavery As It Is: Testimony of a Thousand Witnesses*. New York: American Anti-Slavery Society, 1839.

Weld, Theodore Dwight. *The Bible Against Slavery: Or, an Inquiry into the Genius of the Mosaic System, and the Teachings of the Old Testament on the Subject of Human Rights*. Pittsburgh: United Presbyterian Board of Publication, 1864.

White, Laura A. *Robert Barnwell Rhett: Father of Secession*. Gloucester, Mass.: Peter Smith, 1965.

Whitman, Walt (unsigned). *The People and John Quincy Adams*. Berkeley Heights, N.J.: Oriole Press, 1961.

Whittier, John Greenleaf. *The Conflict with Slavery: Politics and Reform, The Inner Life, Criticism*. Boston: Houghton Mifflin, 1866.

Whittier, John Greenleaf. *The Poetical Works of John Greenleaf Whittier.* 4 vols. Vol. 3, *Anti-Slavery Poems, Songs of Labor and Reform.* Boston: Houghton Mifflin, 1892.

Whittier, John Greenleaf. *The Prose Works of John Greenleaf Whittier.* Vol. 3. Boston: Houghton Mifflin, 1892.

Who Was Who in America: Historical Volume, 1607–1896. Chicago: A. N. Marquis, 1967.

Wiecek, William M. *The Sources of Anti-Slavery Constitutionalism in America, 1760–1848.* Ithaca, N.Y.: Cornell University Press, 1977.

Williams, T. Harry (ed.). *Selected Writings and Speeches of Abraham Lincoln.* New York: Hendricks House, 1980.

Wilson, Clyde N. (ed.). *The Essential Calhoun: Selections from Writings, Speeches, and Letters.* New Brunswick and London: Transaction Publishers, 1992.

Wilson, Clyde N. (ed.). *The Papers of John C. Calhoun.* Vol. 13, *1835–1837.* Columbia: University of South Carolina Press, 1980.

Wilson, Edmund. *Patriotic Gore: Studies in the Literature of the American Civil War.* New York: Oxford University Press, 1966.

Wilson, Henry. *The Rise and Fall of the Slave Power in America.* 3 vols. Boston: Houghton Mifflin, 1872–77.

Wiltse, Charles M. *John C. Calhoun Nullifier, 1829–1839.* Vol. 2. New York: Bobbs-Merrill, 1949.

Wise, Barton H. *The Life of Henry A. Wise of Virginia 1806–1876.* New York: Macmillan, 1899.

Wise, Henry A. *Seven Decades of the Union.* Philadelphia: J. B. Lippincott, 1881.

Woodward, C. Vann. *The Burden of Southern History.* Baton Rouge: Louisiana State University Press, 1968.

Wyatt-Brown, Bertram. *Lewis Tappan and the Evangelical War Against Slavery.* Cleveland: Press of Case Western Reserve University, 1969.

Young, James Sterling. *The Washington Community: 1800–1828.* New York: Columbia University Press, 1968.

Acknowledgments

One sometimes hears that historians, like other scholars, and perhaps other professionals of all kinds—for that matter human beings of all kinds—are not hospitable to outsiders who poach on their territory. A political scientist at an institution other than my own reported that when he asked a historian how it would be received if he wrote a history of Congress, he was told, "We will chop you off at the knees!" And of course there are good reasons as well as bad ones for the wariness of professionals about those who lack their specific training and continuing discipline.

I want to report, though, that my experience has been the opposite of all of that. Although this is the third book in a row of a historical sort that I have written, I am not by training or identity a professional historian. My academic identity involves a slightly confusing crossing of lines. My degree, long ago, was in religious social ethics; most of the time that I was writing this book I held a chair called "Ethics and Institutions." But the historians whom I have asked for help, and those, known to me and not known to me, who read and appraised my productions, now including this most ambitious effort, could not have been more gracious, generous, and constructive, in some cases at some cost in valuable time to themselves. It all goes to restore one's faith in the scholarly community—conceivably a little bit in the human community.

Specifically, with respect to this book, I want to thank three of my University of Virginia colleagues, all historians, who read the manuscript at different stages, and not only saved me from errors but also proposed particular, in some cases major, improvements. Robert C. Cross read large pieces of the earliest version of the manuscript, to my considerable benefit. Edward Ayres, the historian of the South, read the manuscript in its penultimate version and made a number of valuable comments. Most of all I want to thank Michael Holt, the leading scholar on the American Whigs, who made valuable suggestions early in the project, as I was beginning; read the manuscript in two big doses thereafter; and wrote two lengthy and detailed letters of comment, correction, and criticism. I benefited very much from this help. The usual disclaimer is particularly to be underscored in Professor Holt's case; he is not in any way to be held accountable for errors of fact and interpretation that remain. Neither are any others; the faults, of course, are mine.

I spent some pleasant days at the Adams Papers project at the Massachusetts Historical Society in Boston. Richard Ryerson, the director, and, particularly, Celeste Walker, who is the chief editor for John Quincy Adams, were most cordial and encouraging; Celeste Walker constructed for me a convenient list of Adams's letters.

Once again on this book I had the benefit of the discerning and conscientious editing of Corona Machemer, going far beyond the usual work of modern editors. She gave of her time and exceptional editorial intelligence to help the writer make his book better, and her influence has helped to shape it in important ways. I am grateful to her.

Much of this book was written, across nine years, at the Miller Center for Public Affairs at the University of Virginia. I want to thank the center, its board, its staff, and Kenneth W. Thompson, its director, for the support and the setting that enabled me to write it. In particular I am grateful to Robin Kuzen, the center's administrator and editor, for her help of many kinds, going beyond the call of duty. She read the manuscript and, together with Parthie Shields of the center, offered editorial advice and counsel, and continuing support, from which this book profited, and for which I am grateful.

As he has with other writings of mine, Andrew Miller read parts of this book and offered very helpful criticism. So did Cindy and Scott Coffel, who gave me memorable encouragment at a critical moment.

Jennifer Bernstein helped more than any other person to bring this book into being. The long file drawers of folders which are its source and ground are full of memos, notes, underlined pages of the *Globe* and the *Register of Debates*, answers to long lists of questions, and quotations copied in her handwriting, from "JCB," an extraordinarily quick, thorough, and intelligent researcher and all-around assistant.

Her predecessor, Holly Redmond Spiller, had assisted me with several other projects, and gave essential help in getting the basic work for this one done, too, including much copying of the *Globe* and trips to Washington to look at the petitions. I want to thank Holly for her excellent aid on many projects, including this big one.

Other graduate students also gave able support: Jennifer Shepherd, an experienced editor; Brian Menard, whom I thanked also in another book and who contributed some items that can still be found in this one; Wendy Holliday, who dug out copies of the *Tribune* and other papers in New York; and—a versatile assistant on many projects—Scott deLong.

My gratitude to, and other feelings for, Linda Miller go far beyond anything that could possibly be said in these acknowledgments, and far beyond her support on this book. But that is included, too.

William Lee Miller

Index

A NOTE ABOUT THE AUTHOR

William Lee Miller, now Thomas C. Sorensen Professor of Political and Social Thought at the University of Virginia, has also been a Commonwealth Professor, and a Professor of Ethics and Institutions, at that institution. He has also taught at Yale University, Smith College, and Indiana University, and at the last-named was founding director of the Poynter Center on American Institutions. He was at one time a writer on the staff of *The Reporter* magazine, and has written numerous articles and essays for other publications. He has served as an alderman in New Haven, Connecticut, and as a political speech writer and ghost writer. His most recent books are *The First Liberty: Religion and the American Republic* (1986) and *The Business of May Next: James Madison and the Founding* (1992).

A NOTE ON THE TYPE

The text of this book was set in Sabon, a typeface designed by Jan Tschichold (1902–1974), the well-known German typographer. Based loosely on the original designs by Claude Garamond (c. 1480–1561), Sabon is unique in that it was explicitly designed for hotmetal composition on both the Monotype and Linotype machines as well as for filmsetting. Designed in 1966 in Frankfurt, Sabon was named for the famous Lyons punch cutter Jacques Sabon, who is thought to have brought some of Garamond's matrices to Frankfurt.

Composed by ComCom, a division of Haddon Craftsmen,
Allentown, Pennsylvania
Printed and bound by R. R. Donnelley & Sons,
Harrisonburg, Virginia
Designed by Robert C. Olsson